The
PRESIDENT'S
HOUSE

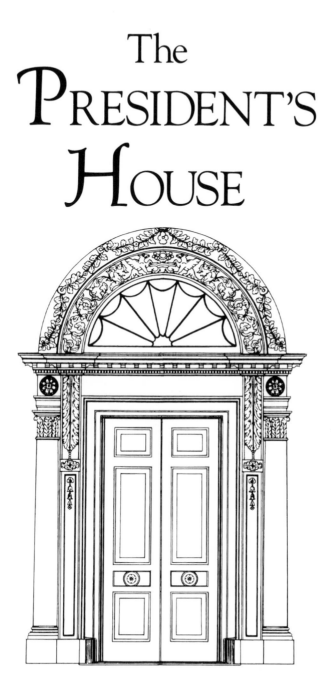

VOLUME TWO

The
PRESIDENT'S
HOUSE

A History

by
William Seale

White House Historical Association
with the cooperation of the National Geographic Society
Washington, D.C.
and Harry N. Abrams, Inc., New York

Copyright © 1986 White House Historical Association
Washington, D.C.

All rights reserved. Reproduction or other utilization of the whole or any
part of the contents without written permission is prohibited.

Library of Congress CIP data: page 1224

ISBN 0-912308-28-1

ISBN 0-8109-1490-5 (Abrams)

FIRST PRINTING

Contents

VOLUME II

Contents: Volume II

Illustrations

Part II, following page 746

Part III, following page 842

The
PRESIDENT'S
HOUSE

VOLUME TWO

26

A Recollection of Roses

By the beginning of the 20th century the Presidency had shaken off the subservience to the Congress that had characterized it since the late 1860s. Cleveland's unprecedented reelection in 1892 demonstrated the desire of the electorate for a leader who would take command. By the presidential standards of the 20th century, Cleveland had not been an especially powerful chief executive in the first term; but in the context of the '80s, his Presidency had been strong, and his special concerns, such as his campaign for the workingman, had gone against the political stream. Whether the American people agreed with him or not, they admired his grit.

Through the 1880s, popular resentment had welled up against congressional favoritism toward big business and established wealth. By the '90s, the rich had begun to acknowledge the role of politics in the accumulation of private fortunes. Millionaires all across the country lined the streets of Washington with palatial mansions, for use when the Congress was in session. The grandeur of these mirrored the palatial houses of the bourgeois bankers of Paris, equipped with every luxury. Measured by this new standard, the White House seemed inadequate. In the early '90s this was seen as a shortcoming in need of correction; in the next century, however, the house was soon renovated to preserve its traditional appearance. Its very unpretentiousness had come to seem the perfect and natural symbol of the Presidency.

Going and Coming

The Harrison family descended in the elevator on Cleveland's inauguration day, March 4, 1893, the men in black suits, the women in mourning costumes, with black veils. They were glad to be leaving the White House. Their four years had not been happy. The elder members of the family would attend Cleveland's inauguration, while the children would be taken directly to the railroad station to wait with servants in the private car. By early afternoon the whole family was on the way home to Indiana.

At 11:30 Mrs. Cleveland entered on Colonel Crook's arm, beaming from her fur wrap and big veiled hat. She was followed by a nurse in white, carrying baby Ruth, the Cleveland's first child. The Blue Room's window and jib doors were opened to admit her, and she walked over the flowery carpet as familiarly as though four years had not intervened since she had last seen the room where she had been married. Apparently none of the Harrisons greeted her, although they were still there. Passing through the Red Room and across the hall, she entered the elevator the Harrisons had left only moments before and ascended to the vacated family quarters. She saw bare tabletops, empty drawers and wardrobes, and sensed that chilly stillness that goes with uninhabited places. In haste she settled Ruth and the nurse in a bedroom and prepared to leave for the inauguration.

At about the time Mrs. Cleveland was riding the elevator to the second floor, Cleveland arrived at the north portico. Harrison appeared on the porch promptly. Protected by the portico from the icy mist, the two men uncovered their heads and bowed, then shook hands and took their places in an open landau for the ride to the Capitol. Both had aged in four years, but Cleveland more noticeably. His thinning hair was almost all white. The tight skin was now pale, sagging around the eyes and in the cheeks. A walrus moustache drooped from his upper lip, and he touched it frequently enough to show his concern that it look neat. He and Harrison talked pleasantly, as they acknowledged the cheering throngs on either side.

Cleveland's inaugural address was forceful, reiterating the principles he had stood for in his first administration. The spirit of his text was optimistic. He pledged honesty and hard work, but made no allusion to history. As before, he considered the Civil War over, and he directed his remarks to a younger generation, who, according to one editor, "have come on the stage since the reign of passion and prejudice came to an end, and the era of discussion has opened."[1]

Aboard the *Oneida*

It is difficult to appreciate fully the high hopes that came with Cleveland's second inauguration, in light of the severity with which they were dashed by the stock market crash the following summer. Certainly the spring was a happy season. So much the center of attention were the Clevelands that they considered moving out of the White House in search of privacy. The state receptions were mobbed. Mrs. Cleveland's daytime receptions, intended only for ladies, now attracted large numbers of men, and the doors were usually closed before the line had ended. On Easter Monday 1893, the egg rolling coincided with a routine daytime reception. Two thousand were received in the house, while on the south lawn an estimated 20,000 pushed and shoved and trampled lawn and flower bed until dark.

Mrs. Cleveland, fuller of figure and looking most of her 28 years, was a bright and pretty hostess. She was expecting her second child in early autumn, although this was not yet known to the public. During the four years in New York she had been sought after as a dinner guest. She was admired alike by artists, whom she enjoyed, and businessmen, the preferred companions of her husband. Women praised her elegant costumes, many of them designed along "colonial" lines and trimmed with antique lace, which she collected. She confided to a reporter that she remained well within a budget of $2,000 per year for clothes, even though the expense for ball gowns alone was great.

On May 1, 1893, the President traveled to Chicago to open the World's Columbian Exposition, which celebrated—one year late—Columbus's discovery of the New World. The "White City," a spectacular assemblage of neoclassical buildings set in a formal park lighted with electricity, enjoyed great public acclaim for the high ideals it symbolized; it was often compared to Cleveland's vision for the nation. But the President's hopes, like the temporary plaster architecture of the fair, stood in danger of destruction from outside forces.

The economic picture had been alarming since the late winter when the failure of the Philadelphia & Reading Railroad threw the New York Stock Exchange into the wildest selling period it had yet known. This happened ten days before Cleveland took office. Other setbacks occurred in the following months, but it was generally believed that the new President would stabilize the situation by building up the gold reserve to create what he called a "sound and stable currency."

On June 27, however, the stock market crashed. Lending institutions began calling in their loans, and business houses began to fall, more than 16,000 of them ruined in the first year of the Panic of 1893. Some 600 banks closed, and an estimated four million citizens were out of work. President Cleveland was determined that the root of the evil had to be the Sherman Silver Purchase Act, which had caused the depletion of the government's gold reserve. He called the Congress into a special session to open in August, and ordered his Democratic colleagues to formulate plans to destroy the offending laws.

As lines were being drawn for one of the bitterest congressional battles since the Civil War, Cleveland underwent a medical examination at the White House on June 18, after suffering sharp pains in his mouth. His doctors discovered a tumor in the roof of his mouth and ordered surgery performed at once. With the nation shaken by the panic, Cleveland insisted that the tumor with its terrible foreboding of cancer be kept secret. He hesitated to leave his work, yet he knew any surgery performed in the White House would be found out. His pain sharpened, and he decided to go elsewhere immediately for the operation.

The planning was left entirely to Colonel Lamont, now the Secretary of War. He had asked Cleveland for Cabinet rank and received it, with the understanding that he would remain the President's confidential adviser. The new private secretary, Henry T. Thurber, an excellent office manager, was never intended to enjoy the same special closeness to Cleveland. In organizing the President's secret operation, Lamont outdid even his own previous record for cunning.

From his office on the morning of June 30 Cleveland issued the order for the Congress to go into special session August 7. Just before noon he left the White House in an open carriage with Mrs. Cleveland and little Ruth and the nurse, boarding a private car at the station for the trip to New York. Ostensibly, the family was going to their summer place at Buzzard's Bay on Cape Cod, for the five weeks before the opening of the special session of the Congress. Cleveland would take his accustomed cruise with his close friend Commodore Elias C. Benedict of New York. The two shared a joint bank account for purposes of investment—since Cleveland did not engage in business while in office. The millionaire Benedict had made the President a rich man.

Nothing about Cleveland's plans seemed out of the ordinary, particularly considering his wife's advanced pregnancy, which according to the conventions of the time demanded seclusion. Cleveland's presence was not required in Washington until August, so Lamont's plan unfolded easily. In New York, Cleveland bade his wife to proceed alone to Cape Cod, and he and Lamont were driven quietly to the port, where they boarded Benedict's yacht, the *Oneida*. A party of doctors was already aboard, including Cleveland's doctor, Joseph D. Bryant. The President stood on the deck puffing a cigar in silence, as the *Oneida* set sail.

The operation was performed at sea, just after noon the following day. Cleveland was given nitrous oxide (laughing gas) and when the cutting was over, was given opium. The extent of the tumor was greater than any of the doctors had imagined. It was malignant, and thus a large area had to be removed, "the entire left upper jaw . . . from the first bicuspid tooth to just beyond the last molar, and nearly up to the middle line," as well as a part of the soft palate. An artificial device made of rubber replaced the palate and filled the cavity left by the surgery.

For five days longer the *Oneida* sailed along the New England coast, dropping anchor at last at Buzzard's Bay, in view of the rambling, shingled cottage Mrs. Cleveland called Gray Gables. The President was hurried ashore and into the house, where he was put to bed, becoming the most difficult of patients. Lamont complained that Cleveland suffered "from an excess of medicine . . . . He always believes that if a little will do some good, a bottle full must be of great advantage indeed." Mrs. Cleveland caught him in the act of eating a peach: "Wouldn't you think a *child* would have had more sense . . . ?"[2]

Only once did the secret come close to being exposed. An article appeared in the Philadelphia *Press* saying that the President had undergone surgery and implying that it was far more serious than anyone would allow. A battery of reporters descended upon Gray Gables. One of Cleveland's executive clerks, Robert Lincoln O'Brien, feared "that if ever one reporter got inside 'Gray Gables' and detected the hospital odors and caught sight of Cleveland, who was just then beginning to sit up in a bathrobe, the jig would be up—for the President looked like a very sick man." Lamont intervened calmly, telling the press that the President had merely suffered the removal of a few teeth, but being a coward about dental work of any sort, had put off the pulling until the need was acute. Naturally he was a little weak as a result. In the immediate circle of the Clevelands' friends at Buzzard's Bay the operation was common knowledge. The President enjoyed a rapid and complete recovery, but the secret of the surgery was otherwise well kept for 24 years, until 1917, when the principal doctor wrote a full and detailed account, in the interest of history, for the *Saturday Evening Post.*[3]

Cleveland was back at the White House the day the Congress convened, and on the following day, August 8, he sent a formal message in which he asked bluntly for the repeal of the Sherman Silver Act. The battle ran on for nearly three months; on November 1, in his White House office, Cleveland signed the repeal into law, and believed that the first definitive step had been taken toward ending the Panic of 1893. Repeal did not end the panic, however; it ran on for four years. Nevertheless, Cleveland pushed ahead with characteristic directness, championing his policies. Even the soothing Lamont could not calm him, as he pounded the desk, making demands of powerful politicians. If the congressmen and senators would not play his game, he withheld patronage; as a result, by mid-autumn of 1893, Cleveland had lost his political base, and his party was crumbling from dissension. By the beginning of 1894 Cleveland was alone at the top, his main claim to power lying in the fact that he happened to hold the office of President.

Endless Lines of Callers

Cleveland's White House was no less bright and lively for the decline of his political power. Crowds continued to stream in daily to inspect the state rooms. Public receptions were never long enough to admit everyone, and some people went away disgruntled as the Metropolitan Police closed the iron gates against them.

The public was admitted to the general evening receptions at about nine o'clock, which was considered "after-dinner," entering the grounds at the northwest gate. They walked up the driveway to the north door, in sight of the large awning-sheltered "bridge" slanting from the driveway to a window of the East Room, by which they would eventually exit. Light glowed from the windows and the colored glass transom of the north door; the strains of the Marine Band sounded within. One visitor remembered that the doors opened with the first notes of the band: "I took a step, those back of me took a step, and then the great procession, several thousand strong . . . began to move. We were all going, rich and poor, old and young, noted and obscure, black and white, to be the guests of the man who guided the destinies of the country, which in our own minds we were pleased to term the 'greatest country on earth.'"[4]

The guests entered the President's House in three columns. At the north door these were reduced to two, then at the center doors in the stained-glass screen they shrank to one for admission across the hall into the Blue Room. Each caller was stopped by doormen at the Blue Room door, then allowed to enter. As a visitor entered, the public buildings officer, once more Cleveland's friend Colonel John M. Wilson, bent forward to hear the name, then repeated it clearly to the President, to his right. The President, in shaking hands with the caller, said firmly: "Happy to meet you," and addressed the guest by name.

The President, with a slight southward movement of the hand he

was shaking, passed the caller to the First Lady, who was more accomplished than he at the reception business. She took the caller quickly by
the fingertips and warbled, "So glad to see you," repeating the name.
Thus each person, though never stopping, had a sense of conversing
pleasantly with the First Lady.

The callers flowed on, thousands in number, through the double
mahogany doors into the Green Room, where an array of official guests—
Cabinet members and wives and sometimes others—stood to be stared
at, arranged like long-stemmed flowers, and at last into the East Room,
stripped of its furniture, its curtains closed, its gilt and white aglow from
the light of the three great chandeliers. To all but the earliest visitors,
entering the East Room must have seemed like walking into a crowded
railroad station during wartime. A reporter noted, however, "The crowd
was the most orderly crowd I have ever seen; good nature and good
temper everywhere prevailed." When a guest desired to leave, he moved
toward the north end of the East Room and found the window to the far
left; through the window and over the bridge to the driveway and his
evening at the White House was over.[5]

Only a few full-scale public receptions, open to all without invitation, were held in a given year. Other evening receptions required invitations; while cards were not difficult to come by, the events were
smaller, with guests numbering in the hundreds instead of the thousands.
That the costumes tended to be more elaborate, the jewelry more profuse, and the general manner more formal seems to have discouraged
most ordinary citizens from requesting invitations.

The logistics for the smaller receptions enhanced their elegance. If
they had drivers, callers could ride in their carriages all the way to the
north portico, where the vehicles either departed after they alighted, or
were parked by number along the driveway and the small paved court
before the house. Although carriages were numerous, many White
House guests took the streetcar or walked, resplendent in full dress.

Upon entering the house, guests checked their coats in the entrance
hall. Men then went to the East Room, while women were directed to
the ushers' room, to the right of the north door, and through the service
and transverse halls to the Red Room. As well as being a shortcut to the
parlors, this was apparently a device to acquaint them with the small
toilet room, which opened off the service hall. To beautify the route,
Mrs. Cleveland had the ushers' room, a simple office, redecorated as a
smoking room, with imitation morocco on the walls and heavy, dark
"Jacobean" furniture. This was only for looks; the desk that normally
occupied the office was returned after the receptions.[6]

Since the rule of punctuality was supposedly unbendable, the guests to invitational receptions were usually a little early. The women might thus take their time admiring what they saw while walking from the Red Room through the Blue Room and Green Room, to join the men in the East Room. Wine or punch was sometimes passed to the guests, as they awaited the President's arrival. At the precise hour stated on the invitation, the Marine Band, stationed in the transverse hall, struck up a rousing "Hail to the Chief," and the President, his wife, and their guests descended the grand staircase at a rapid pace, trotted down the transverse hall, and formed a receiving line in the East Room. After about an hour the line broke up, and the President and First Lady mixed with the company for perhaps an hour and a half. Then the presidential couple departed in the elevator, ending the evening.

Society in Washington did not end with social functions at the White House, but did to some extent center on them. There were far grander private houses within walking distance, having larger numbers of servants, more splendid drawing rooms, and doubtless better chefs. Beginning in 1893 Washington had full ambassadors, replacing the ministers who had previously represented foreign countries in the United States. This rise in the rank of diplomatic representation foreshadowed the nation's emergence from long years of relative isolation. The ambassadors' style of entertaining was generous and sophisticated, and they were housed in handsome embassies. But for all its comparative seediness, the White House eclipsed all rivals. When invitations were mailed to a function there, society tensed, waiting to see who was in and who was out. In the world of Washington politics, being left out was a bitter pill, even though omission, while sometimes a reprimand, more often simply reflected the limited space the White House had to offer.[7]

One of the most glamorous social events of Cleveland's second administration was the entertainment for the Princess Eulalia of Spain. Visits of state were rare in the 19th century, and a quarter of a century was yet to pass before an American President—Wilson—would leave the United States on an official trip. The visit of the king's daughter was a goodwill gesture on the part of Spain, an attempt to soothe the rising American resentment of Spain's activities in Cuba. Princess Eulalia, accompanied by 19 Spanish nobles, called formally at the White House on May 22, 1893, and was received by the President and Mrs. Cleveland in the Red Room. Several hours later, Mrs. Cleveland returned the call at the infanta's rooms in the Arlington Hotel.

A state banquet was held in honor of the infanta and her consort, Prince Antoine, on the following evening; 60 cards were sent out for eight o'clock. The event was excruciatingly formal, with every detail planned, down to the fold of the napkins. It was arranged that the infanta and her party would meet the Clevelands upstairs in the oval room, then descend the grand stair with them. Thus the luminaries would all appear in the East Room at the same time, and one would not seem to be awaiting the other. Instructions became confused, however, and instead of going upstairs, the princess went directly to the East Room. The doormen and ushers were too awed to stop her. In the East Room she looked around for the President. The Clevelands, informed of the mix-up, hastened there, and in the midst of their cheerful greetings, a crash of music announced the march to dinner. Cleveland, with Princess Eulalia, and Mrs. Cleveland, with Prince Antoine, led the guests to the State Dining Room. Once at table everyone relaxed, and the evening ran smoothly.

The dining table was in the usual I-shape, with the President and Mrs. Cleveland facing each other at the center. Like a long pond, the gilded plateau shimmered between "trees" of red and yellow roses, honoring the Spanish colors. They made an allée with garlands of white roses swagged between each tree. When the company sat down, the gaslight was dimmed, and several hundred candles illuminated the room. The infanta wore white brocade, with a full court train; long ropes of pearls extended from her neck to her waist and from her waist to the floor. Mrs. Cleveland's attire was almost the antithesis, a simple satin gown, pale yellow, almost white, with a corsage Pfister had made for her from pink camellias in the glasshouse.[8]

State dinners usually lasted about three hours. Guests could not rise before the President, who stood to signal that dinner was over. Everybody then followed, and the men remained standing while the ladies left the room, led by Mrs. Cleveland and the female guest of honor. The men dispersed or talked informally until about half an hour later, when all the guests assembled in the Red Room for liqueurs and coffee.

The White House social season had become shorter in the 1890s. Once opening in the autumn, it now commenced with the traditional New Year's Day reception and concluded late in May. On New Year's the reception for the diplomatic corps began, as always, at 11 o'clock and lasted for about an hour; at noon the doors were thrown open to the public for two hours, sometimes more.

Three state dinners were the highlights of the season: the Cabinet dinner, the dinner for the foreign ministers and the diplomatic corps, and the dinner for the Supreme Court. The Congress and the military were honored with large receptions, but some individuals were also included in smaller presidential dinner parties. Three of the "card," or invitational, receptions were traditional with every season, as well as several Saturday afternoon receptions, whenever the President wished to hold them, usually from three until five. According to Robert L. O'Brien, Cleveland realized the political value of White House entertainments and took an active role in planning the guest lists. If his wife's sparkle made the dinners and luncheons in-between appear personal in character, they were also political occasions. Smaller dinner parties averaged from 15 to 25 guests, and a safe estimate is that Cleveland entertained about 600 people in this manner in any given season.

Most of the burden of orchestrating the social events fell on Octavius L. Pruden, who devised the seating charts according to the rank of the guests and drew them in India ink on large cards, to be displayed on easels in the State Dining Room. Warren S. Young helped Pruden with the planning, down to the details of the invitations. In 1895 an additional clerk was hired as Mrs. Cleveland's social secretary and to assist Pruden and Young with the guest lists. He was George B. Cortelyou, a 33-year-old lawyer, who was to have a distinguished career at the White House. These employees devised the menus, bearing in mind the preferences and even the allergies of the guests. They satisfied any requirements for calligraphy and, with Mrs. Cleveland, decided on the colors of flowers and other decorations. For state banquets they specified the type and vintage of the wines.[9]

At the outset of the administration William Sinclair dealt directly with the merchants and caterers, when caterers were used, but none of the planning seems to have originated with him.

Perhaps because of personal limitations, perhaps because of the negative attitudes of white tradesmen and merchants in the 1890s toward a black man in such a position of authority, Sinclair became less and less involved in the business aspects of his stewardship. Whenever the Clevelands left town he went with them, so he was absent too much to be an effective administrator. According to the surviving household accounts, the steward's duties in the second Cleveland administration were seldom more complex than routine housekeeping. His substitute in purchasing and making business arrangements became an official described on the payroll as the "chief usher," a white man named William Dubois, who was employed by Cleveland in 1893. The title did not become official until about 1897.[10]

The work of Pruden and Young was significant as the beginning of a White House social "office," which would one day be very large. Pruden had started it in the '70s, when he began drawing fancy invitations for Mrs. Grant's parties. Social matters were then still considered the responsibility of the women of the house. When Young joined Pruden ten years later, in the Arthur administration, many of the social details were delegated to their office. The two showed such talent in this area that President Arthur made it part of their jobs.

After Mrs. Grant's time "theme" parties and decorated social functions—the "rose" teas, the "nautical" breakfasts, the "Japanese" luncheons, and the "flag" dinners—became passé. They were considered in bad taste or, worse, bourgeois. Under Arthur the White House had turned back to traditional black-and-white formality, and this trend became more pronounced in the '90s, influenced by the advent of full-rank ambassadors. Pruden and Young were the obvious candidates to sail the unknown and treacherous waters of international etiquette. A hundred questions of procedure arose in the planning of every state function, most centering on the recognition of rank, but some involving personal or political animosities between guests.

Strict social conformity suited the Clevelands not because they liked formality, but because following prescribed rules permitted shorter entertainments and made it possible to delegate most of the minutiae of planning. They cherished their private hours and were more than pleased to be relieved of any decisions not directly involving politics or the President's official duties. When Pruden and Young were in doubt concerning some issue of procedure, they no longer went to the President or his wife, but to the State Department, where Alvey A. Adee, second assistant secretary of state, had been considered for 22 years the final word on procedures. There was as yet no office of protocol, but Adee was its seed. While Ike Hoover was to recall much later that entertainments under the Clevelands were more brilliant than they had ever been at the White House, Cleveland parties lacked the personal touch that had often been associated with such seasons in the past.[11]

Roses

Few personal events at the White House have attracted warmer interest than the birth on September 9, 1893, of the Clevelands' second child, Esther. She appeared healthy and bright-eyed in the Clevelands' bedroom, the large room second from the northwest corner, still sometimes called the Prince of Wales Room. Esther Cleveland was the only child of a President to be born in the White House. She might have become more popular than Baby McKee, had her parents permitted it, but neither was willing to have a "public" child. There were some good reasons for their protectiveness. Once on the south lawn a party of tourists had tried to wrench Ruth from her nurse for a better look, as Mrs. Cleveland watched in horror from an upstairs window. The Clevelands quickly ruled that the public would not see the children at all. Speculation began to arise that Esther was deformed, but the Clevelands were so adamant about the privacy of their children that they did not even attempt to correct the stories.[12]

In their second term, the Clevelands showed more interest in the White House than they had as newlyweds, even though they acquired another suburban house, Woodley, where they spent a lot of time. At first Mrs. Cleveland made a faint effort to promote Mrs. Harrison's plan for expansion, remarking at opportune times how much she liked it, and now and then ordering the sketches by Frederick Owen set up in the entrance hall. She was encouraged by the Corps of Engineers, but the subject was not mentioned much after the crash in the summer of 1893.

More interested in houses and furnishings now than she had been as a bride, Mrs. Cleveland did make changes. She ordered the Red Room redecorated late in 1893, and in 1894 had all the state rooms repainted. The Red Room remodeling continued to feature the mantel Tiffany had installed for Arthur. The original pine woodwork at the doors and windows was torn out and replaced by trimmings of mahogany, milled to imitate the mantel's flowing wave-like volutes and foliation, which the architect Glenn Brown, who knew the room, described as "modern Romanesque." The color was made uniform and lighter, a shade called at the time "bright crimson." The walls were scraped to the bare plaster and washed down. Tiffany's subtle confection of copper and silver stars and his abstractions of stripes were replaced by neoclassical borders and decorations in shades of gray against red, flecked with gilt. Between wainscoting and frieze the walls were covered with solid-red wallpaper. The window overlooking the south portico was cut down to make a full doorway. For the center table of the Red Room, Mrs. Cleveland purchased a kerosene oil lamp made of cut glass. It had a deeply ruffled silk shade that looked like a hoopskirt, through which the light glowed rosily.[13]

The other major change in the state floor was the refurnishing of the transverse hall with oak settees and chairs bought from the A. H. Davenport Company in Boston and upholstered with a lavish use of brass-head tacks. Paintings were hung on the walls, gallery style, including some presidential portraits. Presumably the painting "Love and Life" was intended to go there also. The painter George F. Watts had shown the work with great success at the World's Fair in Chicago, where Cleveland had admired it, even though its liberal display of nude females had aroused controversy. When the fair closed, Watts presented his picture, valued at $7,000, to the White House. So great was the protest from morality-minded organizations, especially the Women's Christian Temperance Union, that on January 2, 1895, "Love and Life" was carried unceremoniously across the street to the Corcoran Gallery of Art, where it was placed on loan.[14]

Upstairs, Mrs. Cleveland repainted and repapered every room. The little boudoir she had reclaimed on the northwest corner was decorated in sky blue, and the presidential bedchamber adjoining it was colored red. The room across the hall, the accustomed bedroom of the Presidents, was converted into a nursery for Ruth and Esther Cleveland, and the corner dressing room became the bedroom for their nurse. Mrs. Cleveland purchased a suite of heavy Louis XIII style parlor furniture covered in fashionable cretonne, probably for use in the oval room, which served frequently during the day as a meeting room for the President.[15]

The White House under the second Cleveland administration was ample and comfortable, but not as fully occupied as it had been under the numerous Harrisons or even the widower Arthur. Life for the Clevelands centered on the west end of the second floor hall, with the master bedchamber on the north side, the nursery on the south, and an informal sitting room in the hall between. Beneath their windows on the west were the vast glass and iron conservatories, with their banks of flowers and palms. The lovely fragrance of the glasshouse flowers always flavored the air of the family quarters, where Mrs. Cleveland spent most of her days with her children. At the other end of the long hall Grover Cleveland labored with his staff in rooms stacked with papers and pungent with cigar smoke. The contrast in appearance between home and office was striking, and it seemed odd that two places so different could be contained under the same roof.

The First Lady took Ruth on long walks in the conservatory. She had enriched it with many varieties of orchids, ferns, and palms. It seemed remote from the pressures of the White House; its lemon and lime trees were laden with fruit; the rose house smelled sweet and was bright with summer color year-round. Frances Cleveland's favorite flower was the pansy, and when she happened to remark on an especially pretty one, Pfister made a mental note, then returned and plucked it, so Octavius Pruden could paint it in watercolor as a memento for the President's wife. Such excessive attentions changed Mrs. Cleveland as little as the flattery accorded the President changed her husband. The life they preferred was interrupted by the second four years in the White House, and they were to take it up again with relish in 1897, when they left.

Esther would retain no vivid memories of the place. As a grown woman she went there as a guest; the house had been greatly changed, and the conservatories were gone. Nothing she saw made her recall anything about her first four years of life. But when she entered the family quarters on the second floor, she was struck by a strong recollection of the fragrance of roses, together with mustiness. Back home she asked her mother if she remembered anything curious about the smell of the upstairs of the White House. Mrs. Cleveland thought back over the years and replied yes, "That one floor had the smell of an old house by the sea, a musty scent, overlaid with roses."[16]

27

1898

At the Democratic Convention of 1896, the party was wrenched from the hands of conservative Easterners by a new and liberal coalition of agrarian reformers from the South and West. The candidate nominated for the Presidency was the 36-year-old orator William Jennings Bryan of Nebraska. As his rival the Republicans selected William McKinley of Canton, Ohio, known for many years as an effective congressman, and more recently as governor of Ohio. Backed by a shrewd manager, Mark Hanna, and what was at that time by far the largest campaign fund ever raised in the United States, the conservative McKinley won.

Transition

In her last moments in the White House, standing before the great lunette window at the east end of the upstairs hall, with all the staff assembled to bid her farewell, Mrs. Cleveland broke down and cried. It was not so much that she regretted losing her position as First Lady; it was the idea of leaving a life enriched by so many memories that was painful to her. The couple had disliked the White House; now it was hard to say good-bye. Soon the moment came, and she descended the south stairs to the lawn. She was driven across Lafayette Square to the Lamonts' house to await her husband.

For Cleveland there were no tears, nor did the least expression of sadness seem to lie behind his smiling countenance. As practically all Presidents do, he took a final walk through the state rooms, letting his thoughts return to great scenes in his life. In the Red Room he stopped before the big portrait of himself, painted by Eastman Johnson. Quietly he paused; gazing, doubtless wondering at the contrast of his unpopularity that day to the bright prospects of four years before. When he turned to leave, he asked William Sinclair to take the picture down and store it in the attic, for he saw no reason to impose the Cleveland image upon the new President.[1]

Cleveland preferred McKinley over Bryan, the nominee of his own party and a man he considered an irresponsible Moses of rabble. The inaugural ride from the White House to the Capitol and back again was almost jolly. When the two finally arrived at the White House, where the corridors and parlors were filled with McKinleys and McKinley friends, President McKinley and Cleveland sat alone for a while in the Blue Room and continued chatting. At length the doors were opened to admit a crowd to view the final scene. President and ex-President rose and shook hands cordially.

Hardly had Cleveland passed through the Blue Room door before the silence was shattered by a "frail little lady" dressed in rustling black silk who scampered into the room calling, "Major! Major, where are you?" She stopped, oblivious of the presence of others, "Oh! *there* you are! We'd better start now, the luncheon is announced and all are ready." Colonel Crook, who was there, reported that McKinley calmly stepped forward and went with his wife to the State Dining Room.[2]

McKinley took office under the best of circumstances, replacing a man the people had grown to dislike. Although the depression lingered, the economy improved in the early months of his administration and while this was not the result of his efforts, it gave the public a good feeling about him. The return of prosperity brought with it a surge of building. Washington was no exception; in step with the trend, the Army Corps of Engineers unrolled its drawings of the proposed expansion of the White House. But in grim parallel to good times at home, international affairs were in turmoil. A course of events had commenced which would lead to war with Spain.

The President and His Wife

William McKinley was 54 at the time of his inauguration. The last veteran of the Civil War to hold the office of President, he was tall, distinguished, gentle, patient, and courtly. Something in his face reminded people of Napoleon, a comparison that amused McKinley's close friends, who knew the President's unwarlike personality, but one that

was not overlooked by the press during the Spanish-American War.
Even in candid photographs McKinley looks like a diplomat, comfortable with strict formality. Yet nothing in his demeanor was cold or
distant. He was described as friendly and approachable, democratic by
nature, with wide interests and a firm grasp of the issues of his time.
McKinley came to be nearly universally loved and respected.

His sparrowlike wife, on the other hand, was seen by the few who
ever got close enough to form an opinion as the cross he bore gallantly.
Ida Saxton McKinley was a striking contrast to Mrs. Cleveland. Though
not an old woman—she would pass her 50th birthday three months after
moving to the White House—she was always described as old. She was
small and pale; were it not for her lovely skin and hands, she would have
seemed gaunt. Her heart had been broken by the loss of two children, a
daughter who died in infancy and another who died in her third year.
Like Jane Pierce, half-forgotten in the White House past, Ida McKinley
reasoned that the deaths of her children were punishment from God.

Her outlook had turned sour with her misfortune. Self-pity had
honed her tongue into a sharp defensive weapon, which she used impul-
sively, keeping people always on edge. An epileptic, she was cursed by
illness. She was visited by every passing malady and suffered dark periods
of depression. Together with her personal tragedies, this appears to have
made her draw back emotionally to such an extent that only her husband
could really reach her.

Mrs. John A. Logan, widow of the Civil War general, thought she
was sweet and kind. Her love of children was well known. But she was
spoiled by flattery; this, coupled with anxiety over her epilepsy, made her
irritable. She snapped at those who displeased her. The congenial newspaperman Whitelaw Reid, for example, described as a "misfortune" his
victory over her in a card game. Besting her was not the supreme offense:
Any woman who gave a special smile to McKinley or took his arm would
find a stern judge in Mrs. McKinley, whose tiny body would tremble in
anger as she scolded the guilty lady then and there with a cold glare, if
not with words.[3]

Those who knew McKinley well knew that his attentions to her
were deeply sincere. At social affairs he seldom left her side for fear that
she might have a seizure and need him. When this did take place—
always without warning—he covered her face with his handkerchief or at
table with a napkin, until the attack had passed and she relaxed. "The
relationship between them was one of those rare and beautiful things that
live only in tradition," said their cherished friend Jennie Hobart, wife of
Vice President Garret A. Hobart. And McKinley, in private moments,

1. *In working attire, one of four messengers attached to the President's White House office sits astride his horse near the north portico, ca. 1890.*

2. In William McKinley's War Room, 1898, Benjamin F. Montgomery, at left, mans the telegraph desk. The two men at right are unidentified.

3. Telegraph operators work in the War Room, 1898.

4. President McKinley
dictates to his secretary,
J. Addison Porter,
at the Cabinet table,
where he liked to work.

5. William H. Crook,
1898, executive clerk,
began work at the
White House as a
doorman in the time of
President Lincoln. He
later wrote an account
of his years there.

6. *Flower beds and close-cropped lawn surround a "French glurg" fountain on the north lawn, ca. 1890. Plants from the conservatory were placed about on the lawn from May to October.*

7. *Jerry Smith stands on the north portico in the white "duster" that protected his dark, brass-buttoned livery while he performed house-cleaning duties, ca. 1900.*

8. *Ida Saxton McKinley, in a ball gown with a long train, sits in the first court of the conservatory, just beyond glass doors from the State Dining Room, ca. 1898.*

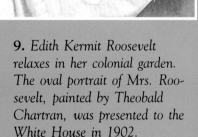

9. Edith Kermit Roosevelt relaxes in her colonial garden. The oval portrait of Mrs. Roosevelt, painted by Theobald Chartran, was presented to the White House in 1902.

10. *Colonel Theodore Bingham's grand scheme for expanding the White House, 1900, with large public spaces, state guest rooms, and press rooms in the wings.*

11. *Edith Roosevelt drew this plan in a letter, September 29, 1901, designating the rooms her family members were to occupy upstairs at the White House. The plan is in most respects accurate, but she included one more bathroom than was actually there.*

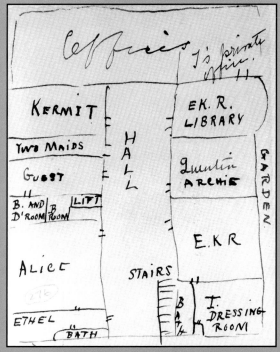

12. *The entrance hall being dismantled, 1902.*

13. *The basement hall, after 1902, shows the original groin vaulting and the new stair to the main floor.*

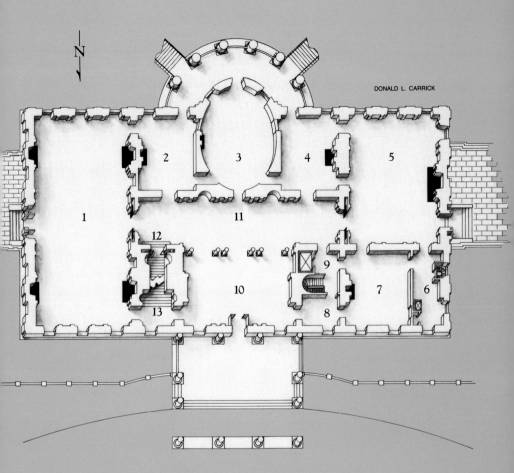

DONALD L. CARRICK

14. Plan of the state floor as remodeled by Theodore Roosevelt in 1902: 1) the East Room; 2) Green Room; 3) Blue Room; 4) Red Room; 5) the enlarged State Dining Room [see plates 16 and 17]; 6) main floor pantry, with its dumbwaiter and a small stair in a window reveal linking it to the family kitchen below; 7) family or private dining room; 8) ushers' office; 9) service hall with elevator and stair; 10) entrance hall; 11) transverse hall; 12) new grand staircase [see plate 20]; and 13) the new stairs from the basement [see plate 13]. Only in the expansion of the dining room and the shifting of the grand staircase did the plan change from Hoban's original [see plate 4, section following page 74].

15. *The State Dining Room as it appeared about 1900.*

16. *The old grand staircase, 1869–1902.*

17. The State Dining Room as redesigned in 1902, with walls paneled in oak waxed to a mellow dark brown. The electric lighting fixtures were silver plated.

18. *The Blue Room as redecorated in 1899.*

19. *The Blue Room after the renovation of 1902.*

20. *The new grand staircase, relocated in 1902,*
provided a striking stage for the President's entrance.

21. *The west side of the White House, showing the conservatory and greenhouses, ca. 1900.*

22. Executive Office Building under construction, 1902, with the last of the doomed greenhouses (right).

23. *The east side of the White House served as the formal entrance to the south grounds, 1869 to 1902.*

24. *The east side became in 1902 the social and appointments entrance to the White House proper. The rooftop terrace opened from the East Room.*

25. *Theodore Roosevelt in the President's Room in the Executive Office Building, 1904. He conducted his most important conferences in the White House.*

used to say to Mrs. Hobart, "Oh, if you could have seen what a beauty Ida was as a girl!"[4]

Mrs. McKinley's habitual weakness usually kept her in her room in the White House, the large Cleveland bedchamber on the north, with its adjoining corner dressing room. She furnished it with several rosewood pieces from the Lincoln bedroom suite, an upholstered lounge and chairs, and a pair of bright brass beds placed side by side. Her favorite "colonial" rocking chair stood near the center table, upon which rested in neat stacks her favorite books and her writing materials. Overhead, the old gas chandelier was a tangle of electric wires and light bulbs, while on the table directly below it stood an electric lamp with a colored-glass shade.

Here, according to her admirer, Mrs. Logan, "Her busy fingers were constantly at work for charity. Before she left the White House she had finished more than three thousand five hundred pairs of knitted slippers for ladies and children, all of which had been given to friends or for charity and invalids." She continued the custom established by Mrs. Hayes 20 years before of sending flowers in place of making personal calls. On each card she wrote a sentiment or signed her name, then dispatched the coachman to deliver the gifts. The wife of George Cortelyou of the office staff, recalled receiving so many White House orchids on the birth of her child that she had not enough vases to contain them.[5]

Occasionally Mrs. McKinley received women callers in her room on the second floor, when she did not feel well and a reception could not be avoided. The ladies presented their invitations at the door and were permitted to wander around in the state rooms until an usher came to escort them up in the elevator. Once in the upper corridor they could expect a brief visit with the First Lady and a glass of ice water.

The young wife of a Texas congressman described one of these visits in her private journal. "The first glimpse of Mrs. McKinley," she wrote, "made me ashamed of coming. She sat propped with pillows in a high armchair with her back to the light. Her color was ghastly, and it was wicked to have dressed her in bright blue velvet with a front of hard white satin spangled with gold. Her poor relaxed hands, holding some pitiful knitting, rested on her lap as if too weak to lift their weight of diamond rings . . . . Her voice was gentle and refined, and her face almost childishly sweet."[6]

Except for her love for the roses from the conservatory, Mrs. McKinley took little interest in the White House. For the palms and the tubbed fruit trees for which the glasshouse was also famous, she had little use. The gardener, Henry Pfister, expanded the collections in the rose house and made rose arrangements for the First Lady every day when she was in residence. She scattered vases of flowers everywhere, often several to a room. When there was a dinner party, the table was always furnished with masses of Mrs. McKinley's favorite blossoms, whether she was to be there or not.

Feelings Against Spain

The year 1898 was not introduced by the usual White House reception because of the death of the President's mother. McKinley observed as long a period of mourning as official etiquette permitted, which was 30 days. The diplomatic community was disappointed by the cancellation of the New Year's event, for the tension between the United States and Spain over Cuba had electrified the international scene, and the diplomats were naturally curious over what might be said and done at a great White House reception.

Revolutions against Spain had been tried in Cuba without success for many years. The latest in the series began in 1895, when Spain suspended the constitutional rights it had granted to the Cuban people 17 years before. Since then, there had been internal peace; now the Cuban countryside once again erupted into guerrilla warfare. By the spring of 1896, 200,000 Spanish troops were suppressing the insurgents and cruelly relocating parts of the peasant population. Accounts of this grim work in American newspapers horrified the public and offended its sense of justice. Americans with property in Cuba were angered for reasons less altruistic. A cry rose for Cuban independence.

Five months after the inauguration, McKinley's minister to Spain, Stewart Woodford, persuaded the queen-regent to stop the ravages. McKinley spoke of Woodford's action to the Congress in December, describing it as a victory. Not wanting war, he asked the usually isolationist American people to stand back and give Spain a chance. For the moment this had a calming effect, but the "yellow press" did not cease to inflame the public with sensational accounts of terror in Cuba.

As a result, the Washington diplomatic community became profoundly interesting to the press and the American people. Flaunting their newfound celebrity in spite of the mourning White House, the ambassadors and ministers made the first weeks of 1898 a joyous season of dinners and balls. Crowds gathered outside the embassy mansions in the evenings to watch the guests arrive. The Spanish minister, the patrician Enrique Dupuy de Lome, was sometimes greeted with hisses. This diplomat had the misfortune of looking rather like a villain, although in the private circles of Washington society some found him warmhearted and charming. Henry Adams wrote that his personal relations with Dupuy de Lome were "so friendly that I cannot openly embrace his enemies."[7]

Under some pressure, the White House at last announced a reception for the evening of January 19. The mourning period was over. As a presidential reception, this event was to be without precedent, there being no general admittance at the door; heretofore most of the great nighttime receptions had been at least in part "public." Two thousand invitations would be issued, and only the holders of these cards would be admitted. The idea for this was Colonel Theodore A. Bingham's, the brilliant though straitlaced and imperious new public buildings officer. A leading member of the Army Corps of Engineers, Bingham had observed for years that the confusion and inconveniences of White House receptions came largely from the liberal policy of admitting the public. He had noted six thousand in attendance at one of Cleveland's receptions; floors had sagged and the President had been exhausted by handshaking. Bingham's solution was to have only invited guests.

McKinley, no stranger to democratic Washington, hesitated at first, fearing the new admission policy would bring accusations of snobbery. But Bingham argued that the receptions were business affairs, held for the benefit of people who counted, and they must no longer be ruined by "such as butchers, cabmen, market and grocery clerks, and the scum of the city." McKinley, who would never have made such a remark himself, let Bingham have his way.[8]

The reception on January 19, 1898, was therefore the smallest in many years. Festive party decorations had not been possible before, because of the crowds. This time the White House was dressed up by the Corps of Engineers, following Bingham's elaborate designs. Few of the diplomats can have been unaware that blazing patriotism inspired the decorations. A wire mesh laden with smilax was suspended from the entire Blue Room ceiling, making sort of a green canopy from which red, white, and blue light bulbs glared down like tawdry stars. Sēnor Dupuy de Lome passed through the line, greeting President and Mrs. McKinley, then Vice President and Mrs. Hobart; the glare of Old Glory's colors shone on the Spanish minister's face.[9]

The brilliance of the occasion would have been remarkable even without Bingham's light bulbs. Two orchestras serenaded—the Marine Band in the conservatory, and the Sixth Cavalry Band in the transverse hall. Guests went first to the Red Room, then they passed into the Blue Room, where the President stood before the windows, with Mrs. McKinley seated in a chair beside him. Court uniform was worn by the diplomats who represented crowned heads, and the attire of many representatives of republics rivaled them in the display of gilt braid and jewels. The women wore court trains at least four feet long. Diamond tiaras held egret feathers and ostrich plumes. Ropes of pearls, white kid gloves, the textures of silk, satin, and velvet filled the state rooms. The White House was a "veritable palace last night," reported the *Washington Post* the next day.

Although the local press praised it, criticism of the restricted guest list was hot and immediate in the out-of-town newspapers. McKinley was accused of exclusiveness, of playing favorites. Bingham was advised later by the President that for most future receptions the White House would revert to tradition.

On February 9, two days before the great reception honoring the Army and the Navy, the New York *Journal* published on its front page a letter written by Enrique Dupuy de Lome to a friend in Havana. It had been intercepted at the Havana post office. In the letter Dupuy de Lome denounced McKinley as a weakling, a "bidder for the admiration of the crowds." That same day the Spanish minister called at the State Department for his passport, and boarded the train to Canada.

The Army and Navy reception at the White House was thus held in an atmosphere of excitement. War fever was building everywhere. Patriotism was once again symbolized in Bingham's decorations—hundreds of American flags were draped over tables, around lamps, on the stair, on the walls; they were clustered like carnival balloons on standards, and tied back at the windows like curtains. Pfister's floral pieces included a great anchor of roses, and a mass of stars made from white roses laid on clouds made of pink roses. Mrs. McKinley descended the grand stair on her husband's arm; against the fury of color from the flags and flowers her costume of white brocade and white lace with a very long train made her seem even paler and older.

The *Maine*

In February, McKinley became distressed by the hovering threat of war. "I have been through one war," he said; "I have seen the dead piled up and I do not want to see another." The newspapers made it seem that the people wanted war, but the President's mail revealed that a large number favored peace with honor. McKinley puzzled over the course he should take. He invited to the White House a succession of old and trusted friends to use as sounding boards for his ideas for maintaining peace. They found him looking worried and were astonished at how much he had aged in a mere year in office. The meetings were nevertheless warm and cordial, held in privacy in the Cabinet Room or the oval room, which was used more for office purposes than as a library. At mealtime, the President led his friends to the central corridor of the family quarters. There he and Mrs. McKinley had created an everyday dining room, with its own oak table and chairs and a sideboard, in the abundant daylight from the great lunette window on the west. In the evenings McKinley, himself fond of scotch, served drinks there to friends. Food was brought up hot on teacarts in the elevator, and the servants left once they had unloaded it.

In mid-February the White House was being prepared for the last public reception of the season. In the newspapers of February 14 the procedures for those planning to attend the next day were announced: where the carriages were to enter, where the coats were to be hung, which path guests were to follow once within the house. Bingham supervised the busy preparations. The state rooms were emptied of most of their furnishings; the bridge and its awnings were set up to the north window; guard stations were established for the Metropolitan Police, as well as plainclothes Secret Service men from the Treasury; palms planted in tubs were hauled from the conservatory into the house.[10]

Early in the morning of the reception day, about three hours after midnight, as everyone else in the disheveled house lay sleeping, a lone usher made his way down the darkened hall and into the McKinleys' bedroom. At the President's bedside he whispered that Secretary of the Navy John Davis Long was on the office telephone with an urgent message. The President ambled, half-dressed, through the series of inner doors to the office, clicking on the electric lamps along his path. The secretary informed him that the battleship *Maine* had exploded and sunk only hours before. Few details were known beyond that; telegrams were arriving by the minute confirming the disaster. McKinley, with the waking nation, would ask who was to blame.[11]

At daybreak, fully dressed, McKinley was again in his office, puffing what was probably not his first cigar of the day. Before him on the table was his telephone. The principal members of the staff had been notified, first his secretary, John Addison Porter, then George Cortelyou, one of Porter's two assistants. The reception scheduled for that night was canceled. Before he had gone down the hall for his breakfast with a nervous, anxious Mrs. McKinley, the President could hear the rumble of many voices in the waiting room outside his door. Senators and congressmen were arriving. Already the cry for war rang in McKinley's ears.

The office staff was assembled early, all but Crook. It had not seemed necessary to call either him or Pendel, the only two members of the White House staff who had been there since the last American war 33 years before. When Crook did arrive, at his accustomed time, he had not seen a newspaper, or talked with anyone on the street. "As soon as I set foot in the White House," he wrote, "I knew that something terrible had happened. Clerks and messengers were hurrying to and fro; the rooms fairly buzzed with excitement; additional emergency operators were swarming into the telegraph room, where messages addressed to the President were arriving from all over the country . . . . Reporters and correspondents were crowding the hallway upstairs."[12]

The Cabinet convened, believing that the sinking of the *Maine* would hurl the United States into war. But McKinley was still determined that there would be no war. While the Cabinet on a vote might well have gone to war, it supported him faithfully.

Joe Cannon Comes To Call

The President made few public statements in the weeks that followed the destruction of the *Maine,* and his popularity suffered. The nation burned with rage, fired by the press and a thousand impassioned orators. McKinley appeared to be blocking the natural course with his pleas for prudence and peaceful actions. Eventually the President began to realize that war was probably unavoidable. Spain's conduct was incompatible with peace, and McKinley's own Republican Party overwhelmingly favored war. Facing the inevitable, he began to prepare.

How to pay for the war was a pressing concern. On Sunday evening, March 6, the President sent a messenger to the hotel of Congressman Joe Cannon of Illinois, with the request that Cannon join him at once. A shrewd political strategist, "Uncle Joe" Cannon was one of the most powerful members of the House, chairman of the House Committee on Appropriations. Ushered to the dark, damask confines of the oval room on the second floor, Cannon recalled that McKinley met him at the door and in his first words came to the point: "Cannon, I must have money to get ready for war. I am doing everything possible to prevent war but it must come, and we are not prepared for war. Who knows where this war will lead us; it may be more than war with Spain. How can I get the money for these extraordinary expenses?" The President, wrote Cannon, "had the matter on his mind to the exclusion of everything else."

At length the congressman was offered a chair, but the President remained standing and "paced the floor with quick nervous strides" while the conversation proceeded. The two agreed that the Congress could

raise the money through an extra tax or a bond issue. "I agreed to introduce a bill," Cannon wrote later, "if he would prepare it." Then, the
congressman recounted, "The President walked over to the table and
wrote on a telegraph blank a single sentence: 'For national defense fifty
million dollars.'" Cannon put the paper in his pocket and left. "It wasn't
a bill nor a Message nor an estimate, but it was the President's memorandum as to what he wanted done . . . ."[13]

The meeting of President and congressman that Sunday evening in
the oval room was to have far-reaching repercussions. Cannon did his
work well; the bill became law three days later, on March 9. Fifty millions were placed at the disposal of the President, to be used for the
defense of the country, with no conditions or committees attached. The
first significant step had been taken toward war, and ultimately toward
the transformation of presidential power.

Peace Before War

A rapid succession of events led to war with Spain. McKinley
courted support among congressmen and senators by having small meetings and "family" dinners at the White House. Mrs. McKinley attended
many of these. Those she could not attend were usually presided over by
Mrs. Hobart, whom she trusted.

There were many visitors at the White House as the weeks of March
passed by. During the day reporters crowded the office stair, leaving
runners or messengers with bicycles stationed outside on the north portico, awaiting reports to rush to the Western Union office. When an
especially exciting event was expected to take place, reporters flowed
into the waiting room upstairs. The President could hear their shuffling
and murmuring through his office door and often took refuge in the
Cabinet Room or the oval room.

Officially the office closed at four in the afternoon, at which time
the office doorman, Charles Loeffler, ordered everyone out. A handful of
reporters sometimes lingered at the northwest gate until long after the
electric lights had blinked on behind the closed linen window shades.
McKinley and his staff worked often into the night. They broke briefly
for supper; the secretaries were served downstairs, and the President
joined his wife for a quiet dinner in the west hall. At about eight McKinley rose from the table and went to his office; he rarely left it before
half past 11. A telegraph operator and usually one other man remained in
the office all night.

Now and then an evening was completely taken up by visits from officials with information or messages. When the secretary of the Navy left town, the assistant secretary, Theodore Roosevelt, seldom failed to find an excuse to call on the President. A vigorous, earnest man in his late 30s, Roosevelt was popular in Washington. McKinley liked him, perhaps admiring the forcefulness that he himself had once displayed.

Ike Hoover remembered that Roosevelt called most frequently during the weeks before the war, usually bringing a satchel of dispatches to show the President. McKinley would sit with him on a sofa in the corridor upstairs, out of hearing of Mrs. McKinley, and discuss the papers. But, as Hoover wrote, "Mr. Roosevelt did most of the discussing, at first merely rising to make his words more forcible, and then striding up and down until his route took in the entire corridor . . . . Never once did he stop talking." As Roosevelt took his leave one night McKinley asked him, if he were President, "in view of all the circumstances," what would he do? "Mr. President," responded Roosevelt, "I would order the whole American Navy to Cuba tonight if I had my way." Roosevelt then turned and walked out the door, "without any pretense of saying good-night."[14]

President McKinley, in no such hurry, continued to deal with the Spanish through the State Department. On Friday, March 25, the report of the findings of the court of inquiry investigating the destruction of the battleship *Maine* was brought quietly to the White House, under guard. The court of inquiry claimed that the explosion was the result of a "submarine mine" outside the ship's hull, but concluded: "The Court has been unable to obtain evidence fixing the responsibility . . . upon any person or persons . . . ."

McKinley made another plea for peace in a message to the Congress accompanying the report on the *Maine*. Late in March, McKinley and the Cabinet made one last proposal to Spain in the interest of peace. The rejection of this offer arrived by telegraph several hours before sunrise on April 1; McKinley then announced that his war message would be sent to the Congress on April 6.

Concern for the safety of American citizens in Cuba and Spain made him delay for five days, during which time there was a last-minute drive to end the controversy peacefully. The diplomatic corps asked permission to call on the President. He received them in the Blue Room; all parties stood. The dean of the corps, Sir Julian Pauncefote, ambassador from Great Britain, read a joint address. He alone among those of the corps who were present had sympathy for the Americans; all the others favored Spain. In his response McKinley observed that he too wanted peace, but they must understand that if the Americans went to war it would be not for themselves but for "humanity's sake."

The war message was delivered to the Congress on Monday morning, April 11, 1898. It was a long and dry recounting of the causes, culminating in a request that the Congress authorize the President to direct a military intervention in Cuba, should it be necessary. The resolution passed on April 20, and McKinley signed it later in the morning in the Cabinet Room, noting the time as 24 minutes past 11. Outside, the waiting room was packed with newsmen, a crush of humanity that extended down the office stair and filled the entrance hall before the glass screen. On the portico the contingent of messengers with their bicycles stood ready. The principal document was placed in what Cortelyou described as a "perfectly plain white envelope of usual size, addressed . . . in handwriting." This was sent by messenger to the official residence of the Spanish minister, Don Luis Pole de Bernabi. Meanwhile, the signing of duplicate documents continued in the Cabinet Room. Several of the Cabinet members wondered whether "ultimatum" was a word preferable to "resolution" in the message.[15]

The President did not look up, or stop writing, when the messenger returned with Don Luis's request for his passport, as well as the minister's wish to know how much time he had. "Judge" William R. Day, the assistant secretary of state and an outspoken war hawk, said he was curious about how much time McKinley had in mind. The President answered, "Until Saturday," then smiled, "Why, judge, I suppose you would like to give him only fifteen minutes." For the first time in many days the tense group in the Cabinet Room relaxed and laughed.[16]

As expected, Spain rejected the ultimatum, and on April 25 the Congress formally declared war. That afternoon at four the war resolution was brought by a congressional delegation to the White House. The President received the men in the Cabinet Room. All day he had moved about nervously, and sleepless nights showed in his face. In constant company with Webb Hayes, son of his Ohio mentor, McKinley went at last to the Cabinet Room, where he sat at the table and surveyed the document lying before him. No one spoke. He signed "William" with one pen, and then, taking a second pen, wrote "McKinley." The two pens he presented to Webb Hayes as souvenirs.

The fighting began in the Pacific, less than a week after the declaration of war. Admiral George Dewey crippled ten Spanish ships at Manila Bay in the Philippines on the first day of May. Nineteen days later Spain's Atlantic fleet arrived in Cuba, where it was harassed by United States naval forces stationed in Key West, Florida. Actual landing of American forces took place on June 6, when 100 marines went ashore at Guantanamo Bay and established Camp McCalla.

As these events were taking place, the war fever had spread to every part of the United States. Volunteer forces sprang up, and drills, parades, and patriotic rallies suddenly became a part of life. On May 21, Saturday, the President reviewed the First Regiment, District of Columbia Volunteers. He stood with his secretaries on the north portico as the regiment, interrupting its march along Pennsylvania Avenue, entered the White House grounds at the northeast gate, rounded the driveway, and departed by the northwest gate.[17]

McKinley's Staff

The President's office force at the White House braced itself for longer hours and heavier responsibilities. Chief over the office staff was the tall, stately John Addison Porter of Connecticut, who styled himself "secretary," instead of the traditional "private secretary," insisting that he was equal in rank to a member of the Cabinet. Porter held his job by virtue of his yeoman service to the McKinley campaign in Connecticut. He was a brilliant political organizer and had political ambitions of his own, hoping one day to be governor of Connecticut.

In most respects Porter was a highly capable man as secretary, but he also had crucial failings that would ultimately lead to his undoing. He was pompous and curt, which made the newsmen, remembering friendships with the genial secretaries of Cleveland and Harrison, detest him. He was not liked by the other members of the office staff, because his relish for his high position made him inconsiderate of them. On April 20, for example, when the resolution was signed, Porter appeared before the reporters in the halls to make the announcement. He praised himself, not the excellent staff support, for moving matters along. The other office workers sat by in annoyance, remaining silent because they realized any public indication of dissension in the office would reflect unfavorably on the President.[18]

Even more serious was his incompetence as an administrator. McKinley, kind and tolerant, did not call him to account, in part from a feeling of gratitude to him for past service and in part because Porter's health, like that of his wife, was failing. But it was to George Cortelyou that President McKinley soon began to turn when he wanted prompt and efficient action. Serious and analytical, Cortelyou had first come to the White House in 1895 as secretary to Mrs. Cleveland. He had proved himself both resourceful and disciplined, and Cleveland had recommended him warmly to McKinley. So attached was Cortelyou to his work that he bore his superior, Porter, in silence, although he confided to his shorthand diary after the events of April 20 that to remain friendly with him "has required all my patience and diplomacy."[19]

Though a man of few words, Cortelyou had a businesslike manner touched with a spirit of camaraderie sufficient to keep the office machinery in happy and constant operation. Where Porter seemed to have no interest in the feelings of his subordinates, Cortelyou was almost as sensitive to them as was McKinley. For example, he once refused a pay raise because his fellow assistant secretary, Octavius Pruden, who had been working in the President's office at the White House far longer, was given none. Gradually more and more responsibility was put in his hands. In 1899 he would replace Porter as secretary to the President.

In theory the office structure was simple, beginning at the top with the President. Below him was Porter; then came Pruden and Cortelyou; next were the eight clerks and six ushers; and at last the five messengers. In practice the hierarchy was often jumbled. By the advent of the war, Cortelyou was the President's principal secretary, in all but name. The balance of the staff members performed many duties outside their assigned areas, often taking on responsibilities meant for others, simply because it was expedient.

Crook, chief disbursement officer, had become venerable by the time his country went to war with Spain. Photographs show a wizened little man with a kindly, comical face, a bald head, and a thick salt-and-pepper beard trimmed neatly in the Prince Edward manner. Visitors delighted in his tours of the East Room and state parlors; he recounted his memories of Lincoln with practiced dignity, proud of being longest at the White House. In fact, Tommy Pendel, who remained in relative silence as an usher, had been there almost as long.

Warren S. Young and Octavius Pruden managed most of the President's official functions. Young looked the part of a social secretary, dapper and bright-eyed, with the smile of a roué. Photographs suggest that he wore a toupee, carefully melded into his own black hair. Pruden was tall and pale, with a thick black moustache. Some of their social powers were usurped by Colonel Bingham during the war, but they had sweet revenge in Bingham's having to return to them constantly for advice. It is probable that no men in Washington were better versed in the personal habits and preferences of the mighty.

Below these officers were anywhere from 12 to 20 clerks, depending upon the need. For the most part, they performed the function of stenographers. Like all male employees of the White House who were not servants, the office staff wore formal morning attire. The only employees of the office who did not were the messengers, whose work took them constantly outside the house, so they wore business suits. "Morning coat"—an ensemble consisting of black cutaway coat, gray-and-black striped trousers, and silk tie—amounted to a White House uniform. Even the President dressed that way when in his office, and visitors calling for the first time at the White House quickly recognized who was "house" and who was not by his manner of dress.[20]

During the war the office was open all but six or seven hours a day, yet it was not nearly as accessible to outsiders as it had once been. Idle callers were admitted in smaller numbers, and members of the press were asked not to use the waiting room as a lounge. Secret Service men from the Treasury Department were stationed on both the first and second floors and in the grounds. That McKinley was probably in danger was known to the inner circle. The mail desk at the White House received many letters threatening his life. Cortelyou recorded some 73 for the months of March and April alone. He looked out from the west windows of the family quarters and worried lest a sniper find a roost on one of the many porches of the State, War, & Navy Building. In the rambling glasshouse he found rattling windows without latches, and called carpenters to secure them with locks.[21]

The press noticed the tightened security and wrote that the President was surrounded at all times by armed guards because he was afraid. Cortelyou dismissed this as a "silly story," noting that the President liked to go on long walks, and did so frequently with friends. More guards, however, served at the White House than ever before. When the Secret Service operatives left the house at the end of the day, they were replaced by a night shift, consisting of a policeman in the transverse hall on the main floor and another in the corridor upstairs. The grounds were patrolled. There were no large public receptions, because the Secret Service feared danger might lurk in the great crowds. Even at the small dinners the guests were scrutinized, and no one was admitted beyond the entrance hall without first presenting the card of invitation he had received and then being identified in person by Octavius Pruden, Warren Young, or someone else on the staff. While the last requirement may at first have appeared inhospitable, it became a matter of course.[22]

The War Room

The office section of the second floor consisted of rooms which had been built for domestic use but which had long since been adapted to business. They looked like converted bedchambers and dressing rooms, each with its fireplace, long windows, and ornamental woodwork.

Everything about the offices seemed temporary. Only the oval room pre-sented a cohesive decor. Beneath a ceiling painted in flowers and gar-lands, with allegories of Reading, Drawing, Writing, and Knowledge, comfortable chairs and sofas were scattered over a fine Wilton carpet. The heavy damask window curtains and those on two inner niches on the opposite walls matched the upholstery of the furniture. Shoulder-high bookcases of mahogany ringed the walls. McKinley sometimes did his late-night work here by gaslight or kerosene lamp, even though Edi-son's incandescent lamps peeked self-consciously from bronze "bouquets" mounted on the wall above the bookcases.

Light bulbs also bristled crazily from the gas chandelier installed by Grant, a large fixture encrusted with gilded leaves. Beneath it was the bizarre center table, upon which McKinley had written his famous note to Joe Cannon; it was richly carved with animal forms. The *Resolute* desk presented to Hayes stood with its back to the central window. Over the mantel hung one of Pierce's great mirrors with a gilded frame, tilted to reflect the densely patterned carpeting, the mahogany, the damask, the soldier-like lines of richly bound volumes on the bookshelves.

McKinley did not use the presidential office, preferring instead the Cabinet Room, which was between the oval room and the office. The south end of the great Cabinet table, the same one used by Grant, was arranged as McKinley's desk, complete with blotter, pen-and-ink stand, clock, calendar, and a row of mounted buzzers for calling his staff. Appar-ently because he used this room so much, McKinley ordered some changes. Since 1865, when it was remodeled as a Cabinet meeting place, the big room had been very plain. At McKinley's request, the Healy portraits of the Presidents were hung in staggered lines on two of the walls, and a French style parlor suite bought by U.S. Grant was reuphol-stered in black leather to match the chairs around the Cabinet tables.

Outside the oval room and Cabinet Room, the business part of the White House was purely functional. The surroundings of Porter, Cor-telyou, Pruden, Young, Crook and others were not in total disarray, but their orderliness was appreciated largely by their occupants. Their desks were in tall chambers, crowded with people and furnishings. In the north rooms rows of matching clerks' desks lined the walls, each with its type-writer and its wire wastebasket. The ceilings were cat's cradles of electric wires, drop light bulbs, and jury-rigged lamps. On the south, the room that had previously served as the office of the President was occupied by Porter, who found it less than private.

One of the office rooms assumed particular importance during McKinley's administration. The narrow chamber on the southeast corner was known officially as the Telegraph and Cipher Bureau, but called the War Room. Between the terms of Andrew Johnson and Rutherford B. Hayes, this had been a telegraph room; otherwise it had served as office for the private secretary. The War Room was a top-secret communications center; access to it was carefully restricted by Loeffler, a German with a heavy accent and a penchant for defying the office dress code by appearing in gaudy—and not readily identifiable—military uniforms. In devising the War Room, McKinley brought the lifeline of war communications under his own wing at the White House, removing it from its traditional place in the War Department. The room itself was ordinary enough. Cortelyou thought it looked like a "telegraph headquarters," being "fitted up with additional typewriters and other paraphernalia." But the French ambassador noted that the work of the War Room was far from ordinary, and that "much of the rapid success of the United States" in the war was because of "the facilities for quick communication afforded by this marvelously equipped department."[23]

Benjamin F. Montgomery, office clerk and official telegraph operator of the White House, presided over the War Room from an oak rolltop desk in the middle of the floor. A little beyond middle life, "Major" Montgomery was overweight, with thick dark hair and a handlebar moustache. He performed his work perfectly, and thus his little realm expanded. New assistants were frequently sent to him from Western Union, as the demands upon the War Room increased. Montgomery had on his desk the principal telegraph keys—the confidential keys—that connected the White House to the various departments and to the Army and the Navy. Lesser receivers were housed in a tall console nearby, which resembled an upright piano. The major alone received the messages that came in on the keys on his desk, and he personally handed them to the secretary, who took them directly to the President.

With time the glass bookcase that lined the north wall of the War Room filled with volumes on history, geography, and international law. The walls themselves, papered in a solid green color, were eventually obscured by rows of maps dotted with round-headed pins locating troop and ship movements. At the time the war began, even as Dewey's Asian fleet sailed to Manila Bay, McKinley had asked that the Philippine Islands be pointed out to him on the large map of the western Pacific. Soon pictures joined the maps on the walls. Stretched across the front of the mantelpiece, a panoramic view of the harbor of Havana showed the mangled hull of the *Maine*. Photographs of all the ships of the fleet were pasted in rows on cardboard backing and hung on the wall or stowed in a print trough brought in from the library.

Porter insisted that he alone move the pins about on the maps, signaling the latest news. The President was likely to pop in anytime, and he might have a dignitary in silent tow. He always took his guests first to the largest of the maps, and the pins helped him to explain the state of the conflict. Wires came in at all hours from Cuba, noting the advance of the Americans. Of interest also were other maps not immediately relevant to the war. Among these was a map of the Hawaiian Islands. In June, McKinley surprised Cortelyou by saying, "We need Hawaii just as much and a good deal more than we did California." The President had not been so pronounced on expansion before. But McKinley went on to add that to expand beyond the continent was America's "manifest destiny." The term had been at rest for many years.[24]

The War Ends

July 1, 1898, early in the morning, the news came to the White House of the Battles of San Juan Hill and Kettle Hill, which ultimately meant the triumph of the land forces, and the fall of Santiago. On July 3 the President was called from his bed by another early morning telegram announcing that the Spanish fleet, which had lain at anchor in Santiago harbor, had challenged the American blockade. Telegrams through the day told in vague terms of a great sea battle. McKinley gathered a group of old and trusted political friends in the War Room. The news did not come until after daybreak the next day, from Admiral W. T. Sampson: "The fleet under my command offers the Nation a Fourth of July present, the destruction of the whole of Cervera's fleet, not one escaped."

The War Room came alive with celebration. "At two o'clock in the morning of July 4th I walked home," wrote one of the company, "with the newsboys crying in my ears the joyful tidings of 'Full account of the destruction of the Spanish fleet!'" By midmorning cheering crowds pressed to the White House fence, calling McKinley's name. Inside the mansion the President spent much of the day alone, but was from time to time with his wife and secretaries. He looked old and tired, his eyes encircled in black.[25]

Diplomacy

Great events came in rapid succession. Acts of imperialism mingled with military victories through the month of July, beginning on the first with the news of San Juan Hill, and the creation of a new hero, Theodore Roosevelt. On July 3 came the destruction of the Spanish fleet;

on July 7 McKinley signed the resolution of the Congress annexing the Hawaiian Islands; on July 17 the city of Santiago surrendered; on July 21 the city of Nipo fell; and on July 25 an expedition ordered by McKinley reached Puerto Rico, the last Spanish colony in the New World.

In the month of July the war thus provided a continuing barrage of fireworks, culminating in its closing days with the beginning negotiations for peace, most of which took place at the White House. The scenes were dramatic in their austerity, centering for the most part on the Cabinet Room, which survives today, to commemorate these events, as the Treaty Room. On July 22 Jules Cambon, ambassador of France, called at the White House and transmitted to the President Spain's overture of peace. The Cabinet was in daily session until July 30, when at two in the afternoon the President returned alone to the Cabinet Room from lunch with Mrs. McKinley, picked up from the table the freshly typed copy of the American response, and passed through the door into the oval room, where the French ambassador and his secretary waited.

The doors were closed and locked and no one emerged until 5:30 p.m. Reporters again filled the waiting room and poured out onto the north portico. They were silent. The afternoon was extremely hot and still. At last, the ambassador and his secretary appeared, threaded through the crowd in silence, and walked out the northwest gate to the sidewalk and toward the French Embassy. George Cortelyou watched them depart from an upstairs window, noting that the reporters stood by, all "Good natured."

The President and the ambassador held a second meeting on August 3, again in the oval room. An agreement was reached between the Spanish and the Americans over the protocol of the peace conference. All that was lacking was the formal signing of the protocol. When this was announced for August 12, the President invited Porter, Cortelyou, Pruden, Montgomery, and Loeffler. It was his way of thanking them, and, as he reminded Cortelyou, "it would be an historic occasion."

The day was dark and rainy, but no less hot, for it was August in Washington. Wind blew the downpour against the windows and jerked the awnings outside like sheets on a clothesline. Electric light shone from the chandelier, dimly illuminating the center part of the room and particularly the Cabinet table, which was empty and polished, save for a blotter and inkstand at the end nearest the corridor. Gilt framed portraits looked down from the walls; books were neatly lined on their shelves, and flags were in place flanking the door to the hall. The signing was to have taken place at the State, War, & Navy Building, but McKinley changed the location to the Cabinet Room in midafternoon, perhaps because of the rainstorm, perhaps because he wanted it to be in the White House. The Cabinet and the invited staff members rose when the ambassador entered. Promptly at 4:30 p.m., to the noise of the furious storm outside, the signing began.[26]

In Paris the peace conference convened on October 1. Through that month and November the commissioners were in constant touch with the President by telegraph, their messages arriving in the War Room at Major Montgomery's desk. McKinley was succinct in his demands for territorial gains, insisting in late October that the United States have the Philippines. The agreement was reached on November 28, and the news was received that day at the White House. December 10 the treaty was signed, removing Spain from the Western Hemisphere.

Six months later on Saturday, June 3, 1899, at 11 a.m., the Spanish minister, the Duke of Arcos, presented his credentials at the White House. He was met at the door by the new Secretary of State, the same John Hay who as a young man had served Lincoln. They walked to the Blue Room door, where Hay presented the minister to Colonel Bingham, who escorted him and his secretaries into the Blue Room. Hay went upstairs in the elevator to the Cabinet Room, to fetch the President.

Soon they were all assembled in the center of the Blue Room. The duke read his address to McKinley in Spanish. McKinley responded by reading a statement in English. They shook hands and remained together briefly, the President asking after the health of the queen consort and King Alphonso. The minister of Spain then took his leave.

28

Grand Schemes

cKinley's skillful assumption of authority during the Spanish-American War had changed the Presidency subtly but effectively. Professor Woodrow Wilson of Princeton University wrote: "The President of the United States is now . . . at the front of affairs, as no president, except Lincoln, has been since the first quarter of the nineteenth century." The President had been granted fifty million dollars with which to defend the country as he saw fit; he had ordered troops to Cuba and the Philippines and at last to Puerto Rico; the President, not the Congress, had dictated the terms of peace, successfully demanding possession of the Philippines. In 1900 he ordered 5,000 American troops to Peking, as part of a joint effort by the Western powers to end the Boxer Rebellion. The newly forceful Presidency had thus not subsided at the close of the war.

Like all Presidents, McKinley had his detractors. Still he was a popular man. He seemed fatherly; gentlemanly and straitlaced, he could make any podium his own, speaking of old American values, family, and honor. Because he seemed to belong to an earlier time, it was ironic that he should be the one to orchestrate the end of long years of American isolation. A major biographer describes him "not as the old-fashioned chief executive nor as the first modern one, but . . . something in between, trying through his policies of conservative conciliation to ease his country and his people into the new position their responsibilities demanded." Those who followed McKinley in the White House would develop and expand the new Presidency. McKinley would die by an assassin's bullet, idolized and lamented.[1]

Colonel Bingham Revives a Plan

The presidential campaign of 1900 was in progress by early summer. McKinley led the Republican ticket, with Theodore Roosevelt, the hero of San Juan Hill, as his running mate. The President's principal opponent was the Democrat William Jennings Bryan, but there were six other parties competing, including the Socialist Labor Party, the Social Democratic Party, the People's Party, the Prohibition Party, the Union Reform Party, and the United Christian Party. McKinley spent most of the summer at his home in Canton, leaving the stumping to others.

With the President away, Colonel Theodore Bingham busied himself in Washington planning a celebration. November 1 would mark the 100th anniversary of the day John Adams took up residence in the White House. The year 1900 was also the anniversary of the official removal of the capital to Washington, and a commission had been entertaining ideas for a suitable commemoration. Bingham envisioned a monument he thought the commissioners would find difficult to resist: a revival of Caroline Harrison's project for expanding the White House. Such an expansion had been a goal of his for several years. An associate had written him the autumn before: "Don't forget that I have been keeping locked within my bosom for more than a year the fact that you had drawn plans for a White House Extension."[2]

Bingham laid his groundwork carefully. Before the President left for Canton, the colonel got him to agree to support a bill that became an act on June 6, 1900, appropriating $6,000 "or so much thereof as might be necessary" for "continuing plans for extending the Executive Mansion." The law placed Bingham in charge. With his encouragement, the Corps of Engineers, which had been involved in all previous plans to reconstruct the White House, began to press its case again in the late 1890s. It was surprised to confront a rival plan promulgated by the Washington philanthropist Mary Foote Henderson. A forceful and erratic woman backed by power and wealth, Mrs. Henderson was the wife of former Senator John Brooks Henderson, the author of the 13th Amendment abolishing slavery. She loved Washington and had envisioned her city for years as a new Paris; she had spent a fortune over two decades spangling it with elegant mansions, many of which she eventually sold as residences and embassies. Mrs. Henderson's interest in a new White House went back to Reconstruction days, when her uncle, Vermont Senator Solomon Foote, had taken her to Meridian Hill and described the presidential mansion that he hoped would one day be built there.

In 1898, responding to the wishes of her long-dead uncle, Mrs.

Henderson engaged Paul J. Pelz, one of the two architects of the Library of Congress, to plan a magnificent executive mansion for the crest of Meridian Hill. She published a brochure in December of that year showing Pelz's drawing and announcing her idea, which it reflected. The Corps of Engineers was being challenged by its own scheme of 1867.[3]

Through the next year, Bingham emphatically furthered the cause of the corps, while Mrs. Henderson and Pelz politicked for their plan. No open conflict took place, although there were hard feelings between Pelz and the corps. The Army engineers had taken over his Library of Congress project, making alterations and elaborations of which he did not approve. In February 1900 Bingham, determined to prevail, obtained official endorsement of his projected expansion from the District of Columbia Centennial Commission. With this in hand he went to the McKinleys for approval, which he received only in halfhearted nods. Mrs. McKinley had "served notice" on the aged Senator William Boyd Allison of Iowa that there would be "no hammering" while she lived in the White House. Bingham nevertheless proclaimed the presidential consent a triumph: Mrs. Henderson had labored in vain.[4]

The colonel went to Frederick D. Owen, the engineer who had drawn the project for Mrs. Harrison, and together they studied the original plans. Ideas concerning architecture had changed since 1882, and Bingham ordered many alterations. The prevailing taste in government architecture ranged from the massive Richardsonian Romanesque post office to the Library of Congress, which, though neoclassical, was heavily ornamented. Colonel Bingham, like his fellow engineers in the corps, considered the library the paragon of beauty. In a sense it was the corps' own, having been superintended and in part redesigned by Colonel Thomas Lincoln Casey, a mentor of the Corps of Engineers and, under President Hayes two decades before, the distinguished occupant of the post now held by Bingham.

Since the outbreak of the Spanish-American War, Frederick Owen had been assistant draftsman in the Navy's Bureau of Construction and Repair. On July 6 he transferred to Bingham's office to pursue the White House project full time. He began his task that day, increasing the richness of materials, while trying to reduce the size of the additions. Mahogany and oak were to be the main finish materials inside, used in profusion; the exterior was to be white marble; state guest suites would be added, each with bathrooms and dressing rooms; ballrooms, drawing rooms, and promenades were to be designed to hold great crowds; the service areas, beneath the west end of the principal floor, were to be equivalent to those in a grand hotel.[5]

Silk for the Walls

Some remodeling had already taken place at the White House, necessitated by wartime wear and tear. The state rooms needed redecorating at the close of the season in May of 1899. E. S. Yergason, now on his own in New York, was called in once again. His work for Mrs. Harrison when he had been employed by the William H. Post Company in Boston had placed him in good stead with the ushers at the White House, and in April 1899 he called on Mrs. McKinley with samples of fabrics, most of them silk. Fabric was to be stretched on the Blue Room walls, a custom which prevails in some of the state rooms today.[6]

While the other rooms received only gilding and some paint, the Blue Room was fully redecorated. Yergason did the planning, and Bingham saw that the work got done, using the local furniture and upholstery house, W. B. Moses & Sons, which had performed such services for the White House since before the Civil War. The completed Blue Room was described as being in the "colonial" style.

A surviving fragment of the damask for the walls and furniture shows a robin's-egg-blue background, with large cartouches of leaves and little roses, all in darker blue, highlighted in beige. Long rectangles of the same damask were framed on the walls by plaster molding, outside which the walls were papered in a darker blue. The "colonial ivory" wainscoting and deep frieze were heavily textured papier mâché embossed to suggest 18th-century garlands and wreaths. Increased electric light allowed the use of softer colors, which would have been dull under gaslight. The number of light bulbs in the glass and nickel-plate chandelier was doubled; the walls were lighted from above the damask panels by brackets of cast bronze representing sprays of roses, each flower containing a light bulb. In the incandescent light, the damask gave off a sheen, in contrast to the matte finish of the wallpaper and the low gloss of the ivory trimmings.[7]

The redecoration of the Blue Room was the McKinleys' principal mark on the White House. The bedroom they used, the large, square room on the northwest, had been freshly painted by President Cleveland as a friendly gesture. Alas, he selected yellow. Upon seeing it, Mrs. McKinley turned abruptly and left the room. She demanded that it be repainted in pink before she would enter it again, for she loathed yellow. Inventories and photographs show the second floor family quarters as uncluttered, well dusted, starched, polished—and plain. The only bed made of wood left on the second floor was the Lincoln bed; the rest were either polished brass or painted iron, both considered at the time to be more sanitary than wood. Chairs were scattered about, some stuffed, some of wicker with loose cushions. Dresser scarves and doilies adorned most of the flat surfaces, as they doubtless did at the McKinleys' home in Canton. All the floors, like those downstairs, were carpeted wall to wall, and the patterns were simple.[8]

One Hundred Years Old

The McKinleys were in Canton for the election in November 1900. His victory did not come as a surprise, although the President had certainly not been sanguine. He interpreted his reelection as a milestone in history. The first President to succeed himself in office since Grant, he proclaimed: "I can no longer be called the President of a party. I am now the President of the whole people."

Meanwhile, Colonel Bingham finalized plans for the centennial celebration as he polished his campaign to enlarge the White House. Because of the presidential election, the centennial could not be staged in November, on the true anniversary of the first occupation of the White House. Instead the colonel chose December 12, 1900, which made his event a part of a longer celebration being held elsewhere in the capital to commemorate the centenary of the government's removal from Philadelphia to Washington. He had hoped for a groundbreaking; when this was denied, he scheduled a midday luncheon and ceremony at the White House, at which he planned to make a formal announcement of the transformation to come.[9]

For the occasion, Frederick Owen supervised the construction of a scale model in white plaster, showing the old White House and the proposed additions. This project had been modified considerably from Mrs. Harrison's. The house was to be given two-story wings on the east and west, each with a heavy wing projecting to the south, forming a U-shape, as opposed to Mrs. Harrison's quadrangle.

Mrs. Harrison's semicircular colonnades on the sides, suggested by the arcades at Mount Vernon, had become large colonnaded rotundas, full-scale buildings instead of connecting passages to wings. This modification seems to have come not from Mrs. Harrison's plan, but from research Bingham had done on Leinster House, widely acknowledged as the model for the White House. During the winter of 1900 Bingham obtained both photographs and drawings of Leinster House through the American consul in Dublin. After being sold by the Fitzgeralds, the old palace on Kildare Street had served for many years as the headquarters of the Royal Dublin Society, gaining in the process two forward-projecting wings with monumental circular colonnades. These were designed in 1884 by Thomas Manly Deane of Dublin and his father, Sir Thomas. The younger Deane sent tracings of his plans and elevations to Colonel Bingham, and it is obvious that they inspired the rotundas of Bingham's White House plan.[10]

Bingham's rotundas were crowned by domes and lanterns patterned on those on the Library of Congress. To the south of the rotundas were relatively short projections meant to serve as official entrances, with heavy marble stairs, porte cocheres, and a profusion of carved ornament. The most prominent architectural features on the south ends of the wings were great half-moon windows, copies of the original lunettes on the ends of the White House, both of which would be lost when Bingham's additions were carried out.

Inside, the plan seemed in some respects more like a state capitol than a house, but its size and arrangement handsomely fit White House needs. The west rotunda was to become an extension of the family quarters upstairs, while on the same level on the east there would be a large office suite. Public access to the office would be through a lobby on the main floor of the east wing. Nearby, there would be an ample press room. Otherwise, all the first story was to be the state floor, with the old parlors and East Room intact, but with a new dining room and reception rooms. The new State Dining Room, large enough to seat more than 200 guests, filled the circle of the west rotunda.

Bingham believed that the quadrangle projected by Mrs. Harrison would ultimately be constructed, for in 25 years or so the need for space would require further additions. He had traced the history of the White House through federal documents and saw it as a building that had always been interesting: "It was a delightful study to trace up the sources of Hoban's inspiration, and see how, point by point, he had improved on his first idea." The colonel considered his plan not only a practical solution to the problem of space, but also historically legitimate. He believed the White House should grow, as Washington had intended.[11]

On the day of the anniversary ceremony, the 100 guests began to arrive at the White House just before noon. Owen had set up his model in the center of the Blue Room. The curtains were drawn back to help the guests better sense the site, with the idea that while enjoying the beautiful views they could imagine the enlarged mansion. President and Mrs. McKinley entered the Blue Room at 11:45 and greeted everyone warmly. He made no official remarks, but he closely inspected the model, walking all around it with his spectacles on, before he led the company to the State Dining Room for lunch. Later, as coffee was passed, Bingham was introduced in flattering terms, and he rose to present a history of the White House, the main feature of the occasion.

"Mr. President, Ladies and Gentlemen," he began, "in the spring of 1792 the commissioners of public buildings and grounds, under the immediate direction of the President, undertook the preparation of plans for the President's House . . . . In December, 1900, the commissioner of public buildings and grounds presents to you a plan for enlarging the President's House." The history became a sales pitch, with the text covering some six pages in small type. It is persuasive, even over the distance of years, for Bingham was no stranger to getting his way.[12]

Opposing Views

Opposition to Bingham's plan was apparent before the centennial luncheon, although the newspapers reported his presentation as a success. A man less isolated in his own sphere than Bingham might have been more cautious in his treatment of inquiring architects, even as the plan was being drawn. Daniel H. Burnham, a powerful and beloved figure in the architectural profession, offered to leave his busy practice in Chicago and journey to Washington to study Bingham's scheme, making suggestions without cost. At first Bingham agreed, then changed his mind; Burnham was on a train en route to the capital when he received the telegram canceling his appointment. If the father of the Columbian Exposition of 1893 was annoyed, his colleagues, who had pressed Burnham to go, were furious.

Bingham made it clear that the White House was his turf. He determined to abide no interference. One week before Christmas of 1900, he moved the model from the Blue Room to the East Room so the public could view it. Very likely Bingham's opponents would have taken stronger stands had the officer in charge of the public buildings not made it so conspicuous that the President had approved the plan. No one wanted to offend McKinley, but objections to the taste shown in the plan had been privately voiced among those attending the centennial luncheon. The movement to stop Bingham involved local arts clubs in Washington, including the Public Art League, as well as the Washington chapter of the American Institute of Architects. Ignored by Bingham, they were forced to seek support from outside, and it was the American Institute of Architects, which had useful national connections, as well as having its professional standards at stake, which led the attack.

The most vocal of the architects was Glenn Brown, a 46-year-old colonial revivalist with an active, if not flourishing, practice in the city.

Brown devoted much of his time to professional organizations in the arts, and he ably served the A.I.A. as its national secretary. The Virginia-born Brown—proud great-grandson of Peter Lennox, the principal carpenter and joiner of the original White House—felt deep family roots in the old mansion. He further had a grudge against Colonel Bingham. Only a year earlier Brown had produced a set of plumbing drawings for Bingham under contract, only to have his name removed and the drawings published under Bingham's name. As the officer in charge of public buildings, Bingham was a department head and his act was not unusual at the time either for the government or for large architectural firms. But Glenn Brown resented it, and 30 years later he expressed his regret at not having taken the matter to court.

The profession of architecture was changing, and Brown's sensitivity reflected it. Throughout the last quarter of the 19th century, but especially by the 1890s, American architects had been trying to gain recognition as professionals apart from engineers, who usually claimed to have the same skills at design and building. Private architects had virtually no chance at all to get government work; while a large architectural office flourished under the Treasury, much of the government work was carried out by engineers. From an architect's point of view the situation at the White House was classic: An engineer, Bingham had employed another engineer, Frederick Owen, to do work that should have been in the hands of an architect.

"Col. Bingham," wrote Brown years later, "was ambitious to have his name prominently connected with the White House. With this end in view he employed some mechanical draughtsmen to make plans . . . he did not employ an architect or architectural draughtsman as to them credit might have to be given; and it would not be his production." Brown was not always fair in his criticism of Bingham, and he sometimes misrepresented the colonel's views; but not all his criticism was aimed at Bingham. He loathed the centennial project which "called for additions to the east and west, each of them larger than the present White House . . . . It was a mongrel, unrecognizable contraption, out of harmony with and destroying the individuality of the old building." Brown was elected chairman of a local union of art clubs, suggested by him as a means of opposing the Bingham plan.[13]

Scattered local forces gradually began to come together and spread through the members of the A.I.A.; by the close of 1900 Brown was leading a movement of greater extent than he could likely have anticipated at the outset. Nationally the cause of the architectural profession had lost its luster. By appearing to be on a quest to rescue the White

House, the A.I.A. set itself up as the leader in a heroic undertaking, which had implications for Washington beyond the design of only one building. Chicago's White City, the great World's Fair complex of 1893, had done more than anything else to illustrate the high standards of beauty the architect had to offer, and it had been gone for six years. Why not make in Washington a permanent monument to take its place? By no coincidence, the national convention of the A.I.A. was scheduled during the centennial celebration of the city of Washington. Brown planned every detail, making the centerpiece of the meeting a historical symposium on early plans for the city. This was highly successful.

At McKinley's luncheon, when Bingham announced his plans for the White House, the Centennial Commission, which was in charge of the commemorative activities in the city, unveiled an additional plan for an ambitious "Centennial Avenue," to be built down the center of the Mall. Bingham claimed that it had been inspired by L'Enfant's original design. A small group of architects, invited to represent the convention at the luncheon, made it their business to leave after the ceremony in company with Senator James McMillan of Michigan. Chairman of the Senate's Centennial Committee, McMillan was known as the father of Detroit's model system of public parks. He was interested in seeing Washington likewise beautified, and for that reason he had gone along with Bingham's plans for the White House and Centennial Avenue. The drawings presented by the engineers had disappointed him, and in conversation he expressed himself sufficiently for the architects to realize that they had at last a friend at court.

At professional meetings in the course of the A.I.A. convention, the architects expressed dismay over Bingham's plans. George B. Post of New York, one of the most prominent men in the field, worried that the plaster model would win popular support for Bingham's project. Other architects criticized the design because they did not consider Owen an architect. Back at the convention, the subject was abruptly brought to the floor. Glenn Brown was ready and waiting to set the architects aflame with his denouncement of the project. And, as will be seen later, wheels of opposition had already started grinding at the Capitol.

A few days after the centennial had ended, and the architects had gone home, Bingham received a letter from the art critic for the *New York Times*. Montgomery Schuyler urged him not to build so soon, but to work toward establishing a congressional arts commission, which could draw an overall plan for the city. The White House could then be remodeled in harmony with the improved landscape of the capital.[14]

The colonel feared the press enough to be courteous in his response to Schuyler, but said that such arts commissions had proved "dismal failures" in the past. "I can tell you of a number of cases," wrote Bingham. "The average Congressman says, 'to hell with art.' I find that there is a general disinclination among Congressmen to deal with 'art commissions,' just as the honest ones shirk from anything involving a real estate purchase . . . . if the White House is to be extended in the immediate future, I venture to say that the only way will be to take my plan, appropriate money to carry it out, directing and authorizing me to have it criticized by architects 'of conspicuous ability,' leaving the final decisions in the hands of the Chief of Engineers, U.S. Army."

Bingham's letter did not hide his contempt for those he saw as his adversaries. To him the protests represented further efforts on the part of private practitioners to win work on government projects, efforts that he had resisted through the previous decade. "I have declined to be made use of for the purpose of the architectural guild here," he wrote. "I should be glad to see and talk to any reputable architect who may desire to discuss the question in a perfectly open way without ulterior motives."[15]

Last Words

There was no White House season of 1901, or the colonel's model would doubtless have been banished to the basement for need of space. Festivities at the inauguration in March were dampened by Mrs. McKinley's sudden lapse into bad health, which, according to Tommy Pendel, required that she be moved about in a "rolling chair." She was unable to receive as First Lady. The President, always her loyal protector, stayed near her at the White House, and early in the summer when she rallied enough to wish to go home, he took her to Canton, where they spent many leisurely days together. Late in June she felt well enough to accompany McKinley to California. Private cars were fitted for her, and the trip went well until, in San Francisco, she fell desperately ill and was thought to be dying.

She improved, however, and traveled back to the White House, where the McKinleys entertained a small group of friends on the Fourth of July. The next day, bundled up in spite of the midsummer heat, Mrs. McKinley accompanied her husband to the railroad station, once again to leave for Ohio. They spent the rest of the summer in Canton, then traveled to Buffalo, New York, in early September to attend the Pan-American Exposition.

The White House was quiet during the balance of July and August, and by the sultry days of early September many little projects such as adding electric wiring and killing rats had been accomplished, which might have been more difficult with the President in residence. On September 6, at about 4:30 p.m., Major Montgomery was sitting idly at his desk when one of the telegraph keys "snapped out a few words." Crying out in horror, he jumped to his feet and read again the words he had so automatically transcribed.

The message was from the chief operator at Western Union in Buffalo: The President had been shot "by an American Anarchist." Montgomery now put his key into operation, wiring direct to the exposition grounds for more information. Meanwhile, Crook remembered, the news "flew like wildfire through the White House." Tommy Pendel, who was in the entrance hall at his post, heard Jerry Smith shout down the office stair, "The President is shot!" In the War Room, now filling with people, Montgomery tried to keep his voice calm, while he wept openly. Colonel Crook scanned the telegram once again; "Good God!" he cried to himself, his thoughts racing over 35 years, "First Lincoln—then Garfield—and now McKinley!"[16]

The President had been shot by Leon F. Czolgosz while standing in a receiving line at the exposition. The assassin had concealed his pistol from the guards by wrapping it with his hand in a handkerchief, so that the hand appeared to be bandaged. Mrs. McKinley was not present. The President was taken by electric ambulance to the infirmary at the exposition. After emergency surgery failed to locate the bullet, he was transferred to the private residence where he and Mrs. McKinley were guests.

Cortelyou, by now promoted to private secretary, had been at McKinley's side when he was shot, and he held the President in his arms. The secretary took control, issuing regular bulletins on McKinley's condition. While there were days with optimistic reports, the President's death early in the morning of September 14 came as no surprise. The end had been coming slowly throughout the day before. "Nearer my God to thee," McKinley had said, before drifting into incoherence.

The next morning the office staff arrived early at the White House. The flag on the roof flew at half-mast. A sign had been hung behind the glass front door: "Closed." Bingham was already there, giving orders and making plans; he worked effectively under pressure. The East Room was closed and darkened, the White House model removed. Crape was being threaded through the globes and prisms of the three great chandeliers.[17]

McKinley's funeral train arrived in Washington in the evening of Monday, September 16, 1901. The coffin was lifted out the window of the palace car and taken to the East Room, where an honor guard surrounded it through the night. It was banked in flowers. Masses of flowers lined the transverse hall, floral tributes from the states, from clubs, from citizens; Pfister interspersed palms and fruit trees among the baskets, crosses, and wreaths. Mrs. McKinley went to the East Room alone to pray at the coffin, holding up with remarkable strength. Those close to her knew she had at first said that she wished God would take her as well.

On Tuesday, the coffin was removed to the Capitol for the state funeral. That day Mrs. McKinley descended in the elevator, frail and stone-faced, veiled in black. George Cortelyou and his wife and several others were with her. At the conclusion of the funeral she followed the flag-draped coffin down the long east steps of the Capitol and joined the funeral procession to the train depot. Looking neither to the right nor the left, she boarded the funeral train for Canton, leaving Washington forever.

When Cortelyou returned from Ohio he went to the White House family quarters, where he spent two days emptying the drawers and wardrobes, stripping from the tops of the dressers and mantels the collections of perfume bottles, souvenirs, pincushions, knitted fancy-pieces, and family pictures. These effects, carefully wrapped in tissue paper, were packed in trunks and crates and marked for shipment to Mrs. McKinley.[18]

Signs

The train that bore Cortelyou back to Washington the day after McKinley's burial also carried as a passenger McKinley's successor. Theodore Roosevelt had remained quiet and contemplative since taking the oath of office in Buffalo. His wife and family had remained in seclusion at their summer home on Long Island, near Oyster Bay. The train from Canton arrived in Washington on September 20, 1901, having traveled all night. Soon Colonel Crook was looking at his watch and recording 9:30 a.m., the moment Roosevelt entered the White House as President of the United States.

Without formally meeting the office employees, Roosevelt stayed close to Cortelyou. The Cabinet met for several hours. Roosevelt then went to the home of his sister Bamie, wife of Commodore William Sheffield Cowles, and for several days commuted from there to the office every morning. At the White House he worked in peace and quiet, for the flowers on McKinley's grave had not yet wilted, nor had the eulogies ceased in towns and cities across America.

Two days later, at dusk, Roosevelt concluded his office work, but this time remained at the White House. It was his first night there, September 22, 1901, and he had as dinner guests his two sisters who

lived in Washington, Bamie Cowles and Corinne, Mrs. Douglas Robinson. The sisters and their husbands ate with the President in the family
dining room. Roosevelt reminded them that it was their late father's
birthday—he would have been 70 years of age.[19]

"I have realized it," said Roosevelt, "as I signed papers all day long,
and I feel that it is a good omen that I begin my duties in this house on
this day. I feel as if my father's hand were on my shoulder, and as if there
were a special blessing over the life I am to lead here."

Later in the Red Room, when coffee was served, special notice was
taken of the customary rosebud from the conservatory placed on each
saucer. This was a tradition begun probably by Mrs. Cleveland, but its
special charm that night was that the buds were of the saffronia rose. "Is
it not strange!" the President said. "This is the rose we all connect with
my father." The sisters were also touched, Corinne remembering how
"whenever we gave him a rose, we gave him one of those."

"I think," said Roosevelt, "there is a blessing connected with this."

29

An Image Refined

Theodore Roosevelt soon possessed the house. On the morning after the dinner party, he assembled the office staff and lined the men up in military fashion. The President greeted them, expressing his delight that his work force was so large. Everyone then set to work and, according to Colonel Crook, they did not break the pace for the 7½ years Roosevelt was President.

The Roosevelts

Mrs. Roosevelt, the children, many maids, and the baggage arrived on September 27, 1901, with a contingent of pets that ranged from birds to a pony. For the White House, the incoming procession had no recent precedent. The youngest of the six Roosevelt children was almost 4, the oldest 16. The last children to live in the White house had been Cleveland's, mere babies; before them there had been the infant McKees, Harrison's grandchildren. Garfield's sons and daughter had been the last children old enough to play ball, ride horses, and generally enliven the sedate White House.

No one on the staff could remember when a family had so completely occupied the place. Storage in the attic was shifted to make bedrooms for personal maids; the eight rooms in the private quarters overflowed with children. In the dining room set up by the McKinleys in the west hall, the Roosevelts ate hearty breakfasts, in full view of the wardrobes, trunks, and cabinets that crowded along the walls all the way down to the office doors. Two maids slept in the small passage that led to the window over the north door. Only two bathrooms served the family quarters. One was for the presidential bedchamber; the other, a "family bathroom" for everyone else, including guests, had three doors in addition to having partitions only head-high, making compartments for lavatories, toilets, and bathtubs. Bingham was certain these inconveniences would bring his grand scheme ever closer to acceptance. He was always present with assistance and advice. [1]

Despite the cramped quarters—and although relationships within the Roosevelt family had not always been harmonious—their lives at the White House were charmed from the start. Any reluctance about living in so visible a place was well concealed, for they were present everywhere, and thoroughly enjoying it. The sedateness of the south lawn was broken by a grazing pony, ducks in the fountain, an abundance of dogs and cats, and numbers of frolicking children. Tourists in the somber East Room were startled when the littlest Roosevelt, Quentin, burst up like a jack-in-the-box from one of the palm vases sunk in the center of the circular divans, to audible giggles from fellow conspirators hiding behind the curtains. Stories of the antics of the Roosevelt children in the White House are legion. But for all the fun and frolic, the President and Mrs. Roosevelt were too conscious of their public responsibilities to permit appearances of lax home discipline. It was an era in which strongly defined family roles were considered important, and the Roosevelts wanted to be models of domestic propriety.

Roosevelt was a little more than a month short of his 43rd birthday when he took office, the youngest yet to hold the job. His small stature surprised people when they met him for the first time. He carried 50 or 60 pounds of excess weight, made less obvious by skillfully tailored clothes. He loved to eat, and he matched his big appetite with strenuous exercise. His gregariousness was infectious; his boyish personality disarmed those who expected a President to be formal and dignified, as were McKinley, Cleveland, and Harrison.

Like his children, Roosevelt delighted in living at the White House. A student of history, he was fascinated by historical relics. He ordered the brass beds removed from the presidential bedroom and replaced by what he called the "Lincoln bed." Lincoln was his hero, and the high-backed rosewood bed, long used in the state guest room, was thenceforward identified with the Civil War President. He enjoyed the presidential portraits as had Andrew Johnson before him. Anecdotes of the White House past interested him, as they had Hayes, and he liked to mingle them with his own adventures in the narrative stream with which he dominated the dinner table.

Mrs. Roosevelt, Edith Kermit Carow, was just under three years her husband's junior. They had known each other nearly all their lives, and had married in London in 1886, two years after the death of Roosevelt's first wife. Family friends would later say that their real happiness together began after they moved into the White House. Edith Roosevelt was pretty, but not beautiful; she was freckled and red-haired, without delicate features, but with an engaging, sunny disposition. Her judgments of people were valuable to her husband, for she was far more shrewd about them than he. With no interest in personal recognition, she was the ideal helpmate for President Roosevelt.

She was often photographed in white, nearly always carrying a parasol and wearing the crisp puffed sleeves and big hats of the day. She loved gardening and books and looked upon the strict maintenance of the social forms as a duty. Relatives and friends were numerous, and guests were frequent, both at Sagamore Hill, the Roosevelt farm, and at the White House. The Roosevelts enjoyed people and had company nearly every day. She arranged most of her entertaining around lunch and dinner, leaving the rest of each day free to accommodate the President's schedule and their private family life.

The Roosevelts made a marked change in the White House image. Their family backgrounds and their personal natures contrasted sharply with those of most of their predecessors. They were both from long lines of distinguished Americans of wealth and settled circumstances, reflecting a class system growing older; blood or cherished family ties connected them with the urban East and him, through his mother, to the plantation South. Roosevelt had always been financially independent enough to pursue whatever attracted him. None of the Presidents before him had been born to such complete freedom.[2]

A Dinner Party

For the first year Roosevelt left the White House more or less as he found it, but made hard use of it. The early months were a period of tense trial and error. He had not been sent by the voters to live in the White House, but moved in only after the death of the elected President. Therefore he lacked the public and party power to support the new international Presidency that McKinley had created. Roosevelt never seems to have doubted his ability to build a following, yet he knew time was of the essence. To help firm his grip on the Presidency, he set out to make the White House his stage. On it he would make his life a performance dramatizing himself and his ideas.

As soon as October 19 had passed, ending the official mourning period for the slain McKinley, the white damask tablecloths were unfolded again over the long table in the State Dining Room. The Roosevelts were ready to thrill the world with their style. An air of naturalness, even innocence, gave their entertaining special flavor. They were fond of dinners and held them nearly every night during the last two months of 1901. Genial hosts, they carefully constructed each guest list with a shrewd eye to politics.[3]

One of these early dinners put White House hospitality on the front pages, surprising the President with a controversy that made him step more cautiously thereafter. This dinner was actually held before the mourning period was officially over, and was the kind of quiet affair that Presidents often call "family supper." On October 16, Roosevelt had among his guests the educator Booker T. Washington, whose autobiography, Up From Slavery, was then highly popular.

The invitation was issued as soon as the President heard Professor Washington was to be in town. Roosevelt liked to ask such callers as were in his office at noontime to accompany him downstairs to lunch; often he scheduled appointments with this in mind. When the day was too full to allow for a useful visit during office hours, he often invited people he wished to see on business to dinner with him and his family. The dinner invitation was awaiting Washington when he arrived in the city, and he called at the north door of the White House promptly at eight. In the Blue Room he joined the other dinner guest, Philip B. Stewart of Colorado. Dinner was probably in the State Dining Room since the party was in evening dress. The guests remembered a simple, cordial evening.

Next morning the dinner was announced in the press in various parts of the country through a news release sent out by Cortelyou. Most, though not all, White House guests were published in the same way: "Booker T. Washington, of Tuskegee, Alabama, dined with the President last evening." The press reaction was nearly instantaneous; the dinner guest made the hottest news since McKinley's assassination. Editorials in the South—but not only in the South— were sometimes harsh in their criticism. Where details of the evening were concerned—insofar as this mattered— the press could say nothing substantial, for no one present at the dinner issued a single word on the subject.

"Probably the First Negro Ever Entertained at the White House," speculated the Atlanta Constitution. Most of the other papers said the same, and to some extent they were correct. Mrs. Lincoln is supposed to have received a party of black women and a white minister in the Red Room; Lincoln signed Sojourner Truth's autograph book at the White

House when she came to see him; Hayes had Frederick Douglass preside at concerts of black performers in the East Room. People in 1829 had been astonished by the boldness of the blacks who entered the White House during Andrew Jackson's inaugural festivities. But in the last quarter of the 19th century, as a policy, blacks were not admitted to the receptions. The writers of occasional accounts suggesting that blacks may have been in attendance probably confused guests with menservants wearing formal attire. From all indications, no Negro received a social invitation to the White House before Booker T. Washington in 1901, nor did any thereafter for many years.

The nationwide furor over the dinner provided a strong indication of growing bigotry. It also gave the President a clear illustration of the power of the White House to symbolize. No documentary sources suggest that Roosevelt himself even suspected that the dinner would have such an unfortunate result, although he must have known that his extending the invitation was out of the ordinary. At the close of the administration, one of the Cabinet members confided to his diary: "The President, in speaking of his actions while in office, mentioned the inviting of Booker Washington to a meal at the White House as a mistake on his part; not in the action itself, but the effect on the South was injurious and misinterpreted."

Roosevelt assured a friend at the time that he had given little thought to the matter beforehand, and said to someone else that it seemed to him a perfectly natural thing to do, to "show some respect to a man whom I cordially esteem as a good citizen and a good American." The affair is the most conspicuous example of the difficulty the young President had now and then in adjusting to the impositions of White House life. Political repercussions from the Washington dinner were of long duration; for the rest of the administration it was often pointed out as an example of Roosevelt's insensitivity and imperiousness. It may well be that the incident gave rise to the strict, sometimes self-conscious social decorum that the Roosevelts imposed upon social life at the President's House in the years that followed.[4]

Bingham on the Defensive

When Theodore Roosevelt became President, the controversy over the proposed White House expansion had been pushed from the papers by more immediate news. The new President was too much occupied with more pressing work to be concerned with remodeling. Nevertheless, both sides hoped he would intervene at once; opinions were tossed at him from afar. Letters opposing Bingham's plan began to pour in. Glenn Brown vented his wrath against the plan not only in professional publications but also in *Century* magazine, which Roosevelt read avidly and for which he had written.[5]

Still Roosevelt was occupied with other things. Only once in the early months did he turn his attention briefly to the White House: Before the close of 1901 he issued an executive order changing the official name of his new residence from the Executive Mansion to the White House.[6] Letterhead, envelopes, and invitations were inscribed accordingly from that time on. Colonel Bingham was determined to see his plan fulfilled, but was not entirely realistic about it. Behind the scenes, and perhaps not really understood by him, his "centennial plan" had already suffered what was probably a fatal blow. This had happened before McKinley's centennial luncheon on December 12, 1900. Perhaps in his haste, perhaps as an oversight, Bingham had alienated a powerful potential supporter by circumventing in his lobbying on the Hill Senator James McMillan, chairman of the Centennial Committee.

So eager was Bingham to get his appropriation that he had gone first to personal friends among the members of the committee. Senator McMillan's previous experience in urban improvements had inclined him to favor funding for an evaluation and reconsideration of the entire parks system of Washington, but he would have supported the White House expansion as well. Fearing that the planning—endorsed by the architects—would take priority in a time of limited funding, Bingham intervened and even wrote a bill for his friends to sponsor. Initially McMillan, though angry, let the matter lie. But at the centennial luncheon he was further offended when he saw Bingham's elaborate model and drawings. In this state of mind he talked after lunch with the representatives of the American Institute of Architects and realized that they felt as strongly as he that the first priority was a master plan for the federal city parks. The architects soon had reason to consider the chance meeting a hinge of history.[7]

Further cementing a relationship between the A.I.A. and McMillan was the happenstance that the senator's political secretary was one of Glenn Brown's closest friends. Charles Moore, former Detroit newspaperman, had been in Washington for more than a decade as McMillan's aide and adviser. In the community, he was known as historian, antiquarian, and enthusiast of architecture and the arts. He made sure that the A.I.A. officials and McMillan kept in touch. Brown gave typescripts of the convention proceedings to Moore, along with copies of the historical papers which had been read. Senator McMillan was so pleased that he ordered the papers published as a Senate document to rally support for an evaluation and master plan for a comprehensive parks system to be developed in Washington. On March 8, 1901, the senator introduced a bill at the executive session of the Senate which authorized the Committee on the District of Columbia to address itself to the city's public lands, with the power "to secure the services of such experts as may be necessary for a proper consideration of the subject."[4]

When McMillan's resolution passed, the senator asked Charles Moore who the consultants should be and was given first the name of Daniel H. Burnham. McMillan agreed and added a second expert, Frederick Law Olmsted, Jr., whom he did not know, but whose father had designed the Belle Isle park for Detroit. He would accept the younger Olmsted sight unseen, out of respect for the deceased father. A third party could then be decided upon by the first two. Before the close of March, Burnham and Olmsted had selected Charles F. McKim of New York's McKim, Mead, & White. The sculptor Augustus Saint-Gaudens became the fourth and last commissioner.

In June, when three of the experts set sail for a tour of inspection in Europe, McMillan saw to it that Charles Moore went along as his representative. They traveled for seven weeks, visiting chateaus, palaces, and great gardens, and studying city plans with relevance to Washington. Already in late July, when they sailed for home, the experts were making sketches for a revised Mall. They discussed the problem of a suitable residence for the President. In his diary entry written aboard the *Deutschland* on July 30, 1901, Burnham noted, "Spent the morning with McKim . . . and suggested that we place the President's House on the site of the old (Naval) Observatory." A new White House?[8]

Colonel Bingham did not know it yet, but his grand scheme for the White House had turned to dust. The experts engaged by the Park Commission paid no attention to his plan, but focused on the federal city as a whole. Under the astute patronage of Senator McMillan, the Park Commission projected a Washington of the future that would be rooted in the original plan. After the period of mourning for McKinley ended, the commission presented its plan to the Congress. The name Pierre Charles L'Enfant was now uttered with reverence.

For the engineer, it was a curious turn of events. L'Enfant had long fascinated Bingham, who studied his city map and read his letters; he even sought out his grave among the cedar trees on an old Maryland farm and went there to contemplate the Frenchman and his glorious dreams. Much of what was known of L'Enfant had come from Bingham's researches, and he had kindled an appreciation for the early design of the

federal city. He liked to say that his proposals for the White House and
Centennial Avenue had grown directly from the ideas of L'Enfant and
President Washington. But a far grander resurrection of L'Enfant's plan
was now drawn on paper. The architects had won the war.

The President Will Stay

President Roosevelt did not take up the matter of the White House
until the spring of 1902. Since January, large crowds had visited the
Corcoran Gallery of Art to see an exhibition planned by McKim on the
McMillan Commission's ideas for Washington. Models, photographs,
and drawings had been prepared at the New York offices of McKim,
Mead, & White. When the President arrived to view the exhibition he
was "interested, curious, and at first critical and then, as the great consistent scheme dawned on him, highly appreciative." So wrote Charles
Moore, who was present.

Roosevelt's reaction to the commission's neoclassical proposal for a
grander Washington seems to have been typical of that of most people
who saw the exhibition. It was beautiful as the World's Fair had been
beautiful, and it recalled the dreams of the Founding Fathers. While
most of the earlier monuments of the city were neoclassical, like the
White House and the Treasury, Washington public architecture since
the mid-19th century had taken a strong turn to the picturesque in red
brick and quarry-faced stone. Towers and bay windows adorned many
private houses adjacent to the public places; vines climbed up their
walls. Great open areas in the public domain were often still marshes or
ragged meadows, and anyone could easily gain a permit to graze livestock
in some of them. The McMillan plan projected a remarkable transformation that would give dramatic emphasis to a greatly elaborated series of
axes, based upon those planned by L'Enfant. Each vista was to terminate
in a fine example of neoclassical architecture. As in L'Enfant's plan, the
principal feature was to be the Mall, the Capitol at one end, a memorial
to Lincoln at the other, and along the sides large neoclassical buildings
for the federal offices. The cross-axis, having the White House at its
northern end, was lengthened south of the Mall, with space reserved for
a monument of an undesignated character.

The commission had rejected Burnham's suggestion to turn the
White House into an executive office and build a new mansion, recom-
mending instead that the White House remain a residence. Roosevelt,
who took an interest in the history and the associations of the old house,
was pleased. And when Charles Moore read a statement to the contrary

in the press, he went to the President for a confirmation or denial: "You tell the newspaper men," said Roosevelt, "that Mrs. Roosevelt and I are firmly of the opinion that the President should live nowhere else than in the historic White House."

"Do you mean, Mr. President," asked Moore, "that you desire to be quoted directly?"

"Yes," replied the President, "you are to quote me."[9]

Money

The McMillan plan—known in its time as the "plan of 1901"—was to ride rough political seas for nine years before it received authorization. Time can never be spent so freely at the White House. Even after they had settled down, the Roosevelts lived in great discomfort in the family quarters. The shortage of bathrooms, the absence of closets, inadequate lighting, a grease-laden, antiquated kitchen, floors that trembled when one walked on them—all these shortcomings added up to one final verdict: The White House needed drastic remodeling. Conditions in the office were even worse.

No President in recent history had made such extensive use of the house. Roosevelt held receptions, dinners, dances, garden parties, and ladies' teas. When more than 40 came to a seated dinner, the East Room had to be used, instead of the State Dining Room. Experiments with putting overflow crowds of from 40 to 60 in the transverse hall, behind the glass screen, merely created problems about who would be in the dining room with the President and who would not. In addition, the structural weakness of the old wooden floors was disquieting. Before large events Bingham brought laborers to the basement to shore up the floors of the East Room and State Dining Room with rough 10-by-10-inch timbers. This practice had been followed since the 1880s for New Year's receptions, but by 1902 an affair with a large attendance would have been unthinkable without the safety measure.[10]

The Roosevelts were perplexed about the White House. It was at once too big for a house and not big enough. They loved it, but it was inadequate to the demands imposed upon it; besides, it looked seedy, even tawdry. Certainly it was no stage for the performances they had in mind, and they began to consider changes. An appropriation of $16,000 was requested to cover repairs and redecorating. The amount was drawn out of thin air, with no specific categories for its use. Well before the bill became law, Mrs. Roosevelt invited Charles McKim to the White House to advise her informally.

As one who looked to New York as the center of fashion in America, Mrs. Roosevelt was unlikely to think of anyone but McKim when a question of taste arose. She wanted the house to reflect her husband's Presidency, and McKim was known for providing glorious results. Her call to him altered the course of White House history. He rode down from New York on the train on April 15, 1902, and the First Lady showed him the White House top to bottom. All the architect could say in honesty was that the appropriation might clean the house in part, but it would cover neither repairs nor improvements. A builder of costly mansions and public buildings, McKim was a perfectionist in a field that celebrated the ideal of perfection. He was not one to suggest patching up.

McKim said that nothing short of a renovation would properly serve the Roosevelts. According to Charles Moore, McKim had "reverence" for the historic White House. On the Park Commission's European tour he had swung the commissioners from Burnham's vision for a new White House, to the idea of keeping the President where he was. "Let me take it down stone by stone and rebuild it," said McKim while on the trip, "and not an architect in the country can make a finer or more appropriate residence for the President of the United States." Both Burnham and McKim had agreed that the President's offices should be removed from the White House proper and placed in an annex of some sort.

On his way back to the railroad depot from the White House, McKim stopped at the Capitol to visit with Charles Moore. He told what he had seen at the White House, relaying the Roosevelts' interest in having things improved. As he spoke, McMillan came in from the Senate floor and began to listen. Moore saw opportunity in this, if McKim did not, and asked abruptly: "How much would be needed to make a beginning—would $100,000 do it?"

"Yes; that would make a beginning," McKim replied.

"And how much would be required for an office building, separate from the White House?"

"I can only guess from the cubage," McKim answered, and calculated an estimate on the basis of what might be the cubic footage of space necessary: "say from $10,000 to $15,000 for a temporary structure to last until Congress shall provide for adequate offices and determine on a location outside the present White House grounds."

Moore later remembered how unceremoniously McKim departed to take his train, and how McMillan also left the room without comment. An hour later, McMillan reentered Moore's office, and said casually, "You might telegraph McKim that the Senate Committee on Appropriations has agreed to increase the House item from $16,000 to $150,000 for repairs to the White House and to provide $15,000 for an office building." The senator had gone directly to the Appropriations Committee, where he had delivered a dramatic oration that "painted a black picture of deplorable conditions, amounting to squalor, at the White House."[11]

McKim

When he received the telegram, McKim said he went into "a frame of mind of a man more likely to go off on a spree than home to dinner." He wrote a long letter to Moore in Washington, demonstrating that he had no doubt that the White House project would be his: "The whole thing is so exciting and full of possibilities that another day will have to intervene before I can tackle it with a sober mind." A second telegram followed from President Roosevelt asking the architect to meet with him several days later at a private house at 4 West 57th Street.[12]

At this meeting on April 19, 1902, McKim was given the responsibility for the work. The money was not yet appropriated, but it was well along in the process. McKim would need to stay in close touch with McMillan about final figures; meanwhile, Roosevelt wanted the planning to get under way. McKim declined to accept the job personally, but took it in the name of McKim, Mead, & White. But although he insisted that the work be attributed to his firm, McKim in fact was always in charge. Early in the following week, he traveled to Washington, where he was joined by O. W. Norcross, president of the Norcross Brothers construction company of Worcester, Massachusetts, the leading contractors on the East Coast. The collaboration between Norcross Brothers and McKim, Mead, & White went back nearly 30 years.

It fell to the lot of the defeated Colonel Bingham to show McKim and Norcross around the White House. Details of the tour are not recorded, but it must have included the shabby rooms to which the relatively fresh Blue Room offered contrast, and the grimy basement with its groin-vaulted corridor, beautiful even though crossed by pipes. The ceilings had cracked plaster, and the sunken floors sometimes shuddered with the footsteps of even so small a party. On the human side, McKim and Bingham might have patched up their personal difficulties immediately by shaking hands. It would have been businesslike. Bingham was capable of doing it: Soon McKim's partner, William Rutherford Mead, the wise businessman of the firm, was to establish a cordial relationship with him. But the arrogant McKim apparently saw no reason to try to make Bingham like him. He treated the colonel not as the officer in charge of public buildings, but as a clerk.[13]

McKim entered the project with somewhat unrealistic expectations. Placed in charge by the President, he demanded subordination from everyone else involved in the work. He had been the principal figure in many great projects, but the White House offered the greatest popular notice. It must be all his. And McKim was also eager to shed a favorable light on his profession. He had labored much of his career for the public and legal recognition of architects as professionals. McKim was thus too much occupied to trouble himself with obstinate men like Bingham. If brushing him off did not keep him in his place, he would go over the colonel's head to a higher authority. Naturally he made an enemy who would give him trouble along the way.

The architect further strained relations by refusing to acknowledge that anyone involved in the government had the slightest expertise in architecture. Reciprocally he made a great point of not understanding the particulars of governmental procedures. He kept his distance from Bingham, who represented bureaucracy, while he privately pursued a personal friendship with Roosevelt. When the President did not respond he turned to the First Lady, in whom he found, if not the close personal friend who would have been the most useful, certainly one who would listen to his problems.

To end the bickering between McKim and Bingham, George Cortelyou prepared a memorandum for the President specifying everyone's area of authority. McKim was in command of the renovation, the President the client, and Bingham the payer of bills. The work was to be done by private contractors, with federal employees on hand to see that the government's interests were properly served. Once McKim's position was secure, the architect made an appointment that must have irked Bingham. The superintendent of construction and Washington representative of McKim, Mead, & White was to be Glenn Brown. Bingham appointed Frederick D. Owen as record keeper of the project.[14]

Meanwhile, the cost estimates became more precise, and the figures were sent to McMillan, with increasing concern. The $150,000 proposed appropriation would not be adequate, according to the research of McKim and Norcross. As a result, McKim suggested doing the work in stages, over several years, a concept readily adopted by the President. A step-by-step procedure was devised that would allow the work to be financed through a series of appropriations. McMillan agreed to support the effort, and Charles Moore represented him at a meeting with "Uncle Joe" Cannon, whose support in the House was essential. Moore made his presentation, and Cannon grumbled, "Those damned *arch*-itects have been fooling Senator McMillan again."

"They never have fooled him," snapped Moore. During the uncomfortable silence that followed, Cannon began to soften.

"I don't care," Cannon said, "and the people of this country don't care, how much it may cost to put the White House into proper shape." He was even willing for the price to be high, but he wanted a total figure at the start. "I am not going to have those appropriations come dribbling in year after year. I've got to know the whole cost and it must go into this one bill. In short, I've got to know the color of this baby's hair before the baby is born!"[14]

Within the hour, Moore telegraphed McKim in New York that he and Norcross must provide a firm estimate by the following day. To save time, the estimate was transmitted from McKim's office by telephone early the next morning and transcribed by Moore's stenographer. The total of $369,050 for the White House alone so astonished Moore that he hurried to the White House to get the President's approval.

He found Roosevelt in the oval library upstairs in a great rush to begin a busy day. "Do you mind my being shaved while we talk?" asked the President. Moore sat down, while the barber lathered his customer's face. When Moore reached the total, President Roosevelt—to use Moore's words—"almost jumped out of the chair."

"That is three times what you first told me!"

"True," Moore said, "but this is the complete estimate; it is what Mr. Cannon wanted."

"Very well," said Roosevelt. "Tell Uncle Joe I approve."

Moore hesitated, then said: "You are the one to tell Mr. Cannon." The President shouted for an assistant to enter from the adjoining Cabinet Room and asked him to schedule an appointment that day with Cannon. The powerful chairman of House appropriations not only accepted the figure, but also agreed to a provision for a temporary office building on the White House grounds. McKim sent further figures for furniture which brought the total to $475,445 for house and office, and an item for removing the glasshouses on the west terrace. It was made a part of the "Sundry Civil Act," which passed the Congress and was signed by Roosevelt at the White House on June 28, 1902.[15]

The Architect's Concept

Since before his appointment as architect, McKim had been sketching furiously to finalize a White House plan. He found the labor irresistible. When in Washington, he was usually with Augustus Saint-Gaudens, his friend and colleague on the McMillan Commission. The two dined sometimes at the home of Glenn Brown or Charles Moore, and often with a party at the Cosmos Club. On those occasions, McKim spoke of little other than the White House project. "Like most architects," wrote Moore, "McKim talked better with pencil than with tongue." He always called for paper. Lacking paper, he was likely to use the tablecloth or a napkin in its stead.[16]

He used the word "restore" continually as a sort of tag for his plans, but in its strict definition, a restoration of the White House was not at all what McKim had in mind. The idea of comprehensive, scholarly restoration had little meaning to architects of the beaux arts persuasion. They felt no obligation to relics, nor did they wish to re-create what actually had been. The past was theirs to use as they pleased, as they designed modern architecture for their own times. Armed with this philosophy of design freedom, McKim had no interest in restoring what Hoban had completed for the first time in 1800, or the second time in 1818, or the house as Andrew Jackson or Abraham Lincoln had occupied it. The only historical obligation he acknowledged was to retain the external image and the general layout of the rooms inside. Beyond that his challenge was to improve the building.

All obstructions to the view of the original block of the White House were to be removed. The glasshouses were the primary offenders; McKim detested them as reminders of Victorian utilitarianism and vulgarity. He meant to bring back the side terraces as President Jefferson had built them, reconstructing the missing eastern terrace to match the one that survived on the west, beneath the conservatory. He planned a clean sweep of any other of what he judged to be ill-planned intrusions—trees, gardens, fences.

The revised White House was to display varied faces adapted to varied functions. Both north and south facades were now to be considered private, for the exclusive use of the President's family and guests. On the west, the new temporary office would provide the business entrance, while the east face, with its porte cochere, would be the entrance for parties and social callers.

With regard to the interior of the White House, the second floor, divested of its offices, presented few problems. The architect needed only to create ranges of bedrooms and bathrooms. So McKim concentrated his attention on the state floor, which was familiar to the public; the prospect of making changes there was a delicate matter, yet some change was necessary. In the creaking vastness of the old parlors and dining rooms, cushioned by carpeting and heavy hangings, McKim saw possibilities for what the architects of his era termed true elegance: clarity of design, with strong historical associations in architecture, richness of materials, and dramatic contrasts of color with white.

McKim wanted the plan to change as little as possible. Practical considerations demanded an enlarged State Dining Room, and he considered several possibilities. To annex the Red Room was of course unthinkable; to build out onto the west terrace, where the glasshouses stood, would ruin the external appearance of the house. The only recourse was to extend the dining room into the west end of the hall, where the grand stair stood. By this means the State Dining Room gained about 30 percent more space; its rectangular shape was preserved, but the main axis had rotated 90 degrees north-south, instead of the original east-west. As expanded, it was second in size only to the East Room. McKim would make a new and grander architectural scheme for it.

A new grand stair would have to be built elsewhere, and McKim tried various solutions. Charles Moore preserved a rough sketch made by McKim showing what appear to be two new stairways, one in place of the office stair and a second in the area occupied by the elevator and the ushers' office, both opening into the transverse hall. In the end the chamber containing the office staircase was opened to the transverse hall through an archway, and a new grand stairway was put there, to provide formal access to the family quarters above.

As the design work proceeded in the offices of McKim, Mead, & White, McKim drew sources for architectural details on the interior from the monuments of 17th- and 18th-century England and to some extent from France. These motifs he believed suitable to an enrichment of Hoban's White House, itself a product, British-style, of the 18th century. Because he wanted the external shell to be undisturbed, McKim had to take additional space where he could, mainly in the attic and basement. From the vast area beneath the roof he carved servants' quarters, closets, and workrooms, leaving one-third for storage. McKim redesigned the basement so that part of it could be put to use for social functions. Since the early days the basement had been strictly utilitarian, and by 1902 it presented a double row of dark, crowded work and storage rooms. In spite of several major cleanings over the past 20 years, it was as gloomy as a dungeon, its two kitchens crisscrossed with pipes and exposed wires, all covered with grease.

By shifting the service functions into the west end of the basement and extending them into the west wing, McKim made way on the east side for several formal rooms. He planned the reconstructed east wing as an entrance with security station, long glazed hallway, and coat room. The oval room of the basement, beneath the Blue Room, had been a furnace room since the 1840s; call bells hanging in rows on the wall evoked an original use as a servants' hall. McKim saw beyond the furnaces and pipes, the broken plaster and dank concrete floor, envisioning yet a third White House oval, the Diplomatic Reception Room.

The ground floor of the house was to extend from wing to wing through the basement. McKim appreciated the groin vaulting of the central basement corridor, and made highly architectural use of it in his revised basement. Guests were to enter this basement corridor through the east wing, then climb an inner stair to the state floor, seeming loftier than ever as it opened once again east and west to promenades or terraces on the roofs of the wings. With the exception of the family dining room on the north side, the state floor was given over entirely to official purposes, allowing a formality never before possible. The third level, the family quarters, seemed quite secluded.[17]

For the temporary executive office building, McKim selected a site that lay to the west, between the White House and the State, War, & Navy Building. The new structure would be added to the end of the old west wing, set back a distance from the front of the house so as to recede from the central feature of the complex, the White House itself. Architecturally it would harmonize with the earlier structure; he did not want it to compete. In every sense it was to be temporary. Burnham, when consulted, disagreed with the location, suggesting that the office building be placed instead squarely in the center of Lafayette Park, because that would assure its being temporary. The west side location prevailed, and McKim set to sketching a rectangular block with long windows and a parapet. He never once considered that the building would stand for any length of time, but, though rebuilt several times, it remains today as the Executive Office Building, commonly known as the West Wing.[18]

McKim's concept for the White House was clean and uncluttered. The traditional simplicity was preserved and enhanced; the reorganization of the spaces was brilliant, promising to make the White House better serve its varied functions. But for all his claims to "restoration," the proposed alterations were to bring in most respects radical change.

Clients

Already by May of 1902, McKim realized that while his colleagues praised his ideas, the Roosevelts' approval might not be so easy to get. They were hesitant to do anything that might endanger the White House, much less call down public disapproval. McKim thought about the best way to approach his clients, feeling perhaps that there was no rush. But on May 10 he knew that getting their approval had become urgent, when he received the following letter from the President:[19]

Personal!

My Dear Mr. McKim:

> *One thing I want definitely understood before we go into this work, and that is the question of expedition. Without fail we must have the last piece of work completed by December first, and we must have the office building and all of the present living apartments finished completely by October first. It may be wise to give to the local Washington people as much as can properly be given, consistent with doing it as well and as quickly and cheaply as possible.*
>
> *Sincerely yours,*
> *Theodore Roosevelt*

The transformation must take place in six months. Though unrealistic, the time was firm. Happily the Roosevelts had some knowledge of the designs McKim had in mind. Moore had already taken sketches to the White House, at Mrs. Roosevelt's request. While she studied these, apparently understanding very little of what she saw, Moore shared a great armchair nearby with little Archie Roosevelt and a collie dog. The First Lady described improvements that she wanted. Most of her wishes involved small details, and they did not indicate that she had given much time to the subject. Moore remembered that the First Lady raced from topic to topic during the discussion.

Most of all, she was hesitant about removing the conservatory, not so much because she admired it, but because it provided palms and fruit trees, as well as cut flowers, on a moment's notice. The gracious custom of sending bouquets to visitors in Washington would be an impossible drain on the President's purse without the glasshouses. Many worthy purposes were served by the conservatory, and Mrs. Roosevelt seemed convinced that these outweighed the argument that it made an awkward appearance from outside—a judgment to which she may well have taken exception. Moore already knew that the subject had been discussed beforehand by the Roosevelts; mention of the proposed demolition had been necessary in the appropriations act. Yet to Moore's surprise later that day, as he stood with Mrs. Roosevelt looking out the great lunette window at the spreading roofs of the greenhouses, the President burst into the hall and loudly exclaimed, "Smash the glass houses!"

"But," said Moore, surprised. "Mr. McKim understands that you want to save the glass houses."

"When you come to know me better," said Roosevelt, "you will understand that I sometimes speak before consulting the head of the house." Mrs. Roosevelt had apparently made up her mind, only to reconsider on second thought. She said little else, and the issue of the greenhouses seemed settled, at least for the time. Knowing Edith Roosevelt's habit of changing her mind frequently, Moore hastened to depart. At the elevator, she stopped him with a new request: "Tell Mr. McKim to make the new elevator door wide enough to admit a stretcher." With the memory of McKinley's murder not a year old, Moore was struck by the parting statement, and brooded about the fear that must haunt those who live in the White House. As the ancient elevator began to descend, it stopped abruptly between the floors and refused to move in either direction. Ike Hoover came to the rescue, freeing the balky elevator and sending Moore at last on his way.[20]

Several weeks later, McKim came to Washington with more precise plans and sketches. On a Sunday evening in late May, he was invited to make his presentation to the Roosevelts after dinner. Shown to the oval room at nine, he was soon joined by the Roosevelts and several guests. Mrs. Roosevelt and her sister Emily Carow were interested only in the new arrangement for the State Dining Room, for Miss Carow's ears still stung from a remark made by a British dinner guest about the President's serving large crowds in the East Room because his dining room was too mean for a gala party. While the two women discussed this, the President unrolled the basement plan, which he proceeded to mark vigorously with a red pencil, only to be reminded by his wife that the "housekeeping end of the establishment" was her business, not his.

He stopped his marking, but moved to the plan of the principal floor, where he saw and disliked the way in which McKim had expanded the State Dining Room. When Mrs. Roosevelt questioned his objection, the President assured her that his only concern was that the flooring over the well where the grand stair had been would disrupt her part of the house. She assured him that she would bear the momentary discomfort gladly to have a larger dining room. Everyone nodded approval, and McKim concealed his astonishment over Roosevelt's statement about disrupting the house. It was clear now that the President had no idea how torn up things would really be. McKim later wrote to Moore in confidence: "I am thinking that our noble President will find himself in such bedlam as he never dreamed of, even at Santiago."[21]

The Treaty of Oyster Bay

All plans were at last in order by about the first of June 1902. The President had made a few minor changes, as though determined to leave his touch; Mrs. Roosevelt had removed any closets which cut off the corners of the rooms or marred their shapes in any way. In New York, in McKim, Mead, & White's offices at 160 Fifth Avenue, draftsmen were busy making working drawings, while William R. Mead, the business-man of the firm, put the books in order and formulated schedules in cooperation with Colonel Bingham. McKim, who had no interest in management, worried over even the smallest part of the designs, be-moaning the close timing. He was particularly irked when his partner Mead pressed him to finalize his detailing for the East Room, so that the draftsmen could begin producing the required working drawings.

"It makes me sick to think," he wrote, "that [the East Room] has to be done in so short a time, and that right or wrong, it must go into construction. One would think it was a bill of goods to be delivered by Adams Express! Can you order a hen to hatch on time?" The architect wisely kept his complaints among friends. "Some one near the President ought to tell him that it is ten times more important to have the [East Room] right, whether he holds his first reception at a certain date or not." But "to have assumed this ground with him . . . would have imper-iled the whole work, and I dared not say what I felt."[22]

Despite McKim's restraint on this point, trouble appeared again at the White House. On June 28, the day the Sundry Civil Act passed and only two days before the beginning of the fiscal year during which the White House was to be renovated, a letter that had originated in the greenhouses revived once more the issue of the vast conservatories loathed by McKim. It had been written directly to Mrs. Roosevelt by the venerable gardener Henry Pfister, who had come to the White House with President Hayes a quarter of a century before. He protested humbly and piteously that his plants not be banished; the glasshouses were his life.[23] In his years at the White House he had built a remarkable and valuable collection of plant material, as Mrs. Roosevelt well knew. There were great palms and fruit trees in tubs, always at hand to turn the East Room into a tropical garden. Cut flowers were available every day, and First Ladies had taken particular pride in the bounty of the rose house, in the south ell of the west wing.

Mrs. Roosevelt, alarmed, asked her husband to intervene in defense of the glasshouses. The President turned the problem over to Bingham with his wife's observation that "though the green houses in my opinion

[are] no pleasure, it is absolutely essential that they should exist for the sake of the decorations. You can realize how expensive [flowers] would be to buy, while it would be impossible to do without them. I cannot submit to the architects spending every penny on the house until such a point as this has been met." To the bottom of his letter he added the following postscript in black ink: "I desire the present green houses kept unless the needed provisions can be made."[24]

Colonel Bingham's cordiality in relaying the President's directive to McKim betrayed his pleasure, and he dragged the matter out through a series of letters, either as a last-ditch effort to assert the authority he believed was rightfully his, or for revenge. He wrote to Mrs. Roosevelt that there "seems to be a misunderstanding all around about the green-houses." The solution to the problem was obvious: "If you wish as [many plants] as last winter, there must of course be as much glass covered space as we have always had."[25]

The President, however, had not actually given McKim an ultimatum. He had left a way out, if McKim were willing to sacrifice enough time and money to put as much greenhouse on another site. Eager to take advantage of this alternative, McKim wired Mrs. Roosevelt on July 1 requesting an appointment. She had taken up Pfister's cause, and was the final authority in the matter. The First Lady, summering at Sagamore Hill, responded by asking McKim and Charles Moore, who was in Washington, to luncheon the next day. The President was not there, and they would have time to talk.

McKim and Moore met at the railroad station in New York early the next morning for the commute to Oyster Bay, from which they hired a hack to Sagamore Hill. A large number of people were assembled at the farm for a party, dressed in the cool whites of summer. Mrs. Roosevelt apologized that she had been pressed to entertain in the middle of the day which she had designated for the study of the White House proposals. It had been too late to wire and cancel. Moore remembered that he and McKim, with no choice but to wait, took rocking chairs and enjoyed "the breezes on the piazza at Sagamore Hill, in the midst of a company of children and dogs."[26]

Mrs. Roosevelt finally found time for them, and an agreement was reached, doubtless aided by the fact that she was weary from her guests. The old conservatory was to be disassembled slowly and carefully, with every possible care given to the plants. Any wooden glasshouses would be sold or scrapped, but the iron-framed ones were to be taken to a place to be designated on the grounds and put together again as new greenhouses, to be officially called the White House Greenhouses. Pfister was to be accommodated in every way during the transfer. Mrs. Roosevelt seemed pleased, and when the business was done, McKim and Moore rose and departed. On the train back to Manhattan, discussing the day, they named their agreement with the First Lady the Treaty of Oyster Bay.[27]

Construction

The exact day demolition commenced in the White House is uncertain. At the end of June, Charles Moore wrote that all parties were stalled, waiting for the Sundry Civil Act to be signed into law. But on July 1—the day he asked Mrs. Roosevelt to meet with him about the greenhouses—McKim spoke of the demolition within the house as having been in progress already for several weeks. The Washington *Evening Star* of June 25 describes the state floor as looking like "a cyclone had passed through it. . . . It is in a state of demolition that is almost thorough." So the work was begun before the act financing it had passed.

The President still intended to remain resident in the White House through it all, although his offices were moved to the Townsend house, a large row house on the west side of Lafayette Park. Roosevelt kept his office hours there for the first time on June 23. Meanwhile, Bingham began to strip the interior of the White House, sparing only the President's bedroom and dressing room and several adjacent rooms necessary to his continued use of the building.

Curtains and cornices were laid unfolded in long boxes and wrapped in muslin scattered with bits of camphor. Pictures and mirrors were packed in pine crates stuffed with straw. Then followed the furniture and the carpets. Last to go were the chandeliers. Most of them were large nickel-plated-and-glass gas fixtures which McKim abhorred, but most people seem to have considered at least their heroic scale rather wonderful. Photographs taken on Bingham's orders show the great fixtures being dismantled. Their parts were numbered and carefully stored.

In early July, McKim wrote, "The house is torn to pieces . . . . bedlam let loose does not compare with it." Even the hardy Theodore Roosevelt could not stand it. Soon the President moved to a third floor bedroom at 22 Jackson Place, and Bingham's workmen cleared out the mansion's last remaining furnishings. Plaster dust alone would have made the building unbearable for Roosevelt. On July 3 he and Cortelyou departed for Oyster Bay, the President comfortably optimistic that he would return October 1 with his family to a completed residence, with little interruption in his schedule. Everything was to be accomplished during his summer sojourn away from the Washington heat. McKim did not tell him otherwise, but confided to a friend that whether or not the three-month schedule could be kept "remains to be seen."[28]

During the silent and sultry capital summer, the White House was to a great extent dismantled. Initially only those elements were to be removed which appeared to have been added to the neoclassical block of the house, except, of course, for the west wing and the porticoes. The conservatory was cut back as far from the White House as possible, leaving it in full operation as a greenhouse. Short work was made of the east porch, added by Andrew Johnson. Inside the house the demolition process dug deeper. Decisions were not based upon historical research and analysis, but upon the dictates of the eye of McKim. He knew very little White House history, and seems not to have cared; Bingham, the historian of the group, was not consulted.

One of the first Victorian offenders to go was the murky colored glass screen in the entrance hall. It was removed to a storage place, to be sold later with the other unwanted effects. A photograph preserves the appearance of the reopened entrance hall, with its arcade of marble Ionic columns, placed there by Hoban in 1818. Even with mounds of debris lying about, the hall was lofty and grand.

Charles McKim did not hold the interior in esteem, even as an interesting specimen of late 18th-century Georgian architecture. He planned to leave few of the ornaments, moldings, and the like inside the house. McKim's artistic eye became a sort of inquisition, before which every facet of the physical White House had to pass in judgment. Glenn Brown recalled an incident that took place at midnight, on the north lawn. He had accompanied McKim from the Cosmos Club across Lafayette Park to sit on a pile of stones and study the house in the wash of moonlight. The architect was disturbed that night by the presence of the iron railing that ran out from the sides of the north portico, fencing the deep north areaway from the driveway. A fine specimen of ironwork from Andrew Jackson's time, it had been wrought in 1833 in New York; its motif of great anthemia echoed Hoban's original "Grecian honeysuckle" cornice in the East Room.

History, however, did not enter into this discussion. McKim thought the black iron railing clumsy: "Would not an iron railing affect the lines of the house behind it and attract undue attention to the railing? Would not a stone balustrade obtrude itself in the same way, only in a less degree? Would not a solid wall of the same color be merged into the house without attracting undue attention?" Old Hickory's anthemia fence that night received its ticket to the scrap heap, to be replaced by a parapet wall.[29]

A large part of the interior was gutted to its wooden framing. The White House had been reconstructed in 1816–18 as a stone shell thickly lined with clay brick, many of its floors and partitions framed with large timbers; structurally, it was a house of wood. By mid July 1902 the interior skeleton was in places fully exposed, and at that point interior demolition stopped and reconstruction began. McKim could stand in the oval furnace room and look up through the floor joists of the Blue Room to the ceiling of the oval room in the family quarters two floors above him. The basement rooms beneath the East Room, their walls still thick with whitewash over layers of grease, gave a distant view up two stories into the now floorless chambers where the offices of the chief executive had recently been. On the south the room where Lincoln had signed the Emancipation Proclamation was a gawking, hollow shell, with fluttering wallpaper shreds dancing in the summer breezes. Mule-drawn wagons hauled the wooden parts to the marshes at the western fringe of the Mall, where they were burned.

Had there been time, much less of the old fabric of the house might have survived, for the builders complained of having to do too hasty a job. The project did not receive the usual thorough treatment accorded most works by McKim, Mead, & White and Norcross Brothers. Every shortcut possible was made in the push to complete the work. As a result, the 1902 renovation was largely cosmetic, not structural, and this shortcoming would come to light dramatically in the near collapse of portions of the house only 46 years later.

What was torn out of the White House in the summer of 1902 was what would have obstructed the new construction. Everything else was covered over and left among the bones of the transformed house. In the East Room, for example, though the protruding chimney breasts were cut out and the new fireplaces built on a plane with the walls, the Grecian decorative cornices and pilasters were chipped away only enough to allow for the introduction of wood paneling. Most of the plaster architectural decorations of James Hoban's East Room remained more or less intact, behind the new walls. Where walls did not have to be removed, the moldings and wallpapers on them were simply covered by new surfaces and left hidden. Modern steel lath or mesh was nailed onto old plaster walls, which themselves had originally been laid on split-wood lath; the plasterers troweled their mud and topcoat on the steel mesh, leaving the original walls beneath, peeling wallpaper and all. The fresh plastering was well under way at the close of July.[30]

McKim's solution for strengthening the structure was to introduce a large number of steel I-beams among the floor joists and socket them into the brick inner lining of the stone walls. This later would prove disastrous because the old clay bricks were not strong enough to hold the heavy steel members securely. Concrete blocks, another modern material, were introduced to a large extent, particularly in the basement, for supporting walls. None of the existing flooring of pine and mahogany was kept. All of it had been covered by wall-to-wall carpeting throughout its existence, except at rare times during the summer when straw matting was not available. The boards were unfinished and raw-looking. In the course of installing the steel I-beams, McKim ordered new floors of bleached northern oak for the entire house, most of it meant to be left exposed, at least in part, around the edges of large rugs. The entrance hall, which had a tile floor, and the transverse hall, where the floors were wood, were given new flooring of Joliet stone.

The old groin vaulting in the basement hall had been originally commenced in sandstone to support stone or marble planned for the floors above. When high costs made it seem prudent to stop the stonework, the vaulting, by then well along, was finished in brick. The groin vaulting had never been necessary to the strength of the house, and while it might have been repaired to support the new stone floors, McKim's floors were built on a bed of concrete and steel footed in the thick sidewalls of the basement corridor. New technology had rendered heavy groin vaulting archaic, but McKim liked its massive grace and called for its restoration as the principal architectural feature of the revised basement corridor. The utilities—wiring and plumbing—were run into a tunnel beneath the corridor floor and out of sight. Any plaster left on the vaulting was removed; weak spots and holes were repaired with brick, and the whole surface was plastered anew. The finish coat was being applied in late September 1902.

From the chaos of demolition the White House emerged transfigured. But so secure was McKim's hand that the building looked as though it had always been meant to be as he had designed it. Through late August and into September, the wreckage began to vanish. The house stood now at once familiar and strange to those who frequently passed the iron fence at the street. In September the last of the glasshouses was taken away. The portion reconstructed was placed not on the White House grounds, as agreed upon in the Treaty of Oyster Bay, but on the propagating grounds near the Washington Monument, out of the way, as McKim had been determined it would be.

With the glasshouses gone, the renewed White House could be appreciated from the street. Stripped of the long range of glasshouses, it seemed naked and exposed. The solitary house seemed suddenly more distant from the great hulks of the Treasury on the East and the State, War, & Navy Building on the west. Between the White House and the latter, close to West Executive Avenue, the new temporary office building had been revealed by the removal of the glasshouses. Of a single tall story, it was chaste of line and long of window, simple in every way; the structure of white-painted brick in no way competed with the White House, yet it did not recede into anonymity.

McKim had the west wing remodeled, replacing storage space with service rooms. Less demolition was done here than anywhere else. Heavy growths of vines on its north wall were carefully preserved and clipped. Dead paint was knocked from the stone walls, and holes were patched. On the east side, the original wing was to be reconstructed to match that on the west. Workmen preparing the ground turned up the early foundations and some old brick pavement. Although Roosevelt's extreme distaste for Jefferson was well known, McKim made quite an issue of rebuilding the East Wing on Jefferson's original foundations.

On October 1, a crisp day, the President and Cortelyou rode from the railroad station in an enclosed carriage, and were taken along the avenue in front of the White House. The building was by no means ready for the President. But Roosevelt was so pleased with what he saw that he accepted this without complaint. Except for the work on the east and west wings, and the chaos of holes and mounds on the usually smooth landscape, the house almost looked finished.[31]

Purse Strings

Within, the White House seemed nowhere near being finished. Much of the plasterwork had been completed; on the second floor the whitecoat was already being polished with pumice. Unconnected electric wires poked from holes in the ceilings and from openings in the walls, the locations for light brackets, chandeliers, service bells, and telephones. The new hardwood floors, neither sanded nor bleached nor varnished, were covered with the plaster dust, which had settled upon them like snow. Around the fireplaces the marble mantels were being set, and the smells of grout and mortar mingled with the smells of plaster and new wood. Stone pavers on the hearths and the floors of the great entrance and transverse halls had been likewise set, and could be crossed only on planks laid down to protect them.

What the house would soon be was easy to see. Anyone who had known the old, dingy basement, for example, could only marvel at its new magnificence. Unencumbered, the long series of groin vaults and arches, all lighted dramatically by electricity, added surprising beauty. On the east end were lounges, reception rooms, and offices; on the west were the new kitchens and service rooms, extending into the west wing, where Thomas Jefferson had originally had his icehouse and other facilities. The old kitchen had been converted into a furnace room; a great steam system had been lowered down into it while the floors of the entrance hall above were torn out. It was neat and clean, like the engine room on a small Navy ship.

When Mrs. Roosevelt returned on October 4 she was dismayed to find a house farther from being finished than she thought. She realized that not only was the building still being completed, but that it also lacked carpets, hangings, furniture, and a thousand things needed to make it function. Before she would go to sleep she insisted upon seeing Bingham, who presented a gray picture of the project's finances. He wondered if the house could be finished in time for the social season's beginning in December.

The White House always opened the season, and Mrs. Roosevelt would have it no other way. McKim had kept her busy all summer with a steady stream of little problems—from New York he had sent fabric swatches by the dozen, samples of wallpaper, and samples of rugs. She had spent hours contemplating these materials, often asking the advice of friends and young Alice. Back in Washington she realized that unless she assumed a personal role the house would not be furnished within the constraints of the budget. She was worried about McKim. Colonel Bingham had convinced her that "we can't depend upon him [to help save] a single dollar." On the day after her return, she wrote to the architect: "Since yesterday I have been thinking seriously of economizing in these last days of the White House renovation." She assured McKim that she was committed to the excellent project, but that it must be finished and presentable by December and the only certain course was to spend every penny from that moment on with the object of containing the overall cost within the congressional appropriation.

McKim's free spending was thus curtailed. He had designed for her a small and elegant greenhouse retreat, a sop to compensate for depriving her of the big greenhouses, which she had so admired. "The first thing that occurs to me," she wrote to McKim, "is that it would be wise to give up the little greenhouse on the grounds. . . . [it] is needed only as an adjunct to the White House—a little pleasure palace—and not of any great assistance in the decorations." One by one she went through the rooms, modifying the previous plans for interior decoration. "I prefer . . . to do nothing further to the President's study, not even to get new curtains. . . . The library comes under the same head. I do not think we ought to do one single thing in it, beyond putting up the paper that we agreed about. I don't think the mantelpiece ought to be changed this year, nor ought there to be new curtains or coverings for the furniture." Mrs. Roosevelt wanted a "reserve fund" kept, to ensure that "when everything is done, we have moved into the White House, set the furniture about and are living there . . . we could apply that money to cover the most glaring deficiencies."

She anticipated McKim's disappointment, realizing that he would cringe to think that the McKinleys' heavy brocade curtains, the lace, the stuffed "French" furniture that he so openly detested were to be returned to the upstairs. "Please, dear Mr. McKim," wrote Mrs. Roosevelt, "don't think me very fussy and interfering; but I am very timid about money and I know what an enormous amount has been done on the White House beyond what strikes the eye, and the money must have gone like water. I do hate to write this, because I know how much you have the perfection of your work at heart, but I have felt that I must do so and I hope you will forgive me."[32]

The First Lady's was a good plan from a practical point of view, but McKim was not one to surrender before he had to. Within the week he had met with the Roosevelts, captured them in the web of his enthusiasm, and from then on, both the First Lady and the President accepted nearly everything he said. Mrs. Roosevelt had, however, made a difference, for once McKim was finished with his decisions on the building, his extravagance waned.

Just where he would economize was unpredictable. He would not agree to make do with furnishings which had been there before. Any old pieces which returned to the house did so over his vociferous objections. The rosewood bed purchased by Mrs. Lincoln and since then— with its accompanying bureau, wardrobe, and elaborate center table carved with birds—the feature of the state guest room, McKim would have sent out as trash. But Mrs. Roosevelt, who had a taste for rich carving, loved its flamboyance, and the President loved its historical associations. By now it was believed that Lincoln had actually slept in the bed during the Civil War, this being the only bed that had survived the nearly 40 years that had intervened. Mrs. Roosevelt described the furniture to McKim as being of "rosewood, carved with big birds, I should say about fifty years old," and ordered that a matching writing desk be designed and made for her own use. When McKim attempted to circumvent this with a new design he thought she could not resist, she was emphatic: "I think the drawing of the writing table is ugly and inconvenient."

It was to be drawn again, made to look like the Lincoln furniture.[33]

Most of the interior decoration was carried out by three decorating companies from Boston and New York, which sent their own workmen and materials, as well as in some cases crates of furniture they had made in their shops. Through October and November, the house was virtually taken over by employees from two famous Fifth Avenue establishments, Herter Brothers and Leon Marcotte & Co., which had been furnishing American mansions for at least 30 years. Although they had worked under pressure for many a rich man before, their past experiences must have seemed easy in comparison to the rush demanded in a "political" house. Bingham watched these luxury tradesmen with a suspicious eye, but he was helpful in every way.[34]

Herter and Marcotte had been the two most creative designers among the manufacturing companies of the 1870s and 1880s, and while they continued to serve the richest clients, the handsome abstractions of their earlier furniture designs had yielded by 1902 to fine reproductions and adaptations of English, French, and, to a lesser extent, Italian antiques of the 17th and 18th centuries. Marcotte provided this and stuffed furniture as well to the White House in 1902.

A. H. Davenport & Company of Boston was the third of the prominent firms. This venerable manufacturing company was the best known business of its kind in the United States; it was less a decorating house than a large-scale producer of catalogue furnishings for both residences and public buildings. Part of the furniture Davenport built for the State Dining Room remains today, two neo-Georgian tables, one large and one small, with pedestals and broad cross-banded borders. Along the walls McKim placed a heavy sideboard and a pair of serving tables, all three with marble slabs supported by carved wood eagles, a style of furniture McKim, Mead, & White had used elsewhere. On one of Davenport's original drawings is noted simply, "copy of an English table."[35]

Though McKim divided the work of interior decoration and furnishing among the three firms, Marcotte received the lion's share. Davenport provided only furniture, and Herter's work lay almost exclusively in the architectural embellishment and decoration of the state rooms. From McKim's designs Herter built the rich paneling of the East Room and the State Dining Room; Herter stretched fabric on the walls of the Red and Green Rooms. With the exception of minor projects in other parts of the house, that was the extent of Herter's involvement in the renovation. Over the years the work of the other firms was to disappear, but Herter's paneling in the State Dining Room remains today.

Davenport manufactured mahogany neocolonial furniture for the

Family Dining Room, and Adamesque sofas and chairs for the Green Room. This last was delicate to the eye, if heavy to lift. It was painted cream, with woven cane backs and seats; there were 15 pieces, the seats covered in flowery chintz, reflecting high British Edwardian taste. Although Davenport's designs were usually less stylish than those of the New York firms, the Green Room suite seemed a generation ahead of the crimson-covered overstuffed and tufted furniture made by Marcotte for the Red Room. More in keeping with Marcotte's usual production was the furniture the firm made for the Blue Room, a matched suite supposed to imitate on a larger scale the French furniture purchased for the room in Paris in 1818. None of the chairs or sofas from the original suite had been at the White House since before the Civil War, although Glenn Brown had discovered the marble-topped pier table in 1902 when the attic was cleaned out. In place of the original gilt, the furniture was enameled white and trimmed in gilt.

Edward F. Caldwell & Company of New York, the outstanding manufacturer of "electroliers" in the United States, made all the light fixtures. With the decline of gas illumination and the rise of electricity, Caldwell had achieved broad recognition with a line of handsome "period" devices that were convincingly historical, yet accommodated electric wires and bulbs. For the White House, McKim collaborated with Caldwell to create, according to Glenn Brown, "probably the most artistic [electric fixtures] that have been designed in this country." None of the old wall brackets or electrified gasoliers were retained. Even the few remaining gas fixtures, kept for use in service areas when the electricity went out, were replaced with new ones. The luxurious sconces and chandeliers suggested 18th-century candle fixtures; they ranged from nickel-plated wall lamps in the bathrooms to gilded brass or silver-plated chandeliers in the state rooms. The parlor chandeliers were showers of prism-cut glass beads and pendants. The neo-Georgian dining room chandelier was sterling silver; a vertical version was installed first, then soon replaced by the horizontal fixture still in use, although since gilded. When McKim saw the huge brass and glass chandeliers Caldwell had produced for the East Room, he ordered them taken down and reduced in size, and while they would be cropped a second time a half-century later, they too remain in place today.[36]

At the insistence of the President and Colonel Bingham, McKim grudgingly included some local Washington firms in the work, but only under pressure. Faced with a difficult deadline, he was naturally inclined to do business with New York firms he trusted through experience. It was nevertheless the source of great annoyance to Washington businesses that they were overlooked, when for years they had been asked constantly for favors by the White House and had been traditionally rewarded with contracts when a project came along. Of the three Washington firms called to the work, W. B. Moses & Sons, which had provided furniture and decoration for the White House for half a century, received an almost obligatory invitation, and a job of some substance. It supplied much of the bedroom furniture, some of the less important office furniture, curtains and shades, various rugs and carpets, and most of the equipment for the kitchen. In addition, Moses was granted small contracts for painting ceilings with calcimine upstairs and in the new office building. The other two Washington firms did little more than wax floors and set bathroom fixtures.

No direct fee was paid to the architects. McKim, representing his firm, claimed a 5 to 10 percent commission from each of the subcontracting companies. The commission was negotiated on an individual basis, but the result had to conform to the 5 to 10 percent allowed the architects by the government. A complete accounting of costs and the commissions to McKim, Mead, & White, compiled to assuage Bingham's suspicion that the firm was accumulating undue profits, shows, for example, that of the $276,502.31 paid to Norcross Brothers, the architects took a commission, which was added to that price, of $14,256.87. Doll & Richards of Boston sold a mirror to McKim for the White House for $325; McKim added to it his fee of $32.50. For the entire work of renovating the White House, McKim, Mead, & White received a total of $31,635.65 out of a project cost of $467,105.60.[37]

Family Quarters

The White House moved toward completion at a slow and steady pace. In the first days of November 1902, most of the work was directed toward the family quarters, for the Roosevelts were eager to move in; the Townsend residence was uncomfortable and inappropriate. Either the President or Mrs. Roosevelt, or both, called Brown or Bingham every day. Their presence stimulated the tradesmen's labors to a frantic rate. With all hands upstairs, the bedrooms and private sitting rooms were soon suitable for occupancy.

On November 4 the Roosevelts moved in, and served dinner in the family dining room to a party of friends. In their room stood the Lincoln bed, draped once again from its high corona fixed to the wall, just below the ceiling. The old suite of furniture must still have smelled of varnish, and the lavish grain of the rosewood stood out all over it, from the panels at the head of the bed to the beaks of the exotic birds carved on the center table. Elsewhere, the upstairs seemed as modern as a new hotel, with suites of bedroom furniture varying from "colonial" to other period styles, some of it painted cream. Block-printed linen, floral chintz, and cretonne were used in window hangings, upholsteries, and bedspreads. Broadloom carpeting in dark colors was laid both wall to wall and as rugs that left a border of polished hardwood flooring.

McKim retained the second-floor plan; although he had opened the long transverse corridor the full width of the house, the sections were still distinct—west hall, central hall, and the east hall, which was raised, as always, several steps above the rest. All the rooms of the second floor opened off the long hallway. Large bathrooms were built into the dressing rooms on the four corners of the house, and elsewhere fitted into the corners or across the ends of rooms. Each of the seven bedrooms had its own bath, gleaming with white ceramic tile and shining with nickel plate, and in most of the rooms this new feature, however convenient, · threw the fireplaces off center.

Each member of the family found a special place for his special purposes. Alice Roosevelt commandeered the east hall for her private sitting room, ordering her brothers and sisters to stay out; the boys and Ethel took rooms on the north side; the room between the President and Mrs. Roosevelt's bedchamber and the oval room, designated as "Mrs. Roosevelt's sitting room," became a family sitting room with overstuffed furniture and the First Lady's desk. Here the Roosevelts would set up their Christmas trees, and the children would hang their stockings on the Victorian marble mantel. As a family they grew to love this room more than any other.

McKim's improvements to the second floor made the family quarters not only large, but also comfortable and private. The great arches that divided the hall were like the originals, but they had been equipped with sliding doors. The west hall, no longer crowded by the grand staircase, became a family living room, dominated by the great lunette window. North and south of it were bedrooms, that on the south being the President's, as it had usually been. Mrs. Roosevelt's sitting room and the adjoining oval room, the library, opened onto the center hall from the south. The two bedrooms across the hall from them were shaded by the north portico; McKim had left the narrow hall between them intact. The small elevator passage opened off the central hall, and most of the traffic to the family quarters—family, guests, and servants—came this way.

On the east of the central hall, one crossed the vestibule at the head of the new grand stair, in place of the original office stair. Double doors screened the stair landing, and heavy iron gates protected the stair on the state floor. Opposite the stair the former Cabinet Room was now a study for the President, its walls covered with tan burlap and lined with bookcases, many of them from the library. The east hall, decorated sparsely but formally, was a sitting room serving the guest bedrooms on each side, of which that on the north, the "Rose Bedroom," was the larger. The color had been opposed by McKim—by 1902 "ashes of roses" was unfashionable—but Mrs. Roosevelt would hear of no other, and she found just the shade she admired on a soft printed linen. It became one of the favorite rooms of the First Lady and of her sister Emily Carow, who occupied it whenever she visited the White House.

The family quarters contained little that was old or antique, nor much that bore any previous reference to the White House. They were handsome in the modern way, their colors muted, their furniture deeply cushioned. Most of the rooms were sparse, with the clutter of daily living concealed in closets. Luxury was symbolized in an abundance of tiny push buttons made of mother-of-pearl; set in the wall beside fireplaces, beds, desks, dressing tables, and bathtubs, these activated the call box downstairs and brought a uniformed maid or footman to the scene within minutes. The new quarters left little to be desired, except for a past. In their letters, both the President and Mrs. Roosevelt seemed troubled by the stark impression of newness, of Englishness and Frenchness, where America's heroes had walked.[38]

They seized the slightest excuse to keep furnishings McKim intended to send out. When McKim declared that the historical portraits and some other presidential memorabilia of the White House would ruin the decorations of the state rooms and must go, Mrs. Roosevelt refused, designating the basement corridor as a place for presidential busts and the portraits of the First Ladies, "including myself." The President put General Grant's old Cabinet table in his study and commissioned a bronze tablet for the mantel displaying these words: "This room was first used for meetings of the Cabinet during the administration of President Johnson. It continued to be so used until the year MCMII. Here the Treaty of Peace with Spain was signed."[39]

The Push

By November 4, 1902, only the second floor and basement were functioning. Bingham pushed the grounds crew on the work of landscaping. Trees and shrubbery were hauled in on mule-drawn wagons; stakes and strings marked the outlines of a geometric "colonial garden," which

Mrs. Roosevelt ordered on the precise spot where the glass-covered rose house had once stood. The grounds began looking more orderly, as Bingham and his workers took full advantage of the autumn planting season.

Inside, the state rooms were still far from complete. At Thanksgiving 1902, a reporter found "The lower floor . . . littered with lumber, paint, and plaster, the walls stripped of their hangings for redecoration, and not an apartment fit for habitation. Everywhere the mason, the carpenter, the electrician, and the decorator are creating the chaos that such people can create, and from morning until night the sound of hammer and saw arises in the clouds of lime dust and other dirt."[40]

Roosevelt's presence in the house seems to have made the wheels move faster. He was not opposed to making demands. Weary of dining in the west hall upstairs, he insisted that the family dining room below be readied, and it was—with remarkable speed—even though plaster dust from the other rooms of the state floor proved so dense as to render the room unusable. The furniture was repacked in Davenport's crates; the chandelier and curtains were "bagged," and the room was locked. Roosevelt's pushing also hastened the completion of the new Executive Office Building. The Cabinet sat there first on November 6, 1902, two days after the Roosevelts moved into the White House. Handsome and even elegant in the neo-Georgian mode, with snowy white woodwork and dark burlap on the walls, the new office—known as the "temporary office"—suited the complete revision of the administrative procedures of the Presidency then under way in the able hands of Cortelyou.

Roosevelt became unceasing in his urging onward, unyielding in his deadlines. Toward the close of November, with the house still nowhere near complete, he ordered invitations sent out for a Cabinet dinner to be held in the State Dining Room on December 18: With this he would inaugurate the restored White House. Workmen and supervisors shrank at the thought of what lay before them, but attacked their labors even more assiduously. Mrs. Roosevelt calmly spoke with the chef about the menu, while the President, in good spirits, wrote to his son Kermit on December 4, "You will be delighted with the White House. The changes have improved it more than you can imagine."[41]

The Finished House

The goal was met. In the morning of December 18, the workmen of Herter and Marcotte packed their tools and departed for the railroad station. The work of the renovation was done and even the most dubious observer could still recognize the result as being the White House. On the state floor the plan remained the same, except for the enlarged State Dining Room and the new grand stairway. Beyond the layout, however, there was little similarity between the new and the old. Gone was the heavy, upholstered look; the thick curtains, the patterned wallpapers and carpeting. The carved furniture was at Sloan's auction rooms awaiting public sale. McKim's new image of the White House was sophisticated and upper class in tone, where the traditional aspect had been bourgeois; it was cosmopolitan, where the decoration of the White House had usually been as insular as the American nation itself.

McKim had changed the traffic patterns dramatically. The north door had become the private, or family, entrance. Office callers went to the Executive Office Building, and social guests were admitted from East Executive Avenue to the East Wing, which was the main entrance for callers and for guests at social events. The East Wing, rebuilt, seemed perfectly natural to the White House; its south colonnade was enclosed with glass, and gave a view of a garden, while a coatroom called the "hat box" extended along the north side. Callers proceeded directly through the East Wing into the vaulted basement, or "ground floor," corridor of the house, where an ample stair, directly beneath the grand stairway, led to the state floor.

The public complained about having to enter the White House through the cellar, but it soon became clear that the new way was more convenient and simplified security. Politicians who objected at first to making business calls at an outbuilding eventually became reconciled to the new arrangement, for the temporary office required less of a walk from the street and offered a comfortable waiting room. The President himself grumbled now and then about the new ways of doing things. Secretary of War Elihu Root related how Roosevelt had insisted that in connecting the offices of the White House by way of the west colonnade, "Mr. McKim was forcing him to walk past the servants' quarters." To this the wry Root replied, "McKim was not counting on always having so decrepit a President."[42]

People who had known the White House for years found the revised interiors strange. Though more "architectural" than previously, they were chilly and barren. All the woodwork and plaster ornament were new, and, except for the frames of the doors, were wholly different from what had been there before. The simple Federal interior of the original house was replaced by a more elaborate Georgian style. It appeared in the entrance hall in a heavy Doric cornice, tall pilasters, and enriched ceilings, and climaxed in the richly carved paneling that encased the East Room and State Dining Room.

McKim unified the state floor by painting it white, warmed slightly with yellow and brown. The ceremonial areas where people would stand or form processions were entirely in this color; it was carried from the entrance hall the entire length of the transverse hall and into the East Room, and appeared on the door framing and wainscoting of the three parlors and the family dining room.

The East Room was the same only in the number of its windows, fireplaces, and chandeliers. Nothing original survived. The lofty walls, 22 feet high, were organized into long rectangles, worked into the design of the enameled wood paneling; rectangles repeated themselves all around the room, from windows to wall panels to tall mirrors over the fireplaces to the slender Corinthian pilasters interspersed along the walls. Highly polished oak flooring in the "Versailles" pattern parquet was left uncovered for the full 40-by-80-foot expanse.

In designing the paneling, McKim had called on his friend Attilio Piccirilli, a decorative carver of New York. A theme for low-relief wood carving had been found in the fables of Aesop, and this was put over the doors in 12 panels executed by Lee Lawrie, who assisted Piccirilli. The only color in the room was in the flooring, the red-marble mantels, and the yellow silk damask at the windows. McKim had wanted red hangings, but Mrs. Roosevelt insisted upon yellow. This most magnificent of the state rooms made a brilliant setting for large crowds and grand occasions.

At the far end of the transverse hall, the State Dining Room, also rich in neo-Georgian paneling, produced an opposite effect. Herter Brothers' elegant paneling here was natural oak, stained dark and heavily waxed, designed to glow in candlelight. According to contemporary period notions, this room suggested a dining hall in a great English country house. The two original fireplaces were replaced by a single large fireplace of stone carved with lions' heads.[43] A series of silver wall sconces holding clusters of electric bulbs matched the chandelier. The "India" carpet was all one color, and green velvet hangings complemented two Flemish-type tapestries, believed to be 17th century. Completing the great-hall theme, stuffed animal heads mounted high on the walls encircled the room. Most of them, if not all, were purchased from the Hart Decorating Company in New York. No sooner had the Cabinet dinner taken place than President and Mrs. Roosevelt began using the State Dining Room daily. They complained about Davenport's rectangular dining table. Before the New Year, the old round table, acquired probably in the '90s, was returned to its former place.

The state parlors were simpler than the ceremonial areas. Each proclaimed its name in luxurious wall coverings of silk; the red, blue, and green were very dark and glossy, set off with wood trim painted the same slightly yellowed white as in the East Room and halls. When McKim spread the swatches before him, Roosevelt had objected to the dark colors, but McKim prevailed. The Red Room was comfortably furnished in upholstered chairs and sofas, all in matching red damask with deep fringe around the bottom. McKim moved here from the State Dining Room one of the marble mantels brought to the house in 1818; he put the second in the Green Room. The Green Room, cool and seemingly remote, was fashionably English period, its Sheraton-type furniture painted cream and upholstered in flowered chintz. Central to this suite was a sprawling sofa, a white frame stretched with cane mesh and piled high with goose-down cushions. Abundant small side chairs were a dubious exception to the English theme. They were copies from an antique in the possession of Frank Millet, a painter and a popular member of the Roosevelt circle, who had been assured that it was a former possession of Marie Antoinette. Placed around the walls in the Blue Room were the imitations of Bellange's Empire chairs and sofa, painted white and gold, covered in blue and gold silk. The Blue Room mantel was white marble and bronze designed after that in the queen's boudoir at the Petit Trianon; on its shelf were some of the original ornaments bought in Paris for Monroe.

The transformed White House was captured in a series of drawings commissioned by McKim from the American painter Jules Guerin. He placed blurred images of the White House in dreamlike landscapes; Guerin's White House shimmers, suspended between reality and fantasy.[44] The pictures evoke a romantic past unencumbered by history. The same was true of McKim's renovation: He stripped from the White House the scars and tracks of time, creating a pale reflection of the house that had been, and a strong, new image that would endure.

30

Protocol

T he Cabinet dinner that was to open the 1902 social season was only 11 days away when the workmen of Herter, Marcotte, and Norcross assembled in the great entrance hall for a ceremony of their own devising—the burial of a time capsule. Although the press was to belittle the occasion of December 3 as a "pretty event," the President had enthusiastically approved the workmen's idea. The hall was vacant of furniture, and some of the light fixtures were still wrapped in protective cardboard and muslin. In the precise center of the hall's screen of columns there was a neat opening in the stone floor. Beside it stood a marble box, a polished slab of marble, a hod of fresh mortar, and a few tools. A hundred men crowded close to witness the burial of the box. When the slab had been set in place and tapped level with the floor, it was rubbed until the brass numbers "1792–1902" shone bright in their surrounding ellipse of brass stars.

According to the newspapers, the contents of the box included the President's message to the Congress, presented only the day before, as well as American coins, autographs of Roosevelt family members, and a chisel worn from use in the renovation. Like many vessels, however, this ark had its stowaways. While it lay unattended during the day, several of the ushers signed their names on its underside. Glenn Brown at one point slipped in a paper certifying that he had been project manager of the restoration and was the descendant of Peter Lennox, principal carpenter on the original building. A representative of McKim, Mead, & White inserted several letters written on his firm's letterhead. An unknown hand soaked the label off a bottle of rye whiskey and deposited it.[1]

When the artifacts saw daylight again half a century later, the most ordinary item in the box was Roosevelt's printed message, available in any public library. Yet the words breathed life into a time that seemed lost, showing the optimism of an era when Americans did not yet wear the scars of two world wars and a great depression.

"We still continue in a period of unbounded prosperity," wrote President Roosevelt. "This prosperity is not the creature of law, but undoubtedly the laws under which we work have been instrumental in creating the conditions which made it possible . . . . The wave will recede; but the tide will advance. This nation is seated on a continent flanked by two great oceans. It is composed of men the descendants of pioneers, or in a sense, pioneers themselves; of men winnowed out from among the nations of the Old World of the energy, boldness, and love of adventure found in their own eager hearts. Such a nation, so placed, will surely wrest success from fortune."

Cortelyou's Turn

The renovation and remodeling of the White House produced an impression of reason and order. Previously it had been added to and patched up as wear and tear required; it was often overdecorated for state affairs, to compensate for its seediness. From being the handiwork of many, the White House became, in McKim's hands, the creation of one.

To fit the new rationality of the place, the White House was reorganized. George Cortelyou devised a formal framework of rules and procedures that better suited the expanded Presidency. He began with the President's office, which, in the summer of 1902, included 27 secretaries and clerks, 5 doorkeepers, and 7 messengers, all of whom had served in the White House. To preclude unnecessary questions or grumbling from seasoned employees who might think themselves above change, the President made certain that the reorganization included the household; Cortelyou also supervised the "ushers, doorkeepers and police officers stationed in and about the White House, the Executive Office, and the grounds," as well as the steward of the White House, and the employees at the stable.[2]

He was charged with putting the presidential organization on a businesslike basis. His time was short, for unknown to all but the intimate presidential circle, Roosevelt planned to appoint him head of the proposed Department of Commerce and Labor, then making the arduous journey toward congressional approval. Probably no man in the country was as qualified as Cortelyou to reorganize the executive establishment.

Having worked in the presidential office since 1895, he was familiar with both its requirements and its peculiarities. Cleveland and McKinley had noted his great ability as a manager, and McKinley had elevated him from assistant to private secretary to the President in 1900. Beginning then, Cortelyou's touch was felt in everything.[3]

His ability as a manager is best illustrated in the way he altered the character of presidential tours. Through the last decades of the 19th century, Presidents had traveled in small parties, going usually by private railroad car, occasionally by private train, taking the White House, as it were, to the people. With the Spanish-American War and the new emphasis on the President, large numbers of journalists began to accompany official tours. At first they simply bought tickets and rode aboard the train that pulled the President's car. To prevent the disruption of routine in their regular passenger cars, the railroad companies began to add an extra car for the press. For a major tour, of which there were from one to three a year by 1900, the party might number as many as 150, including the President's guests and aides. In such cases three or four cars served the tour's needs. Sometimes a wealthy friend of the President's added another private car. It became practical, as the number of cars increased, to assign them their own locomotive; thus a "presidential train" threaded its way across the landscape.

Managing a large tour was complex. Cortelyou had watched mayhem at the railroad depots more than once, with luggage, papers, coats, hats, and frantic people flying about. His response was to publish a little book of instructions for each trip. The first appeared in 1900; by the beginning of Roosevelt's administration, providing such books for presidential tours was customary.

"This book," began the introduction of the first and all that followed, "is issued solely for the information of members of the party, and is not intended for publication or for general circulation." Then followed an hour-by-hour schedule of train stops, speeches, dinners, and any other relevant information. A paragraph was supplied about each stop along the way; it included the name of the place, what it was best known for, and the population. The guide promulgated strict rules about appropriate press conduct; access to the President, for example, was rigidly limited.[4]

Such detailed planning established Cortelyou's expertise. Roosevelt assigned to him the revision of White House procedures in 1902 and early 1903 with full confidence. Only a few days after the executive order, Cortelyou presented the doorkeepers at the White House and Executive Office with a new booklet: *Special Instructions to the Chief Doorkeeper and Those Under His Immediate Supervision.* This enumerated rules of conduct, down to clothing and the appropriate manner of receiving visitors. The casual habits of the doormen were to end; they had been to some extent a law unto themselves, sometimes leaving their posts to run errands or to help with the housework. Not since Mrs. Grant put them in dress suits and white gloves had they endured such a shake-up. Cortelyou's rules reminded the doormen that they were not domestic servants, but plainclothes guards inside the house.[5]

In January, Cortelyou's second volume rolled off the press: *White House and Executive Office: Organization and Rules.* It may well have been awaited with some fear. Fourteen pages long and printed in small type, it contained what today are called job descriptions. The office staff and doorkeepers were listed by title and name, each with a clear outline of his duties and a list of those employees who answered immediately to him. At the top of the column was the private secretary to the President. The second in command, assistant secretary William Loeb, Jr., supervised the telephone and telegraph departments, all purchasing for the office, and maintenance. Answering to him were the chief doorkeeper, chief messenger, sergeant in charge of the police at the White House, and the head of the stable. Each reported to him in writing every week, while he, in turn, reported to the private secretary. Third in line was B. F. Barnes, who managed confidential papers and was responsible for any document bearing the President's signature, as well as any letters and papers the President needed to see. And Barnes would take over the task of transmitting presidential messages to the Congress, formerly the responsibility of the private secretary.

The job descriptions continued down to the last clerk. Cortelyou even spelled out the manner in which work would be conducted in the Executive Office. The work day would begin at nine in the morning, "punctuality required." If his work was done, an employee could leave at four in the afternoon, but if work remained at the close of a day, he "will be expected . . . to remain as much later as required." Sunday hours became official, from 10:30 in the morning until four. This did not mean that Sunday was a regular day of business, but it did mean that a minimum staff was always to be present; this had been so unofficially since the start of the war with Spain.[6]

Night duty would be rotated among all staff members below the rank of assistant secretary. Except for special circumstances, night work had been the responsibility of telegraph operators. Since the late 1880s, the key had been manned only until 11, except in times of crisis, when around-the-clock operators were assigned temporarily. The telephone, presenting more opportunities for personal communication, had created the need for a larger night staff. Night duty usually required one tele-graph operator and two clerks. The office was open from 9 p.m. until 11 to receive callers with appointments and to take telephone and telegraph messages. To the communications system Roosevelt added an overseas wireless, inaugurating it in his office on January 19, 1903, with a message to King Edward VII of England.

The balance of Cortelyou's instructions explained procedures of var-ious kinds and included even a brief manual of style to govern all docu-ments that came from the Executive Office. Employees were to leave their desks in the Executive Office Building absolutely bare at the end of the day; there was to be no disarray of papers and books, such as the clerks could remember from the cramped upstairs quarters in the White House. Major Loeffler and Major Montgomery, who were detailed from the Army, were to abandon morning coats for military uniforms; the others were to wear dark suits. The cutaway coat and striped trousers—dating back to Arthur's time—were ruled out for everyone but the Presi-dent and the principal secretaries. The President approved Cortelyou's program, and all staff members signified their acceptance by initialing a letter of agreement.

To symbolize his reorganization, Cortelyou redesigned the official printed matter. The President and the upper-echelon members of the staff received new calling cards. Roosevelt's was oversize and very thick, with "The President" engraved on it in plain block type. His own read "The Secretary to the President," and he had a second, smaller card bearing his name, "Mr. George Cortelyou." The card for the First Lady said simply "Mrs. Roosevelt." All invitations, announcements, pro-grams, and menus followed the same style of type on heavy stock, far simpler than the embellished script that had previously been customary. The revised stationery appeared well in advance of the remodeled house. First used in October 1901, the letterhead read simply: "White House, Washington." It showed dramatic restraint, and the common name for the mansion suited the new Presidency.[7]

On February 14, 1903, the Congress officially established the De-partment of Commerce and Labor. Two days later, Cortelyou was ap-pointed its head, and was replaced at the White House by the first assist-ant, William Loeb. Cortelyou was to be postmaster general and secretary of the Treasury, before moving to New York and entering private business. His mark on the White House was as indelible as that of McKim, although it was made in procedures, not in brick and stone. Cortelyou established an organizational structure where there had been only personal prerogative.

The Executive Office

The new building was called by its official name "temporary office" for only about six months after it was occupied. The Executive Office, as it was subsequently styled, was not a large structure. It was tall, airy, gleaming white, elegant, and trim. It faced Pennsylvania Avenue but was normally approached on the side, from West Executive Avenue. In Roosevelt's time it was rather Spartan. The woodwork was painted ivory; the plaster walls were covered with burlap dyed dark olive. Floors were of waxed hardwood with close-pile broadloom area rugs; clusters of light bulbs hung overhead in nickel-plated fixtures, with globe brackets spaced along the walls. One writer observed that the "superior . . . decoration" and "simple comfort" were what a business executive might enjoy anywhere in the United States.[8]

McKim's plan for the executive structure placed the private secretary's office ceremoniously on the central axis of the building. From an architectural point of view, this was the position of prime symbolic importance. McKim thus showed that the Executive Office was conceived more as the domain of the staff than of the President, who remained associated with the symbolic White House. Theodore Roosevelt's office in the new building was called the "President's Room." Here he did some of his paperwork and interacted with the executive staff. But office work was not perceived as his major task. His principal role was to receive callers and hold important conferences, and the place for that was in the White House, upstairs in what he called the "study," which had once been the Cabinet Room.

So effective was the distinction in status between the two places of work that Roosevelt suffered the heated objections of congressmen and other leaders when he received them in the new building. They felt that they had a right to call where they had always called, at the White House, and Roosevelt generally accommodated them. The President's study was a handsome, ample room adjoining the oval room. Furnished as an office, it contained Roosevelt's papers and books, and the carved *Resolute* desk that Queen Victoria had sent to President Hayes. It was a cozy room, with full south sun and a comfortable feeling of privacy. Speaker Cannon remembered "sitting about the fire" talking things over "until Midnight or later."[9]

The President's suite in the new office building looked somewhat like the double parlor in a large private house; it may have been modeled on Roosevelt's office arrangement in the double parlor of the Townsend residence. The north room—the Cabinet Room—was the larger of the two; directly behind it, to the south, was the President's Room. Sliding doors, usually left open, divided the rooms. Two great fireplaces gave the suite an intimacy uncharacteristic of offices. Roosevelt often held his small weekly receptions here, instead of in the East Room.

Except for the arrangements for the President and the secretary, the design of the new building was based upon the staff functions as carried out in the old office. Cortelyou's reorganization had not been made in time for McKim to take it into consideration. Most of the building was taken up by big rooms designed to hold many office workers. The entire west end, for example, was a staff room, with rows of desks and space in which to move about with ease; its predecessor had been the large chamber upstairs on the north side, today's Queen's Bedroom. Major Montgomery and his assistants no longer had to share the telegraph room with clerks, but had an office apart.

White House Beat

The single functional innovation of the Executive Office was a small press room to the right of the front entrance. There had never been an actual press room at the White House, but during the war McKinley had permitted reporters to work at tables in the east hall upstairs, in part as a means of keeping an eye on what they wrote. Bingham had a fully equipped press room in his elaborate plan for enlarging the house. Roosevelt owed much to the press, and enjoyed a friendly relationship with reporters. One year after assuming office, he had united his party and was assured of the Republican nomination in 1904, all due in large measure to his favorable treatment in the newspapers.

Creative press relations at the White House did not, however, begin with Roosevelt, but with Cleveland's secretary, Daniel Lamont. His expertise in managing and charming reporters had protected the gruff, spontaneous Cleveland, who loathed newsmen. McKinley's natural charm and frankness made reporters like him, and he was acutely aware of the value of favorable stories. Part of his magic was the work of his first secretary, John Addison Porter, who to some extent institutionalized the White House news procedures of Daniel Lamont. Porter's successor, Cortelyou was clever and well organized, producing "briefing papers" on complex issues. Having learned important lessons under President McKinley, Cortelyou ably promoted the early goodwill between Roosevelt and the press.

"Newspaper men nowadays have access to the President," reported W. W. Price in the Washington *Evening Star* not long after the press room in the new building was put into use, "but they do not intrude upon his privacy, except in cases of absolute necessity. They usually get all the information that is to be had by talking with the secretary or an assistant." Nevertheless, he noted, some information was less available in the new quarters. In the past, visitors to the President had been easily seen coming and going from the White House because they entered on the north and climbed the stairs in open view. Now they could pass through the south entrance, continuing through the ground floor corridor and along the colonnade of the west wing into the Executive Office. All those areas were off limits to everyone but the President's family, guests, and confidential callers with passes. Newsmen learned the value of keeping a vigil in the press room and lobby, not only noting all who came but also listening for clues to who might be calling privately. "Thus the White House," wrote Price, "has become a regular assignment for reporters . . . who remain at or near the building during the business hours of the President and keep in pretty close touch with what is going on."[10]

Chief Usher

The domestic arrangements of the remodeled house were altered even more than was the organization of the Executive Office. McKim seems not to have troubled himself much about how the house had traditionally functioned for entertaining. He answered to the Roosevelts only, and their knowledge of backstairs operations was probably vague. Many small White House customs were thus rendered obsolete by McKim's changes. When the Roosevelts moved back in, Cortelyou counseled Mrs. Roosevelt about the inevitable reorganization. She was interested in domestic management and worked amiably with Bingham, who was in charge of the building and its grounds.

For many years the structure of the White House domestic staff had remained generally the same. At the top was the steward, a federal employee who was bonded; the Congress had created this position to provide a public official who would protect the silver and furnishings in the house. The steward thus had gone on the government payroll, but he continued to function as the stewards had before, as manager of the house. He served two masters. The job required patience, administrative ability, shrewdness as a purchasing agent, and a deep sense of discretion. Beneath him were maids, footmen, cooks, and "laborers."[11]

About one-third of the servants lived in the White House when the Roosevelts moved there. Their homey rooms were in the basement, some dormitory, some private. The thick-walled plastered interiors, with their iron-barred windows, had been given wooden floors at least 70 years before, over Hoban's brick pavers, to make them less dank. Fireplaces and coal stoves provided warmth in winter, and there were separate baths for men and women.

At the White House, Roosevelt found little of the strict domestic organization usual in great houses. The steward dealt with each employee individually; there was no specified hierarchy. Most of the servants were southern blacks who had entered the President's service after similar experience in a hotel or private residence—or through a family connection, as a sister, brother, parent, or aunt already there. The tone of the house was therefore distinctly southern; the pace was slow, the relationships personal, and the social life characterized by comfortable elegance.

Traditionally, domestic management had been the prerogative of the steward. But by the late '80s such an arrangement was no longer efficient. As always at the White House, the circumstances revolved delicately around personalities. Cleveland had appointed William Sinclair as steward. He had little managerial ability, and thus the effectiveness of that crucial position was lessened. At last, early in McKinley's administration, the stewardship virtually collapsed. Others stepped in to discharge the vital responsibilities, and what began as interim rearrangements were ultimately formalized.

During the Cleveland years, whether by agreement or simply through necessity, the doorkeepers who served in the entrance hall began to assume many of Sinclair's responsibilities as steward, while he spent most of his time with the Clevelands. The doorkeepers met the market carts; they directed the maids and footmen in their daily work; they supervised the caterers. During the late 19th century, this group usually consisted of from three to five men, most of them recruited from among members of the Metropolitan Police.

Sinclair left with Cleveland in 1889. Two men followed him under Benjamin Harrison. Although the second of them, the gentlemanly butler Philip McKim, was an excellent steward, he found that he needed the help of the ushers. The extended functions of the doormen were recognized when Harrison appointed from among them a "chief doorkeeper." The salary of this official—usually called the "chief usher"—was $1,800 a year, the same as that of the steward; the regular doormen were paid $1,200. Edson S. Dinsmore, a member of the Metropolitan Police and a former doorman, was the first to hold the job.[12]

During Cleveland's second administration, Sinclair returned, and was given his old post again. A new chief usher was appointed, apparently with the full knowledge that the steward would take little of the general responsibility for the house. When Cleveland left in 1897, he asked that Sinclair be retained as steward. McKinley agreed, and Sinclair stayed on for the duration of the McKinley administration, but it was clear that the chief usher was in charge. The decline in importance of the steward's post was confirmed by Theodore Roosevelt. On September 28, 1901, six days after moving to the White House, he studied the typewritten document entitled "White House Staff—Regular and Detailed." One of only two changes he made was the dismissal of William Sinclair; he put in the position of steward his valet, Henry Pinkney. According to one member of the staff, the "Negro Pinkney . . . performed none of the duties of that office. His principal occupations were seeing that the Roosevelt children got to and from school and doing a little personal messenger work."[13]

The reorganization of the house, commenced in December 1902, was completed during the winter of 1903. Because Mrs. Roosevelt retained for herself the main responsibility for managing the White House, the first chief usher did not carry the authority his successors would have in later years. The revised organization of the house reflected her preferences, yet provided in the chief usher an official who could shoulder all the responsibility himself, should Mrs. Roosevelt be followed by First Ladies of different inclinations.

Thomas E. Stone of Washington was employed as chief usher early in 1903. The city directories list him in 1900 as a railroad conductor, and federal records show him to have been a native of Maryland. At the White House, Stone oversaw marketing as well as special contracts and agreements for services; he also carried out Mrs. Roosevelt's wishes concerning the operation of the house. The Roosevelts made severe and constant demands on the staff, and while they were profuse with compliments when things went well, they were also remembered as intolerant of mistakes. It was Stone's responsibility to make sure there was smooth sailing at the White House.[14]

Male servants—at least those who were white—aspired to become ushers. The ushers were close by at the most interesting activities, and usually had warm relationships with the President and his family. The eldest among the ushers was Tommy Pendel, by now a fixture in the East Room, telling his stories about the days of Lincoln. When the household electrician, Ike Hoover, learned in 1903 that the ushers' force would be increased, he applied for a place and got it, resigning his old job on June 24 and allowing himself one week's vacation. He appeared in frock coat on July 1, the beginning of the new fiscal year, to commence a long and colorful new career.

Under the new rules, ushers no longer carried firearms. They were easily identifiable as functionaries, wearing frock coats from 8 a.m. until 6 p.m., when they changed to white tie and tails for the evening. This pattern was repeated seven days a week, except when the family was gone in the summer. Then, business suits were worn all day.

At the beginning of the summer of 1903, the number of ushers was increased from five to nine. These men, all of them white, answered directly to the chief usher. He moved them about within the system, placing them in charge of different endeavors as the need arose. There were two shifts a day, with only three ushers off duty during any one shift; the ushers kept their headquarters in the small room to the right of the north entrance. The chief usher had his desk and cabinets there, rather than in the large steward's room in the basement, doubtless in part for convenience but also because he did not wish to be identified with the servants.

Beneath the ushers in rank were the waiters and footmen, and the maids and kitchen workers. All wore the Roosevelts' blue and buff livery. Henry Pinkney answered only to the Roosevelts, as did Mrs. Roosevelt's maid and the family governess. Other servants were responsible to Thomas Stone. Exactly how many there were is unclear, although records suggest probably 12 or 14. In theory, most of the servants were paid by the President, but his accounts indicate that many received federal salaries as "laborers."[15]

There was no organizational chart, no book of rules such as Cortelyou's. There seems to have been only a vague ladder of rank among the servants, and one person was likely to perform several tasks. Jerry Smith—known by this time as "old Jerry"—served both as a waiter and a butler, as well as a footman in the house and office, broom or feather duster in hand. If the title "doorman" meant nothing, and referred to ushers, then other titles were even more vague. Andrew Jackson Kennedy, for example, who managed the logistics for the large state occasions beginning in 1903, was not listed on the roll of White House employees for that year, but his name appeared in 1905. His title on the government books was "laborer." Reference is made to a "head butler," who was in charge of the dining room, the table furnishings, and the serving of meals. Ladies' maids, laundresses, and footmen are also mentioned in the various papers of the White House in the early 1900s.[16]

Beginning during the Spanish-American War, executive protection was in the hands of a mixture of ushers, policemen, and a detail of Secret Service agents who had come on duty at the White House during the war and remained. Security tightened following McKinley's assassination, and while the number of agents on duty is usually vague in the records, it is clear that Roosevelt was more heavily guarded than any previous peacetime President. At least two Secret Service men were always at the Executive Office, moving about quietly in street clothes. While they were ordered to be cordial to everyone, they were prepared to get tough should it become necessary.[17]

Roosevelt was uncomfortable with guards around, and he refused to have more than one or two with him at a time. Mrs. Roosevelt was not so casual about his safety, often secretly requesting additional agents, who were to conceal themselves from him. Her letters reveal that the President often had no idea of the extent to which he was guarded.

The official population at the White House was increased considerably by the guards. Including servants, office staff, gardeners, stablemen, Secret Service men, and ushers, approximately 57 people worked in and around the White House six days a week. The number was somewhat less on Sundays. The chief usher was to maintain an overview of all that was going on, and through him the wishes of the President and First Lady were to be carried out. In the beginning years this did not work as well as perhaps had been expected, and the Roosevelts assigned a military aide to attend to the more complex tasks. But the system gradually came into its own and by the advent of Roosevelt's successor, William Howard Taft, it was well established.

Immovable Rules

In her office, the family sitting room between the oval room upstairs and the presidential bedroom, Mrs. Roosevelt worked at a small desk designed to her specifications by McKim and built by Davenport; it had a flat surface and deep drawers, into which she fitted household papers. In theory she inspected all accounts, and although many certainly escaped her scrutiny, she was well aware of expenditures. The chief usher usually met with her several times a day, and other members of the staff were likely to be called to her office at any time. Mrs. Roosevelt shared in the social decisions once made by Warren Young. Seating charts, colors of china and flowers, types of foods and wines were her fascination, and she had particular ideas about entertaining. Her side of White House life was managed like a business.[18]

Previously, most First Ladies had passed the bulk of the letters along to someone in the Executive Office. Mrs. Roosevelt recalled that several of her own letters to Mrs. McKinley had never been answered and determined that things would be different under her. She arranged for all correspondence to be answered in one way or another. Now and then she wrote a personal note; to a stranger she usually sent one of her calling cards with an autograph, and, if the person was in Washington, she would likely send an invitation to a large function. Calling cards left at the north door always received a response. But she could not attend to all this business by herself.

Not long after moving into the White House in 1901 Mrs. Roosevelt arranged to have Isabella L. Hagner, a clerk in the War Department, detailed to her as a social secretary. Belle Hagner first worked only a few hours a day, then went full time, while remaining on the federal payroll. The secretary, a tall, buxom, engaging young woman, came from a prominent Washington family. She had served as a part-time social secretary to a group of local women, including the President's sister Mrs. Cowles. She was perfect for Edith Roosevelt's needs, being both discreet and well-versed in the social ways of the capital. Of her new job Belle Hagner later wrote, "I cannot say that I felt entirely at ease, but I do know that I felt very thrilled."[19]

She reported six days a week, sometimes seven, to the second floor sitting room. It was an uncomplicated office indeed. Papers were stacked on sofas and tables. Here she and Mrs. Roosevelt prepared the invitation lists, made up the seating charts, designed the floral decorations, and planned the menus. Appropriate employees were summoned as needed by means of speaking tubes that ran through the walls to the ushers' room and the service area of the basement.

"The season" at the White House focused on eight events of state: five receptions, and three seated dinners. Invitations to the dinners were among the most coveted in the world, for the guest lists were small, the largest being about 100 and the smallest about 30. Beyond these prescribed functions, the Roosevelts entertained heavily, not so much because they loved parties, but because a major component of the President's success was his personal popularity. As he won over the public with his speeches and by being good newspaper copy, he wooed more constricted circles with White House hospitality.

In support of him, Mrs. Roosevelt planned small dinners, luncheons, and sometimes breakfasts, and presided at weekly teas during the social season, serving hundreds of women tea, coffee, and cakes. Musicales and dances enlivened the winter nights. In Edith Roosevelt's time, it was not as difficult to decline a White House invitation as it is today, and out of a list of 600, perhaps 120 would regret. In response, the lists were made large, to guarantee a crowd.[20]

Under the Roosevelts, state entertaining became a combination of almost severe simplicity and showy ceremony. State functions had always had a gaudy side: overabundant decorations and a certain awkwardness in the way the President moved through his crowds of guests. What transpired early in the Roosevelt administration was a complete recasting of the social procedures to give a new image of presidential glory. Mrs. Roosevelt may have had advisers in this work, but she must be credited with making most of the changes herself.

Since 1834 the strict rules that governed state receptions and dinners had been set by the State Department and were usually based on the judgment of the secretary of state. Procedures in 1902 were not really so different from those of Andrew Jackson's time, although more nations were represented and the advent of full ambassadors had made the diplomatic scene more complex. At all White House social functions, proper recognition of rank was of the utmost importance. Colonel Bingham's notes detailed the hierarchy that determined the order of procession and reception, as well as the configuration of guests on seating charts:[21]

The President

The Chief Executive of Another Nation

The Vice President

The Next in Succession to the Headship of Another Nation

Grandson in Line of Succession of a Reigning Sovereign

Ambassadors

Supreme Court—component part of the US government

The Cabinet—cab members in their homes give foreign
    ministers the precedence

Foreign Ministers

Governors of States & Territories of the US

President Pro Temp of the Senate

Speaker of the House

Senators

Representatives

Officers of the Army & Navy
    1. grade
    2. in each grade, according to date of commission

Such was the basic framework Mrs. Roosevelt, Colonel Bingham, and Belle Hagner had to use in reshaping social functions.

After the Roosevelts returned to the White House in 1902 they began the social season as usual. The first two state events, the Cabinet dinner and the New Year's reception, were held according to the way things had been done before McKim's renovation. Guests entered in the old way, on the north, and left by way of the covered bridge set over the north areaway. The first time the transformed White House was employed in its entirety for a state function was on January 8, 1903, for the diplomatic reception. This event was the most magnificent one of any year, and the Roosevelts wished their first to be no exception.

There would be two entrances. For the first time, the new access through the east wing would be used for most arrivals, while special guests were to enter beneath the south portico, passing into the resuscitated basement oval room. It made an elegant entrance, glowing white, its walls ringed with side chairs. The 200 special guests left their coats in the dressing rooms to the right and left of the windowless oval chamber, and proceeded into the long, vaulted corridor. Rising in the elevator to the state floor eight at a time, the honored persons crossed the transverse hall into the Red Room.

Other changes were apparent to those who knew the house well. In place of servants and Secret Service men, there were quiet and composed military aides. In their full-dress uniforms they appeared almost luminous. The presence of the gallant-looking young men was Colonel Bingham's idea, and followed precedent set in the residences of high officers in the American military services and in some official households abroad. The justification for the aides was the same as for the Marine Band; the military men were serving their commander in chief. These nine men acted as social aides only in addition to performing regular military duties. At the diplomatic reception, as at most other White House festivities, they served as "floor managers."22

By 8 p.m., the stream of special guests was divided between the Red Room, where the early arrivals gathered and conversed, and the transverse hall, near the elevator passage. No food or drink was served; the conversation was low, for the guests anxiously awaited the performance to come. Those in the hall were among the few who witnessed President Roosevelt's entrance. Promptly at eight, just after the White House clocks had chimed, the blast of two trumpets and the rolling back of the iron gates at the foot of the grand stairway announced the descent of the presidential party.

It was a substantial procession, two abreast, and striking to see against the background of pale stone and white plaster. The first to appear were Bingham and a Roosevelt favorite, the dashing Major

Charles L. McCawley, a marine described in the press at the time as "the most popular young society man in Washington." Both were arrow-straight, solemn-faced, a vanguard of polished leather, shining brass, and gleaming gilt braid which in turn yielded to the flat and gloss, black and white, of men's dress suits and the sheen of silk and satin, the brilliance of diamonds, and the toss and flutter of tall feathered head ornaments. The presidential party followed, including house guests and a few invited from outside; they had assembled earlier in the oval room. In the upstairs corridor Bingham had arranged the marchers, allowing about 30 inches front and rear between each pair, and instructed the women to loop their trains over their arms.

The pace was not slow, but a healthy walk to music that kept those who had not practiced it shooting anxious glances at their feet lest they trip and the whole line fall like tin soldiers. About midway in the procession, the President descended with Mrs. Roosevelt at his side. She did not link her arm with his, but kept the pace with no support, handrail or otherwise. The official party crossed the transverse hall between two lines of aides and passed into the Green Room. Here the President stood for a short time, awaiting Bingham, who would come and stand beside him after he had placed the 20 or 30 people from the procession in the three parlors. The 200 who had arrived earlier then swarmed into the Blue Room, and as many as could packed themselves into its north end; those who found no room had to go to the north ends of the Red and Green rooms, standing behind the ones Bingham had stationed there. As the last squeezed into place, the military aides drew velvet ropes in front of them; any departure from that confine for the duration of the reception was absolutely prohibited.

Immediately after the ropes were in place, Bingham escorted the President and Mrs. Roosevelt into the Blue Room, where they stood with their backs to the south windows. He then took his position at the door to the Red Room, awaiting the line of callers. When all was in readiness, he nodded to an aide, who passed the nod to yet another aide, who signaled to the conductor of the Marine Band, which, with 40 pieces, was stationed between the columns of the entrance hall.

Strains of music were now audible to those waiting at the front of the basement stair, beneath the grand stairway. Two by two the line stretched from that stair east into the vaulted corridor to the glazed colonnade that ran out to East Executive Avenue. At the head of the line were the dignitaries and representatives of foreign nations, invited to the reception not by the President but by the secretary of state; they were received according to their rank, the ambassador of Great Britain at the

head. Other guests, with invitations direct from the White House, completed the line to the rear.[23]

Guests checked their wraps and hats in the coatrooms that opened
off the long east hall. All had been required to present special cards at
the door for admittance. Some had come in coaches or carriages, either
their own or, as was more often the case, rented. Their drivers were
required to take numbers printed on cards before proceeding to the parking lot improvised in the meadow south of the house. There on cold
winter nights campfires were built, and the drivers huddled around them
and talked; no matter how vehemently Bingham demanded that they
stay with their carriages, he was never able to crush this custom.

In the White House, at the first sounds of music, the two aides at
the foot of the basement stair removed the velvet rope that held the line
back. The waiting guests advanced, climbing to the entrance hall, where
smiling aides urged them to keep moving. On they pressed into the
ushers' room, which was stripped of most of its furniture and banked with
palms, turning left into the small elevator and service stair hall, and right
into the family dining room, where a temporary configuration of curtains
had created a little vestibule off the State Dining Room.

Moving south through the State Dining Room, then east through
the Red Room, the line narrowed to single file as it approached the Blue
Room. The first of the honored guests were posed about the Red Room,
smiling but saying nothing; nor could even the ambassadors stop and
admire, for they, like the ordinary guests to the rear, were kept on the
move. A brief pause was allowed at the door from the Red Room into the
Blue Room, where Bingham bent slightly forward to hear the visitor's
name, then repeated it as he passed the visitor's hand to his right, into
the grip of the President.[24]

Roosevelt seemed to enjoy himself. He had a word for everyone,
whether a jolly grunt or a happy phrase, or an entire sentence. He never
said enough to stop the line, however, for without really pausing he
shifted the caller's hand to that of Major McCawley, who introduced the
First Lady. Mrs. Roosevelt normally did not shake hands, although she
may have tried it at this first diplomatic reception. McCawley indicated
her preference by a gentle downward push on the visitor's hand. The
First Lady thought handshaking ungraceful for women, and resorted to
the usual device of carrying a bouquet, usually a mass of pink roses.
When bouquets became passé, by her third social season in 1904, she
finally yielded to the demand for her hand.[25]

The crowd at the diplomatic reception continued to move beyond
the receiving line through the Green Room for another display of

honored guests, then scattered as it poured into the East Room. Newsmen waited in the East Room, but they had been warned not to be obtrusive, lest they be ordered to leave. The diplomats in their formal attire were accompanied by ladies in court regalia, with jeweled tiaras, ostrich feathers, long ropes of natural pearls, and often six-foot court trains, which they carried over the wrist, except when standing still.

Though the diplomatic receptions were the most celebrated social occasions of high political and diplomatic society, they were universally considered dull. The diplomats usually lingered in the East Room only long enough to be seen by the majority of the other guests. Perhaps it was curiosity over the new forms that made them stay a little longer on January 8, 1903. That night they waited until the trumpet blasts announced the return of the Roosevelts to the second floor. Once the President was out of sight—he departed this time by climbing the grand staircase, but most times thereafter by the elevator—the gathering became confused and noisy, as people puzzled over what route they must follow to their coats and carriages. But the new procedures were soon put into effect. The military aides urged people to the basement stair, through the northernmost door of the East Room. Once below, the company headed for the glazed colonnade on the east. On the other end of the state floor the honored guests left in the elevator and found their carriages pulling up to receive them on the south driveway.

In the east wing, as hat and coat checks were received, an usher took the carriage number from the guest. Another usher flashed the number on the electric machine set up temporarily in the parking lot south of the house. Having been summoned, a coachman then took his place in the line on East Executive Avenue and, following the directives of the Metropolitan Police, made his way at last to the east porte cochere, where he was allowed ten seconds to wait for his passengers. If they did not emerge he was ordered to go to the end of the line, back at the parking lot. This rule particularly annoyed the drivers. For insolent coachmen, no matter how weary or drunk, there was little toleration. According to written instructions, they were to be treated firmly by the police, but with courtesy to avoid incident. Their names and addresses were to be taken down, however, so they could be arrested at their homes the following morning.[26]

The procedures of the diplomatic reception became customary at all state functions. Abundant criticism inevitably followed, for the Roosevelts had given an entirely new tone to White House hospitality. The President's style was called kingly, his "court" dubbed "imperial." Always before there had been the strained effort to make great events seem homey; this exercise was at last omitted, and the style which replaced it was slick and elegant. But the new pomp also had a refreshingly pragmatic side: The state receptions no longer masqueraded as entertainments. They were now seen as what they were, ceremonial performances, serving to bring the guests—in this case the diplomatic corps—into personal contact with the head of state. The moment of contact was the only significant part of any ceremonial occasion, and so the events were trimmed of everything superfluous to them.

Good-bye Colonel Bingham

In general the procedures instituted at the diplomatic reception had worked well, although there were rough spots. The stairs had been too crowded; for a 15-minute period there had been a carriage jam in the parking lot; and it had been difficult to manage the line when, after threading through the small rooms and passages, it scattered in the vastness of the great State Dining Room. Bingham gloated over these details, noting the next day that "the old problem has been no more solved by McKim than it ever was, namely, to accommodate two thousand people in a House which has space for only one thousand."[27]

The colonel's grudge against the new White House was stronger than ever, and that soon led to his downfall. Until this point, he had gotten along well with the Roosevelts. The President thought highly of him and praised his helpfuness in making a success of the new official ceremonies. Bingham, however, was negative about many of the innovations. He was unhappy with the changing definition of his job, having less power and exercising less creativity than he had under McKinley. Always imperious, he became imprudent.

His final misstep came about a month after the diplomatic reception. He had asked the Congress for a large appropriation for White House expenses; seeing to this had long been part of the commissioner's job. Receiving little encouragement, the impatient Bingham wrote a long letter warning Speaker Cannon that the renovated house cost twice what the previous mansion had cost to operate. In his zeal to convince the speaker, he became so angry that the letter he wrote seemed to characterize the house as a monument to presidential extravagance. When the document was shown to Roosevelt, Bingham was dismissed.[28]

On February 13, Bingham's job was filled by another West Pointer, Colonel Thomas W. Symons, who served about a year before poor health forced his resignation. He was succeeded on April 26, 1904, by the amiable Colonel Charles S. Bromwell. The first non-West Pointer to serve as officer in charge of the public buildings and grounds, Bromwell, a friend of Roosevelt's, held the position quietly until the end of the Roosevelt administration.

Charles Bromwell seldom participated in the planning of social events. He introduced the President on ceremonial occasions and accompanied him in public whenever necessary. Otherwise his White House work centered on the maintenance and improvement of the building and grounds. Society at the White House was run entirely from the sitting room on the second floor.

Roses for Roosevelt

If state entertaining was the most grandiose spectacle at the White House, the most frequent entertainments offered by the Roosevelts were private parties—insofar as any White House party can be "private." Older members of the staff were awed by the frequency and the gala air of the Roosevelts' parties. Social life, wrote an usher, was "A continual two-step and spirited waltz for seven and one half years. The music varied, but the pace never ceased."[29]

Most meals, beyond the breakfast eaten in the tall, airy west hall upstairs, were festive, because there was usually company. Lunch was served in the private dining room on the north side of the house, while most dinners were in the State Dining Room. The Roosevelts loved to eat. With a taste for plain food, the President consumed repasts fit for a farmhand three times a day, without surrendering for an instant his control over the conversation.

For routine meals the food was prepared by the resident kitchen staff, a cook from Sagamore Hill and two assistants. Waiters served it, and when the meal was over they cleaned up, washing the dishes in the main floor pantry where they were kept. Large dinners were prepared by caterers under contracts arranged by the chief usher. The principal caterer, who produced all but a few of the Roosevelt dinners, was Charles Rauscher, owner of an establishment at L Street and Connecticut Avenue. He had been chef at Louis Sherry's in New York, and had recently moved to the capital to compete with Jules Demonet, head of the venerable Demonet family, still the leading caterers and confectioners of the city. Rauscher replaced Demonet in favor at the White House after the renovation of 1903.[30]

Rauscher gave an urbane character to the menus, which he planned in council with Mrs. Roosevelt. His repasts were greeted with delight and talked about for days. Rauscher catered the dinner given for the Cabinet during the Christmas season of 1903. The menu, which survives in pidgin French among notes made by Bromwell, offers a sample of his culinary practice:[31]

White wines Blue Point Oysters on Ice Plates
Boston Brown Bread
*
Sherry Potage Créme Columbia with Croutons
*
Stuffed Olives, Curled Celery, Salted Almonds
*
White Wine Potomac Bass à la Pécheur
Cucumber Potatoes Hollandaise
*
Stuffed Celery au Jus, Bouchees à la Mocelle
*
Red Wine Filet of Vanaison Grand Vensiur
Cassolette Nesselrode Sauce Chasseur
*
Champagne Terrapin à la Baltimore
*
Sorbet
Spoon au Kirsch (fancy candy pieces)
*
Champagne Roasted Quails à la Lucullus Salad Rachel
Cheese Pull Bread
*
Glace
Apollinaris Fastaisie Mousse Merveilleuse
Petits Fours Asortis Marrons Glascés
Certises Marquises Bonbons fourres
*
Cafe
*
Ht. Sauternes. Sherry Amontillado. Claret Chat.
Langoiran. Champagne Ruinart Brut.
Apollinaris. Liqueurs.

For this particular dinner there were 22 waiters—one for every two guests—all but eight hired for the occasion. Fourteen was a more typical number. Rauscher, however, only advised on serving, so that he could concentrate on the food. Some dishes he brought with him, putting on final touches and rewarming them at the house. Such cooking as he did at the White House involved foods, such as soufflés, that had to be prepared at the last minute. The state floor pantry in the northwest corner had been thoroughly modernized with gas ovens, counters and sinks, and an electric dumbwaiter opening directly into the adjoining kitchens on the ground floor. All food service centered on the pantry. A little curving stair built into a deep window reveal linked the pantry with the smaller of the two kitchens. On the day before a dinner Rauscher and his assistant usually moved into the larger kitchen and remained until the event was over.[32]

The work of preparing the house for a large dinner began immediately after breakfast. Andrew Jackson Kennedy, in charge of all extraordinary arrangements, attended to awnings, chairs, platforms, temporary or makeshift tables, carpet runners, and the like. Much of the party equipment was stored at his brother's electric shop on Connecticut Avenue. For dinners of 20, the dining room could be left as it was, with the round table in place. Larger numbers required the return of the rectangular table from storage, and sometimes the inclusion of the table from the adjacent private dining room. For a dinner with more than 40 guests, the regular tables were carried to the basement, to be replaced by the so-called "white pine table tops" which sat on trestles in the shape of a large horseshoe. The horseshoe table was first used at the Cabinet dinner on December 18, 1902. An alternative, introduced during the winter of 1903, was to use small tables seating six to eight guests each.

White damask tablecloths were the invariable rule, spread over white flannel silence cloths. Mrs. Roosevelt took particular interest in the floral decorations. The void left by Pfister was soon filled by George H. Brown, who styled himself a "landscape gardener." Together he and Mrs. Roosevelt designed the centerpieces and other adornments for the dinners. Like most of her predecessors, Mrs. Roosevelt loved roses. There may have been more to this than mere preference, for the President considered the rose a family emblem. He displayed a family crest which featured them prominently on china and bookplates, but many years later his daughter Alice said puckishly to an inquiring scholar, "the crest is a fraud. Our ancestors were gardeners!"[33]

Roses tended to dominate the table decorations. Brown usually divided the Monroe plateau into several separate sections and mounted each one with a low, full arrangement of roses of the same color mixed with asparagus ferns; between the sections he placed tall, trumpet-shaped vases of silver or crystal, with more roses and ferns. Floral table adornments were seldom more elaborate than this, except for the "art pieces," which tended to appear on special occasions. After Mrs. Roosevelt had approved the flowers, she positioned on the table's surface a series of white Sevres porcelain figures, classical statuettes presented to the

Rochambeau commemorative commission by the French government and given by the commission to Mrs. Roosevelt.

The call for flowers was great; the greenhouses could not supply it, and Brown had recourse to a florist. At the diplomatic dinner on January 15, 1903, the color theme was red and white, with green ferns. Brown collected 600 red roses, 736 red crane carnations, 528 white carnations, 2,000 white Roman hyacinths, 252 white lilies of the valley, 250 asparagus sprays, and 1,000 cuttings of maidenhair fern.

For small, informal dinners the parlors and the State Dining Room remained much as they were, decorated with a few big, loose bouquets and bud vases holding roses or lilies. By "informal" the Roosevelts meant "unofficial," as opposed to "state." About a week before such an occasion, engraved invitations with the guest's name and the time added in elegant script were hand delivered. On the specified evening, the company arrived at the east entrance, leaving wraps in the coatroom. If there were more than 20 guests, each male received a small engraved seating chart showing the outline of the table with the seats around it numbered. A check mark added in ink identified his place, and he would be responsible for the woman assigned as his dinner partner. Military aides directed the company to the elevator, from which, once upstairs, they passed to the Red Room, where Bromwell greeted them.[34]

The colonel introduced dinner partners. At the time stated on the invitations, Bromwell went upstairs to get the President and Mrs. Roosevelt, accompanying them in the elevator to the main floor. The President passed down the transverse hall, unseen by the guests in the Red Room. The Marine Band waited silently in the entrance hall.

While the President, Mrs. Roosevelt, and Bromwell placed themselves in the southwest corner of the Blue Room, adjacent to the closed door into the Red Room, the band struck up the national anthem. Then an aide opened the door, and the line began to form. The leader, or "senior guest"—selected in advance by age or rank—began the line, and the other guests followed his cues. When Roosevelt had greeted the last guest, Henry Pinkney, in white tie and tails, appeared in the north door of the Blue Room to proclaim "Dinner is served!" Bromwell presented Roosevelt's dinner partner to the President, and Mrs. Roosevelt's to her. He then stood aside, and they passed into the hall, the other partners falling into line behind. The colonel, with his dinner partner, was the last to seat himself at the table.[35]

These informal dinners were more relaxed than state banquets. When the rectangular table was used, the President and his wife sat directly across from each other at its center. Conversation was often clever and sometimes personal, although Henry Adams complained that Roosevelt talked too much in the first place and in the second place talked too much about himself. In this same vein Governor Samuel W. Pennypacker of Pennsylvania observed, "Hardly an observation was made by anyone else at the table, and in fact, it would only have been possible by the exercise of a sort of brutal force." Many conversations usually went on at once, but when the President raised his voice, other conversation faded in deference. [36]

When coffee was finished, the President rose to his feet. Bromwell went immediately to his side and led the way to the room designated as a smoking room—usually the private dining room, with its table removed or set aside and a circle of comfortable chairs in place. More coffee was served, and cigars were passed. The women guests, meanwhile, followed Mrs. Roosevelt through the door to the Red Room. For about half an hour, they, like the men, were free to descend in the elevator to the basement "dressing rooms." From the smoking room, after the last cigars were extinguished, the President and the men went to the Red Room to join the ladies. Liqueurs were poured. After about 15 or 20 minutes, the senior guest bade the President and Mrs. Roosevelt goodnight, the signal for all others to do likewise.

Left alone in the Red Room, the Roosevelts and their house guests ascended to the second floor, while the machinery of departure was still grinding for the guests in the east wing. Already the regular household staff had begun to clean the state rooms. At daybreak the house would look as though no activity had taken place. With a policeman as escort, the extra waiters and maids went to the west gate, surrendering their temporary passes as they walked into the street.

Tea and Music

Social functions of another sort served large crowds. The need had arisen since the war for entertainments which were neither like dinner parties—with highly selective guest lists—nor like public receptions that required no invitation. Mrs. Roosevelt designed for this purpose teas and musicales. Teas were weekly events during the social season. Obtaining an invitation was easy: a letter was written requesting one, or a lady sent her card, or went to the White House and left it, dog-eared, to show she had appeared in person. From these names Belle Hagner composed a list for Mrs. Roosevelt's approval. There was no way to scrutinize every entry on the list, but she and the First Lady did the best they could. Mrs. Roosevelt was determined that no person of bad reputation receive the hospitality of the White House, knowing that for many years prostitutes had considered it sport to attempt to enter the great receptions. Occasionally this worked, but not as a rule. The police were on the lookout; they knew who most of the women were, and the intrusions were few.

Invitations to the teas might number as many as 600 or as few as 300. About 80 percent of the invitations sent were accepted. Women presented themselves in afternoon costume at the east entrance, wearing hats and gloves. After leaving their coats, parasols, and similar encumbrances in the hat box, they ascended to the main floor, where Mrs. Roosevelt stood at the head of a receiving line in the East Room. With her were Cabinet wives, and usually some female relatives.

The teas lasted from two until four. Coffee, tea, punch, and cakes were served in the State Dining Room, and the ladies were free to wander over the state floor, enjoying whatever music was provided. The teas were democratic affairs in a way. Members of the house party were encouraged to mingle with the guests. Although Negroes were excluded, most others were admitted regardless of ethnic origin, if they were able to solicit an invitation and dress appropriately. Clerks in the departments and salesgirls in shops mingled with women from the palatial houses on Massachusetts Avenue. Washington women took visiting lady relatives to the teas. Strangers in the city were advised to leave their cards at the north door, so that their Washington stay could be climaxed by tea at the White House.

Mrs. Roosevelt's teas echoed a practice followed in private Washington mansions since at least the mid-1880s; her musicales were a larger version of another local custom. She learned early that an evening of music, scheduled well after the dinner hour, was an elegant and inexpensive way to entertain large groups. The musicales were introduced to the White House on December 3, 1903, and the form prevails today. In Roosevelt's time, there were usually two a month, from December to April. The invitations never varied:[37]

MRS. ROOSEVELT

Requests the Pleasure of Your Company
on _____ *evening*
at ten o'clock

Music

From 200 to 600 were invited each time. Musicales lasted about an hour and a half. During the last half hour light refreshments were served on a large round table placed in the transverse hall outside the Blue Room.

Preparations for the events were fairly simple. Gilded bentwood chairs were brought down from the attic. A platform was set up in the north end of the East Room and covered with carpeting. The room was decorated with palms, and the curtains were closed. The guests entered through the east wing, ascending by the stair to the state floor, where aides showed them to the East Room. Except for the first two rows, seating was general. The Roosevelts entered to trumpets immediately before the entertainment.

Various sorts of entertainers appeared—choirs, violinists, singers, quartets, dancers. The Marine Band occasionally played. But Mrs. Roosevelt's favorite performers were pianists, and when she began her program of musicales, Steinway & Sons in New York presented a concert grand piano to the White House. It was an elaborate instrument, the wooden case richly carved with symbols of music and eagles with outstretched wings, all covered with greenish and yellowish gilt. The painter Thomas W. Dewing decorated the inside of the lid with a scene of the nine Muses adoring the allegorical figure of the American republic. Such symbolic splendor had not been seen since the days of Monroe.

Favor and Disfavor

Since the Roosevelts were holding court in a way not seen in the White House before, they were naturally anxious that every event be perfect. Mrs. Roosevelt considered herself the social arbiter of Washington. Remembering the snide treatment accorded her predecessor, Mrs. Harrison, she demanded, and in many respects won, the authority to set the city's social pace. Washington society, with its essentially political character, had been since Dolley Madison's day liberal in accepting persons whose private and sometimes public conduct would have rendered them unacceptable elsewhere. This tradition Mrs. Roosevelt rejected. Morality, restraint, and good manners became prerequisites to receiving White House invitations, even for many politicians.[38]

Not content with scrutinizing the guest lists for teas, she was determined to purge the social scene of unacceptable names. To this end, she turned the Cabinet wives into a sort of genteel secret police, charged with bringing her news about people who were likely to be invited to the White House. She met with them every Tuesday during the winter. They called at 11 in the morning, and were dismissed promptly at 12, only occasionally remaining with an invitation to lunch. Ushers showed them to the second floor, where they were taken to Mrs. Roosevelt's sitting room. From all accounts it was a formal occasion. The First Lady sat in a large armchair near the windows, and the Cabinet wives sat on two long sofas on each side of her. Mrs. Roosevelt introduced all subjects. Individuals, especially women, were the predominant topics, and the judgments were sometimes severe. Now and then a guilty party was notified and given a chance to reform, but the condemned faced the agony of anticipating, but not receiving, the invitations.[39]

At the Tuesday meetings the First Lady also discussed current events and made announcements about social procedures. Despite their snobbishness, the meetings served an important purpose. Entertaining was a vital part of the President's general scheme for promoting the glory of his office and thus America's new world power. Cabinet wives found the meetings useful in keeping up with the fast Roosevelt pace. For Mrs. Roosevelt the Tuesday circle seems to have helped her battle the isolation that always threatens those who live in the White House, and thus to have helped her perform effectively in the world around it.

Suppers

In the interest of making fewer mistakes, the Roosevelts tried to remain close to the established patterns of White House entertaining. Where they departed from the norm was in their small parties; notable among these were the suppers in the corridor of the family quarters upstairs, after state receptions. These began more or less on a whim of the Roosevelts to assemble a small party of friends, but they were so popular that they were repeated again and again, becoming part of the regular social scene. No entertainment seemed more intimate than these; beginning in 1904, all state receptions were followed by small dinners upstairs. For the staff, they were among the most difficult of all social functions. Few details of the setting up could begin before the President and his entourage descended to the reception, and the moving of tables, chairs, food, and decorations up from the basement was a horrendous chore. When the President returned upstairs with his supper guests, they lingered in the west hall in full view of the central corridor where dinner was to be served. Any preparations by the servants had to be conducted with speed and silence. The elevator and the service stair were the only routes between the kitchen and the family quarters, and when the supper company was gone, the cleaning up was made more arduous by the need to accomplish it without disturbing the family or the overnight guests, whose bedrooms opened onto the corridor.

The guests at these small dinners, invited by handwritten note, attended the reception, lingered, and eventually followed the President and Mrs. Roosevelt upstairs when the receiving line closed. They climbed the stairs, since the elevator was needed by the staff. Their ascent, with throngs of departing people watching, was not without its own satisfaction. On the second floor, military aides directed the guests, usually about 30, to the west hall, where they were served whiskey, wine, or Apollinaris water. The center hall was filled with tables for four and six, each with its floral arrangement.

Food was sometimes served as a dinner, sometimes as a buffet. There was only one wine with the alternative of Apollinaris water or plain water for those who did not drink alcohol; the men were likely to request scotch-and-water at table, instead of wine. There were several reasons for the Roosevelts to serve one wine at these private dinners, as opposed to the six or seven usually featured at state dinners. One was the relatively new custom of serving alcohol before dinner, which made it unnecessary to pour so much wine at table. The restriction to one wine may have been an economic measure as well; one wine could be poured in abundance, without the waste that always accompanied the serving of many wines. Decanting during the meal made it certain that every drop was used before new bottles were opened.[40]

The food was brought up in the elevator from the basement. Portable electric warmers were placed in the elevator hall upstairs and in the central corridor near the serving tables. A minimum number of waiters were enlisted, seldom including more than the resident staff. Everything took place in the west hall and the center hall. There was no withdrawing room or smoking room. The men lighted their cigars at table, as coffee was served.

Other special parties usually took place in the more convenient rooms of the state floor. One of the most memorable was the children's party the day after Christmas of 1903, an afternoon occasion meant to honor children who lived in Washington year-round. The idea probably came from Belle Hagner, a devoted Washingtonian. Mrs. Roosevelt, her social secretary, and the Cabinet wives, with suggestions from the Roosevelt offspring, composed a long guest list, and 550 of those invited accepted. The Marine Band played carols, stationed in its usual place in the hall. Children, mothers, maids, and nannies were admitted at the east entrance. Maids and nannies were seated with refreshments in the lower hall; the mothers were sent to the three parlors; the children, all under 12, were led to the East Room. There, a platform with Christmas trees had been set up against the north wall. The children were entertained by a lively singing and dancing company from Chicago known as

Toney's Boys, who kept their audience entranced for an hour, inviting the children to join in song from time to time.

At the instant Toney's Boys made their exit, President and Mrs. Roosevelt appeared at the hall door to the East Room and invited the crowd to march with them to the dining room for punch and cookies. The band played, and the scramble began. Chairs were overturned as the mob surged toward the hall, following the President's prancing steps in glee to the State Dining Room, where they found the table piled high with sweets. When the children had eaten their fill, the Roosevelts began to wonder what to do with them, for the party had yet an hour to go. Urged back to the East Room, now emptied of the chairs and plat-form, the little company ran wild across the great polished floor until the nurses and nannies had to be called up from the basement corridor to put a stop to the carnival and calm down their charges. Promptly at 6:30 the aides scattered among the adults, suggesting that they and the children begin moving toward the coatrooms.[41]

The only other exceptions the Roosevelts made to the usual social schedule were the spring garden parties. Several were held each year, beginning in 1903, and Mrs. Roosevelt made this an opportunity to show off her colonial gardens, which were south of the east and west wings, nestled close to the colonnades. They were intimate gardens, with inter-secting graveled paths and flower beds outlined with boxwood and privet and often filled with roses and lilies.[42]

Guests entered the gardens through the east wing, much as they did for any affair at the White House, then proceeded along the basement corridor to the oval room, and outside through the archway under the south portico. A small receiving line greeted them in the paved area immediately outside, between the two stairs to the porch above, where the Marine Band was stationed playing popular music. Mrs. Roosevelt received alone, unless the President joined her. She carried her gloves and wore a wide-brimmed hat. After passing though the receiving line, the guests were allowed considerable freedom to wander about on the south grounds. Secret Service men were stationed in various places throughout, and walked along the fences outside. The gardens, a hobby of Mrs. Roosevelt's, were of much interest to the guests, and the paths were always crowded.

Most of the people, however, collected on the broad lawn south of the house; most wore white, the women in big hats, their bodices often delicately embroidered in flowers or ribbons or butterflies. Refreshments were served in two open-sided canvas tents with single tables down their centers. "A White House garden-party in the spring is a pretty sight," said the leading published guide to manners and society in the city in 1906. "The bright dresses of the ladies, with their gay parasols, and the tents for refreshments, make a pretty and picturesque scene against the background of the well-kept lawns. . . ."[43]

Princess Alice

Entertaining at the Roosevelt White House was climaxed on February 17, 1906, when Miss Alice was wed to Nicholas Longworth, a junior congressman from Ohio. She was 22 and the most celebrated young woman in the United States, for her position, her beauty, and her daring in breaking some of the rules by which polite society lived. She smoked cigarettes and drove an automobile, even though her father disapproved of both, the first understandably and the second because he believed the Roosevelts should remain a horse family apart from the new machines. Miss Alice was mentioned in the social columns far more often than her parents and most other equally stern judges deemed appropriate.

Despite the publicity, most of the plans for the wedding celebration were kept secret. But the bride remained very much in the public eye. Alice and her stepmother were usually entertained once or twice daily when they were in Washington. Luncheons, teas, and tea dances consumed most days, and most evenings were taken up by dinner parties. Shopping trips to New York were often in the press. Purchases there, however, were held in the strictest confidence.

Invitations to the wedding were in demand. The list was carefully prepared by the President and Mrs. Roosevelt, in council with Alvey Adee, the State Department's expert on official procedures. Belle Hagner attended to the details, with assistance from Warren Young and two other members of the President's office staff. After the announcement on December 14, 1905, an avalanche of gifts descended on the White House, some doubtless sent in hope of drawing an invitation in return; hundreds of letters requested invitations outright. But neither ploy guaranteed an invitation. One thousand guests were invited, and for an event of such universal fascination, the number was small.

Charles Rauscher was engaged to provide two breakfasts, one in private for the wedding party and a second for the 700 guests whose invitations contained a special card allowing them to remain after the wedding. Floral arrangements were planned by Mrs. Roosevelt and George Brown. Crowd management was left to Colonel Bromwell and Chief Usher Stone. It was a complicated task, in that there were several classes of guests, all of whom must be made to feel welcome and, as much as possible, equal. That there would be a large extra force of Metropolitan Police and Secret Service men was taken for granted, but the number was never revealed. Three different entrances were used for the guests, the north door for family friends, the south for the highest ranking diplomats, and the usual east entrance for everyone else.

Enthusiastic crowds began collecting on the sidewalks and in Lafayette Park early in the morning. It was a radiant day, with full sun and clear air. By 11 the streets around the White House were mere aisles dividing throngs of spectators, and at that hour the first carriages began to make their way onto East Executive Avenue and toward the east entrance, which opened promptly at 11:15. Wedding guests who came on foot had to walk in the street, for the sidewalks were blocked by people. They paraded past in their furs, feathers, and black broadcloth, eliciting applause and the clicking of Kodaks.

Once inside, the guests were directed to the East Room, a few to reserved seats but most to places where they would stand. Ribbons stretched between standards over the vast, polished floor marked off sections for family, officials of various sorts, and the wedding party. Against the wide east window was the rounded platform usually used for performances in the north end, its surface now covered by an Oriental rug. The window and its yellow draperies formed the background for a wall of palms; swagged garlands of Easter lilies and asparagus ferns decorated the mantels. Window curtains were left open, with clusters of palms screening the view from outside. On the pier tables between the windows were porcelain tubs brimming with white rhododendrons.

All one thousand guests crammed uncomfortably into the East Room to witness Alice Roosevelt's wedding. The press had a good vantage point in the transverse hall. The guest list was fairly democratic, including people from many different walks of life. Diplomats, who had been told not to wear official regalia for this "private" occasion, were hardly distinguishable from the others. There were reminders of times gone by. Present, for example, was that White House bride of three decades before, Nellie Grant Sartoris, now 50 and divorced.

Shortly after Mrs. Roosevelt was escorted to the front line by her son Ted, the gongs and bells of the clocks clanged noon, and two trumpeters in the Marine Band stood and delivered a rousing fanfare. Then the band struck up the march. Alice and her father had already descended in the elevator and were waiting behind the closed hall doors of the State Dining Room. Two ushers rolled the mahogany doors aside. The entire wedding party marched together, behind the President and his daughter, down the transverse hall, passing before the Marine Band

and the reporters and at last into the bright sunlight of the East Room.

Alice wore a luxurious dress of white satin trimmed in lace handed down by her mother, Alice Lee, and her grandmother. The dress was low waisted, with large bows on the short sleeves. A wreath of orange blossoms held the veil, which covered the long train. The diamond necklace she wore was her wedding present from the groom. Her large bouquet had depleted the supply of orchids in Washington, accounting for the absence of the usual orchid corsages among the ladies. When the service ended Alice went to her stepmother and embraced her. She and Longworth and the President stood on the platform for an official photograph. Her cousin Franklin Delano Roosevelt arranged her train.

The wedding party then went into the transverse hall and walked to the rose-laden private dining room to dance and eat a light breakfast. Meanwhile, President and Mrs. Roosevelt and the bride formed a receiving line in the south end of the Blue Room; the 700 guests asked to remain came from the East Room through the Green Room, shook hands and, without stopping—for the military aides kept them moving—went from the Blue Room to the Red Room to the State Dining Room. In the dining room, the guests found white and red roses massed against the dark paneling.[44]

When the receiving line ended, the bride and groom went to the State Dining Room to cut the wedding cake. The newspapers made a great issue of her commandeering Major McCawley's dress sword for this performance, but she corrected the story many years later: "Any news accounts of the day which say I *seized* a sword and brandished it aloft before slicing the cake are certainly not correct. That makes me sound like a rude hoyden. I certainly did not leap on Charlie McCawley and take his sword. He was standing beside me and politely offered it, and so I used it to cut the cake."[45]

The Longworths departed in an automobile, slipping away almost unnoticed by the wedding guests and the crowds that remained along the streets. They spent two weeks in Cuba, then in June sailed to Europe, where crowned heads and chiefs of state received them as royalty from the new star among great powers.

31

Chronicles

Roosevelt fit the Presidency of his time, and he was always quick to affirm that the job suited him. Though McKinley was highly popular and had made major changes, he had been unable to impress upon the public mind that the new position of the United States in world affairs called for a new definition of presidential leadership. Roosevelt dramatized the changes by dramatizing himself. The presidential image designed by Roosevelt was dubbed "imperial," both in praise and scorn. If George Washington had once collared an aide for announcing him in too kingly a manner, and if Cleveland had blushed crimson when once he had to descend the grand stairway between two lines of military officers standing at attention, Roosevelt was perfectly comfortable when he entered a room to trumpet fanfare. He delighted in his entourage of uniformed military aides, most of them representing distinguished American families.

The first "imperial" White House was Monroe's, symbolizing the Era of Good Feelings. Monroe had worn knee breeches and powdered hair long after both were passé; his wife had dressed in rich style and received while staying seated; they had filled the state rooms with princely furnishings from Napoleonic France. Polk's "imperial" White House was next, symbolizing Manifest Destiny. Somber James K. Polk had marched to his dinner table to rousing band music, through state rooms made rich once again with gilded furniture. But Roosevelt's White House shouted imperial magnificence, where Monroe's and Polk's had merely suggested it. In his wake the stage could no longer be changed by a mere replacement of furniture. When he came into office, the White

House was far more complex, and thus more pliable, than it was when he left. His radical alterations trimmed it to a simple, indelible statement with which all who followed him would have to come to terms. Presidents through history had imposed their personal styles upon the White House. Now the White House would begin to impose a presidential image upon them, and they would sometimes be measured according to how well they fit it.

Authors

The fact that many people believed the White House had been destroyed by Roosevelt's renovations was seen in an upsurge of public interest in the old mansion. Conspicuous among the articles written to supply this demand was a historical essay by Abby Gunn Baker that appeared in *The Independent* in 1903. A resident of Washington and known to Mrs. Roosevelt, Miss Baker would be for 50 years the authority on White House history and memorabilia. Her article was a nostalgic journey through the past; when she referred to McKim's "restoration" she always used quotation marks. "It cannot but be regretted," she wrote, "that the Congress of the United States has not pursued a more far-sighted policy toward [the White House]."[1]

Abby Baker believed the Congress would have been better off had it left the historical White House untouched and built a new house for the President, "instead of providing for the present unsightly executive office building and the repairs to the mansion last year." A new residence would have made it possible for the White House to have "remained unchanged, the building intact as it was when all of our Chief Executives lived in it (with the single exception of Washington) during the first century of our history. As such it would have been preserved as Mount Vernon is preserved—a shrine for the American people."

Despite Miss Baker's disapproval, Roosevelt continued to be enthusiastic about his new home. He admired the appreciative assessment of McKim's work by Charles Moore that had appeared in *The Century Magazine* the previous April and that likely had inspired Abby Gunn Baker's rebuttal. Though Roosevelt's reaction to her article is not known, he was in general infuriated by negative criticism of the renovated house. To the president of *Outlook* magazine, his friend Lawrence Fraser Abbott, Roosevelt wrote a long letter defending himself: "It was not on my recommendation, for I 'made' none whatever, and did not think of making one. It was done because in Congress democrats and republicans alike agreed that it was absolutely necessary."[2]

"The changes," he continued, "were carried through by McKim, Mead & White, the effort being to restore the White House to what it was originally planned and designed to be in the days of Washington and Jefferson. Every competent architect in the country will tell you that it was genuinely patriotic service thus to restore it to its old simple and stately dignity." He then referred Abbott to Moore's article in *The Century Magazine* for the real facts of the case. "Only a yahoo could have his taste offended," Roosevelt concluded, "and excepting a yahoo, only a very base partisan politician would complain of it."

Nevertheless, the White House had lost—along with its sagging ceilings, its scaling walls, its cumbersome greenhouses, and the wood floors that creaked beneath the carpets—the evocative visual quality of its accumulated past. To the ordinary person, it no longer provided touchstones to history. Instead, it looked like the product of a uniform concept of design; it seemed new, like an exhibition hall at one of the great fairs of the time, or perhaps a public library. Where was the house of Jefferson, Jackson, Lincoln, and Grant?

Citizens turned to books as well as articles to assuage their curiosity. The historic home of the Presidents had already been an important part of many books about Washington and the political scene, the best known being the two-volume *Reminiscences of Sixty Years in the National Metropolis* written by the newspaperman and antiquarian Ben Perley Poore and published in 1886. Mrs. John A. Logan's *Thirty Years in Washington,* published in 1901, originally stopped with McKinley, but McKinley was assassinated when her book was still in galleys, and she hastily updated it with a chapter on the Roosevelts.

At the turn of the century there were few books by residents or former residents of the house. The memoir by Paul Jennings, *A Colored Man's Reminiscences,* published in 1866, was the earliest, recounting the burning of the White House by the British as he had seen it half a century before. Papers and letters of various Presidents had been published through the years, but none of them said much about life in the White House. Similarly the letters of Abigail Adams, published in 1840, and those of Dolley Madison, published in 1886, the only relatively complete papers of Presidents' wives in print by 1901, were thin on detailed descriptions of the White House, although much concerned with what went on there. A sampling of letters from Tyler's two First Ladies that appeared in 1884 was equally uninformative.

In some respects, John Hay and George Nicolay's *Lincoln: A History,* a ten-volume work published in 1890, is a White House memoir, for the two former secretaries drew on their personal recollections in telling the story of Lincoln during the war years. No other histories were so closely tied to the experience of the authors, although recollections of presidential administrations found their way now and then into such popular magazines as *The Century*. But public interest in these matters was not particularly strong before the Roosevelt renovation. Mrs. Grant completed a memoir in 1891, the first ever written by a First Lady, and she hoped it would make money as a companion to the best-selling Civil War memories of the late general. To her disappointment, a publisher could not be found, nor even a buyer for the manuscript, which she offered to select collectors for $125,000. The book was not to be published for more than three-quarters of a century.

The author of the first memoir by an intimate of the White House since Paul Jennings's *Reminiscences* still waited quietly in the wings at the time Theodore Roosevelt took office. His pen, however, had been busily calling up the past as he remembered it. The tall, lanky doorman Tommy Pendel—he never called himself "usher"—finished his manuscript in 1901 and it was in print early the next year, before Roosevelt's renovation began. At 78 Pendel was a familiar character to anyone who called regularly at the White House. Not only was he older than any of the other doormen, but he also had escaped the edict issued by Caroline Harrison a decade before and still in effect in 1901, that no beards were to be worn by members of the household staff. Tommy Pendel's was thick and wavy, his badge of venerable dignity.

His tours of the East Room and parlors had been popular with White House visitors since at least the '80s. No official tours were provided, but in lax times the doormen and ushers obligingly led interested callers through the state rooms and told them stories of the Presidents. Pendel's tours, which he embellished with moral reflections, doubtless gave him the idea of writing the memoir, which he entitled *Thirty-Six Years in the White House*. He apparently wrote the book himself, with assistance and advice from his friend Rosalie O. Goulding, who had "experience," he noted, as a journalist. A frontispiece poem celebrated the old doorman in four stanzas, of which the following is the first:

> The sacred task of personal care
> As portal sentry, standing there,
> Protecting him who bore the weight
> Of flashing Mars, and Chief of State.

Tommy Pendel lived until 1911, still serving at his post; at the age of 86 he was fatally stricken while on duty.

Although Pendel concluded his reminiscences by referring to himself as the only member of the staff who had been employed since the Civil War, this was not entirely accurate. There remained in the office, now apart from the White House proper, Colonel William H. Crook, who had come to the Executive Mansion only a few months after Pendel. He might never have written a book, had Pendel not written his. But the shortcomings of Pendel's narrative, his sometimes odd choice of subjects, left the door open to a second try by someone else.

Like Pendel, Colonel Crook had been a guard detailed to the White House by the Metropolitan Police, although he had advanced to the office staff under Andrew Johnson and gained a different vantage point on White House life. But Crook found himself unable to write, strapped between the pressures of his work as a disbursement officer and anxiety over his sick wife. Instead, he collaborated with two different journalists, who wrote his memoirs for him. The first, and probably less accurate, was serialized in *The Century Magazine* in the fall of 1908 by Margareta Spalding Gerry, who apparently did most of the work herself. Three years later, in 1911, the newspaperman and editor Henry E. Rood published a more authoritative account in the book *Memories of the White House: The Home-life of Our Presidents from Lincoln to Roosevelt.* Rood intended his as a serious work, and tried to get as much text as he could from Crook, but he confessed years later: "Crook's autobiography I wrote from notes he'd made on the backs of envelopes, etc."[3]

Both Crook and Pendel gave us a wealth of detail about the White House as they had known it. Their focus was on personalities; their paramount character, Lincoln. Anecdotes they recalled of private lives preserved stories which might otherwise have been lost. If the actual words were sometimes not theirs, they nevertheless approved what was written, and each remained in his job, standing by his facts, when the books came out. Their memoirs, in many ways simple and harmless, provide interesting glimpses behind the scenes in times when particulars of family life were usually not made public.

Why did so few put their White House recollections on paper? The footman Jerry Smith had a wealth of memories, yet he went to his grave about this time, leaving nothing on paper. Octavius Pruden and Warren Young wrote nothing, nor did Major Loeffler, and the scenes of their lives were often thrilling. Men in such positions are often silent out of respect for the privacy of those who benefited them. Through the White House past, those who have known the most usually wrote the least. Presidential employees high and low learn one truth from the outset, or their time at the White House is brief: Only one public figure occupies the White House, and that is the President; even his family members enjoy the spotlight only at his pleasure.

Roosevelt's renovations were not the only inspiration for the heightened interest in the house. The upsurge of fascination with national history that began after the Spanish-American War played its part as well. In the early 1900s, the nation was studied from nearly every angle. In 1907 the impulse produced a full-fledged history in two volumes: *The Story of the White House*. It was written by Esther Singleton of New York, a popular author of books on music, history, travel, and American antiques. Miss Singleton concentrated on the building and its furnishings, using federal records and newspaper and magazine accounts. Her work, still a useful source, had a slight tone of protest.

"We have seen," wrote Esther Singleton at the end of the second volume, "that every President impressed his taste, more or less, upon the White House. . . . Whatever changes he made were, however, temporary, and were swept away by his successor, who in turn arranged the house to suit himself. During President Roosevelt's Administration the historic mansion had undergone complete repair and restoration—so complete, in fact, that the vexed question of an appropriate home for the President of the United States is, in all probability, settled forever." Of the massive changes made in 1902 she had little to say, except to quote long passages from the report of McKim, Mead, & White. At last she conceded, "the President's house has been restored to something of its olden time appearance."[4]

The Chronicler

The White House had only one chronicler, a bright, dedicated recorder of details and personalities. While he did not actually reside in the house, he was there constantly between 1908 and 1912. His vision of the presidential circles of Theodore Roosevelt and William Howard Taft was as penetrating, though not as bitter, as Saint-Simon's of the Versailles of Louis XIV. Archibald Wellingham Butt—Captain Butt, usually called Archie—was a prolific writer of letters that successfully captured the White House and its people.

In all, his letters fill three volumes, about 1,200 pages. They are the work of a careful observer, a journalist by training who, at least after the first few months of his labor, became aware that the world might one day be interested in what he had to write. Soldier, socialite, southern gentleman, horseman, amateur sportsman, and occasional fop, Archie Butt was ordered to the White House as military aide in the spring of 1908.

His letters commenced on his arrival, when he wrote to his mother in Georgia. "Everyone congratulates me most warmly on being ordered to the White House, seeming to think it an exceptional honour. I presume it is, but I am not over enthusiastic. It means being very conspicuous in a small way . . . many people will try to pump one dry of White House news, and work their little schemes through me, but I am too old a drake to swim readily into such shallow ponds."[5]

He was 42 when he went to the White House, tall and formed somewhat like one of Tiffany's tulip-shaped wine glasses, only topped by a large head with moustache and hair neatly parted in the middle. Several things about him appealed to Roosevelt. He was a Georgia aristocrat, just as the President saw himself; he was an expert horseman; his social gifts were legendary among military men and their wives. Archie Butt had been one of those called to assist the regular aides at Alice Roosevelt's wedding.

He kept bachelor hall with several of the other military aides for a while, then settled into an old house with his friend Frank Millet, a Washington painter who was involved with the City Beautiful movement of the time. Captain Butt's letters were probably written late at night, for his days were packed with activities at the White House, and his evenings were devoted to dinner parties and dances. The letters were first addressed to his mother. After her death he wrote to his sister-in-law Clara, Mrs. Lewis F. Butt of Augusta, Georgia. To each of them he stated that he wrote no other letters.

He was a faithful correspondent throughout his White House years. In 1912, before he left on the last trip he ever took, he wrote to Clara, "I always want you to bear in mind that the letters which I wrote to Mother and those which I have written to you are valuable, and in case of my death I have left a provision in my will that they are to be published. Don't ever make the mistake, either, of cutting out names; for letters, if they have any historic value, must be printed as written . . . ."[6]

A View From the Inner Circle

In early May 1908, when Archie Butt reported to work at the White House for the first time, the grounds were already sweet with flowers, and for him spring had flowed uninterrupted from his warm winter assignment in Havana. To him the new green of the old elms was no less splendid than the splashes of yellow forsythia and jonquils in Mrs. Roosevelt's colonial garden.

"I called on the President this morning and had a most hearty welcome," Butt wrote his mother. "He expressed a great pleasure in having me on his official staff. . . . Nothing could have been more characteristic of this first meeting. He came into the office, laid one hand on my shoulder, and with the other wrung my own . . . . He went back to his desk, where he picked up a large picture which he found there, read the note with it and then jerked out: 'How I hate to accept presents from people I dislike. And this man has sent me a Madonna; more pity, for I cannot use it to break over his head.' "[7]

Within moments, Captain Butt, a southern Democrat, was a captive in the magical web spun by the Republican Roosevelts. "I then called on Mrs. Roosevelt," he continued, "who is just as gentle and lovely as he is vigorous and emphatic. She was delighted at my coming and begged me to get into harness at once. So tomorrow night I assist at a dinner party of seventy, including Mr. [William Jennings] Bryan and most of the governors of the states."[8]

This dinner, on May 13, 1908, was part of the National Conference on the Conservation of Natural Resources, which held daily sessions in the East Room. From the conference was born the National Conservation Commission, one of President Roosevelt's greatest achievements and strongest personal interests. For the dinner, all the machinery of White House glamour was set into motion. By 1908, the ceremonial procedures that had been introduced by Roosevelt were into their sixth year of use. Imperial ceremony seemed natural, and the awkward moments that had sometimes accompanied it at the outset had become rare; a bold self-confidence came from the roll of the drums, the blast of trumpet fanfare, the rousing "Hail to the Chief," to which the official party walked briskly down the grand staircase.

Archie Butt, who loved ceremony, was enraptured. The spectacular presidential entrance was the sort of thing Butt himself enjoyed creating. Unlike most military officers of his time, he liked the Army's dress uniforms, wearing his as often as he could find an excuse to do so. A fellow aide remembered that Butt took "frank and unabashed pleasure" in his uniform, "the gaudier . . . the better, the broader and yellower the stripes the better."[9]

The work of a military aide was to mix with the guests, keeping people happy and talking. Much of the social exchange was naturally political, and aides had the responsibility of redirecting some of the conversations. They were also scattered through the crowd to get it moving when necessary, to start applause, or to make certain that no problems arose. The aides were guests at dinner, with their dinner partners assigned, like those of everyone else, by Mrs. Roosevelt and Belle Hagner.

Captain Butt was a master in his role, having both charm and curiosity, which made him a good listener. A fondness for innocent gossip is evident in his letters. He remembered names easily, liked to talk, eat, and drink—and was a good dancer. What was more, he made quick "connections." He could nearly always link himself to strangers through some ancient blood kinship or a mutual friend.

The topic at the conservation dinner, as it was elsewhere in Washington, was the presidential succession. In ten months a new President would go to the White House, and there was no doubt that if a Republican were elected it would be William Howard Taft, Roosevelt's Secretary of War. Soon Archie Butt would be able to write that the nomination of Taft "is largely conceded." But on the night of the dinner it was hard for anyone to imagine Roosevelt in retirement, much less another man in the White House. The place and everything about it had been tailored to him and to what *Harper's Weekly* was to call in the following month his "monarchial instinct."[10]

In the Red Room after dinner, the President concentrated almost entirely upon Bryan, the two talking over coffee and cigars, as Butt stood listening. He was thrilled to think of where he was and in what exalted company. Bryan would be the Democratic presidential candidate in the autumn election, having been previously beaten by McKinley in 1896 and by Roosevelt in 1904. When Bryan rose to leave, Roosevelt took his hand and spoke: "When you see me quoted in the press as welcoming the rest I will have after March 3rd take no stock in it, for I will confess to you confidentially that I like my job. The burdens of this great nation I have borne up under for the past seven years will not be laid aside with relief, as all presidents have heretofore said, but will be laid aside with a good deal of regret, for I have enjoyed every moment of this so-called arduous and exacting task."[11]

Butt memorized the remark and transcribed it in his next letter home. "This is really his feeling on the subject," he added, glowing with admiration for his chief. A few days later he wrote again, in apparent response to his mother's admonition that he vary his social activities and begin leading a more well-rounded life: "You must realize that I cannot let anything interfere with my duties at the White House this winter except sickness. If I undertake this [assignment] I must make a success of it or else hopelessly fail."[12] The time left for Roosevelt's Presidency was short, and behind the unruffled demeanor of his imperial White House, his concern over the succession and the continuation of his policies made everyone close to him tense. And Archie Butt was his frequent, if not constant, companion.

The Man in Office

No one could remember an administration anything like that of Theodore Roosevelt. He was the first President to dominate the White House so completely. If his visible presence was not especially heroic, his symbolic stature was more powerful in its time than Jackson's or Lincoln's had been. In part this reflected the power of Roosevelt's personality, but it was even more the result of calculated strategies. In every particular he made himself the center of the political universe. He pushed backstage any subservient player who shared in the slightest his political spotlight.

His means varied. A first step, in which he was assisted by Cortelyou, was to alter the public position of the private secretary. Often the secretary had stood between the President and the public, a prominent figure in his own right. Cleveland's Lamont and McKinley's Porter had been classic examples. The redefined position was that of administrator and occasional spokesman; the secretary was rarely seen in public. Since his removal to the Executive Office Building, he was seldom involved in official social activities. Those responsibilities had been absorbed by the new military aides. Cortelyou, inherited by Roosevelt from McKinley, was the last private secretary to work in the White House itself. His successor, William Loeb, was the first of the new breed, operating almost entirely behind the scenes. The elegant Executive Office, designed by McKim as the headquarters and place of work of the President's secretary, projected an image grander than the job it represented.

Another of Roosevelt's moves to enhance the Presidency was his removal of intermediaries between himself and the press. His most important step was his attempt to cut off direct communication between the Cabinet and the newspapermen. For many years it had been customary for Cabinet members to pause outside on the portico or driveway after meetings to discuss with reporters what had gone on upstairs with the President. In 1904 Roosevelt requested that this practice cease; when it began again in 1905 he interrupted a Cabinet meeting to deliver a lecture on the subject, and had no problem again until 1907, when once again he found it necessary to make his feelings emphatically known.

Official utterances were to be made by the President. The President feared leaks from the White House staff, and while they were almost unheard of, they did occur now and then. Cabinet members were required to submit to the secretary any news they wished to announce. The secretary would in turn give it to the President for a decision on how it would be made public. When this policy began, the press was usually informed by the secretary, but as time went by Roosevelt increasingly made the statements personally, summoning the reporters by telephone to his office. Often as many as 40 appeared. Moving around the room, he talked informally, bringing up topics great and small, speaking to the reporters as though they were close friends. When he observed that a remark was "off the record," he meant it. Lincoln Steffens, Oscar K. Davis, Mark Sullivan, and other outstanding journalists almost idolized the man. They received their stories from his lips, colored by his particular viewpoint, and they often reported the news as he wished them to. Roosevelt's way of dealing with reporters, and his friendly relationship with them, made up an important part of his strategy.

The White House of his time was a Roosevelt machine, a smooth-running institution that did not tolerate incompetence. About a month after his arrival, Archie Butt became the chief military aide. He was immediately given many of the managerial responsibilities formerly held by the aging but beloved chief usher Thomas Stone, the "old factotum of the Executive Mansion," who was no longer as aggressive as was necessary. Butt met with Mrs. Roosevelt and Belle Hagner to plan the events of a full calendar. When the menu was determined, he went to Charles Rauscher's to make the arrangements. Under Stone, a price per plate had been obtained for Mrs. Roosevelt's approval; the new emissary told Rauscher the amount the First Lady was willing to pay, and negotiations ensued. Butt, the expert in the saddle, was also a shrewd horse trader who readily adapted his abilities at negotiation to the White House budget, and for the First Lady he made highly favorable deals. The usual rate per plate had been ten to eleven dollars, but under him the price was pulled down to seven dollars, including food, wine, and the rental of tableware. The White House supplied only champagne and dinner plates.

Entertaining highlighted Theodore Roosevelt's domination of the White House. He often added little touches to social occasions in order to give them his personal stamp. Sometimes his wife rescued him from his own enthusiasm. On one occasion, delighted by a kinetoscope performance showing a federal marshal in Oklahoma capturing wolves by sticking his fist into their mouths, Roosevelt decided that the marshal should attend a dinner the following week and afterward narrate the moving picture show. To this idea, Mrs. Roosevelt responded, "How would you like to be asked to sit through a kinetoscope performance of a lady showing antique fans?"

"Why, Edith, I cannot understand being so tortured."

"It would not be worse than your wolf pictures to the average dinner guest in Washington," she said. To Archie Butt she added later, with emphasis: "I do not want dogs and wolves introduced to my dinner guests. These pictures may make my guests sick, especially after eating a big dinner. You can't tell what will happen."[13]

Roosevelt kept his towering image before the public by showing himself frequently. He liked people to see him informally, whether at home or while traveling. Both the citizens of Washington and the city's increasing temporary population of tourists saw him often, walking briskly along the street, detectives in tow, or riding on the Mall or in Rock Creek Park. He was recorded many times by photographers, including one motion-picture cameraman who caught his bouncing walk for a few seconds, with the south portico in the distance. "Photograph fiends" was the household name for news photographers, but Roosevelt never hid from them. Indeed the Roosevelts posed themselves and their children frequently for portraits both formal and informal.

He occasionally rode in automobiles, but generally disliked them. Roosevelt's was the last administration to have no motorcar. The President's main carriage was a black Studebaker brougham with glass windows, purchased with federal funds in 1902. Relatively small, the brisk coach was a far cry from the big, low-slung, cushioned equipages of his predecessors. His coachman, Charlie Lee, who had come to the White House with him and replaced H. C. Harris as head of the stable, wore livery of dark blue trousers, striped blue and buff waistcoat, and high black boots; in his high silk hat he wore a bright cockade of red, white, and blue. The uniform was copied from that worn years before by the coachman at Theodore Roosevelt's boyhood home, with the addition of brass buttons engraved "T.R."[14]

Horseback rides were the delight of the President, who mounted daily at the south portico. Rarely was the weather too severe for him; he relished testing himself against hardships. Toward the end of the administration Secret Service men took stations along a route he specified in advance, although he could not be depended upon to ride where he said he would. While the presence of the guards comforted Mrs. Roosevelt, the system was lax. Archie Butt sometimes came upon guards napping in the grass while on the bridle path detail; on occasion the President sent them home, with orders to stay out of Mrs. Roosevelt's sight. For most of Roosevelt's Presidency, several military aides went along, but after Captain Butt joined the staff in 1908, the President seldom had other company. He liked the challenge and the freedom of riding with an expert horseman. When Butt realized that he would be the only aide on most occasions, he bought a pistol and tucked it away in his coat.

Strict rules governed the conduct of any guest who might ride along. Called officially *Rules of the Road For Those Invited to Accompany the President on Horseback Rides,* the typed sheet was distributed to the guests with their invitations. It went as follows:[15]

First. The President will notify whom he wishes to ride with him. The one so notified will take position on the left of the President and keep his right stirrup back of the President's left stirrup.

Second. Those following will keep not less than ten yards in the rear of the President.

Third. When the President asks anyone in the party to ride with him the one at his side should at once retire to the rear. Salutes should be returned only by the President, except by those in the rear. Anyone unable to control his horse should withdraw to the rear.

Roosevelt Style

All Presidents had taken pains to plan the public aspects of their lives, but before Roosevelt only Washington had made so strong an effort to project himself as a symbol of national ideals. Washington had dramatized himself through ceremony as the head of state. Roosevelt built his imperial Presidency somewhat the same way, symbolizing through ceremony and grandeur his country's new position as a world power.

Roosevelt was especially eager to represent the "new America" to foreign nations. Diplomats expected state splendor in the chief of a great nation, and Theodore Roosevelt gave it to them. He was stern in asserting American equality in their presence as well as in the presence of the increasing number of distinguished guests from abroad. Early in his administration, when Prince Henry of Prussia visited the United States and called at the White House, great consternation arose behind the scenes over the manner in which prince and President would be introduced. Who would be presented first: an elected official or the brother of the emperor of Germany? Roosevelt's solution was for him and the prince to enter the empty Blue Room from opposite doors, shake hands and introduce themselves before admitting the rest of the company. The performance was widely praised as an example of Roosevelt's ability to handle delicate matters of that kind.

In instances where his private life became public, the President consulted, but often overrode, the State Department's venerable expert on official form, Alvey A. Adee. He seldom took the advice of anyone other than Mrs. Roosevelt, whom he considered the last word on all matters of taste. Both she and the President realized that their private activities at the White House could not be entirely separated from their official life, so they mixed the two somewhat, with the happy result of giving their private functions some magnificence, and taking the pompous edge off the public affairs.

A brilliant example of the softened official style was the debut of the Roosevelts' younger daughter, Ethel, on December 28, 1908. Ethel had wanted her debut in the White House; this meant, however, that it could not be as informal as it might have been at Sagamore Hill, or as lively as it might have been at a hotel. There was an all-night dance with a midnight supper. No married people were invited, although many married relatives were present to assist with the receiving. President and Mrs. Roosevelt received in the Blue Room, where they introduced Ethel. Other members of the family moved through the parlors speaking to the guests and thereby stimulating conversation.

The party began at ten. Ethel was presented in snowy white, standing in a simulated garden shelter at the south end of the Blue Room; the bouquets she had received as gifts, as well as the corsages and boutonnieres to be given out after dinner as favors to the guests, were pinned over the structure's latticed walls. After being greeted by the Roosevelts at the door, the guests went to Ethel, who was thus seen against a background of flowers. From her gazebo the young guests passed through the Green Room into the East Room, which was to be the ballroom. The receiving line ended after half an hour, and the doors of the Blue Room were closed. Ethel went alone to the East Room, and her parents remained behind.

The floor of the East Room was waxed for dancing. At the north end a stage covered with green carpet and banked with palms had been set up for the Marine Band, which was divided into two orchestras of 20 musicians each, for continuous music. The transverse hall and two of the three parlors were open for promenading; the doors to the east terrace were open and, although the night was cold, the guests liked walking among the clipped bay trees that were lined up in tubs against the parapets. Punch was poured from an elaborate floral setting in the State Dining Room. The midnight supper took place in the basement, where the rooms were decorated with additional electric lights spaced on standards around the walls at five-foot intervals and massed with smilax. Round tables for six, with gilt bentwood chairs, filled the three rooms below the parlors and part of the lower corridor. Rauscher served the following menu at six dollars per person:[17]

Hot consommé in cups
*
Sweetbread cutlets Perigordine
fresh mushrooms
*
Galatine of Pheasant (Bellvue
cold Smithfield ham slice)
*
Dessert
*
Biscuits Neapolitan Glacés
*
Petits fours assortis bonbons fourres
marrons glacés
*
café demi tasse

White wine was poured, a dry wine left over from Alice's wedding, and there was champagne with dessert. Notes in the official record say eight cases of wine were consumed. Butt insisted that the figure was ten, and observed: "I did not see a single youth show any effect from it."[17]

Ethel's party was a great success, or, as the President liked to say of his parties, a "grand time." During the dinner, the curious parents stayed back as long as they could bear it, then walked once through the dining rooms, stopping here and there to chat briefly, asking the guests not to rise. It was their sort of party, elegant, with a short menu and one table wine carefully chosen and profusely offered.

Thus, even with a party for young people, Roosevelt artfully melded his style to both his public and private life. In retrospect, it is often difficult to determine if there was much difference between the two. The family cherished being together at the White House. Their 7½ years there were extremely happy, by their own accounts, and the ceremonious existence cost them no warmth at all. On the day of Ethel's debut, Archie Butt and Alice Longworth, close friends, walked through the state rooms looking at the decorations. Two months remained for the Roosevelts, before they were to leave, and Butt wrote that Alice was "unutterably sad . . . . We went from room to room and each one had some sweet memory for this girl whose career at the White House has been the most dramatic of any in its history. 'Princess Alice,' she was called . . . she seemed to realize just what the change would mean to her. She was not complaining, for she has too much of her father in her for that, but she did not hesitate to give voice to the note of sadness."[18]

Roosevelt had a more constant interest in the White House even than Jefferson. As he was about to move out he ordered the stone lion heads McKim had put on the mantel in the State Dining Room recarved as bison, believing the American buffalo more appropriate to the President's House.[19] In his letters he showed a warm affection for his official home. To Joel Chandler Harris he wrote: "Last night Mrs. Roosevelt and I were sitting out on the porch at the back of the White House, and were talking of you and wishing you could be sitting there with us. It is delightful at all times, but I think especially so after dark. The [Washington] monument stands up distinct but not quite earthly in the night, and at this season the air is sweet with the jasmine and honeysuckle."[20]

Successor

Facing the rather forbidding prospect of retirement at 50, Roosevelt made a characteristic decision. He would go to Africa for a year, to disappear on the savannas hunting big game. But before he left he wished to ensure that the next President would be inclined to continue his policies. As early as 1906, he had settled on William Howard Taft, his Secretary of War, as the most promising candidate. While no two men could have seemed more unlike, they were close friends, and their families were on good terms. In contrast to the brisk and bouncy Roosevelt, who called men to follow him, the heavy—indeed immense—Taft poured over them affectionately, "like a huge pan of sweet milk." At least that was the way Archie Butt saw it.[21]

During the spring of 1906 the Roosevelts had the Tafts to dinner at the White House. Given the familiar high sign as the other guests were departing, Taft and Mrs. Taft stood back, and when everyone else was gone joined the Roosevelts upstairs in the oval room. The President began to speak, imitating the mysterious droning voice one associates with the tellers of fortunes.

"I am the seventh son of a seventh daughter," he said; "I have clairvoyant powers. I see a man weighing three hundred and fifty pounds. There is something hanging over his head. I cannot make out what it is. . . . At one time it looks like the Presidency, then again it looks like the chief justiceship."

"Make it the chief justiceship," said Taft.

"Make it the presidency," said his wife.[22]

Taft was nominated at the Republican Convention in Chicago on June 18, 1908, and was elected President in November, reaping a margin of more than a million votes over his opponent, William Jennings Bryan. The Tafts came briefly to Washington after the election, and left in early December, not to return until February. Roosevelt was elated over the victory, considering it a triumph for himself.

The weeks that followed the election, however, brought indications that relations between Roosevelt and Taft were cooling. Taft was naturally much in the news, playing golf daily, first in Hot Springs, Virginia, then, when the weather got bad, on the sandy links of Augusta, Georgia. The President was concerned by some of the President-elect's utterances, as well as by the company he was keeping. Roosevelt's old friend Senator Henry Cabot Lodge was stirring up unrest between the two men, in the interest of preserving his own power. Archie Butt sensed changed feelings in December when, after a brief visit with Roosevelt, he wrote, "I could not help but wonder if he does not, way down in his heart, fear that big, generous, unsuspecting heart of Mr. Taft."[23]

To the public, however, there were still no greater friends than Taft and Roosevelt. Intimates saw indications in the two families that the truth was otherwise. Mrs. Taft began to assert herself even before she left Washington. On December 10, Butt was summoned to call on her at the Boardman residence near Dupont Circle, where she and Taft occupied a series of upper floor rooms that had been set aside for their use.

Butt had known the Tafts when Taft was governor of the Philippines, and had also known them later when he became a part of Roosevelt's official family. The tone of his meeting with them that December morning in 1908 surprised him. When he appeared, the couple was in an animated exchange over the proposed appointment of a certain man to the Cabinet. Taft was rocking with laughter, having told Mrs. Taft the man's name, and her having verbally "wiped him off the face of the earth." The President-elect explained the situation—and Helen Taft's motivation—to Captain Butt: "The personal side of politics has always been funny to me, but nothing has been quite as funny as to have a man's career wrecked by a jealous wife."

"Not jealous at all," said Mrs. Taft, "but I could not believe you to be serious when you mentioned that man's name. He is perfectly awful and his family are even worse. I won't even talk about it." Having ended that discussion, she turned to the subject of changes she wished to make at the White House.[24]

She was inclined to dismiss most of the staff, objecting particularly to the ushers in frock coats standing in the entrance hall, or lounging about in their room to the right of the north door. Accustomed to the abundant staff of servants in Malacanang Palace in Manila, she determined to replace the familiar ushers, who were white and not servants, with liveried black servants. Butt had gone to the meeting expecting this, with Mrs. Roosevelt's urgent plea that he do what he could to change Mrs. Taft's mind and save the men's jobs. "It will hurt them so," Mrs. Roosevelt had said.[25]

Archie Butt did his best. He had already been informed that he was to remain, for the Tafts liked him, and his responsibilities had increased to such an extent that he had by now, as Mrs. Taft observed, "supervision of the White House and all functions." Taft, an astute administrator, knew that it had never been intended that the chief military aide be a majordomo, and that Butt was loaded with work because in the first place he was resourceful and efficient, but also because Thomas Stone, the chief usher, was too old to be either. It was not Taft's plan to restore authority to the chief usher. He intended to divide Butt's present work with another military aide, and dispose of ushers entirely.[26]

Determined to keep his promise to Mrs. Roosevelt, Butt set out to save those of the ushers he could. He described the post of usher as being too entrenched in tradition to be removed entirely; liveried servants, he said, "would certainly look much better," but their presence might appear snobbish; some of the ushers also had political importance, by virtue of long tenure. Mrs. Taft agreed to compromise, apparently with reluctance. She would keep two of the present ushers to supervise the servants, and the other ushers, including Thomas Stone, would be "promoted" to the Executive Office.[27]

Later, Captain Butt reported on the conference to Mrs. Roosevelt, who was "tremendously relieved," and complimented him on handling the matter with delicacy. In her enthusiasm she told Butt to telephone Mrs. Taft with an offer of a meeting, at which the two women could sit quietly and discuss the staff one by one. Mrs. Roosevelt wanted to make it perfectly clear that if Mrs. Taft did not wish to do so, she "would not feel the least offended." She was soon informed that Mrs. Taft did not wish to do so. Mrs. Roosevelt was less offended than hurt, and Archie Butt, a little annoyed himself, presumed to suggest that Mrs. Taft thank Mrs. Roosevelt for her kind offer. This Mrs. Taft agreed to do at a luncheon she was soon to attend at the White House.[28]

Such were the discomforts that arose on the domestic scene as the result of politics. On the surface, most of the problems between the families seem to have come from Mrs. Taft, although she may suffer in the record more than she should, for the most detailed accounts come from Alice Roosevelt Longworth and Archie Butt. She was a woman of broad experience, who had been more directly involved in politics than Mrs. Roosevelt. Determined that she and her husband not appear as mere surrogate Roosevelts, Mrs. Taft believed she knew what to do. And she knew the White House well enough to realize that she could not tolerate a minute's delay but must put her plan into effect, with the changes concealed by the glitter of the inauguration.

Bitterness

In the months between the election and the inauguration, Mrs. Taft faced the staggering challenge of taking Mrs. Roosevelt's place in the White House. Archie Butt read in her attitude a hostility that may have been only the outward manner of a woman inwardly bewildered by the big job she had to perform. The President-elect respected her mettle. He attributed much of his success to her, and her conduct at this time had his approval.

By New Year's the unpleasantness between Mrs. Roosevelt and Mrs. Taft over the household staff found a parallel in their husbands' coolness toward each other, after Taft declined to make some of the appointments suggested by Roosevelt. For example, Roosevelt's secretary, William Loeb, wanted a Cabinet position, like Cortelyou before him. Taft humored Roosevelt only so far as to offer Loeb a temporary appointment of several months, to give him the distinction of having served in the Cabinet. Roosevelt felt obliged to demur because it seemed to him that the Cabinet was being used in that case for the personal benefit of Loeb. The secretary was made collector of the Port of New York.

Bad feelings between the Tafts and the Roosevelts cast a pall over the White House. The men and women who worked there had been told prematurely by Roosevelt that their jobs were secure. Now they realized that they were not, and they knew that only the good graces of Captain Butt had kept them from being ordered out come March 4. Those in close daily contact with the Roosevelts sympathized deeply with the anguish the President and First Lady suffered.

As if to increase the gloom of her last days in the White House, Mrs. Roosevelt was exposed to embarrassment in the press. She asked if she might take home to Sagamore Hill a small sofa she had purchased with a few dollars of public money at an antique shop in 1901 and used in the upstairs hall. The request got into official channels, ultimately finding its way into the hands of Speaker Cannon. He gave it to the press, and it was widely reported as an example of the Roosevelts' appropriation of White House property. This angered and hurt the First Lady, who had been heretofore exempt from political mudslinging. Her entire feeling toward the White House seemed to change; she even ordered the remains of the pets buried in the colonial garden exhumed and taken to Sagamore Hill for reburial.[29]

Meanwhile, Archie Butt, William Loeb, and Belle Hagner concealed from the President and First Lady large numbers of threatening letters that began to arrive daily. Hate letters were nothing new at the White House, but an avalanche came in the last months of Roosevelt's administration. Many of them threatened the Roosevelts with physical harm, once the Secret Service men were no longer guarding them; others alluded to plots to kidnap and murder the younger children. The letters were turned over to the Secret Service, and presumably each was dealt with on an individual basis.[30]

The weeks of January and February passed miserably. It rained often, and the air was cold, frequently with strong winds. Gradually the strained relations between Taft and Roosevelt found their way into the press. The full extent of the problem, however, was known only to those who were closest to the two men involved. "It can be truthfully said," wrote Ike Hoover many years later, "that there has seldom been such bitterness between an incoming and an outgoing administration. This applies to the entire families."[31]

Friends

To assuage rumors of discord, the Roosevelts invited the President-elect and Mrs. Taft to eat dinner and sleep at the White House the night before the inauguration. It was a snowy evening, but clear skies were expected the next day. The Roosevelt children were not included in the invitation. Dinner was for 12, black tie as usual, in the State Dining Room. "I think we all dreaded this dinner," wrote Archie Butt, who was one of the guests. Yet the evening went as well as could be expected.

From the dining room the party adjourned to the second floor, where the men went with Roosevelt into his study and the women convened in the oval room next door. At 10:30 Taft left for the Willard Hotel to attend a smoker given in his honor by the Yale Club. Soon after, in the oval room, Mrs. Roosevelt stood up, took Mrs. Taft's hand, and warmly bade her goodnight.

In the Blue Bedroom, Mrs. Taft was wakened just after daybreak by a crackling sound outside. She raised the shade to see ice-covered trees swaying noisily in the wind. The city had been surprised after midnight by a storm. The President-elect, occupying the Rose Bedroom across the hall, slept through it all.

At nine Mrs. Taft went to the west hall upstairs to join Mrs. Roosevelt, who, moist-eyed, was saying good-bye to the military aides. They were the first of the staff with whom she had made appointments that morning to say farewell and convey her thanks. She spoke to each one warmly, by name. Now she turned to Mrs. Taft and presented the aides to her. The session was brief, and Mrs. Taft returned down the hall to the Blue Bedroom. Sitting there waiting to be called downstairs, she let her eyes rest on the bronze plaque on the mantelpiece; it told how in that room Lincoln had signed the proclamation freeing four million slaves.[32]

Taft joined Roosevelt in the entrance hall at ten. The brougham was parked beneath the shelter of the north portico, with Charlie Lee on the box, wearing Roosevelt livery for the last time. There were to be no more coaches or carriages. The Taft administration was changing over to automobiles. Behind Lee's vehicle, extending out into the avenue, was a line of carriages filled with officials and other dignitaries; before him, stretching down the driveway and as far east on the avenue as the Treasury, were orderly rows of mounted soldiers, their dark uniforms powdered white by falling snow.

In the entrance hall, the President and President-elect puzzled with inaugural officials over whether to hold the ceremony inside the Capitol. Taft dreaded trying to deliver his address in the cold, and he worried about the well-being of spectators braving the elements to see him. Finally, Taft and Roosevelt entered the brougham. A network of signals got the procession going, creeping along the snowy avenue to the Capitol, where Taft directed that the ceremony be moved inside.

In the crowded Senate Chamber, William Howard Taft was sworn in as the 27th President of the United States. Roosevelt congratulated him with a hearty "bully" and went back to the brougham, thence in a small procession to Union Station. Mrs. Roosevelt awaited him in the warm seclusion of the train. At three o'clock they began their journey home to Oyster Bay. Meanwhile, leaving the Senate Chamber, the Tafts joined hands in the rotunda, then walked into the open air of the east portico, where they were greeted with a sudden explosion of sunlight. A roar swelled from the crowd and continued as they descended the long east staircase. Taft ordered the top of the carriage folded back, and for the first time in American history a new President was accompanied by his wife on his inaugural ride from Capitol to White House. The papers the next day would point out this exception to tradition as a further example of the rift between the Tafts and the Roosevelts. (It was actually suggested in advance by the inaugural committee, probably because Roosevelt disliked the former custom and favored the innovation.)[33]

Archie Butt made a note that it was 2:22 p.m. when the Tafts' carriage stopped beneath the north portico. The President and his wife mixed informally with about 80 friends in the State Dining Room and private dining room, hurriedly picking over a buffet of bouillon, oyster pâté, chicken croquettes, ham, and sandwiches. Twenty-three minutes after their arrival, the President and Mrs. Taft climbed onto the reviewing stand on Pennsylvania Avenue to watch the inaugural parade. It was a time of singular triumph.

To everyone's surprise, a lone member of the Roosevelt family suddenly appeared to share Taft's glory. It was Quentin, the youngest, playing hooky from Episcopal High School over the river in Virginia to be with his friend Charlie Taft. The son of the President and the son of the ex-President, both 11, shared a single chair, huddled against the wind, apparently oblivious of the bitterness between their parents.[34] They remained with all the others until the last band had played its last note, and night had fallen.

32

Summer Days

Seven days after the inauguration, as Taft and Archie Butt were motoring near the Potomac, the President invited a friend to leave his own vehicle and join them. "Well, Mr. President," said the visitor, "how do you like it?"

"I hardly know yet," Taft responded. "When I hear someone say Mr. President, I look around expecting to see Roosevelt, and when I read in the headlines of the morning papers that the President and Senator Aldrich and Speaker Cannon have had a conference, my first thought is, 'I wonder what they talked about.' So you can see that I have not gone very far yet."[1]

Although Roosevelt was in retirement, his presence hovered beyond the door of every room Taft occupied, the unseen figure at the conference table where Taft sat in council with his political family. Taft continued to remark upon this from time to time, and the idea has lived on in history books, where Taft's administration is usually treated as a relatively unimportant interlude between the years of Theodore Roosevelt and Woodrow Wilson.

Under William Howard Taft the income tax made its debut with the 2 percent tax on corporations; troops were sent to the border of troubled Mexico; the first significant reduction in protective tariffs took place; and rival conservative and liberal forces within Taft's Republican Party caused the fatal split which would clear the way for a Democratic victory in the election of 1912. Domestic problems interested the public, drawing attention to the Congress. Most citizens were unconcerned about diplomacy; that a war might erupt in Latin America did seem possible,

739

but not even a premonition of war in Europe clouded the sky when Taft began his Presidency.

During Roosevelt's years in the White House, the American people had learned to expect their President as daily fare in the newspapers. Taft made little effort to promote himself while President, virtually ignoring reporters who had been privileged favorites since McKinley's time. A journalist complained to Archie Butt over lunch one day that the press corps was "getting angry with President Taft for withholding news from its members." When Butt repeated the conversation to the President, Taft dismissed it, saying, "The people of this country elected me," not the press. He intended to give his news directly to the people in his speeches, not in releases to the newsmen.[2]

Nor was that the only marked difference between the presidential styles of Taft and Roosevelt. Taft seemed slow and soft-spoken, and while he praised Roosevelt's flamboyance for its arousal of the public "conscience" to change, he believed that the time had come to work behind the scenes for "affirmative legislation" to perpetuate Roosevelt's principles. Taft held the law as sacred, while Roosevelt did not hesitate to stretch it to achieve his ends. To Roosevelt, the main function of diplomacy was to strengthen national power, but Taft viewed national power as an asset to be used through diplomacy, to create treaties that would help American commerce all over the world. The "big stick" of Roosevelt yielded to Taft's "dollar diplomacy."

Shipshape

For all his uncertainty in some matters, Taft did not hesitate to make quick changes at the White House, beginning a trend that would replace the leisurely transfers of the past. The 20th-century White House would usually adjust to new occupants on inauguration day, between the departure of one President and the arrival of the next. Hardly had Mrs. Roosevelt's carriage rolled out of sight when, across the square, Mrs. Elizabeth Jaffray, her luggage borne by a White House footman, her face veiled, her importance marked by a high-cocked, feathered hat, began her walk through the snow to assume her new post as housekeeper to the presidential family. No housekeeper had been employed at the White House for many years, and never again would there be one quite like Mrs. Jaffray. Taken to her rooms upstairs in the family quarters, she paused only to remove her hat before returning downstairs, to prepare for the new President and First Lady.[3]

While the erect, wasp-waisted Mrs. Jaffray inspected the house she was to manage, the members of the existing staff hurriedly shifted to their new positions. Chief Usher Stone moved to the Executive Office with all but two of the other ushers, Ike Hoover and Tommy Pendel; two black footmen in blue livery appeared in the entrance hall. The transformation of the staff ordered by Mrs. Taft took only a few minutes. That spirits remained high was due to the diplomacy of Archie Butt, who carefully orchestrated everything before departing for the Capitol.

Suddenly it was no longer the "Roosevelt White House." Mrs. Taft, knowing what she wanted, made her mark in a hurry. Helen Herron Taft, born during the first year of the Civil War, was 47 at the time of Taft's election. Quick-witted and energetic, she was less a charmer than her husband, and more of a pusher, when it came to having her way. Like Mrs. Roosevelt, but unlike most other First Ladies since Sarah Polk, she was well informed on the political details of her husband's activities; she knew who were his friends, who were his enemies, and how to approach them all with some caution. Her everyday influence on Taft may not have been as strong as Mrs. Roosevelt's was with Roosevelt, but in major decisions she made her views known. There can be no question that she wanted very much for Taft to be President, nor any doubt that her desires helped direct his own ambitions. Once in the White House she determined to make every minute count, and began to transform things from the bottom up.[4]

She had spent sufficient time observing the house during the Roosevelt years to note the areas she thought needed change. Unlike Mrs. Roosevelt, she wished to spend as little time as possible on the routine details of household management. She had learned at Malacanang Palace that a strong administrative structure would free her from day-to-day obligations. No previous First Lady had brought such broad experience to the White House.

Her arrangement with Mrs. Jaffray proved successful. Elizabeth Jaffray—"Ella" to the few who knew her personally—was found through "an exclusive employment bureau" in New York, where she had been looking for work. "Fate had turned a trick on me," she later wrote of her life. For her six married years she had lived happily in Montreal, the wife of a young army officer. "I found that with the death of my husband I had to earn my own living," she wrote, "instead of having my own home and my own servants." She was a lady, and intended to live and be treated as such. In New York she had found employment as housekeeper in a large Manhattan establishment, then for one year was a social secretary, a role she apparently found unsuitable. Disquieted, she searched for a better position, more security, and new scenery.[5]

At first she hesitated to take the post at the White House. Mrs.
Taft's manner was abrupt, yet her promises were appealing. "For two and
a half hours we talked. Before we were through I liked this rather outspoken, determined lady who in less than ninety days was to be Mistress
of the White House." Mrs. Taft had an ability to sweep people up in her
projects, and a way of not hearing "no" when it was said.

Mrs. Jaffray's suite, adjacent to the second-floor service hall and
elevator, consisted of a small, squarish room and a large bedchamber,
both looking out on the north portico. In the first room she kept her
office; the bedchamber, with bath, was her living quarters. For 17 years
she occupied these rooms, serving four administrations, holding what to
many seemed unbendable authority. Her sometimes abrasive manner
betrayed a burden of bitterness over her early widowhood, making her
generally unpopular with the staff. But those she cared to try to please—
the President, his wife, and his children—usually liked her. It is probably
a testimony to her coldness that her very name is omitted from the
memoirs of the time, including, oddly enough, those of Mrs. Taft, who
called her merely "the housekeeper."[6]

She did her work to the satisfaction of the new First Lady. The two
women met daily. Parties were planned, flower arrangements designed,
new servants hired and others dismissed. It was understood that Mrs.
Jaffray was to be the one responsible for making certain that the furniture
and corners were dusted, curtains laundered, rugs mended, floors waxed
glossy, and that slipcovers were crisp, cushions plump, pots shiny, prisms
and mirrors polished, and linens in perfect order. In short, wrote Mrs.
Taft, "just like employés in other homes," those at the White House
needed a woman's guidance. Previous First Ladies had always had to
point out details to the "gentlemen ushers," as Mrs. Taft called them:
Men were no good at housekeeping.[7]

Mrs. Taft's children accused her of making her domestic responsibilities "three times" as hard as necessary by insisting upon her own methods. She denied it, and, although she claimed that her "very active
participation" in her husband's career came to an end the minute she
entered the White House, she remained his devoted, if unofficial, adviser; her eye for political implications and motivations was usually
sharper than his. Thus she depended heavily upon Mrs. Jaffray. It is
probable that neither the President nor Mrs. Taft ever intended Mrs.
Jaffray's authority to be absolute, but their reliance upon her made this
inevitable. She controlled the White House from her shadowed sitting
room, becoming the terror of the lower servants and inspiring both contempt and fear in the upper household staff. Her subordinates were not

permitted to sit down in her presence, nor to address her first. Elizabeth Jaffray built her little empire in a few short months.

There were 25 full-time servants in the White House, with part-time servants brought in for special purposes. All but the Tafts' two personal attendants were paid by the government, but their federal wages did not give them benefits and protections enjoyed by civil servants. They could be hired or fired at the pleasure of the President. The dozen live-in servants were black and occupied the ten servants' bedrooms, five in the west wing and five in the attic.

Twelve servants generally worked in the basement and on the state floor. Excepting the female Swedish cook, most were black. Among them were four footmen who alternated in pairs on duty at the north door; one parlor maid in royal blue ankle-length dress and white organdy cap and apron circulated through the parlors, the East Room, and the State Dining Room, primping curtains and pillows and pinching wilted flowers from the arrangements. The State Dining Room and the private dining room were presided over by a white butler, a "second man," and the pantry man, both black. The last two were usually stationed with the silver and china in the basement storage room or in the pantry, the northwest corner room on the state floor. Upstairs in the family quarters were five servants, two men and three women, most of them white. They answered electric bells which sounded on three call boxes, one in the ushers' office one floor below, the second in the sitting room of the servants' area in the attic, and the third in the servants' dining room, which was also a sitting room, the easternmost room of the west wing.

Mrs. Jaffray "rules them all," wrote *Good Housekeeping* magazine of the staff at the White House.[8] But she had no authority over Mrs. Taft's maids, first Ethel Clark and later Annie Anderson; Arthur Brooks, a black man Taft had ordered detailed from the War Department, and Monico, Taft's Philippine valet, were in theory under the family and not responsible to the housekeeper. Mrs. Jaffray eventually had her confrontation with the latter two. The temperamental Monico fell under her thumb immediately, while Brooks, a shrewd man who was really more an aide than a valet, was adroit enough to become her trusted ally, holding at last the keys to the silver closets and wine cellar. He had traveled the hard road from janitor in the War Department to messenger, a position coveted by black employees of the government, and was no novice at getting what he wanted.

It becomes clear in observing Taft's readjustments in the domestic establishment that over many years a pecking order had developed among the White House employees; the result was a strange hierarchy that defied any comparison to other large household staffs. It was based first on personalities and only second on job status. The White House "backstairs" operation revealed itself most clearly at mealtime. A perquisite of employment was at least one meal each day. The cook, Alice Howard, with her two assistants, prepared plain but substantial food for the servants' dining room. The mealtime rituals were highly ordered. The top-ranking men ate separately at a table in the pantry of the state floor and were served food left over from the President's table. This intimate repast was shared by the chief usher, the butler, the head of the stable, and several others, both black and white.[9]

The maids from the second floor and the parlor maid from the state floor joined the footmen in the servants' dining room. This meal was also seated without regard to race, and also served by a waiter or waitress. Lower kitchen help, laundry maids, and scrubwomen served themselves and ate at another table, probably in the large kitchen, which adjoined the smaller one and was used only for special occasions.[10]

Mrs. Jaffray was displeased by this etiquette. "I immediately ordered that all the colored servants, regardless of rank or position, should eat at a single table and at a given hour," remembered Mrs. Jaffray. "The white servants were to have their own table—but there was no other distinction of any kind." Loud and angry were the objections of the servants. "I promised dismissal," wrote Mrs. Jaffray, and "the revolt died."[11]

Mrs. Taft's eagerness to make changes did not carry over into the interior decoration. To most people the house looked as it had under Roosevelt; after she left it, Mrs. Taft recalled making very few alterations. She had more "modern" taste than Mrs. Roosevelt, and she loved the open airiness and the bright colors of the tropics. Some curtains she modified by taking away the valances. The coronet and side curtains, carefully restored by Mrs. Roosevelt to the Lincoln bed, were removed, as were all the bed draperies in the house; sunny chintz was substituted here and there for McKim's muted brocades. "Colonial" furniture was put in conspicuous places; pieces in what Mrs. Taft characterized as the "scarcely-to-be-called beautiful style of the Victorian era" were stored or put in secondary locations. The simple, gold-rimmed china selected by Mrs. Roosevelt pleased Mrs. Taft sufficiently for her to order the set increased, and she often mixed it on the table with the historic pieces collected by Mrs. Harrison and Mrs. Roosevelt. Into storage went the fanciful Hayes china—"about as ugly," wrote Archie Butt, "as it is possible for china to be."[12]

To everyone's surprise, the President took a personal interest in the first social season. He pored over the guest lists with Warren Young, giving thought to each invitation. "Archie, I am rather proud of these lists," he told his military aide, with a tone of discovery. "The White House is a big political asset when used wisely." Dinners began with the traditional Cabinet dinner on March 26. Guests commented that the house ran more smoothly than most could remember.[13]

The Tafts

The Tafts were a bright and busy family. Charles, the youngest of the three children, was already familiar to the existing staff at the White House because of his friendship with Archie Roosevelt. Robert, the eldest son, age 19, was in his junior year at Yale. The only daughter, Helen, was 17 and a student at Bryn Mawr; although close to her parents, she was seldom at the White House. Both of the older children corresponded faithfully with their parents, and Mrs. Taft's letters to them were numerous and chatty. "This week has been noted for having our *first two entertainments,*" she wrote Helen not long after the inauguration, "a tea to the Congressional ladies and a large dinner also to Congressmen—both of them went off fairly well, however, I think we shall improve as we all become more accustomed to things. I fixed on Monday for your dinner with Alice Longworth . . . . If you can think of enough people for a little dance, we will have it on Tuesday night as we cannot do it in Holy Week very well. . . . "[14]

Archie Butt liked the Taft children. "I have never seen people more natural and wholesome," he said. "Not one of them shows the least signs of what might be called the 'swelled head.' They have inherited the kindly genial nature of the President and the hard common sense of the mother. The President says that Charlie is the only grafter in the family who feels that what is the government's is his and is ready to accept any gift which comes his way."[15]

Taft indulged his children during his Presidency as he never had before. They were given parties, luncheons, and trips; they wore the best clothes, in spite of Mrs. Taft's constant admonition that the costs were too high. "Let them have a good time while they can," the President said, " . . . I want them each to look back upon this portion of their life with the keenest relish." Then he added affectionately, "They are not children to be spoiled by a little luxury now."[16]

The Tafts took the traditional presidential bedroom on the southwest for their suite. "The windows of this room," wrote Mrs. Taft, "look out on the White House gardens where the large fountain plays, and, beyond, on the Washington Monument, the Potomac River and the distant Virginia hills." She remembered the view as it was when she prepared for the inaugural ball, "the most glorious vista in Washington . . . seeing it that March night by the long line of lights which stretch across the Potomac bridge and meet the lights of Arlington, it was, indeed, inspiring." The Tafts loved the room for its "intimate and personal association" with former Presidents, in contrast to the state rooms, "the scenes of great historic events and . . . magnificent hospitality." In the upstairs rooms, "the Presidents of the United States have really lived and been at home."[17]

The next room, going east, was Charlie Taft's, opening into the oval room, thence into the President's private study. This range of rooms comprised the family's daily living quarters. Their oval living room was furnished with a suite of heavily carved furniture made for the Tafts while they lived in the Philippines. A reporter described this room as "an Oriental interior with all the cunningly carved teakwood chairs and tables and Cabinets, wonderful Eastern fabrics for curtains and brilliant splashes of gold dragons on rich backgrounds, a screen of soft wisteria bloom, and wall panels of the tender grays of Japanese art; a tea-table covered with an exquisite piece of embroidery and Oriental pottery."[18]

The west end of the upstairs hall contained a baby grand piano, with stacks of music, comfortable chairs, and a desk for the social secretary, Belle Hagner first, then her successor in 1911, Alice Blech. No dining room furniture remained there, for the Tafts preferred the state floor for dining. They used the state rooms more regularly than any family since Grant's. Breakfast and lunch were served in the small dining room; dinner, usually black-tie, was in the State Dining Room. They found the Blue Room too dark and barren for a sitting room, yet here the President placed his Victrola. His collection of records ranged from grand opera to ragtime. For his guests he personally ground the crank, placed the thick Edison disks on the turntable, and filled the Blue Room with the tenor of Caruso or the soprano of Melba.[19]

The Green Room was the Tafts' favorite sitting room. Mrs. Taft kept its air sweet with cut flowers, its windows often open to welcome summer breezes. Her principal portrait photograph, taken in 1909, shows her seated in one of the painted armchairs in the Green Room. She is clothed in heavily embroidered evening dress of dark crepe, her hair in deep waves and crowned by a diamond tiara.

She wore clothes with an elegance not usual to women as diminutive as she. At 49 she was still trim. Taft urged her to spend all she needed on clothing. Many of her formal dresses were made in China or Japan from luxurious silks and brocades. They were trimmed with pearls,

26. *The Tafts on the south portico, June 18, 1911,
the day they celebrated their silver anniversary. From
the left, Charles, the First Lady, Helen, the President, and Robert. The day ended with a reception in
the south grounds amid thousands of electric lights.*

27. President Taft and Archie Butt take a ride in the great White Steamer, an automobile so long and large that to turn it around the chauffeur had to drive it to one of the city's circles.

28. *The Oval Office, as built in 1909, became the President's workplace in the Executive Office Building.*

29. *Cary Grayson, devoted friend and doctor to Woodrow Wilson, rides in the President's Park, 1917.*

30. *From left, Ellen Wilson, Jessie, Margaret, and Nell, beside a sandstone column, south portico, 1913.*

31. *A statue of Pan climaxes Mrs. Wilson's rose garden west of the White House, 1913. High costs prevented completion of the garden project, which called for an outdoor picture gallery.*

32. *The East Room, bagged in white linen for the summer of 1920. Air-conditioning ended this custom.*

33. *Laundry room in the west terrace, ca. 1917.*

34. *Woodrow Wilson's private study, ca. 1917.*

35. *The Oval Office, July 1, 1918: Wilson signs the Army and Navy Bill into law. Such ceremonies had previously taken place in the White House proper.*

36. *President Wilson and Edith Bolling Wilson, 1916.*

37. *Woodrow Wilson's bedroom at the White House, with the Lincoln bed, 1917.*

38. President Wilson, suffering from a burn on his hand, watches the Liberty Day Parade of April 28, 1918, from his limousine. At this moment, flier Ruth Law is performing high above the White House.

brilliants, or the embroidery which was her trademark.[19] Taft thought his wife magnificent in every way. The two were devoted to each other, she ambitious for him, and he willing to do her bidding. The main difference between them was in their outlook on people: He loved and trusted humankind and she did not. Neither perceived the other's trait as a bad characteristic, only perhaps a weakness. One evening as the Tafts prepared to go out for dinner, Mrs. Jaffray chanced upon them in the second floor corridor and was struck by Mrs. Taft's remarkable appearance in a scarlet gown "shot with gold, with slippers to match." "My goodness, you look like a queen," said Mrs. Jaffray. "She is a queen," Taft said, patting his wife affectionately.[20]

Good Living

The President was content that he lived, if not like a king, certainly well enough for the head of state. His wife liked to quote him as saying, "the country treats its President exceedingly well."[21] On Taft's inauguration day the Congress had raised the presidential salary to $75,000. This was only the third raise since George Washington's time. The original salary was set at $25,000 in September 1789; it had been doubled at the beginning of Grant's second term in 1873; it remained at $50,000 for 36 years, until March 4, 1909.

The cost of the Presidency did not, of course, stop with the salary. A tally provided for Taft by Roosevelt showed $210,544.56 spent by the government on the presidential office and household in fiscal year 1908. This amount included the salaries of full-time and part-time servants, higher household staff, clerks, secretaries, and other employees of the Executive Office. Since the Civil War the Congress had begun to approve more and more presidential expenses. Appropriations were made for certain social costs, for basic interior decoration and repairs, and for necessary purchases of household goods. Of the figure given to Taft, the costs associated with the White House alone—not counting travel, the office, or the stable—amounted to $122,152.56, more than half the total. Gone was the need for the President to spend his own money to run the White House, but being President was still costly, and services were borrowed heavily from the departments, as always.

Taft's statement that Presidents were treated well could not have been made as smugly by many of his predecessors. The President was provided with virtually everything. At state dinners Taft paid only for hard liquor and wines other than champagne. The cost of entertaining for private or political purposes, and of meals for the staff, came from the

President's own purse. Food for all occasions was bought in huge quantity at wholesale, in exchange for exclusive patronage. Every effort was made by Mrs. Jaffray to keep the costs down, but food remained one of Taft's biggest financial obligations.

Mrs. Jaffray calculated that an average of 2,610 individuals were served at the White House each month. Taft ordered a breakdown of food costs on a three-month average in 1909: meats, fruits, and vegetables—$336.62; fowl—$93.97; groceries, including champagne—$155.37; butter and eggs—$103.63; milk and cream—$51.75 (even though the Tafts kept a cow); bread and rolls—$21.88; oysters and fish—$102.97; ices—$12.50; with a total of $878.69, a figure approximating at the time the annual salary of female clerks in the federal government.[22]

The White House budget was managed by the officer in charge of public buildings, in this case Colonel Spencer Cosby, who replaced Colonel Bromwell the week after Taft came to office. Cosby also kept the White House accounts. He was still nominally the chief ceremonial officer of the house as well, although in practice the function had been taken over by Archie Butt. This arrangement was never official, but it worked well because Butt was suited to it and close to the President. Heretofore the commissioner had dealt with the chief usher; for the time, his main White House contact was Butt.

Paid by the Army, Butt was detailed to the office of the chief of the Corps of Engineers, and early in Taft's administration he was promoted to the rank of major. He really had little to do with the corps, for the White House was his full-time assignment and the President his superior. By the time Taft came to office, Butt was so much in control of the operation of the house that Taft came quickly to depend upon him. Even the fearsome Mrs. Jaffray never questioned his position. In the interest of those who would follow him, he continued the scrapbooks of White House events, reporting on the good and bad points of each dinner, dance, or presidential tour. With impeccable judgment, Butt planned receptions and parties, escorted diplomats, smoothed over difficult predicaments, and, as those who remembered him always recalled, was an ambassador of goodwill from the White House to everyone he met.

Potomac Drive

In his few quiet hours, Major Butt wrote faithfully. "The President is very complacent," he noted of Taft after several months. "He is so complacent that sometimes people fall into the erroneous opinion that he is soft. He is only complacent so far as it is convenient to do so. He puts up with a lot of dictation from me apparently, but it is convenient for him to do so. I make things easy for him, but I do not fool myself that I am necessary to him or that he continues this connection with me for any deep affection he has for me . . . . I may be over modest, but it is better to err on this side than take myself too seriously."[23]

As for Mrs. Taft, "you have no idea how lovely she can look," Butt wrote to his sister-in-law. "She really looks ten years younger since she entered the White House, and I think she has become more gracious and kinder toward all the world. She has always had a struggle, and she possesses a nature which I think is going to unfold and enlarge itself as it adjusts itself to new and broader surroundings."[24]

Curiously, the sedentary Taft had a love for the out-of-doors, and customarily took afternoon automobile rides. There were four White House automobiles, under the management of the chauffeur, George H. Robinson, a civilian employee of the Army detailed to the White House. Automobiles were still relatively new, and they mixed with horse-drawn carriages in the streets of Washington. The carriages at the White House stable on 17th Street were put under canvas covers and rolled into storage areas, with one exception. Roosevelt's brougham was turned over to Mrs. Jaffray, who was afraid of automobiles. Each morning she appeared on the north portico to be assisted into the brougham. Wearing a large-brimmed hat with veil, and carrying a parasol, she would ride off to do the marketing.

The Tafts' favorite automobile was a seven-passenger White Steamer, purchased by Taft from the manufacturer, the White Sewing Machine Company of Cleveland, Ohio, shortly before he moved to the White House. In this vast coach of black-laquered metal, silver plate, and glass, the Tafts spent many happy afternoons bumping along country roads in Virginia or gliding over the smooth streets of the city. Like most Presidents, Taft loved fast driving. Remembering cool evenings in Manila, and pleasant carriage rides through tree-lined parks there, Mrs. Taft had dreamed early of having a promenade and drive appropriate to the federal city.[25]

This wish led to the first public project ever undertaken by a First Lady. In this Nellie Taft was the precursor of First Ladies yet to come. Washington's favorite spot for testing an automobile's capabilities was the paved "Speedway," a drive that ran through Potomac Park, at the foot of the ellipse and along the river. Mrs. Taft, determined that this would be her promenade, renamed the Speedway Potomac Drive. Summoning Archie Butt, she made her views known; for Commissioner Cosby she drew a plan. With both men in tow, she went to the park, where she selected a site for a bandstand. Belle Hagner let it be known in town that the Marine Band would give concerts in the park on Wednesday and Saturday afternoons from five until seven. A crew of carpenters soon set to work.

Potomac Drive was an immediate success. Opened on April 15, 1909, it attracted what Major Butt described as a "terrible crush" of people. He had personally teased the press with morsels of news, giving out word that Taft would appear on horseback and Mrs. Taft would ride in the steamer with the top removed. For weeks, Mrs. Taft "worried herself almost sick" that no one would show up on opening day.[26] But Potomac Drive became the most fashionable place in Washington on warm afternoons from April until late October. In 1911, also through the efforts of Mrs. Taft, the drive would be given its famous cherry trees, presented by Mayor Ozaki of Tokyo. The mayor's wife, Theodora, wrote in a personal letter to Mrs. Taft that the trees were intended as a "memorial of national friendship between the U.S. and Japan."[27]

In Teddy's Footsteps

The Tafts loved the active social life required by the Presidency, in spite of its harsh demands on their stamina. But they tried to adjust it to their own personal styles. Neither of the Tafts liked the "imperial" entrance ceremony, he because he believed it made him look foolish (Cleveland, also a large man, had felt the same) and Mrs. Taft because "'The Star-Spangled Banner' . . . is almost as difficult a tune to walk to as Mendelssohn's Wedding March." Where Roosevelt's military experiences seemed to justify the formal march down the grand stairway to trumpets, with a parade of officers, Taft's smiling, good-natured appearance led him to seek a less theatrical alternative. The change he devised, however, had an unhappy result.[28]

The new procedure was inaugurated at a dinner in late March, called in the press a "harmony" dinner, for President Taft had invited the principal figures from both sides of the aisles in the Congress. As a result, the nerves of many of those in attendance were strained. The Tafts elected to have the guests assemble in the East Room, then simply to enter themselves, without flourishes, procession, or announcement.

After the first guests had arrived, the Tafts sent their house party downstairs to the East Room to join them. The Vice President and his wife had been asked to arrive early to mingle with the company. At the dinner hour, the Tafts descended, probably in the elevator, and walked alone down the transverse hall to the East Room doors, where Taft instinctively stepped aside to let his wife enter. "Mrs. Taft should have allowed the President to enter first," confided Archie Butt later, "instead . . . she bolted in ahead of him and was almost halfway around their guests before he had finished shaking hands with the first couple." The confusion might not have been noticed in an ordinary house, but at the White House it made the guests ill at ease, besides demonstrating a disorder unbecoming in the home of the chief of state. Both the Tafts and their guests, particularly the official party, were mortified. "I thought you would enter with trumpets and the band," explained one guest to Mrs. Taft. "Instead . . . you came in like anybody else."[29]

"I was never so nervous and upset in my life," Mrs. Taft told Major Butt the next morning. "You can imagine how much so when I went ahead of Mr. Taft and rather assumed his place as host, but I was not more so than he was, for he talked all night in his sleep and this morning told me that he did nothing but dream of that dinner the entire night."[30]

"Confound it," said Taft to Archie still later, "had anyone told me that such a thing as a dinner could make me nervous, I would have laughed at it, but I assure you I was nervous as a young girl of sixteen. The fact of the matter is, the White House is a bigger proposition than one imagines. The moment you enter it you realize how necessary it is to have every detail go off in perfect order. One or two breaks and you become a laughing stock. Then, too, the aides being with us and uniforms and the music—all makes one nervous. It is the first time in my life I have ever felt stampeded. I was not nearly so nervous the day I took the oath of office."[31]

Archie Butt, who was not present at the White House that evening, could not help being pleased that they were upset. He had done all he could to curb the change in advance; he realized that most of the ceremonial was far from vain showmanship. The President did business at the state functions; they were not "parties" in the same sense as entertainments held by private persons, but a means of exposing the President to certain persons he needed to be with, on the most comfortable terms possible. Butt observed that Presidents and First Ladies might well make their innovations, but they would learn soon enough that "after all, they are only a part of the machinery and cannot interfere with it beyond a given point."[32]

The Tafts did prevail in their wish not to march to music, reserving their marching for large receptions, not for dinners. The compromise finally reached, though odd, worked well. Under the careful supervision of Major Butt, the guests were arranged in a particular formation before the President arrived. He and Belle Hagner had worked out the plan,

with Warren Young's approval. The guests were placed according to
rank, with the highest ranking member nearest to the door the President
would enter. Butt stood at the door and, when the President appeared,
announced him in a loud voice. Taft then entered the room, with
Mrs. Taft a few steps behind. The presidential couple went to the guests,
one by one. When the last guest had been greeted, the butler appeared to
announce dinner. The President was at that point with his dinner partner, the last woman he greeted. Butt escorted the male guest of honor to
Mrs. Taft, and the procession to the dining room began, with only serene
dinner music, no marches.[33]

Gardens, Food, and Drink

The Tafts also made many small changes in the White House style
of entertaining. These Archie Butt duly noted in his scrapbooks labeled
"Social Functions." Food and drink were served at the large receptions;
only ice water had been available for more than 20 years. Now the table
in the State Dining Room was filled with cookies and cakes, fruits and
nuts, and a punch bowl. Punch was also available in the transverse hall
and in the East Room. It was usually nonalcoholic, in the interest of
keeping the crowds from lingering.

Entertaining under Taft was notable for its variety. In the beautiful
spring of 1909, Mrs. Taft gave wing to her love for the tropics by banking
the interior of the house with palms. For dinner parties and dances, she
opened the terraces to the east and west. The globes of the electric lamp
standards spaced along the balustrades were covered with red silk, and
glowed in the dark like strange bright cherries. The tubbed bay trees,
clipped in large balls and cones, were intermingled with potted palms
along the parapets of the terraces. After dinner, the guests wandered
along the red tile floors under the stars. For dances, the Marine Band
played on a platform at the north end of the East Room. The music could
be heard through the open windows on the east terrace, where those who
wished could dance outside.

Musicales, begun by the Roosevelts, were continued by the Tafts.
Their musicales were often smaller, making use of the Blue Room. A
handsome, cream-colored concert grand piano, which matched the
neo-Empire furnishings, was installed there, and from January until May
musicales were usually held twice a week. Mrs. Taft, who played the
piano herself, tended to prefer that instrument, with either strings or
a flute and frequently a female singer.

Mrs. Taft held her first garden party in early May 1909. This had been one of her favorite ways of entertaining since her cherished years in the Philippines. Her garden parties were more elaborate than those of Mrs. Roosevelt, with increased floral decorations. At her first, she had an allée of flowers made from the archway beneath the south portico, where the guests entered the party, to the spot where she stood to receive, in the shelter of blooming pear trees.

Heavy rain drove the first garden party into the house, where it continued in the East Room and State Dining Room. At dusk the rain ceased, and the doors to the terraces were opened, allowing the company to walk out and enjoy the rose-pink end of day. "All my life the elements have been unfriendly to me," wrote Nellie Taft, remembering the day. Guests at her second garden party enjoyed sunny skies and dogwood in full bloom; the fountain on the south lawn "made rainbows and diamond showers in the sun." This party became the standard of perfection by which every subsequent garden party was judged.[34]

The military aides attended the garden parties, dressed in summer whites. They served a security function, although there were also Secret Service men stationed throughout the house and grounds. Archie Butt always stood with the President, unless he was announcing for Mrs. Taft. When he walked with the President or First Lady, he was usually directly behind them, but as close as possible. The eight junior aides scattered far apart, circulating constantly among the guests. At the slightest signal from one of them, plainclothesmen would converge quickly upon an offending guest. While this swarming occurred at least once at each of the great receptions, it took place at only one garden party, when a guest was taken from the premises for noisily demanding that his card be carried to the President. "The secret service men, like the poor," sighed Mrs. Taft, "we had with us always."[35]

State dinners were not very different from similar events under Roosevelt. Butt's meticulous records show that the horseshoe table was used almost exclusively, with the innovation of an additional rectangular table within the horseshoe, which increased the dining room's capacity by 30 percent. As she wrote of this in her memoirs, it dawned on Mrs. Taft that a star-shaped table inside the horseshoe might have held even more, "but I'm glad it never occurred to Mr. Taft," she wrote. "With his expansive disposition he certainly would have had it tried."[36]

On pleasant late spring or summer evenings, the west terrace was sometimes arranged for dinners. Secluded in the embrace of large trees, it was an elegant setting, with the wash of electric light on tall "walls" of shimmering green leaves. The east terrace was kept permanently outfitted as a promenade from April to late October and was frequently in use.

It provided more dramatic vistas than did the west terrace; at its eastern end rose the heroic colonnade of the Treasury Building, and the east pool and fountain lay at its feet; on the south the lawn swept down to the ellipse, bordered by groves of trees. Most dinner guests ended up on the east terrace when the weather permitted. With its tropical plants, it was more characteristically Taft than any "room" in the White House.

White House hospitality centered on the dining table, where the Tafts' taste was regal. The preparation of the dinners, large and small, continued generally as it had under Theodore Roosevelt, except that no caterers were engaged. Mrs. Jaffray supervised the cooking, and Butt oversaw the other details. In the absence of the traditional caterers, Major Butt, Mrs. Jaffray, and the chief usher developed a list of part-time waiters, maids, police, and others approved by the Secret Service. Guest lists were developed by the President and Mrs. Taft, with advice from the State Department. Only personal invitations were issued from the White House itself; all other invitations were sent from the Executive Office by Warren Young.

The areas of the house devoted to food preparation were in the west end of the basement. McKim's white tile, nickel plate, and gloss white paint gleamed in these rooms. Pantries for vegetables, flour, sugar, and preserves were located in this part of the house and stretched into the west terrace, behind Jefferson's colonnades. The everyday kitchen, west of the larger kitchen, was beneath the main floor pantry and had glass-front cabinets, stove, sink, and a great dumbwaiter set into the wall. The larger kitchen contained four gas ovens and two hotel-size gas ranges, the largest an Imperial French Coal Range 12 feet long, purchased in 1912. At the same time, Cosby selected a "Forty quart Peerless Ice Cream Freezer," with a direct current motor, complete with copper can.

Across the west end of the basement hall, itself a pantry fitted with cabinets, was a nest of little rooms called the "steward's closets" or "steward's rooms." Here the silver and much of the china that was infrequently used were stored, the silver in its original leather trunks, compartmented to fit each piece. Mrs. Taft had the area remodeled into a silver vault and an office for Arthur Brooks. This displaced the china. Twenty or thirty pieces then considered historic remained on exhibit in glass cases that Mrs. Roosevelt had placed in the vaulted basement corridor. The rest was stored in the tall cabinets of the main floor pantry, under the care of the pantry man, James Walker. Everyday flat silver was kept there as well, in special drawers. Pantry and small kitchen were virtually in full-time operation every day, from just after daybreak until at least ten at night. When a major dinner was being prepared, the large kitchen operated simultaneously with the small kitchen, beginning a day or two before the event. The permanent staff of six men and women were joined by as many as ten temporary workers, making the two kitchens, the pantries, and Arthur Brooks' rooms the scenes of busy activity.

A Sudden Illness

As the frantic pace of the Presidency began to take its toll on the Tafts' peace of mind, they increasingly sought rest. One special pleasure was provided by the *Sylph,* the smaller of the two Navy boats used as presidential yachts. Particularly enjoyable to the Tafts was the trip down the Potomac to Mount Vernon late in the afternoon, but they often took longer trips. On the larger vessel, the *Mayflower,* they ventured out to sea, or to New York, or to their summer home in Beverly, Massachusetts.

On May 17, 1909, en route to Mount Vernon, Mrs. Taft suffered an attack aboard the *Sylph* which was to curtail the couple's fast pace for more than a year. She and the President had invited a small group of friends to meet them aboard the yacht at 4 p.m. for a sail down the Potomac. It had been a trying day for Mrs. Taft, spent in large part with young Charlie in the hospital, where his adenoids had been removed. She had dropped everything at the White House, insisting upon being with her son, and had been very worried.

The *Sylph* had hardly left the dock when Attorney General George Wickersham, seated on deck beside Mrs. Taft, noticed she had suddenly ceased responding to his conversation, and had become very still. "Mrs. Taft has fainted," he called out. He and Archie Butt carried her into the saloon, where she was revived, but could not speak. Muscular control of her right arm and leg was gone. Major Butt ordered the *Sylph* back to the dock. In an enclosed automobile they rushed to the White House, where Mrs. Taft was carried through the south entrance along the corridor to the elevator. No word was said to anyone about what had happened until after the doctor had examined her. "The President looked like a great stricken animal," Archie Butt recalled, "I have never seen greater suffering or pain . . . on a man's face."[37]

While it is generally accepted today that Mrs. Taft suffered a stroke, it was not acknowledged at the time. The most the family would admit was that she had a "nervous disorder." Doctors seemed to confirm this at first. She made a speedy recovery, and was able to take drives in the open car in May, but her face was veiled. During the summer, while at Beverly, she refused to allow reporters or office staff to enter the big, shingled house. Only the closest family friends could see her.

She remained weak for at least another year, and was not herself again until well into 1911. Until then, she moved about with difficulty; a part of her face was relaxed, temporarily disfigured. But social life at the White House could not halt. Unable to act as hostess, she called on her sisters at first and then upon her strong-willed daughter, Helen, even though Helen had not yet made her debut. When an entertainment was large enough to justify the traditional presidential entrance down the stair to music, the President descended alone. He insisted that no woman, not even his daughter, would be allowed to take the place of the First Lady in any official ceremony.

Mrs. Taft had to live for the time in the shadows. It was a painful sentence of fate, for she had dreamed of being First Lady. She longed to be engaged with people and politics. She remained very much involved in all that took place at the White House, but appeared in public only rarely. While Taft held dinners in the State Dining Room, Mrs. Taft sat alone and silent at the table in the adjoining small dining room, the banquet food before her, listening to the mingled conversations in the great room beyond the mahogany doors.[38]

Oval Office

In a flurry of activity on Taft's inauguration day, the Congress had appropriated $40,000 "for additional accommodations to the building erected for the offices of the President, and for each and every purpose connected therewith." The name "temporary" had been dropped from the title of the office wing, in favor of Executive Office Building, or, in common parlance, "the EOB." Taft did not address this project until the following month. Colonel Cosby had by then become accustomed to his job, so the President met with him, and with his private secretary, Fred Carpenter, and gave his ideas about how the money might best be spent in filling the need for additional office space.

Either wings or a second story were the obvious solutions. Taft concluded that a second floor would create a mass which would detract from the White House, so the answer seemed to lie in a southward extension, built on the Roosevelt tennis court, immediately behind the existing building. In the proposed addition the floor space would be increased by approximately four-fifths. A plan was sketched, apparently under the President's immediate direction. Cosby had a clearer drawing made from it, and this was blueprinted for distribution.

Taft had a personal interest in architecture and was a strong political supporter of the profession. Having learned his lessons well from the

American Institute of Architects, he concluded that the best way to approach the addition was to stage a competition among architects. Colonel Cosby was dispatched to New York with the sketch plan and a list of questions for McKim, Mead, & White, with the idea that they would know how to carry out the President's competition. But ill health prevented McKim from attending the meeting; White was dead, and Mead was living in Italy. Cosby had to discuss his problem with the new generation of the firm. After they later consulted with McKim at his home, they prepared a letter to Cosby stating their views. All the architects agreed that Taft's plan was excellent, and saluted his idea of expanding to the south, realizing not only that the existing structure, being "temporary," was too weak for a second floor, but that a second floor would be a "serious detriment" to the setting of the White House. Because the architectural problem was "already solved except in its minor details," McKim, Mead, & White advised against a competition.[39]

The advice was not taken. Taft did modify his original intention and asked Cosby to select two local architects to compete for the work. Each firm was to be paid $250 for sophisticated sketch plans and elevations, preliminary to working drawings. Cosby selected two architects who had designed and built successful additions to major buildings. Waddy Wood of Wood, Donn, & Deming, had transformed the gangly old Providence Hospital into an acclaimed Spanish mission-style edifice only five years before; Nathan C. Wyeth had added a fourth floor to the Lemon Building, where Cosby worked every day, and while the job had been done 18 years before, it was still considered an enhancement to a fine building designed in the modern mode associated with Chicago.

Contact with the architects was made on April 17, 1909. The drawings were deposited in the commissioner's office in the Lemon Building 12 days later. Great pains were taken to evaluate both works systematically, so that the best would win. An official "government" opinion was solicited. In the office of public buildings the architect Frederick D. Owen, friend of the late Mrs. Harrison and a former protegé of Colonel Bingham, still labored. Owen, who had once dreamed of following in Hoban's footsteps, was asked for an appraisal of the merits of the two designs. He reported that Wyeth's was by far the best. "Favorable consideration," he wrote, "is respectfully urged. . . . His estimate of cost seems low, yet I believe he can execute what he undertakes." Nathan C. Wyeth was informed that he had won the competition.[40]

Although the original competition drawings do not survive, written documentation makes it apparent that both competitors followed with only minor variations the plan of rooms established by the President,

Fred Carpenter, and Colonel Cosby. This plan changed the symbolic character of the Executive Office Building from a staff office into an office for the President, in the same sense that the "West Wing" is an executive office today. The main alteration was relocating the President's office on the central axis, where the secretary's office had been. Where the office of the secretary had featured a bow on the south wall, the new office added for the President was fully oval, like the Blue Room.

Taft was revising the building to make it conform to his idea of its new purpose, an actual business office for the use of the President. McKim had hesitated to move the business function entirely from the White House, where it had been since 1800. The historically minded Roosevelt had used the upstairs study in the White House, the old Cabinet Room, as an office. Taft, too, was unwilling to abandon the association completely. When on August 3, 1911, he needed a place to consummate what he considered the high point of his administration, he turned to the same study for the signing of the Arbitration Treaty between the United States, Great Britain, and France. Most of the actual work on the treaty, however, had taken place in the new Oval Office.

The Oval Office began to take form during the summer of 1909, and the White House complex gained the first new state room since its building in the 1790s. Of his Oval Office design, the architect Nathan Wyeth had this to say: "I have endeavored to show a dignified treatment in keeping with the high purpose it is to serve."[41] The remainder of the plan was less enduring. None of it survives except the Oval Office itself, which was relocated a quarter of a century later. Taft's changes had little effect on the 1902 building, except to put reception space where the central office had been. Across the rear Wyeth added a long transverse corridor running east and west, separating the new addition from the original office building. Waiting rooms and offices were put in the old structure, and the new part contained the Cabinet Room, secretary's room, and Oval Office. Double doors at the east end of the transverse corridor gave onto the colonnade of the wing, providing covered access to the house, somewhat protected by the vines and shade of the colonial garden. On the west this same broad hall terminated in a new telegraph room, which also connected with the secretary's office. The Oval Office was in the center of the new addition, with the Cabinet and the secretary's rooms flanking it to the east and west. For reasons of privacy and security it was not entered directly on axis, but from the sides, through alcoves equipped with desks for doormen.

Construction started on July 1, the beginning of the new fiscal year. By mid-August, the shell and most of the interior partitions were nearly complete. In early September, the stucco worker united the old and new parts of the Executive Office Building with a smooth layer of his cement, which he scored to resemble ashlar, then painted white. The finished building competed very little with the White House, although it was larger than it seemed. By creating slopes and planting hemlock screens to the south and southwest, the architect made the heavy, horizontal mass seem unobtrusive.

Edward Caldwell, who had provided light fixtures for the McKim renovations of 1902, returned to produce fixtures for the office building. John C. Knipp & Son, marine woodworkers and interior decorators of Washington and Baltimore, was given the contract for furnishings and hangings. Taft chose deeply upholstered chairs and heavy tables of oak and mahogany. His most innovative requirement was an air-conditioning system, in which electric fans blew over great bins of ice in the attic, cooling air which was then forced into the air ducts of the heating system. This never worked and was soon abandoned.[42]

The President probably occupied his new office in early October. The color scheme of this first Oval Office, chosen by Taft and Carpenter, was largely an olive green, including curtains of silk velvet, a rug, and "Tapestrolea," trade name for the burlap-like material that covered the walls. Rich neocolonial woodwork had been executed from Wyeth's designs; the doors were pedimented, the wainscoting deeply paneled, and the trimming painted white. The floor was of mahajua wood from the Philippines, mixed with lightly bleached oak and set in a diagonal checkerboard parquet pattern with broad borders. Most of the seating furniture was covered with caribou hide, embellished with brass studs and rubbed to a high sheen with dark red pigment.[43]

The Oval Office functioned as the President's office from that time on, notwithstanding Taft's occasional hesitation over its symbolic importance. In its creation, Taft placed the President, metaphorically as well as physically, in the middle of his day-to-day office operations, and therefore made him more of a presence in the running of the government. His administrative practices as President supported this change. An example of his tightening of controls was his edict requiring all departments to secure his approval before honoring congressional requests for important documents. He took an active interest in the minutiae of finances, ordering that all estimates for appropriations come to him before being sent to the Congress. By such unprecedented personal monitoring, the President cut millions from the estimates. His calculation of money he trimmed at the close of fiscal year 1911 was $42,818,000. He went further and proposed a national budget, but the plan came to nothing.

He instituted civil service reform through the Committee of Efficiency and Economy, composed of successful businessmen and lawyers. They found the governmental service flabby from overemployment and inefficiently managed. Taft's ensuing reform programs extended to the very doors of his own Oval Office, in a general tightening of the operation. His office workers saw him every day, and dealt with him on a closer basis than they had with any of his recent predecessors. In some respects, Taft revived the old spirit of camaraderie that had not been known since the President's staff occupied cramped rooms upstairs in the White House. Now the office force was five times the size, yet the President was once more among them.

As part of this restructuring, the prestige and power of the secretary to the President was considerably reduced. Under Roosevelt the secretary had been a prince in his own realm, as reflected in the central position of his office in the new building. Taft put himself at the head of the Executive Office, as his remodeling of the building soon illustrated, and considered the secretarial post an assistantship, to carry out the management of the office. Fred W. Carpenter, who had served as Taft's secretary since 1901, did not object to this. He found the pattern of their relationship too well established to change and was uncomfortable with high rank.

Carpenter was appointed minister to Morocco in 1910. When Charles D. Norton replaced him, the title was informally changed to "assistant to the President," which more accurately described the managerial character of the work. Norton remained less than one year, before moving to New York to enter banking; though an able businessman, he had not been enough of a politician for the job. His successors were experienced politicians. The first, Charles Hilles of New York, left temporarily in 1912 to serve as chairman of the Republican National Committee. In his absence the position was filled by Carmi Thompson of Ohio. Both of those men, but especially Hilles, were powerful Republicans, and served the President as advisers on political strategy, in an effort to save the crumbling Republican Party.

Night of Electric Light

The one brilliant event that the Tafts cherished for the rest of their lives was the celebration of their silver wedding anniversary on June 19, 1911. It was a magnificent party. All Presidents entertain old friends, as a way of sharing with them the more obvious pleasures of being President. Whether house parties, dinners, or even dances, the occasions are usually small, and are always remembered by former tenants of the White

House as the most joyful, reminiscent of simpler times in their lives but staged in the full glory of the presidential scene.[44]

Taft's was held on the grandest scale of all, and has yet to be rivaled. By the late spring of 1911, Mrs. Taft was her old self, perhaps not moving as fast, but again visible in public. For their 25th anniversary celebration the Tafts decided upon a large evening garden party, a brilliant reception and illumination of the sort they had loved in Manila. The guest list would be large, including everyone the Tafts could think of who had ever done them a favor or had been a special friend.

In her memoirs, Mrs. Taft refused to guess how many invitations were sent. Archie Butt recorded that there were 8,000. Some of those invited were friends; some had been the Tafts' hosts in distant places; some were relatives, some mere acquaintances, and some official guests. All would have the chance to visit with the President and his wife, if only briefly, and all would have good food and drink.

On the south grounds, night was to be turned into day by means of multicolored electric lights. On June 18, after dinner, the President requested a preview of the lights, on which the electricians had been working for four days. Strands with hundreds of bulbs covered the great elm trees and the Jackson magnolias, and the glittering spectacle extended all the way to the ellipse. But the President wanted even more: Why not light the flag on the roof? Why not the fountain down on the lawn? Taft ordered twice as many spotlights as were there. Aides telephoned the naval bases at Norfolk and Annapolis to borrow strands of lights used on ships. These were on freight cars by early morning, en route to Washington; still the President thought there were too few lights. He paced the flat platform atop the roof of the White House, issuing orders for more strands, more spotlights, more paper lanterns.

Archie Butt, in charge of the evening, designed the special invitations, substituting silver for the usual White House gold. He emptied the White House greenhouses, then went to florists and private greenhouses to borrow blooming trees, fruit trees, palms, and tropical plants to mass in the house and through the grounds. Seven temporary aides joined the usual nine in standing in close formation near the Tafts at all times. Butt approved the china and silver and flowers and tasted the punch. When the time came it was described as "one of those balmy nights that come in June," perfect weather for a tropical fête. Much was in bloom on the White House grounds, delayed by a late winter; honeysuckle was at its fragrant peak on the stairs that led to the south portico. The gates were opened to the invited guests at 8 p.m. Thousands of spectators crowded the streets and the ellipse, as daylight fell and the electric lights rose.

The White House itself was completely illuminated, perhaps for the first time in its history. Over its roof a giant American flag floated horizontally on the wind made by electric fans concealed among the chimneys. All the trees were covered with strings of lights, and from their lower limbs bulbs shaded by paper lanterns were strung from tree to tree; the lanterns "diffused the light and softened the whole into a maze of dreamland." So read the official account, written by Archie Butt.

Music came from the Engineers Band, seated on the south portico, and the Marine Band, on the new tennis court, half concealed in the trees on the west side of the south lawn. The two played alternately, with no intermissions. Guests were allowed an hour to walk through the grounds before the appearance of the Tafts. According to the press, the company did not have the "the slightest conception of the elaborate preparations," and stood in wonder at what they saw. It was "a scene beautiful beyond description. All around the outer edge of the acres of level, short-clipped grass . . . were Chinese lanterns of fantastic designs, blocks upon blocks of them, barely 6 inches apart, swinging in the light breeze and casting their queer shapes and shadows on the lawn."[45]

At nine o'clock the Engineers Band played the "Star-Spangled Banner," and the Tafts descended the grand staircase to the crowded state floor. Down the transverse hallway, side by side and not pausing, through the well-wishers, the couple walked to the Red Room, from which they stepped out onto the south portico. A great cheer rose from the several thousand people by then on the lawn, and the cheering spread to the estimated 15,000 outside the fences. The President smiled, took his wife's hand, and nodded to the band; and as the band played the Wedding March, the Tafts walked down the stair to the lawn, Mrs. Taft in white satin embroidered with silver roses and carnations.

For several hours, they shook hands beneath a tall arch of trees and boughs, crowned by "1886-1911" written out in light bulbs. The guests had freedom to move at will through the state floor and the grounds. At 11 p.m. the State Dining Room was opened for the buffet supper, and food was also served in the East Room and in small tents scattered throughout the groves flanking the south lawn. As the guests ate, the Washington Saengerbund Society, concealed in the Jackson Magnolias, sang "My Old Kentucky Home" and "The Last Rose of Summer."

At midnight, Mrs. Taft, exhausted, went upstairs in the elevator. She could not sleep for a long while, but turned out the lights in the bedroom, opened the window, and watched the scene on the grounds below. At 1 a.m., the leader of the Engineers Band sent a note to the President, asking if he should strike up "Home Sweet Home"; no indeed, responded the President, keep the music playing. Taft then went into the grounds to mix with the company, talking informally. When at last the music stopped, at 2 a.m., the crowd began to leave. The President ordered the lights turned off in the Blue Room and on the south portico, where he seated himself, and remained until the last guest had gone, watching the evening end, as though—in Archie Butt's words—"he loathed to see it pass."[46]

Before he retired for the night Taft decided that the magic of the evening must live once more. He ordered that the grounds be open to the public the next night from 8 until 11, and that the music and lights remain exactly as they were the night of his silver anniversary.

Major Archibald Butt

Taft depended heavily upon Archie Butt, and the major was showing signs of breaking under the constant pressure. Besides his fast pace at the White House, he was probably the most popular bachelor in Washington. At the large old-fashioned house he rented several blocks from the White House, he and his artist friend Frank Millet gave open houses and suppers with some regularity. As a rule his friends seem to have been prominent and wealthy, people who lived more in the Roosevelt tradition of active leisure than in the Taft's circle, where intellectual growth and good deeds were what counted. Photographs in the official records show that he had become pale and weary looking, with bags under his eyes. Some of the newcomers at the White House he classed as rivals.

His doctor advised a trip for relaxation, and during the winter of 1912, Archie determined that spring would find him in Europe, where he would join Frank Millet, who had spent the winter in Rome at the American Academy. The President thought this a good idea. Major Butt's last dinner party at the White House was less a duty than a farewell affair for him, complete with gifts and slaps on the back. Everyone loved Archie Butt. He sailed from New York in March, intending to stay for two months. But the President received a wire in early April that his aide had changed his mind and would be back early, as he and Millet had the opportunity to sail home aboard the new *Titanic*.

Taft heard the news of the disaster on April 15, the day after it happened, but took heart when told that most of the passengers had survived. At the theater that night he was told otherwise, and immediately returned to his office, where in the cold emptiness of the place, he wired the White Star Line for word of Archie Butt. The next morning he was informed that Butt and Millet were not on the list of survivors.

"He was like a member of my family," wrote Taft, "and I feel as if he had been a younger brother." In preparing her memoirs later, Mrs. Taft leafed through the scrapbooks Archie Butt had meticulously kept during his four years as military aide at the White House. "It amuses me to find," she wrote, "that Captain Butt in the Official Diary has carefully recorded all my mistakes as well as my successes. . . . "[47]

Departure

Taft's early biographer, Henry F. Pringle, observed that Taft's great "personal tragedy" as a statesman was that he did not communicate publicly the ideas that enriched his letters. The American people never really perceived the great mind of William Howard Taft. "The fine, brave words he uttered, " wrote Pringle, "were to lie covered with dust in locked files for decades. Only his mistakes—and his timid uncertainties— reached the headlines."[48]

In the winter of 1912, Theodore Roosevelt, who had been very much in the newspapers since his triumphant return from his travels nearly two years earlier, announced that he was available for nomination by the Republican Party. At the convention in June, he lost overwhelmingly to Taft, although a large number of the delegates refused to vote either way. Two months later, the Progressive Party, a liberal split from the Republicans, nominated Roosevelt at its national convention. He was a candidate for President in the election of 1912, and the bitterness between himself and Taft paralleled that between two other former close friends, Jefferson and Adams, more than a century earlier. Those earlier rivals, however, mended their differences.

Meanwhile, the Democratic Convention in Baltimore that summer erupted in more constructive turmoil, with the mighty William Jennings Bryan looming over its deliberations. Through a series of unexpected turns, the Democrats produced a surprise nominee in Governor Woodrow Wilson of New Jersey. Former president of Princeton University and a professor and political writer of note before that, Wilson had only entered politics in 1910, when he ran for governor. He had been mentioned as a presidential possibility as early as 1906, both because of his published essays and his academic reforms at Princeton, which had received wide coverage in newspapers and popular magazines.

For all the political furor, the White House was a quiet place during the summer of 1912. Mrs. Taft and Charlie were vacationing in Massachusetts. The President played golf regularly at the Chevy Chase club, and took daily drives in the new Pierce Arrow limousine, which had taken the place of the steamer. Charles Norton, the secretary, had convinced Taft that it was absurd to use a car that had to be driven to one of Washington's circles to be turned around. When Taft reluctantly agreed to auction it off in 1911, Norton was the winning bidder![49]

Taft refused to stay alone in the White House. He often invited members of his political family to move there while his own family was away, so the bedrooms were sometimes filled with Cabinet members, department heads, or members of the office staff. Now and then the house party was so large that guests had to double up in the sleeping quarters. Working sessions over piles of official papers sometimes ran to midnight in Taft's study. The President delighted in both work and company, and could not bear to dine alone. He provided for his company bright conversation, heavy grilled food, and scotch and soda.

Taft knew that summer that the chances of his winning were slim. At dinner one evening with Charles Hilles, who had returned from his unlucky stint as chairman of the Republican National Committee, Taft discussed the dim picture. Hilles, who knew the Tafts well, asked if Mrs. Taft would be deeply hurt if he were defeated. The conversation that ensued so impressed itself in Taft's mind that he repeated his response the next day in a letter to his wife, more as a question than a statement: "I told him the contrary was the case, that you had for a long time not expected me to be re-elected, and that you were most gratified, as we all were, in the accomplishment of the more important purpose of defeating Roosevelt in Chicago. I hope that I stated your views with exactness."[50]

"I wanted him to be re-elected," Mrs. Taft later insisted in her memoirs, "but I never entertained the slightest expectation of it and only longed for the end of the turmoil when he could rest his weary mind and get back into association with the pleasant things of life." She recalled that after the fatal split of the Republican Party, "I began to make plans for the future in which the White House played no part. I stopped reading the accounts of the bitter political contest because . . . I was in a state of constant rage which could do me no possible good."[51]

After Wilson's election in November, the Tafts prepared for their return to private life. The President seemed relieved that the mudslinging was over; Roosevelt had not beaten him, even though he had pulled more popular votes. William Howard Taft would not retire, but would accept a chair of law at Yale, and this new challenge he anticipated with great satisfaction. During his last months in the White House, he put on a series of small dinner parties to honor his old and close friends. Mrs. Taft, though troubled by a small setback in her health, was at his side. The big parties were over.

The morning of March 4, as Taft and Woodrow Wilson departed for the inauguration ceremonies, Mrs. Taft and Helen watched from Helen's bedroom upstairs, over the private dining room. For Mrs. Taft it was a sad occasion. Deep inside she could hardly bear to leave the White House, and she lingered almost until the last minute, when the Wilsons were expected to return. The house staff was afraid that she would not be gone in time. Mrs. Taft calmly penned letters to each of her sons, away at school. It was the last time she would be able to use the heavy paper engraved "White House," and perhaps the boys might one day enjoy showing the letters to their children. When the clocks began to chime noon, she rose and put on her furs and a hat. She at last appeared alone and unsmiling on the state floor, the two letters clutched in her fingers, her arms filled with magazines.

After a last look at the state parlors, she walked into the ushers' office. When she handed the letters to Ike Hoover to mail, the magazines she was carrying slipped to the floor. She stood motionless as others scrambled to pick them up; not one word was uttered by anyone. Packed up again, Mrs. Taft walked in silence to the waiting Pierce Arrow. As soon as the car moved away, Helen came down to the entrance hall. She walked cheerfully along the driveway in the bright March daylight, and out the front gate, where a young friend was waiting for her. The two, talking animatedly, disappeared up the street.[52]

33

Thresholds

Woodrow Wilson described himself as the only true Democrat to be President of the United States since James Buchanan. Cleveland he dismissed as a Republican in Democrat's clothing. For his own election, Wilson could thank the Republican split: As a candidate he had offered an inspiring alternative to a portion of the predominantly Republican electorate. The election of 1912 showed a transformation in the Democratic Party, dominated since the mid-19th century by southern interests. Wilson had attracted a strong, young, middle-class following; he had turned it away from regionalism and toward exalted national ideals, in a time when Americans were still somewhat confused about the implications of being a world power. By affirming his faith in the people's good judgment, he had revived the Everyman spirit of the party's early days.

His inauguration displayed an almost sanctified sense of beginning not seen since Abraham Lincoln took office. Though Wilson was not flamboyant, his deep intellectual commitment inspired respect, and he had a teacher's instinct for casting a spell over a crowd. He knew how to set the scene. At the podium on his inauguration day, about to begin his address, he looked down and saw a police barricade holding back the eager throng. "Let the people come forward!" he commanded, and as the guards dropped their hands, the crowd rolled in like a tide to the base of the platform. Wilson began to speak, and his pretty, bright-eyed wife, seemingly oblivious of thousands of watching eyes, left her seat and descended the steps to the ground, where she could better see her husband in his great hour.

The Democrats Move In

Colonel Cosby knew that with the new administration—especially as it was Democratic—his days as officer in charge of public buildings and grounds were numbered. As he left for the inauguration, he asked a member of the White House staff to go to the roof, wait until the precise stroke of noon, remove the flag for him, and replace it with another. Within a few minutes after the hour, Cosby's souvenir was in the ushers' office, while a score of employees stood by, in hallways, pantries, and at windows, almost as motionless as the folded flag.

Ike Hoover found such odd, suspended times among the most interesting in his White House career. Normally the staff had little idea of what an incoming administration would do; the change of political party increased their uncertainty. The actual transfer was ultimately simple: One presidential family left in the morning, and a second arrived at or soon after noon. Upstairs, the Tafts' dresser drawers were empty; the tabletops were bare; the oval room was practically vacant. Messengers were taking Wilson luggage up in the elevator, but the new President had to sleep in his underwear that night because the suitcase containing his pajamas had gone astray.

Every employee, wrote Hoover, "sees some particular reason why he should be retained," but on this Democratic inaugural day, the staff was naturally "just a little worried." Hoover probably felt safer than most, because after the death of Archie Butt the management of the house had fallen again to the chief usher. The post had been restored to its former status with fiscal year 1913, and Hoover was given the job. Still he had not yet been in touch with the Wilsons.[1]

Mrs. Jaffray alone had been in contact with the incoming family. Asked to call on the Wilsons in Princeton several weeks after the election, she went, with Mrs. Taft's blessing. In later years the housekeeper recalled the Wilsons' "comfortable" living room, and Mrs. Wilson, a "rather plump, sweet brown-eyed woman," who received her cordially. Cosby had supplied Mrs. Jaffray with plans of the state floor, the basement, the chamber or private floor, and the servants' room in the attic. These Mrs. Jaffray described completely, in the course of explaining how the house was managed.

"My! What a difficult house," said Mrs. Wilson. "We certainly want you to stay on and take care of things. . . . You will, won't you?"

So Mrs. Jaffray was the only one who had no reason to worry that inaugural day, as she attended to the details of the lunch Mrs. Taft had planned for the Wilsons. At one o'clock she stood in the small service hall on the second floor, awaiting the elevator, when Wilson walked up, hat in hand. "Welcome to your new home, Mr. President," she ventured, thrusting her hand forward.

He took her hand and bowed. "Oh! You are Mrs. Jaffray, aren't you?" he said. "I am so happy to meet you." Mrs. Wilson then joined them in the hall. "Mrs. Jaffray and I are already friends," said the President of the United States to his wife.

Downstairs, Ike Hoover was amazed that he could recognize so few faces in the crowd gathering in the East Room. There was, he wrote, "an entirely new lot of people." To confuse matters, Taft had accepted Wilson's pro forma invitation to lunch. This he did to the great consternation of the aides accompanying him, and to the subsequent annoyance of his wife, who was standing by at the Boardmans', waiting for him to go to the railroad depot. Taft insisted that he had a minute for a sandwich, and remained for about half an hour. It was an uncomfortable time for almost everyone but him, because ex-Presidents, as a rule, have no place at the White House. Too much history accompanies them.

A familiar face from the old days did appear, that of Belle Hagner, returned now to be social secretary to Mrs. Wilson. She had stayed on for nearly two years with the Tafts but at last had taken a job as a clerk at the State Department, reporting daily to a desk situated among dozens of others. Clerking had made a dull two years for her; she worked alongside men whose jobs were duplicates of hers, only they were paid twice her $750 per year salary. She would have quit, but needed to earn a living. Not long after Wilson's election, she received a wire from Mrs. Wilson inviting her to Princeton. A note from Mrs. Roosevelt at Sagamore Hill had already signaled that Mrs. Wilson might seek her out. Belle Hagner took the train to Princeton, where she found a small, unprepossessing lady with "sweet, gentle manner" and a "charming southern voice," proposing that she return to the White House as social secretary. Mrs. Wilson admitted freely that she "knew nothing of Washington," and had been there "only once in her life." She wanted to perform properly, maintaining the traditions surrounding the Presidency. In particular, she wanted her three daughters "to take their place in the social life of Washington as well as continuing to carry on their own individual interests."[2]

Unlike Mrs. Jaffray, who had responded to Mrs. Wilson's offer with a counteroffer of a mutual three-month trial period, Belle Hagner quickly grasped the opportunity. Wilson's office had made the announcement of her appointment on Christmas Eve. She was in the news; the women of Wilson's household did not speak with reporters, so the reporters, hoping

Miss Hagner would be less reticent, followed her about during the winter. She knew no peace, but gave no stories. When Mrs. Wilson moved to the Shoreham Hotel from her Princeton home, Belle Hagner was with her constantly.

Inauguration day was gloomy and overcast. The jubilant crowd inside the White House could see many thousands of spectators beyond the iron fences that bordered the lawns to the north and south. Band music sounded in the distance. A great number of the Wilsons' guests at lunch were relatives, for both the President and Mrs. Wilson were from large and close families. Tall and dapper, the new President, still carrying his top hat, moved through the company shaking hands, bowing, sharing a memory with one of the Woodrows, his strong-willed Presbyterian cousins from South Carolina.

Toward midafternoon, the President began asking officials if it was not time for him to go to the reviewing stand. When a definitive answer was not forthcoming by three o'clock, he spied General Leonard Wood in the dining room eating lunch. Wilson scratched out a message and handed it to a servant, telling Wood to hurry up, the President of the United States was ready to start the review. At 3:10 p.m., Wilson, officials of the inaugural, and several others passed through the north door and made their way to the great reviewing stand that had been built along Pennsylvania Avenue, the guests following close behind. That evening personal friends and relatives were invited to tea, upstairs in the oval room. The youngest Wilson, Nell, remembered how dark the second floor seemed when she first saw it. A considerable group, mostly women, were in the library with her mother, drinking tea and talking. Nell entered the room, which she had never seen before: "At first I thought the room very grand and uncomfortable. It was done in rose color and the proportions were exquisite, but . . . it looked as if no one had ever lived there." Furniture had been pulled in from the west hall to compensate for the absence of the Tafts' Philippine mahogany. Nell noted that after a few days her mother had warmed the chilly oval room with family pictures and favorite books, "making it look almost as home-like as any room we had ever lived in."[3]

Colonel Brooks Is Heard

Three days after the inauguration, the diary-writing wife of Congressman James Luther Slayden of Texas was invited to tea. "To suit the era of democratic simplicity," she wrote that night, "I meant to walk . . . but time was so precious I ordered a cab and buttoned my gloves on the way." At the White House she was met by two doormen in livery, one taking her card on a silver tray, the other opening the door into the entrance hall, where she was met by a uniformed military aide. Once her name was checked off the list, she was ushered to the Green Room. The Hannibal clock there announced to her dismay that she was a quarter-hour early. She passed the time in idle talk with other guests, including Alice Roosevelt Longworth, "tossy and hoydenish," striving to be noticed. The company was oddly mixed, Ellen Slayden thought, and she was amused by it, "some earnest and dowdy, but many of the ultra smart who profess to scorn the Wilsons and anticipate a Wednesday-night-prayer-meeting social atmosphere."

An usher announced that Mrs. Wilson would receive in the Blue Room. Into the dark blue-and-white oval the guests marched, women in the lead, then the few men, to find the new First Lady standing before the windows with her eldest daughter, Margaret, age 26. "Mrs. Wilson, short, round-faced, round-pompadoured, red-cheeked and not so becomingly dressed, gave each of us a limp hand and passed us on to Miss Wilson, blonde and chill, but refined and intelligent looking." Belle Hagner was seated at the far end of the room behind a silver tea service. The congressman's lady graded the event as boring. Miss Hagner's familiar face was "comforting" by contrast to those of the Wilson women. "I don't question the Wilson breeding," she wrote, "but they certainly lack manner and cordiality."[4]

This was a far cry from the receptions of the Roosevelts and Tafts, the lively open houses with bright conversation and imperial elegance. The almost daily innovations in form, the masses of artistic flower sprays, romantic promenades on the breeze-swept terraces—had all gone! Mrs. Wilson was not ignorant of the fine points of social performance, but society meant very little to her; because it was of even less consequence to the President, glamorous entertaining did not enjoy a high priority at the Wilson White House.

Even before Wilson assumed office it was speculated that he might alter the White House procedure, to allow for a more informal—democratic—style. His abrupt decision not to permit an inaugural ball was taken as a harbinger of impending modifications. But no such reversal transpired. Belle Hagner remembered that apart from the departure of imperial glamour, the modes of entertaining and receiving under Wilson were "practically the same" as those of the Roosevelt years. One obvious reason was that those plans worked. Whatever they may have illustrated about the character of the Presidency, they were also excellent means of organizing and moving crowds with minimal confusion.

The presidential entrance march, made dramatic by Roosevelt, was sorely missed when Taft abandoned it, because it had been the means of setting the President immediately apart. Under Archie Butt's tutelage Taft restored a pared-down version of the march, descending quietly in the elevator and allowing the band to play a few moments before he entered through the reception room door. Wilson followed a similar procedure, though the guests were no longer arranged around the room by rank. Music was played in order to inform everyone that the President would soon enter. Once in the room, the President and the First Lady formed a receiving line.

It took awhile for some of the staff to get to know the Wilsons. They seemed in many ways odd, bookish, and quiet, yet given to teasing among themselves. They liked to be together in private. Belle Hagner remembered Wilson at home: "I was so unaccustomed to seeing a man so completely surrounded by women folk," that she "mildly" suggested to a member of the family that when the President went to play golf it might be well if someone were to seek out interesting men companions for him. "I soon realized," wrote Belle, "that he did not mix with men except in a most formal way." She could recall only a few men ever being with the President in casual moments.[5]

It was the question of the President's appearance that concerned another member of the staff. When Wilson's baggage had finally arrived at the White House, Arthur Brooks, retained as presidential valet, was shocked to find that the President possessed only a small number of inexpensive, ready-made suits with which to cover his slim frame. Wilson felt that the ready-made suits sufficed; he was not difficult to clothe "off the rack." Brooks—known universally as Colonel Brooks, for he was a lieutenant colonel of the National Guard—found the new President's wardrobe so demeaning that he convinced him to go to a tailor, of Brooks' choice. With Mrs. Wilson's approval, Brooks selected fabrics he thought looked properly presidential. He supervised the fittings, and the professor's ready-mades soon gave way to trim wool suits in winter and natty white pants, blazer, and boater in summer. Woodrow Wilson became a style setter, with Colonel Brooks as mastermind.[6]

Wilson Women

The quiet, unassuming Ellen Axson Wilson was in many respects the head of the house. She was 52 when she went to the White House, and she bore only traces of her earlier beauty, for she had taken no pains to hold back the clock. Mrs. Jaffray was deceived in thinking her "a little unsophisticated," but got somewhat closer by giving her the label "day-dreamer." Wilson himself would doubtless have been more amused than insulted by these appellations, for he credited his wife with much of his success. She was wise and compassionate, and although she was content to appear domestic and retiring, those close to Wilson knew her to be not only a woman of great mental gifts but also Wilson's closest adviser. She had the ability to sift through and evaluate the advice Wilson got from others. She shared his deep moral values, and his belief that human life could be improved.

In contrast to some other First Ladies, Mrs. Wilson cared nothing for the glamour of public position. She was essentially a private person, a lover of art and reading, a woman who cherished time spent alone. Among the possessions she brought to the White House—and the Wilsons brought very little—were her paints and brushes. In the servants' area on the third floor she found a room with a skylight, and this became her studio, where she painted flowers and landscapes, which were somewhat better than Mrs. Harrison's parlor art. In her art, as in everything else, she was not especially competitive, though neither was she passive. She painted for her own pleasure and that of her family.

A stern, dedicated educator and thinker, Wilson aptly likened himself to a Presbyterian preacher. The scion of distinguished Presbyterian clergymen, he took a serious stance before the public as President. Yet in the sanctum of home, Wilson often seemed the opposite of the seldom-smiling public character already familiar in the press. His daughter Nell, who was 23 when he became president, remembered his waking up inauguration morning in their suite in the Shoreham Hotel and doing an impromptu vaudeville dance around her mother singing, "We're going to the White House—*today!*" He liked to dance and sing and tell stories, and all the family liked parlor games. They went frequently to the theater and enjoyed the "moving pictures." Dedicated readers, all the Wilsons collected books; the President was interested in political history and poetry, while Mrs. Wilson and Margaret favored music and painting.[7]

Wilson and his wife were close and demonstratively affectionate in the circle of family and friends. Their surviving letters express such tender thoughts that to read them in print is to feel like an intruder. In the loneliness of his first summer in the White House, with the family away on vacation, Wilson wrote to his wife: "How shall I tell you what my heart is full of? It is literally full to overflowing with yearning love for you, my incomparable darling, and for the sweet daughters whom I love with so deep a passion, and admire as much as I love! I dare not pour it out today. I am too lonely. I must think quietly and not with rebellion.

The big house is very still: I must copy its stately peace, and try to be worthy of the trust of those whom I try to serve and those who make me happy by their wonderful love!"

That same summer of 1913 Mrs. Wilson wrote to the President: "Oh, how I adore you! I am perfectly sure that you are the greatest, most wonderful, most lovable man who *ever* lived. I am not expressing an opinion, I am simply stating a self-evident fact. Certainly such love is the real source of youth and renewal for women—for me—and it is a joy too deep for words to hear you say and feel that it is the same for you."[8]

Such letters were more the rule than the exception. President Wilson considered his family unit sacred and private. Nevertheless the mother and three daughters received constant publicity, though they tried to avoid it. Some of what appeared in print about Margaret, Nell, and the middle sister, Jessie, age 25, had no foundation in truth. Most annoying to the Wilsons were the reports allying the daughters romantically with various men around the country. Nell told proudly in her memoirs how her father finally had his fill of the sensational news. "I am a public character," he said suddenly at a press conference, " . . . but the ladies of my household are not public characters, because they are not servants of the government. I deeply resent the treatment they are receiving at the hands of the newspapers. . . . If this continues, I shall deal with you not as President, but man to man." The offending news reports became fewer after that.[9]

Ellen Wilson's Remodeling

Most of the changes the Wilsons made in the White House were in the family quarters, which had been altered very little since 1902. A decade is a long time for paint, wallpaper, carpeting, and fabrics at the White House. During May and early June 1913, before she departed for summer vacation, Mrs. Wilson worked with Colonel Cosby, who remained in office until late summer, on plans for extensive alterations and decoration in the family quarters. A special appropriation of $9,500 had been made by the Congress for remodeling the third, or attic, floor, converting part of it to the use of the family.

Every effort was made to begin work by the start of the fiscal year July 1. Robert S. Talmadge, an interior decorator and merchandiser with offices in New York, was invited to the White House in June to consult with Mrs. Wilson. Her taste seems to have been surprisingly "modern" and uninhibited by the predilection of her two immediate predecessors for the "colonial." She disliked, for example, the dark colors selected by

McKim and Mrs. Roosevelt; McKim had wanted dark walls, to play up the architectural elements of the rooms and to accommodate by sharp contrasts the hard glare of electric light. His judgment had often been imposed upon the Roosevelts, who acquiesced because they believed McKim could give them the setting they required. Mrs. Wilson ordered the dark green burlap peeled from the walls of the long upstairs corridor and replaced with Japanese grass cloth, dyed amber and shot through with heavy thread in a mahogany color.

Talmadge showed Mrs. Wilson a wide selection of materials, papers, and fabrics, and made recommendations. He also brought photographs of some of his stock, and particularily delighted Mrs. Wilson with a bedroom set of imitation Louis XVI furniture painted with glossy white enamel. For this he offered her "special summer prices." She selected other modern French-style pieces, suggesting 17th- and 18th-century antiques, for the new bedrooms upstairs and the guest room on the north side, across from the oval room. With an artist's eye for color, the First Lady mixed chintzes, cretonne, and some hand-woven "craft" materials for curtains and upholstery.[10]

Plans for the third floor were developed by Nathan C. Wyeth, after conversations with Mrs. Wilson. The work was to be far more extensive than a mere redecoration of the six servants' bedrooms in the west end, clustered around the elevator. The rest of the vast attic was set aside for storage, its walls unplastered, its floor of rough boards. Mrs. Wilson wanted to use this space to increase the family quarters from six to eleven bedrooms and to add more bathrooms. The family quarters would now have a second story. She had visits from relatives in mind, for not since the Benjamin Harrisons had so many kin come to call. Some remained for several weeks or even months.[11]

Downstairs in the state rooms, Mrs. Wilson made few permanent changes, although she ordered many minor repairs. None of her family liked the dark walls of the state parlors. "I thought the Red Room one of the ugliest I had ever seen," remembered Nell. "Paneled in magenta-red velours, with a hideous rug on the floor, heavy velvet curtains, overstuffed furniture, and lots of gilt everywhere, it was gloomy beyond words." Even the Gilbert Stuart portrait of President Washington, hanging over the fireplace, did not please her, for, as she wrote with characteristic irreverence, his false teeth looked as if they "were about to leap out of his mouth."[12]

Mrs. Wilson was not one to waste, however, having lived frugally as an academic wife. She did not like the dark velour either, but it was still in good condition, so she covered it up, for the summer at least, with slipcovers and summer curtains. She also ordered pleated white dimity covers to fit over the upholstered silk walls of the state parlors. Thus she had her bright rooms—"ghosts," the President called them—if only for part of the year.

The president seems to have endured the tearing up in good spirits. A busy and eventful summer kept him close to Washington, although he joined his family several times at the summer home in Cornish, New Hampshire. Cornish was an artists' colony of a serious though well-fed sort. The Wilsons had leased the summer home of the novelist Winston Churchill. Mrs. Wilson enjoyed the informal mixture of professional and amateur artists, the lectures and long conversations beneath the spreading shade trees. A busy Wilson endured the sizzling summer weather in Washington, noting that he occupied only his bedroom, dressing room, and sitting room, hardly venturing into the rest of the house, which was dirty with the dust of remodeling.

The seemingly constant delays in rebuilding the third floor may have hurried Colonel Cosby's replacement by Colonel William W. Harts, also of the Corps of Engineers. Talmadge's contract for the decorating was signed in late June, but the contractors, Boyle-Robertson Construction Company of Washington, were not put under contract until two days after Harts took over, on August 19. Construction began immediately; but when the new furnishings and curtains arrived from New York in September, they had to be sent to storage. Demolition was still under way on the third floor and no new construction had begun.

Mrs. Wilson returned in mid-October to find the second floor complete and the decoration of the third floor guest rooms well along. One of the second floor guest rooms overlooking the north portico, a dark and shadowy room, had been finished in varying shades of bright, clear yellow, an echo, no doubt of the decorative taste of J. A. M. Whistler, Mrs. Wilson's favorite painter. Most of the wall-to-wall carpeting of the bedrooms was replaced by large area rugs, leaving exposed a border of polished oak flooring. McKim's white woodwork was now softened to ivory, and the dark walls were supplanted by pastel colors in paint and paper. The master suite was delft blue and white, with twin beds, sofa, and chairs covered in chintz. "It looked like an indoor garden," wrote Nell Wilson. In the adjoining sitting room, between the bedroom and the oval library, was the Lincoln bed, and perhaps with a "rail splitter" theme in mind, Mrs. Wilson ordered rugs and upholstery in the "double chariot wheel." The room was sometimes called the "Blue Mountain Room," after the locality where the crafts originated.[13]

Upstairs, the new attic rooms were odd-shaped, some with slanted ceilings. Mrs. Wilson took such delight in this quaintness that she outlined them with wallpaper borders. The windows which faced the massive stone balustrade outside were curtained in ruffled chintz. On the west side several interconnecting rooms with one bath became known as the Bachelors' Suite, presumably because visiting beaus of Margaret, Jessie, and Nell sometimes stayed there. The daughters, like nearly everyone else who saw the new third floor, thought it the best part of the house, admiring the coziness of the guest rooms with their high-windowed views of the city and the Virginia hills.

The minor work on the state floor had been completed early in the summer, leaving only one conspicuous change: The stuffed animal heads in the State Dining Room had been removed. Though most of them had in fact been bought from a New York decorator, not shot by Roosevelt, they were beloved symbols of the former President. If their removal seemed to express Wilson's dislike of Roosevelt, it was not deliberate; Mrs. Wilson banished them because she thought them gruesome. All were stored at the Smithsonian.[14]

The smaller dining room on the north side, used customarily for daytime meals, was too dark to suit the Wilsons. As had Theodore Roosevelt after 1902, the Wilson family used the State Dining Room almost all the time, setting up a small table and chairs in its southwest corner, which had strong natural light, and which, when the windows could be opened, was breezy. Dinner, served at 7 p.m., was black-tie, a custom of the White House, not of the Wilsons. The family and guests were always expected to appear for dinner, but could eat other meals in their rooms. On lovely days in May and June or October, the Wilsons often dined at noon on the west terrace, in a makeshift grove made by clustering the tubbed bay trees that lined its parapets.

Gardens for a Gardener

Perhaps the most significant changes made in the early months of the Wilson administration were in the gardens. Like many creative people, Mrs. Wilson loved gardening. Her gardens at Princeton had been much admired, in a town noted for its handsome gardens. The colonial garden planted for Mrs. Roosevelt did not satisfy Mrs. Wilson's horticultural urges. Laid out in parterres shaped like great four-petal flowers, the colonial garden was more quaint than artistic, with its winding paths of grass, its crazy-quilt colors, and its white wooden settees. Mrs. Wilson's artistic eye longed for the geometrical clarity of the new formalism in landscape design.

The First Lady studied the west garden most assiduously, for it lay just below her dressing room windows. On inauguration day, the first day she noted the view, she began making plans in her mind. The girls came upon her late that afternoon, standing at the windows looking down. "Come and look, children," she said, and showed them the now-barren colonial garden, its earth turned up, awaiting the green of spring. "It will be our rose garden with a high hedge around it."[15]

She also came to dislike the walk by which the President communicated with the Executive Office. Normally he descended to the basement, walked out through the pantry in its west end, and progressed along the southward colonnade until he reached a modest doorway in the southern ell of the old wing, which gave access to a short passage to the office building. He passed servants' rooms, laundry, gardener's office, and flower arranging room; like Theodore Roosevelt, Mrs. Wilson believed it inappropriate for the President to take a backstairs path to his office. She began to design what she styled the "President's walk."[16]

In the early fall of 1913, well before her return from Cornish, she put her ideas on paper. Her objective was to redesign and replant the gardens close to the White House. She invited two New York landscape designers to assist her, both of whom catered to clients like the members of Mrs. Wilson's artistic circle in Princeton and Cornish. Beatrix Farrand and George Burnap were among the most highly respected practitioners of the new formalism in landscape gardening. To Miss Farrand, Mrs. Wilson assigned the east garden, for which she may not have had ideas of her own; Burnap was given the west garden. Surviving sketches make it clear that Mrs. Wilson knew exactly what she wanted on the west side. But she needed a professional to give form to her ideas.

The garden on the east was known sometimes as the "southeast colonial garden." Seldom actually used, it was nevertheless constantly viewed through the windows of the east colonnade. The objective seems to have been to create a pretty picture, a green garden that would stay attractive all the year. Beatrix Farrand prepared a simple, uncluttered plan consisting of beds around the four sides, with four L-shaped parterres in the center, framing a rectangular lily pool. Ivy borders, mostly evergreen plantings, and expanses of carpet-like lawn completed a tranquil, unchanging scene.[17]

After a conference with Mrs. Wilson, George Burnap made sketches incorporating her ideas for a west garden and a President's walk. The plan made the garden appear to flow from the Executive Office, not the White House. Burnap referred to the garden as "raised"; his sketches suggest that the grade was elevated to the level of the colonnade. In plan the garden showed long parallel lines of beds and sharp-edged, flat-topped hedges running east and west, with a secluded nook in an apse made of high hedges at its eastern end, echoing the bay of the Oval Office. Built into this semicircular retreat was a wooden seat that followed the curve, with a round table before it. On the opposite end of the garden, the southward ell of the old west wing was extended by means of an elaborate latticed pergola, which was climaxed by a niche for a statue of Pan. Mrs. Wilson seems also to have intended the lattice walls as a place to hang her pictures on sunny days.[18]

The President's walk was conceived by George Burnap as an elaborate allée of trees—probably clipped beech trees—running parallel to the colonnade of the west wing, and screened from both that and the garden by shoulder-high boxwood hedges. Pleasantly shaded in summer by the arching, entwined branches of the trees, the President's walk was designed to culminate at a new and ornamental entrance to the Executive Office Building, a stone tribunal mounted by a stair on one side and framing a richly carved stone doorway.

For lack of money, Mrs. Wilson's garden plans were only partially realized. Since Beatrix Farrand's plan presented no major expense except the lily pool, it was probably under way during the late summer. Then the prohibitive bids came in for the west garden. Disappointed, Mrs. Wilson met with Charles Henlock, the gardener, and modified the scheme into something they could execute themselves. This plan she took with her to Cornish, where Burnap studied it and added touches; Mrs. Wilson finally gave her approval on September 29, 1913. The west garden was greatly simplified, although the original plan could still be easily recognized in the long parallel lines, made with narrow beds and hedges, in the vistas, and in a simpler version of the lattice and pergola. The President's walk was built, but flanked by hedges, not trees, and without the elaborate tribunal as its terminus. At the eastern end the bow was converted into a semioctagon. Burnap designed a bench and table for the shady nook, both of them in the "honest" craftsman mode of the time, painted white and looking handmade.

By Christmas 1913 the colonial gardens had been replaced by the "southeast" and "southwest" gardens, names simplified soon enough to "east" and "west" gardens. Mrs. Wilson loved them both, and she spent hours looking down on the garden on the west side. Nell Wilson remembered that west garden as being especially close to her mother's heart. It had "a suggestion of Italy," to Nell's thinking, with its vistas, tall clipped trees, "roses in profusion, and masses of small multicolored flowers bordering the paths."[19]

President Wilson

Success in office came remarkably early for Woodrow Wilson. His moral sensitivity attracted a warm response, and his enemies soon learned that he was resourceful at politics, even in the unfamiliar Washington scene. From the beginning he seemed aware of his limitations, as well as his abilities. Better at politicking before a crowd than one-on-one, he took his first message to the Congress in person rather than sending it to be read, according to the procedure established by Thomas Jefferson. Breaking with this tradition helped his cause with the Congress, while capturing the public's imagination and illustrating the new President's commitment to change.

Through the summer of 1913, with his family away in Cornish, Wilson labored over one of his major objectives, the reduction of the tariff. His work culminated triumphantly in the fall with the Underwood Tariff Act. As the Congress, in special session, was besieged by lobbyists opposing the program, it also found itself much lobbied by Wilson, who called meetings at the Oval Office and paid surprise visits to politicians at the Capitol. When at last the legislation was signed into law, Wilson staged the event in the Oval Office, inviting the 50 men he considered key figures in his battle. "It was really most impressive," wrote the President to his wife, describing the scene, "I was very much moved. . . . "[20]

Early victories in tariff and finance fulfilled the basic planks of the New Freedom platform of Wilson's campaign. The public was impressed; Wilson's administration was high-minded and fast-moving. The President seemed to be giving substance to a nationalism which had been expressed too often before by empty ceremony. By early 1914 he was able to say that most of the work of the New Freedom was done, and what remained was merely to manage it.

Wilson used the administrative machinery of the White House in a manner somewhat different from that of Taft; but Taft did create circumstances Wilson could accept, and he made no changes of substance. Though unaccustomed to a large staff, Wilson nonetheless retained Taft's entire office force of 35 to 40 people. This was something new, for heretofore in a change of administration there had always been some replacement of personnel. The office setup Wilson inherited reflected changes Taft had made. The President's secretary had become a political manager, and was no longer the chief administrator in the office. Taft had identified the need for someone to manage day-to-day activities, and recognized that this person need not be personally loyal to him. He appointed the veteran White House official Rudolph

Forster as his executive clerk, the chief administrator over his staff.[21]

Time would show that creation of the permanent post of administrator would mark the end of major shifts in the rolls of employees when new Presidents came in. Around the President's secretary would slowly develop a "political" staff, appointees who were quite apart from the more durable body of "career" employees in the Executive Office. Wilson's secretary, Joseph P. Tumulty, a witty, buoyant man of 33, had been an important figure in Wilson's campaign for governor of New Jersey. He had served as secretary to the governor, then had become a conspicuous worker in Wilson's ascent to the Presidency.

Wilson used the Oval Office even more than Taft as his principal place for work, but he also spent time in the upstairs study at the White House. His typewriter was hastily shuttled between the two places, behind the scenes. He wrote from time to time of how he and the machine had gone through many thoughts together, and many emotions. He typed most of his own letters, at least in draft, and practically all of his important papers and addresses.[22]

Quite unlike Taft and Roosevelt, who were usually in company with their official circle and political associates, whether at work or play, Wilson drew a sharp line between his public and private life. In private he kept close to his family. It was a custom he had developed during his years in academia. Unlike most Presidents, who, coming from more strictly political backgrounds, intermingled business with everything else, Wilson tried to make certain that politics did not consume his life. He met most official appointments in his office, drawing a sharp distinction between residence and place of business. It was a rare honor for a caller to receive an invitation to eat lunch with the Wilson family.

Except for his relatives, Wilson had few companions, although the few were as close to him as brothers. The most famous if not the most enduring of these friendships was with millionaire Edward M. House of Austin, Texas, and New York. "Colonel" House was a ruddy, small-boned man who had devoted himself to political kingmaking in Texas before going east in search of bigger game. He joined the Democratic campaign only one year before the inauguration of Wilson, was without question the one most responsible for his victory, and became the new President's chief political adviser. The two were extremely close, Wilson showing great deference to House whenever the opportunity presented itself, personally meeting him at the train and allowing no other appointments to take precedence over his. House usually stayed in the Rose Bedroom at the White House, and most of his visits were spent with the President, either in the study or among Wilson's family.

Wilson had a closer personal friend in the Navy doctor Cary Grayson, whom he met the day he moved to the White House. Unofficially, Grayson had served as White House physician for most of the Taft administration, pinch-hitting for the august Surgeon General Presley Marion Rixey. Appointed by McKinley, Rixey had been the first White House doctor; he had stayed on to serve Roosevelt, but his insolence had annoyed Taft and he had become persona non grata at the White House. Cary Grayson was listed in the records only as a military aide. When Wilson's sister Mrs. George Howe, from South Carolina, had gashed her forehead in a fall on the marble stair during the inaugural day lunch, Grayson managed the situation masterfully and earned the gratitude of both the President and Mrs. Wilson. Soon he was a fixture in the family, confidant of the senior Wilsons and their three daughters.[23]

Grayson was small and athletic, an expert horseman and a popular bachelor in Washington's best social circles. He was attractive and witty, speaking with a slow Virginia drawl that Wilson liked, for it reminded him of his boyhood in the South and of his days in school. Where others failed, Grayson was able to lure the President from his typewriter and office papers onto the golf course. Grayson took inventory of how Wilson attended to his health. He cast out a stomach pump and many medicines, replacing them with exercise and diet, to ease Wilson's frequent abdominal pains and headaches. To a great extent, Grayson's efforts met with success, and he became an ever present shadow of the President, eventually gaining the rank of admiral.

Wilson's circle of confidants was small and, except for Grayson and Joe Tumulty, consisted entirely of relatives. Tumulty was more an associate than a friend; devoted to a large family of his own, he had little time to participate in the President's leisure activities. The Wilson relatives came to the White House in a constant stream. All were welcome, and certain ones, such as his brother Joseph Ruggles Wilson, Jr., from Tennessee, were special friends. Fitz William Woodrow—a cousin—was brought in as a military aide, to remain resident in the White House for nearly the entire duration of the two Wilson terms. This was the beloved "Fitz," whose name appears in the family letters. From New Orleans the rosy Smith sisters, Lucy and Mary, both childhood friends of the Wilson girls, came and stayed months at a time. Their departure always drew a pall of sadness over the house.

"The White House?" said one cousin nearly 70 years later, "Why, it was like a great and good family home! Cousin Ellie would write and ask, 'Why not come and see us?' When you would go, there would be no limit on time. The family was often together in the big oval room upstairs. I had breakfast by myself with Cousin Woodrow from time to time, in the big dining room downstairs. So soft and gentle, his voice always had a soothing effect. He took a great interest in what we young people were doing and what we thought. I must say we all loved him very much. Some of my happiest memories are of those lovely and peaceful times I spent with Cousin Ellie and Cousin Woodrow and the girls. They had a warm *family* home, don't you know?"[24]

First Lady's Crusade

The piano used by Mrs. Taft in the west hall on the second floor was taken to Margaret Wilson's room, the Blue Bedroom, and replaced by a desk for Belle Hagner. Her back to the great fan window, a telephone before her, and neat note boxes and boxes of engraved stationery all around, the tall, gangly Miss Hagner resumed her position as social secretary, as though the intervening years as a lowly clerk in "State" had never been. She liked to say that things had remained the same at the White House, but knew that this was not strictly true. There was less laughter, almost no swagger. When she saw former colleagues like Charlie McCawley, conversation turned nostalgically to "the days of the empire," their name for the Roosevelt years.[25]

Belle Hagner played a more dominant role under Mrs. Wilson than under Mrs. Roosevelt. Often Mrs. Wilson had to be urged to hold social affairs, where parties had been the delight of Edith Roosevelt. The Wilson girls, too, sometimes alarmed Belle Hagner with their reckless independence, their hardheaded refusal to obey the stiffer rules of capital society regarding costume and where they should and should not go. This she attributed to their father, for she felt that he did not understand the social side of White House life. Though fond of the secretary and in her office frequently, the Wilson daughters feared her reprimands, which she always clothed in teasing or in laughter.

The business side of Mrs. Wilson's life was managed by a second secretary, Helen Bones, a first cousin of the President. Small and delicate, with beautiful blue eyes, Miss Bones had been intimate with the Wilsons all her life. She would probably have lived with them at the White House in any case, so she was given an official position. She lived in the family quarters, and she was constantly with one or another of the family. One of her principal duties was to maintain warm relations between the Wilsons and their Wilson, Woodrow, and Axson relatives in Ohio, Tennessee, South Carolina, and Georgia. Always in the past the Wilsons had kept up a lively correspondence with the family; now Helen

Bones became a sort of family social secretary. She put together interesting combinations of relatives to invite to state dinners, garden parties, and other events in the social season. She kept the new guest rooms on the third floor fairly well in use through 1913 and 1914.

In addition, Helen Bones attended to practically everything else which did not fall under the social jurisdiction of Belle Hagner. A thrifty shopper, Mrs. Wilson sent Cousin Helen anonymously to scout fashions which might be of interest to her. Hats, bags, gloves, and the other articles needed by the First Lady were nearly always selected by this "confidential secretary." Helen Bones made arrangements for automobile drives, the theater, and countless other pastimes enjoyed by the President and Mrs. Wilson. But state social occasions were Belle Hagner's exclusive preserve. She renewed her association with Warren Young of the Executive Office, whose wisdom in social questions was matched only by that of Alvey Adee of the State Department, the wizened expert on protocol who, like Young, had come to work for the government in the time of President Arthur.

Mrs. Wilson gave Belle Hagner her support, because the social secretary made it possible for the First Lady to pursue interests of her own. These sometimes surprised Belle Hagner: To her horror, Mrs. Wilson's avocations soon went beyond the arts to include social reform, an area which, except for the temperance cause espoused by Lucy Webb Hayes, had been avoided by Presidents' wives. "Slumming parties" was what Belle Hagner called the ventures by automobile through Washington's notorious "alley slums." Begun by Mrs. Wilson in April 1913, these morning tours made the First Lady a budding champion for better housing in the District of Columbia. To a Washington native like Belle Hagner the alley slums were simply part of the scene, "Negro shanties" located conveniently for domestic servants. They offended Mrs. Wilson's alien eyes and her sense of humanity, and she set out to use the power of her position to correct the situation.[26]

The slums had come into existence in the second half of the 19th century, the result of dense residential development in the heart of the city. Some had been stables and servants' quarters to the rear of big houses on the street; many more were built as cheap rental units for the poor, out of sight, yet near the centers of work, in a day when most people still went home for the midday meal. By Mrs. Wilson's time most of the slums were shabby places of brick or wood, worn by use and overcrowding, and occupied almost entirely by blacks. Since the 1870s, agitation for reform had come to nothing. In 1904 a congressional report on the subject interested Theodore Roosevelt enough for him to mention it in his annual message, ànd when it seemed that the government would take over, the citizens relaxed their own efforts. The movement started up again about the time Mrs. Wilson arrived in Washington, this time in the hands of socially prominent citizens, the intellectual and artistic kind who appealed to the new First Lady.[27]

Meetings were held at the White House about the alley problem. In the fall of 1913, Mrs. Wilson herself, with Mrs. Archibald Hopkins, was taking prominent citizens and politicians through the narrow alleyways in the White House Pierce-Arrow, pointing out the flocks of half-clad children playing on the bricks and cobblestones, and the dirty, shabby houses where they lived. Mrs. Wilson had no interest in beautifying the alleys, but she wanted to eradicate slum life. She was outraged by what she saw as close as four blocks from her White House doorstep; she believed that demolishing these rental dwellings would force the occupants out, into the more ample and airy Negro neighborhoods, away from the center of the city.

That the First Lady took to the soapbox surprised her family, although they were familiar with her strong moral sensibilities. "I wonder," said Mrs. Wilson, "how anyone who reaches middle-age can bear it, if she cannot feel, on looking back, that whatever mistakes she may have made, she has on the whole lived for others and not for herself." Such a sensitivity made Ellen Wilson a likely champion for those who wished to fight the alley blight. Her participation gave impetus to the movement, and she became central to the coterie of local reformers. "The philanthropic women would not let her alone," remembered Nell Wilson angrily. "I grew to hate the sight of one of them, a tall, angular woman who was constantly arriving at the White House, and pounding at mother, tearing her tender heart with tales of woe."[28]

Weddings

Belle Hagner was therefore the first White House social secretary to have to cope with the correspondence and press interest provoked by a First Lady's humanitarian cause. As if that were not enough, a frazzled Hagner was informed in June that there would be a White House wedding in November. The engagement was announced in July, at a garden party in Cornish. Jessie Wilson's fiancé was Francis Bowes Sayre, a young assistant district attorney for the City of New York. He planned to assume a teaching position at Williams College after their marriage. While the family liked Frank Sayre, they were uncomfortable with the idea of Jessie's being married, and would have felt the same about either of the other daughters. Most of the planning for the wedding was left to Belle Hagner, for the mother and sisters found the impending event painful to think about, let alone to plan for.

There having been no wedding at the White House since Alice Roosevelt's, the social secretary decided to re-create that celebrated event. Searching through the thick social scrapbooks of the officer in charge of public buildings, she learned every detail, from where to put platforms to the order of guests. That source exhausted, she contacted Charlie McCawley, now a colonel in the Marine Corps, and he provided notes still in his possession on the Roosevelt-Longworth wedding.

Preparations for Jessie Wilson's elaborate wedding were well along when Nell Wilson's friendship with William Gibbs McAdoo, Secretary of the Treasury and one of Wilson's most important advisers in the Cabinet, turned into a romance. A widower with children, McAdoo was 26 years Nell's senior; no two worlds could have seemed farther apart than those of the President's fun-loving daughter and the rugged self-made corporate lawyer turned politician. He was a strong political figure, and Wilson trusted him. Though he had made his way in New York, his southern background showed in his gradual introduction of strict racial segregation into the government service; he made the Treasury Department the pilot of an entire movement. The Wilsons seemed less than overjoyed with the match between Nell and McAdoo. Mrs. Wilson argued that Nell knew nothing of housekeeping. The President felt that things had moved too fast.

Nevertheless, within a short time after Jessie's wedding, an announcement of Nell's engagement was made from the White House. Coinciding as the wedding news did with the triumph of Wilson's New Federalism, the couples became much in demand, reflecting the President's popularity. Jessie and the scholarly Sayre went quietly to the Georgetown boat club for daylong canoe trips; picnic baskets were prepared for them in the White House kitchen. News reporters tried to follow them but seldom with luck. Nell, more tolerant of the press and very much in love with the publicity her position attracted, went openly to lunch and to the theater with McAdoo, himself already a public figure.

The two weddings, Jessie's on November 25, 1913, and Nell's on May 7, 1914, were quite different. The first was large and glittering, the other small and intimate, in part because the groom had been married before. Both were styled family weddings and not state occasions, but the Wilsons took care to design them in high style. In the flood of press coverage, each unmistakably made its statement about the Wilsons as "private" people of refinement. The two weddings wholly possessed the

White House. For Jessie's the house was filled with cousins. One of the Woodrows felt privileged that her attic room was adjacent to the great cedar closet Mrs. Wilson had ordered built above the north portico. "I was dressing when the maids came in to get Jessie's dress," she later remembered. "So I saw it first, and oh a more magnificent wedding dress there never was!"[29]

Blonde and angelic-looking, the bride wore white satin with a long train and veil. The bridesmaids wore silk in as many different shades of rose as there were bridesmaids. The dresses had short trains, with a bit of silk-stockinged shin showing in front. Silver lace wired into high Russian-style crowns framed their faces. The wedding party descended in the elevator, to assemble in formation in the State Dining Room just before six o'clock. On the hour of six the mahogany doors rolled back. The Marine Band, stationed in the entrance hall, struck up the march. Two by two the wedding party proceeded down the transverse hall along an aisle that ran through the thick crowd to the altar before the great east windows in the East Room.

At the conclusion of the ceremony, the wedding party returned by way of the transverse hall to the Blue Room. President and Mrs. Wilson stood at one of the doors between the Green and Blue Rooms, while the bride, groom, and the bride's attendants stood in the Blue Room's southern bow. Within about ten minutes, the several thousand guests began to file from the East Room, through the Green Room, to be received in the Blue Room, then pass on through the Red Room to the State Dining Room for refreshments.[30]

Nell Wilson's wedding was managed as it might have been in a private home. The bride and her father descended the grand staircase and walked down the hall to the Blue Room, where the ceremony took place. Belle Hagner, standing near the Blue Room fireplace, saw McAdoo's eldest daughter, Nona, burst into tears, then erupt into hysterical cries as the Marine Band played the Wedding March. Quickly Belle and another guest took the girl to the basement cloak room, where they comforted her until they could summon her father's carriage to take her home. The bride apparently knew nothing of this, the girl having been removed by the time she entered the flower-banked Blue Room. Nell took her place beside her two sisters, her only attendants, who carried tall shepherd's crooks adorned with festoons of roses and lilies of the valley. The marriage ceremony took place just at dusk; by eight, when the couple was to depart, reporters pressed en masse on the southeast gate, through which the McAdoos were to pass. Four different automobiles pulled up to the south portico, and four couples appeared at intervals and climbed inside; the cars sped away at once, through gates thrown open by the police. Forced back by the gates, the reporters soon recovered and followed in pursuit.

Then the bride and groom walked quietly out onto the south portico and entered a smaller car, in which they left unnoticed, enjoying the trick. Nell looked back to see her parents, hand in hand, standing on the porch. All through the excitement of the two weddings, she had increasingly sensed that something was wrong with her mother. Now this concern overtook her, and that, together with the thought of leaving home, caused her mood to change abruptly. "I horrified my husband," she said, "by dissolving into tears in the darkness of the car."[31]

Mrs. Wilson's Death

In late May when she and McAdoo returned to Washington, arriving late at night, Nell called the White House to speak to her mother. Ike Hoover was "slightly evasive." Nell was puzzled. Hoover asked if she would mind calling again in the morning, as her mother had gone to bed, her father was in conference, and Margaret was out of the house. At the White House early the next morning, Nell stood before her mother, who was in bed. "My heart sank when I looked at her. She had changed—she looked very small and white, and all her lovely color was gone."

Was Nell happy? Mrs. Wilson asked, then said, "I needed only to see your face, as I did Jessie's, to know that you are happy."[32]

The household knew that the First Lady's illness was serious. It had begun with a fall in the upstairs corridor, a slip on a throw rug; put to bed, she began to weaken. At first it was believed that she was merely exhausted from the weddings, which had begun and closed a rigorous social season. Dr. Grayson asked her to remain in bed for hours at a time. This she did through June and early July. In July, Grayson made the grim diagnosis that Mrs. Wilson had tuberculosis of the kidneys, a form of Bright's disease, "so far advanced that it was incurable."[33]

Wilson was struck hard by the news. While with his daughters at lunch in the small dining room on July 28, 1914, the conversation hinged on the day's report that Austria had declared war on Serbia, in retribution for the murder of their heir to the throne of Austria-Hungary. "It's incredible—incredible," he said. "Don't tell your mother anything about it." Nell asked if her father thought implications were far greater than a war between Austria and Serbia. He did not respond at first, but put his hands over his eyes, showing great strain, and said, "I can think of nothing—nothing, when my dear one is suffering."[34]

Mrs. Wilson died on August 6 in the presidential bedroom. She lived out her last weeks in terrible pain. Toward the end she asked about her alley project, and she was assured that a bill was going to be passed to rid Washington of alley slums. Wilson was disconsolate over her death. At first he would not allow her body to be put in a coffin. He ordered that the remains be placed on the sofa in the bedroom, as though she were still alive. Mrs. Jaffray remembered when the undertakers laid her out. Wilson was there. "With his own hands he placed around her shoulders a lovely white silk shawl. Her golden brown hair was braided and twisted around her head. She was a beautiful Madonna."[35]

For several days Wilson hardly moved from beside his dead wife. The curtains were drawn, the lights kept low. At last he permitted the body to be placed in a coffin in the center of the East Room, where palms and flowers from the greenhouse lined the walls. The brief funeral service had no music; Wilson wept when the minister took his hand. Later in the day the family boarded a special train to Ellen Wilson's hometown, Rome, Georgia. Wilson rode in the compartment with the coffin. A funeral was held in Rome in the Presbyterian church where 30 years before Wilson had first beheld the woman who was to be his wife. She was buried in Myrtle Hill Cemetery among her ancestors.

The Transient

Back at the White House, no official mourning period was observed, nor were there the usual black draperies on the mirrors. The flag on the roof was not flown at half-mast. It must have been the President who stopped the tradition, perhaps because it did not reflect his or his late wife's attitude toward death. Mourning was restricted to a cancellation of all social functions until October. Margaret Wilson became the President's hostess at that time, a responsibility she somewhat resented. Her mother had always encouraged her inclination to follow a career in concert music. Being the President's daughter had opened many doors for her, and to turn from these opportunities was difficult. Nell would have been the natural hostess had she been free from the duties of her own home and McAdoo's children. Jessie was pregnant.

The Wilson daughters came to the President's aid as best they could, as their mother would have wanted. When they fell short, little Helen Bones compensated, staying at the side of a man she had idolized all her life. But Wilson's unhappiness as a widower in the White House transcended all that those around him could do to compensate. Cary Grayson felt that "anyone who was with him constantly" could see that "an undercurrent of thought" removed him from full participation in any conversation. Some months before Mrs. Wilson's death, the President had spoken to Colonel House of "not feeling at home anywhere," even going so far as to add that he "had no home." He had occupied the official residence of the president at Princeton, the governor's mansion in New Jersey, and now the White House, another public place. His family circle had been home to him, wherever he was. That was essential to him, and now it was broken.[36]

In the White House the staff walked softly and whispered. Only Margaret, playing her piano in her room, or sometimes Theodore Roosevelt's big Steinway in the East Room, gave life to the house through the autumn of 1914 and the winter that followed.

34

1917

As Mrs. Wilson lay dying in the White House, the great world war broke out in Europe. Insisting that his wife know nothing of the events of the day, President Wilson stayed at her bedside, comforting her with a drone of talk about scenes and friends dear to them both. Important papers were brought to him there, and he mulled them over, making marginal notes, writing out memoranda. While she slept, he wrote his letter to the warring nations of Europe, offering the "good offices" of the United States as a mediator for peace. During the agony of her last days, he issued the first of ten proclamations firmly declaring American neutrality.

Years afterward, the President remembered Ellen Wilson's death as her salvation from the chaos that followed. She became a symbol to him of a gentler time, before life as they had loved it had gone. "She was so radiant, so happy," he said to one of his daughters. "We must be grateful for her sake that she did not see the world crash into ruin. It would have broken her heart."[1]

The Widower's Household

His grief dimmed the official social season, when it finally opened in October 1914. A grim-faced President dutifully appeared, white-tie, before his dinner guests with the tall, blonde Margaret. Of the three Wilson daughters, she liked such duties the least, but was the only one available to help. Nell, because she was a Cabinet wife, usually ranked as a guest, while Jessie, living in New England, was not expected to attend

791

the President's events. She returned to the White House for the birth of her first child, Francis B. Sayre, Jr., on January 17, 1915.

Wilson's dinners were long and dull, with little laughter. After the meal, Margaret usually played and sang for the guests in the Blue Room or, when there were big crowds, in the East Room. The buoyancy of much of contemporary American life must have made the morose house seem even sadder by contrast. The years before the war were characterized by optimism: "We all felt that America had already stepped across the threshold of a great future," remembered Nell Wilson. "Idealism, altruism, all the fine hopes and dreams that fill men's hearts seemed realities. . . . " Though movements for various reforms were part of this optimism, Americans seemed on the whole lighthearted, a busy people. Cocktails and cigarettes were common at fashionable parties, although less so at the White House. The fox-trot and the tango were current, except at the White House, even though the President did permit dancing parties before Mrs. Wilson's death.[2]

Holding to his traditional privilege, the President accepted few invitations. This was an advantage to others as well as to him, for even the good-hearted Taft had inhibited people by his presence "out in company," no matter what honor he might have shed on his host. Normally, the President went only to the homes of the Vice President and the Cabinet officers. When he did accept another invitation, the host was required to submit a guest list in advance, before the President made his final decision to attend.

Though isolated within the White House, those who ran it participated in the life of the town. Ike Hoover, Warren Young, and the others belonged to Washington's middle class, enjoying comfortable circumstances and a quiet sort of celebrity. Black employees of the White House were likewise prosperous members of their community, within which they formed part of a social elite. For most of them above the lowest rank, politeness was a professional prerequisite. In private life they called on one another on Sunday afternoons.

The black male employees celebrated themselves once a year with a dance called the Chandelier Ball. Invitations were engraved, and to receive one was an honor. The Chandelier Ball, named for the chandeliers of the East Room, was probably begun about 1910, although the date is uncertain. Like many other romantic customs, it continued only until the war. "I went first when I was a girl of 18," remembered one guest 60 years later. "The Chandelier Ball was the finest dance in town, and the food was fabulous, though my mother would not let me go up to the dining room because of the wine. Everything was done just like at the

White House," she continued. "The palms were from the greenhouse, the little gilt chairs, I guess the white damask tablecloths and napkins, and even the coatracks from the coatrooms." This function was held at the Oddfellows Hall, 16th and M Streets, where the ballroom was on the first floor and dinner was served on the second. Music was provided by the Marine Band. Favorite White House dignitaries were always invited, and always attended, including most of the top officials and family intimates up to, but not including, the President and his wife.[3]

The prestige of the Chandelier Ball generated a kind of rivalry among the white employers of the blacks who attended. When the dance was new, Mrs. Taft had given her maid, Annie Anderson, a beautiful silk gown with a fan-shaped train and artificial roses made of silk chiffon. Belle Hagner's cook, Alice Green, received an invitation at last in 1914, having been passed over before as not being of sufficient rank. Not to be outdone by other employers, Belle Hagner produced for the cook a black-and-white evening dress with pearl beads, and when the ensemble still did not suit her, Belle finished the costume off with a net veil. A pleased Alice Green reported the next morning that the Chandelier Ball was a "very high toned affair." In writing down this summation, Belle Hagner observed: "The distinctions in the colored world of Washington are most clearly drawn."[4]

At the head of the White House organization, the chief usher presided in a way that can be likened to the winder of a clock, not a one-day clock, but one which, well wound, would run many days without further winding before anyone noticed that the mechanism needed fresh energy. Ike Hoover delighted in order, and gradually the widower President let him again take up old customs. Just before the social season began in the fall of 1914, the house was transformed. Slipcovers came off the furniture they had covered since before Mrs. Wilson died. The white linen dust covers of the walls were removed, the tacks extracted around their edges, and the silk gimp edging restored to frame the velvet and damask wall coverings. Heavy curtains and cornices were brought down from the "cedar room" over the north portico; the rugs arrived from storage, including the shaggy white vicuña upon which both Jessie and Nell had stood when they were married.

The servants swapped their summer whites, which had been designed by Mrs. Taft, for the cool-weather livery designed by Mrs. Wilson. The uniforms consisted of bottle-green jackets and black-and-white-striped vests spangled with large gilt buttons. Likewise on the streets of Washington, white breeches and sport jackets, popularized by President Wilson, were replaced by dark suits.[5]

Coast to Coast

As life went on around him, President Wilson absorbed himself in work, making as few public appearances as possible. The war in Europe dominated the front pages of the newspapers. Reacting to the growing hostility of Americans toward imperial Germany, the President urged moderation in thought and action. The war, fought thus far only on land, seemed not much of a threat to the United States.

Happier events also made the front pages. On January 25, 1915, a bit more than a week after the birth of his first grandchild in the White House, Wilson held a ceremony to inaugurate the first transcontinental telephone line, from New York to San Francisco. The telephone was installed in the Oval Office, where Wilson assembled guests to witness the historic call. Ike Hoover, the former electrician, had convinced the telephone people to install an extension in the ushers' office. Into that small room the staff crowded on the cold and windy January day to eavesdrop on the first east-to-west call.[6]

About ten days later, in early February, Germany announced the beginning of submarine warfare in the seas around the British Isles. Wilson attempted to mediate, with no success; at last he delivered a formal warning, reminding Germany of the rights of neutral ships. Fearing that this was only the beginning of American involvement in the war, Secretary of State William Jennings Bryan protested the President's statement, but Wilson stood firm.

Mrs. Galt

The exact day in March 1915 when President Wilson met the widowed Mrs. Galt was forgotten in the rapid progression of friendship, romance, and marriage that took place before the close of the year. Only seven months had elapsed since Ellen Wilson's death. The President became utterly captivated by the new love, throwing aside his mourning to pursue Mrs. Galt to the altar.

It began with Cary Grayson's concern about the loneliness of Helen Bones, the only female family member resident full time in the White House. She seemed to Admiral Grayson to be unhappy, spending all her time with the morose widower; the doctor underestimated her worship of her cousin, yet he had kindly intentions. Helen Bones was shy, but not withdrawn, and she was well liked by the people who got to know her. She enjoyed walking, but had lost her favorite companions when Nell and Jessie moved away. Grayson, keeper of health in the household, asked his fiancée, Alice Gertrude Gordon—called Altrude—to draw from their own circle some women Helen Bones might enjoy.

Among these she grew to like a widow named Edith Bolling Galt, who also enjoyed walks. Mrs. Galt was 42, tall and buxom, with soft gray eyes, ivory skin, and and a sensual quality that enhanced her good looks. Though witty and talkative, she had a melancholy side that seemed to appeal to Helen Bones, who liked to take care of people. Edith Galt's marriage of 12 years had been cut short by her husband's death when she was 35. From him she had inherited the venerable family jewelry store, Galt & Brother, one of the oldest businesses in Washington. Suffering financially at the time of Galt's death, the company had been revived through the efforts of loyal employees and provided the widow with a comfortable income. She lived in a style befitting a Virginia Bolling, and though hers was not an uninteresting life, it was, by her own preference, removed from the livelier elements of "society."

On the now-forgotten day in March, after Mrs. Galt and Helen Bones had been walking in a muddy Rock Creek Park, Helen invited her companion to the White House for tea. Neither of the women was dressed suitably for a formal tea, but since Mrs. Galt had never been to the White House, and Helen Bones assured her that she would see no one, she accepted. As they stood in the little elevator hall of the basement, preparing to ascend to the family quarters, President Wilson entered with Dr. Grayson, returning from a golf game. The result was a foursome at tea, shabby walking clothes and all, seated before the great arched window of the west hall. Reporting the event to a cousin later, Helen Bones observed that the President had smiled: "It is the first time I had seen him smile since Cousin Ellie's death!" And many months later, asked how long it took the President to become interested in Mrs. Galt, Miss Bones replied, "About ten minutes."[7]

During the balance of March and through April, the President took drives with the two women. In April, Mrs. Galt was an occasional dinner guest within the President's family circle. Dressed in cream-colored satin and white lace, she appeared at the White House for her first formal dinner on May 3, when the President entertained his sister and other relatives from South Carolina in the State Dining Room. After dinner Wilson led her away from the party to the south portico, to drink in the spring night. He told her that he loved her and wanted to marry her. Taken by surprise, she responded, "Oh, you can't love me, for you don't really know me, and it is less than a year since your wife died."[8]

Without hesitation, President Wilson countered, "in this place time is not measured by weeks, or months, or years, but by deep human experiences. . . . " The loss of his wife had made him miserable; he said he was ready to live again, and would not wait, nor should she expect him to. She said she would continue to see him, if either her sister, or Helen Bones, or some other suitable chaperone were always along. Wilson, not entirely pleased, reminded her that the courtship could not be entirely orthodox, because of "the spotlight that is always on this house." Their relationship would have to be kept secret. "I cannot come to your house without increasing gossip," he said, "you . . . will have to come here." She agreed.[9]

Edith Galt was at first confused by Wilson's pursuit. Marriage seems to have been remote from her thoughts in her seventh year of widowhood. Perhaps she had thought for so long that there would be no second chance that its sudden appearance frightened her. Did she love Wilson, or was she fascinated by the glamour of the Presidency? She asked herself this question again and again as the summer passed. At least three times a week she joined the President for dinner, either at the White House or aboard the *Mayflower*, always ostensibly as the guest of Helen Bones, or Cary Grayson and Altrude Gordon. But she was Wilson's guest, and the others acted accordingly. Leaving the dinner table, she and Wilson went to his study, not to be disturbed. They were left alone likewise on the yacht, when the signal was given.

The Marriage

When the two were apart they sent letters by special courier, carefully avoiding the ordinary mails, or even the usual White House messengers. The letters were long and passionate, some sounding as though they were already married. "All the household is asleep," wrote Wilson on an early morning late in May, "the study door is closed, and here I am alone with my darling, free to talk to her and think only of her, the tasks of the day unable yet to exercise their tyranny over me. . . . I can turn to her here in this quiet room as to my own sweet comrade and lover, no barrier any longer between us, my heart thrilling with pride and fairly melting with tenderness, dream that her dear, beautiful form is close beside me and that I have only to stretch out my arms to have her come to them for comfort and happiness and peace, my kisses on her lips and eyelids. . . . I venture to say my Lady, my Queen, that never in your life have you looked so wonderfully beautiful as I have seen you look when the love tide was running in your heart without check, since you came to understand yourself and me. . . . "[10]

Political intimates began to worry lest the romance become public.

Colonel House returned from a secret European mission for the President early in the summer, only to be greeted suddenly by the turn of events in Wilson's personal life. Reasoning that marrying again might be good for the President, he encouraged it, though he urged that out of respect for Ellen Wilson the marriage be postponed for a year. To this Wilson strongly objected, and House argued back, with no hesitation. The colonel's observations in Europe had convinced him that the salvation of world order might well lie in the person of Woodrow Wilson. Nothing could be allowed to happen that might endanger the nearly universal respect of people for the President.

House was certain some of Wilson's anxiety—and apparent unwillingness to listen to reason—came from emotional exhaustion, and suggested that he vacation at the house in Cornish during the summer of 1915. Wilson agreed, if Mrs. Galt would come for a long visit. It proved to be such an idyllic holiday that by autumn House and others of Wilson's friends began to fear a sudden marriage, which they were certain would lead to defeat in the presidential election the coming year.

The result of the unrest among Wilson's advisers was a little scheme to break up the romance. Wilson was told that an old friend, Mary Allen Peck, to whom he had written for many years, was displaying some of his letters in California and causing a riot of gossip. While his relationship with Mrs. Peck was innocent—Mrs. Peck had also been a close friend of Mrs. Wilson's—she was a divorcée and the sort of unorthodox person that the political enemies of the President could easily use to his disadvantage.

The news came to Wilson by way of McAdoo, who later blamed the idea on House. Wilson went into a deep depression, not because of the threat of scandal, but because he knew the situation would hurt Mrs. Galt. He tried to prepare a letter to her, explaining what had happened and warning of the possibility that she might have to endure unfavorable publicity. Unable to put his thoughts on paper, he sent Cary Grayson to tell her what had happened and to offer to sever the relationship. Depression soon sent him to bed sick, where he sank into gloom. When Edith Galt's response was brought to him in a sealed letter, he would not open it because he feared a rejection.

The President sank lower and lower, until Dr. Grayson, ever concerned about his health, asked his permission to fetch Mrs. Galt. Ignoring the President's negative response, Grayson soon appeared in the bedroom with Edith Galt. Wilson lay in bed, pale and troubled; Grayson and Colonel Brooks quietly departed. She remained until the matter between them was settled. The President was soon in touch with Mrs. Peck in

California, and while neither he nor Edith Galt nor Mary Peck was to know for the time that there had been a hoax, the problem was ended. Wilson then went to House and said he wished to marry Mrs. Galt. Exploring every political angle, House at last conceded that it would be well to wait no longer. The President began to tell those close to him, beginning with his relatives. Then he informed his favorites at the White House, receiving them one by one in his study. "I want you to be one of the first to know that I am going to marry Mrs. Galt." On October 5 he sat at his typewriter and tapped out a news release. This he showed to Edith Galt, then gave to his secretary, Joseph Tumulty, to distribute. On October 7 the announcement was made to the world that the wedding would take place in December.[11]

Secrecy was no longer necessary. Wilson dined often at her house on 20th Street, arriving by limousine, and accompanied by an extra car carrying Secret Service men. One of those guards, a tattletale Kentuckian named Ed Starling, wrote that President Wilson "was an ardent lover. . . . He talked, gesticulated, laughed, boldly held her hand. It was hard to believe he was fifty-eight years old." The guard or guards always waited outside Mrs. Galt's house, and the President seldom reappeared before midnight or one in the morning. Sometimes he insisted upon walking home. "I remember those October and November nights," wrote Starling, "the air was clear, and just cold enough to make me conscious of my skin and the tip of my nose. . . . We walked briskly, and the President danced off the curbs and up them when we crossed streets." When it became necessary to pause at street corners, he "whistled softly, through his teeth, tapping out the rhythm with restless feet, 'Oh, you beautiful doll! You great big beautiful doll!' "[12]

December 18, 1915, was the wedding day. Ike Hoover, in charge of all arrangements, coordinated his efforts with the Secret Service. Taking President Tyler as his model, Wilson decided to marry in the bride's home. The row house on 20th Street was not large, having only a parlor, a dining room, a stair hall, and a kitchen on the main floor. Hoover ordered the furniture removed from the parlor and dining room and hauled to the second floor, then he called Charles Henlock. The two of them decorated for the wedding, making Mrs. Galt's rooms bowers of orchids, heather, ferns, and palms.

By 8:30 p.m. the hall and parlors were packed with wedding guests. The Marine Band struck up the march, and the President and Mrs. Galt descended the staircase, taking their places at an improvised altar. After the ceremony, the couple turned and mingled with the crowd. A buffet wedding supper, brought from the White House, consisted of Virginia ham, oyster patties, chicken salad, cheese straws, and other southern dishes, as well as a strong punch.

At ten, the President and Mrs. Wilson stepped out on the stoop of her house and walked arm in arm down the steps. One block distant, thousands of spectators crowded the streets beyond the police barricades; a line of motorcars idled at the curb before the house. The couple entered the Pierce-Arrow, and the shades were drawn; the car moved away slowly through the crowds, then, clear of people, began to race from the dark city, the Secret Service cars fast behind, followed by a scattering of automobiles and taxicabs containing news reporters. Some 40 minutes later, the official party of four cars arrived at the railroad station in Alexandria, where the Wilsons boarded a private train for West Virginia.

Dangers

During the 16 months between the death of Ellen Axson Wilson and Wilson's marriage to Edith Bolling Galt, the President guided the nation over a hazardous road of neutrality. It was clear that America could tip the bloody scales in one direction or the other. Her stance philosophically was to avoid the war, to scorn it as the predictable product of rivalry among degenerate political systems. But popular emotions were aroused by the European conflict. At the helm, the former professor showed himself to be presidential in every way, playing his part to the satisfaction of most of the voters, who reelected him their chief in 1916, with the slogan, "He kept us out of war."

Still, through 1916 the public grew increasingly hostile to Germany. The loss of American lives aboard the *Lusitania* and the *Arabic*, torpedoed by German submarines, offended the Americans' sense of justice; war propaganda from abroad and, increasingly, at home inflamed this feeling. Early in 1916, Wilson was forced to cut short his wedding trip in Hot Springs because of the sinking of the British liner *Persia*, with a great loss of lives, including that of one American. By the summer his program of "preparedness" would begin, with the opening of military training camps and the buildup of the Army and the Navy.

When the President returned to the White House from Hot Springs, an excited Joe Tumulty confronted him with reports of the loud cries for revenge against Germany. "I have made up my mind," said Wilson, "that I am more interested in the opinion that the country will have of me ten years from now than the opinion it may be willing to express today. . . . I will not be rushed into war, no matter if every last Congressman stands up on his hind legs and calls me a coward."[13]

The Newlyweds

Few changes were made at the White House by Edith Bolling Wilson. She had her own bedroom furniture placed in the sitting room west of the oval room, and the Lincoln bed moved to the adjoining presidential bedroom, replacing the twin beds put there originally by Taft and used by Wilson and his first wife. Those members of the staff who set down their views were unanimous in approval of the new First Lady. "Mrs. Wilson was what I would call a perfect wife," wrote Ella Jaffray. "She was a wonderful companion for President Wilson, sympathetic and understanding and very gentle."[14]

Ike Hoover found her "nervous and hesitant," but a "lovely character." She was not a political pusher like Mrs. Taft, who entered all conversations and gave her opinion, but neither was she shrewd about people as the first Mrs. Wilson had been. Edith Wilson dealt entirely in personalities; this was not merely an inclination, but a strong emotional trait. Clearly lacking the wisdom and depth of insight of the first wife, she was nevertheless kept equally informed by her husband, who, even during their short courtship, gave her important papers to read. The President was accustomed to taking his problems home with him; Ellen Wilson had been a strong adviser. Whether to the good or not, Edith Wilson was prepared early for a similar role.

The couple demanded privacy, using the two rooms of the presidential suite almost as a separate apartment. In the smaller of the rooms, the sitting room, they ate breakfast, drank tea, and occasionally had lunch or dinner. It was an awkward, crowded room; the bathroom and closet, added in the renovation of 1902, threw the mantelpiece off center. The chintz put there by Ellen Wilson remained, the lone continuity in a mixture of family photographs, framed coats of arms, lamps, books, "handwork," pillows, and the other odds and ends with which Edith Wilson surrounded herself.

Her day centered on her husband; all other duties were secondary. The Wilsons began their mornings early, when he rose and got a tray which had been placed on a table in the hall outside their bedroom. From this he obtained a sandwich and a thermos bottle of hot coffee, all of which he consumed while he dressed in the southwest corner dressing room, assisted by Colonel Brooks. Soon he was off for a round of golf at one of the public courses, in company with several Secret Service men and Dr. Grayson. When he returned to the White House at eight, his wife and a full breakfast awaited him in the sitting room. She had by that time dressed for the morning.

After breakfast, the Wilsons crossed the oval room to the study, where the President opened what he and his wife called "The Drawer." If urgent matters had appeared after closing time the day before, a memorandum and related papers would be found in The Drawer, situated in the center of one side of the historic *Resolute* desk. But even if The Drawer were empty, there were papers enough on the desk to keep the President busy. Many of the documents he read to his new wife, inviting her comments, perhaps placing himself in the role of teacher to this woman he loved. Her memoirs suggest that she was not especially interested in the business of state, but accommodated her husband by reading and discussing whatever he wished.[15]

In those early months of their marriage their patterns of daily living were established quickly, to the obvious pleasure of them both. They spent the better part of an hour in the study alone, then were joined by a stenographer from the Executive Office, usually Charles L. Swem. Wilson sometimes dictated for several hours, but not the very important letters, for those he still typed himself. Swem opened Wilson's regular mail early in the morning, bringing to the study those letters which required a ready response from the President, dispatching elsewhere the correspondence to which others could attend. Wilson was a great letter writer, who insisted upon performing the principal function in all his correspondence, no matter the convenience of assigning some of the work to subordinates. He always signed letters personally, where many of his predecessors had allowed secretaries to imitate their signatures.

Household duties usually called Mrs. Wilson away before the dictation was finished. She crossed the corridor and the elevator hall to Mrs. Jaffray's office overlooking Pennsylvania Avenue. Given the menu book by the housekeeper, she studied the plans for the day's meals originated by the cook and approved or corrected by Mrs. Jaffray. At this session Mrs. Jaffray was informed of the number of guests the Wilsons expected for meals. Plans were made late and always subject to change. Margaret Wilson's many causes, in addition to her interest in music and religion, kept her busy holding luncheons of her own, sometimes upstairs in the east hall. For the large weekly dinners, to which guests were invited by formal invitation, Mrs. Jaffray had the figures well ahead of time. From the housekeeper's office Mrs. Wilson returned to the sitting room—often called the boudoir—where she and the President had eaten breakfast. Her social secretary awaited at about ten o'clock. Only in the first month did Belle Hagner fill this post, for the secretary announced her own engagement soon after the President announced his, and married Norman James of Baltimore, a widower with children. Belle Hagner's replacement was Edith Benham, daughter of Admiral Benham, and a young woman alert to the social ways of the capital.

Mrs. Wilson planned the day with Edith Benham, then the two sat in the west hall and attended to correspondence. The First Lady usually took the window seat, her back to the great lunette window; her social secretary sat at the desk with the papers. All letters to Mrs. Wilson received a response, even requests for autographs. Bold requests for invitations to the White House were sometimes courteously dismissed with a response from the secretary, sometimes honored with an invitation to an afternoon reception, of which several were held each week during the social season. Letters which were unkind or threatening were usually turned over to the Secret Service. Belle Hagner had proved to be expert at evaluating the mail, and Edith Benham became a worthy successor, holding the job of social secretary intermittently for more than 23 years under three First Ladies.[16]

Mrs. Wilson kept a watch for the President down the long central corridor. When he emerged from his study, heading for the elevator, she joined him and they walked together to the Executive Office, passing through the basement to the colonnade, and into the little "President's hall" that led through the west wing into the office building. At the end of the hall they kissed and parted, she returning to her letters and to her social secretary in the west hall.

The Wilsons met for lunch at half past noon in the private dining room. Unlike her predecessor, Mrs. Wilson found this room "more homelike" than the State Dining Room with its dark oak paneling. While there were nearly always guests, the President and Mrs. Wilson did sometimes dine alone in their sitting room upstairs or, in nice weather, on the west terrace, screened by the tubbed bay trees. As usual, the house was open to visitors from ten to four, with no break at midday. Luncheon was therefore served behind closed doors. The faint rumble of the tourists could be heard now and then over lunchtime chatter. At 2 or 2:30 Mrs. Wilson walked back to the Oval Office with her husband, sometimes remaining at his side for an hour or more, making no comments, only listening to the men talk.

In the early evening the Wilsons usually took a long drive. Particular about the routes he took, like Taft, Wilson planned the excursions with care. The automobile trips occupied about an hour, and the President could relate the advantages of each of his routes. One was a ramble in northern Virginia; another followed the dirt river road that hugged the Potomac opposite Washington; still another took the presidential couple and the accompanying Secret Service car through Rock Creek Park to the site where the new Washington Cathedral was under construction.

Another amusement, always eagerly anticipated, was the weekend river trip aboard the *Mayflower*. This handsome vessel, gleaming white and shining with polished mahogany, had served the Presidents beginning with Roosevelt. It was comfortable without being as luxurious as some private yachts. There were decks lined with wicker lounge chairs, an ample suite for the President and First Lady, a salon, and guest rooms, in addition to a dining room, presided over by a Chinese chef. Mrs. Wilson remembered the dreamlike weekends when they sailed down the Potomac, leaving from the Navy Yard on Friday afternoons at about dusk and returning Sunday night.[17]

"We both liked studying the charts," she wrote, "to see if we could find some little tributary of the river to explore." Fond of old houses and villages, they often went ashore to view the relics of Virginia and Maryland. Sometimes they took guests, but often it was only the two of them, with servants, some office staff, and Secret Service men.[18]

Just as Cary Grayson watched the health of the President, urging him into a routine of eating—when he had little interest in food—and practically forcing him to play golf every day, Mrs. Wilson saw to it that he relaxed. The drives, the boat trips, movies in the East Room, and a night or two at the theater during most weeks were all part of her program, devised in council with Dr. Grayson. It was an incredible schedule, but Grayson believed that Edith Wilson had saved the President. "With dynamic vitality and sheer joy of living," wrote Grayson, "she showed him how to take hold again of life and happiness."[19]

End of an Age

The President labored under inconceivable pressure, which more than counterbalanced the bliss of his private life. Apart from troubles in the Caribbean and Mexico, Wilson watched the European war intensify. German submarines plagued the seas; Americans died or were wounded. The cry for revenge grew loud. A large and vocal opposing element wanted neutrality sustained. Wilson warned the Germans in stronger terms, threatening, in April 1916, a severance of diplomatic relations. The distant war seemed ever closer.

In the light of this, Wilson, in long and arduous hours alone with his thoughts, began to refine his ideas on the future place of America in the world. Should his country go to war, he believed, the war must be fought on principles higher and more universal than those which had started the fighting in Europe. Wilson knew that his convictions, though commonly held by others, demanded that the United States make a commitment which many Americans might at first suspect and resent. He wanted his views to be perfectly understood from the outset, to attract the greatest following possible. Encouraged by Colonel House, he determined to state his views in that presidential election year, expressing the ideal he believed the United States should try to achieve as a world power. The first opportunity to speak out came in an invitation, arranged by Colonel House, to address the first national assembly of the League to Enforce Peace.

Before the speech Wilson tried out his ideas on a small scale in an informal talk before the National Press Club. In spite of negative editorials, cartoons, and news reports on his neutral stand, Wilson generally enjoyed good relations with the press. To the Press Club he sketched out in plain language the logic of his "new nationalism," wherein men thought not of themselves in a heat of "party passion . . . and personal preference" but "in terms of America." President Wilson saw America's mission expand from spreading democracy over a vacant continent to bringing its blessings to the crowded, weary world; the United States was now the peacemaker, the one nation left with both strength and uncorrupted moral values.[20]

Satisfied with his reception at the Press Club, Wilson crafted his speech to the League to Enforce Peace with the greatest care and in more precise language. This was to be a formal address, which he would read. He typed his speech in his White House sanctum, spending many hours at the task. On May 27, 1916, he stood before some 2,000 people at the New Willard Hotel and began with a short but eloquent survey of the basic rights of Americans, established by the Founding Fathers; he then reasoned that other nations great and small deserved to enjoy the freedom to be governed as they wished, to have the same rights, if they wanted them. "I am sure," said Wilson, "that I speak the mind and wish of the people of America when I say that the United States is willing to become a partner in any feasible association of nations formed in order to realize these objects and make them secure against violation." The United States wished to be the peacemaker in the present war in Europe. "We have nothing material of any kind to ask for ourselves. . . . Our interest is only in peace and its future guarantees." His conclusion confirmed the moral, indeed the spiritual, tone of his quest: "God grant that the dawn of that day of frank dealing and of settled peace, concord, and cooperation may be near at hand!"[21]

In his address the President laid out the road he planned to follow. The speech was generally well received, but few realized its historical significance. President Wilson had announced an end to isolation, the dominant theme in American foreign policy since the administration of George Washington.

Only days later Wilson was again busy at his typewriter drafting new speeches, in which he further clarified his objectives, his philosophy of the position America must assume in the world. He gained new confidence. Though campaigning for reelection, he seemed more concerned with selling his ideas, and he performed with youthful vigor. He and Mrs. Wilson, who were vacationing in New Jersey during the election, returned triumphant to the White House in mid-November. From the nightly dinner parties the President went to his study, where in a pool of light from his desk lamp he labored at his typewriter until the early hours of morning. On the 25th, Mrs. Wilson wrote in her diary that she had helped her husband work in his study until midnight. "He is writing what he says 'may prove the greatest piece of work of my life'; and oh if only it is so, for it will mean so much."[22]

A Plea for Peace

What Wilson produced was a message to the warring nations of Europe, asking them to lay down their arms, accept American mediation, and work together for a "league of nations to ensure peace and justice throughout the world." Just before Christmas, the message was sent. House considered it a masterpiece. "There are some sentences," he wrote in his diary, "that will live as long as human history." In early January the British delivered a negative reply. Britain intended to defeat Germany. Germany's response was also negative, or at least had so many conditions attached to a frail acceptance as to make the reply insulting.[23]

To draw the bewildered President from his worries, Mrs. Wilson kept the house filled with favorite relatives. Quiet dinners were held every evening, with the days left open for the cousins to explore Washington. In the bitterly cold, snowy month of January 1917, suffragettes demonstrated before the White House day and night, huddled against the terrible northwest wind, holding their yellow banners high. Wilson had slight sympathy, but did worry that the demonstrators were cold. When he sent Ike Hoover out to invite them in for tea before a warm fire, the motive may have come more from Wilson the humorist than Wilson the humanitarian. The invitation was declined.

On the last day of January, Wilson received word that Germany would resume unrestricted submarine warfare. On February 3 he made good his warning of the previous spring and cut off diplomatic relations.

More British ships were sunk by German submarines, the first being the *Laconia,* a Cunard liner, with two Americans aboard. Headlines proclaimed the news, and war cries filled the editorial pages.

Still Wilson attempted to pursue a course of peace. The day before his second inaugural, the Capitol rang with the debates over armed neutrality. The President, abstracted and troubled, went for a long walk with Mrs. Wilson on the glossy wet sidewalks and along the muddy gravel walks in the park. The inauguration was held the next day, Sunday, in the President's Room of the Capitol, the parade and public ceremony having been put off until Monday. The sun shone that second day, although the glittering ceremonies were marred for the Wilsons by the knowledge of several bomb threats and assassination plots. For that reason there was an unusually large military and police presence, with guards stationed even on the rooftops. Secret Service agent Ed Starling, assigned to the presidential car, wrote, "The mile from the White House to the Capitol was the longest I ever rode."

On March 18 German submarines sent three American vessels to the bottom. Rallies were held in the streets of the cities. Crowds collected at the White House fences. War propaganda seemed to be everywhere, and the military spirit was in the air.

Newsmen stalked the President in greater numbers than ever before. A group seemed always collected near the north portico, ready to swarm the car when it came for the President. They plagued officials as they left the confines of the Executive Office Building after a visit to the President. When official callers entered from West Executive Avenue they found newsmen along the walkway to the office building, and at night reporters stood in clusters and talked in the light of the porch lamps. Important visitors, hoping to avoid exposure, could enter secretly beneath the south portico.

March 20, after a brief bout with illness, the President met with his Cabinet in the Executive Office. The nation was shaken over the sinkings two days before. Crowds stood in the streets, and reporters filled the entrance to the Executive Office. The moment was tense; the decision to enter the war or not was Wilson's. The American people waited for the President to lead them. To a man, the Cabinet favored war. So vociferous were several of its members in stating their opinions that Wilson asked them to modulate their voices, lest the reporters and staff outside the doors hear what they were saying.

At four Wilson dismissed the Cabinet without committing himself. The next day he summoned the Congress to a special session, to convene April 2, and began preparing his message in virtual seclusion in the study. He asked no advice on the text from the members of his Cabinet, who resented their exclusion. Only House advised the President as he struggled with his task. Their conversations were long and often personal, an uncertain Wilson gaining strength from his close friend.

Wilson made various drafts of a war message and on April 1 showed House the finished address, which House admired. When House suggested he give it to the Cabinet for review, the President declined. "He preferred to keep it to himself and take the responsibility," wrote House. The colonel did not approve, and to his diary confided: "I have noticed recently that he holds a tighter rein over his Cabinet and that he is impatient of any initiative on their part."[24]

Message and Proclamation

Still Wilson could not sleep. In his study early on April 2, the day the Congress was to convene, he nervously pondered what was to come. He telephoned his friend Frank I. Cobb, editor of the *World.* Cobb was there by one in the afternoon and found Wilson depressed and "worn down." The President told him that he had never been so uncertain of anything in his life. "I think I know what war means," he said, insisting that he had tried every possible way to avoid one. Now there would be a war; Germany would be crushed, and "a peace-time civilization" reconstructed with "war standards." America would be hardened by the experience. She would lose her gentleness, her human grandeur, and go "warmad, quit thinking, and devote [her] energies to destruction." Perhaps she would never again be the same: "Once lead this people into war, and they'll forget there ever was such a thing as tolerance. . . . the spirit of ruthless brutality will enter into the very fiber of our national life. . . . every man who refused to conform would have to pay the penalty."[25]

After golf in the morning of April 2, he spent a part of the afternoon walking in the fine, misty rain to several of the department buildings. The Congress was to receive the President at 8:30 that evening. Dinner was served in the State Dining Room at 6:30 to House, Dr. Grayson, and several members of the family who were in town to hear the message. At 8:20 President and Mrs. Wilson and Dr. Grayson entered the Pierce-Arrow. Thousands of spectators had come out that night, nearly all to cheer Woodrow Wilson. They stood shivering, visible only in the pools of light made by the electric street lamps.

Little American flags had been distributed through the crowds, and their fluttering enlivened the edges of the streets. "How well I remember that night," wrote one of the guards who accompanied the President's car, "the soft spring rain falling on us as we moved down Pennsylvania Avenue. . . . Cavalry, foot soldiers, and marines were abroad; pacifists had gathered in groups, silently protesting. . . . " The exterior of the Capitol was illuminated for the first time that night, and the great building seemed to float over the city.[26]

In the gallery of the House Chamber, Colonel House kept a careful eye on his watch during the President's message. The address began at 8:40, and was finished in 32 minutes. Wilson and his party left the Capitol immediately; as he entered the car, Ed Starling found him "very tired." He and Mrs. Wilson climbed at once to the oval room upstairs, where they were joined by Margaret Wilson, Grayson, House, and the visiting relatives for a family evening of about two hours, discussing the message and occasionally going to the windows within darkened rooms to look out and see the cheering people lining the streets.

Early in the afternoon of April 7, the Wilsons and Helen Bones were having lunch in the State Dining Room when word was whispered to the President that the joint resolution of the Congress declaring war had arrived for his signature. Wilson ordered it brought over from the office, and when Rudolph Forster arrived with it, excused himself from the table and went directly to the ushers' office, where Ed Starling and Ike Hoover sat in idle conversation.

Wilson, followed by his wife and Helen Bones, came in from the dining room. "How are you, Rudolph? Have you the proclamation?"

"Yes sir," responded Forster, "shall I take it to your study?"

The President decided that he would sign the proclamation then and there. Seating himself at Ike Hoover's mahogany rolltop desk, which was usually nosed against the south wall of the room, he asked for a pen. "Use this one," said Mrs. Wilson, handing him a little gold pen he had given her as a gift.

"Stand behind me, Edith," said the President. She looked over his right shoulder, Helen Bones at her side. Rudolph Forster took his place immediately behind the President's chair. Forster, almost 19 years earlier, had stood in the old Cabinet Room as McKinley signed a similar document against Spain. On the President's left stood Starling; Hoover drew close, holding a blotter.[27]

Wilson carefully read the printed document that lay before him. Daylight from the window was largely blocked by the little tableau that had formed around him, so his paper was illuminated by the desk lamp. He took the pen and signed "Woodrow Wilson." After a pause the President rose from the chair. Forster took the telephone to a corner and called the Executive Office, where a mass of newsmen waited; Ike

Hoover pressed a button on the desk, the signal to someone somewhere else in the house to call and advise the Navy Department. Oblivious of these things, or seeming so, Wilson walked from the office to the elevator in the adjacent hall, the women close behind him.

That same day the White House was closed to tourists, as part of a program of heightened security. It was not to be opened again until after the President departed for Versailles. An announcement was issued through the press canceling all receptions, garden parties, and dinners. Additional guard stations were established in both house and grounds. Access to the house and the office building was stringently controlled. Idle callers, heretofore admitted at certain hours to meet the President, were stopped at the gate on West Executive Avenue and sent away. The tradition of leaving calling cards at the north door of the White House was suspended.

The President was again the commander in chief of a nation at war, and the White House once more a guarded fortress—for the fifth time in 117 years.

35

Distant Drums

As the machine of war was built and as it began to operate with furious speed, the White House remained tranquil and timeless, seemingly apart from anxiety and change. The President had time to think and plan, for the nation was as isolated by sea from the action as the White House seemed by time from the growing wartime frenzy beyond its iron fences. In the soft glow of the carpeted halls, and in the quiet rooms with their fresh bouquets, one found no symbols of an international upheaval; indeed Woodrow Wilson's White House was the very picture of peace. Even the decorative thunder of the imperial Theodore Roosevelt had been modified in little ways by artwork, chintzes, cream-colored silk lampshades, and gauzy white undercurtains that billowed at the open windows.

Great change, however, had come to the Presidency. The Congress, through a series of emergency acts, had bestowed upon Woodrow Wilson greater power than had ever before been held by a President. At his typewriter Wilson wrote private memos to himself, in which he contemplated how best to use this power. He knew that the diplomatic potency of the Presidency had been tried very little. That power would increase as a result of America's intervention in the war; perceiving this, he meant to make the most of it.

The President passionately believed that the nations of the Western world must sacrifice their chauvinism and unite to bring about permanent peace. Nothing in the European tradition suggested a voluntary yielding of prerogative. But Wilson determined that moral right would prevail over the darker forces of history.

Loyalties

As always, the White House staff adjusted quickly to wartime circumstances, although this time there were rough spots. Oaths of loyalty
were required of all employees, as they had been during the Civil War
and the Spanish-American War. Additional guards were placed in and
around the house. All arriving carriages, cars, letters, and parcels were
inspected in the East Wing before being taken inside. Obtaining entry
was difficult for anyone outside the President's family and his close political and official circle. Since interest in the President is highest during a
crisis, people stood daily at the iron fence on Pennsylvania Avenue,
waiting for a glimpse of him. In the war's first weeks protestors sometimes
appeared bearing banners.

A crowd always collected at the northeast gate between five and six
in the evening, when the Pierce-Arrow emerged from the north portico
with the President, his wife, and Dr. Grayson, followed by a car with
three or four Secret Service men. A Secret Service man sat beside
the chauffeur, George H. Robinson ("Robbie"), or Edward P. White
("Doc"), while the President traditionally sat on the right rear seat, his
wife to the left, and other passengers before them in jump seats. Once in
the street, the cars moved at fast speeds, obeying no limits, stopping at
no intersections, turning where the President pleased.

Anti-German feeling made its appearance at the White House early
in the war. A feature of the almost holy quest to cleanse the world was
the Espionage Act, which gave the government power of censorship and
other regulatory authority over anti-American activities. A great popular
fear of subversion was most dramatically manifested in a suspicion of
Germans. Wilson repeated at a Cabinet meeting certain rumors against
the German-born furnace fireman, William Strauss, an employee at the
White House since 1888. The President concluded that the stories were
unfounded, but the staff regarded Strauss with suspicion throughout the
war. The head cook, the Swede Sigrid Nulsson, was "quite pro-German"
at the outbreak of the war. Her two assistants, Olive Ceaveu, French,
and Elizabeth Colquist, Irish, were ardent supporters of the Allies and
celebrated the entry of the United States into the war. Mrs. Jaffray soon
heard that the cooks were bickering almost constantly both in the
kitchen and in the west end of the third floor, where they lived. One day
the housekeeper descended to the basement and walked unnoticed to the
door of the kitchen, where she listened to a lively argument, which soon
became a brawl. The small, plump, blonde Sigrid Nulsson fought the two
Allies furiously, until Mrs. Jaffray appeared in the doorway. A sharp

lecture was followed by a warning to the entire household staff that the subject of the war was not to be mentioned, on penalty of dismissal. Apparently there were no more incidents.[1]

Those who remembered the Spanish-American War found the White House a quieter place during the world war, in part because the office was in a separate building.

The functions served by the old War Room were discharged in the Executive Office Building. Housed there were the telegraph, telephone, and the equivalent of a map room, along with some 60 to 75 clerks and other personnel. The office was open round the clock, as were many of the offices in the State, War, & Navy Building next door. Galaxies of lighted windows greeted Mrs. Wilson when she looked from her southwest corner dressing room into the dark nights.

The President's Study

Freed almost entirely from the details of administration, the President spent most of his time in his study. There he received his intimate associates, although he met ceremonial callers, some reporters, and others formally in the Oval Office. Now called the Treaty Room, Wilson's study was a large square chamber with two long windows on the south, a fireplace on the east, and two doors, one connecting it with the oval room, and another opening on the hall.

Few changes had been made in the study in the 15 years since McKim had decorated it. Buckram still covered the walls, a yellowish beige material showing the texture of its heavy weave. At the two windows hung the same heavy curtains of brown velour. On the floor lay the same blue Wilton rug, sized to leave a border of white maple flooring exposed. The walls were banded at about chest height by interconnecting mahogany bookcases, their shelves filled tightly with President Wilson's books. To anyone who had known Wilson well, his different signatures on the flyleaves of these volumes were a time line of his life— "Thomas W. Wilson," the name he used in young manhood, through Thomas Woodrow Wilson, T. W. Wilson, T. Woodrow Wilson, and, at last, Woodrow Wilson.

The tops of the bookcases formed a stage for memorabilia. Wilson's personal collection was relatively small: a few family pictures, a scattering of framed political photographs, and neat piles of letters. Above the bookcases on the buckram-covered walls were hung a variety of pictures, with little apparent regard for symmetry. Most prominent was the large canvas by Théobald Chartran, *The Signing of the Peace Protocol*, depicting

President McKinley and the other principals of that event, which had taken place in this room in 1898. The picture had been acquired for the White House in 1902, the year the same artist had painted Mrs. Roosevelt in her colonial garden.

Near the center of the room, squarely on the blue carpet, was the *Resolute* desk at which Wilson worked. A photograph of the room taken in Wilson's time shows the desktop neatly arranged, with blotter, inkwell, clock, calendar, pens and pencils, and papers all in place. To the left of the desk chair a small table contains additional papers, suggesting that Wilson swiveled in the chair between two work surfaces, or used the second table for his typewriter, which was not photographed. Also absent is the kerosene student lamp, referred to frequently; he liked to work by this relic of his college days, even though the room had electric fixtures. Four leather armchairs and one of the three round mahogany tables Andrew Jackson had acquired for the East Room completed the inventory of Wilson's sparse White House study.[2]

Among Ike Hoover's papers at the Library of Congress is a small volume, rather more a notebook than a diary or journal, in which he described Wilson during the war. The President had told him in 1913, "If a man knew his job he did not have to work hard." It was true that before the war Wilson spent more time with his family than any President Hoover could recall. But in 1917, "when the Great War came on," Hoover wrote, "he spent more time at his desk, abandoning the practice of going to the Executive Office except on Cabinet Days. He worked in his study where he could do so undisturbed."[3]

Wilson himself set down his reasons in a letter: "I have found by experience that the only place I can get things done is the White House. We are so safely (almost annoyingly) guarded here nowadays that we, as a matter of fact, have a great deal of seclusion and privacy. . . ."[4]

Public and Private

As a result of wartime security, life at the White House underwent a marked change. One of the most powerful figures in the world became more isolated than ever from life beyond the iron fence that enclosed his official residence. No longer did the President mix on the streets of the city; except from the windows of the White House, the windows of his automobile, over the rostrum, or over the edge of his box at the theater, he saw only those with whom he had special business, his staff, and the few people he cherished.

To a large extent, Wilson allowed this to happen. His was not a public personality. He did, however, complain about his isolation. On evenings together he and Mrs. Wilson often dreamed of what they would do after the Presidency. He said he wanted to go on a bicycle tour of Europe, as he had done when he was younger. Mrs. Wilson heard the stories of his bicycling adventures again and again "over the roads of Scotland, England and the Continent, stopping at little wayside taverns and striking up acquaintance with farmers, townsmen and all manner of folk." He bought her a bicycle so she could prepare herself by learning to ride. The long basement corridor was where she practiced.[5]

With the valid excuse created by the war, the Secret Service, the Army, and the White House staff may have made the President more remote from the everyday world than any American President has ever been. In times to come, radio and television would somewhat reduce the danger of this sort of isolation; in Wilson's case, the situation seems eventually to have affected his outlook. His wartime living conditions encouraged his tendency to bury himself in his thoughts. Most of the people who saw him either wanted something or were his subordinates. His wife became more and more central to his life, and she reinforced this by gradually excluding the flock of friendly and outspoken relatives that had earlier surrounded him and had meant so much to him.

Sometimes the enormous pressure of work, together with the isolation, nearly got the best of him and he did seek escape, but as it always turned out, to isolation of yet another kind: "Edith and I are on the MAYFLOWER to-day," he wrote to one of his daughters, "to get away from the madness (it is scarcely less) of Washington for a day or two, not to stop work (that *cannot* stop nowadays) . . . but to escape *people* and their intolerable excitements and demands." On the same river trip he wrote to Colonel House, "A point is reached when I *must* escape . . . for a little while."[6]

Several circumstances contributed to the President's increasing isolation. McKinley's assassination was the great catalyst, spawning a constant fear that the President might be harmed. The Secret Service accompanied him everywhere. A certain paranoia went with the assignment. Threatening letters were in nearly every mail delivery; cranks frequently called in person and had to be carried away bodily; crowds of thousands, no matter their smiles and cheering, seemed sinister, for it took only one eye, one hand, one gun, one bullet to make a fatal strike.

The protection of First Ladies had begun with Mrs. Lincoln, who was accompanied by a member of the Metropolitan Police force on her shopping trips to New York. Those who had accompanied Presidents' wives before that had been more in the nature of footmen than guards. Mrs. Lincoln's "footman," though in plainclothes, carried a pistol. Children of Presidents had begun to receive full-time protection with the advent of William Howard Taft. Threats to the children were rare before the early 20th century, but began to appear in the hundreds late in the Roosevelt administration.

In addition to keeping a vigil against assassins, the Secret Service guarded the President's privacy. Americans had always been bolder than Europeans in approaching public figures. Wherever the President appeared, a crowd was certain to collect, becoming without much provocation a pushing, shoving sea of people, all eager to shake hands with their chief. Caught in the middle, the President became vulnerable to indignity and danger. The reporters, likewise direct, were constant in their pursuit of the President and his family. The newsmen who called daily at the Executive Office were usually orderly, for fear of being banned. On the street it was otherwise. They waited with cameras for any opportunity to find some kind of story connected with the White House. Only the Secret Service held them at bay.

When the war began, the Secret Service agents at the White House were urged not to join the Army, being told that guarding the President was "more important than being a soldier." Most of them stayed. During the war their duties were narrowed to include only the personal protection of the President, his wife, and daughters. External protection for the White House and Executive Office was now provided by the Army, not the Treasury. Military display in the presidential enclave, carrying a connotation of power by force, is always reserved for wartime. During Wilson's wartime tenure, men in uniform stood at the gates and patrolled the grounds. The same had been true, to a greater or lesser degree, during all the wars except for the Spanish-American War, when McKinley, fearing public objections, refused to allow patrols.

Only upstairs at the White House was Wilson able to be alone. The great corridor and large rooms gave him a sense of space, where he could move about unobserved. Elsewhere guards were at hand or just beyond the doorway. A kind of etiquette was established to provide the President with at least the appearance of privacy. When he played golf, he might see only one or two guards, but in the woods adjoining the course six or eight more moved through the trees. He liked to go for walks. He never saw most of the guards accompanying him. Nevertheless, their presence was hard to deny. People on the street or in stores or theaters were not allowed to approach him, unless he asked them to do so. Groups that gathered along the sidewalks or in lobbies were watched by a Secret

Service man who carried a pistol in his shoulder holster and was prepared to halt any undue movement toward the President.

Wilson never understood the public's fascination with his private life. His secrecy about it made him appear aloof. Edward W. Bok, editor of *The Ladies' Home Journal,* and a good friend, pronounced Wilson the "poorest kind of a publicist" of himself. Wrote Bok, "He was resentful of any personal exploitation." One evening during the war Bok was invited to call on the Wilsons. They sat in the oval library, Wilson thumbing through a book and Mrs. Wilson sewing, while they talked. Bok, who knew Wilson well enough to be fairly candid, opened the topic of the President's relative obscurity as an individual, doubtless comparing him with his predecessors, Roosevelt and Taft. The editor "cautiously suggested" that he would like to get Wilson "more into the picture."

"That's an inspiring thought," Wilson responded. "Had an idea I was very much in the picture—more than some people like to have me, I should judge. How do you mean?"

"I want to give a double page of photographs depicting your personal side."

"Why?"

"Well, I think the people should know better the man behind the official."

"How solicitous you are that I should be correctly understood, as you call it, aren't you?" asked Wilson. "The trouble is you can't see that you want to put the emphasis on the wrong side of me. That part belongs to my family."

"Not altogether," Bok persisted. "The trouble with you is, Mr. President, if you will let me paraphrase your statement, you won't let your friends put the emphasis on the side the public wants to know about. Your fine distinction between your private self and that of the President of the United States satisfies you, but not the people."

"I think he is right, dear," said Mrs. Wilson. "He wants a picture like this, for instance, you reading and I sewing. Why not?"

"Two to one," said the President.

"Well, can you beat the combination?" Bok asked.

"No," said Wilson, "I don't think I can. What do you want?" The conversation continued, and Mrs. Wilson produced old pictures, one an especially amusing snapshot of the President riding a donkey in Egypt. Wilson cringed at the thought of this going into print.

"No one has seen it outside the family," begged Mrs. Wilson.

"Nor should anyone," said the President. Then he threw up his hands in mock resignation: "I see it's no use. I don't expect either of you to use discretion because I don't think you have any. I suppose all I can expect and ask is mercy! Be sure to add a list of my favorite one hundred books, the poems I love best, my favorite dishes, my favorite chair and how I like to sit when I am reading, how many hours I sleep, and on which side I sleep. These details will add to the unusual quality of the article and give it literary distinction. If you don't know any of these points, come to me, and having nothing important to do in these war-times, I'll take a day off and devote myself to deep thought on all these important points of my life, and, if necessary, I can go to sleep for an hour or two, and you can photograph me and get the exact angle at which I commune with Morpheus."

Satisfied, the President returned to his book. Mrs. Wilson and Bok went to the table and began shuffling through the old pictures. At length Wilson looked up and said to his friend Bok, "Doesn't your hotel close at all at night?"

"Don't mind what he says," said Edith Wilson. "Upstairs here he is just like anyone of us, and we pay no attention to him."[7]

Protest

Washington was strikingly altered by the war. Thousands of war workers moved there within a few months, and huge temporary structures built to house them mushroomed on the public lands, in defiance of the City Beautiful. "The khaki of our Army and the blue of our Navy uniforms began to give color to the streets of Washington," wrote Mrs. Wilson, "and to these were soon added the various hues of the uniforms of the Allies as their official Commissions reached these shores to discuss the tying of our efforts with theirs."[8]

Commissioners of the Allied powers were received with military pomp, which heightened the already soaring war spirit to near frenzy. The British commission was the first to arrive, followed through late April and May by the French, Italian, Belgian, Russian, and Japanese. Each was fêted with parades; each was received at the White House and honored with luncheon or dinner. In May the glittering hero of the Marne, Marshal Joseph-Jacques-Césaire Joffre—"Papa Joffre"—arrived in splendor to the wild enthusiasm of the American public. This French-man was less personally interesting to the Wilsons than the genteel and intellectual English diplomat Arthur Balfour, head of the British com-mission. He was invited to conversations over teacups upstairs in the study. On a sunny afternoon Mrs. Wilson took him to see the spring blossoms on the south grounds, which "cheered him." She later recalled his saying that "after the gloom and shadows of London to see our lighted streets, lighted houses and gleaming white buildings was like being transported to another world."[9]

The tranquillity of the White House was shattered by demonstrators during the first months of the war, and they aroused the President's anger. Protesters took advantage of the arrival of the foreign commissions to crowd at the gates with specially prepared banners. Most noteworthy was the performance of the suffragettes on the arrival of the Russian delegation, which represented the brief democratic interlude after the revolution. The legend on the suffragettes' banner accused the President of deceiving Russia by appearing to support democracy, while women in his own country could not vote. For about two years the suffragettes had been familiar figures at the White House, demonstrating from time to time on the sidewalk beside Pennsylvania Avenue.

Wartime shrank the general toleration for such groups. During the demonstration before the Russians, a party of enraged spectators rushed forward and tore the banner from the iron fence. Several days later the Wilsons returned to the White House from a wedding to find on the fence another suffragette banner, and this so angered the President that the arrest of those who had put it there soon followed, together with stiff sentences to the workhouse.

To some the sentence of the suffragettes was a shocking violation of freedom of speech. But the general public, fired by the war spirit, heartily approved. While the President finally pardoned the offenders to keep them from becoming martyrs, he had no sympathy for them; suffragettes had been a thorn in his side since long before the war. Mrs. Wilson, "indignant" over the event, objected to her husband's act of mercy, for she could not forgive the women's affront. The secretary of the Navy observed that she was a good hater. Protest at the White House became less evident for the duration of the war.

The White House Staff

The quiet couple in the wartime White House was served by some 30 employees, counting the chief usher and his assistant and Mrs. Jaffray. Because of the war, the White House threw up ever stronger walls against intrusion. Within, it seemed more than ever a planet unto itself. Thirty percent of its population lived in the town, and the rest commuted, entering daily at the southeast gate.

For the most part the names of the minor members of the staff are lost. When they do survive, as did that of the Negro undercook Alice

Howard, they are simply "Alice" or "Joe" or "Brown" or "Mays," scribbled on a scrap of paper, with some notation in Mrs. Jaffray's elegantly illegible hand. Most of the principal servants are known either through payroll records or through the private correspondence within the tight presidential circle.

About two-thirds of the servants saw the President or members of his family every day, so the association was rather close. Edith Wilson had cordial relations with the staff, if she did not inspire the genuine affection in them that Ellen Wilson had. Wilson was usually described by the employees as cold and unyielding, especially since the death of his first wife, whose gentle influence had softened him. Had Colonel Arthur Brooks been the sort to speak out, however, he might have taken issue with those who said Wilson was cold. No member of the staff was closer to Wilson than Brooks, and President and valet held each other in high regard. Quite possibly, Wilson was consciously bestowing a personal honor when he ordered the colonel's beloved First Separate Battalion to stand by in defense of the capital, soon after the declaration of war.[9]

Three black men presided over the dining room, headed by James Coates, head butler, with Adolph Byrd and Arnold Dixon second and third. They were responsible to three chiefs: Colonel Brooks, over table linens, china, and silver; Mrs. Jaffray, over food and the manner of service; and Ike Hoover, who, as chief usher, held authority over all. Besides service in the two main floor dining rooms and occasional coffee or tea service in the Executive Office, the butlers were charged with the delivery of any meals eaten in the family quarters. Wearing the bottle-green jackets and black-and-white-striped vests designed by Ellen Wilson, they were frequently seen moving about in the second floor corridor with tea carts and trays.[10]

Annie Anderson, an Irishwoman, had been maid to the first Mrs. Wilson. Tall and gaunt, her pale face was rendered ghost-like by the contrast of black-dyed hair and black winter uniform. She was assigned to Helen Bones and replaced in the First Lady's dressing room by Susie Boothe, a short, fat black woman who had worked for Edith Wilson since her marriage to Galt. That connection, said Mrs. Jaffray, was Susie Boothe's "principal call for consideration," for she had few qualifications, having been more a housekeeper at the Galts' than a lady's maid. The only black assigned regularly to the family quarters, Susie Boothe demanded special favors. Mrs. Wilson heard complaints about her regularly, but remained loyal, which she would one day regret.[11]

Lilly Carter was mentioned in Mrs. Jaffray's notes as the "charwoman," although her title was "upstairs maid," responsible for the ten bathrooms of the second and third floors. She kept the linen organized in the "linen room" on the third floor, and she spent her spare time in the sewing room doing fancy mending of curtains and women's clothing. Her agility with the needle was remembered with awe 60 years later by a little girl, grown old, whom she had taught the mysteries of her art. Elsie Dufan was a laundress and Isabel McIntosh was a cleaning woman, and both spoke with heavy brogues. Maggie Rogers and Jennie Crowley were the two chambermaids; Ragna Halusen was a ladies' maid assigned either to the Rose Bedroom on the northeast or the Blue Bedroom across the hall when they were in use as guest chambers. In the absence of female guests, Ragna Halusen was "sempstress of the government linen," as designated by Mrs. Jaffray.[12]

Once the staff had been small for such a big house of grand purpose. It was no longer small, nor were there any longer many private establishments august enough to make it seem mean and understaffed by comparison. A few Washington houses were staffed with from 15 to 35 servants. The rich in New York, Chicago, and other large American cities often lived on a similar if not more expansive scale. But for all their grandiosity, the elegance of their servants' livery, the affected foreignness of their customs, life in even the grandest American mansions was no more luxurious in terms of service than that in the White House.

Wilson lived in the relatively silent midst of an army of servitors eager to please him. The "extra" services provided by the government agencies became so extensive during the war that to achieve the same in a private house would have required several hundred employees. Chauffeurs, gardeners, repairmen, orchestra, yacht and crew, carpenters, painters—all came from the departments, not costing the White House a cent. Employees considered themselves on a very high plane as the personal attendants to the President. The pay was low, the work demanding; utter devotion was required, as well as painful discretion and perseverance. Far from crushing the employees, however, the hardships seem to have heightened their sense of status. Royal palaces inevitably create such people behind the scenes. At the White House, in the course of carrying out their duties, the employees produced yet another barrier isolating the President.[13]

The intricacies of White House management had not changed much through the years. From the first, the big house had patronized a wide spectrum of Washington tradesmen. A clock-winder and repairman, for example, made his rounds regularly, and by Wilson's time only two men, both local jewelers, had held this post over its duration of more than 100 years. As often as was necessary, the clock-winder called and wound some 35 or 40 clocks—the number was never clear. The simpler clocks hung on the wall or stood on tables and shelves in service rooms and offices. In the principal rooms the fine clocks—such as the venerable Hannibal and Minerva clocks, which had kept time at the White House since 1818—had originally stood on mantels and could not be wound until heavy protective domes of glass were lifted aside.

Since Jefferson's time, through gentlemen's agreements between shop owners and the officials in charge of the White House, tradesmen had come in May and late October to disrobe and redress the rooms. Firewood had been provided by means of the same sort of unwritten understanding, but if he did well, a woodman could depend upon a steady income from the White House from year to year until he wished to retire. Much the same had been true of grocery suppliers, whose wagons almost every day threaded the service roadway from the east gate to the areaway beneath the north portico, where they showed their produce to the cook and housekeeper. Chickens, ducks, wild game, turtles from the Chesapeake Bay, and a variety of other provisions had entered the house by that means from at least the early 1820s. Mrs. Jaffray's only change in this process was to go first to the market to select the meat and vegetables herself, then have her purchases delivered.

Knife sharpeners, tinsmiths, electrical repairmen, ironmongers, glaziers, carpenters, painters, varnishers, floor polishers, chimney sweeps, plumbers, and part-time servants had come regularly in the past. But wartime security ended this in 1917, and the freedom of access from outside never entirely returned. Clocks were subsequently wound by a houseman; the maids took over the seasonal task of robing and disrobing the furniture; market delivery wagons were met by soldiers or Secret Service agents, or a White House automobile with guard accompanied Mrs. Jaffray and her carriage to the Central Market, where she did most of her shopping, and brought home the meats, greens, vegetables, and other perishables that she selected. The absent tradesmen were replaced wherever possible by civil or military personnel, culminating in a process that had been developing slowly, since before the Civil War, when clerks were "borrowed" from the departments and doormen were detailed from the Metropolitan Police.[14]

Within the house this shift did not produce much change. That which should be polished was polished, and the rooms were kept fresh and inviting. Little customs were continued. "The whole house was a mass of bloom," remembered Nell Wilson McAdoo. "Every morning the 'flower man,' with his little rubber-tired wagon, passed quietly from one room to another, watering the ferns and plants and replenishing the vases with fresh-cut flowers from the White House greenhouses. On his heels came another little wagon with wood for the fireplaces. The 'wood man' was a genius—his fires were laid with geometric precision and skill; they always burned cheerily and never smoked or sulked."[15]

The dying remains of one of those wonderful fires smoldered in the fireplace of the State Dining Room one cold winter night during the war when Secret Service agent Ed Starling, on late duty, saw that the coast was clear and took himself to the hearth to benefit from the last rays of warmth. He was in a melancholy mood. "It is my job to go over the whole house at times, say once or twice a week," he wrote to his mother. "I wish you could see the rooms—they are lovely, but haunted, I think . . . . We are very careful now and watch everything that goes on, and it is therefore hard on me both physically and mentally, but especially physically. I pray every night for the President's safety, and for courage and wisdom for myself in performing my duty."[16]

Life During the War

The war at sea began quickly, for the Navy, unlike the Army, had been built into a considerable force during the Roosevelt and Taft years. Mines laid in the North Sea crippled Germany's underwater campaign. An extensive convoy system linked the United States and Europe, allowing the effective transport of troops.

Americans became involved in the fighting on land more slowly. The first troops landed in France two months after Wilson's war message, and in the autumn Americans began to arrive in large numbers. Still they saw little significant action until the next year. On June 5, 1918, some 27,500 American soldiers plunged into a counteroffensive against a part of the mighty thrust of the Germans toward Paris. The battle took place at Belleau Wood, 56 miles from Paris; more than half the Americans died in this signal victory for the Allies.

To the citizens at home, that sudden bloodshed followed a winter and spring of relative calm. Wilson had opened the new year with his Fourteen Points Address, which evoked nearly universal praise. These were his personal requirements for peace. Through the spring American troops poured into Europe, 300,000 by March, 1,750,000 by the close of summer. They shored up Allied forces weakened by the withdrawal of Russian troops by the new Soviet government.

When the President was at the White House, which was most of the time, he was usually at work in his study. There with the assistance of Colonel House he wrote the Fourteen Points, and there he carried on his private conferences with officials of his wartime regime. He relaxed in several ways, the most regularly with golf. Walking was a special pleasure. To the despair of the Secret Service he walked frequently in the ice and snow of the winter of 1918. When the weather warmed he spent time on the *Mayflower*, traveling up and down the Potomac, sometimes going ashore with Mrs. Wilson. The two were nearly always together or within calling distance of each other.

"Washington society has given itself up to war and charity work," proclaimed the *Washington Post* just before Christmas 1917. "The President and Mrs. Wilson have shown a keen and active interest in all these benefit affairs, Mrs. Wilson not only lending her name for many, but frequently attending them in person, the President accompanying her when his time permits." When they went to these charity parties they remained only briefly, normally about 15 minutes. The President shook hands and walked through the company, while Mrs. Wilson, arm in arm with the hostess, did the same. They apparently grew quite proficient at these short appearances, for they were reviewed in the press with considerable praise. To their custom of presenting themselves at patriotic functions they soon added the theatrical element of taking everyone by surprise when they entered, a twist that frustrated the usual advance security measures of the Secret Service. [17]

At the White House, entertaining remained rather simple, although it increased in 1918. Wilson, having announced his Fourteen Points, started at once selling them to the politicians. Small luncheons and dinners took place at the White House several days each week, through the winter and spring. To keep the mood intimate, Mrs. Wilson sent to storage the great dining table in the State Dining Room and resurrected from the kitchen an old circular dining table probably dating from the administration of Ulysses S. Grant. Around it, the President's company enjoyed cozy meals.

The principal diversion for Wilson during the war was the vaudeville theater, Keith's, where he and a party of friends were likely to be found any Saturday night. Always the audience made a great show of affection as he entered, and the orchestra played in his honor. At home later he sometimes amused his companions by imitating the actors he had seen, taking particular delight in mimicking the tap dancers and singers. Moving pictures were regularly shown, usually in the East Room. Wilson was a movie fan, an admirer of Charlie Chaplin and the other comedy stars of the early days of film. Not even the small furor over his screening of *Birth of a Nation* in the White House during his first term dampened his enthusiasm for movies. [18]

What might be classed as great entertainments were not held at the White House during the war. Even the traditional New Year's Reception was called off in 1918, and, according to the press, "The Chief executive and his family spent a very quiet New Year's day, with only the members of the family about them, and no official glamour." To combat rising complaints that the lack of activity showed a negative attitude about the war, the First Lady resumed her teas late in 1917 on a reduced scale. She used the Red Room, inviting the wives of prominent visitors to the city and also women who had left their cards at the northwest gate. Wartime security prohibited the traditional leaving of cards in the entrance hall. [19]

Mrs. Wilson stood at the Red Room door with the buildings commissioner, who announced for her. A tea table was set up before the window to the south portico, so that the porch could provide access for the butlers to replenish it. Edith Benham, the social secretary, poured tea and coffee. Some effort was made to hide the fact that the guests were carefully watched from the moment they entered the gate until their departure. The teas seldom lasted more than an hour. By most standards they were somewhat odd; the women liked them, however, because a glimpse inside the White House during wartime was rare.

Helping the War Effort

It was the Wilsons' wish that they be seen as a model American family. If he opposed seeing his family in the newspapers in peacetime, he made no opposition to their participation in public programs during the war. Margaret Wilson sang to raise money for the troops; the other women of the family took part in activities of a more domestic nature. Mrs. Wilson was asked by Herbert Hoover, one of Wilson's wartime dollar-a-year-men and head of the Food Administration, to demonstrate publicly her support of his programs to conserve food. She readily and proudly agreed, taking the required oath and displaying the colorful card signifying her acceptance in one of the windows of the entrance hall. Mrs. Jaffray was accordingly informed, and the White House observed "wheatless Mondays" and "meatless Tuesdays," whether for formal dinners or family meals.

There were also "gasless days." Thus the Pierce-Arrow and other White House cars were temporarily stored on blocks. The coaches, long unused except by Mrs. Jaffray in her expeditions to the Central Market, were rolled from the stable and polished for service. The President greatly enjoyed afternoon drives in the open carriage. Carriages had by no means vanished from Washington's streets, for high government officials still used them, and many people preferred them to cars for afternoon drives. In Wilson's case the carriage was always followed by a motorcar filled with Secret Service men.

The carriage was not the only wartime symbol to appear at the White House. A flock of sheep was installed on the south grounds to save the manpower that was required to keep so large a lawn mowed. The sheep became at once perhaps the most frequently photographed creatures on earth. At its peak the flock numbered 18, producing enough wool to provide two pounds for auction in each of the states, Kansas paying the top price of $10,000. The total of $52,823 was presented to the Red Cross. As for the flock's use in cutting grass, the gardener, Charles Henlock, grumbled to a reporter years later that "the best thing those sheep ever did was to eat up Mrs. Taft's hedge, along with a few other things." He had no use for them: "They were a nuisance, those sheep—but they were very pretty."[20]

On quiet evenings the family gathered in the oval room upstairs, described in the *New York Tribune* during the war as "large, with massive furniture, upholstered in rose color . . . the real 'living room' of the family, and made cosily livable by a hundred intimate touches, of books and family pictures and friendly oil lamps on the tables and a cheery wood wire crackling on the hearth." The reporter, who supposedly had entrée to this intimate place, found the Wilsons' private life to be "as domestic as any in America."[21]

As ever, home life revolved entirely around Woodrow Wilson. Mrs. Wilson doted on him, and his daughters vied for his affection. Jessie, his favorite, had two children, Francis and Ellen; Nell had a daughter, Eleanor. Cary Grayson was ever present, now with a young son, Gordon, in whom the President took delight. Helen Bones suffered a nervous breakdown in the winter of 1918; this was kept quiet, and she recovered under the devoted care of Maggie Rogers and Jennie Crowley. Fewer cousins visited, both because of the complications created by the war and because some of them did not get along with the new First Lady, but Wilson could not be happy without relatives nearby. His brother Joseph was a frequent visitor from Baltimore. The Axsons of Georgia were more or less replaced by the Virginia relatives of Edith Wilson. Secure and comfortable among his kin, Woodrow Wilson read the Bible aloud, and Mrs. Wilson soothed him by reading selections of his favorite poems. The assembled women knitted socks and sweaters and helmet covers for the Red Cross, while the men talked of war, family, and public affairs. From this happy domesticity the President often removed himself late at night for hours of work in his study.

Armistice

The summer of 1918 was a summer of horror and victory. After the Battle of Belleau Wood in June the tide turned in favor of the Allies. Bloodbath followed bloodbath as the Allies, strengthened by nearly two million American troops, hammered away at the Western Front. The drive was climaxed beginning in late September with the 40-day battle along the Meuse River and in the Argonne Forest. One million two-hundred thousand American soldiers took part, and 177,000 were killed, wounded, or captured.

In the second week of November, the Germans requested a cease-fire. This was followed by the abdication of the kaiser and the establishment of a democratic republic. Courting American favor, the Germans wished to save their country from invasion by reaching a peace through the least painful means, Wilson's Fourteen Points. When the reports reached Washington about midmorning on Thursday, November 7, they were misinterpreted as meaning the end of the war. One citizen remembered "the false report of peace" and how the capital became a "riot scene, with shouting celebrators pouring from every building, as if on a pre-concerted signal. The streets were filled with battalions of marchers shrieking their joy to the accompaniment of whistles and bells."

The maids called Mrs. Wilson to the windows just before noon to see "a jubilant throng" storming the White House, "with bands playing and hats thrown into the air." She hurried to the President's study, threw open the doors, and told him that he was being called out by the people to celebrate the armistice. Wilson assured her that there was no armistice, which she later said she already knew, but she was disappointed that he would not present himself to the people. Later in the day she went for a drive in an open car and was mobbed by well-wishers.

When the mistake became known, the memorable Thursday of triumph was followed by three days of tense silence, as the representatives of Germany and the Allied nations met aboard a railroad car in the Forest of Compiègne. Sunday evening, after a family dinner, Wilson retired to his study. A nervous Edith Wilson followed him there and asked for something to do, whereupon the President handed her a stack of messages that he had found in The Drawer. Since she often decoded official messages for Wilson, this was easy work, and she and her brother Randolph Bolling went to the west hall, where the lighted office windows outside spangled the dark autumn night.

Seated at the large work table where Edith Benham wrote her notes and addressed White House invitations, they began their decoding, taking each completed one in turn to the President down the hall. They finished at 1 a.m., the calendar having turned to November 11, 1918. Two hours later the husband and wife were wakened with the message announcing that the armistice was signed. "The guns were stilled!" Mrs. Wilson wrote. "The World War has ended!" But she never forgot that at the time, she and the President "stood mute—unable to grasp the full significance" of what they had been told.[22]

Later, at the breakfast table, Wilson wrote in pencil a message transmitted to the American people: "The armistice was signed this morning. Everything for which America fought has been accomplished. It will now be our fortunate duty to assist by example, by sober, friendly counsel and material aid in the establishment of just democracy throughout the world."

The Quest Begins

Faced with the imminence of a peace conference, Wilson stood fast in his commitment to achieve the high goals of justice for which the war had been fought. In the week prior to the armistice his party suffered disastrous defeats in the congressional elections. This was brought on in large measure by Wilson himself, who had made an impolitic personal appeal to the people to vote Democratic to demonstrate to the nations of the world that the American people had faith in their President. Edith Wilson had advised him not to issue the statement. His biographers consider it the beginning of the tragic course his life was now to take.

As early as the summer of 1918, when the American troops made their first impact on the front, Wilson had debated whether or not to go in person to the peace conference or send diplomats, in the traditional way. By the time of the armistice he had decided to go, in spite of opposition from some of the advisers he trusted the most. He had always had great faith in his ability as a salesman of ideas; he thought he had a mandate to go, in defense of humankind.

At a dinner party on November 18, 1918, at the home of the secretary of state, Wilson announced his intention to attend the conference in Paris. Four days later the secretary of the Navy authorized $10,000 for "fitting up appropriately" the USS *George Washington*, a confiscated German liner of the same name, which had been converted into an American troop-transport vessel. She had carried 50,000 troops to Europe. Many repairs were needed in the passenger quarters. On the 25th the presidential flags were transferred from the *Mayflower* to the *George Washington*. Captain Edward McCauley, Jr., in command of the

George Washington, reported "feverish activity" in preparing his ship for her "most historic voyage."[23]

Rumors flew through the White House. Who would be asked to go along? A small number were selected in confidence, Edith Benham and Cary Grayson being probably the first to be asked. Ike Hoover was invited to go and manage the official residence in Paris; Colonel Arthur Brooks was to be the President's valet, and Susie Boothe would be Mrs. Wilson's maid; Charles Swem, the stenographer, was on the list, along with Gilbert F. Close, also from the Executive Office; Joseph E. Murphy and Ed Starling were among the eight Secret Service men who would remain close to the President.

In spite of Wilson's request for simplicity, the preparations were elaborate. Three orchestras were signed on, and Captain McCauley ordered some 200 reels of popular movies; a hotel chef, assistants, and great quantities of fine food and drink came aboard, but the Navy drew the line when an ice-cream freezer was requested, because no official policy justified the presence of ice-cream freezers aboard Navy ships. Although the President probably had little idea of the extent to which his ship was being fitted out, his detractors condemned the luxurious arrangements. A congressman's wife wrote in her diary of the "amazing trip to Europe . . . preparations for which exceed in grandeur those for the Field of the Cloth of Gold or the Queen of Sheba's visit to King Solomon. The apes and peacocks alone are lacking, and there are people unkind enough to say that even they will go along in one form or another."[24]

Toward opposition to his going to Paris, Wilson increasingly turned with an anger approaching righteous indignation. He was resolute in his mission. On December 2, 1918, he addressed the Congress in advance of his departure and received a chilly reception. Had he sought the advice or counsel of the legislators, the reaction might have been different, but his aloofness made many enemies, who accused him of being drunk with the special wartime powers they had granted him, of thinking that the peace was his alone to achieve.

To Wilson the grandeur of distant horizons overwhelmed most of the concern he might normally have had over the volatile political debate growing around him. He addressed himself to the work ahead, determining to attend to the home fires later. The greater challenge lay over the ocean. Sustained by deep religious convictions and a faith of iron, Wilson maintained his course.

On the evening of December 3 the Wilsons, Dr. Grayson, and the most intimate members of their party dined in the State Dining Room. When the coffee cups and liqueur glasses were set aside in the Red Room, the group left in automobiles from the north portico and proceeded to Union Station along streets crowded with spectators. They went to their berths aboard a private train headed to Hoboken, New Jersey, where the *George Washington* lay at anchor.

At 8:10 a.m. on December 4 the President and Mrs. Wilson stepped aboard the ship, waving to tens of thousands of spectators on the shore. Captain McCauley marked the time, 10:17 a.m., when the *George Washington* left the pier. He soon ordered a 21-gun salute. Other ships and smaller craft turned the morning into a jubilee, shooting up sprays of water, blowing whistles, cranking sirens, and ringing bells. Six airplanes flew overhead, diving playfully like airborne dolphins, until the *George Washington* met her sea escort at 11:30 a.m.

Suddenly the mood became serious. The flagship *Pennsylvania* and 15 other ships stood in formation to receive the presidential vessel. All but five of the ships would accompany Wilson to Europe. Eight hours later, at 7:30 p.m., as the President sat down to dinner in Mrs. Wilson's suite, Captain McCauley, on the bridge, wrote in his log, "Last lighthouse vanishes from sight."[25]

The Statesman

In an age of rapid transportation it is difficult to imagine the President being away from the White House for long. Wilson was gone two months on the first trip to the peace conference and four months on the second. His extended absence eroded his political base and undermined the power his Presidency had developed during the war. No subsequent President would repeat the mistake of appearing to abandon the home fires.

On June 28, 1919, the peace conference at the Palace of Versailles ended, and the President boarded the *George Washington* to return home. On July 8 he received a hero's reception in New York, and that evening an estimated 10,000 people greeted his private train at Union Station. Photographs show the effects of fatigue and a bout with illness in Wilson's face. Mrs. Wilson found the reception back home "exhilarating"; but she also felt, "how good it was to reach Washington and see the White House limousine, with Robinson at the wheel. And how good to be surrounded, once more, by the simple dignity of the White House, spick and span with cool linen on the chairs and flowers everywhere."[26]

Significant opposition to the peace treaty, and particularly to the part establishing the League of Nations, was reported to Wilson in Paris before the treaty was signed. When he got home he found his enemies not only well organized, but also strengthened by circumstance: The country was suffering from inflation; industry was cursed with strikes; in parts of the North, where the manufacturers had reduced their labor forces, there were race riots against the southern blacks who had swelled the labor supply during wartime, then remained to compete with whites for the jobs that were available. Fear of the Bolshevism that had taken over Russia gripped the American people, inspiring a general distrust of foreigners and encouraging a return to isolationism, the antithesis of what President Wilson espoused. Wilson's archenemy, Senator Henry Cabot Lodge, tied up the treaty ratification process with long hearings in his Senate Foreign Relations Committee.

Wilson's efforts to hurry the Senate along met the immovable wall of the "irreconcilables," four Democrats and six Republicans who led the fight against the treaty. In desperation, Wilson decided to assemble the Senate Foreign Relations Committee at the White House. This would be the first time the committee had ever been privileged as a body to question the President of the United States. That the President did not select the Executive Office for the meeting is not particularly surprising, for he seldom went there, but his use of the East Room made it clear that his meeting was to be a spectacle, of the sort he had experienced in France during the peace conference.

It was considered a historic event, and numerous reporters attended. Joe Tumulty offered comfortable accommodations for the newsmen, providing desks along the walls of the transverse hall outside the state parlors. The committee members began to arrive at ten. Assembled in the East Room, seated on the gilt chairs, they awaited the President, who entered and stood before them. He presented his argument for the treaty and the League of Nations; they listened without uttering a word. When he had finished, questions came from the floor. After 3½ hours, Wilson invited the senators to join him at the other end of the hall for lunch.[27]

Little was actually accomplished, and the President lost some credibility when, during the question period, he revealed a lack of communication with the Department of State in vital areas. Alarmed over the apparent growth of the opposition, Wilson determined to take his cause to the people on a cross-country speaking tour. Dr. Grayson protested, reminding the President that he had not yet recovered his strength from the peace conference. No man of 60, said Grayson, could totally ignore his health, and Wilson's had never been strong. The President remained steadfast. The admiral was so disturbed by this that he confronted Wilson one last time, rapping on the study door early one morning. As he entered, Wilson spoke first: "I know what you have come for. I do not want to do anything foolhardy but the League of Nations is now in its crisis, and if it fails, I hate to think what will happen to the world . . . . I cannot put my personal safety, my health, in the balance against my duty—I must go."

The President then put down his pen, rose, walked to the window and looked out toward the Washington Monument. When he turned around, his eyes were moist. Grayson remembered, "There was lead where my heart ought to be, but I knew the debate was closed, that there was nothing I could do except to go with him and take such care of him as I could."[28]

Wichita

A private train was assembled at Union Station, with Pullman and dining cars to accommodate some 100 reporters, in addition to presidential staff. The President and Mrs. Wilson occupied the last car, which contained its own kitchen, two bedrooms, and a drawing room outfitted with stuffed chairs, soft carpeting, and a galaxy of silk-shaded electric bracket lamps. In addition to the cook, the Wilsons' immediate personal staff consisted of Colonel Brooks and Sigrid Nulsson, the former White House cook, who had replaced Susie Boothe as Mrs. Wilson's personal maid. Space was tight, with the attendants sleeping in the car where they could; Brooks bedded down on the drawing room sofa, the others on pallets on the floor, while Wilson and his wife occupied the two bedrooms. Glass doors divided the drawing room from the rear platform from which Wilson was to make his speeches.[29]

The President boarded the train in the evening of September 3, 1919. Dr. Grayson was already in open conflict with Joe Tumulty, trying to make him trim the heavy schedule of speeches. But Tumulty had his orders from the Democratic Party and would not yield; Grayson never forgave him. On Grayson's orders the train halted now and then in the countryside, and the doctor accompanied the President and Mrs. Wilson on a walk along a quiet road. Grayson knew very well that the journey was "a prolonged agony of physical pain," and he believed Mrs. Wilson knew it, too. Still the train moved on. The local committees crowded into the presidential car at every town; for about half an hour handshaking, cigar smoke, picture taking, and noise pervaded the drawing room. Then the President appeared on the platform and delivered a speech, into which, each time, it seemed he poured his soul.

In Montana, Wilson began suffering asthma attacks and splitting headaches. By the time the train rolled into Colorado his headaches had become so severe that he was almost blinded by them. On the tracks late one night at Wichita, Kansas, Grayson was awakened to go to Wilson's room in the next car, where he found the President "on the verge of a complete breakdown." Neither the doctor nor the First Lady had any intention of permitting Wilson one further speech. The President at last admitted that he had stretched his endurance to the limit.

At 11 o'clock, on the Friday morning of September 26, 1919, the train left for Washington at top speed. All speeches and other appearances had been canceled, and newspapers everywhere learned that the President was ill. Exactly 48 hours later, as the church bells of Washington tolled 11 a.m., the train slid into Union Station. Wilson heard the bells and decided to go to church. Grayson and Mrs. Wilson, close at his side, persuaded him otherwise. They hurried him to the Pierce-Arrow, where Margaret Wilson waited.

Ike Hoover, at the White House when they arrived, observed that the President "appeared no worse than when he left, except that he looked a little peaked and seemed to have lost some of his spirit. . . . there was apparently nothing alarming about his condition." But Hoover and others who had been in the household with him in Paris had already been noticing since spring certain peculiarities in his conduct, such as loss of memory and talking to himself, which they later identified as signals that something was wrong.[30]

Doctor Grayson prescribed a strict regimen of walking, golfing, and resting. At first the President responded favorably, and a rapid recovery was predicted. But four days after the return from Wichita, on the morning of October 2, 1919, Ike Hoover, at the big rolltop in the ushers' office, answered the house telephone and heard Mrs. Wilson say in a soft but urgent voice, "Please get Doctor Grayson, the President is very sick." The chief usher called Dr. Grayson, then went upstairs in the elevator and found to his surprise that every door into the long central corridor was closed. This he had never seen before. He had been able to tell from the mechanism on his own desk that the telephone call had been made from Edith Benham's desk in the west hall, but there was no sign of Mrs. Wilson there. Several of the maids went about their dusting of tabletops in the hall, unaware that anything might be wrong. "I was helpless," wrote Hoover, "so far as being of any assistance was concerned," for he dared not rap on the bedroom door.

When Grayson arrived he went directly to that door. Without knocking he attempted to turn the knob, only to find the door locked. He knocked softly. The door opened to admit him, then closed again. Grayson found Wilson prostrate on the white-tile floor of his bathroom, his head resting on a pillow brought there by his wife, and his form covered by a blanket she had spread over him after his collapse. "We lifted the President into his bed," remembered Edith Wilson. "He had suffered a stroke, paralyzing the left side of his body. An arm and one leg were useless, but, thank God, the brain was clear and untouched."[31]

Surrogate?

Woodrow Wilson was to be an invalid for the rest of his life. From the morning of his stroke at the White House until the middle of November he lay helpless in the Lincoln bed, as his beard grew full and white. Every need was attended to by Dr. Grayson, Mrs. Wilson, or the nurse, Ruth Powderly, for whom patient, wife, and doctor soon developed a genuine affection. A few weeks after Christmas 1919, Wilson began the arduous task of learning to walk despite the impaired left leg. His speech returned, although at first he had mumbled. Even at his lowest ebb, he yearned to reenter the battle for the treaty. In exile from the reality of that fight, he coldly rejected his colleagues' pleas for compromise. The isolation of the White House worked at its full power.

Told by Grayson that any excitement would be like "turning a knife in an open wound," that his nerves were "crying out for rest," Edith Wilson placed herself firmly between her husband and the world. She began what she later called her "stewardship," one of the strangest episodes in the history of the White House. On her orders, all presidential business was brought first to her. "I studied every paper, sent from the different Secretaries or Senators, and tried to digest and present in tabloid form the things that, despite my vigilance, had to go to the President. I, myself, never made a single decision regarding the disposition of public affairs. The only decision that was mine," she wrote, "was what was important and what was not, and the *very* important decision of when to present matters to my husband."

What she did was perfectly natural for a pragmatic, if not remarkably wise, woman. A crisis was at hand: Her husband needed rest, yet he could not reveal his deteriorated condition to the world. He must remain President and see the treaty through. He expected to recover completely. Mrs. Wilson had witnessed enough of politicians to know that any of Wilson's political allies would readily grasp a regency if he could—and she soon saw proof of this when the secretary of state called a Cabinet meeting on his own. She had to act alone, although she knew she would be criticized for acting as if she were an official of the United States government. His life was hers to save; she would not let others kill him in the name of duty. In her memoirs she is candid in justifying herself: "Woodrow Wilson was first my beloved husband whose life I was trying to save, fighting with my back to the wall—after that he was the President of the United States."

So conspicuous was Wilson's absence from the public eye that an official inquiry became inevitable. This emerged when the hostile Senate Foreign Relations Committee debated the troubles with Mexico. The secretary of state testified that he had not discussed Mexican affairs with Wilson since his return from Paris. In the resulting furor, Senator Lodge questioned whether the President was competent to deal with the situation. The committee requested that it be allowed to send representatives for an interview and to its surprise received an appointment for the next day. Wilson knew that if he denied this visit he would fan an already dangerous fire of curiosity.

The afternoon of the appointment, December 5, 1919, the White House seemed to be under siege by newsmen. No pretense masked the purpose of the committee's visit. The Mexican question was virtually irrelevant. The two representatives arrived promptly, one Wilson's esteemed ally, Senator Gilbert M. Hitchcock, Democrat and Senate manager of the fight to ratify the treaty; the other was Senator Albert Fall, Republican, a colorful and extravagant Westerner who was no friend of Wilson's or of his policies. Mrs. Wilson led the delegation to the foot of the Lincoln bed, where the President lay carefully banked in pillows, with the covers arranged to conceal the useless limbs while displaying the able right side. Edith Wilson took notes with pad and pencil. The interview was brief. As the senators left, Senator Fall squeezed Wilson's hand and said, "Well, Mr. President, we have all been praying for you."

"Which way, Senator?" was Woodrow Wilson's famous reply, at which Fall laughed heartily, wrote Mrs. Wilson, "as if the witticism had been his own."[32]

The Wilson Era Ends

In 1920 the League of Nations became a reality, meeting first in Paris on January 16, while the Senate of the United States still furiously debated whether or not to approve American participation. Wilson followed the proceedings from the sidelines. Those whom he received were warned not to excite him; allowed relative peace, he gradually improved. He walked only for exercise. Most of the time he was moved about in a high-backed "rolling chair," not the kind used by hospitals but an ample wicker vehicle from the boardwalk at Atlantic City. Most days he was wheeled from his study at noon into the elevators, then to the East Room, where the curtains were drawn for the screening of a movie. Douglas Fairbanks had presented a large theater-type projector to the President. After the show—sometimes after several of them—Wilson was wheeled back to the elevator, then ate his lunch upstairs. When spring brought warm days, he ate downstairs in the State Dining Room, and spent time after lunch on the south portico, where the canvas awnings were drawn up to admit abundant sunlight. When Prohibition became law in 1920, he obediently banished alcohol from the White House, depriving himself of the occasional scotch he enjoyed.

Political allies in the treaty fight were calling daily by late January. He enjoyed advising them and hearing them report on the battle in the Senate. But when the treaty failed on March 19, 1920, a pall of gloom fell over the White House that even the efforts of the First Lady could not lift. One year less a few days remained of his Presidency; seldom a week went by that he did not make some move in behalf of the League. When the Democratic Convention assembled, he was not there, nor did he speak for the candidates James M. Cox and Franklin D. Roosevelt, beyond giving them an old man's blessing, and issuing to all the voters an appeal to cast their ballots only for men who would support the treaty.

"He was a figure pitiful beyond words," remembered Mrs. Jaffray of Wilson in his last year in the White House. "I can shut my eyes now and see him being helped down the corridor by Mrs. Wilson and one of the doctors, each step a silent and painful one, as wooden and lifeless as if a mechanical man were walking through the hall." Hoover remembered that Wilson "never had any more actual initiative" after his stroke. "We conspired in every way," wrote the kindhearted Ed Starling, "to give him comfort and solace. When he was to go for a ride some of us organized a group to stand at the gate as he returned, and we told them to cheer as he passed through." Looking out the car window, Wilson studied the figures on the sidewalk, and his eyes glistened with tears.[33]

36

Limelight

The Republicans returned to power in the presidential election of 1920, with the victory of Warren G. Harding of Ohio, one of the senators who had vociferously opposed the treaty. Isolated more than ever in the confines of the White House, the Wilsons waited out the year 1920 and the first two months of 1921. The President's condition had stopped improving. He was feeble and much occupied with his books and papers, though lacking the mental power that had been the key to his greatness. In December 1920 he was awarded the Nobel Peace Prize, and his spirits rose. Remorse yielded to genuine gratification, in which even in good times he had seldom indulged himself.

Edith Wilson found diversion from this almost oppressive situation by planning to remodel the house they had acquired on S Street. She had little money to spend. The Blue Room curtains were being replaced; she and Lilly Carter, the White House seamstress, salvaged enough of the dark blue damask from the old ones to upholster a suite of furniture for the new house. Her bedroom furniture from the *George Washington*, cream-colored reproductions of Louis XVI pieces, were presented to her, and she acquired a low-post bed that she said was like the Lincoln bed, so that her husband's room would seem familiar to him.

As these things took place, the world seemed to pass the Wilsons by. March 4, 1921, inauguration day, came at last, a sunny, cold Friday. Years later, when writing her memoirs, Mrs. Wilson barely concealed her bitterness toward the new President and his wife, painting them as *déclassé*, and through her icy words, herself as tense and confused.

Wilson struggled through the day's festivities, hobbling along with his cane on one side and the strong arm of Dr. Grayson on the other. When the ceremony was over, he joined Mrs. Wilson in the Pierce-Arrow for the ride home. The car moved away from the crowds, and was suddenly alone, speeding down a vacant Massachusetts Avenue. Wilson laughed as his wife vented her anger over the Hardings and over the fact that so little had been done to honor Woodrow Wilson. But his laughter, so rare of late, remained as infectious as ever, and she too was laughing by the time the car turned into S Street, where, to their deep satisfaction, a large crowd waited, cheering.[1]

Every Inch a President

At the White House, President Harding and his wife entered the north door at 2:45 p.m. With 21 friends they sat down at the table in the State Dining Room and quickly devoured a chicken salad luncheon ordered by Mrs. Wilson, then rose and hurried out through the north portico, across the lawn, and onto the reviewing stand on Pennsylvania Avenue. It was a smaller parade than usual. "If I were to have wholly my own way there would not be any inaugural celebration at all," Warren G. Harding had written as President-elect. "I would prefer to go to Washington simple, then go to the Capitol and take the oath of office and proceed to the Executive Mansion and go to work." All the festivities of the day were modified to suit him. Rather than the traditional inaugural ball, a late-night dance and supper were held in Georgetown, private affairs limited to the official family and the Republican circle.[2]

At sunset the President left the reviewing stand and returned to the White House, where he found the state rooms thick with people. Republican triumph was hard to conceal; Harding's wishes had imposed only a flimsy lid on the bubbling pot. He was tall and handsome, age 55, with silver white hair and a brilliant smile, the worldly antithesis of the Princeton professor, the stern Presbyterian. Moving among the guests, the new President might have known them all personally, so genuine seemed his warmth, so consuming his friendliness. In the electrical shimmer of the chandeliers, he confirmed what was often said about him: He looked every inch a President.

Harding had been sold to the American people like a vacuum cleaner or an automobile, through the newspapers. A newspaper publisher himself, he appeared rather suddenly as a candidate, and his freshness was a good measure of his appeal. From the partisan fury of postwar debate he had emerged calm and optimistic, appealing to his fellow citizens with a promise that he would return the United States to what it had been before the war. He patterned his campaign, like his public image, on McKinley, the last old-style President, and greeted the world at home on his front porch. Newsmen flocked to listen at his feet.

Few Presidents have gone to the White House with such adulation as was heaped upon Warren G. Harding. Born poor, he had struggled to achieve success in business; he was typical of what Americans liked to think was "American" in a man. He was neither blue-blooded nor intellectual but a log-cabin sort of President, and his speech writers developed his public stature along that line, giving him words to deliver in his rolling, resonant voice: "America's present need is not heroics but healing; not nostrums, but normalcy; not revolution, but restoration; not agitation, but adjustment; not surgery, but serenity; not the dramatic, but the dispassionate; not experiment, but equipoise; not submergence in internationality, but sustainment in triumphant nationality."[3]

In the edge of the limelight stood the "Duchess," as Harding called his wife. The sharp-eyed Florence Kling Harding was unable to conceal her aggressiveness by genteel manners, any more than she could mask with powder, rouge, and a wavy frame of marcelled hair the fact that she was five years her husband's senior. Mrs. Harding was unmistakably 60. That she idolized her husband was clear, and it was widely believed that she was perpetually suspicious of his moral strength, at least where other women were concerned. She was a good talker—a valuable talent in the political world—and could make herself known in any company. But her boldness was balanced by uncertainty, particularly in society. Easily offended, she confided to Alice Roosevelt Longworth that for years she had kept a little red book of names of people who had crossed her or her husband in Washington and that this would be consulted in all social planning for the White House.[4]

Florence Harding had been preoccupied with Warren Harding for half her years. She had met and married him at 30, when she, the daughter of banker Amos Kling, the richest man in Marion, Ohio, was a divorcée living with her young son in rented rooms in her hometown, teaching piano. Nor had she strayed from Harding's side for the three decades prior to his election to the Presidency. She helped him run the Marion *Star*; she managed their big, cheery house on the best street in Marion, and was a highly accomplished hostess. Perhaps merely to tease him, she claimed considerable credit for his success. Soon after Harding arrived at the White House, a member of the office staff overheard her quip, "Well, Warren Harding. I have got you the Presidency; what are you going to do with it?"[5]

Standards

As personalities, the Hardings were more like the presidential couples of the 19th century than like their 20th-century predecessors. They were ordinary people, not distinguished by aristocratic pretensions or sanctified by ideals any more exalted than the patriotism one might expect from any President. History often has been unkind in appraising them, and the usual primary sources are sometimes undependable. Memoirs written by their contemporaries are seldom harsh, and they are negative only if recast in the light of the scandals that surfaced after the President's death. In this sense, as sources, they are misinterpreted. The Teapot Dome oil schemes and the other activities of his associates tainted Harding's reputation. His dignity suffered further from stories of his extramarital love affairs.

The Hardings survive most vividly in the pages of the newspapers and magazines. In a postwar America hungry to know itself, journalists found that Harding in the White House provided an excellent subject for analysis. Often the view is close up, enriched by examples of presidential home life, which in other administrations had been carefully screened from newsmen. The famous newspaper columnist Mark Sullivan remembered him in later years as "conscientious according to his own standards—which is the only way anybody can be conscientious; and he was irked, a little shamed, by the compromises he had frequently to make between what he liked to do and what his office obliged him to do, or what he felt was due to his office." Sullivan liked to cite an example of the dichotomy of man and President in an anecdote that would have been shocking had it been reported at the time: The two were sitting in rockers on the south portico, Sullivan recalled, when the President "wished to offer me a drink. He, with Mrs. Harding, took me into their bedroom, saying they felt that since the national prohibition was in effect, they ought not to drink in the ordinary rooms of the White House, nor offer drinks to their friends, but that in their bedroom they might properly follow their personal standards."[6]

One of Harding's earliest acts was to open the White House to the public—it had been closed since the beginning of the war. People came in droves, entering daily at nine through the East Wing and ascending from the basement corridor to the main floor, where they viewed the great ivory and gilt East Room. There, after the renovation of 1902, the tours had usually stopped. But under Harding the doors to the state parlors and the dining room were opened. Visitors were allowed to peer into them across velvet ropes, as they had sometimes been able to do in the 19th century. Harding revived another custom practiced intermittently throughout the 19th century—that of going to the state floor just before lunch on weekdays, except when the Cabinet was meeting, and making an unannounced visit to the East Room to greet the tourists there. Crowds usually collected, hoping the President would appear. A record was kept of the number of people he met each time.

The state rooms had not changed essentially since McKim's renovation of 1902, when the ideals of the beaux arts movement were still fresh. Twenty years later the rooms seemed relics of the imperial White House of the prewar era, and visitors found them cold and forbidding. Small table lamps, sofa and chair pillows, footstools, and a few comfortable chairs added through the years contrasted to everything else. The earlier sparse furnishings were still placed in the same stiff configurations, constantly renewed by obedient hands.

Broadloom carpeting and heavy draperies of dark damask lined with sateen and interlined with flannel muffled voices and footsteps, contributing to that silence which outsiders always find remarkable in the White House. Although visitors sometimes strained to hear voices from other rooms, they also perceived nearly complete absence of animation. There were no guides unless one of Ike Hoover's assistants could spare a few minutes. Visitors wandered along a more or less prescribed path, with a policeman stationed in the entrance hall, but only one or two circulating elsewhere, usually out of sight.

The Hardings left the state rooms as they found them. Most of the glossy white woodwork was freshly painted, and only a few months before, Mrs. Wilson had replaced soiled window hangings and upholsteries with the same dark patterns and hues. She had been sensitive to criticism that implied that the White House had become run down and been turned into a hospital. President and Mrs. Harding, who found it spick-and-span, let it be known that "no reasonable expense should be spared in furnishing and maintaining the public rooms on a scale befitting the dignity of the Executive Mansion." But they had no plans to change things.[7]

Upstairs, the Hardings' views coincided: Economy was the first consideration. The family quarters were furnished by the government in only a basic way. Presidents had always brought furniture of their own to the White House to supplement what was there. The oval room and the blue sitting room (or "West Parlor") immediately west of it were almost empty. Ten days after the inauguration, the New York Times reported that Harding would use "home furnishings" both from his house in Marion and the one then being closed in Washington, as an "example of

Government economy." The usual congressional appropriation of $20,000 for an incoming administration would not be spent (although in fact the amount was transferred to the fund for official entertaining). Most of what came to the White House was from the Hardings' house on Wyoming Avenue. Most of the china and silver and many other small items were never to be unpacked; they were found still sealed in the same crates some years later when the Harding Memorial Association took inventory of the couple's belongings. The furniture seems to have been the usual variety of neo-Jacobean, neo-Queen Anne, and overstuffed "club" chairs such as one might have found in any upper-middle-class residence of the time.[8]

The Lincoln bed was moved from the presidential bedroom where Woodrow Wilson had used it to the guest room across the hall, and was replaced by the twin beds brought by President and Mrs. Taft. The gilded crown and blue damask side curtains that had graced the Lincoln bed were left hanging over the pair of smaller beds. For the first time, the press emphasized that the presidential bedroom was "their room," not just the President's. Note was taken of the "coziest davenport" pulled up to the fireplace, and of miniature portraits of Florence Harding and the President's parents on the mantel.[9]

Mrs. Harding's expensive clothing filled the closets of the dressing room adjoining the presidential bedroom. Additional shelves and cabinets were built for bags and hats. The bookcase in the bedroom was made into a shoe closet, with silk shirred over its glass doors to hide its contents. The rest of the First Lady's clothing was stored in tall Victorian wardrobes, which had long been hidden in the rooms and corridors of the attic floor. Mrs. Harding moved two of these to the blue sitting room to hold dresses and furs.

Through the most private part of the family quarters—the four rooms along the south side, beginning with the President's bedroom and ending with the study east of the oval room—the Hardings scattered their memorabilia, along with their furnishings. Pictures on tables, walls, and mantels depicted Harding giving speeches, receiving individuals and groups, playing golf, and walking along streets before adoring crowds. Here and there were mementos, such as a souvenir pipe in a stand, or an engraved loving cup. Mrs. Harding's memorabilia took the form of a few collections, particularly statuettes of elephants. Friends sent her elephants carved in ivory, or cast in brass; some were cheap souvenirs of distant places, others fine examples of craftsmanship. They paraded single-file in great numbers across mantel shelves, among the Hardings' pictures, and over tabletops.[10]

On Stage and in the Wings

Both the President and his wife enjoyed entertaining. Their political family and friends came to know the upstairs very well during Harding's time in office. If being invited to an official party downstairs was an important event in most people's lives, an invitation to the family quarters loomed even larger. The Hardings knew that their friends liked to go to the White House, and they extended their hospitality generously.

Entertaining upstairs usually took place in the central corridor, for a large crowd, or in the oval room, for the usual company of from 6 to 15. Oval room gatherings might spill over into the adjoining study. The President did not use the study as an office, although he sometimes scheduled private appointments there, or visited it in early morning to write letters. Normally, however, the study was simply another sitting room, still containing the furniture accumulated since 1902. Not even the carpet had been changed.

The library was furnished for comfort, its south windows shaded by green-striped awnings as well as the deep overhang of the portico. In the context of the laws of the day, some of Harding's conduct in the oval room was wholly illegal. Beside his poker table was a makeshift bar for mixing cocktails, or serving ale or wine; liquor was plentifully supplied, but the President's sources are not known. Harding's poker parties usually took place several times a week, with the men playing cards and the women chatting elsewhere in the room. The President liked one scotch in the evening, followed with ale if the night grew long. Mrs. Harding, sitting not far from the poker table, served the President's drinks. Harding was moderate with alcohol but not with tobacco. He smoked pipes, cigars, cigarettes. Sometimes his urge for tobacco was so strong that he would toss a whole cigarette into his mouth and chew it up. Much was written later about the seamy aspects of the poker parties. Secret Service agent Ed Starling, who was usually present or nearby, dismissed them as harmless, like the activities of small-town Elks clubs.[11]

Social life under Harding helped symbolize the return to "normalcy." Every abandoned White House tradition was revived, from the New Year's receptions to the Easter-egg rolling to garden parties in May. Weekly receptions brought hundreds of people to the house, under more democratic circumstances than ever before. The staff stood by in astonishment as Mrs. Harding added the names of heretofore unacceptable people; all First Ladies had included personal friends on their lists, but Florence Harding's guests were in some cases people of wealth who were snubbed by Washington society as being too racy or flashy. Notable

39. *President Warren G. Harding and Florence Kling Harding make a public appearance, ca. 1921.*

40. *Human interest news coverage: Harding and Laddie romp for the camera, south portico, 1922.*

41. *President and Mrs. Coolidge greet conventioneers, ca. 1924, on the grounds of the White House.*

42. *Grace Coolidge, by Howard Chandler Christy.*

43. *Calvin Coolidge, with his sons, Calvin, Jr., left,
and John, sits for a portrait on the south portico, 1924.*

44. *Steel and concrete replace Hoban's old attic story of wood in the spring and summer of 1927.*

45. *The central corridor of the new third floor. The railed opening let daylight into the family quarters.*

46. *Relics and reproductions: The Monroe Room upstairs, created by Mrs. Hoover in 1932.*

BOTH WHITE HOUSE COLLECTION

47. *Period interior: The Green Room, as decorated in 1928–30 by the furnishings advisory committee.*

48. *Lou Henry Hoover stands beneath the arched entrance to the rose garden, 1929.*

49. Beginning a tradition that prevails today, Herbert Hoover chooses the rose garden for his appearance at a 1932 conference of humanitarian organizations.

among these were the millionaire Edward B. McLean and his wife, Evalyn Walsh McLean. They were close friends of the Hardings', but not from among what Washingtonians—and White House servants—called the "made" people.[12]

In theory anyone who left a card on the silver tray at the north door soon received an invitation to a reception, tea, or some other event. This was not entirely true in practice. The lists were carefully composed by the social secretary, Laura Harlan, who culled calling cards. Miss Harlan, the daughter of Supreme Court Justice John Marshall Harlan, knew Washington society and had many means of tracing unfamiliar names. Having gone to work as an assistant under President Wilson, the tall, dark-haired Miss Harlan had been on hand while Mrs. Harding was trying to decide whom she wanted as secretary. Applicants eager for the post had worked on Harding's campaign, but Miss Harlan shortly had rendered herself indispensable to the First Lady. By mid-April 1921, she was social secretary of the White House.

Anyone who entered the northwest gate to call on the President or the First Lady had to be an innocent soul indeed to expect to see either. The caller on foot entered the north door, where a butler came out into the hall or even onto the porch and held out a silver tray, into which the caller dropped a card. The caller then departed. Making the call in an automobile was somewhat different. When an unexpected car entered the gate—which was always open except at night—it was likely to be that of a caller. Signaled from the ushers' room, a butler took the card tray out the north door and descended the steps to the driveway. The car halted beneath the portico. The silver tray was thrust through an open window to receive the card. Often the sole occupant of the automobile was a chauffeur or perhaps even a taxi driver, and it was perfectly acceptable for him to deliver several cards at once. Coachmen had done the same in other times. Sticklers for correctness still dog-eared the upper left corner of the cards when delivering them in person.[13]

Though the President and Mrs. Harding were informal, even playful, they fit comfortably into the social framework provided for them. This may be more a comment on the system than on the Hardings themselves. Underlying all forms of White House social events was the need to cope gracefully with large numbers of guests in such a way that the President suffered no awkward moments or indignities. Since the renovation of 1902, the staff had been able to accommodate new Presidents almost instantaneously. To some extent the White House began to mold the presidential image, as earlier Presidents had shaped that of the White House. The ceremonies of state entertaining had altered little since the time of Taft. The Hardings seem to have had little idea of how their dinners and receptions were prepared and conducted, but took the chief usher's advice and did what had been expected of previous Presidents.

The procedure for setting up events involved a temporary alteration in the roles of approximately half the staff of 27. For example, preparations for a state dinner began about 32 hours in advance. Housemen changed from dark livery to overalls to retrieve the props of official entertaining that local merchants stored as a favor in their attics, for then as now, storage at the White House was scant. Brought in by truck, the materials were unloaded out of sight in the areaway on the north side and taken up through the house.[14]

At state dinners the State Dining Room was usually used to its full capacity of 104. That meant bringing in the pine horseshoe table made for Roosevelt in 1902, to replace the mahogany dining table. Once the sections of the horseshoe table were connected, the housemen laid a silence cloth of two thicknesses of flannel over the unpainted surface and unfolded a damask cloth on top of that. A maid then gently sprinkled it with water and pressed out the creases.

A space of about 26 inches was allowed for a single place at table. The last act in the arrangement was the placement of the gilt bentwood chairs on both the sides and the ends of the horseshoe. Harding, like most of his predecessors, sat with his back to the fireplace, the First Lady directly across the table from him, inside the curve of the horseshoe. As the table was being prepared, the serving tables against the walls were set as well, for dishes were served, never passed. Desserts were lined up on the pantry counter. Vegetable and meat platters were prepared in the kitchen, and the food began to rise in the electric dumbwaiter.[15]

These elaborate and orderly preparations were often complicated by the need to accommodate other activities. There was frequently a smaller dinner on the eve of the state dinner, and there might be one of Harding's large stag breakfasts the next morning in the private dining room, and possibly a luncheon, then a reception in the afternoon, only hours before the state dinner was to begin.

As the stage was being set, the cooks labored under somewhat more tranquil conditions in the large kitchen, used only for major events. Taft had improved it, directing that caterers no longer be employed at the White House. The rules had stuck, but the kitchen, for all the glories of its giant gas range and deep warming drawers, was not large enough to serve the many functions assigned to it. Family meals still had to be prepared, no matter that cooking for a great dinner was under way; even with the two kitchens in full use, the cooks and assistants felt cramped.

At a great wooden table in the center of the large kitchen the work of mixing, grating, rolling, and chopping began on the afternoon before the dinner was to be held. Sometimes an extra work table was set up in the pantry at the west end of the ground floor corridor. Tradesmen brought the supplies Mrs. Jaffray had purchased for the occasion. Following a menu drawn up by Mrs. Jaffray and approved by Mrs. Harding, the kitchen workers would stay busy late into the night, and start again early the next morning. They seem seldom, if ever, to have required any additional helpers.[16]

Colonel Brooks opened the basement vault and released the silver when the butlers were ready for it. The florist got from him the vases for flower arrangements. In the colonel's domain on the south side of the basement was a long table covered with oilcloth. Light came from dangling overhead bulbs and from two squatty windows with iron bars. The walls were covered with key racks, all duly labeled to identify which of the more than 200 closets, drawers, cabinets, and rooms each key fit. At the table the century-old White House silver was polished, its surface gloss rich from years of hard use and loving care. Carefully counted in advance by Brooks, the silver was sent across the hall to the dumbwaiter and assigned to Thomas Roach, principal of the three black butlers. Upstairs, assisted by fellow butlers Adolph Byrd and Arnold Dixon, the tall, stately Roach set the table and made all the serving arrangements in the State Dining Room and pantry.

At about 5 p.m. on the day of the dinner, extra help for the butlers began to arrive. The procedure for hiring outsiders had changed with the war. In Roosevelt's day, and probably before, the head butler had kept a list of men and women in Washington who were available to assist at large functions. Security considerations, heightened by the war, restricted this list to people actually employed in the government. Of the sometimes 40 extra workers, only the butlers were in direct contact with the President. They therefore formed something of an elite corps and styled themselves the "butler's club."[17]

At 30 minutes before the dinner hour, eight o'clock, the butlers descended to the West Wing locker room to don black tails and white gloves; the military aides arrived in dress uniform; the Marine Band made its appearance at the stand in the entrance hall, resplendent in red jackets. Ike Hoover, in full evening dress, walked alone through the unoccupied state rooms, closing the appropriate doors, examining the flower arrangements, inspecting the places where the dignitaries were to stand, looking for anything which might not be as it should. The servants believed he could smell error. On the state floor all other staff members had vanished. A moment of quiet, then the first guests were heard on the stair that led from the basement corridor.

From the arrival of the guests in the East Room to their departure, the staff carried the state dinner through a course that seemed smooth and effortless. At about eight, the buildings commissioner, first Colonel Clarence S. Ridley, a Wilson appointment, but soon Harding's Colonel Clarence O. Sherrill, arranged the guests in a long oval to be received by the President. He followed a list prepared by the social secretary and approved by the President and the State Department. When all was ready, the colonel signaled an aide in the hall, who in turn signaled the leader of the Marine Band. The bandleader looked up to the stair landing for Ike Hoover's nod to begin the drumroll.

The Hardings descended as instructed by the chief usher, much in the manner of Roosevelt, only with less fanfare. They walked around the oval of guests just as Taft and Wilson and their wives had done; along the same path trod first by the Polks more than 70 years before, they led the way to dinner; they sat at table as presidential couples had for generations. The only novelty was the absence of the traditional arc of wine glasses at each plate. No wine had been served at an official dinner since 1920, when Wilson banned it at the beginning of Prohibition.

Beyond the dark-oak enclosure of the State Dining Room, the house was an anthill of activity. Food on platters, in bowls, on trays, and on plates was packed according to careful plan on the pantry counters. When its time came, it was borne through the upholstered swinging door into the dining room. Happily for the staff, it was customary for guests to remain seated until the President ended the meal by standing up. This freed the elevator for food service, and food-laden tea carts were hauled up to the state floor, then rolled to the pantry or private dining room. Dishes and tableware were stacked on carts in the smaller dining room when removed from the table.

At the conclusion of the meal, men adjourned to the Red Room to smoke, women to the Green Room, many of them also to smoke. With ample "dressing rooms" below, and with women now accustomed to smoking, at least one of the principal reasons for the after dinner separation was gone, but the custom prevailed. After about half an hour, the party adjourned to the East Room, where they found as many as a hundred more guests waiting to join them for a musicale. The late company was admitted just as the dinner guests rose from the table.[18]

In the empty dining room, the evening was already over before the strains of music began down the hall. The mahogany doors to the Red Room and hall were drawn shut, and the work of cleaning began.

Approximately two-thirds of the full-time staff could now relax, away from the eyes of the guests. Tail coats were relegated to the pantry closet and, in white aprons, with sleeves rolled to the elbows, the butler's club was in session. The cleanup had traditionally been festive, and while horseplay and repartee survived, Prohibition precluded the strong punch of other times, which the butlers had made from leftover spirits mixed on ice with squeezed citrus fruits.[19]

The dishes, glassware, and silver were washed in the pantry and dried by hand. Taken below in the dumbwaiter, or down the little twisting stair that connected pantry and small kitchen, the silver was received by Colonel Brooks in the vault. He thoroughly inspected each item, knife or fork or soup tureen, and checked it off his list. Most of the dishes remained upstairs in the pantry, with the glasses. President Monroe's great plateau was taken from the table so that the cloth could be removed, then returned to its place stripped of the evening's flowers.

When the last guests departed, around midnight, other parts of the house were restored for the coming day. The gilt chairs from the East Room and the State Dining Room were stacked along the walls of the lower corridor. Other props were similarly made ready for their return to storage early the next morning. At the southwest gate, near War & Navy, the extra servants turned in their passes and departed. Ike Hoover, after a final inspection, went home by limousine. The lights were turned out by one of the two watchmen who patrolled the house throughout the night. They would push mother-of-pearl buttons along the way to signal the central guard station that all was well.

Friends

Harding's administration was marked by early and dramatic successes. In April 1921, the month after his inauguration, the President addressed the Congress, requesting legislation for a series of steps that would lead to the "normalcy" he had promised. Besides reduced taxation, a revival of protective tariffs, and a national budget, he asked for an end to the state of war that still technically existed with Germany. The wheels began to turn without delay. May saw the passage of the Emergency Tariff Bill, June the establishment of the Bureau of the Budget and the Office of Comptroller General; on July 2, while he was vacationing at a friend's home in New Jersey, the President signed a joint resolution of the Congress making peace with Germany official. Also in July, Harding signed an appropriations bill providing for a disarmament conference. Hailed as a major move toward world peace, the Washington

Disarmament Conference opened November 12, 1921. Staged to be moving and spectacular, it was called Harding's most triumphant achievement. At that juncture, he was probably as popular as any past President other than Washington. Great crowds greeted him at public appearances. His picture was on practically every front page several times a week, playing golf, walking his dog Laddie on the south lawn.

Change began to come in the spring of 1922. The coal strikes that plagued the Midwest turned violent by early summer. Already in April an event had taken place that would have far more significance than Harding would ever know. On April 7, one of three mighty naval oil reserves, Number 3, Teapot Dome, Wyoming, was secretly leased by Secretary of the Interior Albert B. Fall to oilman Harry F. Sinclair. This was done without the requisite competitive bidding. Eight days later there was an inquiry into the Fall transaction on the Senate floor, followed after two weeks by a Senate resolution to investigate the lease. The matter was turned over to the Public Lands Committee.

Meanwhile, the White House doctor, Charles E. Sawyer, an old friend Mrs. Harding brought to Washington with the administration, began to warn the Hardings privately that he suspected graft in the sale of goods in a Veterans Bureau warehouse. The agency was headed by Harding's friend Charles R. Forbes, whom Harding supported loyally until at last, in late November, he could avoid an inquiry no longer and temporarily closed the warehouse in question. In mid-March 1922 the Senate ordered an investigation of the Veterans Bureau.

Both Fall and Forbes submitted resignations on January 2, 1923, Fall's to be effective in March, Forbes's in February. By then, the President had looked around him and had begun to suspect the motives of some of those who had come with him to this pinnacle of success. He began to retreat from his friends, except for Attorney General Harry M. Daugherty, to seek the advice of the remainder of his Cabinet, such honorable public servants as Herbert Hoover, Secretary of Commerce, Charles Evans Hughes, Secretary of State, and Andrew W. Mellon, Secretary of the Treasury.

One friend, Jess Smith, who had lived like a member of the family, was ordered back to Ohio. In his despondency, he shot himself; another close friend, Charles F. Cramer, having resigned from the Veterans Bureau, was also found dead, an apparent suicide. Both deaths greatly disturbed the Hardings, and helped turn their sweet life at the White House sour. At this turning point the journalist William Allen White asked Harding a question about his enemies, and the President of the United States made his famous reply: "My God, this is a hell of a job! I have no trouble with my enemies. I can take care of my enemies all right. But my damn friends, my God-damn friends, White, they're the ones that keep me walking the floor nights!"[20]

Nevertheless, the President seemed to enjoy undiminished popularity. He and Mrs. Harding were out often in public, happily obliging anyone with a camera by posing with scouts, dogs, cats, visiting teachers and nurses, wounded veterans, and a parade of celebrities. When Mrs. Harding, who suffered from a chronic kidney ailment, drew perilously close to death in the autumn of 1922, the entire nation watched for hourly reports on her condition. Their affection for her had not lessened, any more than their love for him.[21]

Precautions

Harding was a dynamic performer before an audience, the bigger the better. He held press conferences in his office twice a week and made speeches more frequently than any President before him, keeping a speech writer and two assistants busy in the Executive Office. Acutely aware of image in his symbolic role, he was careful about his clothes, his manner, and his appearance. In the earlier Republican tradition, he believed that the Congress was the giver of law and he was merely the one to carry it out. He therefore felt that public appearances were a major responsibility of the Presidency. One part of his carrying out the dictates of the Congress was to sell its ideas to the people. While Presidents as early as McKinley had realized that the Chief Executive could no longer simply remain at the White House, Harding took this part of his job more seriously than had McKinley, Roosevelt, Taft, or Wilson. Mingling with his fellow citizens was what he did best.

Already in 1922 plans were well under way for a cross-country tour by train, culminating in Alaska, which had not yet received a presidential visit; the trip would also include a goodwill junket into Canada, and stops along the Pacific Coast. Harding had been showing some strain, and his doctor urged him either to stay at home or trim his itinerary, pointing out how such a journey left Wilson in broken health. Neither the President nor his Republican advisers would hear of changing the plans. The time was right politically.

Extensive publicity accompanied the "Voyage to Understanding," as the trip was billed. The presidential train was named the *Superb,* and included the usual accommodations for press, staff, and Secret Service. The last car, with a platform on the rear, was reserved for the President. Sixty-five guests joined the party, in addition to staff and press. Every effort would be made along the way to restore the now-dwindling public faith in the administration.

The train was scheduled to leave Union Station June 20 at two in the afternoon. Ed Starling, advance man for the Secret Service, left eight days before to try the planned path of the train, attempting to coordinate events and cut the numerous ceremonies to the minimum time. Mrs. Harding was worried by a premonition of danger. She spoke to Starling privately before he left to ask him to make certain that the doctors who went along slept as near the President's room as possible. Ruth Powderly, the nurse who had cared for Woodrow Wilson, would also be close at hand. "You understand?" said Mrs. Harding to Starling.

"Perfectly," he replied.

"Are you *sure* you understand? It is not for myself that I want this done but for Warren."[22]

San Francisco

The trip commenced precisely as planned. Harding crossed the Midwest, and relatively small audiences yielded to ever larger ones, until by the time he reached Alaska and Canada he was attracting great and adoring crowds and was on every front page in the country. It was a marked political victory at the grass-roots level; Harding stumped gloriously before millions. But on the morning of August 3, 1923, the headlines announced that he was dead. The end had come the evening before in his room at the Palace Hotel in San Francisco, where he had lain ill for several days. He died at 7:35, while his wife was reading to him. The doctors agreed that the cause of death was apoplexy, but Mrs. Harding would allow no autopsy.

The news astonished the American people. Telephones and telegraph stayed busy between San Francisco and the Executive Office at the White House. Rudolph Forster and Alvey Adee, the two venerable experts on official procedures, united the efforts of White House and State Department in planning the upcoming ceremonies. The *Superb* was decorated as a funeral train. A special car was outfitted as a hearse, with a bier to elevate the coffin so that it could be seen through the windows. Abraham Lincoln's body had been transported in the same way, from Washington home to Illinois.

Approximately 24 hours after the President died, the train left San Francisco, pulling the lighted car, with flag-draped coffin, honor guard, and banks of flowers. Once out of the city, the engineer opened up to full speed; a moist-eyed Mrs. Harding, looking out from her darkened car, was touched to see multitudes of people gathered along the tracks in towns and villages; she asked that the speed be reduced so that plain citizens could take a final farewell of one who had loved them.

The outpouring of sorrow for Harding rivaled that expressed for any other President. "The spectacle of the funeral train," observed the *Washington Post,* "transversing the entire breadth of the United States, is not to be forgotten. In ancient times the death of an emperor resounded far and wide . . . but nowhere else on earth, in ancient or modern times, has a funeral cortege traveled for thousands of miles under one flag, meeting with the solemn greetings and tears of millions of persons speaking the same language and instantly equally informed, as if by magic . . . . The solidarity of this nation is a fact that stands out conspicuously upon such a melancholy occasion as the passing of a dead President's train, conveying him to the Capitol for a national funeral. The people . . . are of equal mind and heart, affected by the same events and sharing a mutual sorrow."[23]

37

Hearth and Home

News of President Harding's death had come to the White House by telephone. Ike Hoover had been trying to keep a diary, but at important times he never seemed to make a record. "President dies," he wrote, and wrote no more. His little book is otherwise merely a series of blank pages for the early days of August 1923. Hoover's job was to run the White House, not keep chronicles. From Alvey Adee and Rudolph Forster he got his bearings, then quickly set to work. Crape was hung over the chandeliers and mirrors of the East Room; little funerary drapery was put elsewhere. The shades were drawn, and the house was closed to the public.[1]

The Stage Is Cleared

For all the restraint shown at the White House, the public mourned its dead leader extravagantly. Flowers began to arrive as soon as the florists opened August 3. Ike Hoover ordered them banked along the sides of the transverse hall and around the walls of the East Room. A stenographer kept a running account of the donors' names, also noting the form of the arrangement—bouquets, crosses, wreaths, anchors of hope, and many other traditional symbols of mourning. The Lincoln bier, housed in the basement of the Capitol, was brought again to the East Room, repaired, and made ready to receive Harding's coffin.[2]

The funeral train pulled into Union Station at 10:30 p.m. on a hot, still August 7. It had held the world transfixed during its five-day trip across the nation. While an honor guard transported the coffin from the train with great ceremony, Mrs. Harding and her small party hastened from the presidential car unnoticed, crossed the President's Room of the station, and were hurried by automobile to the White House. Friends and relatives awaited her upstairs. At 11:35, the flag-covered coffin arrived on a horse-drawn caisson at the northeast gate. The faces of Harding's close friends and relatives peered from the upstairs windows of the White House. Throngs of spectators stood silent outside the fence.

As the coffin was carried through the north door, the sobbing of the gardener, Charlie Patton, broke the quiet. "I never thought I'd live to see this day," he said. The undertaker, a volunteer, tied a black crape decoration on the front door, in ignorance—or defiance—of the official policy of decorative restraint. Harding's body was placed in the East Room with the head to the south. The procession soon withdrew, leaving an honor guard stationed at each corner of the bier. Mrs. Harding then descended to the East Room and selected the flowers she thought her husband would like, dispatching the others to the Capitol for the funeral. Better composed than might have been expected, she asked to be left alone in the East Room for a while that night and the next morning. For the top of the coffin the widow designed a spread eagle made of red, white, and blue flowers.[3]

At ten o'clock the next morning the coffin was mounted again on the caisson and taken in a long and somber procession to the Capitol, where a funeral service was held before the Congress, the Cabinet, and a large group of invited dignitaries. At the conclusion of the service the public was admitted to the rotunda to view the silvery metal coffin, with its flag and floral eagle. Mrs. Harding slipped away to her car, once again unnoticed by the crowd. Stopped for more than half an hour in a traffic jam on Constitution Avenue, she finally arrived at the White House at noon, where she received the Cabinet wives in the oval room upstairs, the scene of many happy occasions.

The funeral train departed for Marion late in the afternoon. During the night Mrs. Harding, traveling alone in the private car that had borne her and the President to the West, kept her vigil, immaculately dressed, her marcel flawless. The final funeral service and burial were held two days later. When Mrs. Harding returned to Washington, Mrs. Coolidge met her at the station and they were driven to the White House, where Mrs. Coolidge assured her she could remain as long as was necessary. That evening the Coolidges dined alone with Mrs. Harding in the private dining room.

The widow remained for five busy days, during which she saw only a few intimate callers; her main task was to cull the President's papers. Hot as the weather was, she had a fire built in the fireplace of the study, where she began burning those papers she determined should not survive. Through the desk drawers she shuffled, dropping some documents into boxes and bags and others into the fire. The late President's secretary, George A. Christian, Jr., stood by helpless during this process. On his own authority he did order most of the papers he found undisturbed in the Oval Office packed up and safely hidden under Colonel Brooks's eye in the pantry in the basement, where they remained, supposedly forgotten, until after Mrs. Harding's death, when the Library of Congress was told to come and get them. No others of President Harding's papers are known to have escaped her purge.[4]

By and by an urgency to leave overtook the widow. The remaining papers were ordered packed in boxes and removed to Friendship, the home of the Ned McLeans in Georgetown. There she soon resumed her burning at a slower pace in small fires built on the lawn. Back in Marion still later, her archival pyres would grow higher as the "Harding scandals" surfaced. All of that was yet to come. On the fifth day after her return from Marion, she walked around the family quarters one last time, viewing rooms now divested of the little elephants, the pictures, and all that had belonged to her. At six in the evening Mrs. Coolidge called for her at the north portico. Accompanied by Nurse Powderly and George Christian, Mrs. Harding went by automobile to Georgetown to join the McLeans for dinner, never again to return to the White House.

Man, Woman, and Decade

The Coolidge era had already begun. While the Harding obsequies were taking place in Ohio, the Executive Office was being prepared to receive the new President. He was, of course, the greatest curiosity in town. Clerks on their way to the departments gathered in the mornings to catch sight of him emerging from the side entrance of the Willard Hotel, turning westward and rounding the Treasury Building, then walking along Pennsylvania Avenue before the White House and entering the grounds on the west side.

Spare and pale, Coolidge had a plain, boyish, freckled face crowned by thin sandy hair combed down close to his scalp. His smile was not a ready one; his wit seldom came through in great utterances, but often in remarks made under his breath. If Warren Harding had looked every inch a President, Calvin Coolidge did not look like a President at all. He seemed the direct opposite of his predecessor, and all the more so as unsavory details of the Harding administration began to surface.

Born on the Fourth of July in 1872, in the Gilded Age of General Grant, Calvin Coolidge became President one month after his 51st birthday. The circumstances of his oath-taking in the farmhouse in his native Plymouth, Vermont, underlined the simplicity of his style of living. A lawyer by training, Coolidge brought to the Presidency a more comprehensive political background than any President before or since. His career had begun at the grass roots in Massachusetts in the late 1890s and continued in state politics to the governorship in 1919. His nomination to the Vice Presidency had been dramatic, marking an open defiance of his state's once-powerful party machine, which did not support him. Thrust suddenly into the Presidency, Coolidge concealed any difficulties in adjustment behind closed doors. To the public the transition appeared smooth and easy.

Although Washington bristled with construction—the new President encouraged the building of monuments, roads, and bridges—it was a small city, and he treated it as a hometown, to the great delight of the permanent population. By today's standards, the White House was so lightly guarded in the 1920s that it seemed, if the biggest, also the friendliest residence in the neighborhood. The public moved freely in and out during calling hours. Guards stood at stations along the way, leaving their posts regularly to guide visitors about. The President sometimes was seen emerging from the elevator hall or from the Executive Office Building. When he went walking he took a Secret Service man along. In the limousine the guard rode up front with the driver. Without the wartime barriers of security—which Harding had greatly cut back—the people of Washington thought of the White House once again as a family home. And their affection for the Coolidge family was genuine.

It was easy for the average American to identify the White House with his own home. The old mansion of the Presidents sheltered husband and wife and two young sons. In the midst of the requisite presidential formality, the Coolidges lived without ostentation. Their domesticity meant more and more to the public as revelations appeared about the evildoings of Harding's associates.

The Coolidges moved to the White House unannounced at three o'clock on the afternoon of August 21, 1923. Mrs. Coolidge stepped from her car, from the glare of the hot sun, into the shadowy house; she would always remember the coolness and fragrance of the rooms that day, enshrouded in their white summer covers. She paused to listen to the leaves of Andrew Jackson's magnolia trees rustling in the breeze outside the Red Room. The tall, elegant Grace Goodhue Coolidge was one of the most beautiful and gentle of the First Ladies.[5]

During 1924 Howard Chandler Christy painted two portraits of
Mrs. Coolidge, one for her family and one to remain at the White
House. In the first she wears white satin and is seated in a Victorian
chair. The second shows her full length, standing on the south lawn
dressed in red silk, beside her white collie, Rob Roy. The Grace Coolidge
in white is a handsome matron, an image cherished by her husband and
sons. She could have been the wife of a successful banker. An overblown
peace rose is cradled in her hand, while her eyes reveal that she is about
to flash her famous smile. The portrait in red shows a different Grace
Coolidge. Here she is a mature beauty, a well-made soignée figure. Her
expression at once sensual, mysterious, and distant, she commands the
large canvas, as the background of the south portico and gardens recedes
into a dreamlike indistinctness.

Her personal appearance was dominated by big gray-green eyes and
the smile. She carried herself regally, and the fashions of the day suited
her so well that her frugal husband urged her to abandon her plain cot-
tons and woolens and buy dresses with rhinestones, feathers, and fur.
Now and then on one of his walks he happened on a dress he liked in a
shop window and brought it home as a surprise for his wife, who sometimes liked his selections and wore them.

Mrs. Coolidge's secretary, Mary Randolph, usually called Polly,
remembered how "Very sweet and alluring she was in her gay spring
dresses . . . . Very few things were unbecoming to her; white, pink,
yellow, blue, red, orchid, old rose, and certain carefully chosen shades of
gray and taupe suited her equally well." Polly Randolph, who also
worked for Mrs. Coolidge during the Vice Presidency, observed that only
after going to the White House did fashion become a real interest of the
First Lady. Widely praised in the press as a beauty, she sensed a responsibility to look her best. "Fashions changed a good deal while the Coolidges were in the White House," Polly Randolph wrote. She delighted
in the First Lady's growing interest in beautiful costumes. "There were
gorgeous lamés with long court trains of gold lace—a *robe de style* of
bright pink taffeta, the skirt bordered by a deep flounce of silver lace, and
with a spray of silk flowers appliquéd across the front. For the morning,
she was fond of simple knitted dresses which were very becoming to her
trim figure, and she had them in several colors."[6]

Always meticulously groomed and attired, Mrs. Coolidge wore her
hair in a striking "horseshoe marcel" popularized first by the Broadway
star Elsie Ferguson. The wave was born anew every Tuesday at the Washington Hotel in Miss Belle Pretty's beauty parlor. With a Secret Service
man close behind, Mrs. Coolidge often walked to this appointment

several blocks from the White House, then toured the neighborhood shop windows once her coiffure was complete and under a net. Sometimes the President met her at the beauty parlor and they walked together, a practice that depended upon the season, for in spring or fall unpleasantly large crowds were likely to gather. As a couple, they were not especially handsome because Mrs. Coolidge made a considerably better appearance than he.

The Coolidges cherished their close family circle. When they moved to the White House, their eldest son, John, was one month from his 17th birthday. Calvin, the younger, was 15. John was shy and sometimes the unhappy object of his father's incessant teasing, which Calvin was able to brush away by teasing in return. These were the first teenage children of a President to live in the White House since Charlie Taft moved out a decade before. Public interest in the Coolidge boys was natural, but from the start the President had no intention of allowing his sons to become youthful celebrities. They were to be neither spoiled nor were they to claim too much limelight. Both boys were accompanied outside the White House by Secret Service men, and both quietly returned to boarding school in the fall of 1923.

There was an aura of calm about the house for the first four months of Coolidge's administration. The President was in no hurry to present himself to the public in a statement of policy, and spent his time mending fences within the Congress and becoming known himself in the capital. Summer passed into autumn with no official activity at the White House. Congressmen and senators were invited to breakfasts. Small dinners frequently occupied the evenings. Coolidge spent some of his time giving interviews to newsmen.

By December, Coolidge was well established; he was ready to make his first public statements. On December 6, 1923, the President made his first major address, 129 days after he had taken the oath of office. The speech aroused enormous interest, and though the political critics denounced it as mere party rhetoric, the public gave it wide acclaim. From that point he was President of the United States in the minds of the people, not a pinch hitter for Harding.

Keeping Traditions

That same December the social season was launched at the White House, thus opening "the season" in Washington. White House dinners were always anticipated both by those who knew they would go and those who hoped they would be invited. The Coolidges, who had proceeded with extreme caution, wanted entertaining carried out precisely according to tradition. Ike Hoover was placed in charge.

Throughout the administration, social forms remained more or less the same. Coolidge wanted constancy, both because that is what he wished to represent to the people and because he and his guests were likely to be more comfortable following familiar rules. The social season was structured around four state dinners, each followed by a musicale for additional guests; five large receptions; two musicales during Lent; and several garden parties in late April or early May. Many more parties took place at the White House than the official ones prescribed by custom. But the "official functions" were the main ones and were always widely reported because they assembled the most important people in the government in a setting of state formality. State dinners were nearly always held on Thursdays; the season opened with the Cabinet dinner early in December, followed by the diplomatic reception the next week and the diplomatic dinner in mid-December.

A state reception usually included about 3,500 guests, while a seated dinner in the State Dining Room was held for about 100. The New Year's reception was followed the next week by the judicial reception, and several weeks after that came the Supreme Court dinner. February saw the congressional reception at the beginning of the month, the House speaker's dinner one week later. The season of great dinners and receptions ended with the glittering Army and Navy reception, usually held about mid-February. Other White House dinners were more like private parties, with black tie, as opposed to the white tie specified at the state affairs, and fewer guests.

All guest lists were drawn with the greatest care. Each autumn the President's ceremonial officer, a State Department functionary assigned to the White House, wrote to an extensive list of officials, asking for the names of their spouses and members of their households and, in the case of children, their ages. This information was placed on cards in duplicate, to be kept by the ceremonial officer for use by himself and the First Lady's social secretary. In addition, a sort of social register of "unofficial persons" who might be invited to the White House was maintained. In theory, to be in this group, one had only to have paid a social call at the White House "at least as recently as the preceding winter." In actuality, however, "unofficial persons" were usually members of society, primarily Washington society.[7]

Foreigners were excluded from White House entertainments, unless their diplomatic representative succeeded in gaining admittance for them from the Department of State. "School girls" were to be excluded whenever possible, in spite of the strong pressure brought to bear to admit them to receptions of all kinds, so they could benefit from the experience of going to the White House; secretaries of the members of Congress were to be invited only on request from their employers; no one outside the "clearly defined categories" of official guests was to be invited to more than two functions each season; no transfers of invitations could be made to other events; and any guest lending his official card of admission to another was to be "permanently black-listed."

The order of precedence for officials at state functions was prepared by the State Department. Before Coolidge's time the process of making these decisions was somewhat informal, largely in the hands of Alvey A. Adee. The frail-looking man with his encyclopedic mind supervised Coolidge's first year, but died on Independence Day in 1924. He had already organized a ceremonial office in 1919 to shoulder some of his burden. Nevertheless, his absence was strongly felt, and the need arose for a more comprehensive system. This led in February 1928 to the formation of the State Department's Division of Protocol. The then-current ceremonial officer, James Clement Dunn, a protégé of Adee, became its first chief. "Protocol," as the division was commonly called, became the last word on social precedence at the White House.[8]

Outside official protocol, most of the social forms were really no more than efficient means of moving large crowds. At receptions President Coolidge stood at the south end of the Blue Room, receiving a moving line of people that snaked across the entrance hall to the State Dining Room, and on around through the Red Room. Without really stopping, the line inched on through the Green Room—where Cabinet wives and other honored guests stood in formal attire, usually without speaking, but nodding—and finally into the East Room. The crowds at receptions were so thick that on hot days both hosts and guests experienced considerable misery. When the receiving line closed, the President and Mrs. Coolidge went into the East Room to stand briefly beneath the central chandelier before retiring.

The Coolidges received universal acclaim for their performances in the social season of 1923–24. No President since Theodore Roosevelt had attracted so much attention as a personality. An apparently endless flow of news copy praised the First Lady's charm and her beautiful dresses. The President received approbation for successfully filling Harding's shoes. Although the intelligentsia did not like Coolidge, the President's general popularity grew steadily, fed in part by economic good times. Calvin Coolidge likened himself to an executive running a business. From all indications that is exactly what the people wanted.

Victory and Tears

Through the winter and spring of 1924 Coolidge had to cope with the Harding scandals, which erupted full force, presenting the Democrats with the opportunity to attack the administration. When accusations of complicity against him failed, the President was denounced as stupid and incompetent. Stirred to anger, the Congress neglected all the requests Coolidge made in his December address. By April, however, the persecution of the President backfired in an unexpected outburst of public favor for Coolidge. The Congress was widely condemned for its ill treatment of a blameless man.

At the Republican Convention in June 1924, Coolidge and his supporters achieved a crowning triumph, effecting a revolution within the party. Coolidge was nominated without hesitation, even though his earlier nomination for Vice President had been opposed by Republican leaders even in his home state of Massachusetts. The nomination marked the overthrow of most of the old political figures who had dominated Republican politics since Roosevelt's time, a notable casualty being Senator Henry Cabot Lodge of Massachusetts. A new structure of party power was built under Coolidge, based on principles more conservative than the Republicans had ever known.

The President did not attend the convention, held in Kansas City, but remained at the White House with his family. So happy for him was the turn of events, and so busy was he with politics, that he decided to remain onstage at home rather than spend the summer in seclusion. He canceled plans for a family trek to his father's farm, planning instead hot-weather diversion in the form of weekend river trips aboard the *Mayflower*, with parties of relatives and friends.

The summer proved to be hot and rainy, the worst sort Washington has to offer. Privacy became a problem even at the White House. The President was no longer able to relax on the south portico because tourists and the press now kept vigil at the fences on the east and west and in the windows of nearby buildings. Neither awnings nor vines offered sufficient screening to satisfy the Secret Service. Not for nearly 25 years would the Presidents again have their southern porch, with the building of the Truman balcony, too high to be visible from the ground and concealed by trees from the side streets.

Coolidge gave himself to the press willingly, exerting every effort to make his newfound popularity serve his political objectives. But he wished to shield his family. No interviews were allowed with Mrs. Coolidge or the boys. When they were mentioned in print, the President was usually tolerant. He resented, however, the reporting of any details of their private lives, and when household intimates talked to reporters about his loved ones it made him angry. The color of Mrs. Coolidge's dresses, the sorts of flowers with which she decorated the dining room table, perhaps a new dance or song she seemed to like—such things might be found out easily, but staff, as well as friends and acquaintances, soon became careful to repeat nothing they saw or heard within the family circle.

The house was filled with young people in the summer of 1924, for both boys were at home. John Coolidge, just graduated from Mercersburg Academy in Pennsylvania, would enter Amherst in the fall. The younger son, Calvin, still in prep school, was the lively favorite of the White House staff and newsmen. It was not a house suited to entertaining youth, yet there were amusements to keep active boys busy, with baseball on the south lawn, and the tennis court south of the Executive Office. Tragedy struck in the innocent form of a tennis game.

On the court in late June, playing in shoes without socks, Calvin developed a blister on the top of his right toe. Thinking nothing of it, he sought no treatment, assuming that it would heal of itself. By the time he showed it to his parents, it was giving him pain, making him feel weak and tired. The White House doctor put him to bed in his room on the northwest corner, diagnosing the blister as infected. July came on hot, and a weakening Calvin, lying with his foot propped up, listened to the Democratic Convention on the radio.

He began to sink rapidly. On the Fourth of July it became clear the infection had led to blood poisoning. That Independence Day the President gave a speech under conditions of almost unbearable emotional stress. The next day Calvin drifted into periods of unconsciousness and hallucination, and doctors seemed helpless to ease his suffering. His mother stayed close beside the twin bed where he lay. The staff could not remember which of the twin beds had been the deathbed of the first Mrs. Wilson, or which one Mrs. Taft had occupied when she was close to death. Mrs. Coolidge proved stronger than the President, who seemed half sleeping, half waking. Starling saw him capture a rabbit on the south lawn: "I watched him take the little animal in his arms and carry it inside to show Calvin." Pacing in and out of the boy's bedroom, watching the pale face, Coolidge was stunned by his own helplessness. "In his suffering," he wrote, "he was asking me to make him well. I could not."[9]

Early in the morning of the sixth, the doctors pronounced the boy's condition hopeless. Pressed, they offered to try removing the poison through surgery. Calvin was carried on a stretcher down the grand staircase and on to the south entrance of the basement, from which he was taken by ambulance to Walter Reed Hospital. His mother followed in a White House car. President Coolidge remained in the Executive Office until he could bear the anxiety no longer, then joined his wife at Walter Reed. The doctors failed in their effort to save the boy's life. Unconscious in his last hours, Calvin died in the presence of his parents at 10:30 at night, July 7, 1924, at the age of 16.

At the White House, social secretary Polly Randolph hurried down the hall to find John Coolidge as soon as she received word of Calvin's death. He was alone in the blue sitting room adjoining his parents' room upstairs. "He bore the blow like a soldier," Miss Randolph wrote in her memoirs, "but I felt like a murderer as I told him, for I knew that some of the light of youth was taken from him forever. . . . " The two went to the north side to stand at a window and await the return of the parents.

The intense heat finally lessened in the deep of night. "For what seemed an eternity, John and I stood together at the window over the front door, waiting. At last the headlights of the President's car turned in at the northwest gate, and drew up beneath the portico. Wearily up the steps and into the house they came—Calvin and Grace Coolidge; worn, exhausted by days and nights of watching and of grief—but still courageous! John's only thought was for his father and mother. He ran to meet them."[10]

Shortly after daybreak the remains of Calvin Coolidge, Jr., arrived at the White House in a gray metal coffin, which was placed in the center of the East Room. Newsboys were already on the street with the headlines proclaiming his death. An honor guard marched solemnly in and stationed itself beside the coffin. The funeral was held in the East Room the following day, summer sun streaming through the tall windows onto political, military, and diplomatic leaders, many weeping openly. Through the service the three Coolidges sat motionless, their arms linked tightly together.

When the ceremony was over, the family departed by special train to Vermont for Calvin's burial among his ancestors. Weeks later the correspondent John T. Lambert, an acquaintance of Coolidge's since his years in Massachusetts politics, called at the Oval Office to express his sympathy. "I am sorry," he said at last; "Calvin was a good boy." President Coolidge turned his chair around in silence and looked outside through the windows behind his desk. "You know," he finally said to Lambert, "I sit here thinking of it, and I just can't believe it has happened." He repeated himself, his eyes brimming with tears, "I just can't believe it has happened."[11]

Diversion

After spending the balance of the summer in near seclusion in New England, Mrs. Coolidge returned to the White House in the fall of 1924 less interested in the upcoming election than in restoring her spirits through a worthy project. John was away at Amherst; seeing him go had hurt more this time, and the Coolidges had consoled themselves by sending as bodyguard Colonel Ed Starling, who had become a family favorite. At Amherst he shared John's quarters, pledging to guard both the boy's safety and his morals.

In looking around for a project, Mrs. Coolidge decided to improve the White House by redecorating and furnishing the family quarters. The rooms were drab and sparsely furnished, having been filled and emptied four times since McKim finished them in 1902. McKim had run out of money, leaving the Roosevelts and those who followed to furnish their living quarters as best they could. Both Mrs. Taft and the first Mrs. Wilson had done some redecorating, largely with their own possessions. A little furniture was bought from public funds during each administration, to finish this or that room. The guest rooms at the east end of the second floor were comfortably furnished, in the manner of bland hotel rooms; some of their mahogany beds and dressers had been made in 1902 by Davenport in Boston. But the family's rooms lacked the cheerful and homelike abundance one might expect in the private rooms of a President of the United States. Especially bare and uninviting were the four rooms in the heart of the family quarters, beginning with the oval room on the south side and moving west.

The Coolidges had little furniture of their own, for they had always rented either partially furnished houses or furnished apartments in hotels. Since they had not surrendered their rented house in Northampton, most of what they had was still there. After the Hardings' possessions were moved out of the White House, the Coolidges borrowed so much furniture from other parts of the house to supply the family quarters that the central corridor and several bedrooms were left bare. Mrs. Coolidge found this making do an unwelcome burden. In her project for the family quarters, she intended to improve her own surroundings, while at the same time creating something truly worthwhile that she could pass on to her successors.

By the fall of 1924 the First Lady had decided to furnish the family quarters in "colonial" style. Many influences swayed her decision. Since the war the so-called "American colonial" style in interior decoration had become the most popular mode in domestic furnishing. Examples poured from the factories—wing chairs, camel-back sofas, candle stands, footstools, dropleaf tables, grandfather clocks, and four-poster beds. Meanwhile, the American Wing at the Metropolitan Museum of Art, which opened to great public admiration on November 10, 1924, doubtless helped persuade Mrs. Coolidge of the connection between colonial antiques and the historic White House. Mrs. Coolidge's concern that the furnishings selected for the family quarters not become obsolete may have attracted her to the American Wing. The historical rooms displayed there, taken from actual old houses and furnished with antiques that complemented the architecture, were widely praised for having stood the test of centuries. Mrs. Coolidge wrote some years later: "I had a strong desire to refurnish some of the rooms of the Mansion with furniture of the period in which it was built."[12]

The First Lady kept her program to herself until after Coolidge's election in November, then she got to work. On the advice of Mrs. Harold I. Pratt of New York, a Republican and a furniture collector possessed of Standard Oil millions, Mrs. Coolidge took unusual steps to raise money for her project. Instead of asking Congress for funds, she tried an approach used successfully by museums: seeking donations of money and furniture from private sources. Such tactics had been highly successful for the American Wing. The legal framework for this strategy was provided late in February 1925 when a joint resolution of Congress permitted the White House to accept gifts of furniture and artwork. This was the first legal recognition that the President's house also functioned as a museum. In addition, to assist the First Lady, the Congress raised the traditional redecorating appropriation it gave each incoming administration from $20,000 to $50,000.

One month after the inauguration, Mrs. Coolidge was happily absorbed in her project. Guided by Harriet Barnes Pratt, she appointed experts to an advisory committee, the first ever established for the White House. It was practically the same committee that had overseen the American Wing; the chairman, Robert W. De Forest, was president of the Metropolitan Museum of Art and the donor of the American Wing. Mrs. Pratt was a member, as was the Baltimore antiquarian and collector Mrs. Miles White, Jr., remembered for the restoration of the Hammond-Harwood House in Annapolis. The Manhattan architect William Adams Delano, designer of Long Island estates, agreed to serve on the committee, beginning a long professional association with the White House. An older and more famous architect, Charles A. Platt of New York, designer of the Freer Gallery of Art, which had been completed on the Mall two years before, represented the traditional beaux arts persuasion. Francis C.

Jones, an acknowledged expert on American art, was the delegate from the Commission of Fine Arts in Washington, which governed architectural planning in the city.

Had the list stopped with those members, the commission might have succeeded in its task. But the inclusion of two distinguished experts on the American decorative arts, R. T. Haines Halsey and Luke Vincent Lockwood, made things difficult. Both were also successful businessmen, Halsey a stockbroker and Lockwood a lawyer. They had collaborated at the Metropolitan in 1909 on the first major museum exhibition of American antiques. The American Wing was essentially Halsey's creation, but it also expressed the knowledge, as well as the ideals, of many others, including Lockwood. If the architects had built their showcase at the Chicago Fair, then the antique collectors had built theirs in the American Wing. Halsey and Lockwood were fervent proselytizers, and they joined Mrs. Coolidge's advisory committee with goals far beyond the First Lady's rather simple domestic objectives.

Window Dressers

Antique collecting had been a popular American pastime since the late 19th century, and the tastes of the collectors who were to work with Mrs. Coolidge were rooted in that era, but they would have considered the label "Victorian" an insult. They scorned their parents' ideas about antiques as unscholarly and inaccurate. Rather than merely accumulating relics, they demanded in each piece excellence of design and authenticity to the last wooden peg; experience had taught them what made an antique object "right" or "wrong."

In the aftermath of the World War, their work seemed to gain a new significance that transcended aesthetics. Many collectors began to look back to times they viewed as purer and happier, when old standards prevailed and the United States had not been contaminated by influences from Europe. The flow of immigration and the shaken structure of society since the war were seen as threats to what they supposed were traditional values in American life. The desire to symbolize the colonial epoch as a lost Eden provided part of the zeal that went into the creation of an image of early America through the decorative arts. Mrs. Coolidge probably did not understand these implications entirely, but like many others, she found something reassuring in the colonial style. Again and again she described the furnishings as warm or homelike or appropriate for such American rooms as those in the White House.

Although the First Lady's advisory committee was eager to begin, she did not summon it for two years. The Coolidges were at the height of their popularity during the spring of 1925. His inauguration in March was the emotional peak of an absorbing social season; his first address after that was the first radio broadcast by a President to an unseen audience of millions. A surprisingly sunny Mrs. Coolidge reigned at the White House, where her days were often occupied with teas and lawn parties, and her evenings with receptions, large dinners, and small suppers. She had time only to sketch her redecoration plans on paper. In June she and the President sailed aboard the *Mayflower* to Massachusetts for the summer. Before she left, Mrs. Coolidge told Colonel Clarence O. Sherrill, the officer in charge of public buildings, that she wanted the family quarters painted and plastered; all the "French" moldings were to be removed from the walls to gain a simpler, more colonial effect. She did not consult her committee about these modest changes; she planned to consult them only about furnishings. The redecoration of the family quarters reflected her personal taste, which she knew her successors would modify to suit their own preferences.[13]

Colonel Sherrill was the only other person authorized to contact the committee. He seems not to have called the advisers about the remodeling. His busy spring had included politicking for an act on February 26, 1925, separating his office from the Corps of Engineers, where it had been for nearly 60 years. The change was to take effect when the new fiscal year began in July, and Colonel Sherrill was concerned with the details of reorganizing his office and hiring new assistants. For the work at the White House, the First Lady's notes and verbal directions seemed sufficient; he felt no need for expert advice.

In any case, Sherrill's main concern was structural rather than stylistic. He feared the upper structure might be near collapse. An engineering survey ordered by Harding had called the roof unsafe; Sherrill knew he could convince Coolidge that the situation was serious, if the engineers were willing to commit themselves in strong language. In the interest of economy, however, Coolidge agreed only to authorize the redecoration planned by Mrs. Coolidge. Sherrill complied, yet was unable to get the engineers' warnings off his mind, and he determined to investigate the structure further on his own authority.[14]

The colonel began the project in mid-June, allowing plenty of time to be certain that everything would be completed when the President returned in September. As he commenced work on the second floor, the advisory committee—or rather some of its New York members—began meeting on their own and issuing statements about the White House to the press. They had heard about the remodeling and were piqued that they had not been consulted. The remodeling was well under way when Sherrill received word in early July that a delegate from the committee would call on him at the White House. He probably received this news with apprehension, for he realized that the committee had already thrust itself too far into public view. Announcements had been made in the press that the White House would be redecorated in the "colonial" style. "Gifts of Historic Furniture May be Asked for White House," proclaimed one headline in June. None of these statements had been approved in the Executive Office.[15]

While the *Mayflower* was sailing toward Massachusetts, a controversy began to stir at home over the remodeling. In its newspaper comments the advisory committee had thrown down the gauntlet, and the challenge was taken up by the American Institute of Architects. Still strongly committed to beaux arts classicism, the institute protested that Charles McKim's work was being threatened by a group of antiquarians. A cherished letter, framed and hung on the wall at the A.I.A. headquarters in the Octagon House, was taken down and read again. It was from Theodore Roosevelt, written in December 1908 to the then-president of the A.I.A., Cass Gilbert. "If I had it in my power as I leave office," the letter read, "I should like to leave a legacy to you and the American Institute of Architects, the duty of preserving a perpetual 'eye of guardianship' over the White House to see that it is kept unchanged and unmarred from this time on." President Roosevelt's words became a battle cry in an architectural holy war.[16]

On July 8, R. T. Haines Halsey called on Sherrill at the White House, where he toured the upstairs rooms then being painted. Halsey then inspected the state rooms. To the reporters perpetually waiting outside and hungry for news in the slow summer season, Halsey denounced the living quarters as "horrible and frightful." But he assured them that the White House was at last in good hands. The advisory committee of experts had already contacted leading manufacturers, and arrangements were being made for them to reproduce "linens, rugs, and other furnishings" based on historical examples. Plans, said Halsey, would be ready for the President's approval within two weeks.[17]

Now the A.I.A. was furious. During the ensuing row it was revealed that the advisory committee also planned to change the Green Room. Private quarters were one thing, but the state interiors were quite another, and the architects were more offended than ever. The Green Room, though worn and faded, still presented the elegantly Edwardian setting completed by McKim in 1902. Harriet Pratt recalled in later years that the state of the Green Room had inspired the entire redecorating project. While the rest of the evidence suggests that the inspiration sprang from the family quarters, it is certain that after the idea of redecorating the state floor was broached in the summer of 1925, the debate gained for both architects and antiquarians the mystical appeal of a crusade. To help the cause, Harold I. Pratt, who managed his family's financial interests—established a fund for the redecoration of the Green Room. This nest egg was increased by donations from Mrs. Dwight Morrow, Mrs. John T. Pratt, and Mrs. George Whitney.

In August the advisory committee made another announcement: A renovation was planned for the Red Room as well. The angry A.I.A. could not bear this in silence. Up until now the President and his staff had not dignified the controversy with any public notice. Sherrill kept quiet, hoping perhaps that the storm would pass. Representing the architects, E. C. Kemper, executive director, took his grievance directly to the President in a rather presumptuous letter, requesting a "hearing" before any decision was made about the remodeling of the rooms. At the Executive Office someone scrawled "some nerve" across the face of Kemper's letter; but this should not be interpreted to mean that the advisory committee had support in the President's office. It did not. Obviously the newspaper articles had been read in the confines of the White House and by Coolidge in Massachusetts. The negative reaction is easy to imagine.[18]

In the heat of the quarrel one editor compared this furnishings controversy and that during James Monroe's administration, when critics objected "to so much foreign furniture in the White House." In fact, the "foreignness" of the beaux arts interiors was a large part of the issue; the antiquarians did want more "American" furnishings at the White House. Nor was this an elite predilection. The Literary Digest polled its readers about the choice of a White House style. A majority of those responding preferred American colonial furniture, by which they probably meant anything old, but not "foreign" or recognizably "Victorian."

Leaders in the art world gave their views. C. C. Colt, the art editor of the Boston Transcript, hoped the White House would not be "museumized Colonially," although he liked the idea of using colonial furniture, both because it was comfortable and ornamental and because "it fits the architectural style of the house." Reginald T. Townsend, editor of the American magazine Country Life, took the "eminently nationalist" view that the American Wing's period rooms were excellent models for the White House. Peyton Boswell, the editor of Art News and International Studio, thought that "The fact that the national consciousness has been pricked by the realization that the 'first house' of the land is a hodge-podge so far as its furnishings are concerned" was a good sign: "The fact that the newspapers have considered it good editorial policy to print columns about the White House controversy is an indication that the people as a whole are concerning themselves with a question that pertains to art, for the newspapers keep a knowing hand on the nation's pulse and do not bother to print news that has no interest to their readers."[19]

The architects found their adversaries considerably more formidable than the engineers they had battled in 1902. They were on the defensive and received much less serious attention in the press than did their opponents. It was a hard comedown. The architects' heroic image had diminished since the war. Grandiose buildings rich with borrowings from the architectural motifs of the Old World now bespoke internationalism, an idea widely mistrusted and even feared. McKim's White House interiors had been designed to evoke a romantic, if not especially accurate, 18th-century mood. Although through longevity they had become themselves historical, this proved to be their downfall, for the real past they represented was the unfashionable "imperial" time before the war. Had there been no Halsey and no advisory committee to speak to the press on the subject, change would have come quietly.

Presidents are uncomfortable when even minor domestic disputes become public and suggest that all is not well at the President's House. He who leads the nation must at least appear to be able to rule beneath his own roof. A debate about furniture style might have seemed harmless enough, but as the average American was unlikely to appreciate the fine points of the argument, the incident was perceived as simply unpleasant. Thus the feud over furnishings in the summer of 1925 offered the curious spectacle of public bickering over how the President should furnish his domicile. News reporters did not miss the opportunity to write humorous accounts; the intemperate behavior of both sides put the White House in an undignified position.

Coolidge decided to take action early in August, while still in Massachusetts. By the second week of the month the subject of redecorating the White House vanished from the newspapers. The President simply stopped the problem at its roots: There would be no refurnishing. In mid-August it was made clear that the work would not include the state rooms except for repainting the entrance hall and the ceilings of the Red and Blue Rooms. The remainder of the work was to be upstairs in the family quarters; by order of the President, no details were to be given out as to the character of the decoration.

As summer drew to a close, even the smoke of battle was gone, and the White House project came to a peaceful conclusion. "Changes Are Few in White House," a small headline advised in late August, with the accompanying statement, "When the President and Mrs. Coolidge return to the White House next month they will find no sharp changes in the appearance of their historic home." The advisory committee and the A.I.A. were silent.[20]

Habits

Most days when he was in residence, President Coolidge could be found in the Oval Office. He made less use of the study in the White House than had any of his predecessors. He usually arrived at his desk at nine, leaving at noon for lunch and a nap, then returning to resume work from 2:30 until half past five. This businessman-President wore dark suits, like any company executive, abandoning the morning coat that most previous Presidents had worn.

As always, Coolidge's White House welcomed a daily flow of guests. Counting the President and Mrs. Coolidge, seldom fewer than eight sat down to lunch, ordinarily eaten in the private dining room on the state floor. In pleasant weather, lunch might be served on the south portico, with screens set up to block the view from East Executive Avenue. A typical "company" dinner in the evening consisted of 12 people and was held in the State Dining Room. Mrs. Coolidge tried to soften the stiff formality of her dinner parties by allowing black tie instead of white and simplifying the traditional table settings. She used some of the historic china, often mixing it with the full state service, which was the same simple gold-rimmed pattern ordered by the Roosevelts. Large, loose bouquets of roses from the garden filled cut-glass bowls. There were usually three of these, one large and two small, placed symmetrically on a crisp white damask cloth. Prohibition required that water be served instead of wine; as during the Hayes administration in the '70s, the food was elaborate, to compensate for the lack of spirits.

Guests were not allowed to wander about as they might in a private house. At a dinner party, for example, as the company moved to different rooms of the state floor, doors closed behind them, containing them in the particular room in which they stood. This was done for two reasons: First, unknown to the company, hectic activity might be taking place in the room they had just left, from the vacuuming of the rug to preparations for another event; second, as soon as the doors closed, Secret Service men appeared to patrol the immediate area. Thus the President was also contained, for security reasons.

Purely social guests were relatively few. Many school groups, professional societies, outstanding citizens, friends of politicians, and delegations of every kind had their hours at the White House. For every kind of occasion there was a prescribed pattern. Small groups were taken to the Green Room to await Mrs. Coolidge, who might remain with them for 30 minutes. If the President was with her, the Blue Room was the usual meeting place. Rare callers, privileged either for personal or for political reasons, were offered a coveted look at the family quarters. Large groups were greeted in the East Room or outside on the terrace before the south portico. If the importance of the group merited it, refreshments might be part of the hospitality, but usually they were not. Receptions for wounded veterans always featured punch and cake and occasionally a light lunch. Mrs. Coolidge gave herself wholeheartedly to the role of hostess. Photographs record one Easter egg rolling at which she dressed her dogs in Easter bonnets, the white collie even sporting a black veil. The President was famous for being droll, and seldom disappointed callers privileged to hear him.

The Coolidges made extensive use of the *Mayflower,* which the Navy continued to maintain for the President. Accompanied by a party of a dozen or so, they often left the capital at the close of the working day and spent the weekend on the river. A few musicians from the Marine Band were taken along to provide entertainment, and they were sometimes joined by a string quartet or a pianist. The crew members were Navy men, and the servants were civilians on the Navy payroll. Several members of the White House domestic staff also went along.

The *Mayflower* was sufficiently large to permit privacy for the passengers. An office, fully equipped, was provided for the President, and he and Mrs. Coolidge shared a large suite that opened on the deck. Reporters were never included on the weekend excursions, although groups of them usually awaited at the river villages where the *Mayflower* might stop. Like Roosevelt, Taft, and Wilson before him, Coolidge came to cherish the river trips as a means of escape.[21]

Engineers

"If it is as bad as you say," the President had asked the engineers in 1923, "why doesn't it fall down?" Coolidge had looked over the proposed plan for remodeling soon after he took office, and he was appalled by the estimated cost of half a million dollars. With a policy of government thrift, he had no intention of undertaking conspicuous improvements at the White House.[22]

Two years later, Colonel Sherrill was still worried about the engineers' warning that the upper parts of the house were in poor condition. He had made additional investigations which confirmed the fears expressed in the earlier report. Hardly had the smell of fresh paint subsided in the redecorated family quarters toward the end of 1925, than the President began to see evidence that the attic floor might be in dangerous condition. The recently repaired walls were already so severely cracked that ridges showed in the new wallpaper. Bits of debris fell through similar clefts in the ceilings, indicating trouble in the old wooden framework that laced the interior of the house together. Sherrill once again laid the engineers' reports before Coolidge.

At first the President suggested that the roof and attic be replaced without disturbing the second floor, so that he could remain during the work. In a cautious memorandum of October 1, 1925, Major J. C. Mehaffey, chief of design and construction for the Office of Public Buildings and Public Parks, evaluated this plan. After weighing the pros and cons, he recommended against it. "It is my opinion," he wrote, "that if the replacement of the roof were started as proposed, the President would soon find the conditions intolerable and would either stop the work or decide to move out." Mehaffey estimated that "because of the conditions" involved in his staying there, "the cost of the work would be approximately 50 per cent more than it would be if the White House were vacated." The repairs would require the removal of the entire roof structure and attic floor, including the ceilings of the second story family quarters.[23]

The need for such a reconstruction program was well documented. Engineers had thoroughly inspected the structure during the summer, even crawling into the small spaces between the floor joists to view the old truss system. While work was under way, Sherrill ordered most of the contents of the attic rooms carried away, for fear they would fall through the ceilings below. The wood framing, built by Hoban in the reconstruction of 1818, had been cut into so many times through the years that the engineers reported to their superiors, "truss action no longer exists in those members which are intended to be roof trusses." The circular opening in the attic floor, cut through during the Wilson administration to permit light from a skylight to fall through the attic story into the second floor corridor, had been ripped haphazardly through the inner wood skeleton, with little consideration for the existing structure.

Poor construction was nothing new at the White House, where time was always precious, and where building or remodeling had usually been done in a hurry. In the 19th century this had been seen in the forcings of tiny bathrooms onto stair landings and the careless threading of gas pipes through walls. New paper and paint covered the evidence but could not repair the damage. Roosevelt's renovation had brought apparent order, yet beneath the serene white surface the structural work had been quite as shoddy as the work in the past. By 1925 the problems apparent in the upper parts of the house could no longer be solved cosmetically. Sherrill had every reason to believe that if disturbed the roof trusses might give way, sending tons of material crashing through the interior of the house to the basement.

The White House was a house of brick and wood, enveloped in an outer shell of stone, which had a thick lining of soft clay brick. McKim had run steel beams through the ceilings of the state rooms, binding them into the old external walls. But the wooden skeleton still held much of the inner structure together, and its upper reaches had become overburdened. Mrs. Wilson's expansion of the attic in 1913 had increased the load dramatically. Water tanks, electric machines of many kinds, new bathrooms, and a variety of other conveniences and improvements had been added regularly, as the third floor became increasingly important to the functioning of the second.

The simplest and most obvious course was the introduction of surface supports and braces, but the engineers concluded that in addition to the danger obvious in the visible parts of the structure, problems as yet unseen might offer even greater hazards. Knowing that most of the walls would have to be opened in the process of repair, the engineers advised that the structural wood be torn away entirely and replaced with steel. Presented with the alternatives of patching or reconstructing, Coolidge finally accepted the latter, agreeing to move to temporary quarters while the renovation took place.

The Attic Is Rebuilt

At this point, Colonel Clarence D. Sherrill stepped down as director of parks and grounds; he felt that the office needed a younger man. He could reflect on great successes. To him was due in large measure the revival of the City Beautiful movement, which had been dormant since the outbreak of the war. He had reorganized the parks and grounds office and increased its staff, so that it could function independently of the Corps of Engineers. When Sherrill left, numerous major new building projects loomed on the horizon.

In December 1925 the directorship passed to Major U. S. Grant III. Tall and strikingly handsome, Grant at age 44 had a severe military demeanor. He appeared always busy and had no time for small talk; he was quick to make a decision and unyielding in carrying it out. The grandson of President Grant, the major had enjoyed a successful career of his own in various parts of the United States and in Europe, where he worked with several American commissions during the peace negotiations in 1918. Polished by a lifetime of travel, he was entertaining in company; his intellectual interests made him an agreeable comrade to creative men. The social position of his wife, Edith, daughter of Elihu Root, together with his own Grant connections, gave him entrée to Washington politics as well as a place in society. He got to know the Coolidges by way of the close friendship of Mrs. Coolidge and his sister Julia, wife of the aristocratic Russian emigré Prince Cantacuzène. A promotion to lieutenant colonel in 1926 gave Grant military rank to match the dignity of his new job.

With the blessings of the White House—and a legacy of goodwill from Sherrill—U. S. Grant III set out to secure funding for the renovation. In the spring of 1926 the Congress appropriated $375,000 for rebuilding the attic and roof of the White House, including the ceilings of the second floor. Grant based the designs on a large body of architectural drawings executed in 1923 in the office of the supervising architect of the Treasury. These projected a more or less exact replacement of the wooden upper parts of the house with steel framing. But while he had less money in 1926 than Sherrill had believed necessary three years before, Grant was able to make major modifications in the plans that would render the attic story more nearly like a full third floor. These included a rearrangement of rooms and a general expansion of space, achieved by slightly steepening the pitch of the roof and omitting many of the slanted ceilings in the attic.

It is difficult to assign the title of architect of the remodeling to any one person. After the initial plans and specifications were on paper, Grant engaged as architectural consultant William Adams Delano, the New York architect who was a member of Mrs. Coolidge's furnishings advisory committee. Delano probably was more useful to Grant as a member of the Fine Arts Commission than as a designer, for Grant already knew how he wanted the new third floor to be. The supervising architect, James A. Wetmore, was a lawyer who always insisted that he was merely working as an administrator. Several architects under Wetmore drew the original plans, although their names have not survived in the federal records. Major J. C. Mehaffey, chief of design and construction in Grant's office, is the most likely candidate for the title of architect. He worked intimately with Colonel Grant on the project, the two interjecting what Grant later called their "personal views" somewhat "more than we should have done."[24]

Planning the new upper parts of the White House took the better part of a year. The drawings were sufficiently advanced by the autumn of 1926 that the Office of Public Buildings and Parks could advertise for written bids, which were to be accompanied by a résumé of "large rebuilding or remodeling jobs which are comparable with the proposed work and which have been successfully completed by the Contractor." Final bids were to be submitted by 11 a.m. December 29, 1926. Nine bids were received, the highest, $369,224; the lowest and winning bid, $185,000. N. P. Severin Company of Chicago cited previous work on mansions in suburban Chicago and on schools, churches, and a hospital. As might have been expected, most of the subcontractors they proposed to hire were also from Chicago. Representatives from Severin came to Washington in early January 1927, and the contract was signed in Grant's office on the eighth. Work was to commence in March, as soon as the President assumed another residence.[25]

The question of where to put the President was soon settled, when Colonel Grant leased 15 Dupont Circle, the Patterson mansion. It had been closed for several years while its owner, Cissy Patterson Schlesinger, lived in New York. One of the most magnificent houses in Washington, it had been completed for Mrs. Schlesinger's parents more than 20 years earlier by McKim, Mead, & White. It had a V-shaped plan and an exterior like a Renaissance palazzo, shining in white marble and glazed terra-cotta. For comfort and luxury it had nearly everything; the ample and elegant drawing rooms overlooked Dupont Circle, where the daily traffic of black motorcars framed the tranquil park in the center.

Severin was committed in writing to a tight 125-day construction schedule. When agreeing to move out, the President told all parties that they must not tarry. Coolidge had lunch in the White House on March 2, but at the close of day, instead of walking his usual path home through the colonnade beside the rose garden, he was driven to 15 Dupont Circle, where all was in readiness. Mrs. Coolidge had gone there earlier, and the luggage, pets, and personal possessions went with her.

By sunset that day, packing at the White House was nearly complete. It had not been necessary to take much to the Patterson house, for the building was fully equipped. The furnishings of the second and third floors of the White House were taken downstairs to the East Room and the State Dining Room, where they were stacked and put under heavy dustcovers. Those furnishings remaining in the state parlors were clothed first in their summer slipcovers, then in dustcovers. Special muslin masks

were made for the silk wall coverings; linen bags shielded the chandeliers. Draperies, rugs, pictures, and small objects were packed away in the
basement and in the coatroom of the East Wing.[26]

Construction started early in the morning of March 14, 1927. By
that time the entire building was covered by a temporary roof of wood, to
protect the interior when the real roof was removed. The building of this
enormous structure was the first step in the renovation; removing it
would be the last. Within two weeks the old slate roof and Hoban's
timber framing beneath it were gone, some of the wood salvaged to make
souvenirs. The White House was demolished down to the upper walls of
the second floor chambers. On March 28, the first of the steel construction began, the new members having been made in Chicago under the
direction of Severin.

A construction shack was built at the east gate for the superintendent to use as an office; the drawings and other papers necessary to the
work were stored there. Each morning at 6:30 the workmen arrived from
their boardinghouses—few appear to have been local men—to be admitted by a Secret Service man. They did not pass through the house, all
inner stairwells being closed off at the second-floor level, but went to a
temporary stair on the outside, at the northeast corner, which they
climbed some 70 feet to the work area. One morning Mrs. Coolidge, on
an infrequent visit to inspect the work, delighted the construction crew
by donning a hard hat and climbing the long stair herself.

Nothing kept the rebuilding from proceeding on schedule. After the
steel framework was in place, the hollow concrete tiles which were to
form the walls were hoisted to the top of the house and the work of laying
them, brick-like, began. The plumbers, electricians, and other tradesmen appeared in June. On July 1, Colonel Grant could report that "all of
the steel was in place, all of the roof, floor and partition tile had been
laid, all plumbing and electrical connections roughed in, and the plastering of the new second-story ceilings completed." By the first of August
the interior finishing was nearly done, with the installation of fixtures
and the setting of bathroom tiles half finished. Severin turned the key
over to Grant on August 9 and was soon on his way back to Chicago.[27]

Cleaning and painting were put into the hands of local contractors.
The second and third floors were entirely repainted, the basement and
main floor thoroughly cleaned, their paint surfaces touched up as needed;
the exterior was washed down, repaired where necessary, and given one
coat of paint (two in places where the old paint had been flaking). Mrs.
Coolidge wrote with pride in later years that the employees at the White
House had gotten the job done "by working nights and Sunday of the last

week before we were expected. . . . " She and the President entered the house without ceremony on September 11, 1927.[28]

The most significant result of the work was the creation of a large third floor to serve the needs of the second, which remained the family quarters. No formal staircase went to the third floor, only service stairs, with the single elevator of the house the most frequently used means of access. Makeshift service rooms were replaced by a well-planned series of 14 major rooms, along with many smaller spaces to be used as linen closets and storage chambers. Areas had also been allotted for several new baths, which for the while were only roughed in. The attic of the north portico, where Jessie Wilson's wedding dress had been hidden, was no longer a closet but three commodious storage rooms with skylights.

The large rooms were concentrated in the central section and on the west end, with the east end finished largely for storage. On the northwest, five servants' bedrooms opened on a secondary passage, which connected to two bathrooms, one for men and one for women. The housekeeper was relocated from the second floor to a large suite on the central hall of the third floor. Only two guest rooms were designated in the new plan, although it was anticipated that several other rooms might in the future be adapted for guests. Both were on the south side, small cubicles with high, quaint-looking windows barred from the outside by the stone balustrade surrounding the roof. Daylight fell into the central corridor through a large skylight of ground glass; a second skylight, set into the floor and ringed with an iron railing, allowed the light to pass into the transverse hallway of the family quarters.

The most conspicuous and enduring innovation in the remodeling is attributed to Mrs. Coolidge: the sky parlor. Named for the attic rooms sometimes found in old American houses, this lofty sun room was intended to serve the same purpose as the glassed-in porches popular in private houses of the time. Sunshine and fresh air were believed to cure nearly any malady and to preserve health and good spirits. Built on the roof of the south portico and masked from view by the stone balustrade, the small, squarish sky parlor offered magnificent prospects of Washington, particularly of the Washington Monument and the Mall.

Crochet

After their return in the autumn of 1927, less than two years remained to the Coolidges in the White House. A glamorous aura continued to surround them, although the public's interest in them had lessened somewhat; they were still always in the papers, the improbable couple, droll "Cal" and lovely Grace. At their temporary residence on Dupont Circle they received Charles A. Lindbergh after his transatlantic flight while thousands of spectators packed the streets and park before the house cheering the hero. Now Will Rogers sat at their table; again it was the fiery Queen of Rumania, or a quiet-spoken business or social leader. Everywhere were the reporters, eager for a quotation or a picture. Usually they were obliged.

For all their outward compliance, the Coolidges found public life wearing. She developed poor health, and sometimes his moods varied sharply. Their domestic life was troubled by cruel sensationalism of a sort presidential couples had not faced before. Unfounded stories that they planned to divorce after he retired appeared in the newspapers and both hurt and embarrassed them. They were unable to defend themselves because of their official positions, but they did begin to appear in public together more frequently, to thwart gossip. As if these demeaning command performances were not enough, there was the "Black Hills affair" during their summer vacation in South Dakota in 1927, while work was under way at the White House. Mrs. Coolidge was lost for several hours during a walk in the woods with a handsome young Secret Service agent. The President's annoyance on her return was misinterpreted by some reporters as the rage of a jealous husband.[29]

In reaction the President and his wife tried to separate more sharply their public and private lives. When John visited, great effort was made to set aside time for the three of them. Now and again they spent a few days in Northampton in their old house, which was as it had been when they and John and Calvin had been together. At the White House they spent time in the sky parlor. In it they perhaps unknowingly created the symbol of their retreat, and it has been the retreat of many presidential families since. A quiet and isolated place high above the labyrinthine City of Politics, it was the only part of the White House from which one could look uninterrupted to the distant horizons.

When she moved back to the remodeled White House, Mrs. Coolidge unpacked from a velvet-covered, silk-lined box a coverlet she had crocheted as a gift for the house. She spread it over the Lincoln bed in hers and the President's bedroom. It was a labor of love, undertaken in the hope that she was beginning a tradition for every First Lady to make something for posterity to enjoy and remember her by. It was a large coverlet made of shoe thread, giving the effect of heavy netting, decorated with representations of the American eagle and the presidential shield. At the head of the coverlet the name "Grace Coolidge" was worked into the design.

The coverlet contradicts Mrs. Coolidge's own recollections of one of the most important events in her husband's Presidency. In August 1927, before she and the President returned to the White House, Coolidge issued the political announcement which was to become his most famous: "I do not choose to run for President in nineteen twenty eight." Mrs. Coolidge insisted that she had no previous knowledge of his decision, that she, like the public, had been completely surprised. But in an article published in the New York *Herald Tribune*, Mrs. Coolidge wrote that her "final stitches" were made "on board the U.S.S. Mayflower during the President's review of the fleet at Hampton Roads in June, 1927." On the coverlet are embroidered, together with her name and that of the President's House, the dates that were to mark the beginning and end of the administration of Calvin Coolidge: August 8, 1923, to March 4, 1929.[30]

The Green Room

Staying closer to home, Mrs. Coolidge became interested once again in the furnishings of the house. The rooms looked barren after the remodeling. The members of her furnishings committee were as eager as ever to get to work, although she had neglected them for some time. Several of them had been attempting to push the issue through Billy Delano, the only committee member directly involved at the White House. Probably at their urging, he had asked Colonel Grant in the winter of 1927: "We have in prospect some very handsome pieces of furniture for the White House. As the Committee on Furnishings is now formed, it is a temporary one holding power for only a limited time. It may well be that the next incumbent of the White House would want to dispense with the Committee and all the furniture that has been collected. Is there any possibility of making this Committee a permanent one?"

Delano was apprehensive as a result of the Halsey controversy of two years before. "I think the suggestions," he wrote to Grant, "would have to come from you: no member of the Committee could very well make it and I doubt if Mrs. Coolidge would want to make the proposal but I think you can see how unfair it would be to induce people to give handsome pieces to the White House without the assurance that the work of the Committee was going to be a continuous one."[31]

It happened that after the bills for the remodeling were paid in the winter of 1928, Grant was left with money to spend. Of the original appropriation of $375,000 the remodeling had cost only $296,773.11; from that $25,000 was subtracted for the rental and maintenance of the house on Dupont Circle, and a total of $53,226.89 remained in reserve. The idea of spending this money on furnishings was apparently the result of discussions between Colonel Grant and Billy Delano. In the summer of 1928 Grant agreed to present the idea to Mrs. Coolidge. "In compliance with your request," Grant wrote to Delano in July, "I took up recently with Mrs. Coolidge the possibility of refurnishing one of the first floor rooms with funds now available. She expressed herself entirely agreeable to this proposition, provided she would have a chance to act on the general scheme proposed and on individual pieces of furniture to be purchased." Mrs. Coolidge had already given the subject some thought, and indicated, Colonel Grant reported, "That the Green Room was the one she would like taken care of first and that, if your committee could study the problem and draft its recommendations this summer, she would be very glad to have a meeting on her return to Washington sometime in September."[32]

The furnishings advisory committee at last had permission to proceed. But Grant had no intention of surrendering his authority; he wrote Delano, "I feel that the close contact between this office and the Committee should be re-established. If you will look up the law creating the Committee, approved February 28, 1925, you will see that the Committee is explicitly instituted to make recommendations to the officer in charge of public buildings and grounds. It, therefore, seems most desirable that this office be represented at every meeting of the Committee. May I ask that I be informed in advance of any meeting proposed for the Committee, so that I can be present in person or be represented by Major Mehaffey." There were to be no operations on the colonel's turf without the colonel's participation.[33]

Few details survive of the committee's meetings and other activities. Harriet Pratt was a wise choice for chairman; in her late 40s, she was tall and domineering, with a sure feel for politics. Twenty years later Mrs. Pratt recalled the committee's altered structure in a memorandum to the Fine Arts Commission: "Charles A. Platt, architect, William Adams Delano, architect, and Luke Vincent Lockwood were appointed by Pres. Coolidge to serve with Mrs. Pratt as a temporary committee to advise Mrs. Coolidge." At the same time, "The following were asked to serve in an advisory capacity to the committee in regard to the selection of furniture: Mr. Robert W. de Forest and Mr. R.T.H. Halsey of the Metropolitan Museum of Art, New York." This definition of responsibilities made it clear that the public debates of the summer of 1925 were neither forgotten nor expected to happen again.[34]

Whatever ideas the members may have had for enlarging their

committee's functions, Mrs. Coolidge still considered it an advisory to herself. But even after starting up again in 1928, it seems not to have had a major influence on the First Lady, who proceeded with her decorating on her own. While she pursued her interest in the colonial style, she made no pretense to erudition. With friends or with her secretary, Polly Randolph, she searched through the materials unloaded from the attic before the remodeling and selected objects to be set aside. Discovery thrilled her. First she retrieved a mahogany table, an old brass-inlaid round-topped affair on a pedestal with claw feet. This fine specimen of American craftsmanship in the Grecian taste of the 1830s had been purchased by Andrew Jackson. Mrs. Coolidge was unaware of its provenance. She was simply looking for old things that would give the remodeled rooms a flavor of American history.

Grant, a devoted amateur historian, became interested in White House memorabilia, and was soon searching for treasures elsewhere, on behalf of Mrs. Coolidge. An inquiry at the Soldiers' Home, the vacation retreat of Presidents from the 1850s until the early 80s, brought a list of furnishings said to have been used in Lincoln's time. An old columned clock of black marble trimmed with brass stood in the home's museum room, and an aged employee told officials that the clock had been in the hallway of Anderson Cottage during the time the Presidents spent their summers there. When they took the clock to the cottage they found their proof, for it "fitted exactly" on the brackets that remained on the wall in the hall, its base coinciding "with distinct marks where some objects had set." The clock was taken to the White House, along with four pieces of china and a desk on which President Lincoln was said to have drafted the Emancipation Proclamation.

In the White House, Mrs. Coolidge seemed to take special delight in things Victorian, finding "a number of interesting pieces of black walnut furniture" in her search, "including a pair of beautiful dressers having a mirror in the center extending to the floor and on each side five or six drawers, triangular in shape, which swing out on pivots." Her quest for historical information on this material came to nothing. "There was no record," she wrote, "of any of these pieces."[35]

While the First Lady possibly entertained a passing fancy for the Victorian, her advisers were determined that the house be furnished in styles either of the colonial period or shortly after. These they considered more important, more tasteful, "handmade," as opposed to "machine-made." The industrial age, they felt, had been the beginning of the end of America's innocence. Mrs. Coolidge yielded to their preferences, accepting them as her teachers because of their museum exhibits and books. But when ordering new furniture for the two small guest rooms on the third floor, she selected for practicality newly made beds of maple, "colonial" style. Pine timbers saved by Grant from the roof structure of the original house were made into a Georgian-style bookcase with broken pediment, glass doors, and bracket feet. The whole was waxed, unpainted, so that the ancient tones of the wood could remain visible.

During the autumn of 1928 the nation was occupied with the presidential election. Herbert Hoover, champion of "rugged individualism," was the Republican nominee, and he carried his party to victory in November. Time was running out, and the furnishings committee had not done its work. Some furnishings had been acquired, but by no means a quantity sufficient to furnish even the Green Room. Grant proceeded on his own. He renewed the wall fabric in the Red Room, using the same type of red velour; and to the downy tufted sofas and chairs put there by Roosevelt in 1902, somewhat out of style even then, he restored the same pattern of red damask. The Green Room's walls were covered with new material, a green brocade woven to harmonize with a carpet purchased for the room by Mrs. Coolidge. Grant ordered colonial-style window hangings. Made of the same green brocade, they consisted of deep swags with long tails and side panels tied back.[36]

The delay in the committee's action was the result of disagreement among its members. They were strong-willed, and their tastes were not all the same. Mrs. Pratt—never reticent herself—was by December close to exasperation with her troublesome flock, finding her best ally in Billy Delano. Vigorous and impatient with indecision, she had made several purchases on her own but could not get a consensus from the committee as to whether these furnishings were suitable. Three days before Christmas she wrote to Grant wondering what would happen to the antiques and reproductions she had assembled in her basement in New York. "I am willing to underwrite up to the sum of five thousand dollars," she wrote, "for the purchase of furniture to be placed in the Green or Red Room, providing the supervision of these rooms can be placed under a committee chosen for its knowledge of the needs of the White House."

There was no question that the committee had not functioned well. Mrs. Pratt believed the only recourse in the future was to have a "supervising committee," brought together by the Smithsonian, which would have an appropriation from the Congress "for the purchase of suitable selections of furniture." She hoped the Smithsonian committee would have more power than the one appointed by Mrs. Coolidge. Implicit in her letter was the desire that the future committee on White House furnishings work more harmoniously than the present one. "I should think," she wrote, "that the personnel of the Smithsonian committee would exclude Mr. de Forest and Mr. Halsey, for obvious reasons, also Mrs. Miles White, who was appointed at the request of Mr. Halsey."[37]

In the winter of 1929, as the Coolidges commenced their final round of dinners and musicales, the committee's furnishings for the Green Room finally arrived. At that point, McKim's Green Room passed into history. The large new rug for the room was one of two commissioned by the committee for the White House; the other was predominantly red for the Red Room. Over the green rug's flamboyant Aubusson pattern, frail pieces of furniture, both antiques and reproductions, recalled the antiquarians' image of the drawing rooms of the rich in the Federalist era. "The furniture of the Green Room," went a contemporary account, "is mainly in the Hepplewhite manner, that cabinet-maker who modeled his delicacy of line and his sensitive strength after the architecture of the Adam Brothers."[38]

Against the west wall of the Green Room was a reproduction commissioned by Mrs. Pratt of an old settee known to have been owned by George Washington. This was upholstered in yellow brocade and scattered with pillows, en suite with the other upholstery of the room. A variety of tables and side and arm chairs was elegantly disposed through the lofty space. Between the great south windows a little mahogany desk stood open for writing, its surface neatly presenting several old leather-bound books, letter paper, and a bud vase. Tucked into the deep reveals of the windows were a pair of window seats. Over the sofa hung the Andrews portrait of Jefferson, commissioned by Hayes.

In the completed Green Room, with all the patriotic implications carried by its decoration, the advisory committee had created an appropriate symbol of "Coolidge prosperity." But the committee's work went little further. March came all too soon, and when the Green Room was completed, Mrs. Coolidge had turned her interests elsewhere. In later years, she would reflect proudly on her work in furnishing the White House colonial style. Her effort was the first of many.

Good-byes

March 4, 1929, was rainy and chilly. The chief usher remembered the President as moody and quiet during the weeks before Herbert Hoover took office. Workmen building the great reviewing stand before the White House remarked that the President "acted like a prisoner who had to witness the noise and bustle attendant on the building of a scaffold for his execution." Ed Starling, who was a friendly witness, felt differently.

On inauguration day, as President Coolidge was preparing to leave the White House, he asked Starling, "You're going to the station with us, aren't you?"

"Yes," said Starling, "I am." Starling had been his closest companion during the five years and seven months of his Presidency. "We didn't discuss it further," wrote the Secret Service guard. "A sudden wave of melancholy was rising in me. I knew he was glad to go, and I was happy to see him leave before something happened to him. He was getting away in good health, unworried and unburdened. I should rejoice for him. I fought back the sadness."[39]

The Coolidges bade farewell to the staff, distributing little gifts. The scene was almost tearful. For the most part the White House employees were the same people who had been there when the Coolidges arrived in 1923. Elizabeth Jaffray—"Queenie" to the President—was absent, dismissed when the household temporarily moved to Dupont Circle. The reasons are not clear, but her abrupt manner probably did not please the President. The beloved Colonel Arthur Brooks was dead; he had been taken home sick from the President's summer home in July, 1926, to die in his bed of a heart ailment.

When the Hoovers were announced as being downstairs, Mrs. Coolidge gave a final pat to her coverlet on the Lincoln bed and, with the President, descended in the elevator to the state floor. They joined the Hoovers in the Blue Room. The cars were ready at the north door. President and President-elect departed, followed by the two women in a second car, over rain-slick streets to the Capitol.

38

Irony

If ever a man became President purely to serve the public, it was Herbert Clark Hoover. Mrs. Hoover, in a letter to her children and grandchildren, made clear: "Your father did not want the Presidency himself, or for himself, or for the reputation it might bring him." Even as Lou Henry Hoover wrote, in July 1932, the protesting veterans of the Bonus Army still camped within sight of the Capitol and milled about bitterly in the streets surrounding the White House. Hoover had been in office for 3½ years. Republican prosperity had disappeared long since, its decline beginning with the stock market crash seven months after Hoover took office.[1]

When Hoover had decided to run for President, the skies had been brighter for him. He was recognized as one of the greatest living humanitarians. He had negotiated the rescue of thousands of Americans stranded in Europe at the outbreak of the World War; he had directed the program of relief for millions of Belgians and French suffering in the aftermath of the German invasion of Belgium; he had served as head of President Wilson's Food Administration. During the war the "wheatless" and "porkless" days had made Hoover's name a household word.

Herbert Hoover entered public life as a volunteer in 1914. Born into modest circumstances and orphaned early, he worked his way through school. With an engineering degree in hand, he had built a fortune in mining before his 35th year. For several years after the World War he had continued to fill high positions without salary. He was appointed secretary of commerce by Harding in 1921, and was retained by Coolidge in 1923. Under him the department became a model of effectiveness and good management. By 1928, when he resigned to run for President, the stocky, round-faced public servant, reserved but deliberate, was universally admired. Hooveria, an asteroid between Mars and Jupiter, had been named for him.

To the public his years of selfless labor for mankind were his crown. On the platform he urged the citizens toward "rugged individualism," of which he himself seemed the prime example. Even with only token help from Coolidge he won the Presidency by a large majority. The newspapers printed in the fall of 1928 greeted Hoover as an innovator, in contrast to Coolidge; they expected him to improve American life, bringing prosperity to more people than had ever known it before. "I have no fears for the future of our country," he said in his inaugural address. "It is bright with hope."

Most of the optimism that prevailed then has been forgotten, and Hoover is usually seen as an inept leader who was unable to pull the country out of the Great Depression. The joy of his rainy inauguration day, March 4, 1929, seems almost incongruous in view of the single-term administration that was to follow.

Taking Over

The enthusiasm that accompanied the 54-year-old Hoover into office brought new luster to the Presidency. Public interest in the Chief Executive, which typically had waned in the last years of the Coolidge administration, revived, and there was a rebirth of curiosity about life at the White House. Changes made in the residence by the cosmopolitan Hoovers were noted with interest. Active and ambitious, Herbert and Lou Hoover moved fast, long accustomed to having aides to help them achieve their goals. They seemed to understand sooner than most of their predecessors how precious time was in the Presidency.

"The Hoovers came in and upset the whole private part of the White House," complained Ike Hoover, whose years of service numbered nearly 40. "Never was the place so changed, so torn up, so twisted around." Accustomed to being in virtual command under Coolidge, he resented serving as middleman. The Hoovers increased the number of telephones; they installed 13 radios—the whirl of changes with these energetic people left Ike Hoover dizzy. On the night of inauguration day the new President summoned the chief usher upstairs to the study before he went to dinner. Large numbers of objects were to be removed from the room. The floor-to-ceiling bookcases put there by Coolidge during the remodeling were to be pulled out and replaced by cases only chest high, like those Herbert Hoover had seen there in Wilson's and Harding's times, with plenty of surface room on top for memorabilia and space on the walls above that for pictures and framed documents.[2]

In the days following, no sooner had the Coolidge shelving been torn out and the room painted than the President decided to move his study one room to the east, to the room Lincoln had used as an office. A great admirer of the Rail Splitter, Hoover grew to like the idea of working in the room that had housed his illustrious predecessor. All the furniture—the high post bed, several bureaus, a sofa, and chairs—was taken to another room. Storage areas in the attic and basement were searched for furnishings that might have been used in Lincoln's time. Hoover brought from among his own possessions a favorite print, "First Reading of the Emancipation Proclamation Before the Cabinet."

Meanwhile, other alterations took place, most of them under the direction of Mrs. Hoover. She was a woman with gentle, matronly good looks. Like the President, she was an excellent manager, an expert organizer of people. An eternal wellspring of ideas, she liked to make improvements whether in procedures or, as in this case, in the arrangement of furniture. Mrs. Hoover would be rearranging furniture for four years. She had known the White House well since Wilson's time; she and her husband had tolerated Harding's poker parties on occasion, but, like Andrew Mellon, never really as members of the gang. During Coolidge's years she had had ample opportunity to learn about the private quarters. After her husband's election she began studying floor plans provided by Colonel Grant.

Lincoln's rosewood bed was removed from the presidential bedroom across the hall to the northwest bedroom, the one Lincoln himself had known as the Prince of Wales Bedroom; this was now styled the "Lincoln Bedroom," the first by that name in the White House. For the room Mrs. Hoover acquired an old horsehair-covered parlor suite said to have been owned by Lincoln; hers and the President's collection of Lincoln memorabilia was arranged for display. The presidential bedroom on the south side they furnished with the comfortable furniture they had used for many years in their house at 2300 S Street in Washington. In the adjoining dressing room on the southwest corner Mrs. Hoover placed a daybed for afternoon rest and a desk for personal accounts and correspondence.

The Hoovers also transferred the contents of their S Street drawing room, including two large Chippendale-style sofas covered in black-and-gold Chinese brocade, to the oval room. Mrs. Hoover's piano was put there, and her secretaries later recalled the great effort the First Lady put into finding a suitable shade of green taffeta for the window curtains. She ultimately settled on "lettuce green." One secretary further remarked that Mrs. Hoover "had her own very definite ideas of interior decoration, and when she got things all together, it was very comfortable and lovely." Her bold color scheme for the oval room was black and green.[3]

Shoulder-high bookcases were built along the walls of the central corridor to hold a library of 500 volumes presented by the American Booksellers Association. With the books was intermingled a Hoover Museum: Here the classic book on mining she and Hoover had translated from the Spanish; elsewhere lines of framed photographs—the newly-weds at their residence in Peking, later with their two sons at the London house in Hyde Park Gate or in the country at Walton-on-Thames, still later on the campus of their beloved Stanford University. They had been happy everywhere they had lived, and loved to be surrounded by remind-ers of their life together.

In front of the bookcases awaited rows of chairs, for use when mov-ies were shown to family, staff, and guests. Hoover had a wide interest in film and broadcasting. Among the First Lady's innumerable hobbies was home movies. Before moving to the White House she found time to do all her own film editing; afterward the work was often assigned to one of her three secretaries, who found the First Lady an exacting critic. Her movies of the President and their journeys and pastimes were regularly screened in the upstairs corridor. Now and then the bill was expanded to include a feature-length Hollywood production.[4]

What had been the study, east of the oval room, became the main upstairs drawing room. Furnished initially with belongings from the S Street house, it was later to be the object of a major redecoration. Smaller rooms, once dressing rooms, became bedrooms in some cases, and some former bedrooms became sitting rooms. The Hoovers' manner of receiving required many sitting rooms, both large and small, formal and informal. They tended to give appointments liberally; but the meet-ings were typically short. To conserve time, they had developed over the years a system that involved the use of adjacent or nearby rooms to expedite social and business matters almost concurrently. Visitors were ushered to different rooms, usually unseen by one another, where they met briefly with their host. An extra minute or two might be spared for social callers, but subordinates usually found a five-minute business con-ference with the President a generous portion. Personal contact, how-ever, was too important to Hoover to relegate most of his appointments to aides, as had others before him. Mrs. Hoover, always involved in civic activities, added to her demanding load the streams of callers who came to request favors or just to meet her.[5]

In the west hall, Mrs. Hoover wished to create something different, a special room with a whimsical tropical setting. The plaster walls were painted dead white. Tall palms and ferns in pots were massed along the walls and on a plant stand built beneath the great lunette window, which was stripped of curtains so that the western light poured in. Several suites of wicker furniture, painted ivory, were arranged over a green and straw-colored checkerboard of manila floor matting. The sofas were heaped with colorful cushions; magazines and books were arranged on the tables. Canaries chirped from cages among the plants. It was the most memorable room in the Hoover White House.

In a few weeks the upstairs began to look lived-in. Though Coolidge had built the new third floor, President Hoover was the first to use and furnish its expanded spaces. He was also first to articulate the family quarters as an apartment separate from the state areas. The second floor was more or less self-contained, with most of the departments of personal service housed on the third floor. Dependence upon the central kitchen in the basement was all that tied presidential family life to the rest of the White House. The Hoovers made a point of eating all their meals in the State Dining Room, as if to remind themselves and those around them of who they were. Dinner was always an occasion for evening clothes and full formal service even on those rare occasions—only three, according to the housekeeper—when the President and Mrs. Hoover sat down to dine alone.[6]

Seven Months

The first seven months of the Hoover administration were marked by constant social activity at the White House. Dinners, musicales, receptions—the First Lady's office and the State Department's protocol office were almost melded into one by the constant labor of keeping the social wheels rolling. Polly Randolph remained for more than a year as social secretary, paid by the government, and was joined by two other young women who had served Mrs. Hoover in private life, Ruth Fesler and Mildred Hall. These two remained in Mrs. Hoover's personal employ, doing White House work, as well as that connected with the First Lady's demanding position as president of the Girl Scouts of America. Along with reference books on social procedures, the secretaries always kept the *Girl Scout Handbook* close by, for Mrs. Hoover considered it the final authority on most essential questions.[7]

The three secretaries were the most yet employed by a First Lady. A staff of this magnitude created an office-like environment upstairs that was too busy and noisy for the family quarters. In the interest of privacy for the family, Mrs. Hoover moved her secretaries and files to rooms on the new third floor.

The Hoovers were veteran entertainers, experienced in society in the United States, Europe, and the Orient, and they took their responsibilities as host and hostess seriously. The rituals of White House entertaining, long familiar to the Hoovers, were left much the same. They usually invited larger numbers of guests to receptions than had the Coolidges. The march down the grand stair was reinstated, with all the official family and special guests included, along with an honor guard and blaring bugles. When the end of the receiving line was in sight in the Blue Room, the Marine Band struck up "The Blue Danube Waltz," to signal that the official party should start toward the Red Room. Awaiting his guests there, the President would lead them in a march back upstairs, from whence they descended in the elevator and left in automobiles from the south entrance. The guests who remained in the state rooms could choose either to depart or to remain and dance for several hours to the music of the band.

The Hoovers were sensitive in humanitarian matters. They warmly received the wives and daughters of Mormon senators and congressmen, who had heretofore been excluded. Mrs. Oscar DePriest, the wife of the first Negro congressman since Reconstruction, was invited to tea by Mrs. Hoover, breaking a long White House tradition of racial segregation. No Negro had been entertained at the White House since the controversial visit of Booker T. Washington in 1901. If the new Mormon policy got little attention, the DePriest invitation created a stir. As soon as it was received, Congressman DePriest informed the press. Mrs. DePriest was sought out by reporters. The three social secretaries were besieged with angry telephone calls. Concerned over how some of the guests might act, and sensitive to Mrs. DePriest's feelings, Mrs. Hoover split her tea party into two separate events with two carefully composed guest lists. On the first day, when Mrs. DePriest attended, the company was made up of what the President described as "ladies previously tested as to their feelings." Everything went smoothly, except for a brief case of jitters by one of the black butlers.[8]

But the flood of mail that followed still deeply offended Ruth Fesler when she recalled it many years after the tea party. Wrote the secretary, "it was unfortunate for Mrs. Hoover that she opened and read [the letters]. But she stood her ground; she had done the right thing and she knew it."[9] President Hoover recalled the incident many years later: "The speeches of southern Senators and Congressmen, the editorials in the southern press, and a denunciatory resolution by the Texas Legislature wounded her deeply . . . .I sought to divert the lightning by at once inviting Dr. [Robert Russa] Moton of Tuskegee to lunch with me. The White House was thus 'defiled' several times during my term."[10]

In comparison, the other wave that crashed on the social sands of the White House early in Hoover's administration seemed farcical. Its protagonist was Dolly Gann, a portly woman in her early 60s with a gift of gab and a devilish twinkle in her eye. Photographs show a woman who liked dressy clothes; she sported strands of pearls and the headache bands more familiar on younger women. She had been the popular hostess for her widower half brother, Senator Charles Curtis, for some time, and she occupied her own position in society as Mrs. Edward E. Gann, wife of an successful, easygoing lawyer.

Mrs. Gann continued to serve as hostess for Curtis when he became Hoover's Vice President. Both assumed she would receive official rank at social affairs as though she were his wife. To clarify the point, Vice President Curtis, in March 1929, notified Secretary of State Frank B. Kellogg that Mrs. Gann was to be his official hostess. The secretary responded immediately that her "title" would have significance only in Curtis's own home. At the same time, the secretary made an issue of the matter by notifying the entire diplomatic corps that Mrs. Gann was to be seated in precedence below the wives of ambassadors, being recognized merely as a guest of the Vice President.

Angered by what he considered an affront to his sister, Curtis wrote a heated commentary on this decision. Almost concurrently, Kellogg was replaced as secretary of state by Henry L. Stimson, who recognized a lighted fuse when he saw one, but could not ignore a controversy that had become front-page news. He moved cautiously, putting the question to selected members of the diplomatic corps. Even as the ambassadors huddled, sides were being taken for and against Dolly Gann. One State Department official anonymously told a reporter from the *New York Herald Tribune*, "I think . . . that if Mr. Curtis and Mrs. Gann insist on their present line of attack that they will be the chief sufferers."[11]

Stimson finally got the diplomats to give him the decision he wanted, to grant Mrs. Gann the status due a Vice President's wife, adding tactfully that if some American authority decided otherwise, they would comply. The secretary declared this final. Mrs. Gann had triumphed over the men. What about the women, to whom official rank was often even more important than to their husbands? The Vice President's official hostess was honored with full rank at a dinner on April 11, 1929, given at the Chilean Embassy by Ambassador Carlos Davila. This affair went exactly as Stimson had decreed. Trouble did not come until Mrs. Eugene Meyer, Jr., revealed that she would honor the State Department ruling for a dinner party on May 5, at the end of the social season. Alice Roosevelt Longworth, wife of the speaker of the House, was the first to decline, and others followed.

The matter simmered over the summer, and in October the White House became the battleground. A state dinner was always the ultimate test for anyone whose official rank might be in question. This one, held unusually early, was the most important dinner Hoover had yet given, and honored Prime Minister J. Ramsay MacDonald of Britain. Invitations reached their destinations in late September; responses, always prompt, included an acceptance from Mrs. Gann for herself, the Vice President, and Mr. Gann. She had delayed ending her summer retreat and now returned to Washington. The President, determined to make the final statement and end the war forever, followed protocol to the letter. At eight in the evening of October 6, when the Marine Band played "Hail to the Chief," Mrs. Gann descended the grand staircase on the Prime Minister's arm, and was seated on the President's left. By way of quiet compromise, the Vice President yielded his place beside Mrs. Hoover and sat with the Prime Minister's daughter farther down the table. The Longworths let it be known that they were out of town.[12]

The Great Depression Begins

President Hoover was in the Midwest concluding his first major tour the day the stock market crashed. He had gone to announce a vast federal waterworks project, to be one of the most ambitious public works programs in history. From the platform of his private train, in town after town, he proclaimed prosperity. For seven rainy days he traveled, arriving home in midafternoon on October 24, 1929. Reports on the economy had come to him regularly aboard the train. At a press conference the next morning in the East Room he assured newsmen that the nation's business stood on a solid foundation.

But things grew worse. October 29, Black Tuesday, the market fell sharply to what seemed rock bottom. The President urged the people not to think in negative terms, for he earnestly believed this was only an interlude, like the Panic of 1907. Like most people, he seemed to have had little idea of how bad the worst could be. Prior to the convening of the Congress in December he summoned an impressive list of business leaders to the White House, where they met in ten different groups through the days of November. The telegraph office in the West Wing was busy night and day receiving messages to the President; in the course of the November conferences, some 5,000 telegrams of support came to the White House.

When the President gave his plan to the Congress in December it was surprisingly different from anything that could have been imagined by his Republican predecessors. Where they had put their faith in business, he called on the federal government to save the day through educational reforms, improved housing for the underprivileged, conservation, and jobs in long-range construction work; the government was further to institute lower taxation, more efficient management, and a balanced budget. He called upon the volunteer spirit in Americans to help him pull the ox from the ditch as it had done with success in his great food programs during the war.

His challenge was not understood. Not a politician by experience, or even by inclination, Hoover had proposed a course utterly alien to friends and enemies alike. The congressmen and senators, meeting in the storm of a national crisis, were far more interested in fixing blame than in taking radical steps toward a solution. Hoover did not pause to play or even to understand their game, but forged ahead in the belief that he, being right, would prevail. His successes were to be few. Through the rest of his administration he introduced his programs, only to have them fall or be wounded in the political attacks of his adversaries. He stubbornly believed that sound policies, as he defined them, would free the nation from its troubles, that the governmental framework as it stood could, if managed well, be used to solve the problems. But never again was he able to sell himself to the public after the Depression began. Even his pleasant relationship with the press turned sour.

The Executive Office Building

To add to the gloom of 1929, the Executive Office Building was burned to its walls by a great fire that struck on Christmas Eve. The White House was a jewel box in the snow that night, lighted top to bottom, with the clatter of a children's Christmas party audible to the Secret Service and police guards patrolling the grounds. The night had begun in the entrance hall with a serenade of Christmas carols by a group of Girl Scouts. With their two grandchildren in their arms, the Hoovers had stood moist-eyed in the doorway of the Blue Room, their dinner guests lining the transverse hall. Mrs. Hoover could hardly bear to see the serenade end, and requested more and more carols.[13]

Later, as the President's official family and their children were eating dinner, Ike Hoover hurriedly entered the State Dining Room and whispered to the President that the Executive Office Building was on fire. The men quickly departed. Mrs. Hoover ordered the butler to close the curtains and shepherded the children to the Christmas tree at the south end of the dining room, where, with a combination of stories and presents, she kept them so calm that the New York *World* proclaimed her a "heroine."[14]

Outside, from the elevation of the west terrace, the President, his sons, his secretaries, and his Cabinet watched the blaze rising high before them. Firemen were working toward the fire from West Executive Avenue, but the hottest flames were in the north part of the building and great damage was being done. Hoover's dinner companions scattered across the terrace, down the stair into the wing, and joined the work of pulling files out onto the snow-covered grounds. The youngest son, Allan Hoover, home from Harvard for the holiday, went into the dark Oval Office and, with the assistance of one of the secretaries, removed the drawers from his father's desk. Pictures were pulled from the walls, books from the shelves. Ike Hoover entered the Cabinet Room and covered the great table with a wet tarpaulin.[15]

Fewer materials were saved from the north end of the building, where fire and water hose alike tore at the offices. When the flames spread to the rear, and the rescuers abandoned the Oval Office, the hoses began freezing and yielded no more water until thawed out with heat. Fire could be seen running riot in the Oval Office. Weakened by water and heat, portions of the plaster ceiling fell from its metal lath. Such of the dark green burlap on the walls that was not eaten by fire sagged from the water that soaked it, revealing in places the white plaster behind it.

While the President specified the materials he wanted to save, he apparently did not go into the burning office, remaining instead on the west terrace. Someone brought him an overcoat, which he put on over his evening suit. The bitter wind of the snowy night cut at him, and the yellow glare of the raging fire reflected on his face, and on the faces of more than a hundred men working in freezing temperatures to douse it. At about one in the morning, the fire was out, leaving the Executive Office Building a smoking shambles. New snow began to fall as the spectators departed, and an enlarged detail of the White House Police began to patrol the site.

Melodrama always thrives in the recollections of fires. George E. Akerson, one of the President's secretaries, had bought for his son's Christmas present a wire-haired terrier puppy. To hide it from the boy, he had stashed it away in his office, intending to take it home in its cardboard box after the party. In the alarm and confusion, he forgot the dog. After the fire was over, in the horror of sudden realization, Akerson was happily relieved to discover that the President had remembered the puppy and had ordered its rescue.[16]

Rebuilding and Expanding

The destruction of the Executive Office Building might be seen initially as a symbol of the unhappy tricks history had played on the Rugged Individualist. But the West Wing—as the office building was being called by that time—had a more specific meaning. In most respects it was a better symbol of the Hoover Presidency than the White House itself. He had carried out a major remodeling of the building not long after he took office, converting the simple annex into an administrative center to house his corporation-style staff, which was much larger than any of its predecessors. The remodeled West Wing was a testimony in brick and mortar to Hoover's efficiency.

When he had first arrived at the White House in March 1929, practically all the functions of the Executive Office were carried out on the main floor of the West Wing. The second floor was only an attic, while underground there was a large basement for storage. Working conditions were crowded, with some 40 people in only five rooms. Little had changed since Taft's renovation in 1909, when the Oval Office was created. Besides the President's office, large spaces were allocated for reporters and the private secretary, and for Cabinet meetings and a tastefully appointed lounge where congressmen and senators could wait for interviews with the President or the secretary.

Since Hoover had three private secretaries instead of the usual one, a change of some sort was necessary. Each required a suitable office, with an antechamber for his stenographer. In addition, by Hoover's third month in office, the staff had grown so large that the old building would have been wholly inadequate.

By the middle of March in 1929, Colonel Grant was well along with plans for remodeling. A file of drawings from the original construction under McKim in 1902 recorded the development of the West Wing. It had been built as a temporary office structure, a rectangle of brick subdivided by partitions of wood frame and plaster. Taft's expansion program in 1909 had made it permanent, doubling its size by adding on to the south side. The stuccoed rear wall of the earlier Executive Office could still be seen in a long transverse corridor which divided the plan into two parts. On the north were the clerical staff and the waiting rooms; on the south were the President, his secretary, and the Cabinet meeting room.

Hoover ordered major rearrangements on the north side. Knocking out partitions created two new executive suites, each with a fireplace and other amenities suitable to presidential secretaries. The modest square entrance lobby became a T-shaped space fully twice the size it had been. Except for the few who came over from the White House, all callers were to present themselves in the lobby. One change clearly revealed the President's lack of concern for politics: The special waiting room for congressmen and senators was eliminated. The politicians were required to sit in the lobby like everyone else, in full view of the public and the adjacent press room.

The basement of the Executive Office Building was redesigned. Extensive excavation doubled the space, leaving only the areas beneath the Cabinet Room and the Oval Office at grade level. Telegraph room, clerks' rooms, stenographers' offices, stockrooms, vault, locker rooms, and men's and women's lounges were moved there. The rooms were ample, and some had windows on a western areaway. A broad stair led to the corridor on the main floor.[17]

In its general layout, the new plan emphasized the distinction between the President and his staff and outsiders who called at the West Wing. Visitors and press were restricted to the north side. Only one staff office had immediate access to the lobby and the press room: that of Walter Newton, the President's secretary for political matters, who dealt with patronage. The avenue of communication for the workers in the office became the new transverse corridor, which was cut off from the public lobby, but connected with all offices, including that of the President. Thus the President was in the midst of his staff, instead of remaining apart from it.

The contract for construction was awarded to the N.P. Severin Company, which had built the new roof and attic of the White House two years before. Grant observed confidentially that the "contractor took this work at about cost because of its prominence." The contract was signed April 18, 1929. As always in White House projects, time was short. The West Wing was to be completed by early June, with little or no disturbance of the functioning office. First the basement was excavated by hand to approximately three-quarters of the space beneath the building. Underpinnings were built, and the new rooms were created with wooden partitions and finished; the entire clerical staff was moved there to free the main floor for its rearrangements. Heavy canvas was used to screen the north half of the structure from the executive offices on the south. In terms of both dust and noise, the work was surprisingly unobtrusive. Only the cutting of new doors, the walling in of old ones, and the building of the new basement stair seem to have interfered with the President's schedule. Forewarned, he usually retreated to the study upstairs in the White House when noise or dirt might be a problem. The heaviest of the labor was conducted at night and on weekends, when the President was likely to be out of town.[18]

Grant accepted the finished building June 7. And for 6½ months the revised Executive Office functioned successfully, until the Christmas Eve fire, which left only the brick walls on the north and the severely damaged framework of the Oval Office and the other rooms on the south. Inspecting the ruins on Christmas Day 1929, Grant pronounced the brick walls unharmed. "He was unable to find even a crack," reported the Washington *Evening Star*.[19]

Grant's office at once began making drawings for reconstruction. For political reasons, words were used cautiously in describing the work: The attic was to be rebuilt, the main floor and basement to have "general repairs." Bids were to be in on December 27. There were several, but the contract went to a Washington firm, Charles H. Tompkins Company, the low bidder at $74,880. The finished West Wing, including a central air-conditioning system installed by the Carrier Engineering Company of Newark, New Jersey, was reoccupied in April of 1930.

With the nation in turmoil in 1929 over the "business situation," Hoover was reluctant to make obvious changes in the paraphernalia of the Presidency. The reconstruction of the West Wing in 1930 produced a near duplication of the original as remodeled in 1929. Even at the time it was clear that there were better alternatives. The President's staff hoped that the ruins would be demolished and that they would relocate permanently to the State, War, & Navy Building next door. While Hoover and his office force did move temporarily to War & Navy during the rebuilding of the West Wing, he remained eager to return to his proper office. Even at War & Navy, where he used General Pershing's office, the President ordered all war memorabilia removed and the room furnished and arranged to be as much like the Oval Office as possible.

The need for space was to increase throughout Hoover's administration. Even his telephone records reveal a fast tempo of work: During 1930 calls made from the Executive Office Building totaled 77,055; and 308,220 were received. In 1931 the President commandeered several of the household service rooms in the old west terrace that extended from the side of the White House. Their plaster walls were repaired and their pine floors sanded, transforming them into suitable executive offices. In 1932 more west terrace rooms were converted into offices, sending laundry, maids' dining room, and floral services into cramped make-do spaces in the basement of the house proper. Still the needs of the burgeoning presidential staff were not satisfied. By the close of the Hoover administration in 1933 the West Wing was almost obsolete for want of space. Hoover's last change was to redesign the northeast office on the main floor to accommodate a secretarial pool.[20]

Administration

President Hoover was an exacting taskmaster. The working day in the Executive Office began at around 7:30 a.m., with the President arriving about an hour later to read major newspapers from throughout the country. He dictated his correspondence until 10, then saw callers at 10-to-15-minute intervals until 12:30 or 1:00. Lunch with Mrs. Hoover, and almost always several guests, occupied about an hour. When the President received the credentials of a new diplomat, he usually did so after lunch, in the Blue Room.

Back in the office at 2:30 or 3:00 p.m., Hoover labored until 6, then returned to the White House with papers tucked under his arm. By tradition no employees of the office departed before the President, and there were senior employees in sufficient abundance to keep the others informed of tradition. Among the seniors was Rudolph Forster, the neat, soft-spoken executive clerk who had gone to the White House on temporary detail during the Spanish-American War and had never left. Nelson P. Webster, the executive and disbursements clerk, had also worked for McKinley. Five office employees of Hoover in 1930 had appeared on Theodore Roosevelt's payroll in 1902. Others had accumulated through the administrations of Taft, Wilson, Harding, and Coolidge. Although a woman had first appeared on the payroll in 1889, when Harrison came to office, it was under Coolidge that women came into mild prominence on the White House office staff as stenographers.

Records show 38 employees in the Executive Office in 1930, including the three principal secretaries, who were political appointees and the highest in rank. But this represents only part of a body of well over a hundred people. Arriving at an exact total of employees appearing daily to work in the West Wing is almost impossible, for most of the President's staff was "borrowed" from the departments, particularly from Navy, War, Justice, and Treasury, and the Veterans' Bureau and the Government Printing Office.[21]

Hoover remembered in later years that when he went to the White House the West Wing was "sorely afflicted with time-consuming and nerve-racking customs." When he reorganized and expanded his staff, he attempted to streamline the procedures, particularly those of receiving calls from citizens. The noon-hour receptions in the West Wing, when visitors came to see the President and shake his hand, had grown so that they sometimes involved more than a thousand people. Hoover tried to require an admission card from a high official, or a congressman or senator, only to find that "Congressmen availed themselves of this as an entertainment feature for their visiting constituents." The situation "got worse," and the President "suppressed the noon reception altogether," giving the time thereafter to appointments with people calling to discuss "matters of importance."[22]

Improve what he might, Hoover found much inefficiency that he could not erase, for it was part of the institution. One of his secretaries, George Aubrey Hastings, set down his impression of the demands upon the President: "Supposing you were dealing in your office with matters of vast magnitude and under pressure of time and volume of work and also knew that your anteroom was filled with callers awaiting to see you on business, that you had half a dozen speeches scheduled for the near future, that invitations to speak or attend some public function were pouring into your office hourly, that your daily mail was more than ten men could give personal attention to, that press representatives and photographers were waiting to see you, and that a delegation was waiting to shake hands with you—this would give you some idea of what an average day means to the President."[23]

The White House in Hard Times

Although Depression Washington was sustained to some extent by the stability of the federal establishment, thousands of its citizens lacked work, and evidence of financial disaster was everywhere. Hoover himself wrote of the "dreary no man's land of the depression." Jobs were few, but the applicants many. The West Wing reconstruction was besieged from beginning to end by men needing work. Full-scale wages were paid by direction of the President, who, wrote Grant, made it a policy "not to permit the temporary financial stringency of the country to lower the scale of living of American workmen."

When the White House was painted in the autumn of 1930, the contract was awarded to a company with nonunion employees. A loud protest arose; labor unions wrote to the legislators on Capitol Hill, who passed their letters on to Colonel Grant. Never one to back down or avoid an issue, Grant wrote a lengthy response. The federal government, he said, was not required to employ union labor, and if he restricted his candidates to union shops, he would be in "violation of the statutes passed by Congress." To the charge that the nonunion companies paid slave wages, Grant said that he required the contractors to pay at least government scale.[24]

A servant recalled, "Times were terrible, but we [the servants] could pay our rent and we had good meals at the White House." Gathered at the tables in either the colored or white servants' dining rooms, a large percentage of the 58 household employees—the 32 house servants for the most part—ate one, two, and sometimes three meals a day. The President personally paid for this and more, for meals were often served to part-time help who came on special assignment.[25]

Domestic management of the house was conducted by Mrs. Ava Long, who was in later years to write articles on the subject. Her title, "official custodian of the White House," had been created in 1927, when Coolidge replaced Mrs. Jaffray with Ellen Riley, a Boston dietitian. Mrs. Long had managed large establishments for private citizens and had felt closer to those families than to the occupants of the White House. "I found it much easier to admire the Hoovers than to like them," she wrote soon after the administration had ended in 1933. "Finer people never lived. But the President and Mrs. Hoover rarely broke through the barrier between those who serve and those who are served. During the entire four years that I shared a roof with them, Mr. Hoover spoke to me only four times."[26]

Mrs. Long, living in an apartment on the third floor, seldom left the White House during the Hoovers' four years. In theory, at least, she worked under the supervision of Ike Hoover; their association was usually only by telephone. Ike Hoover handled the day-to-day operation, most of the hiring and firing, and anything regarding ceremony and procedure. In his job, continuity was a valuable asset; his and Mrs. Long's paths of authority were more or less parallel, crossing only in the sense that he was charged with keeping the house in operation and she with translating the Hoovers' wishes and tastes to a well-managed kitchen and a residence that represented them well.

"Each morning I went through a certain routine," she wrote. "At nine, in my office on the ground floor, I met the chief cook, the butler, the head houseman from each floor, and the carpenter. . . . If a party were in the offing, I saw also at the morning conference the head flower man, to find out what flowers were available." By the time of the meeting, she would already have spoken with Mrs. Hoover. When the daily arrangements were made, and everyone was at work, she turned to her accounts. "Because of the peculiar division of expenses in the White House, I had to keep three sets of books. The first accounted for the President's personal share of the household expenses. In the second, I recorded all expenditures for official entertainments. . . . My third set of books accounted for the salaries of servants and for all repairs and re-placements which are paid for out of the general appropriation for run-ning the White House."[27]

In her recollections Mrs. Long does not mention the Depression, although she surely saw evidence of its ravages when she emerged from the presidential enclave. She did all the buying of food, as had Miss Riley and Mrs. Jaffray before her. Driven to stores and markets twice a week, she selected fruits and vegetables, meats and butter. Those of her bills that survive do not reflect the sharp drop in prices that eventually came with the Depression, nor do they show any belt-tightening at the White House. The bills for cigars alone ran into the hundreds of dollars each month; as much was spent for fancy candies and cakes; meat and produce cost staggering sums. Hoover's food bills were usually some $2,000 per month, and this, of course, without liquor or wine.[28]

He ran the White House as though there were no Depression. He wanted it to symbolize optimism and hope. Public visiting hours were extended from a short morning period to 10 a.m. until 4 p.m., except when the state rooms were in use. Annual visitation nearly doubled; 900,000 people went to the White House in 1932. A single holiday might bring 5,000. The increased size of these crowds reflected the na-tional focus on the President during hard times. Mrs. Hoover made some changes in the state rooms, in an effort to enrich the visitors' experience. In 1930 she ordered the portraits of George and Martha Washington moved from the Red Room to the East Room, the most frequently seen by the public. They have hung there ever since.[29]

Receptions were larger than ever, with guest lists including up to 2,500 people. The greatest public event was the colorful and traditional New Year's reception. Although Coolidge had chosen not to continue this custom in 1929, spending the holiday in Florida rather than endure an event which was sure to leave him and his wife exhausted, sometimes with hands bruised and bodies aching, Hoover chose to revive the cus-tom. On New Year's morning 1930, after greeting the nation by radio from the West Wing, the President opened the White House doors to the diplomatic corps at noon, and afterward received 6,348 citizens between the hours of 1 and 3:30 in the afternoon. The reception was held again in 1931 and 1932. In 1933 the Hoovers too fled to Florida, and the historic New Year's reception was never held again.[30]

The Bonus Army

The President put himself before the public as much as possible. A sketch survives of his radio setup in the West Wing, the elevated rostrum with its row of boxlike microphones and the various other equipment placed about on the floor. He traveled frequently, always by private train, making speeches and public appearances. While his relations with the press had deteriorated, the newspapers constantly covered not only his official activities, but also as much of his private life as he would permit. Publicity, together with the sad state of economic affairs, increased people's interest in Herbert Hoover, and his personal appearances drew unprecedented crowds.

Guarding the President and his house became more complicated. Two select groups of guards served the White House, the Secret Service detail, which protected the President's person, and the White House Police, a branch of the Metropolitan Police, which had for nearly a century protected the buildings and grounds. The Secret Service men were under the jurisdiction of the Treasury Department, while the White House Police were under Grant's Public Buildings and Grounds Office. Ed Starling, who was the senior member of the Secret Service detail at the White House, wrote: "The effect of the depression on the Detail was acute. Our vigilance had to be doubled; the worries and problems which ordinarily beset us were multiplied. Crank letters, threats, and eccentric visitors reached a new high. Secret Service agents all over the country were busy checking on the people who felt an inclination to swell the White House mailbags."[31]

Early in 1930 President Hoover determined to unite the two forces that guarded the White House, "in the interest of good administration." This was accomplished by the Congress in February, when it placed the White House Police under the chief of the Secret Service Division. The police were not to be trained as Secret Service men, but, according to the act, were to "possess privileges and powers and perform duties similar to those of the members of the Metropolitan Police of the District of Columbia."

The President and First Lady were more closely guarded at all times. There were between 40 and 50 men assigned to each White House Police working shift; moreover, two Secret Service agents always accompanied the President in town, and eight or ten were with him on trips. These attendants were only the tip of the security iceberg, as numerous other Secret Service men were sent ahead from Washington or recruited locally in the areas in which the President traveled. News reporters had their briefcases and cameras inspected upon entering the West Wing; womens' purses had to be inspected before they could enter the White House to see the President or Mrs. Hoover. No one, no matter who he or she was, could approach the President even at a social gathering in the White House carrying a package of any kind.

Documents relating to security at the White House suggest that the Secret Service in Hoover's time anticipated not only attempts on the President's life but civil disorders as well. A confidential memorandum dated January 1932 is entitled "Riot Call Regulations." It describes 13 key guard positions in the White House and on the two terraces. The agents knew that bitterness was building on many fronts, with the flood of unemployed and the increased bankruptcies. It was a presidential election year, and the Democrats were denouncing the programs that Hoover hoped would rescue the nation. The Republicans nominated Hoover for another term in June.

Later that month the White House security force was certain it would at last have its riot, when the "Bonus Army"—camped in Washington since May—began to make trouble. Some 20,000 strong, this "army" of veterans had come to Washington from all over the nation to try peacefully to coerce Congress into releasing their service bonuses, which were bonds that, ironically, were not to mature until 1945. Broke and desperate, their theme was "Stay till '45" if not paid before.[32]

The thousands of bonus veterans milling about with their wives and children on the Capitol grounds and in the public offices during the worst financial crisis in American history made a compelling scene. This was a demonstration, indeed a threat of a sort not made to the Congress since the 18th century, in the days of the Articles of Confederation. The effect of the Bonus Marchers' presence in Washington on the Secret Service can be readily imagined. Agents feared that the same sort of violence that had shaken some other American cities had now arrived on the President's doorstep. In anticipation of trouble, Secret Service men were called to the capital from all over the United States. The White House was patrolled like a fortress, with scores of plainclothesmen stationed throughout the house and grounds. But the veterans were at first too much occupied with the Capitol and their demonstrations there to give attention to the White House. Beginning about June 24, a lone veteran in uniform, carrying an American flag, began walking back and forth along the iron fence on Pennsylvania Avenue with a sign pinned to his backpack: "Pay the Bonus now."

The stage was thus set for violence at the White House. The last had taken place when Tyler had been burned in effigy some 90 years before. Hoover, still in town and busy with work, felt sympathetic toward the marchers as veterans, but he was suspicious of the small group of professed communists known to be among them. The camps occupied by the marchers, both in Washington and across the river in Anacostia, were on military sites, and the President had provided military supplies, as well as basic campground comforts. Hoover suggested that Congress appropriate funds to pay the marchers for railroad tickets home. Congress complied before it adjourned, without taking any further action for the Bonus marchers.

On the night of the adjournment, June 20, an "On to the White House" movement was proposed by some of the marchers at the Capitol. During the day rumors of this shift had reached the Secret Service, which decided on its own authority to remove the veteran who had been marching in front of the fence, now joined by another marcher, a little man with one hand, carrying a large American flag.

The agents delayed their action until nearly 11 p.m., however, which was about the time the Congress began its adjournment proceedings at the Capitol. Already a crowd of considerable size had gathered in front of the White House, a combination of Bonus Marchers, curious citizens, and the press. When the police attempted to drag the demonstrators into police cars and arrest them on the charge of parading without permits, the two fought back. The jeering crowd surged toward the officers, providing photographers with pictures that assured full front-page coverage of the incident nationwide.

By the following morning the demonstrating was finished at the White House and the Capitol. A large part of the Bonus Army was either on its way home, with the tickets provided by the Congress, or soon would be. Yet some 5,000 or more remained, still provided for by the Army, hoping to convince the President to call the Congress into an extra session in their behalf. By July 20, having no luck, the veterans determined to picket the White House.

The police refused to issue a parade permit for this purpose. Marching over from Anacostia, some 200 veterans were met near the Treasury Building by a contingent of police and told that they could go no farther. The area around the White House was closed for the day. Chains bound the gates; police cars and policemen were everywhere; the Secret Service covered the grounds within the iron fence and patrolled the windows and roof of the house. All traffic was barred from the streets around the White House and Lafayette Park. The veterans attempted to charge through the police barricades in wedge-shaped formations, but were met by the police halfway with countercharges. In each of about seven assaults the veterans fell back, until at last they were transported to the Anacostia camp in Army vehicles.

The marchers never met the President. Hoover had told his aides at the outset: "If they ask you for permission to see me and they are veterans, tell them that I will receive a committee representing them. . . . I won't receive any communists. The committee must be composed of veterans." Despite the President's sympathetic attitude, the police, Secret Service, and Army, alarmed by the incident in the street, were determined to rid the city of the Bonus Army. Several days later, when the police attempted to clear one of the Bonus Marchers' camps to make way for a federal building project, a bloody riot erupted.

A reluctant President, under great pressure from those who surrounded him, finally called out the Army, although he refused to establish martial law. Eager to end the episode, the Army paid little heed to the President's specific admonition to proceed cautiously and respect human life and dignity. Camps were burned and their tenants routed in such a rough manner as to create a national scandal. The President was held ultimately responsible for the ill-treatment not only of veterans, but also of the women and children who had accompanied them. It was the low ebb of Hoover's administration.[33]

Where the Heart Is

Even in the storm of events, the home life of the Hoovers at the White House remained much as it had always been elsewhere. They were used to transience, and knew how to make themselves feel at home. Their permanent residence in Palo Alto, California, was on land leased to them by the trustees of Stanford University. Built just after the war, the large house was Mrs. Hoover's rather severe version of the then-popular Mission style, designed to suggest an ancient adobe pueblo of the Southwest. It replaced the family's two houses in England. They also maintained an apartment in New York as a second lodging.

The size of the Hoover family resident at the White House varied, but was largest in 1930, when their daughter-in-law Margaret and her two children lived there while her husband, Herbert Hoover, Jr., recovered from a mild case of tuberculosis in the mountains at Asheville, North Carolina. Margaret Hoover, little Peggy Ann, and Herbert III soon became White House celebrities. Usually, however, the senior Hoovers were by themselves. Allan, their second son, visited only occasionally in between college and his travels; parties were held for him at the White House, but he said the place gave him the "willies."

Many guests came for short stays. For a visitor, the Rose Bedroom, with its ample northeast corner dressing room, was the choice accommodation. Draped and carpeted in rose pink, it contained the high-post bed, a gift to the house in 1903, which had in the interim acquired the unlikely name of "the Andrew Jackson Bed." Three or four other guest rooms were on the third floor.

The writer Christopher Morley and his wife spent a few days with the Hoovers in the spring of 1932 and slept in the Rose Bedroom. That fall he described what it was like to be a White House guest: "The Government pays a chivalrous deference to ladies. It was evident, by the way the servants laid out garments, that the enormous Rose Room (with Andrew Jackson's vast four-poster) was intended for Mrs. Citizen: Mr. C. found himself arranged for in the cozy small chamber adjoining. . . . On the mantel was an ornate old marble clock, surmounted by a bronze amazon drawing a bow, inscribed ANTIOPE." The writing table—it was the desk Lincoln used, he was told later, was generously supplied with note paper engraved in gold, THE WHITE HOUSE, WASHINGTON.

"There was a silver ashtray with plenty of matches. He admired the beautiful old mahogany wardrobe, and an antique trunk or chest of inlaid woods. On the little table by the bed was a well-polished old bell-push, the three buttons of which were inscribed MAID, BUTLER, VALET. . . . Over the writing table was a painting, the gift of the artist—called WELCOME. It showed an ocean liner coming past the Statue of Liberty. . . . In the bathroom of the suite he admired the solid 19th century fixtures—a wide marble wash-basin, a delicious covered soap dish of old pink china, once cracked and carefully mended. Soaps and toilet waters, he was pleased to note, were duly American in origin. In the frames of the enormous windows were tucked little home-whittled pegs, to prevent the sashes from rattling on stormy nights."[34]

Homebodies of a paradoxical sort, the Hoovers seldom remained in one home long, but preferred to take "home" with them to a variety of houses. Soon after moving to the White House, they began to long for a retreat. They had no interest in the *Mayflower*, which had served the Presidents since 1901. She was outmoded and costly to maintain. Hoover decommissioned the old steam yacht as an economy measure early in his administration, at the same time ordering the seven pleasure horses in the White House stable removed to Fort Myer. With the assistance of the Navy the President began searching for a country hideaway.

Late in the spring of 1929, Hoover purchased a tract of some 164 acres in the Blue Ridge foothills of Virginia, at the confluence of the Mill Prong and Laurel Prong streams, which form the Rapidan River. Marine engineers and the captain of the *Mayflower* accompanied him and Mrs. Hoover to the site, the entire party traveling the last several miles on horseback. The Hoovers knew exactly what they wanted. Work was to begin at once, with the President paying the bills and the Marines doing the work. Camp Rapidan was completed early in the summer of 1929.

Three hours from Washington, the camp was the Hoovers' favorite escape during their White House years. No such presidential retreat had been established since Mrs. Theodore Roosevelt's Pine Knot farmhouse near Charlottesville. The extensive Camp Rapidan—eventually to have even its own school for local children—was reached from the main highway by a steep, winding mountain road built by the Marines and kept open by the military in residence at the camp. Ike Hoover was astonished by what he found when he visited Camp Rapidan in 1931: "I had no idea such a place could possibly exist up in those wilds. . . . As a camp it is just as complete as the White House is as a place of residence. There is not a detail lacking."[35]

Designed almost certainly by Mrs. Hoover, the camp buildings were an eastern version of the adobe vernacular she had devised for her house in Palo Alto, California; logs and rustic boards, rock chimneys and split-shingle roofs evoked the pioneer houses of the Blue Ridge. Camp Rapidan was a cluster of cabins, a mock frontier village. The houses had deep porches and unsheltered decks strewn with rockers and basket-seat chairs. Visitors felt as though they were comfortably placed in the branches of the trees.

The Hoovers lovingly furnished the camp with things they liked, mostly homemade-looking, bought at Clore's Furniture Factory not far away. Some of the furnishings from the *Mayflower* were brought to Camp Rapidan, together with the Navy staff that had served the presidential yacht. Always eager to get away for a weekend at "the camp," the Hoovers happily planned house parties, inviting a mix of friends and people the President needed to see officially. Everyone ate together in a large mess hall. The President's cabin, situated in the middle of the camp, was used only by the Hoovers.

Journeys to the camp usually took place on Friday afternoon or early Saturday morning. The party traveled in a convoy led by White House Car Number One, at first a Pierce-Arrow, then, beginning in the fall of 1930, a 16-cylinder Cadillac limousine, in which the President usually rode either alone or with several of his guests for the weekend. Caravans to Camp Rapidan might include as few as six additional vehicles, or the full thirteen automobiles leased by the White House, as well as some guests traveling on their own. Mildred Hall, one of Mrs. Hoover's secretaries, recalled that when she went to the camp Mrs. Hoover usually asked her to bring along her Ford V-8 convertible. Outside the city the First Lady would find reason to join Miss Hall and ultimately be at the wheel herself, flying on up the road ahead of the caravan.

Historian and Antiquarians

The furnishings of the White House were first studied seriously as historical artifacts during the Hoover administration. This program was more systematic and comprehensive than Mrs. Coolidge's, and in only minor respects a continuation. Both the President and Mrs. Hoover were interested in the history of the White House. Mrs. Hoover realized that the house would have to be refurnished sooner or later, and she seems to have believed the historical study would simplify this task by identifying the important objects among the vast inventory of other material which might not need to be kept.[36]

From the outset, she hoped that her study would suggest ways to give each of the rooms the flavor of the history it had witnessed. Her concept of re-creating the past was quite different from that represented at the Metropolitan Museum of Art. In Palo Alto and at Camp Rapidan she had shown her delight in trying to capture the aura and romance of past eras. Neither of those houses was an attempt at a reproduction. Nor did anonymous "antiques" interest her; she liked furnishings with historical associations.

Idealized interior settings like those in the American Wing were lost on Lou Hoover's pragmatic mind. The First Lady was therefore at odds philosophically with Mrs. Pratt's committee. Still very active, having redecorated the Green Room just before the Coolidges left the White House, the furnishings committee was looking for a chandelier for the room when the Hoover administration began. Mrs. Pratt made contact with the Hoovers through friends, but she was apparently not encouraged to venture beyond the Green Room in her future plans. There was no unpleasantness between her and Mrs. Hoover, but each went her separate way, Mrs. Pratt seeking the chandelier for the Green Room, Mrs. Hoover doing as she pleased in the rest of the house.

Hardly a corner, outside the Green Room, went untouched by Mrs. Hoover. Over a period of a year she examined nearly everything in the house to determine its historical worth. Warehouses were searched for old White House materials. Repeated visits were made to the Soldiers' Home in hope of discovering some hidden Lincoln treasure; furniture from the *Mayflower* was brought in: little dropleaf tables, cigarette stands, leather sofas worn to venerable magnificence by years of use. Being "colonial" or "period" was not Mrs. Hoover's only criterion for being historical. Even some furniture salvaged from the fire in the Executive Office Building passed muster as memorabilia. Most of the First Lady's personal research consisted of simply questioning old household employees about this or that piece of furniture; her time was too limited for much else.

The research did not take on real substance until late in 1931, when Dare Stark McMullin of Connecticut, a former secretary to Mrs. Hoover, was a guest, and Mrs. Hoover invited her along on an excursion to see some furniture that had been found in a remote storage room. In the course of the afternoon the two agreed that a catalogue should be compiled, so that the results of Mrs. Hoover's investigations would not be lost. That the First Lady do the catalogue herself was out of the question, so Dare McMullin took on the task as a volunteer.[37]

Mrs. McMullin elaborated the project until it required her moving to the White House, where she joined the staff. She created a three-way cross-reference file and a large illustrated volume listing and describing White House furnishings, telling when they were bought and what their history might be. Given her resources, she did sound, systematic research, and her catalogue is still one of the most useful sources for identifying White House furnishings. Mrs. Hoover was to assure a concerned Colonel Grant that the catalogue did not contain information that could possibly embarrass anyone: "There is nothing of a personal or private nature in the material. . . . it may all be obtained from various publications or government records, except such as was given us by many individuals in personal reminiscences."[38]

The documentation of the furniture lent a new credibility to Mrs. Hoover's project and uncovered an abundance of historical objects to incorporate into the interior decor. Every room got its share, but the rooms that the public saw on the daily tours profited most, and since the visitors entered from East Executive Avenue, this included both the ground floor and the state rooms. In the newly created Appointment Room, the southeast chamber on the basement or ground floor, was a small table made out of wood from the frigate *Constitution*. A painting of the Liberty Bell was framed in wood authenticated as being from the bedpost of a bed slept in by General Washington. The China Room, the next room going west, had been created by the second Mrs. Wilson to house the ever-growing collection of historic plates, cups, and saucers and other china pieces used at the dinner tables of Presidents. An unofficial curator presided over the collection in the person of Abby Gunn

Baker, the newswoman who had originally presented the idea of a china collection to Mrs. McKinley at the turn of the century and had helped Mrs. Roosevelt carry it out. Mrs. Hoover enriched the room by adding a heavily carved "court chest," or sideboard, made of timbers from Sulgrave Manor, the ancestral English home of the Washington family.

Upstairs on the state floor, the same pattern of historical decoration was continued. Lincoln's portrait by Cogswell was hung on the wall in the State Dining Room in place of the tapestry put there by McKim. In the private dining room, which the Hoovers seldom used, the McKim chairs bought from Davenport were replaced by authentic reproductions of a type of chair once owned by Robert Morris and borrowed by George Washington when he rented the Morris mansion during his Presidency. Portraits of past Presidents were hung in the transverse hall.

In the family quarters, Mrs. Hoover made the east corridor into a gallery for the display of her collection of old pictures of the White House. Furniture from the *Mayflower* was put in the central corridor, which she—like many before her and others to come—hoped to make into a picture gallery with comfortable seating. Her research indicated erroneously that the Lincoln bed had in fact been purchased by Buchanan, but it did not alter her plan for the Lincoln Bedroom, where she put practically any Victorian furniture she could find.[39]

Meanwhile, on March 25, 1930, the Green Room received its finishing touch, a large cut-glass chandelier. The search for the "right" fixture had taken several years. At last in London, at Christie's Auction Rooms, Billy Delano saw the perfect one; measuring a full seven feet, it was a starry shower of glass, from its canopy to the egg-shaped pendant at its lower tip. It was an 18th-century antique, and Delano believed it would fit perfectly the requirement that it symbolize taste in the era of John Adams, when the White House was first occupied. He wired Mrs. Pratt in New York, who by telephone located a sponsor for the purchase, Herbert N. Straus of the R. H. Macy department store fortune, a philanthropist and a close friend of the Pratts. In Straus's name, Delano made the purchase for about $5,000 and sent the fixture on to Edward Caldwell's in New York to be wired for electricity.

Herbert Straus donated the chandelier anonymously in March. Before the month's end, Colonel Grant's men installed it, and the first room decorated by the first furnishings committee of the White House was complete. The Green Room, with its green and yellow silk hangings and upholstery, its brilliant glass chandelier, had that distant look almost universal to period room settings created by connoisseurs. From over the marble mantel, G. P. A. Healy's portrait of John Quincy Adams surveyed an elegant setting compiled to represent the highest taste of his father's era.[40]

When Mrs. Hoover decided to create a period room according to her own idea of what a period room should be, the results were decidedly different. She selected the former presidential study, east of and adjoining the oval room. For more than a year the study had been barely furnished, briefly as a bedroom, then as a sitting room. It was in need of redecoration, and in 1930 Mrs. Hoover decided to make it into a formal drawing room for the family.

First it became the Rose Drawing Room, its windows hung with the old curtains from the oval room and the walls painted a light rose. This sufficed until Dare McMullin, doing research in the files at Colonel Grant's office, found an inventory made in James Monroe's time, identifying this as an upstairs drawing room. Mrs. Hoover was intrigued by the coincidence. Not long after she learned about it, she and friends stopped by the James Monroe Law Office museum in Fredericksburg, Virginia, on their way to Camp Rapidan. The museum had housed since 1927 a remarkable collection of French furniture once owned by the President and Mrs. Monroe and since donated by their descendants. For two hours the First Lady admired the delicate objects, with their dark, glossy wood, pale marble, and polished brass trimmings.

Soon she had decided that her second floor drawing room would be the "Monroe Drawing Room." It seemed obvious: A John Adams Green Room notwithstanding, it was, after all, James Monroe who had first occupied the present White House; the White House of Adams, Jefferson, and Madison had been burned by the British. Faced with the impossibility of retrieving Monroe's original furnishings, Mrs. Hoover settled on having reproductions made of objects known to have been there. Since the room had been in the family quarters, she and Dare McMullin reasoned that the Monroes probably used their own furniture there as well as the government's. It would be valid, therefore, to copy the furniture in Fredericksburg and supplement it with other copies of historical pieces. Wrote Mrs. McMullin, "Mrs. Hoover took delighted interest in filling [the room] with the true types of the period, even though they must be reproductions."[41]

The cast-off chandelier from the Green Room was brought to the Monroe Room. Every part of the house was scavenged for tables and chairs which might seem appropriate. Descendants of the Monroes came forward with family memorabilia, including a small tea table, one of a pair of card tables, and a small terra-cotta vase. A copy was made of a portrait of Mrs. Monroe wearing black velvet. From the Smithsonian came pictures on loan and a small pianoforte from the 1820s, its sounding boards and works English and its case American.

In the spring of 1932, Mrs. Hoover commissioned from the Washington cabinetmaker Morris W. Dove exact reproductions of some of the furniture from the Monroe Law Office Museum in Fredericksburg, including the French desk on which Monroe had signed the Monroe Doctrine. When these furnishings arrived in the summer of 1932, Mrs. Hoover was gratified to see that the Russian-born Dover had done his work to perfection. She hurried to complete her Monroe Room, replicating history as nearly as possible. The rose color scheme was retained. On tables and chests she placed memorabilia that she thought enhanced her theme, including books, miniatures of the Monroes and their friends, and a few possessions of the Monroes' contemporaries, such as a pair of candleholders that had belonged to Dolley Madison.

When finished, the second floor Monroe Room stood in subtle contrast to the Green Room on the state floor directly below it. The furnishings committee had attempted in the Green Room to create a work of art that would symbolize the excellence of an earlier America. Mrs. Hoover had approached her Monroe Room from an entirely different point of view. She regarded it as an opportunity to re-create history, to touch the distant White House past. In the final report on the White House furnishings, this subject is addressed: "The first Adams drawing-room, the Jefferson and Madison, we shall never be able to re-summon in place, their very walls were destroyed and taken down. But a drawing-room of the early Federal period could really be put back in this room that had once housed its original. . . . " In the Monroe Room, with its exact copies, she believed she had made her finest and most enduring contribution to the White House.[42]

A Gathering in the Red Room

In the summer of 1932, when the Monroe Room was completed, Franklin Delano Roosevelt was nominated by the Democratic National Convention in Chicago. On August 11 in Washington, Hoover formally accepted the Republican nomination proffered two months before. The President began instituting strong federal programs to cope with the Depression. But he did not make political hay from it: Absorbed in his work, he stayed out of the public eye for the balance of August; in September he held no press conferences. By October he was ready to proceed with a carefully planned series of campaign addresses. The Democrats were in brilliant parade, two flamboyant months ahead of him. His

Midwest junket began in Iowa, where he had been born 58 years before. On then to Cleveland and the crucial Detroit, where tens of thousands of unemployed greeted him with anti-Hoover banners. Wrote Starling: "For the first time in my long experience on the Detail I heard the President of the United States booed."[43]

The transfer of office from Republican to Democrat in 1933 was the coolest since the days of both Adamses. Soon after the election, President Hoover had made an effort to persuade Roosevelt and his advisers to commit themselves to some of his policies through cooperative agreements. He feared the Democrats had no grasp of the national situation that would soon face them. Late in February, when the bank crisis threatened a virtual economic collapse, the President renewed his push for a partnership. Roosevelt again refused to join hands. At best, the feeling between the two men was by March one of mutual contempt.

So it could not have come as much of a surprise to anyone that the Hoovers had no more intention of giving the traditional March 3 dinner for the incoming President than the Roosevelts had of attending. The respective staffs were concerned over what the press might make of this. Ike Hoover dared to approach the President on the subject, saying he understood Mr. Roosevelt would accept an invitation to tea for himself and his family. "At this hint," wrote the chief usher, "I was instructed to pass the word along that the President and Mrs. Hoover would be pleased to have the President-elect and Mrs. Roosevelt call at that time. The suggestion about the family fell on deaf ears."[44]

The small party gathered in the Red Room to fulfill the obligation. Even at this last minute, President Hoover summoned two of his financial advisers, Secretary of the Treasury Ogden Mills, and Eugene Meyer. Forewarned, Roosevelt brought his own adviser, Raymond Moley. The tea thus became yet another conference, with the two women quite apart from the five men, who talked business for more than an hour. No commitment was made by Roosevelt, who simply said he would take Hoover's ideas back to his fellow Democrats.[45]

Inauguration day was overcast and chilly. Hoover's famous Medicine Ball Cabinet assembled for the morning exercise for the last time. To his companions, the President seemed suddenly relieved, even cheerful. In true form, he had his last day scheduled down to the last hour, and had already changed various details. His plan to leave for California after the inauguration was canceled; he was going instead to New York, to remain for a month or so, to be nearby if needed during the transition. He urged those who had served him to remain with Roosevelt as long as they felt they could do some good.

At about a quarter to eleven he and Mrs. Hoover walked through the north door for the last time as President and First Lady. The Roosevelts were in two open automobiles beneath the shelter of the north portico, not having gone inside to the Blue Room, as was traditional, because of Roosevelt's physical handicap. On the way to the Capitol, Hoover did not join Roosevelt in raising his top hat to the cheering throngs. He believed the ovation was not for him.

39

Full House

The most extreme change in my experience at the White House took place on March 4, 1933," wrote an aging Ike Hoover. "Republicans dropped out of sight overnight. Those that were left seemed to have changed into Democrats." He had known only two Democratic administrations, those of Cleveland and of Wilson, during more than 40 years of service.

For some time the staff at the White House had agreed that the chief usher was too set in his ways, resenting practically everything new. Incorrigible or not, Ike Hoover admired the beginning of Franklin Delano Roosevelt's administration, if not for its changes, certainly for its order and smoothness. Moreover, he had known the new First Lady, Theodore Roosevelt's niece, as "Miss Eleanor" 30 years before. It amused her to allow him the same privilege now that she was in her Aunt Edith's shoes, and he did so on occasion with great delight.[1]

The Curtain Falls, but Rises Quickly

Mrs. Roosevelt had been taken on a tour of the house by Mrs. Hoover. Showing little more than indifference to the formal rooms with their historical furnishings, she had become interested when taken into the kitchen and service areas, about which she had many questions. After Mrs. Hoover had left her, she sat with the chief usher for about 15 minutes; from her satchel she withdrew menus and lists of the people who would move in on inauguration day. She had designated which bedrooms family and guests would occupy.

Some days before Mrs. Roosevelt's visit, the President-elect's chief aide, Louis M. Howe, had come to the White House to study those parts of the house where the new President was likely to be seen by the public. The sickly, wizened little man hurriedly inspected halls, elevators, vestibules, and any parts of the state floor where visitors or an unfriendly cameraman might get a glimpse of Roosevelt in his wheelchair. Throughout the campaign, Howe had carefully kept concealed his candidate's physical state. While it was known that Roosevelt had been stricken with poliomyelitis in 1921, eleven years before, the tense mood of Depression times made Howe cautious, lest the electorate interpret Roosevelt's paraplegia as symbolic of more significant weaknesses. The nation needed a strong and active leader, and Roosevelt had campaigned as the man to fill the bill. With the election over, Howe planned to avoid anything that might undermine the hard-won image.[2]

Apparently not satisfied with what he learned on his visit, Howe ordered a second inspection by press secretary Steve Early. Inquiries led Early to Colonel Ed Starling, who remembered how the White House had functioned when Wilson was confined to a wheelchair. The situation was explained to Starling: Roosevelt was totally paralyzed from his hips down; when outside public view he used a wheelchair, but his major public appearances were carefully staged to hide the full extent of his condition. If he was required to stand, he wore leg braces that locked at the knees, making his legs stiff; he then thrust his weight back against a special high stool or some available support, as a balustrade or wall. When he walked, he gained both support and balance from a cane on one side and leaned heavily on an aide on the other side, who stood very close and more or less carried him along. At these rare times, he walked only a few yards at the most, if possible following a pattern that had been well planned in advance.

Starling's experiences with Wilson also made him useful in planning the inauguration, since he was as familiar with maneuvering wheelchairs at the Capitol as at the White House. Finding himself in great favor with Roosevelt's advance guard, the colonel became less eager to honor Hoover's request that he accompany him to New York as guard after the inauguration. Threats of assassination had upset both him and Mrs. Hoover. In his memoirs, Starling makes an awkward effort to explain why he did not go on the train with Hoover. It is clear between the lines that he was too swept up in the Roosevelt orbit to leave.[3]

On inauguration day Mrs. Hoover poured tea in the Red Room for the chief usher and his two assistants, her way of giving them a special thanks and good-bye. To Ike Hoover's first assistant, the soft-spoken

Howell Crim, she presented a little cactus she had planted in a pot of sand. The living thing was to be a symbol of Herbert Hoover's continuing usefulness to his country. Crim would remember this as one of the most moving of his personal encounters in the White House. Then the Hoovers and the Roosevelts were in two limousines driving out the northeast gate to the Capitol. Members of the Roosevelt staff began to enter the White House as soon as they left. The turnover was quiet and immediate. Below stairs the cooks were preparing the luncheon ordered by Mrs. Roosevelt. The dining room was being set up for the buffet, which would include as a democratic symbol, hot dogs. Not long after the oath was completed at the Capitol, guests began to arrive.[4]

At about 1 p.m. the President appeared on the state floor. He had been driven to the south portico, entering beneath its massive arch. For more than 12 years this would be his usual entrance to the White House. Wheeled in his chair through the Diplomatic Reception Room, he passed down the hall to the elevator. Standing with the support of one of his sons, he moved stiffly and slowly to the Red Room, where he received his guests. Tall, with massive shoulders and chest, Franklin D. Roosevelt had a commanding presence that was embellished by a brilliant smile and a voice that filled the room. The striking good looks of his youth had lingered, though at 51 his face was naturally fleshier, his hair thinner and graying. His flamboyant manner overshadowed his physical limitations.

Roosevelt was rolled in his wheelchair to the reviewing stand outside, which stretched along Pennsylvania Avenue. It had been designed to suggest the Hermitage, the Tennessee mansion of Andrew Jackson, to symbolize Roosevelt as another champion of the people. The President, who loved parades, enjoyed the inaugural review, remaining until the daylight was almost gone and the cold air made it nearly unbearable, even in the glassed-in enclosure. In the White House, Mrs. Roosevelt was already at work receiving a thousand invited guests at tea, moving informally among them in the Red and Blue Rooms.

While the immediate occasion was joyous for those who had worked hard for the President, many were also afraid, wondering what was to befall the country. The Depression had never been darker; millions were out of work, and banks were closing. Roosevelt's son Elliott remembered a half-century later that among his relatives at dinner that night, "A sense of near-imminent disaster dominated everyone."[5]

From the parade Roosevelt was quietly wheeled inside to the elevator. He went to the oval room on the second floor and sat behind the desk in its southward bow, ready to receive his Cabinet for the swearing in. The Hoovers had nearly emptied the room when they removed their personal possessions. Mrs. Hoover's lettuce-green curtains still hung at the windows, but the walls were bare of pictures. A few chairs and sofas had been pulled in from the hall. The mahogany desk was bare except for a lamp and an ashtray, which the President began filling with his almost endless chain of cigarettes.

The Cabinet assembled solemnly. Frances Perkins, Secretary of Labor, the first woman to hold a Cabinet position, recalled the oval room on that historic occasion. "It never looked so tidy again as it did that night. Everything was in perfect order. There were no stacks of papers, pictures and things around." Roosevelt had not yet made it or the White House his own.[6]

Winning Streak

At 2:30 the following afternoon, Sunday, the President held his first Cabinet meeting in the oval room. The subject of discussion was the bank crisis, which demanded instant action. That night after dinner the representatives of four press associations were ushered upstairs, and Roosevelt explained what he planned to do. The desk before him was piled high with papers. In this first press conference, he spoke to the reporters with friendly candor, asking for their understanding and support.

Late Monday morning the President headed for the Oval Office, where he had not yet been. After the long process of rising and dressing, during which he met with intimate aides, he was ready to go to his desk. In his special wheelchair—a narrow, armless chair equipped with wheels—he entered the great upstairs hall, where the work of shifting furniture was under way. Pushed by his valet, Irvin McDuffie, he proceeded to the elevator. As the machine descended, "Duffie" pushed the hall alarm buzzer three times, following a long-established White House tradition—probably dating back to the 1880s and still in practice today—of signaling everyone ahead to duck out of sight, or at least make way, to assure President Roosevelt's privacy.

Usually, no one was to be seen when he entered the basement or when he was wheeled outside onto the open colonnade of the West Wing. He passed along the Rose Garden into the long cross hall of the Executive Office Building, where similar advance warning signals had preceded him. In the Oval Office he pivoted himself from wheelchair to desk chair, slipping behind the great mahogany desk presented to Hoover by furniture makers in Grand Rapids.

Roosevelt liked to recall that first experience alone in the office, after McDuffie had departed. An official of his administration, Rexford Tugwell, later remembered Roosevelt's delight in the story: " . . . there he was, he used to say, in a big empty room, completely alone; there was nothing to be seen and nothing to be heard. . . . Here he was, without even the wherewithal to make a note—if he had a note to make. And for a few dreadful minutes he hadn't a thought. He knew that the stimulus of human contact would break the spell; but where was everybody? There must be buttons to push, but he couldn't see them. He pulled out a drawer or two; they had been cleaned out."

At last he rocked back in his swivel chair and shouted. Suddenly he was no longer alone, but the interlude of silence left a permanent impression. Most people interpreted the story as an illustration of a handicapped man's fear of being left by himself. Tugwell believed otherwise: "What seemed appalling to [Roosevelt] in retrospect was the implication that the national paralysis had struck so nearly to the center, and for that short time, had reached the vital organ of direction. What would have happened if at that instant he had been permanently immobilized?"[7]

Roosevelt, however, was anything but unfit. Feeling healthy after a pre-inaugural cruise, he was ready to tackle his greatest problem, the Depression. Already he had summoned the Congress into special session for March 9. He had announced an economic program that was essentially the same one Hoover had espoused, to no avail. His advisers, together with some of Hoover's former staff, brought forward a banking program Roosevelt accepted. Roosevelt was a practical politician and was neither intellectual nor patient with abstract theories. That the plan had first been Hoover's did not especially concern him.

Roosevelt believed quick recovery would come only through massive federal intervention. Given a Congress predominantly Democratic but essentially conservative, he knew that his liberal New Deal would have to be passed during the "honeymoon" period following his inauguration, or it might never be realized. For the time, his popularity was high; public opinion urged him to act. The day after the inauguration Will Rogers said, "The whole country is with him, just so he starts something. If he burned down the capitol we would cheer and say 'Well, we at least got a fire started anyhow.'"

The special session of Congress convened on March 9 and met for one hundred days until June 16. From the oval room at the White House, the President sent to the lawmakers the building blocks of the New Deal. First he asked approval for the banking bill, which granted him broad powers to control money and banking. On March 9, 1933, eight hours after the bill was presented, the President, at his desk in the oval room, signed the Emergency Banking Relief Act into law. Newsmen and invited spectators filled the long chamber. Shipping crates of furniture and paintings still unopened or half unpacked lay stacked against the gray walls, dramatizing the urgency of the hour.

A program of new legislation unfolded during the next weeks. The Economy Act on March 20 reduced federal salaries and veterans' pensions. National morale was lifted on the 22nd with the end of Prohibition. When he next entertained the press, the President ordered barrels of beer set up in the hall outside the Blue Room. On the last day of March, the Civilian Conservation Corps Reconstruction Relief Act was signed. It was the most radical program yet passed, creating 250,000 federal relief jobs for young men between 18 and 25.

The President's legislation continued to roll through Congress all spring. Roosevelt quickly changed the focus of public interest in government from the Capitol to the White House. No President before had made fuller use of the official residence. Partially because of his physical limitations, and partially because it made an effective stage, the White House was nearly always the scene of his publicized activities. He recognized its great symbolic value at a time when Americans craved security. Eight days after his administration began, he delivered from the White House his first fireside chat.

The astonishing spread of the radio into millions of American homes had made it an attractive and obvious tool for politicians. Hoover had been the first to give regular radio addresses, but his broadcasts, though announced as being from the White House, actually came from the Executive Office. As governor of New York, Roosevelt had explained his policies by means of informal evening speeches on the radio. To the president of the National Broadcasting Company he wrote several months before his inauguration: "I fully expect to give personal talks from time to time on all kinds of subjects of national interest."[8]

For the fireside chats, broadcasting equipment was moved into the Diplomatic Reception Room. Why Roosevelt selected this particular room is uncertain, although it was large, had a convenient basement location, was suitable for a small audience, and expedited the moving in and out of necessary radio equipment.

"I want to talk for a few minutes with the people of the United States about banking. . . . " So the President began at ten in the evening, Sunday, March 12, 1933. He spoke for about 15 minutes, taking up again his inaugural warning against the perils of fear. Witty and conversational, even though his speech was carefully written out, Roosevelt admonished his listeners to trust the banks: "I can assure you that it is safer to keep your money in a reopened bank than under the mattress."[9]

The tremendous success of the first fireside chat led to more, helping establish a warm relationship between the President and the public. Hoover's initial venture into radio notwithstanding, it was Roosevelt, with his compelling media personality, who gave a new dimension to the Presidency through mass communication. It is significant that he set his fireside chats in the White House. By making a point of being there, the President evoked a rich sense of continuity that linked the old house to the Founding Fathers.

Images, Comforts, and a Swimming Pool

Already by the middle of March the White House was gaining the FDR stamp. Externally it remained the same, of course, and the state rooms did not vary even slightly from the way Mrs. Hoover had left them. Upstairs, however, Hoover formality had yielded to a comfort as self-conscious in its disarray as Hoover's had been in its order. Upholstered furniture was mixed with wicker, plain with fancy. Personal memorabilia crowded the tops of tables and bookcases; pictures and collections accumulated in the way of houses where generations of the same family have generated layers of possessions. In the family quarters the Roosevelts' Hyde Park was transferred from the Hudson to the Potomac. Seen in immediate contrast to the Hoovers' rooms, the Roosevelts' manner of interior decoration was not without snobbishness: The White House was not to disturb so ancient a family as they; Roosevelts would live as they always had.

The re-creation was undertaken by the new First Lady. Eleanor Roosevelt, a tall and vigorous woman of 48, had confided to a friend after her husband's election that she had not wanted to live in the White House. "If I wanted to be selfish," she said, "I could wish Franklin had not been elected."[10] Nevertheless, she had a compelling manner and great poise; when people who knew her commented on her appearance, they offered no excuses for her lack of interest in fashion, but seemed invariably to observe that she photographed poorly. She was by nature shy, and had lived most of her married life in the home of her mother-in-law, to whom her husband was devoted. The frustrations of a marriage long troubled had led her to seek satisfaction in teaching, politics, and a partnership with other women in a small furniture factory at her own retreat, Val-Kill, near Hyde Park. She had made a life for herself at Val-Kill, apart from Hyde Park, and the prospect of moving to the White House threatened her hard-won peace.

Mrs. Roosevelt invited her friend Nancy Cook, the artistic partner in Val-Kill Industries, to assist her in arranging the White House. The two women took about a week to transform the second and third floors of the family quarters. As things fell into place, Mrs. Roosevelt began to take genuine pleasure in the effort and viewed the house with increasing interest and affection. Although her views on the household had never meant much at Hyde Park, here she would manage things as she saw fit.

In order to conserve as much of the $50,000 congressional appropriation for "repairs and improvements" as possible, the First Lady tried to reuse what was already available. Such appropriations had been made for nearly every four-year term in the White House as a matter of course, and while the figure had varied several times, it had stabilized at $20,000 until the 1920s, when it was extended to $50,000 to accommodate Mrs. Coolidge's furnishings program. The higher figure had stuck, the same amount being appropriated for Hoover, then Roosevelt. Divided among four years, fifty thousand was small for a house so large and so heavily used. The appropriation never went far.

Six Army trucks hauled family things from Hyde Park. Old White House furniture was recalled from storage. Mrs. Roosevelt emptied the palm room Mrs. Hoover had created in the West Hall, to refurnish it as a sitting room. A storage room yielded red-leather sofas and chairs from the former presidential yacht *Mayflower*. These Mrs. Roosevelt described later as "very comfortable, nice and solid and very heavy, the kind that men like and boys can kick." She had them sheathed in chintz slipcovers. Cigarette tables, bureaus, office chairs, old wardrobes, and many other odds and ends were put in the rooms upstairs to give the informal clutter the Roosevelts liked. Hoover's study, which he had named the Lincoln Study, became a bedroom again, although it was still usually called the Lincoln Study throughout the Roosevelt years, and was often confused with the Lincoln Bedroom in the northwest part of the house. Mrs. Hoover's reproductions of James Monroe's delicate French furniture were removed from the Monroe Room and lined up along the walls of the central corridor, where they stood less chance of breakage. The First Lady strove to show that she was making the White House practical and comfortable.[11]

Elsewhere in the house the Roosevelt mark was seen early in the appearance of the swimming pool. The President was accustomed to swimming frequently as therapy at pools at Hyde Park and in Georgia at Warm Springs, where since 1924 he had been developing the famous center for the treatment of poliomyelitis. On March 14, 1933, the *New York Daily News* announced a campaign to raise money with which to build the President a swimming pool at the White House; 41 other New York newspapers subsequently joined in the effort.

The idea was to honor the fourth native son to become President. And although newspaper promotions in Illinois, Nebraska, and Pennsylvania also netted significant contributions, the pool was largely a gift from the people of New York. Fred Pasley, manager of the project for the *New York Daily News* wrote, "The response continued and gained a volume unprecedented in the history of such movements so far as this newspaper's experience goes."

The tally by March 26 was $22,656.90. When asked how many contributions there had been, Pasley could not answer: "Frequently a whole family would send in $1 without saying how many members were included. Or a class of school children would chip in their pennies for a 25 or 50 cent total. I recall the case of 22 infantile paralysis victims, whose ages ranged from 6 to 12, inmates of the Evelyn Goldsmith Home for Crippled Children at Far Rockaway, L.I. They raised $1.15." As to the general class of Americans represented in these Depression-time donations, Pasley continued, "They were, generally speaking, what we commonly call average folks. The children led the way and I should say that closely following them was the man in the street—the forgotten man, if you'd care to put it that way. However, there was a generous response from the upper stratum, especially in the latter days of the drive, checks of $25, $50 and $100 being not uncommon. In fact one hotel owner in New York wrote his check for $1,000." Counted as part of the total were generous donations of services and equipment amounting to nearly $10,000.[12]

While the money was being raised, responsibility for design was put in the hands of Colonel U. S. Grant III. Although little had been heard of him in the flurry of the Roosevelts' first days in the White House, Grant was an important man in Washington. He had presided over the mighty public building boom of the 1920s, with work still in progress. He supervised a large staff in the public buildings office, which had grown greatly during the Hoover administration; he held power over hundreds of jobs in Washington, jobs for many sorts of people, from professionals to laborers.

Grant found himself too much occupied to attend to the swimming pool project personally. He ordered several sketches made for a large indoor pool with an open-air exercise yard, situated in a new structure south of the Executive Office, resembling a small-scale Florida beach club. This was rejected by the President, the reasons probably twofold: the cost would be high, and the President wanted the site kept free for a possible expansion of the West Wing. A place equally accessible was necessary, and Roosevelt wanted his pool in a hurry. Grant turned the work over to two of his assistants, Lorenzo S. Winslow, a civilian architect, and Major D. H. Gillette, a close friend of Winslow's and an engineer in the Corps of Engineers. For Winslow, tall, personable, with thick, neatly combed blond hair and baggy suits, this marked the beginning of a long relationship with the house of the Presidents. This resourceful team had drawings approved in mid-April 1933, and assured the President the pool and dressing rooms would be completed by June.[13]

The swimming pool was to be a year-round facility built within the existing walls of the old west wing of the house. There was no more convenient site within the White House complex. On March 27, when the Congress passed a joint resolution authorizing the pool, the plan was already well established. The director of Public Buildings and Public Parks of the National Capital was to accept the pool fund and supervise the construction of a "swimming tank" in the "west terrace of the White House, so as not to in any way mar the architectural features of the buildings or the grounds." Lorenzo Winslow in later years remembered the west terrace as he first saw it in 1933: it "contained makeshift laundry rooms, a Bouquet Room [?], black servants' dining room, Servants' Rooms, all of which were in an unsanitary, dilapidated condition." The interior of the terrace wing was gutted up to the west end, where Herbert Hoover's new offices had been added. The digging for the pool itself revealed the floor of the old stable from James Monroe's time about four feet down, its brick pavers and gutters intact. As usual, the White House kept no records of such historical discoveries, but Lorenzo Winslow set down some of his own observations.[14]

Winslow soon learned that the pool project was no exception to the tight schedules of White House building projects. Nor was it lacking in problems. For example, Gillette's complicated systems for steam and water could be built only at night after 11, because the process required turning off the mechanical works of the Executive Office. Most noisy work had to be accomplished at night, but only on nights when there were no dinners or other functions, or on weekends, when the President was away. These constraints were not unusual in White House building projects, but in the context of the Hundred Days, with the world's eyes on the White House and a battling FDR, they made the work exciting to those building the pool.

Gillette produced a wholly modern facility. The pool had not only underwater lighting, but also featured sterilizers, circulators, and practically every other gadget known to contemporary technology. In his design, Lorenzo Winslow successfully preserved existing elements while creating an interior wholly new to the White House. Trained in the beaux arts tradition, he found in the naked shell of the west terrace features that delighted him, particularly the high rows of half-moon windows that banded the north and south walls. Designed originally by Jefferson to illuminate and ventilate the individual chambers of the west terrace, these lunettes shed light into one long, narrow room, once the partitions were torn out.

Winslow created a composition which he might have called—in architectural language of his time—"classical in feeling," but it was the starkly pared-down classicism of the Moderne style of the 1930s. Beneath each lunette on the south wall he cut French doors onto the colonnade overlooking the Rose Garden. Inside the room he arched the ceiling north to south to lighten and heighten its span over the long, shimmering rectangle of water. The walls he wainscoted with terra-cotta blocks colored in various shades of blue, which he set off on the walls above with cream-colored paint.[15]

On June 2, 1933, the workmen assembled poolside to hear the President make a few remarks of thanks from his wheelchair. He admired the completed swimming pool. "I built a pool once myself," he said, "and did all the designing and all the work and when I had completed it the pool fell in. The pool you built will stand up. I want you men to know that this pool will be a big help to me, and it will be about the only air I can get. It will be one of the greatest pleasures for me during my stay in the White House."[16]

Lorenzo Winslow emerged from this project a Roosevelt favorite. Cheerful and accommodating, the architect impressed Roosevelt as a man of ability. Winslow's boss, however, the grandson of an earlier President, treated the Roosevelts with the same highhandedness he showed his subordinates. Instead of seeking to accommodate the new Democratic regime, Colonel Grant, with many Republican friends in the Congress, continued to behave imperiously. The climax came in April 1933, when he refused to allow Mrs. Roosevelt to build a swing for her grandchildren in one of the old trees on the south lawn, lest it damage the bark. The incident got into the newspapers; Mrs. Roosevelt got her swing; and General Grant was replaced. Eight days after the pool was finished, President Roosevelt, as part of his massive reorganization of the government, dissolved the Office of Public Buildings and Public Parks of the National Capital, turning stewardship over the White House and other public buildings in the capital to the National Park Service, where it has remained.

Family and Guests

Family life at the Roosevelt White House was unorthodox; parents and children seemed more intimate than in fact they were. The five grown children felt closer to their father than their mother, whom they found cold and distant. Eleanor Roosevelt had been preempted long since from her rightful role in the household by her mother-in-law, the accomplished Sara Delano Roosevelt, who had directed life closely at Hyde Park. The domination of an old woman over the younger generation was not so unusual at the time, especially when her son's family lived in her home, but a more politic mother-in-law might have seen the problems she was creating and diplomatically yielded some territory. As First Lady, Eleanor Roosevelt thwarted any effort to re-create the Hyde Park situation and insisted upon personally managing the White House, as long as her enthusiasm for it lasted.

The upstairs rooms, however, came to reflect Hyde Park at least in being filled with guests. In the entire 12 years of Roosevelt's Presidency the husband and wife were never in residence alone. In addition to short-term company, there were guests who remained indefinitely. These were either relatives or persons the Roosevelts deemed necessary for one reason or another. Such guests lived more or less as part of the family, although with little privacy, for they were on constant call by one or both of the Roosevelts.

Foremost among the full-time guests was Louis McHenry Howe, who had been the President-elect's liaison with the White House. If the intimacy of a personal relationship had been the measure, Howe would have been the most powerful man in the United States. Roosevelt felt both indebted to him and dependent upon him. Mrs. Roosevelt held Howe in equally high regard, he having discovered her capabilities as a campaigner and promoted her from the background to the forefront of her husband's election effort. Perhaps in jest, Howe asked that he and his wife, Grace, sleep in the Lincoln bed. Since his wishes were usually fairly sacred in the eyes of his patrons, the bed was moved from the Lincoln Bedroom to the small chamber the Howes occupied, shaded by the north portico. The presidential secretary suffered from emphysema, which, with other ailments, eventually turned his room into a sick bay. At that point he was given the Lincoln Bedroom on the northwest, where there was space not only for oxygen tanks and other medical paraphernalia but also for the mounds of papers that always surrounded him. Howe's funeral would be held in the East Room as a tribute to his public service.

Second in rank among the permanent guests was Marguerite LeHand, called "Missy" in the family circle. She was the President's personal secretary and great friend; it was generally agreed by intimates that her power in the Executive Office equaled Mrs. Roosevelt's over the house. Attractive and immaculately groomed, with prematurely white hair, she was an able secretary, a shrewd judge of people, and a good-natured companion to the President. She had already lived in the Roosevelt household for 13 years, moving to Hyde Park after Roosevelt's unsuccessful vice presidential campaign of 1920. At the White House the secretary was given what had been the housekeeper's apartment on the third floor, a tiny but pleasantly remote suite with slanted ceilings, and with high windows looking out toward the Potomac, through the heavy stone balustrade that crowned the house.

The least-known guest, and a full-time resident only at intervals, was Lorena Hickok, an Associated Press reporter who first met Mrs. Roosevelt while covering Al Smith's campaign in 1928. Not until 1932 did they become close friends. Lorena Hickok's usual bedroom was the former dressing room of the Lincoln Bedroom, on the northwest corner, across the hall from Mrs. Roosevelt's suite. A quiet, unhealthy, and rather mannish woman in her late 30s, Lorena Hickok was often sent by the First Lady—presumably in accord with President Roosevelt's wishes—to observe situations in various parts of the country. "Hick," as she was called, was really less a member of the family than Louis Howe or Missy LeHand.

This somewhat odd circle coexisted in apparent harmony. As a group, they liked their comforts. When they got their first taste of the Washington heat, Louis Howe ordered air-conditioning for six rooms on the second floor—those of Roosevelt, Mrs. Roosevelt, Lorena Hickok, and himself—and for the bedroom of Missy LeHand's suite on the third floor. Westinghouse made the installation in May 1933, placing the units in the fireplaces and connecting them through the chimneys to the compressors on the roof. The permanent inhabitants used their bedrooms as offices and sometimes had private guests there for cocktails or meals. Most evenings the entire household was together for dinner, although breakfast and lunch could be eaten in one's room.[17]

There would be other residents at the Roosevelt White House later on, notably Harry L. Hopkins, one of the architects of the New Deal. The Roosevelt children lived there from time to time. Anna, the eldest, was there for the longest periods, moving in soon after the inauguration with her two children, Sistie and Buzz, in anticipation of a divorce from her husband, Curtis Dall. They would remain until Anna's remarriage in

1935, when they moved to the West Coast. In the last months of the administration in 1945, Anna was to return to comfort her dying father. The other children visited for short periods, occupying either the small guest rooms that looked out on the north portico, or quarters on the third floor, so that their children could use the sky parlor as a playroom. At the time of Roosevelt's inauguration in 1933, Anna was 27; the youngest of the Roosevelt children, John, was 17, a student with his 19-year-old brother, Franklin, at Groton. Falling between were Elliott and James, both young men trying to establish their careers.

The President's children were always controversial. Of the five, three were divorced during Roosevelt's Presidency; divorce still carried a stigma in America, perhaps especially in the moralistic climate of the Depression. Public criticism was also aroused by the high-paying jobs taken by the boys, apparently because of their father's position. Many years later Elliott remembered himself and his brothers and sister and explained how they had "reached maturity" in the "rarefied atmosphere" of the White House. "We were left," he wrote, "with scars and some anguish as an inheritance that influenced the course of our lives. For myself, I have no excuses to offer."[18]

Anyone was likely to be invited to the White House, from the man on the street to a youth on a committee which interested the First Lady. As the dinner table was always full, so were the bedrooms. Magazine editors, theatrical performers, old friends, authors, educators, some politicians—the categories of guests were numerous. Relatives were often there, for the Roosevelts cherished their kin. Much of the open-house policy undoubtedly stemmed from the President's need to have the world brought to him, a need which had started at Hyde Park after he was stricken with poliomyelitis. Having seen the sad state of Wilson's Presidency after the war, Roosevelt, and perhaps his wife also, sensed the ever-present danger of becoming isolated in the White House, a danger to which a man in a wheelchair might be particularly vulnerable. For years before his Presidency, Eleanor Roosevelt had played a major role in bringing the world to her husband, and she continued to do so through the years at the White House.

Home Economics

The Roosevelts themselves occupied the usual presidential rooms, the three that comprise the southwest quarter of the second floor. Roosevelt's bedroom, crowded with personal things and odds and ends of furniture, was adjacent to the oval room, which he used for his study. When no White House bed suited him, Mrs. Roosevelt ordered a special one built at the Val-Kill factory. It was a small bed of the "colonial" type, its four low posts surmounted by wooden "cannon balls." The First Lady used the traditional presidential bedroom, west of Roosevelt's room, as a sitting room; she furnished its corner dressing room with the single bed in which she slept. These were personal sorts of rooms, crowded with pictures and memorabilia and comfortable furniture.

Across the upstairs corridor on the north side were four guest rooms, with two more on the third floor, besides Missy LeHand's suite. At the east end of the second floor were the principal guest suites, the Rose Bedroom and the Lincoln Study. The Monroe Sitting Room, directly over the Green Room, was used from time to time as a bedroom, but was finally kept as a parlor with comfortable upholstered furniture.

Mrs. Roosevelt was not an accomplished household manager, lacking both experience and enthusiasm. But she was determined to remain in control. Roosevelt was a free spender who could easily run through both his private income of about $50,000 a year and his $75,000 salary (which, in order to demonstrate his support of federal cost-cutting, he had voluntarily reduced from that figure by 15 percent). To help her keep a tight rein on expenses, the First Lady brought with her from Hyde Park as housekeeper a busy little country woman named Henrietta Nesbitt. Mrs. Roosevelt feared that a housekeeper chosen from the existing staff would not be primarily loyal to the presidential family. Mrs. Nesbitt worked within a strict budget, which, given the President's love of food and the hospitality of both Roosevelts, together with the large staff to be fed, did not give her much room to maneuver. Food in the Roosevelt White House was therefore notorious as the worst in Washington.[19]

In her memoirs of her years in the White House, Mrs. Nesbitt explained the housekeeping system: "Every month the President turned $2,000 of his salary over to Mrs. Roosevelt for the White House food, and she turned this over to me." The First Lady, herself indifferent to food, was a strong pillar of support for Mrs. Nesbitt when the President criticized the disappointing cuisine. A believer in simple "American" foods, Mrs. Roosevelt was immovable on the composition of menus; under her the traditional French cooking produced by the kitchen since it was first occupied was on most occasions abandoned in favor of roast beef and mashed potatoes.

For a while Mrs. Nesbitt also supervised the functioning of the household staff. Soon after the inauguration, she and Mrs. Roosevelt reorganized the servants, dismissing all the whites, hiring some new blacks. "Mrs. Roosevelt and I agreed," wrote Mrs. Nesbitt, "that a staff

solid in any one color works in better understanding and maintains a
smoother-running establishment." Now the "colored dining room" in
the west terrace could be abandoned, making way for the pool. The
servants' dining room in the basement would serve all.[20]

In theory, there were to be no more quarrels over rank within the
staff. The Swedish cooks were replaced by two black women, Ida Allen
and Elizabeth Moore, both of whom had cooked for the Roosevelts in the
Albany governor's mansion. Servants brought to the house or hired anew
by the Roosevelts tended to go along with Mrs. Nesbitt's sometimes
capricious innovations, until more seasoned employees protested. For
example, the housekeeper tried to introduce the practice of filling individual plates for a state banquet beforehand in the kitchen, in an effort to
control the size of each serving, as well as to reduce the need to hire extra
servants at large dinners. The horrified head butler, Alonzo Fields,
shrewdly maneuvered the question to Mrs. Roosevelt. As he had hoped,
she reversed the housekeeper's policy, but at the same time she dismayed
him by radically trimming the menu to fewer courses and simpler dishes.
Never before had the White House table been so spare.[21]

Moreover, the Roosevelts' domestic tone was in general conservative. Mrs. Roosevelt continued to use proper invitations, calling cards,
seating charts, and to follow other long-established customs. Her teas
were formal, with her secretaries or some invited friends pouring in the
State Dining Room or the Red Room, or on the awning-shaded south
portico. Larger crowds than ever attended the teas, garden parties, and
receptions. They were less social affairs than public occasions, although
still by invitation only. Mrs. Nesbitt remembered her first garden party,
where 3,000 sandwiches were required. After much confusion, she
learned to call in extra help: eight women, who started making sandwiches the day before the party, seated around the big mahogany table in
the servants' dining room. Teas were held in two shifts of from 500 to
sometimes—albeit rarely—1,000 each. A receiving line was held if the
smaller number attended. For the bigger crowds Mrs. Roosevelt appeared
and mixed, developing a remarkable ability to make all the guests feel as
if they had spoken intimately with the First Lady.

State dinners were conducted as usual, only with less exciting food.
After the end of Prohibition, wine returned to the dinner table. Mrs.
Roosevelt, the daughter of an alcoholic, was strongly opposed to liquor,
as was her mother-in-law, but Roosevelt, devoted to his evening cocktails, insisted upon having them for his guests. The compromise was that
one glass of champagne was sometimes served before state dinners. That
it was often warm was an accident, but it seemed to guests a statement

against drinking. Wines were served at state or formal dinners, and the refilling process was very slow.

On some "moral" subjects, the First Lady was surprisingly liberal. Smoking, for example, had never been considered absolutely proper for women at the White House. Foreign ladies had started it, in Harding's time, and it had since been tolerated, though female guests in the know usually abstained. Mrs. Roosevelt, concerned about women's freedoms, encouraged women smokers by ordering a butler to bring cigarettes to her in the Red Room after dinner. Though not a regular smoker, she puffed for a while as an invitation to others to join in.

The main way in which the Roosevelts' state dinners and other large White House affairs were different from those of their predecessors was in the gradual abandonment of the "made list." As news of this swept Washington society, it caused more shock than even the more radical measures of the New Deal. No longer would a certain group of people be distributed among the social events of the White House, forming a core of guests. The Roosevelts would ask whomever they pleased.[22]

Belonging themselves to circles which they doubtless considered more sophisticated than those in the nation's capital, the Roosevelts cannot have taken Washington society too seriously. The "cave dwellers," as the Washington natives were termed, were southern in their feelings and often had provincial ways; they affected to take no notice of politics, although this was the town's lifeblood. One of the queens of Washington society was Alice Roosevelt Longworth, a cousin who openly mocked the President and his wife.

The Roosevelt "edict" may have appeared a bold stroke in behalf of democracy, but that was not its main purpose. In making these changes, the Roosevelts' first consideration was the need to make more effective political use of the official functions. Every activity at the White House is, at its roots, political; by disposing of the made list, Roosevelt had room for guests who were invited for a purpose other than social.

Like all other Presidents, Roosevelt realized that the White House was a potent symbol. People could be invited to dinner, and in the glory of the place be converted to his thinking or be convinced to render some needed service. The value of the house in politics was certainly known to Jefferson, and perhaps also to the first occupant. While the made list had given a certain sheen to the entertainments—for no one could deny the social graces of its members—Washington society meant very little to Roosevelt's national constituency. When he needed more glitter than even his own bright personality could provide, he called in movie stars. That the public could respond to.

All's Well

When the noise and joy of the inauguration had subsided, among the many Depression demons facing the new administration was the Bonus Army. Although it had been reduced to several hundred men, it had by no means disbanded, but remained in the camp across the Anacostia River. In May 1933 a second Bonus Army descended upon Washington, responding to the drama of the Hundred Days, to renew the demands for payment of the bonuses which had not yet matured. The regular Army made preparations once again to house the marchers. Fort Hunt, on the George Washington Parkway near Mount Vernon, was outfitted with tents and other supplies. The location, though not as convenient to Washington as the former one, was beautiful that spring, a canopy of redbud blossoms shading a carpet of new green grass.

The President offered the veterans positions in the Civilian Conservation Corps at one dollar a day. This was taken as an insult by some of the marchers. But most of them, tired and anxious, remained close to the camp, peacefully awaiting a better offer, while debating their own next move. An obvious course for the President was to visit them, but, probably on the advice of Louis Howe, he stayed away. Howe's wise afterthought was to send Mrs. Roosevelt. He drove her there himself, turning off the engine at the gate of Fort Hunt and sending her alone to the mess hall, where the men were lining up to eat.

The First Lady spoke to the men simply and affectionately and won them over. She let them show her through the camp, and at the end of the tour led them in singing a song familiar on the battlefields, "There's a long, long trail awinding." Her visit had the desired effect, a tribute to her ability with people, as well as to Howe's knowledge of showmanship. By the first weeks of June the Bonus Army had all but broken up, with more than 2,600 enrolled in the CCC. "Hoover sent the army," remarked one veteran, "Roosevelt sent his wife."

Meanwhile, during the early summer of 1933, Ike Hoover became ill. His responsibilities were assumed by Raymond Douglas Muir, a tall, discreet man of 36, who succeeded him as chief usher when Hoover died on September 14, 1933. Seeing that the end was near, Ike Hoover recalled the diaries he had started through the years and had his children bring his papers to his bed. He had written on the backs of envelopes, in notebooks, in bound journal books; he had souvenir invitations and autographed letters. His plan had been to retire in 1935, at the end of 44 years of service, and write his memoirs. He had actually written a draft covering most of the story through the Taft administration, but the rest was a mass of fragments subsequently preserved at the Library of Congress. A publisher pulled much of it together into a book within a year after Hoover's death, *Forty-Two Years in the White House*.[23]

Hoover had been dead a year when the author Frances Parkinson Keyes, wife of Vermont Senator Henry Wilder Keyes and a close friend of Mrs. Roosevelt's, drove over from Alexandria and called at the White House. She had not been there for a long while: " . . . as I entered the front door I was conscious of some undefined lack which gave me a sense of the unfamiliar. At first I could not identify this. Then I realized what it was: 'Ike' Hoover . . . was not there to greet me with faultless and formal civility."

To the butler who took her coat she said, "How are you getting along without Mr. Hoover? You must miss him very much." The attendant, confusing his Hoovers, "drew himself up straight" and replied, "This President's doing very well, too, thank you, Mrs. Keyes."[24]

40

Sketchbooks

In the Roosevelt '30s the White House looked much like an old family home. It stood out in stark white contrast to its green setting of trees and grass. The gates were left open during the day, the few patrols on duty staying near the house. Most activity was confined to the edges of the scene—on the west the cluster of automobiles and the figures hurrying to and from the Executive Office, on the east the lines of tourists waiting to enter. The area before the building was utterly serene, save for the stirring of the leaves, the fluttering of canvas awnings, and the splashing of the fountain.

Outside the iron fence, the heart of the city of Washington pumped anew. Roosevelt's programs attracted thousands of new civil servants. The large federal buildings, many of them planned in the 1920s to serve the needs of the future, were supplemented with temporary offices. On the streets of the capital, the Depression was not immediately evident. Government salaries, though reduced, were steady; shops and stores were still open, and the busy hotels struck a note of prosperity that set Washington apart from most other cities.

The specter of terrible times, however, was never far off. In 1934 the capital even had a grim taste of the dust bowl, the result of the drought burning the agricultural West. High winds carried a dust storm "from the sun-parched wheat fields"—according to the *Post*—all the way to Washington on May 11, 1934. The sun was blotted out; a gritty haze dimmed the flowery spring morning. Dust sifted onto the President's desk. In other ways only less biblical in dramatic pitch, the city further shared the nation's agonies, in spite of its own apparent flourishing.

A man who loved tradition, Roosevelt sensed deeply that the Depression had brought a sharp break in American life as it had been. He viewed the New Deal as a means of saving what could be saved. He believed that the days of the leisure class to which he belonged were numbered. Before the close of the tumultuous decade he was to deed Hyde Park to the public, anxious that it be preserved, for he felt no assurance that his heirs could ever afford to carry it on.

The White House naturally fascinated a man with Roosevelt's interests and concerns. He delighted in accepting a small medicine chest from a descendant of the British sailor who had taken it as a souvenir during the invasion of Washington in 1814. When he found out about another piece of White House memorabilia he entered it in a special list of things he hoped to acquire. A President as strong as Roosevelt was certain to bring physical change to the house.[1]

President and First Lady

All Presidents and their wives are celebrities, but none before had made news—or gone after it—to the extent that the Roosevelts did. This was especially true of the First Lady; she even eclipsed Mrs. Coolidge as news copy, and her style was so completely different as to bear no resemblance to that of her glamorous predecessor. Obviously the winning of the press was wise politics. Newspaper publishers in their editorials might often espouse the businessman's anti-Roosevelt point of view, but they were businessmen enough to give space to stories that sold papers.

Press conferences were long and informal, usually held in the Oval Office, with the President seated at his desk, cigarette lighted, and the reporters crowded thickly into the long room. Only reporters from the daily papers were admitted, so that the number in attendance could be kept as small as possible. The President knew most of the reporters by name and, as was his custom with nearly everyone, called them by their first names, instead of the traditional "Jones" or "Brown." He had even improved on his uncle's skill at seeming off-the-cuff and confidential amid the clamor of several hundred journalists. Roosevelt's charm was irresistible. To the newsmen's delight, he broke with custom and occasionally allowed them to quote him directly.

To general astonishment, Mrs. Roosevelt announced early on that she too would hold press conferences. Her first was in New York before the inauguration; her initial one as First Lady took place in the Red Room on the Monday after her husband took office. Influenced to a great extent by Lorena Hickok, Mrs. Roosevelt decided to give conferences as a special favor to women reporters, who were not admitted to the presidential press conferences. During the hard times of the Depression years, inability to get good stories could cost them their jobs. "I shall never forget my first press conference," Mrs. Roosevelt wrote. "I could feel the disapproval of the ushers as I went in fear and trembling, trying to cover my uncertainty by passing around a large box of candy to fill in the first awkward moments."[2]

Mrs. Roosevelt did not start a trend of Presidents' wives meeting the press, but she did clear away the old taboo against it. Articles had featured First Ladies since the days of Mrs. Grant. They had not, however, quoted the First Ladies or in any way presumed to record direct interviews. Mrs. Hoover's projects had received wide press coverage through others involved in them, even though the appeal of them really lay in the First Lady's participation. Thus by the 1930s the stage was set for a First Lady who had something serious to say, and Mrs. Roosevelt, advised by her close circle of women friends, grasped the opportunity. She was by any standards a lady, reared in a socially prominent family, and polished by a good education. She became a newspaper personality without compromising her dignity; she believed that her outspokenness encouraged other women to stand up and be counted.

From the start it was made clear that Mrs. Roosevelt's press conferences were not official. In tone they were more like ladies' teas than press conferences. The women reporters—men were not admitted—were warned to ask no questions about politics. Participants dressed properly as for a social call, with hat and gloves. Mrs. Roosevelt sat among the reporters, usually in the Red Room, but occasionally in her sitting room upstairs, working at her knitting as she talked. While she spoke, the room remained in utter silence except for her voice, which one journalist called "gentle, soft, and cultured."[3]

The subjects varied. For the most part the interviews centered on domestic topics—cooking, hygiene, something now and then on interior decorating. Details about White House entertaining, which had traditionally been released only in writing and by the chief usher, now became "exclusives" of the First Lady. As time passed and Mrs. Roosevelt became increasingly involved in humanitarian endeavors, her conferences occasionally turned in those directions. Her travels, nearly constant in later years, provided rich sources of information for the newswomen, as well as subject matter for her own books and articles, many written in her sitting room at the White House.

Like the President, the First Lady sought out the world. When the President was not along, she always demonstrated her unofficial status by rejecting a private train car in favor of riding Pullman. She often carried her own baggage, which experience finally reduced to a small suitcase or satchel. Better still, in her view, was flying. Relatively new in the 1930s, commercial air transportation suited the fast-paced Mrs. Roosevelt. Her enthusiastic patronage of the airlines drew attention to air travel, and eased some of the public's fear of flying. She did not like being accompanied by a bodyguard, and often was not before the outbreak of World War II. A Secret Service man trained her in the use of a pistol, which she reluctantly agreed to carry in her purse, although she confided that she would never use it. In the same mode, the First Lady always preferred private apartments to hotels. Eventually she rented an apartment in New York in Greenwich Village. This was supposedly unguarded, and she used it frequently.

President Roosevelt, like his predecessors, nearly always traveled by railroad. Presidential train excursions, begun by Andrew Johnson in the late 1860s, had been institutionalized under Theodore Roosevelt, and most of the procedures set up by Cortelyou at that time survived more than 30 years later. No official presidential car existed until the *Ferdinand Magellan* was built for FDR in 1940. During the '30s, Roosevelt rode in private Pullman cars selected for him for each trip. His private secretary, Grace Tully, remembered that on an average trip, perhaps a weekend excursion to Hyde Park or a visit to Warm Springs, eight cars made up the presidential train. On a campaign trip or tour, such as the one in 1934 to inspect the dust bowl regions, the cars might number 18 to 20.

The era of grand railroad accommodations had not yet passed, and presidential trains represented the peak of luxury. An avid admirer of trains, Roosevelt looked forward to his journeys with relish; the coordinator of his trips was Dewey Long, and Roosevelt often met with him, taking an active role in the planning. While on a trip, the presidential entourage could use the dining car, the mail room, and the telephone and telegraph facilities any time, day or night.

The *Ferdinand Magellan* had several bedrooms with baths, a study, and an observation room at the back, with the railed platform from which the President made short speeches at stops. During waking hours the train seldom moved more than 30 miles an hour, for the President could not move about freely in his armless wheelchair at higher speeds. After he went to bed the speed increased to 70 miles an hour.[4]

At the urging of Louis Howe, the President asked his wife to report to him firsthand on the conditions she observed in various parts of the country. The First Lady was proud of this role, and in performing it broadened her own horizons. She lectured frequently under contract.

She had had her own commercially sponsored radio program for a while prior to her husband's election. Within a year after going to the White House she signed a contract for her own radio show. Sponsored initially by the Simmons Mattress Company, she commanded a fee of $500 a minute, which was in the same range as those paid to the most successful radio actors of the day. Mrs. Roosevelt went on the lecture circuit in 1935, agreeing with an agency to make at least two talks a year at a fee of $1,000 each, the sponsor selecting from five topics she had prepared. She began a career in writing, producing articles in 1933 and 1934 for the *Woman's Home Companion*. She had an appealingly informal way with words and could command a sizable readership. In 1935 she commenced her chatty newspaper column "My Day," which she continued beyond her White House years. *This is My Story*, her autobiography to 1924, was published in book form in 1937, having been serialized in the *Ladies Home Journal*.

Her conspicuous success made Mrs. Roosevelt a target for her husband's enemies. And she became the first President's wife since Mary Lincoln to develop enemies of her own. They questioned whether the time she spent speaking and writing left her enough to fill the demands of being First Lady. Did she use her position for personal profit? If not an entirely fair criticism, it was also not entirely wrong. Her income was not public knowledge, or the figure might have sparked resentment in the Depression; in 1938 Mrs. Roosevelt made more than $100,000 from speaking and writing, a figure approximating the President's own salary, including his allowance for official entertaining. Complaints against her never carried much weight at the White House, for her work was valuable to the administration in its early years. Had there been cause for alarm politically, her activities would doubtless have been curtailed.[5]

No previous President and First Lady had seemed so omnipresent. Drawing into service newspapers, radio, railroad, and airplanes, they made themselves seen, calming troubled waters, lifting burdened spirits, and selling their views on how America could be improved. They were successful persuaders, releasing the Presidency from the aloofness that had characterized it since the days of McKinley.

The President Likes To Build

If the New Deal had increased the population of Washington sharply, its effect upon the Executive Office Building had been even more striking. Hoover had rebuilt the structure after the New Year's Eve fire of 1929, well aware that the restored building would be inadequate

50. "THE NATIONAL CAPITAL: *Press Conference
at the White House,*" *a cartoon of Franklin D. Roosevelt
in the Oval Office, 1942. The President's informality
masked his tight grip on the news he released.*

51. *Roosevelt, on his 52nd birthday, spoofs criticism that he conducted himself like an emperor, 1934.*

52. *Eleanor Roosevelt, Monroe Room, 1933.*

53. *Oval room in FDR's time, with the desk moved from the center window, perhaps by the Secret Service.*

54. *Guests gather on the south portico at a luncheon for the crown prince and princess of Norway, 1939.*

55. *Roosevelt and Churchill at the White House, 1942.*

56. *Roosevelt's fourth inaugural ceremony, from a window of the Washington Monument, 1945.*

57. *FDR's flag-draped coffin, April 14, 1945.*

58. *President Harry S. Truman, Mrs. Truman, and Margaret Truman visit with relatives, 1945.*

59. *The renovation of the White House, 1949–52.*

60. *Dismantling the paneling of the East Room, 1949.*

61. *Excavating the sub-basements, 1950. Steel braces the walls after removal of the wood and brick interior.*

62. Changed, yet unchanged, the White House prevails as the foremost symbol of the Presidency.

even for his own staff of about 38. But the fire had taken place so soon after the Crash that it seemed a bad omen, and Hoover's eagerness to return to the status quo led him to approve a reconstruction without the necessary expansion.

By the close of 1933 Roosevelt's staff was already approximately twice the size Hoover's had been. On December 13, Louis Howe wrote to Harold L. Ickes, Secretary of the Interior, requesting additional space for the executive employees and suggesting that the ground floor rooms of the east side of the State, War, & Navy Building might be suitable. He described conditions in the Executive Office as "extremely over-crowded." While some of the staff did move into the State, War, & Navy Building, the solution was not ideal, because of the necessity of traveling back and forth across busy West Executive Avenue, which was in the '30s still open to traffic. For a time there was thought of moving the entire office staff, and perhaps even the President, to another location in Washington, but it never received serious consideration. Clearly the of-fice function, or at least its most visible components, belonged at the White House. The President and his closest aides discussed the limited options available. Roosevelt ordered a drawing board and instruments sent to him, and began to sketch.[6]

The President gave architecture high priority among his hobbies. He had supervised many construction projects at Hyde Park, including the remodeling in 1914 of the mansion itself. When in 1925 the con-struction bids on Mrs. Roosevelt's Val-Kill factory and cottages came in high, Franklin Roosevelt took over as "contractor" and built the little complex for his wife and her friends for considerably less than they had expected it to cost.

Roosevelt called Lorenzo Winslow to the Oval Office, probably in February of 1934, where the architect found that his chief had made "several free hand sketches and . . . a plan to scale of the proposed changes." This was a scheme for a completely new building on the site of the old. Winslow had also made some sketches, and apparently his and Roosevelt's ideas were combined into a project which delighted the Pres-ident. Not much is known of this plan, for it was not carried out, and became a delicate subject with the President. It is likely most of it came from Roosevelt's imagination. Winslow was an able architect, as he had demonstrated in his work on the swimming pool. But he seems to have been an even better bureaucrat than he was an architect, and he knew how to get close to the boss. He already understood the President's archi-tectural predilections, and he realized that people who like to build, no matter how amateurish, set great value on their taste. Lorenzo Winslow navigated so successfully through the perilous waters of codesigning with the President that he soon became what might be called Roosevelt's "architectural assistant."[7]

The proposed Executive Office concept was sent to the drafting rooms, where, as Winslow remembered, with "the active advice and interest of the President in all the various details, sketches were prepared for an addition to the building extending southward along West Executive Avenue." It had a full second floor, "over the existing roof," with a parapet to help conceal it. The mass must have been large, for there were numerous new spaces, including an auditorium for press conferences with adjacent lounges.

During the execution of the drawings, Roosevelt was told that the Congress was unlikely to appropriate funds for a new building, because the public works law in effect at the time prohibited new construction. The President bypassed this obstacle with a ploy similar to the one President Madison had used when faced with a Congress disinclined to reconstruct the public buildings of Washington after the War of 1812: Keep a portion of the walls as a token, and call the work a rebuilding or, in Roosevelt's more modern terminology, a "remodeling."

Until early in the spring of 1934 it seemed as though the Executive Office project would enjoy smooth sailing. But up to this point efficiency had been the project's guiding concern; little thought had been given to the aesthetic controversies in which White House building projects were often embroiled. No official application had yet been made to the Commission of Fine Arts, which, in theory at least, had to approve or disapprove the plan. The omission was glaring. Already the commissioners had learned that a new Executive Office was being planned. The silence from the Democratic White House was ominous, especially to a commission which, with some of the same members, had orchestrated the celebration of Republican glory in the capital's public-building programs of the '20s. Turning a President down is not an easy matter. The commission had not yet had to do so, and did not want to be put in that position.

At last, on March 21, the President's uncle Frederick Delano went to the chairman, Charles Moore, and laid the plans before him. Moore showed his displeasure politely, but made it clear that no approval would be forthcoming from the commission. At age 78, Moore was the veteran of many architectural wars in the capital city, not the least ferocious being that seminal one over the White House in 1902. The present Executive Office had been built as a temporary building, and Moore wanted it to go eventually, with the offices moved to the State, War, & Navy Building, which he would have remodeled along neoclassical lines to balance with the Treasury Building on the east. A tunnel would connect the new office to the White House. Delano went home discouraged in his mission, but confessed to the President that he agreed with Moore in principle.[8]

For almost 20 years as chairman, Charles Moore had guided the Commission of Fine Arts according to the principles of the McMillan Plan. Conceived in the era of Theodore Roosevelt and nurtured by architecture's warm friend, William Howard Taft, the plan projected a neoclassical city, a vision of beauty of the sort seen at the Chicago World's Fair of 1893. The White House was a key feature in the plan, and its preservation in 1902 had marked the beginning of a new role for the professional architect in the design of the federal city.

Roosevelt emphatically wanted his new building, and Charles Moore struggled to find a solution to this dilemma: How to stop the President? It occurred to him that he might try to reach FDR through a personal connection, an architect named Eric Gugler, who practiced in Manhattan and had worked with the Roosevelts. The handsome, artistic Gugler idolized McKim, and had studied and even measured some of his finest buildings. Once, after reading Moore's 1929 *Life and Letters of Charles McKim*, Gugler had come to ask Moore questions about McKim. Moore liked the younger man, and had doubtless been flattered by his interest. Now in his 40s, Gugler had studied at the American Academy in Rome on a McKim fellowship, after finishing his courses in architecture at Columbia University. He considered himself a follower of McKim, whom he had never known, and was a committed practitioner of the beaux arts ideal of the past in architectural design.

Charles Moore was certain that Gugler would not be happy to know about the plans for the White House, so he invited him for a visit, ostensibly to talk more about the great days of the beaux arts architects. Gugler later remembered the meeting: "I came to his office promptly. It was about five o'clock. Some of the members of the Commission of Fine Arts were leaving. It was getting dark but [Moore] made no move to go, as I had expected, to the old Cosmos Club. Finally, I remember it seemed to me a long time—he said he wondered whether he could talk to me on a matter that might well at least disturb or perhaps break any possible friendship that might exist between myself and the Roosevelts."[9]

When Gugler heard the story he was, in his own words, "clearly outraged" to think that McKim's concept—itself a modification of what was believed to be Jefferson's earlier idea—should be so blatantly abandoned. "I thought of FDR as a cultivated man," Gugler wrote, "and was sure that he could hardly have understood what it was all about or that he may have been misinformed." Moore asked whether Gugler would be willing to speak to the President. Gugler remembered: "I said that I certainly would."

Moore's ear for politics was still well tuned, and he was also lucky. There were perhaps only three architects in the United States suited to take on his mission. Most obvious was Billy Delano, Roosevelt's distant cousin and friend; he was probably asked initially by Moore and declined. The others were Gugler and his former partner Henry Toombs. Of the two, Gugler may have seemed more appropriate because he was working closely with Mrs. Roosevelt on a pet public works project of hers in West Virginia—the new town of Arthurdale.

As early as 1925 Gugler and the Georgia-born Toombs had collaborated with Mrs. Roosevelt and her partners on the design of the cottage at Val-Kill, on the Roosevelt estate. This project interested Roosevelt very much, and his satisfaction with the architects led to their appointment in 1927 to design and remodel buildings at Warm Springs along "colonial" lines. When in 1931 Toombs decided to return home to Georgia, Gugler remained in practice in Manhattan, where, at the time the Roosevelts went to the White House, he had a small office engaged primarily in the design of private residences.

In his recollection of the Executive Office controversy, Gugler could not recall the whole sequence of events that led him to challenge the President's ideas about the proposed plan for a new West Wing. The confrontation took place at lunch, in the private dining room at the White House. "I started . . . right off," wrote Gugler, "to say that many of his (FDR's) best friends and supporters would be unhappy with unnecessary upsetting of the proportions of the White House. I may have mentioned C. C. Burlingham, Carl Van Doren, George McAneny and others, mutual friends who I thought he might have respected. I thought, I told him, that it would be an unpopular move, particularly to the most sensitive and cultivated of his friends—that it would be made fun of, 'improving Jefferson's work,' etc. and anyway, was it worth risking the public criticism bound to take place?"

Roosevelt, annoyed, fired back at Gugler, saying that the architect was like other artistic people and did not care about the country's government. "He said he was handicapped and so much trouble is involved in running the government without reasonable convenience such as adequate space"—thus an apparently long and rambling essay ensued that Gugler pronounced "Not very pleasant!" Roosevelt pronounced Charles Moore an "old fuddiduddy," to which Gugler boldly took exception, but from which judgment Roosevelt would not retreat.

The storm subsided, and Gugler said that his first preference was to leave the Executive Office alone and spill the extra presidential staff into the State, War, & Navy Building. Roosevelt asked if Gugler would speak to several of his aides on the subject while he was in Washington. A time was set. When the meeting did take place, Gugler was taken to the President himself, who said that he had already spoken to his aides and no one liked the idea, in point of convenience or security: "You don't wish me to get into a hassle among these people with whom I live in the White House family, do you?"

But Roosevelt was listening, and soon became cheerful with Gugler. During the conference the architect said that he could show how the present Executive Office could be made three times as large, "without increasing the apparent size of the building to anyone who might look at it from any side, no change to the eye . . . ." The President could hardly do other than express an interest, at which juncture Gugler asked, " . . . may I be permitted to make you such a study to look at?"

The architect was given about five days to prepare his project. He hurried back to New York, elated about the challenge of his crusade in honor of the great McKim. Mrs. Roosevelt had offered her support, so he felt his cause at least had a chance; his friends urged him on, and helped him with the task as he labored through the weekend. Tuesday night he was on the train for Washington with his precious "drawings and documents." Wednesday morning at about nine he entered the oval room. "I was positively happy," he recalled, "to find that Mrs. Roosevelt was there, too, along with her dear friends, Nancy Cook and Marian Dickerman." Also present was Clarence Pickett, the Quaker leader who had inspired the Arthurdale project. The President was in his wheelchair, and Eric Gugler spread the drawings on the floor before him in sequence, one by one. As the concept became evident, the women exclaimed over the appropriateness and beauty of it. Gugler remembered that the President studied the drawings and at last said, "Yes. OK."

"All of us," wrote Gugler, "were very happy, but I never was quite sure F.D.R. was."[10]

A Fireside Chat

The new scheme was acclaimed by nearly all parties. The Commission of Fine Arts agreed "unanimously and heartily" with the solution, and Moore urged the President to give Gugler the job. Roosevelt hesitated, knowing that the construction of the new office was the responsibility of the National Park Service. Federal agencies are jealous of their turf; the President had been close to Winslow in planning, through the winter and spring. He considered Moore's recommendation, then wrote to Marvin H. McIntyre, his secretary in charge of the project: "Don't you think . . . in order to prevent criticism by [Park Service] architects, we should not employ Eric Gugler as an architect, but on a per diem basis as consultant . . . ." This arrangement was made, but Gugler had the final say on design. He had no intention of being acquiescent, as Billy Delano before him had been in dealing with U.S. Grant III.[11]

Gugler was paid a fee and daily expenses, and other costs he had to beg or pay himself. "There was no money for the necessary draftsmen to get out the drawings, especially the details," he wrote, "but we managed somehow . . . ." Among those who helped him was Ferdinand Eiseman, his representative at Arthurdale and later his partner in New York for many years. The government provided no work space for Gugler, a situation quickly remedied by the American Institute of Architects, which allowed him to use the "major ground floor rooms" in the Octagon, the mansion that served as its national headquarters. Winslow, meanwhile, was a good loser. He would remain involved in the work, acting as surrogate when Gugler was not in town. The architect's office of the National Park Service managed the bidding, the contracts, and other such details, and was in fact the agency in charge, with Winslow as the architect representing that agency.

In governmental matters, Lorenzo Winslow rode the waves; his vivid blue eyes had taken more than one glimpse of the great, and he knew the fickleness of those in powerful positions. But in his memoirs many years later he could not resist dismissing Eric Gugler in this way: "Mrs. Roosevelt had a social worker whose husband was a New York architect . . . he suddenly was the man."[12]

Preparations went ahead full speed. The necessary negotiations with labor representatives were completed in June, with an agreement that there would be no strikes, that all unions—except the electricians— would work on six-hour shifts a day, without charging overtime. A similar arrangement was finally made with the electricians. Meanwhile, Gugler completed his drawings late in the month, and the Commission of Fine Arts quickly approved them on June 25. The next day the drawings and estimates were taken to the Treasury Department, where they were approved for expenditure.

On June 28 Roosevelt addressed the nation in a fireside chat from the Diplomatic Reception Room. He used the Executive Office project as an illustration of his point that his federal recovery programs were not a threat to the American way of life, but a means of strengthening "old and tested American ideals." The text, which shows Roosevelt's gift for plain talk, also reflects his awareness of the public's sensitivity about change at the White House:[13]

> While I am away from Washington this summer, a long needed renovation of and addition to our White House office building is to be started. The architects have planned a few new rooms built into the present all too small one-story structure. We are going to include in this addition and in this renovation modern electric wiring and modern plumbing and modern means of keeping the offices cool in the hot Washington summers. But the structural lines of the old Executive Office Building will remain. The artistic lines of the White House buildings were the creation of master builders when our Republic was young. The simplicity and the strength of the structure remain in the face of every modern test. But within this magnificent pattern, the necessities of modern government business require constant reorganization and rebuilding.
>
> If I were to listen to the arguments of some prophets of calamity who are talking these days, I should hesitate to make these alterations. I should fear that while I am away for a few weeks the architects might build some strange new Gothic tower or a factory building or perhaps a replica of the Kremlin or of the Potsdam Palace. But I have no such fears. The architects and builders are men of common sense and of artistic American tastes. They know that the principles of harmony and of necessity itself require that the building of the new structure shall blend with the essential lines of the old. It is this combination of the old and the new that marks orderly peaceful progress—not only in building buildings but in building government itself.
>
> Our new structure is a part of and a fulfillment of the old.
>
> All that we do seeks to fulfill the historic traditions of the American people . . . ."

The New West Wing

When the President departed in early June for his summer travels, the Executive Office Building was vacated. Under the chief usher's direction, the offices of the major secretaries were moved into the Green and Blue rooms of the White House proper, with their stenographers housed in the basement; the President's office was transferred to the oval room upstairs, while the remaining staff, comprising about half of the total, occupied temporary quarters in the State, War, & Navy Building. Roosevelt left the following memorandum: "While I am away, if any question arises about the plans for the Executive Office, I should like to have my uncle, Fred. A. Delano, consulted . . . ."[14]

The construction contract was awarded on July 24, 1934, to the N.P. Severin Company of Chicago, which had built the new roof on the White House for Coolidge in 1927 and had reconstructed the Executive Office Building for Hoover in 1930. Demolition of the existing structure— which was, for the most part, only four years old—commenced before the close of the month. Little was left: Only the north wall survived in its entirety, and parts of the east and west walls were braced for reuse. Because of the special handicaps associated with doing heavy work in the White House compound, and the sturdy steel construction of Hoover's rebuilt office building, the demolition work went slowly. What might be called the preparation for construction, together with the excavation for the new underground section of the building to the south, took much of August. By then it was clear that the President would not occupy his office in October.

After construction began, in the third week of August, it lasted about 100 days, until the close of November. As with most White House work since the World War, the operation continued around the clock; workers were divided among three shifts. The agreement with the trade unions for six-hour shifts instead of eight had been an effort to achieve greater efficiency through tighter scheduling, lessening the chances that a newly arrived workman would have to wait for his predecessor to finish before he could get started. West Executive Avenue was temporarily closed for use in unloading and loading materials, for storage and as a general work area, so that as little as possible of the White House grounds would be intruded upon.

The roof was completed during the first week in November, and by then the interior was well along. Meanwhile, in October, the Roosevelts had returned to the White House. Except for meals in the State Dining Room, most of their activities were restricted to the family quarters. Steve Early wrote in his diary about the discomforts of having the executive offices on the state floor of the White House: "We work under difficulties due to the fact that Mack [Marvin McIntyre] and I share the same room—the Green Room—while the offices are located in the White House proper—the President's visitors also waiting in this room and, of course, as they come in, engage in conversation with each other and with us who are trying to take care of our regular work."[15]

Painting and some of the interior decoration were near completion by mid-November, although additions would be made by both Gugler and Winslow over the first months of 1935. When the staff began to move back to the Executive Office Building on November 16, Roosevelt went to Warm Springs for a short vacation. On December 4, 1934, before a large gathering of reporters and his own executive staff of 120, the President was wheeled into the building from the east side, to work there for the first time.

In certain respects, the Executive Office Building seemed little changed. McKim's north front remained, with its central entrance door—framed by engaged columns and flanked by rows of long windows—cut into the simple white plane of the facade. Since the square footage of the building had been doubled, however, the rebuilt office would have rivaled the White House in scale, had it all been exposed. Most of it lay hidden. Gugler had tucked away new space everywhere he could, but his principal devices for expanding the original form were the addition of a penthouse, a receding second story, not immediately visible from the ground, and a southward extension of the basement as a subterranean wing under three feet of earth, with grass and shrubbery planted over it.

The principal floor was reserved for the President and his secretaries. Apart from the large waiting rooms, where, said Gugler, "the general effect and spirit . . . should be akin to that of the Entrance Hall of the White House itself," little was seen of the rational planning that had characterized McKim's earlier Executive Office Building. The rooms, connected by narrow, rambling corridors, were placed not for ceremonial purposes, but for their convenient proximity to each other.[16]

Formerly on axis with the front door, the presidential office was shifted to the southeast corner, where it has remained. From the waiting rooms, the Oval Office was reached by a series of halls, terminating at last in a small vaulted antechamber. Now less integral to the plan of the Executive Office than it had been, the Oval Office related more to the White House. It looked out onto the Rose Garden; the colonnade around the garden was extended farther south to provide the porch Roosevelt had requested, with French doors giving onto it from the Oval Office. When entered from that side, the Oval Office seemed to have no relationship to the rest of the Executive Office Building. Quiet and removed, it shared only with the Cabinet Room and Missy Le-Hand's office the shade of the colonnade and the greenery of the garden.

Finished somewhat more elaborately than its predecessor, the Oval Office had rather theatrical neocolonial trimmings, somewhat in the Moderne vein. The most important doors had heavy pediments, while doors of secondary status had shell-shaped niches over them. A color scheme of gray-green walls—this a particular request of Roosevelt's—and white woodwork and ceiling was tried and modified only in the addition of a few drops of green to the ceiling paint, because Gugler disliked the contrast made by the flat-white plaster. He designed curtains for the room in the grand manner of those on the state floor in the house; they were dark green, surmounted by cornices with spread eagles in gilded wood.[17]

Elsewhere, the main floor was also handsomely finished. Following White House tradition, the offices of the most important aides had fireplaces. These were kept freshly laid with logs on a bed of kindling, like all White House fireplaces. The trimmings of the offices were of wood, painted white, and the plaster walls were painted usually in cream, green, or light brown. Floors throughout the building were covered with cork, except in the waiting room, where black and white rubber tiles were laid in a checkerboard pattern.

Major spaces had glass chandeliers, but the most notable innovation in illumination was the indirect lighting on the main floor. Popular with architects because it "washed" a room with light, yet required no visible fixture and made no glare, the indirect lighting was set into troughs that extended around the cornices of the rooms. Representing the state of the art in illumination, the lighting proved successful in the Executive Office. It had been suggested to Gugler by Charles Moore as a means of avoiding what he called the "Modernism" and "bad taste" of lighting devices of the day.

Beyond the principal floor, in the penthouse and the subterranean ranges of offices, the rooms were numerous and finished simply. There were mail rooms, secretarial pools, library rooms, filing rooms, private offices, and offices for two, three, and more employees. One of Gugler's most delightful architectural effects was actually for the less glamorous part of the Executive Office Building. So that the basement offices would not become oppressive in total exile from the light of day, he created a colonnaded atrium, a sunken courtyard cut into the earth and edged above at the ground level with a surrounding parapet. The spaces between the columns were glazed with windowpanes, like the colonnade on the east side of the White House. From what would normally have been a windowless basement, Executive Office workers looked out on a courtyard green with boxwood and English ivy, climaxed by a splashing central fountain.

The only feature of Eric Gugler's design not realized was a roofed iron balcony. This was to have overlooked West Executive Avenue as though it were a tribunal from which to watch parades. Broad and handsomely detailed, it would have had a metal roof—probably copper—that sloped like an awning over its four lattice columns of wrought iron. Even after it was dropped from the plan, Gugler rather wistfully wrote: "The balcony of the Executive Avenue Facade should not be forgotten. In the winter time when the leaves are off the trees the appearance of that facade is decidedly inferior if not unpleasant. The balance of the facade could be beautifully taken care of by the balcony as drawn."[18]

Gugler was praised for his work by newspapers, magazines, and his fellow architects. But what meant the most to him was a letter from Charles Moore, written as the building neared completion: "it was a great satisfaction to go over the new White House Office Building. The fundamentals have been taken care of in [a] most satisfactory manner. You have gained the additional space needed at the least possible expense of the none too abundant areas of the grounds. Moreover, you have kept the spirit of the White House throughout. . . . And you have preserved the charm that Hoban and Latrobe imparted to the original house and that McKim added to when he made it into a residence for the First Gentlemen of the Nation. . . ." Nearly 40 years later, Eric Gugler could quote the letter almost verbatim.[19]

Guardian Angels

At the time Charles Moore first approached Gugler about the Executive Office, Gugler was assisting Mrs. Roosevelt with some minor decisions involving the Red Room. This parlor looked outmoded with its tufted and fringed Victorian furniture, velour-covered walls, and dark red velvet draperies. By 1934 the materials were sufficiently worn out to justify a change. This decoration was to take longer than most.

What of the advisory committee? Established by a joint resolution of the Congress in February 1928, the committee was referred to in the legislation as "temporary." Mrs. Roosevelt can have felt no pressure to call the committee, even though Billy Delano had approached her on the subject in New York well before her husband's inauguration. Activity on the part of the committee had been very slight since Roosevelt's election in 1932. Mrs. Harold I. Pratt, Republican to her marrow, like the other members, had stood by, interested, but acting only through Delano. He was a close friend whom she did not hesitate to prod.

Mrs. Roosevelt's interest was only in refreshing the Red Room. Given the national situation and her growing interest in the plight of the needy, the thought of sponsoring an elaborate program of redecoration may have seemed inappropriate to her. Interior decoration was also an activity closely associated with Mrs. Hoover, and most First Ladies want projects they originate themselves. Eric Gugler was called only because he was close at hand, and Mrs. Roosevelt wanted advice on the design of an Oriental screen she felt would add interest to the Red Room.

The initial meeting took place in the spring of 1934 between Mrs. Roosevelt, Gugler, and Lieutenant E. P. Locke, Jr., who handled White House projects for the buildings office of the National Park Service. Discussion of the screen led to a general appraisal of the room. In mid-June, after the design of the Executive Office Building had been approved, the three met again in the Red Room, and Gugler set down the decisions they made: The walls were to be re-covered in silk, and new curtains were to be made; a different chandelier, similar to the large glass one in the Green Room, was to replace the present fixture; a new sofa, a rug, a small screen, and a table were to be acquired to mix with most of what was already there. To the June meeting Gugler brought swatches of fabrics that he and his wife, the actress Anne Tonetti, had selected from various suppliers in New York. These were velvets and brocades. Mrs. Roosevelt could not decide whether she wished to retain the light-absorbing velvet, or turn to shiny brocade for the wall covering. According to Gugler's figures, the velvet would cost about $5,000, while the brocade was about $1,500 less.[20]

The discussion turned out to be academic, since the Red Room was designated for use as an office during the construction of the Executive Office Building. Nothing could be accomplished before mid-autumn of 1934, when the President's staff would vacate the state rooms and return to the new quarters. As that time approached, and the Roosevelts were back in the White House from their summer travels, Gugler found that Mrs. Roosevelt—having doubtless consulted her circle at Val-Kill—had decided to use damask, less shiny than brocade, for both walls and curtains. Gugler suggested that they begin with this, waiting until later to make the other decisions, and recommended that W. & J. Sloane Company in New York carry out the installation, in part because it had a Washington store. He purchased the dark red damask from Stroheim & Romann, a leading manufacturer in New York.[21]

Mrs. Roosevelt authorized the work on October 31, and it began on Monday, November 19. She retained the final say on materials for chairs and sofas, making her final choices on December 1 to allow time for completion by December 15, the beginning of the White House social season. As a courtesy she asked Charles Moore to join Gugler in selecting pictures from the White House collection to hang in the Red Room.

Reupholstered, but otherwise the same, the Red Room faced a busy schedule in 1935. Mrs. Roosevelt's press conferences assembled there weekly. In was the scene of after dinner coffee and innumerable teas. It became the Roosevelts' favorite of all the state parlors, but something still seemed to be lacking. It was not satisfying like the Green Room. Mrs. Roosevelt decided she wanted a new look, and by late spring Gugler was showing her drawings of "Adam" style furniture reproductions. Soon the screen ordered earlier was in place; a costly object made of wood and silk, it had been created by Mikami Studio of New York, specialists in Oriental-style art objects for architects and interior decorators. While the new wall coverings and curtains of the Red Room had been paid for out of the congressional allowance, high prices made it obvious that the money for the new furniture would have to come from someplace else.

Early in the summer, contact was made at last—and, it seems, hesitantly—with the advisory committee. Mrs. Pratt was invited to a reception, where Mrs. Roosevelt made a point of meeting her and bringing up the subject of furnishing the Red Room. The conversation, though brief, opened the door. On July 11, Eric Gugler wrote to Mrs. Pratt at her summer home in Dark Harbor, Maine: "Mrs. Roosevelt told me last month that you had in mind the possibility of getting an Adam settee, something like the one in the Green Room, for the Red Room. . . . The problem of getting some new chairs, chandeliers, etc. for the Red Room is up now and I am starting work on it. . . . If you should happen to be in New York during the summer I would like to have a moment to go over the problems of furnishing the Red Room with you."[22]

This was the invitation to help. Harriet Pratt wrote to Billy Delano from Maine, "Mr. Eric Gugler wrote me about his plans for the Red Room in the White House. As he expresses it, he wishes to be office boy for you. We have a little over a thousand dollars and with his [this?] money perhaps we can make a start." She returned home, where, shrewd lady that she was, she responded to Gugler's letter very carefully: "My committee is very much interested in the furnishing of the Red Room. . . . We have some money which we may wish to use, providing the furnishings purchased by the Government seem appropriate to us. We think the Green Room is very beautiful and in keeping with the period of the White House and we are happy to know that Mrs. Roosevelt agrees with us."[23]

She was invited to tea by Mrs. Roosevelt, probably in New York at Mrs. Roosevelt's apartment on 11th Street, in Greenwich Village. From Mrs. Pratt's point of view, the meeting seems not to have been entirely satisfactory. Mrs. Roosevelt had some interest in antiques herself, having visited many museums, including the Metropolitan, in search of models for her Val-Kill reproductions. But while this may have provided a common ground for chitchat, Mrs. Pratt had a goal in mind: She wanted the

President to establish a permanent advisory committee to replace the temporary one described in the law, so that she could be assured of the perpetuity of her work. As bait, she alluded vaguely to the fund for White House furnishings, on deposit in a bank—unnamed—in New York. When she got no encouragement in her objective from the First Lady, she felt justified in her suspicion that her committee was wanted only for the money it might provide.

Soon after, Mrs. Pratt called on Eric Gugler at his office at 101 Park Avenue. When she had left, he wrote a memo, apparently for the record, of the substance of the meeting. He was suspicious of her. "I cannot be sure," he wrote to Mrs. Roosevelt, "that there really is money left over." Continuing with his analysis of the situation: "She seems to know that her committee has no real legal standing and, I think, would be happy to have an arrangement worked out whereby it did. I gave her a list of what I thought was needed for the room. . . . She mentioned that the cost of the screen seemed to her to be a lot and I think that if not careful she may, although I doubt it, prove to be difficult in this matter."[24]

Soon two sides were at work, with Mrs. Roosevelt and Eric Gugler caught in the middle. At one extreme was Mrs. Pratt, while at the other appeared Charles Moore, longtime watchdog over White House design and the chairman of the Commission of Fine Arts. Neither admired Roosevelt's politics, but both had decided ideas about his domicile. Moore had no intention of admitting an advisory group between himself and the White House. Admired deeply and sincerely by Gugler, he now asserted all the power he could muster to block the creation of a furnishings committee. To him the Commission of Fine Arts represented professionalism in the arts—architects, sculptors, painters; he resented the creation of an advisory committee of antiquarians and amateurs, fearing, as Gugler put it in expressing Moore's views, that "some time . . . people of doubtful taste might get control of it."[25]

While Moore stood firm, Mrs. Pratt was willing to lay her petition aside for a while, to pursue the more interesting subject of furnishing the Red Room. Everybody agreed that the first needs were for a glass chandelier of the late 18th or early 19th century and a sofa of the same period. Mrs. Pratt had already put Gugler in touch with Luke Vincent Lockwood, who, she said, knew of chandeliers from Devonshire House in England which might be available. Lockwood replied that the time was not right, that "the matter will have to wait for a little while," but directed Gugler to French & Company in New York, who "I think have the largest variety of good things of anyone. Ask for Mr. Mitchell Samuels and see if there is anything there that attracts you."[26]

In this general vein the interactions continued through the autumn of 1935, increasingly cordial on the part of Gugler and the advisory committee. By late September they were considering reproductions of antiques, since they were unable to find or afford the originals. Wrote Gugler that month to Harriet Pratt: "Mr. Delano said that he would take another look at the sofa now in the Green Room to see whether it would be good to have an additional reproduction made. As soon as he returns, if he feels that the reproduction would be good, I would like to proceed immediately to get chairs that would go with it and of course, would like your and Mr. Delano's opinion and Mr. Lockwood's. If the people who made the original reproduction are no longer in business it is possible that Sloan's in Washington could do the job. . . ."27

By early December Mrs. Pratt was so encouraged and eager to proceed that she asked Charles Moore to meet her at the White House to discuss the decoration of the rooms. She found to her dismay that "the furniture which had been given the Government for the Green Room had been scattered throughout the various rooms in the White House." Back in New York, she quickly dispatched Louise Rennie, who had assisted the advisory committee in seeking furnishings for the Green Room, to investigate the situation.

Miss Rennie located some of the furniture, but not all. To her surprise, she also discovered that the upholsteries and other details of furnishings at the White House were not the particular concern of the First Lady: ". . .the housekeeper is now choosing all the renewals of fabric for the furniture." In reaction to Louise Rennie's report, Mrs. Pratt told Billy Delano that it was time for some formal delegation of authority over the state rooms, with the ideal, of course, being that the Advisory Committee have full and undiluted control.

"Mrs. Roosevelt has intimated to me," wrote Mrs. Pratt, "that personally she is not especially interested and only wishes the Red Room to be a gracious room in which to receive her guests." Given the money to do otherwise, it is doubtful that any First Lady would turn the house over to a committee. But there is seldom public money available for the expensive decorating required in state interiors; the appropriation made by Congress for each new four-year term is quickly swallowed up by necessities. Even when the funding exists, most Presidents are reluctant to appear to be spending on opulence, for that course is likely to inspire damaging criticism.28

Mrs. Roosevelt's hope for a special appropriation came to nothing, nor during the Depression could she have been too sanguine in her hopes for it. If suitable redecoration was to take place in the White House, it was going to be expensive, and the only recourse was to turn to private sources—such persons as Mrs. Pratt and Luke Lockwood and others. In exchange for the donations, they would require some say in how the money would be spent. On this point, White House officials hesitated, recalling the difficulties with the advisory committee under Coolidge, nearly a decade before.

Mrs. Pratt, perhaps in desperation, softened to a second-line position on the question of authority in December 1935. She had gotten on well with Charles Moore, finding in the old man a caginess that matched her own. "It would be ideal," she wrote to Delano, "if our committee could work under the Fine Arts Commission." Perhaps in Moore she saw at least a faint glimmer of sympathy for the great works she had in mind. Speaking of her visit with him to the White House, she wrote: "Mr. Moore . . . more or less intimated that [a connection with the Advisory Committee] would be a pleasant association for him if it could be arranged informally."[29]

"He is very anxious, of course," she continued, "to maintain the McKim, Mead & White tradition. I gather that he felt rather badly that the McKim, Mead & White cane furniture was taken out of the Green Room, and he expressed disapproval of the Aubusson rugs. However, I don't think he is very serious. Whatever he would do would be in the spirit of the tradition of the White House as it is expressed by McKim, Mead & White in the Blue Room. Our Sheraton furniture in the Green Room is a little earlier and we should be thinking about what would be appropriate for the Red Room."

On January 18, 1936, Mrs. Roosevelt wrote in her column "My Day" about the work at the White House: "Mr. Eric Gugler . . . and I are trying to pick out some new chairs and a sofa for the Red Room. We have to please the art commission and keep within the budget. We thought we were considering every aspect of the problem, when suddenly I was reminded, after I had sat down on a chair and thought it was comfortable, that I must also be sure that it was strong enough, so that, no matter what treatment it received, it would not collapse under any important guests. . . . I decided it would be wiser to have the chairs made, and not to go in for antiques."

Ideas came from everyone. Through the spring of 1936 Gugler corresponded with manufacturers of fine fabrics and interior decorating companies such as W. & J. Sloane, or furnishings departments within larger companies, such as B. Altman & Company in New York. Fabric swatches flew through the mails; rare documentary silks, possible models to copy, were delivered by hand, then returned to the archives of the manufacturers. It was clear that no one would act until an organized form was established within which to operate. Charles Moore, determined to be the final authority, placed as he was at the head of the prestigious Fine Arts Commission, intimidated everyone else involved. In letters to Gugler he discussed the classic periods of furniture. After a luncheon at the White House with the committee, he wrote to the patient architect, "Of course you know—although the 'Committee' evidently didn't—that there was no Colonial furniture in the White House. After it was restored following the burning by the British in 1814, Monroe completely furnished the house with imported French furniture. . . .the French influence has always predominated at the White House."[30]

Nothing concrete was accomplished until after Moore's retirement in 1937 from the Commission of Fine Arts. At 82 he was the senior figure in Washington's small arts and humanities community, and well connected in official circles. He had served 22 years as chairman of the commission, as well as being for most of that time highly successful as the director of manuscripts at the Library of Congress. Moore had celebrated the beaux arts architects with several important biographies, as well as serving as adviser on the 1932 *Writings of George Washington* sponsored by the Congress. For the Red Room—a minute part of his distinguished career—his departure was advantageous. His successor, the landscape architect Major Gilmore D. Clarke, though a veteran member of the commission, was willing to compromise, and compromise was the commission's theme for the future.

The Red Room work was finally completed later in the spring of 1937. Five reproduction seating pieces were commissioned from W. & J. Sloane in New York, copies from antiques provided as models by the committee. This suite in mahogany, with shallow upholstery, consisted of four armchairs and one long sofa, all in the simple, formal, neoclassical taste of the Federalist era. The crimson damask for the chairs and rose damask for the sofa also came from Sloane, bought at low prices. Wholly transformed from its turn-of-the-century cushioned richness into a serene "colonial" setting, the Red Room joined the Green Room in the "period" look that was to characterize the White House state rooms for many years to come. There was relatively little furniture in the room: a sofa, side tables and porcelain lamps with cream-colored silk shades, arm chairs scattered about, and a bronze clock and old gilt and porcelain ornaments that had been in the White House for at least a century. The tall, full hangings at the windows were a continuation in the same red damask of the walls. A number of presidential portraits constituted the only—perhaps dubious—representatives of fine art.

Not until four years after the Red Room was finished, on March 17, 1941, did Mrs. Roosevelt sign a carefully worded agreement on how the advisory committee would work. The committee would now be cautiously styled the Sub-committee Upon Furnishings and Gifts for State Rooms of the White House, to be appointed by the chairman of the Commission of Fine Arts. Each member was to be approved by the First Lady. Both chairman and President's wife were to sit ex-officio on the subcommittee. A "sharp distinction" was made between the state rooms and the "Apartments of the Family of the President." State rooms included all the rooms of the main floor, "the smaller private dining room excepted." Guest rooms were to be considered state rooms only if "designated by the wife of the President."[31]

The committee was to meet regularly in January and June, but it could be summoned to special sessions by the chairman of the Commission of Fine Arts. Its jurisdiction over existing White House furnishings was vague in some ways: Did the committee have authority over all the furnishings for the White House, or only those in the state rooms? In the agreement the term is "existing furnishings," which implies all of them. Finally, the committee was to advise on the grounds and gardens.

Mrs. Pratt visited the White House regularly through the '30s and early '40s, usually in company with Mrs. Harry Horton Benkard, her Long Island neighbor, a devoted collector and a patron of the American Wing. To Billy Delano she wrote, soon after the organizational structure had been confirmed, "I am sure you will agree with me that we must tread very gently until we become better established. . . .We must feel our way, especially about the changes which are dear to Mrs. Roosevelt, such as the portraits of Grover Cleveland and of Theodore Roosevelt in the Red Room. It is hoped some time that these rooms may only contain portraits of an earlier date."[32]

By the "historical" decoration of the rooms and the presence of the advisory, the museum function was established at the White House. This was in some respects odd. In the past the house had been more monument than museum, although Jefferson had scattered artifacts from the West through the rooms, and over the years others, including many Indian tribal representatives, had brought gifts for display. All had gone, eventually. The public flocked to the White House not to see exhibits but to inspect the place where their President conducted the business of the nation, the rooms where he drank his coffee and talked to his wife and children. Through its long life the house had never been treated in a consciously historical way before the completion of the Green Room during the Hoover administration.

Harriet Barnes Pratt had been the guiding light. Her labors since 1925 were rewarded in the instrument signed by Mrs. Roosevelt in 1941. She had seen her program institutionalized, and her sense of triumph overwhelmed her weariness over past frustrations. The museum impulse throbbed stronger even as the agreement was signed, in the decision by the Park Service to produce a master plan and catalogue to guide the future of all the state rooms. "The development of this plan," wrote Mrs. Pratt to Mrs. Roosevelt, "will be the fulfillment of a hope which I have cherished for many, many years."[33]

The Ground Floor

Roosevelt's alterations continued throughout the 1930s. In 1935, for example, much of the basement was overhauled, under the direction of the President himself, working closely with Lorenzo Winslow. This came about as a result of the rewiring of the house for electricity in 1935. Terrified of fire, Roosevelt had the house inspected frequently for fire hazards, as though issuing a mandate to find something wrong. Winter wood fires in the fireplaces were extinguished if Roosevelt was to be in the room alone. When the wiring was judged faulty, nothing would suit but the installation of a new system. Since the walls of the basement area had to be opened extensively for this purpose, the opportunity arose to make improvements. Principal among these changes was a new kitchen, but there was more.

The first of the President's basement projects was to create a wholly new interior, a library. Probably in the spring of 1935, he hailed Lorenzo Winslow in the Rose Garden and asked him to push him in his chair to the room in the basement immediately east of the stair to the state floor. Theodore Roosevelt had made this into a men's lounge—the "gentlemen's ante-room"—with toilet facilities in the adjoining secondary room on the corner of the building. When, after about 1920, it was no longer needed for its original purpose, the men's room had been given over to storage and the bathroom to use by servants. The large square chamber was "in somewhat deplorable condition," Winslow later remembered. Since the early 1850s the oval room on the second floor had been the library, but an increasing need to use it for other purposes had, in 1929, exiled the books to the central corridor. Thus the White House was without a library, and the President, who loved books, intended to reestablish one.

Winslow looked around the northeast room and quickly agreed: "I thought that it would be an excellent library as it was over 22 feet square with a Victorian mantel of marble that I would remove and line the walls with book shelves enclosed by glass doors." The architect went to his drawing board and produced a predictable sort of library, the kind of neocolonial interior characteristic of expensive Long Island houses of the '20s and '30s; the design featured a "georgian wood mantel" and the book shelves bore a similar motif. On second thought, glass doors seemed unwise for a basement which was sometimes dank, so Winslow designed wood-frame doors with brass mesh. "I made [an elevation] of the wall with the fireplace showing a picture in color of a yacht sailing under a good breeze with full sail . . . when I showed it to FDR he was so pleased and laughed at my small attempt to please him."[34]

The cabinetwork was executed from Winslow's drawings by the carpentry shop at the White House. As the room was nearing completion, Roosevelt objected to the marble facing around the fireplace opening, thinking, as Winslow recalled, that it "might be changed to Delft blue tile with scenes of Washington public buildings." The library was completed without the tiles. Roosevelt later had his Dutch tiles made for Hyde Park, but through a series of circumstances they ultimately ended up in the White House Library.[35]

The Diplomatic Reception Room next received the President's attention. Called by McKim on his plans the "Diplomatic Ante-Room," this had been used as little more than an entrance hall for the south side of the house. It was made famous by the fireside chats. The room concerned the President less because of its stuffiness and windowless discomfort than the fact that the famous fireplace was really a fake, only a mantelpiece with a "hole cut in the wall behind it." Winslow moved the mantel aside and cut into the wall, finding the original fireplace and flue that had served the room more than a century before, when it was the servants' dining room. It was restored to use in 1935.[36]

Neither library nor reception room work was begun when Roosevelt informed Winslow that he had "found $25,000 to put in new electric ranges in the Kitchen." Winslow remembered, "I told him that the Kitchen needed a lot more than electric ranges. I said that it was a very filthy place . . . that the whole Kitchen should be done over in order to clean out the vermin, filth and grease of more than 50 years. . . . " Roosevelt was doubtful, saying, "Our kitchen at Hyde Park has been in use far longer than [the one at the White House] and it is fairly clean and in good condition." A tour of the two White House kitchens, however, changed his mind. They were outmoded and inconvenient.

The service area of the basement was confined to the west end, where it had always been, occupying rooms on both sides of the vaulted central corridor. A permanent partition built across the hall screened movement between the kitchens on the north side and the housekeeper's office and pantry and the doctor's office on the south; the hall space west of the partition had long since been drafted into service for groceries, its walls lined with cabinets and shelves. When the President went to the Oval Office from the house, he passed through this makeshift pantry where, recalled Winslow, "The pleasant spicy smell of groceries, spices, coffee, etc." filled the air.[37]

Both the large and the small kitchens were remodeled. Winslow did the general planning, with Captain Locke as engineer. The result was modern, streamlined kitchens of stainless steel, immaculate and uncluttered; indirect lighting fell on cream-colored walls and on green and cream-colored linoleum floors with black borders. According to the *Journal of Home Economics*, "The lay-out in the new White House kitchen of course embodies the modern ideas about grouping equipment into work centers to save waste motion and keep the different jobs moving along in smooth sequence." Dominated by a hotel-size electric range and ovens, the larger of the two kitchens was to be used for everyday cooking, as well as for the big dinners and parties for which it had mostly served in the past. The small kitchen was converted into a pantry, with refrigerators and warming ovens, serving both the kitchen and the main floor pantry, to which it was linked by electric dumbwaiters and the narrow, twisting stair built into one of the window reveals long years before.[38]

Through the summer and fall of 1935 the basement was under construction. The kitchen work was done last, much of it while the facility was in use. New space was made in the early day kitchen, situated directly below the entrance hall, and once the same size. It had been a furnace room since 1902, its two great stone fireplaces, still exposed but long unused, separated by partitions. Winslow cleared out the partitions and relocated parts of the furnace and elevator machinery, thereby borrowing enough space to wall off a servants' dining room at the west end. Another area gained from the new arrangement was made into narrow locker rooms and a small lounge for off-duty servants.

Linen closets in the basement replaced those on the third floor, although the problem of mildew, which had originally caused the linens to be kept upstairs, soon forced the linen maids to retreat upstairs again. The vaulted space beneath the north portico was enclosed, and excavations were made behind the north wall of the deep open areaway, producing a veritable cave beneath the north drive, containing 4,200 square feet of storage and work rooms and a carpenter shop. This underground addition, though of the simplest design and almost invisible to everyone but the household employees, significantly increased the usefulness of the basement. The whole basement was repainted. Completed at a direct cost of $159,530.25, these were the first major improvements in the service parts of the house since Mrs. Taft had built her pantry in 1909. When the work began, Taft's mighty gas range was still in use, and while the old ice-cooled refrigerators had long since been electrified, most of the boxes were the oak-encased ones installed by McKim.[39]

The Grounds Revised

Roosevelt's landscaping program was ambitious. Known as the Olmsted Plan, this scheme for a revision of the White House grounds forms the basis for the landscape that has remained. When Roosevelt became President in 1933, the landscape was essentially what had been developed during the administration of President Grant, itself a modification of Downing's earlier concept for President Fillmore in the 1850s. This had been modified somewhat by McKim, who conceived the grounds merely as a green setting for the architecture of the house. He had replaced intricate parterre plantings at the base of the house with low, clustered evergreens; numerous trees and shrubs were brought in to frame the facade, especially from the south.

McKim had also created two formal gardens, east and west, which had more varied histories. Mrs. Theodore Roosevelt had quickly usurped the area on the west to build her colonial garden, a geometrical parterre with boxwood-edged beds filled with colorful flowers. The first Mrs. Wilson had brought in two leading landscapers: George Burnap, who designed the formal Rose Garden on the west, and Beatrix Farrand, who designed the "southeast colonial garden," which came to be called the east garden. Mrs. Wilson's innovations had lasted 21 years.

Eric Gugler had made sketches for redesigning the Rose Garden to better suit the new Executive Office. He wanted the garden expanded to the south, to be in line with the southernmost extremity of the enlarged office structure. The ground where the Oval Office was built had been occupied by a drying yard for the laundry, masked by the first Mrs. Wilson with a wall of wooden lattice, which became the western backdrop for her rose garden when it was planted in 1913. After Gugler rebuilt the Executive Office Building, the lengthened colonnade became the garden's backdrop on the west. The architect played with various landscaping ideas, seeming to prefer a series of parallel hedges, which would give each of the rooms on the colonnade its own long eastward vista. The plans were not carried out.[40]

Roosevelt, dissatisfied with Gugler's gardening ideas, became critical of the whole landscape. His doubts were supported—and perhaps even encouraged—by the feeling of the Secret Service agents that the White House was not sufficiently screened from the surrounding streets to make it safe. It was probably during the winter or spring of 1934 that the President happened to meet Frederick Law Olmsted, Jr., and discussed the subject of the White House grounds with him. Olmsted, acclaimed son of a famous father, was with the family firm Olmsted Brothers, Landscape Architects, of Brookline, Massachusetts. As a young man, Olmsted had been a member of the original McMillan Commission that studied the plan of Washington; at the age of 64, he was the leading figure in his profession.

Back at the White House, the President set the wheels turning for new plans for the grounds. With construction beginning on the Executive Office in late summer, Roosevelt wanted a landscaping program to follow close behind. Marvin McIntyre, the secretary put in charge of this endeavor, was told by the President: "It is of the utmost importance that Mr. Olmsted be associated with this project because he is recognized as the outstanding authority." Inspecting the grounds in early June 1934, the landscape architect was struck by the venerable trees and shrubbery. Some of the old presidential trees had grown to enormous size, not least the Jackson magnolias. Some of the buckeye, or horse chestnut, trees brought by Hayes from Ohio had survived; they were tall, with magnificent umbrella spreads of dense foliage. "The White House grounds," Olmsted wrote, "are characterized by many long-established landscape qualities of great dignity and appropriateness. . . . Some of these admirable qualities inherited from the past are very obvious; some have already been obscured by part deliberate or accidental alterations."[41]

His report, submitted in October, dealt "primarily with matters of appearance." He tried to be objective, but as a history buff he found it difficult to suppress his musings over relics. For example, some distance from the south side of the house, along the edge of the driveway, he discovered a "dilapidated rusty iron fence." laden with "rambler roses and clematis." He wondered who long ago had put it there: "Apart from serving to support . . . plants this fence appears to have no function unless it be as a barrier when throngs of people are admitted. . . . " President Grant had installed it for that very purpose in 1873.

Because no body of research existed to tell Olmsted the many things he wished to know about the genesis of the White House landscape, he asked the President if they might not engage a historical specialist. Roosevelt heartily agreed. Morley Jeffers Williams, of the School of

Landscape Architecture at Harvard, was at that time doing research on the gardens at Mount Vernon, preparatory to their restoration. Olmsted found this work "extraordinarily thorough and very illuminating," and approached the professor about the White House work. Well in advance of writing his report, Olmsted informed McIntyre that Williams "has consented to undertake, in collaboration with me, a study much needed as a sound basis for guiding any changes and improvements to be made in the future."[42]

While this research was never finished, it did open windows on the past of the White House grounds that had been closed for many years. The discovery of former locations of driveways and plantings may not have led to their restoration, but it informed the reasoning behind the new designs. That Olmsted was circumspect about altering so historic a landscape is not surprising. The history of landscape gardening was of great interest to him and his circle in the '30s. At the same time, Williamsburg in Virginia was in the infant stages of its reconstruction and restoration. The architects restoring Williamsburg, Perry, Shaw, & Hepburn, of Boston, were both friends and colleagues of Olmsted's. As Olmsted conducted his work at the White House, the intricate walled gardens of the old Governor's Palace were being re-created as they might have been when George Washington knew them.

Having settled his concerns about research, Olmsted turned to determining what should remain and what should be changed in the grounds. He paid particular attention to "increasing the general amenity and the seclusion and privacy proper to the domestic portions of the grounds south of the building." In the main, he called for a more cohesive organization of the grounds. Since President Grant's major redesigning in 1873, they had developed piecemeal, with little regard for the whole. Olmsted found trees planted in unlikely places, curious configurations of shrubbery, and elements such as the flower beds around the fountains, which he found "trivial." He suggested a new emphasis on the great sweep of lawn from the south facade to the south end of the grounds, and a thickening of plantings along its sides, using both trees and yew hedges, to block close views from East and West Executive Avenues.

Olmsted judged the guitar-shaped south drive "a blemish in the landscape," because its curves made a "conspicuous interruption of the lawn and plantations by pavement." The driveway had probably been patterned on the 18th-century one at Mount Vernon; it had been laid out in 1873, when the trees were not so large and therefore did not make such a heavy frame along the sides of the sloping south lawn. This drive, said Olmsted, should be "obliterated," to be replaced by a pair of gently curving roads that joined before the south portico and extended southward to gates at distant entrances on the east and west. A transverse drive was to link these opposite gates, but would be sunk lower than grade, to remove it entirely from the vista from the house or street.

After a radical tree cutting, which would remove all plantings that obstructed a central lawn 200 feet wide, the south grounds were to present an unbroken carpet of grass, flanked by groves. Olmsted described the great lawn as a "look-in" for the public, which was "of marked esthetic importance in the general plan of the National Capital," maintaining "in perpetuity an unobstructed and satisfying view into the White House Grounds from the street."

He discouraged plantings of flower beds and scattered shrubbery, preferring the effect of forests along the sides, with shrubbery screens close to the fences on the perimeter. "In general," he wrote, "the White House Grounds outside of the definitely enclosed gardens next to the building are characterized by a very restrained use of shrubbery and minor vegetation; for the most part confined to a few rather large, massive and very dignified specimens. . . . This characteristic of the general landscape ought to be carefully respected in any efforts to develop the boundary foliage screens so much needed for privacy. . . . " He believed that flower plantings should be confined to the two formal gardens on the east and west of the house. If absolutely necessary, they might also be tolerated in the "lateral wooded areas" flanking the central vista, especially where they would be screened by the so-called Jefferson mounds, which had been thrown up by Franklin Pierce in 1855.

Olmsted envisioned the formal gardens as the most intimate and private areas of the landscape. He decried their "make-shift look," attributing that and other shortcomings to weak design and hasty execution. "What is needed for the two formal gardens," he wrote, "is to work out patiently and skillfully in detail a number of alternative studies for their complete and permanent rehabilitation and for their continuing maintenance, directed toward making them as perfect and beautiful examples of their rather simple and unpretentious kind as they can possibly be made; to subject these studies to careful criticism by a number of people thoroughly well-informed on such questions; and when a plan and maintenance program is finally decided on to hold to their plan and program firmly and persistently year after year except as amendments of the plan and program *as a whole* may be adopted after equally careful deliberation." This made sense to a landscaper, but it was unrealistic for the White House, where new tenants always bring new ideas.

The problem of automobile traffic in the grounds was of long duration. There were as yet no gate lodges with guards, and callers moved in and out of the driveways at will most days, although during special events a guard might be stationed at each gate. Nearly all callers at the Executive Office, including staff, entered the White House grounds through the northwest gate, parking their cars wherever they found space. The horseshoe driveway still followed the path laid down by Andrew Jackson; a spur on the west connected it to the Executive Office, where an asphalt-paved forecourt was used for parking. Guests of the President and grocery delivery trucks entered the grounds by the same road.

Olmsted recommended a reorganization of all traffic and parking. For the use of the Executive Office he would enlist West Executive Avenue; for service and delivery to the house itself he recommended a special driveway lowered below grade and extending from West Executive Avenue to the sunken areaway on the north side of the house, with limited underground parking along its sides. Congestion at the east entrance on social occasions could be easily alleviated by a double-deck driveway, with two entrances that could function at the same time, one underground and the second above. This was not, however, Olmsted's preference, for he hoped to see the north portico revived as the social entrance to the White House. He objected to having guests enter from the side, and was sure that once the north grounds were cleared of everyday business callers, the Pennsylvania Avenue front would once again be appropriate as the main entrance during formal functions.

In general, Olmsted's report, dated October 16, 1934, proposed a redefinition of the grounds, retaining as much of the old plant material as possible. His ideas were accepted by Roosevelt, who directed the National Park Service to prepare estimates of the cost for immediate implementation. The response was presented by Captain Locke 13 days later, projecting a total cost to the government of $289,769.51.[43]

Roosevelt thought the price too high, yet he did approve a contract with Olmsted Brothers to implement the entire project on paper. It was put into effect part by part over many years. The clearing of the vista and the addition of trees and shrubbery along the sides was the first step, commenced in the spring of 1935. In 1937 the iron fences of 1818 and 1873 were removed and the entire grounds enclosed with a modern version of the original; the old gates, however, were allowed to remain between the tall stone gate posts.

Each year some new feature of the plan was introduced. Several of the more elaborate elements, as the westward sunken drive to the basement service areas, were either modified or never realized, while others of Olmsted's original ideas, such as the double-deck driveway on the east, dropped completely out of the plan. The most striking change in the setting of the White House was the broad stretch of the south lawn and the thick screening along its sides; this principal element of the Olmsted Plan was developed fully by the close of the decade.

Royal Visitors

Roosevelt was reelected in 1936 by a landslide, a reward for the success of his domestic policies. The Depression had eased: The New Deal had done its work thus far. The terrible anxiety that had gripped the American people when the President took office in 1933 was largely gone, and the American system had survived.

Writing in *Reader's Digest* in September 1938, Emil Ludwig, a German-born writer of popular biographies, described the President's House as the "House of a Democrat," explaining: "A European would not suspect that the White House is the residence of a chief of state. All our European republics have placed their presidents in the castles of the kings who once governed, and the visitor passes through haughty railings between gloomy guards and is led across scarlet carpets into lofty, ornate inner rooms of the chief executive, even if the latter happens to be a socialist. . . . The White House is different; not splendid enough for a castle, but more striking than a private home, the patrician aspect of this house is at once almost princely and yet private."

"One would say," Ludwig continued, "that here lives the father of a country, for it is evident from the open site of the house that he does not have to be afraid, like a king or a dictator. . . . the fact that the house is white again distinguishes it from all other official residences in the world." To Emil Ludwig the "superb democracy and unostentatious simplicity" of the White House symbolized the "essential differences between a democratic system based on consent, and a dictatorial system based on force. And one is more than ever convinced of the startling and truly unique quality of the American achievement."[44]

Ludwig often wrote in superlatives. But his observations echoed those of many foreign journalists. In the late 1930s, the strength and durability of the United States took on new meaning to the democratic nations of Europe, threatened by the aggressiveness of fascist Germany. Their leaders felt certain that war was coming, and they knew that if it did come, American aid would be critical. Already during the summer of 1938 the arrival of the crown prince and princess of Sweden had begun a succession of visits by foreign luminaries. Like most of the others, this visit had its pretense: the supposed wish of the couple to inspect Swedish communities in the United States. But the real reason for this and subsequent similar visits, as Mrs. Roosevelt later remembered, was to solicit the goodwill of the American people. "It was evident," she wrote, "that the people of Europe were deeply troubled by the general feeling of unrest and uncertainty on the continent, and were looking for friends in other parts of the world. . . ."[45]

The President also realized that war was coming in Europe and, as Mrs. Roosevelt observed, "he wanted to make contact with those he hoped would preserve and adhere to democracy and prove to be allies against fascism when the conflict came." Welcoming the foreign dignitaries, he also welcomed the widespread publicity that accompanied their visits, hoping to kindle public sympathy among the Americans for the imperiled nations.

Of all the visits, the most spectacular was that of the king and queen of England. It appealed to the American fascination with British royalty and built warm feelings toward the British. King George VI and Queen Elizabeth came at Roosevelt's invitation. They had announced that they would tour Canada in June 1939. Aware of their successful visit to France the previous year, the President wrote a warm, personal invitation to the king to extend his visit to the United States. The king accepted, starting preparations for the first visit of a British monarch to the United States. The royal couple would spend a night in the White House.

Money was available for sprucing up the house: Congress had appropriated $50,000 after Roosevelt's reelection, and little of this had been spent. The house of the Presidents underwent such a cleaning as perhaps it had never known. Mrs. Nesbitt—called "Fluffy" behind her back by the servants—was informed in February of the royal visit to take place in June. She spent a busy winter and spring replacing rugs and making repairs. To give freer access to the vacuum cleaners, she cut off some ten inches from the bottoms of the curtains of the state rooms—an innovation Mrs. Harold I. Pratt was to marvel over even into her old age. The Blue Room's silk wall covering, found to be rotted and splitting, was replaced, complete with an embroidered Greek key border like that on McKim's original. The repaired room looked fresh and elegant, down to its lion-skin rug, a gift to Roosevelt from Emperor Haile Selassie. Mrs. Nesbitt had sent this to the dry cleaners.

By June the housekeeper was pleased with the results of her work. "If I do say so," she wrote, "the lovely old house shone like a brand-new stove!" The staff was excited about the coming of royalty. The servants' hall rang with debate over such questions as whether the men were to bow and the women curtsy before the king and queen. As the day approached, recalled one maid, "The kitchen girls broke dishes, the hall men waxed the same floors over again; and 'Fluffy' scolded the maids."[46]

Meanwhile, the First Lady was besieged with advice on how to treat royalty. Having been educated in England and considering herself well informed about English customs, she was impatient with some of this, but was most irritated by a long, confidential memorandum sent to her by William C. Bullitt, American ambassador to France. He had received the king and queen in Paris during their visit the year before, and he felt that Mrs. Roosevelt could profit from his experience.

The Bullitt memorandum was published by Mrs. Nesbitt years later in her recollections, erroneously labeled as an official British document. The following excerpt captures both its tone and its detail:[47]

Suggestions for the Furnishing of His Majesty's Room

Large bed 'de Milieu' (in center of panel) with the head
   against the wall. (Never with the side against the wall.)
No bolster—two pillows.
Special bolster supplied by His Majesty's valet.
Warm, but light, blankets with silk cover.
Very soft eiderdown quilt, which can be accordion pleated at
   the foot of the bed.
On each side of the bed a bedside table with lamp.
In the bathroom or bedroom (according to possibility) and
   preferably in window recess, on account of light, a dressing table with triple mirror, high enough to enable contemplating oneself when standing.
Very comfortable settee.
Ash trays, matches, cigars and cigarettes for guests, His Majesty having his own cigarettes.
Great numbers of hangers; some of them with wide back
   slightly curved; others with a double bar for trousers; no
   special clip hangers for trousers.
On desk an inkstand with two inkwells, one full of blue-black
   and another of red ink.
No toweled bathrobe. His Majesty prefers large bath towels. (I
   bought sheet size.)
To be ready to supply, if requested, garnet-red and white carnations for boutonnieres. . . . "

Long afterward, Mrs. Roosevelt remembered how the ambassador had presumed to advise her on entertaining in her own house. She considered it condescending: "I always wanted to ask Mr. Bullitt, whether, when he stayed in the White House, he had not found in the bathrooms some of the things he listed as essential, like soap, a glass, towels, and the like."[48] She intended to receive the king and queen in the way she and the President saw proper. It was not a personal or private visit; it was symbolic and had to be carefully staged. Consulting with her old friend, Lady Lindsay, the American wife of British Ambassador Sir Ronald Lindsay, she made her plans, taking into account the formality appropriate to such an event. But the First Lady would also have folk songs sung for the king and queen in the East Room, and at Hyde Park they would be served hot dogs cooked outside, picnic style.

The newspapers that early summer covered in detail the progress of the royal couple through Canada; the American people eagerly awaited their arrival in the United States. A stroke of bad luck had come in a disagreement between the Americans and the British over British foreign policy in the Middle East, but even that did not dampen the public's high spirits, and soon the royal visit dominated the front pages. Just after nine in the evening of June 7, 1939, the king and queen crossed the border by train from Canada and were received by an American delegation in Niagara Falls, New York. Through the night the royal train sped toward Washington, arriving at 11 in the morning of June 8. Vast crowds were drawn to the city, hoping for a glimpse of King George and Queen Elizabeth. The President and Mrs. Roosevelt received their guests in the flower-banked President's Room at Union Station. Two open limousines, King George and President Roosevelt in one and Queen Elizabeth and the First Lady in the second, joined a waiting military parade, which included bombers flying overhead.

The June heat was intense and the glare dazzling. King George wore the full-dress uniform of an admiral of the fleet, while Queen Elizabeth was "radiant," wrote one spectator, in an ankle-length summery dress of "powder-mauve," with a wide-brimmed straw hat garnished with feathers. The President wore a morning coat, and Mrs. Roosevelt a yoke-collared, calf-length blue dress and a wide-brimmed hat. The queen soon produced a parasol for shade, but, noted Mrs. Roosevelt, continued to have "the most gracious manner and bowed right and left with interest, actually looking at people in the crowd so that I am sure many of them felt that the bow was really for them personally."[49]

A cheering crowd, variously estimated at 500,000 to 700,000, packed the streets along the parade route, seemingly oblivious of the heat. A White House guest observed, "Washington was a great sight that day—people had brought chairs and in some cases bridge tables which they set up on the grass of the Parks or Circles by which the procession was to pass. . . ." With the royal party was a British newspaper correspondent, who wrote, "The state drive from the station to the White House rivalled in enthusiasm anything Their Majesties had ever seen. . . ." The same newsman claimed that 150 tons of confetti were swept up from the streets of Washington the next day.[50]

The two cars left the procession at the White House and entered the cool green of the south grounds through the southeast gate. Disembarking at the south portico, they passed beneath the arch and into the Diplomatic Reception Room, where the two couples paused for a short time and conversed pleasantly. In the East Room at high noon the diplomatic corps presented itself in full dress, arranged by rank in the long oval known as the Diplomatic Circle. The British ambassador, the dean of the corps, rounded the circle with the king, while his wife, Lady Lindsay, followed with the queen. Each of the diplomats and their wives were presented in turn to the king and queen, in a relatively rapid ceremony that ended with the departure of the guests of honor by elevator to their rooms upstairs. At 1 p.m. they returned for a small, informal lunch with the Roosevelts, then began an automobile tour of the city. Since the route of the tour had been announced in advance, the roads were all crowded, with thousands again struggling for a glimpse of royalty.

Little about the two-day royal visit to Washington could be called "social," although there was a succession of dinners, luncheons, teas, and receptions. Every event was official. The Roosevelts held a state dinner on the first evening, and after it King George and President Roosevelt talked in the oval room until the early morning. Before their night departure for New York on June 9, King George honored the President with a small dinner at the British Embassy. From Washington the king and queen went to New York, where they viewed the World's Fair and spent Saturday night and Sunday with the Roosevelts at Hyde Park. On Sunday evening they embarked by train for Canada.

During the royal visit to the White House, the queen used the Rose Bedroom on the northeast, and King George stayed across the hall in what is known today as the Lincoln Bedroom and was then the Lincoln Study. A movement outside the White House to decorate these quarters for the occasion with American antiques from museums and private collections had been stopped by President Roosevelt. The most embellishment he would permit was the hanging in the queen's room of gilt-framed lithographs of Victoria and Albert and their children, which the Roosevelts had borrowed from a family friend.

Most of the operations regarding the accommodation of royalty were under Howell G. Crim, a lawyer by training, who had been assistant usher under Ike Hoover and Ray Muir, before becoming chief usher himself in 1938. During the 44 hours that the king and queen were guests at the White House, Chief Usher Crim kept the waters calm, sometimes a difficult task because relations between the royal attendants and the White House staff were anything but peaceful. Besides the predictable rivalries over turf, the British servants treated the American blacks with contempt. When a maid was reported to him by a servant of the queen for daring to ask for the royal autograph, Crim summoned the offending woman and told her that people had been fired for less, but pressed the matter no further. The maid, Lizzie McDuffie, would remember Crim as a kind man.[51]

The royal tour was a complete triumph, marking a revived sense of kinship between the American and the British peoples. This was as the President had wanted. The king's visit was the last great public event at the White House in the decade of the '30s, and it prepared the way for the future. Only a few months later, in September, Britain and the Continent entered a war against Hitler's Germany. Two years thereafter the United States would follow.

41

The Castle

December 7, 1941, began quietly as a routine Sunday at the White House. Domestic activities always got under way more slowly on Sundays, with breakfast trays sent up from the kitchen to the individual bedrooms. Mrs. Nesbitt noted on her wall calendar, "One P.M. small lunch, about thirty-four, in State Dining Room." She never knew until just before a meal was to be served exactly how many would sit down at table. Today the President would not be present.[1]

Some of the house guests walked across the park to services at St. John's. The President remained closeted in the oval room. Although he had risen early, he had not been with the guests. He was in the first year of an unprecedented third term in office, in his ninth year in the White House already resident longer than any previous President. Sunlight streamed through the south windows, making it warm, even in December. At a quarter to one the company began to arrive, entering through the East Wing. A close friend of Mrs. Roosevelt's remembered: "We all lined up in the Blue parlour according to the alphabet. Eleanor was quite a little late in joining us and she seemed a bit flustered as she told us she was so sorry but the news from Japan was very bad—that the President would be unable to come down to luncheon."[2]

In the oval room that morning with the doors closed, Roosevelt sat at his desk trying to distract himself with his stamp collection. He was deeply worried: At 9:30 the night before, he and Harry Hopkins had been called away from the dinner table to the oval room to read telegrams sent from the imperial government of Japan to its ambassador. The

971

State Department had intercepted the messages and decoded them. Commander L.R. Schultz, who brought the documents to the White House, recalled that after President Roosevelt read the message, he said, "This means war."[3]

Pearl Harbor and War

That Sunday morning the President called Hopkins to the oval room for lunch. As Mrs. Roosevelt's guests were entering the State Dining Room, a trolley with luncheon trays arrived upstairs, and the two men were finishing their meal at about 1:40 p.m. when the telephone on the President's desk rang; Frank Knox, Secretary of the Navy, had received a radio message from Honolulu reporting: "AIR RAID ON PEARL HARBOR THIS IS NOT A DRILL."

At 2:28 Admiral Harold R. Stark, chief of naval operations, called with confirmation. The President dictated a news statement to Steve Early for immediate release, then gave a second one 30 minutes later. As word of Pearl Harbor spread from the oval room to the radio wires and thereby to the nation, it inspired shock and anger. In Washington people moved out into the streets; throngs collected at the White House. Wrote one presidential caller of the afternoon, "As I approached the White House there were crowds of people in evidence, especially around the entrance. The people were quiet and serious. They were responding to that human instinct to get near a scene of action even if they could see and hear nothing."

The President, Secretary Knox, Secretary of State Cordell Hull, Admiral Stark, and General George Marshall met in the oval room at 3 p.m., in what might be called the first council of war. They sat about on the leather sofas and brocade chairs; the President remained at his desk, taking telephone calls on the first ring. With the day now overcast, the lamps were on. The flow of conversation, largely from Roosevelt, went from defense to diplomacy. Already the President had decided to go before the Congress on Monday with his war message.

During this meeting, Prime Minister Winston Churchill called from England. Hopkins recalled what he heard of the conversation from his chair near Roosevelt's desk: "The President told Churchill that we were all in the same boat now and that he was going to Congress tomorrow. Churchill apparently told him that the Malay Straits had been attacked and that he too was going to the House of Commons in the morning and would ask for a declaration of war."

Monday the 8th at midday the President and Mrs. Roosevelt drove to the Capitol, where the war message was to be delivered. Howell Crim noted in the usher's log that the long line of automobiles departed at 12:05 p.m. The Roosevelt party included the immediate military aides, James Roosevelt and his wife, the closest secretaries and friends, and Mrs. Woodrow Wilson—14 in all. At the Capitol before a joint session, Roosevelt called December 7, 1941, "a date which will live in infamy." The address was otherwise unadorned with drama, in contrast to the fiery oration delivered on the same day by Winston Churchill before the House of Commons.

But the emotional pitch was so high in the United States that a thundering presidential address was unnecessary. The Pearl Harbor attack had fired the anger of the American people, and disagreement over whether to go to war yielded to a consensus that the United States had no other course. On December 8, soon after Roosevelt's address, the Congress declared a state of war with Japan. Three days later, Germany and Italy, adhering to the Axis pact of cohesion with Japan, declared war on the United States, and the President sent a special message to the Congress on that day asking that a state of war with those nations be promptly recognized.[4]

Christmas Tree

On December 22 the White House announced that Winston Churchill and his staff were in residence. The prime minister's visit had been clothed in the utmost secrecy, unknown even to Mrs. Roosevelt until shortly before he arrived. His appearance preoccupied the whole country at Christmas 1941, since he personified the valor of Britain's stand against Hitler. It had been a solitary stand since the fall of France to the Nazis, and Churchill had known that without the Americans Britain would be defeated sooner or later. The prime minister dominated the newspapers during his visit, although he was not seen much by the public for reasons of security.

The White House never adjusted to Churchill, although he was to return several times. The most difficult of guests, his rule was late to bed and late to rise, and he wandered about the house at will, often in an air force jump suit, interrupting the usual decorum of the place. He took for granted more extensive personal service than the White House was used to offering its guests, so more servants than usual had to stand by, awaiting his call. His cigars, his brandy, his general unpredictability kept master and servant alike flustered, and the kitchen staff in fear of what food he might order up and when. He fussed about the high temperature inside the house, giving himself on one visit a touch of heart strain by trying to open a window to mitigate a room's "oppressive heat."[5]

Churchill slept in the Rose Bedroom, having tried without invitation bedrooms in other parts of the house. His valet stayed in the adjoining dressing room. The two principal secretaries occupied the Lincoln Study across the hall, where they also set up their offices, with several new telephones. One of these men, John Martin, could recall years later nothing especially interesting in his White House accommodations except for the "*eggs*—the wonderful eggs. I hadn't eaten an egg in years, times were so hard at home. It seems we did nothing but order up eggs." The visitors had no hesitation ordering second helpings of everything, soup to nuts. Mrs. Nesbitt was flattered at last.[6]

Among Churchill's complicating wishes was to have a work room for his daily use. Since there was no available space in the Executive Office Building, room had to be found elsewhere. Very likely because of a desire to keep the prime minister as close to one part of the house as possible, the Monroe Room was emptied of its furnishings and fitted as a "map room," so-called after that in the Cabinet War Rooms beneath the New Public Offices in London. The walls hung with large maps, the floor crowded with chairs, and the tables heaped with papers, the old Monroe Room was left in disarray.

During the preparations for Christmas, the Secret Service determined not to allow the Community Christmas Tree in Lafayette Park, for it interfered with the nighttime blackout of the city, a key part of the war program of Civil Defense. Moreover, for reasons of safety, the President's traditional lighting of this tree could not be condoned. Roosevelt, thinking this smacked of cowardice, insisted upon having his tree. The Secret Service was adamant, arguing that the Christmas tree would bring danger to the city as well as to the President. Subordinates from both sides huddled. As a compromise, the tree was relocated on the south grounds. Although the security agents had lost in the matter of the lights, they could at least better protect the President this way; only those people invited as spectators would pass through the iron fence, while the thousands of uninvited would remain outside. The tree was now styled the "National Christmas Tree."

On the south portico, just after dark on the eve of the first Christmas of the war, the Roosevelts, Churchill, and guests looked out toward a crowd of some 15,000 whom they, for the darkness, could not see. Before them, toward the far end of the grounds, stood the tree, itself seeming little more than a hulking shadow, set slightly to the east, off axis with the house. It would be lighted, and Roosevelt and Churchill would speak. The President touched a button, which sounded a signal in a dugout on the lawn below the great tree, where an electrician made the tree blaze with light, reflecting colors on the White House and on the faces of thousands of spectators, who burst into singing.[7]

Protection

When Grace Tully reported for work early Monday morning, December 8, she found "already a new 'normality' of routine. The grounds were under guard of a special detachment of Military Police and sentry boxes were being set up at intervals inside and outside the fence." She had only recently become the principal secretary to the President after Missy LeHand had been incapacitated by a stroke. The White House was animated by men and women on official errands.[8]

In the first months of the war, bombs and bullets seemed very near, and the bitter cold weather of the ensuing weeks made even optimists gloomy. Haunted by visions of the London blitzkrieg, military and Secret Service men moved about the White House with notebooks, studying security. Mrs. Nesbitt already had her orders to fit the windows with blackout curtains; when one thickness of the black sateen sent by the Treasury Department seemed inadequate, the housekeeper was told to add a second layer everywhere, including the basement windows. Skylights and bathroom windows—though few White House baths had windows—were painted black. The staff members were given "little dimmed-out flashlights" to help them find their cars at night.

Secretary of the Treasury Henry Morgenthau, Jr., was the liaison between the Army, the Secret Service, and the President. He found the President often inclined to reject the more extravagant precautions proposed by the military because of the poor public appearance they might make. On December 14 a long report was presented by Frank J. Wilson, chief of the Secret Service, and Battalion Chief Daniel A. Deasy of the New York Fire Department, representing the Office of Civilian Defense. So detailed was this document that Morgenthau, protesting its length, ordered it condensed so that he might evaluate it on the following day.[9]

Even after nearly 50 years, the report exudes the fear felt by those responsible for White House security. It was recommended that the several skylights of the house be covered with six inches of sand, topped with a layer of tin. The roofs of the east and west terraces were to be "covered with sand bags and machine guns installed"; the glazed colonnade of the East Wing was to be painted black; the west colonnade, along which the President passed going to the Oval Office, was to be enclosed or equipped with steel rolling curtains; bullet-proof glass was to be installed in the rooms frequented by the family, particularly the oval room; glass in all doors was to be replaced with bullet-proof panes, and all the outer doors were to have "light and air or gas locks" to seal them.

The rooms of the White House were to be studied to determine what "old furniture and other unnecessary articles" could be removed, together with paints and other combustible materials in the carpentry shop. Round-the-clock patrols were to be assigned to the roof, which had a large central deck as well as concealed places behind the stone parapet; these guards and those on the terrace roofs were to be provided with "equipment to combat incendiary bombs." Completely circling the "White House building and Executive Offices" was to be a sandbag barricade 15 feet high.

The investigators suggested that the walls of the White House be painted according to standards of Army Air Corps camouflage, with the slate roof painted black. They further suggested a bomb shelter, for their inspection had revealed that for all the apparent strength of its stone walls and steel-framed roof, the White House was inadequate to withstand an air attack. The part of the report that had the most far-reaching effect on the White House established its structural vulnerability to fire, pointing out the seldom recognized fact that internally the White House was largely of wood. Roosevelt balked at most of the options for security. All he agreed to at first was doubling the White House guard force, insisting over the telephone to Morgenthau, "That's all you need. As long as you have one about every hundred feet around the fence, that's all. . . . What you could do is this: Block off both Executive Avenues . . . . Put up barricades between the White House and the Treasury and also . . . between the White House and State Department."[10]

Because of the President's recalcitrance, most of the official recommendations were not carried out. Bullet-proof glass was installed halfway up in the three south windows of the Oval Office, behind the President's desk; a "bomb barrier" of concrete was poured along the west wall of the Executive Office Building. The house was heavily guarded, beginning within an hour after the news from Hawaii on December 7. Roosevelt did reluctantly permit the sentries and patrols of military police, although normally they were stationed in guard boxes or outside the iron fence. Toward the end of the war, when it became clear that Germany would soon fall, the President ordered the soldiers removed and the blackout curtains taken down.

Some of the wartime security practices became permanent. The guard boxes set up at the external gates began a custom of guarding the

White House at the perimeters of the grounds. Previously the north grounds had been accessible to the casual visitor eight or ten hours a day; the guards had been kept close to the house. Until the war, callers still left their cards at the north door. Often in fair weather people were allowed to stroll in the south grounds, particularly when the trees were blooming in the spring. Never again would admission to the White House grounds be gained so casually.

For all Roosevelt's protests, wartime security was strict. Those at the White House who could not cope with the new way were quickly removed; Colonel Ed Starling was forced into retirement for that reason. Sentries with machine guns were placed on the roof and on the roofs of nearby buildings; White House police patrolled the corridors day and night. Special outdoor lighting was designed and installed by the General Electric Company to dimly illuminate the grounds, while casting no glare on the house. Within the House, every room was supplied with a bucket of sand and a shovel, in case of fire; there were candles and matches on all the mantels. Gas masks were neatly folded on every dresser, with instructions placed beside them. Fire drills were held weekly.[11]

The official White House social season of 1941–42 had been canceled in October, before war was declared, to avoid the unpleasantries that might have resulted from mixing a tense diplomatic community. The President continued to entertain more or less informally, relieved of the prescribed dinners and receptions, with their complex structures of protocol. There would never be a formal social season at the Roosevelt White House again. Tourists had been prohibited from visiting the house since June of 1941, except for uniformed members of the armed forces, who could call during a two-hour period each Saturday morning. The somewhat implausible explanation offered to the public for closing the White House was the laying of a new floor in the East Room and other work, but when the summer's improvements were completed the house was not reopened. War brought a halt at last even to the special tours for the military. The custom of leaving calling cards, though it had been continued through part of the first World War, was also discontinued, never to be revived.

Callers at the Executive Office during the war were received only by appointment, without which persons could not even draw near the building. For what were called "off the record appointments with the President," a Secret Service agent entered the automobile of the visiting individual or group at a point immediately south of the Treasury Building and drove it into the south grounds through the southeast gate. If the appointment was to be kept in the White House proper, the visitor entered through the Diplomatic Reception Room, then rode the elevator upstairs. Callers at the Oval Office were directed to pass through the Rose Garden or, in inclement weather, to walk to the colonnade by way of the basement hall. [12]

Of these changes Grace Tully was to write: "The appointments and office conferences of the wartime years had an electric quality all their own. The urgency and grim temper of the times, security restrictions and all the other elements of war contributed to an atmosphere quite different from that of earlier years at 1600 Pennsylvania Avenue." [13]

East Wing

President Roosevelt took the opportunity presented by wartime upheavals to commence major construction at the White House. On the day of Pearl Harbor, Lorenzo Winslow and his family had taken advantage of the warm, sunny morning to go on a picnic. When he returned to his house in Georgetown late in the afternoon he found that the President's office had been trying to reach him. Having heard the news, he rushed to the car and drove down immediately. "As soon as I arrived I was told to go right up as FDR was waiting for me."

The President, at his desk in the oval room, told Winslow that buildings must be erected in a hurry. A great many people would be coming to work at the White House as part of the war effort. "He [said] that steps should be taken at once to provide space in temporary buildings on the South lawn of the White House and he gave me a detailed list of the people who would be housed in the quarters—we talked together for over an hour." As Winslow departed, the President told him that he wanted the architectural office moved from the State, War, & Navy Building into the new library they had built in the basement. Roosevelt could then drop in as he pleased. The President liked to have his staff nearby, an inclination doubtless influenced by his physical limitations. At seven the next morning an enormously pleased Winslow was setting up shop in the library when he was summoned to the President's bedroom. From his bed Roosevelt told him that he had "given the matter much thought," and added: "Instead of temporary buildings on the South Lawn why not build a permanent East Wing?" [14]

Winslow cannot have been too surprised by this change in plan, for the President had been wanting to build a new East Wing for at least three years—both to serve his growing executive staff and to house a museum. As it stood, the east wing was as Theodore Roosevelt had built it, the "social" entrance. It included a porte cochere, guard stations, a glazed colonnaded corridor, and a long cloakroom called the Hat Box, a name transferred to it after it was finished in 1902; this term for a coatroom entered White House parlance in the mid-19th century when wooden hatboxes were stacked at the Entrance Hall to accommodate party guests.

Roosevelt realized that if his plans for reorganizing the executive department came to fruition, he would need more office space at the White House, and after the successfully unobtrusive expansion on the west, the obvious next place to add to the White House was on the east. In January 1938 he had obtained from Oliver Taylor of the National Park Service a preliminary project for a new "east entrance," which was apparently to be a structure only somewhat smaller than the Executive Office on the west. Taylor had asked Eric Gugler for schematic drawings, but this time Mrs. Roosevelt's friend struck out, criticized by both Winslow and Roosevelt for the high estimated costs of his designs.[15]

The program of 1938 had not materialized, although the President proceeded with his reorganization of the executive department anyway. Immediately after the outbreak of war in Europe, on September 8, 1939, he had issued the Limited National Emergency Proclamation, in which he buried an executive order restructuring and enlarging his immediate staff. Among a number of similar transferrals, the Bureau of the Budget was moved from the Treasury Department to the office of the President, which gave the President what one of his staff members called a "personal intelligence service," a network of federal agents watching the management of public money. The expanded executive staff was supervised by six new presidential assistants, each responsible directly to the President. To satisfy anticipated demands for space, Roosevelt in September 1939 activated a congressional act passed under Hoover in 1930, allowing for the purchase by the government of the private property surrounding Lafayette Park.

The declaration of war provided an opportunity and a need for the new East Wing. The plans Lorenzo Winslow produced in December of 1941 proposed a building not only smaller but also simpler than that envisioned by Gugler in 1938. Winslow described his project this way: "I had made sketches on a new East Entrance, with 2nd floor office space, quarters for the White House police, etc. etc.—The President was keen on a part of the East Entrance being used as a museum space for old White House mementoes that could not well be shown in the White House. He had a list of ancient White House furniture that could be donated by the various owners and, busy as he was, he still had a little time to play with his ideas!"

Monday, December 8, as the President prepared to give his war message, Winslow, in his own words, "immediately changed my plans for the temporary buildings and started the draftsmen taking all the necessary measurements and existing data on the old East Entrance. . . . I made several sketches of what I proposed to do with the whole new East Wing. It was to be somewhat similar to a large theater entrance, with protection from the weather, and yet it could not overwhelm the White House in the background." He took his sketches to the President, who "agreed to every detail," probably having helped set down some of the ideas himself several years before. As the occupants of the architectural office in the crowded library proceeded through Christmas with their working drawings, demolition began on the East Wing. Winslow remembered: "I can truthfully say that I worked 16 to 18 hours a day, as I had a hand in all these projects and was the only means of the President knowing what was going on."[16]

As if to compound his burdens, the Army insisted that now was the time to build the air raid shelter. Roosevelt objected, but finally yielded. The new East Wing was the obvious site, but first a temporary shelter was established in the old abandoned vaults beneath the Treasury Building. In late December a tunnel was dug practically overnight from a knoll on the northeast grounds to the dry moat of the Treasury Building, crossing under East Executive Avenue; this steeply inclined subterranean corridor, its dingy concrete interior lighted by bare light bulbs, led to the basement vaults, which were to serve until a permanent and more suitable shelter could be built as a sub-basement of the East Wing. Grace Tully was surprised to find that one had to cross the roofless moat with "open sky above" before passing through a door into the vaults. The President himself never visited the place.[17]

Roosevelt took a personal interest in the actual construction of the East Wing, meeting with Winslow every morning at 7:30, while still in bed. "He gave nearly an hour a day to all the construction on the way even though the war was starting full swing." Work went on 24 hours a day, Winslow recalled, except for a few days after Prime Minister Churchill's departure, when everyone, including the President, was exhausted. In later years, he remembered "hearing everyone tell how so and so was worn out attending meetings with Churchill. . . . After he left the W.H. went out of business for a few days as there was no one awake to produce anything."[18]

Against a small storm of public protest, the demolition of most of the McKim East Wing got under way in December, the opposition denouncing the construction as extravagant and wasteful during wartime.

Warm weather changed to bitter cold at Christmas, but no halt was called because of the weather. Workmen took short breaks to huddle around fires built in oil drums. During Churchill's visit the rumble of wrecking and earth-moving machinery continued around the clock, clearly visible from the prime minister's dressing room windows. All manner of difficulties impeded progress. The bomb shelter had to be excavated in secrecy; only after the war, in 1945, did the public learn of its existence. This required not only the blocking off of East Executive Avenue from traffic, but also the complete screening of the construction site. Poor records as to the locations of water mains and telegraph cables led to trouble again and again.

In the course of the excavation, workmen unearthed the old sewer line built by James Hoban during the reconstruction in 1816–18. Winslow and others got down in it and found an arched tunnel about three feet at the highest point built of "egg-shaped" brick and surviving in "perfect condition." Its purpose, as Winslow correctly speculated, had been to receive water from the roof gutters and channel it to the plains south of the house, in Hoban's day mostly swamps. Out of sentiment, Winslow put the relic into use again for carrying "storm water" to the river, for ruins he found at the riverbank suggested to him that the sewer had at some previous time extended that far.

Other Lorenzo Winslow discoveries included a cistern, some 15 feet long and 8 feet high, vaulted in brick and wholly underground, looking like a tomb. While he made no record of the precise location of this "reservoir"—wartime had no spare moments for such scholarly activity— he described it and noted the remains of wooden pipes connected to it, before it was destroyed early in 1942. The general area on the southeast in which he found it had been the site of the old presidential flower garden, demolished in the late 1850s to make way for the Treasury extension; the cistern was probably part of a watering system for that garden. Others like it may have existed in the early days.

The East Wing was first occupied in May 1942, oddly enough, by Winslow's architectural office, which, by presidential request, was installed there permanently in large rooms on the south end of the second floor. But the building was not completed until after the war. Final interior finishing was carried out in 1942 only on the second floor, where Winslow, the social office, and part of the Secret Service were to be housed. The upstairs walls were plastered, but the first floor walls were covered provisionally with monk's cloth in grayish tan. Later the plans were carried out and the first floor rooms were finished in wood.[19]

As late as October, Howell Crim was borrowing furniture from the

White House to stock the new rooms of the East Wing. When he began moving the furniture from the temporary bomb shelter in the Treasury vault, however, the Army officials stopped him, protesting that the vault must remain fully fitted out as an annex to the new shelter; if Crim had any reason to object to being ordered about in his own domain, he seems to have decided it prudent to keep his peace. The Army, having established its White House foothold in the bomb shelter, was to hold fast to it.

The new East Wing was finished, insofar as the work carried out during the war, by the close of 1942. In his design, Winslow recalled familiar features of both the Executive Office Building and the old east entrance built by Charles McKim. The East Wing's principal facade was turned east, away from the White House, in some respects like a separate building. The neoclassical mode was here restrained, as on the west. The new wing was essentially a rectangular block, connected to the White House by the surviving narrow glazed colonnade and Hat Box. A tall main story was topped by a low second floor and fronted by a long porte cochere through which a new horseshoe driveway passed from the street, allowing as many as five cars to unload or load at one time. This covered drive for automobiles extended nearly three-quarters of the way across the east facade.[20]

In McKim's east facade, the effect of an open peristyle had been achieved through wide and lofty walls of windowpanes, which carried the eye through the colonnade into the glazed gallery beyond. The new wing did not seem nearly so open. Its porte cochere was heavier, more protective of those who passed beneath it. The eye stopped at the glass doors opening into the building, for the entrance gave onto a long, rather dark hall. McKim's paired columns, borrowed perhaps from the West Front of the Capitol, but also an echo of his revised White House entrance hall, became the dominant theme in Winslow's porte cochere. They supported a long and regular span, weighted at each end by heavy pavilions and crowned by a paneled parapet. The structure was painted white, over smooth stucco. It nestled into grassy knolls and trees, seeming from the outside much smaller than it was. Looking from the north, if one had been able to see an entire east to west elevation of the White House, the second stories of East Wing and Executive Office stood on a plane with the Jefferson terraces themselves. With the thick plantings and old trees, such a view was never actually possible, but the results of this design were admirable: Like the Executive Office Building, the East Wing was unobtrusive; only close inspection revealed the large scale.

Within, the East Wing was simply an office building of its time, perhaps more ambitious than many in its finishes and projected finishes, but certainly simpler than what one would have found in a great corporate headquarters in most American cities. The second floor contained five offices, four of them very large and one of them small, and a photographer's darkroom, all opening on a narrow corridor. The spaces were amenable to later subdivision.

Downstairs were six new rooms, the largest one a conference room; three of the rooms were designated as offices; the other two were linked to the entrance hall by folding doors and were intended to house the museum, but they were converted into offices for Admiral William D. Leahy, Harry Hopkins, and James MacGregor Burns. A small chamber off the long hall, designed to be a parlor-like reception room with a fireplace and mirrors, was instead furnished as an office. President Roosevelt ordered the Hat Box converted into a movie theater in July 1942, and from then on the White House was to have no permanent coatroom, but would improvise in the movie theater or, for special guests, in the rooms flanking the Diplomatic Reception Room. As an economy measure, Winslow decorated the theater by mixing "odds and ends" of the paint used elsewhere in the wing. His efforts produced a color scheme "flaunting walls of vernal green, with cornices of electric blue—accented by draperies of burnt orange."[21]

Soon the wing filled up with staff offices, including the "social" office housed heretofore in the West Wing. Beneath the wartime East Wing was the secret bomb shelter, of which much was said later on in the memoirs of Roosevelt's staff and associates. This took up approximately half of the basement; the remaining half was fitted out as offices, storage, and locker rooms for police and Secret Service men. A new means of access to the tunnel to the Treasury vaults was constructed here, although the original outside entrance remained as well.

The bomb shelter resembled a dungeon, with walls and floors seven feet thick and a ceiling nine feet thick, all of concrete heavily laced with steel. In plan it was originally one large room, 40 feet square, with a tiny island of a presidential bedchamber and bath in the center, encased in walls three feet thick. Several small side rooms contained ventilation machinery and toilets; others served as storage areas for food and water. The common room was a work room, with telephone, telegraph, and radio equipment along the walls and on the desks. Steel sheathed the low ceilings, and the walls were left bare concrete.

Roosevelt went to the shelter after it was finished to satisfy his curiosity. One can imagine his discomfort; during the tedious progress of his wheelchair through narrow descending passages, he was lifted down steps, there being no ramps. At the end lay the low, windowless, concrete hollow, anticipating disasters such as had befallen London. The President's sense of confinement must have been overwhelming, but he never had to go there again.[22]

Rooms

Roosevelt liked to tell about the time Carl Sandburg came to see him. The poet, who was writing his biography of Lincoln, asked the President which window Lincoln had stood before, watching the smoke from enemy cannon across the Potomac. Roosevelt said he had no idea, but he took Sandburg to the second floor and let him walk from window to window. At the center window of the oval room Sandburg stopped, said Roosevelt, "and stood there silently for about ten minutes."

Not wishing to disturb Sandburg's reverie, the President shuffled through papers on his desk, until his caller was ready to talk. "Yes," said Sandburg at last, "that's the one—the center window." When Roosevelt asked how he could be so certain, Sandburg replied, "I felt it."[23]

Roosevelt directed America's wartime effort from the White House. Through it passed Churchill, most spectacularly, and also Hopkins the ever present adviser, and a parade of generals and admirals. The historian Frank Freidel has written that the power concentrated in the executive mansion "in its global dimensions surpassed that in any earlier administration, even those of Abraham Lincoln and Woodrow Wilson."[24]

Because he moved about with difficulty, the President confined his activities to relatively few rooms. In the Executive Office Building, the rooms important to him were clustered in the southeast part, around the Oval Office. There he met some of his appointments and normally held press conferences. Separated from it by Grace Tully's small office was the Cabinet Room, long and narrow, with a fireplace at the north end and a row of French doors giving onto the colonnade overlooking the Rose Garden. A windowless rectangular reception and conference room, situated obliquely near the Oval Office, was occasionally used for staff meetings. Sometimes called the "Fish Room," it housed mementos of the President's fishing exploits, about which he liked to reminisce. It was an odds-and-ends room, containing storage and a motley array of office furniture. Staff members dubbed it the "junk room" and the "morgue," the latter because they sometimes seated hotheaded delegations there to cool off before being received by the President.

The oval room in the White House proper was the most important room of Roosevelt's Presidency. There he worked, there he relaxed, and there he conducted most of the important business of State. To the oval room he brought Winston Churchill on New Year's Day 1942, joined by Maksim Litvinof, representing the Soviet Union, and T. V. Soong, representing China, to sign what Churchill termed "this majestic document," which began the process of binding 26 countries into a "united nations" against the Axis powers. The oval room—usually called the "study" in FDR's time—was the same shape as the Blue Room below it, but because its ceiling was relatively low, it lacked the pleasing proportions of the more famous state parlor. It had become stuffed with maritime pictures, models, books, and stacks of papers. The woodwork was glossy white, the plaster walls painted in a light color Lorenzo Winslow described as "a sort of schoolhouse tan." A dark green chenille rug, cut in an oval several feet smaller than the room, united a miscellaneous group of tables, floor lamps, and chromium ashtray stands.[25]

The tall mahogany bookcases were jammed with books lying sideways on top of the vertical rows. Most of the leather sofas and chairs had acquired a mellow glow; some brown ones and some in green had been around since Theodore Roosevelt had used them aboard the *Mayflower*. Beyond the three windows, the southward vista was framed by the Ionic columns of the semicircular portico, and was terminated in the distance by the new Jefferson Memorial, domed and columned, like a temple-folly in some great garden.

Even before the war years, Roosevelt was eating most of his meals in the oval room, leaving the formal dining rooms downstairs to Mrs. Roosevelt and her guests. Husband and wife seldom dined together, although he did attend luncheons and dinners which could benefit from his presence, if business did not interfere. Normally the President ate with members of his staff or with whomever he happened to be meeting when the lunch or dinner hour arrived. Oval room meals were served on individual trays, Roosevelt seated at his desk, guests at folding card tables set up before the sofas. So great was Roosevelt's dislike of Mrs. Nesbitt's food that in 1938 he ordered a small kitchen built on the third floor and had many of his oval room meals cooked there. Various members of the kitchen staff were detailed to the President's kitchen as needed, until his mother died in 1941, and he brought her cook, Mary Campbell, from Hyde Park and opened his third-floor kitchen full time. This proved satisfactory, and Mrs. Campbell, who knew how to season food the way Roosevelt liked it, remained resident at the White House, leaving only to accompany the President on visits to his home on the Hudson.

An oval room ceremony most evenings was cocktails. The President enjoyed a cocktail before dinner—never before lunch—and he seldom drank wine with his meals. Most of the time, he mixed the drinks him-self. In the early years of his administration, the cocktail ritual often took place in the west hall, with Mrs. Roosevelt sometimes in attendance. During the war it was nearly always in the oval room, usually without the First Lady. The President stayed seated at his desk, before him a tray equipped with what he needed for the cocktail of the day, which he had determined in advance—gin martinis and bourbon orange blossoms being his favorites. "He mixed the ingredients," recalled Robert E. Sher-wood, "with the deliberation of an alchemist but with what appeared to be a certain lack of precision since he carried on a steady conversation while doing it." Clare Boothe Luce recalled the "very dry martinis" mixed in a silver shaker. The oval room cocktail parties were lively and informal, and ended with the serving of dinner.[26]

Roosevelt's bedroom adjoining the oval room could be reached from the hall, from Mrs. Roosevelt's sitting room, and by way of a door near Roosevelt's desk. The bedroom was a square chamber which had been rectangular in the original house; the addition in 1902 of a bathroom and closet on the north end had reduced its dimensions and had left the fireplace on the west side off center. The fireplace had been filled by an air-conditioning unit, and its mantel shelf was used as a depository of clutter. The room was kept entirely by the President's valet, Arthur Prettyman, fourth in a line of succession beginning with McDuffie. Roo-sevelt woke early, but transacted much business from his bed. Frequently morning appointments were held in the bedroom, particularly ones the President hoped would not be noticed in the press. A Virginia congress-man remembered meetings there when the President was "propped up in bed on pillows, with a breakfast tray for himself in front of him and one for me on a card table beside the bed."[27]

Members of his close staff brought papers and questions to him in his bedroom, and occasionally—particularly when the President was suffer-ing from his chronic colds and sinus trouble—Cabinet officers met with him there. Frances Perkins recalled: "I have a photographic impression of that room. A little too large to be cozy, it was not large enough to be impressive. A heavy dark wardrobe stood against a wall. . . . A marble mantelpiece of the Victorian type carved with grapes held a collection of miniature pigs—Mexican pigs, Irish pigs, pigs of all kinds, sizes and colors. Snapshots of children, friends, and expeditions were propped up in back of the pigs."

Any room Roosevelt used, remarked Miss Perkins, "invariably got that lived-in and overcrowded look which indicated the complexity and variety of his interests and intentions." She might also have observed that his inability to move about made him tend to cluster useful materials around him for easy access. She remembered "an old bureau between the windows, with a plain white towel on top and the things men need for their dressing arrangements. There was an old-fashioned rocking chair, often with a piece of clothing thrown over it."

He had discarded the Val-Kill four-poster in favor of what Miss Perkins described as "a small, narrow white iron bedstead, the kind one sees in the boy's room of many an American house. It had a thin, hard-looking mattress, a couple of pillows, and an ordinary white seersucker spread. A folded old gray shawl lay at the foot. . . . A white painted table, the kind one often sees in bathrooms, stood beside the bed, with a towel over it and with aspirin, nose drops, a glass of water, stubs of pencils, bits of paper with telephone numbers, addresses and memoranda to himself, a couple of books, a worn old prayer book, a watch, a package of cigarettes, an ash tray, a couple of telephones, all cluttered together."

"Hanging on the walls," she recalled, "were a few pictures of the children and favorite familiar scenes. And over the door at the opposite end of the room hung a horse's tail. When one asked what that was, he would say, 'Why, that's Gloucester's tail.' Gloucester, a horse owned by the President's father, had been regarded by the family as one of the finest examples of horseflesh in the world."[28]

A third room essential to the wartime Roosevelt was the Map Room, two stories below his bedroom, in the basement. It was a mysterious place of limited access. Completed in January 1942, this "presidential news center" existed only for the duration of the war. Here messages were received, filed, and distributed. Roosevelt's wish to create such a place was inspired in part by the temporary Map Room set up for Churchill during his visit in December 1941 and the descriptions of Churchill's map room in his underground headquarters in London. Fond as he was of discussing the White House past with the perennial executive clerk, Rudolph Forster, the President may also have gotten some ideas from Forster's memories of McKinley's War Room.

The Map Room was a communications center, its purpose, according to an official memorandum, "to make available to the President certain vital and secret information on the progress of the war, and the position of Army and Navy units on the war fronts." In the Map Room the status of the war, the movement of Allied forces, the victories and the defeats were reported to him, usually by the Telegraph and Transportation Division of the Signal Corps, which had served the White House needs for communications and decoding since the Spanish American War. The President's copies of presidential conferences, top secret war plans, and correspondence relative to the war were filed in the Map Room. Commander George M. Elsey, USNR, who was assigned to the Map Room, recalled that it was the "secretariat for all the President's cables to heads of state relating to the war. We filed them, we kept them, we delivered them to the appropriate people."[29]

Roosevelt had selected the White House for his Map Room instead of the more obvious Executive Office Building for reasons of security and convenience. The basement location was remote from the daily comings and goings of the house. It was directly west of the Diplomatic Reception Room, across the hall from the elevator. The low-ceilinged, rectangular room was once a coatroom for women, and pale green paint from powder room days remained on the walls; pipes could be seen where marble lavatories had once extended along one wall. Prismed wall lamps remained. A toilet room lay beyond a door on the south wall.

The Map Room was planned by Lieutenant Robert Montgomery, an intelligence officer who had spent time in Churchill's map room in London. Blackout shades were put on its single window and those in the bathroom, and the door into the Diplomatic Reception Room was sealed. The walls were hung with large maps of the theaters of war, Atlantic and Pacific. Drab-colored desks and tables held local telephones; the largest single piece of furniture was a map case.[30]

A staff of twelve, six from the Army and six from the Navy, was assigned to the Map Room under Captain John L. McCrea, the chief naval aide to the President. The principal responsibilities of these men were to keep all the President's papers relative to the war carefully filed and to keep military placements current on the maps. For this last, Montgomery had devised a series of colored pins whereby ships, airplanes, and troops could be repositioned according to the latest dispatches. To identify the three Allied leaders, also tracked on the maps, he mounted three distinctive pins: one with a cigarette holder, a second with a cigar, and a third with a briar pipe.[31]

Top secrecy was carefully maintained for the Map Room. A White House policeman stood at its only entrance, in the long vaulted hallway of the basement, day and night. Access was highly restricted, with only seven FDR intimates allowed to go there at will. Cabinet members felt affronted that they could not enter freely, but Roosevelt kept to his rules. Even the Secret Service men, including Roosevelt's bodyguards, were not allowed past the door, since the Map Room was considered a military facility. This fanned the rivalry between the Secret Service and the military. The Secret Service retaliated with an irritating rule requiring full security clearance of military personnel working in the Map Room.[32]

Even Mrs. Roosevelt was not authorized to go to the Map Room. When she learned of the maps with pins designating ships at sea, she became curious about the location of the ship of one of her sons in the Pacific. Without permission she walked boldly past the guard, who was afraid to stop her. This raid seems to have gone unreprimanded, and she invaded the Map Room on several other occasions. One afternoon in 1943 she took Madame Chiang Kai-shek there, acting apparently on impulse; warned in advance by the guard, the Map Room staff quickly set the room in disarray, shifting the pins around on the maps. One of them remembered, however, giving Madame Chiang "the full tour."[33]

Roosevelt went there perhaps once a day until his last year. The location was convenient to his route from the oval room to the Oval Office; he had merely to be wheeled from the elevator across the hall. The officers inside borrowed a wheelchair and practiced pushing it around in the crowded Map Room, to avoid bumping the President against the furniture. When he ceased visiting the Map Room about mid-1944, the Map Room in a sense went to him. Materials were selected and put in a leather folder, which he opened in his bedroom in the morning. Later in the day, when he was in the doctor's office next door to the Map Room—the former silver and china pantry—another packet of papers was sent for him to study.

The Map Room was not a part of Roosevelt's executive office. Run entirely by military personnel, it was isolated in a room in the White House—a carefully managed storehouse of information. Messages still came direct to him from the State Department; military leaders and other officials could gain access. But Roosevelt kept the Map Room for his own use. As commander in chief, he meant to make sure that his generals were not interfered with by the bureaucracy—even that represented by his own staff. As President, he, like Wilson, had placed himself at the head of all foreign relations and intended personally to guide the fortunes of his country.

Close Quarters

The isolation of the United States from the theaters of war was less a redeeming factor during the great military buildup in '42 and '43 than it had been during World War I. Mrs Roosevelt wrote to her daughter in the spring of 1942, "I feel he [your father] is more content with the way the war is going, tho' he seems to expect bombings this summer in N.Y. & Washington & perhaps Seattle."[34]

By that time, the Roosevelts' four sons were in service: All would see action, and all would serve with distinction. Robert Todd Lincoln had been the only other son of a President in office to go to war. "I imagine every mother felt as I did," wrote Mrs. Roosevelt, "when I said good-bye to the children during the war. I had a feeling that I might be saying good-bye for the last time. It was a sort of precursor of what it would be like if your children were killed and never to come back. Life had to go on and you had to do what was required of you, but something inside of you quietly died."[35]

Roosevelt, although much occupied with his work, also feared for the safety of his sons. In the Map Room a special pin designated the ship on which Franklin, Jr., served. An officer on the Map Room staff recalled this pin as an exception in itself, for "Space did not allow the use of separate pins to indicate individual destroyers, submarines, and other small ships, and they were indicated in clusters." The officer also remembered that "FDR's first look was always for that pin."[36]

The children were in and out of the White House during the war. Anna, remarried and living on the West Coast, moved her family into the house in 1943, so that she could be of assistance to her father. Roosevelt saw his sons as frequently as he could. When the Allied conferences took place he arranged for one or more of the boys to join him on the trip. Only John Roosevelt had military duties that prevented his taking advantage of this opportunity. Wrote Elliott, remembering the closeness that developed between father and sons during the war: "I felt the strong love and pride he had for all of us children. Above all I learned what a unique mind he had and how formidable was his grasp of the course of human events. All my life I [have felt] irresistible pride that this man was my father."[37]

Franklin and Eleanor Roosevelt often invited relatives to the White House, many of whom they looked upon as lifelong friends. Theodore Roosevelt's son Archie, at age 48, visited early in the summer of 1942; he toured from attic to cellar, noting the changes made since his father was President. A fellow guest remarked how Archie was "terribly impressed by the bathrooms," there having been only three upstairs when he moved to the White House in 1901.[38]

In the early years of the war, the only full-time guest was Harry Hopkins, who, with his young daughter, Diana, moved there in May 1940. The former social worker and ardent New Dealer had become increasingly important to Roosevelt since the death of Louis Howe in 1936. Hopkins's eye had been on the Presidency, with Roosevelt's blessing, and had his health held up, he might possibly have run. A physical collapse in 1939 and a lingering battle with cancer ended this dream.

During dinner on May 10, 1940, Hopkins took sick and was put to bed upstairs. The President would not hear of his moving out for 3½ years. A Roosevelt cousin visiting the White House described Harry Hopkins as looking ghost-like: "he is always a different color—sometimes green—sometimes gray—or white—or pink."[39] Rexford G. Tugwell, one of Roosevelt's officials, wrote, "It was obvious to anyone who looked at Hopkins that he was hanging onto life by the most tenuous threads. He had not lost his sharp wit, his flair for intrigue, or his determination to stay close to Franklin."[40]

Hopkins occupied the Lincoln Study from time to time, one of the two state guest rooms. Diana Hopkins was installed in a bedroom on the third floor near the sky parlor. Her mother had died in 1937, and Diana was a lonely child. She received kind attention from the upstairs maids and from Mrs. Roosevelt, who may have seen in Diana Hopkins a reflection of herself as a child. Hopkins spent many hours with the President. They met daily, often taking meals together in the oval room. Roosevelt liked having Hopkins near, and Mrs. Roosevelt, admiring Hopkins as a great humanitarian, was also glad to have him at the White House, where she could look after him. For the initial year of his residence before the war began, they lived as a happy family.

Difficulties between Hopkins and Mrs. Roosevelt began immediately after the war started. The First Lady believed that the war provided an opportunity for rapid expansion of the social programs of the New Deal. Both the President and Hopkins insisted that the overriding objective was to win the war. The First Lady pressed her case, seeking to reach her husband through Hopkins, but, as she phrased it in her memoirs, "Harry Hopkins could not be bothered."[41]

Nor, after that, did Mrs. Roosevelt want Hopkins in the house. When in the summer of 1942 he announced his intention to marry Mrs. Louise Macy, and Roosevelt invited the couple to live in the White House, Mrs. Roosevelt went to her husband in protest. The President told her that "the most important thing in the world at that time was the conduct of the war and that it was absolutely necessary that Harry be in the house." Mrs. Roosevelt acquiesced, but wrote Mrs. Macy a rather chilly letter establishing the ground rules for full-time guests. The marriage took place in the oval room on July 30, 1942. An enthusiastic Roosevelt ordered the Lincoln Study and sitting room repainted for the bride and groom. The First Lady wrote that she "did not try to develop any great intimacy" with the Hopkinses. But even though she was annoyed by their nightly cocktail parties in their rooms, as well as being jealous of Harry Hopkins's closeness to her husband, she did develop genuine admiration for Mrs. Hopkins, who, said Mrs. Roosevelt, transformed "an almost waiflike" Diana into "a child who really felt she had a family and the security of love."[42]

The names of temporary guests fill the ushers' logbooks now in the presidential library at Hyde Park. Friends and relatives with business in Washington were welcomed to the White House, staying from a night to a month or more. Both they and official guests were required to have a security clearance and to be fingerprinted on arrival, although important dignitaries were spared. Soviet Foreign Minister Vyacheslav M. Molotov arrived May 29, 1942, spending several days under the incognito of "Mr. Brown." Churchill returned in late June of 1942. Winter brought Madame Chiang Kai-shek for a ten-day visit.

Mrs. Roosevelt wrote to her daughter in late spring 1942: "We've had the Dutch [royalty] for a night, all the [Philippine President Manuel] Quezon family for a night & in June await the King of Greece. . . . I forgot the President of Peru." She had political concerns about the presence of the royalty. Press coverage was extensive, and the First Lady feared that the President's hospitality to the royal guests might be interpreted as a wish that they be able to reestablish their thrones after the war. With some hesitation she and her son Johnny finally approached him on this subject; according to a family friend who was there, the response was sharp. This fourth party quoted the President as saying "he realized that 99% of these guys should never go back into power—that they have no realization of why this war is being fought—they are for the most part unintelligent phonies who wouldn't last five minutes if they didn't have control of the armies in their countries and if their people knew how to handle a democratic system." He assured his wife that he welcomed them only because of protocol, that they might one day return to their thrones, and if they did their favorable feelings would be important to the United States.[43]

Two Households

In spite of the great efforts to make the White House seem like an ordinary American home, the similarities were only superficial. Few other homes offered such extensive personal service: Linen maids, fire layers, clock winders, brass polishers—countless little specialties were divided up among about 30 servants and as many part-time helpers. No other home had to be so intricately zoned for use; no other was commanded by members of the Army and Secret Service, always circulating, though largely out of sight. More than a thousand people were likely to pass in and out of the complex during the day. Yet the establishment functioned smoothly.

At the head of the operation was Howell Crim, the chief usher. Promoted to the position in 1938, he had seen his role expand rapidly over the summer of that year, when Mrs. Roosevelt virtually surrendered her participation in the household management in favor of her public pursuits. He became a sort of executive officer over the house and grounds. All the domestic employees came under him, even the house-keeper; he became a liaison between the White House and the government offices, always negotiating to borrow goods and services to stretch the President's household budget. His main federal resource outside the White House was the National Park Service, or, more particularly, the agency known as National Capital Parks. Gardeners, laborers, carpenters, painters, electricians were readily available to Crim through the "Parks Department," and paid for by the Park Service.[44]

The White House has always been vulnerable to criticism. Its occupants may seem to enjoy too privileged a manner of living, on too grand a scale. Nevertheless, in many respects, it has actually been run like an ordinary house. During World War II, for example, all gasoline, though bought cheaply through the Park Service and available without limit, had to be paid for by the gallon and an account kept of how much was used by each car on each trip. Like their fellow citizens, the President and the First Lady were expected to conserve energy. In winter they shivered inside the house under heavy wool sweaters and scarves. Electricity was used sparingly.[45]

The housekeeper was subject to the rules of the Office of Price Administration. Although a stand was made in 1943 against classifying the White House as a residence—it was finally classed as an institution, with hotels, tugboats, and restaurants—Mrs. Nesbitt had to go to OPA officials and negotiate for her "points." In preparation for this, she calculated what quantity of each of the restricted foods was used each month in the year 1942. Her efforts backfired, in that the OPA merely selected the months of lowest consumption for the norm. During those months the Roosevelts had seldom been at home.

Mrs. Nesbitt labored to stay within her allotments, hoarding her ration stamps in her basement office. When a resident member of the household was going out of town for more than seven meals, she had to put together a little package of stamps from her cache. She was surprised to find supplies missing from pantry, kitchen, storerooms, and wine cellar. Complaining to Crim, she asked that the staff be notified that on pain of dismissal they were to cease removing food and drink from her stores. When this failed, she had the Navy bind the refrigerators with straps and padlocks; still food disappeared. At last Charles Frederick, one of the Secret Service men assigned to the President, assumed responsibility for the stores, and there was no more pilfering. His methods of protecting them were not recorded.

In an attempt to conserve supplies, Mrs. Nesbitt conferred with Mrs. Roosevelt about simplifying menus. The traditional dinner of from six to eight courses was a strain on the allotment of stamps, even with the reduction of social activity, which had meant that dinner groups were much smaller than before the war. A typical number of guests was about 30, and the maximum Mrs. Nesbitt could remember for the whole war period was 80.

Mrs. Roosevelt agreed to reduce the menu to three courses, soup, entrée, and dessert. Wines, usually three, were cut to one, if any were poured at all. Soon, shortages limited the entrées to chicken and fish, which alone were available in some abundance. By comparison, the President's kitchen upstairs was the land of plenty. Hunter friends sent gifts of wild duck, goose, and venison. The restrictions of the Office of Price Administration did not limit wild game, but other gifts could not be so gratefully accepted. When Texas oilman Sid Richardson sent magnificent beefsteaks during the depths of the war, they had to be declined for lack of stamps.[46]

Despite the elimination of most official functions, social life remained relatively active. The dinner table or cocktail hour provided good opportunities for President Roosevelt to see individuals and groups. Mrs. Roosevelt entertained practically every day at lunch and dinner, inviting people she wished to consult about her many projects. Joseph T. Lash, a youth activist in the 1930s and the friend and later biographer of Mrs. Roosevelt, wrote that already, in the late '30s, "The White House was in a sense divided into two households," the President's and Mrs. Roosevelt's. This separation was most pronounced at meals, when Roosevelt might be presiding at his table upstairs, and Mrs. Roosevelt at hers below.[47]

Still there were times when they entertained delightfully together. Like many First Ladies before her, she saw the dinner table as a place to bring together interesting people, whose conversation would be both entertaining and informative to the President. She was not always without ulterior motives, using the opportunity to introduce the President to people whom he otherwise was likely not to see—or not want to see. Never particular about rank, the First Lady drew some criticism for her mixtures of guests. "A number of people," she wrote in her defense, "have accused me at various times of having no sense of propriety, because frequently I had what they called 'unimportant' people to meet 'important' ones. The truth is that the 'unimportant' people usually had been asked long before hand, or had standing invitations, and when the important people came I still wanted my friends. . . . throughout the war years the comings and goings of official people were shrouded in mystery. . . . They arrived and they left suddenly and none of us were warned beforehand."[48]

The President's aides constantly searched for diversions for Roosevelt, but these were ultimately few, because he maintained a heavy work schedule. One frequent guest commented on "the inevitable news reel" in the new theater after dinner. Roosevelt took special interest in the film footage of battles; the reels were edited for public consumption so in this respect, at least, he saw the war as did other citizens in movie houses across the country. He liked to read, but had little time for it. Roosevelt's study and bedroom were stacked with books he meant to read. Even the long drives in open cars, so much loved by the Roosevelts in peacetime, were discouraged during the war by the Secret Service. The President's pleasure driving was largely restricted to the country roads at Hyde Park and Warm Springs, where he drove himself.

Admiral Ross McIntyre, the White House doctor, had the idea of finding a nearby place for short vacations, because he was concerned over Roosevelt's declining health. So the recreational scene improved for the President in the summer of 1942, when he made his first visit to a retreat set aside for him in the Maryland mountains. Here he was to find his chief relaxation for the balance of his life. The rustic camp, known today as Camp David, was 75 miles from Washington, with some of the same scenic qualities as Hyde Park. Roosevelt named the camp Shangri-La, after the secret paradise in James Hilton's novel *Lost Horizon*.

Situated in the National Park Service's eight-million-acre Catoctin reserve, Roosevelt's Shangri-La started out as a tourist camp, built in the early 1930s by the Civilian Conservation Corps and the Works Progress Administration for rental to vacationers. Similar camps were built during the Depression in national parks and forests all over the United States; at Catoctin three were built like little "pioneer settlements," small, with squarish cabins of slab oak, situated near central swimming pools. Two of the camps were taken over for military training purposes early in 1942. The third McIntyre reserved for the President.[49]

To make Roosevelt's house, three of the slab houses were pulled together, giving him a combined living room and dining room, four bedrooms, a kitchen and butler's pantry, and two baths, the largest of them adjacent to the President's bedroom. On one side was a screened porch with a flagstone floor and a view of the mountains and the valley that led to Frederick, Maryland. The interior was simple. Framed political cartoons on rough, unpainted walls were scattered haphazardly. White-painted office furniture, salvaged from various government locations, mingled with colonial style pieces from the President's motor yacht *Potomac,* now assigned to combat duty. Elliott Roosevelt remembered that his father found Shangri-La to be a more practical retreat than Hyde Park. "From Shangri-la," he wrote, "he could be back at his desk within two hours, and he had a direct line to the White House. So he tried to get there on weekends, to sit working . . . with Hopkins and others, glancing out at a beautiful view of the Catoctin Valley, keeping a logbook record of each visit. . . . "[50]

Mrs. Roosevelt never visited Shangri-La. To a large extent she went her own way in the war years, emerging as a figure apart from the President. With some families, the confines of the White House help create a closeness that was not there before; not so with the Roosevelts. Living among his advisers, the President lacked the time, and perhaps he also lacked the inclination, to give his family much attention. Upon the death of his mother, he had asked his wife to give up her home at Val-Kill, but she refused to return to Hyde Park. Memories were too bitter. "Of course," she wrote her daughter, "I know I've got to live there more, but only when he is there. . . . Will you and the boys understand it or does it make you resentful?"

The war increased Eleanor Roosevelt's hunger to be useful to mankind. She traveled widely. Soon after Pearl Harbor she went to the West Coast; that fall she was in Great Britain, touring in horror and dismay the bombed-out ruins of London, a city she had loved nearly all her life. Against warnings from military officials, she journeyed to the Southwest Pacific in 1943, stopping at Guadalcanal, where she visited every hospital bed and viewed the scene of the victorious Battle of Guadalcanal, which had taken place a year earlier. "I have never seen her so weary," wrote her young friend Joseph T. Lash, who was stationed there. Often her longtime secretary, Malvina Thompson, traveled with her, but "Tommy" was not always well and at last had to be left at home.[51]

At the White House businesslike continuity was maintained on the social side by the formidable Edith Benham Helm, the former social secretary to the second Mrs. Wilson and the widow of Admiral James M. Helm. Her desk was in the west hall, and she had files in Mrs. Roosevelt's sitting room, a small office overlooking the north portico, and rooms upstairs in the East Wing. Her duties included correspondence, invitations, and social scheduling. She received telephone calls to the First Lady. A woman of experience, tact, and common sense, she never gave her demanding employer cause to complain.

Although not a close friend of Mrs. Roosevelt's in the sense that Tommy Thompson was, Edith Helm had known the First Lady since World War I and had been asked in 1933 to help out at the White House for a few weeks. It was while she was there that Mrs. Roosevelt emerged as a public personality. With the First Lady suddenly occupied by so many other interests, her responsibilities as a hostess became less interesting to her; she was pleased to put the whole "package" into competent hands. Mrs. Helm stayed on, supported by two agencies, one the so-called "social office" in the East Wing, with its calligrapher, who wrote the invitations, and its pool of stenographers; and the other the protocol office, which was always available for discussions concerning matters of form and procedure. Interested in the work, Edith Helm could enjoy it at her own pace, without the usual pressures, because Mrs. Roosevelt was otherwise occupied.

Mrs. Helm's routine was simpler and her days not so harried as those of Tommy Thompson, who remained nearly always at Mrs. Roosevelt's elbow. Both Roosevelts had their devoted personal aides. Many years after her father's Presidency, Anna Roosevelt said this in an interview: "The people who worked with [Mother and Father] had to be just as if they had no lives of their own. I think both of them unwittingly and unknowingly never realized—it never occurred to them—that these people lived their lives through them, and had nothing of their own."[52]

Fourth Term

The turning point in the war in the Pacific came late in 1942 with the victory at Guadalcanal. Early the next year President Roosevelt departed for Casablanca in Morocco, where the first of the wartime conferences was held; on the way he stopped in Brazil and Gambia. In the spring he and Mrs. Roosevelt toured parts of the United States by rail, with a visit to northern Mexico to review Mexican troops and meet briefly with the president of Mexico. Churchill was at the White House in May, attending a conference of the United Nations held in the East Room in June. At a state dinner on July 9, 1943, the President announced the Allied invasion of Sicily.

That autumn, on November 9, Roosevelt staged a spectacle in the East Room. Representatives of the 44 United Nations gathered around a great table and signed the agreement for the United Nations Relief and

Rehabilitation Administration. Mrs. Nesbitt recalled how difficult it was to find enough green baize to cover the vast surface, which was created by pushing together the plain pine dining tables built for Theodore Roosevelt's state dinners. Mrs. Roosevelt wrote of her husband, "He believed in dramatizing special occasions, and he carefully planned that [this] be done with pomp and ceremony. . . . I was particularly glad of the chance to witness the beginning of this giant organization, which was to bring relief to many people."[53]

Toward the close of 1943 the household changed. Anna moved into the President's House with her three children, and the Hopkinses departed for his house in Georgetown to make a home for Diana. Roosevelt's daughter became increasingly attached to her father, and tried to protect him and ensure his peace and comfort. She felt a strong domestic tension, for which she blamed her mother, who she believed nagged her father unmercifully to support her private crusades. On this subject, Rexford Tugwell agreed; even family dinners became opportunities to exert pressure: "Really serious talk at table was avoided if Roosevelt could manage it. Eleanor, so humorless and so weighed down with responsibility, made this difficult."[54]

Roosevelt faced the question of whether to run for a fourth term. Although some of his family opposed the idea at first, the President decided to run again. His health had declined so sharply that closeup photography of him was discouraged; the press complied. Thin and pale, the President announced that his work was not yet done, and urged Americans to elect him again. Among the public there was some opposition and outrage, but a consensus that this was appropriate. Roosevelt had become a symbol of freedom to people all over the world. The war had turned in favor of the Allies; the bloody but brilliantly successful invasion of France had begun on June 6, 1944. The popular wish to have the wartime leader preside over the final victory and the postwar reconstruction guaranteed Roosevelt's reelection.

The fourth inauguration took place January 20, 1945, on the south portico. Roosevelt's previous inaugurations had been held at the Capitol, but his frail health dictated the new location, though the reason offered to the public was "wartime austerity." The awnings of the south portico were drawn up, and shivering spectators stood on the rain-soaked south lawn. An usher called it "by far the greatest assemblage of people ever to gather at the White House." The next day, in the deepest secrecy, Roosevelt left Washington by rail to board a destroyer that would take him to Yalta in the Crimea. Anna was with him. At Yalta the Big Three would discuss the conditions of the surrender of Germany.

Flags Half-Mast

The death of President Roosevelt on April 12, 1945, took the world wholly by surprise. Although those close to him had feared since his reelection campaign that his time was near, the public was not alerted to his condition even by the photographs from Yalta clearly showing his physical deterioration. When on March 1 he had addressed the Congress, reporting on the Yalta conference, the legislators had been shocked by his worn and aged appearance. He had apologized for speaking from his chair instead of the podium, explaining that it was an ordeal for him to stand with ten pounds of steel braces. This was his first and only public acknowledgement of the severity of his handicap.

The news came by telephone to the Executive Office at about mid-afternoon that the President, visiting Warm Springs, had collapsed while sitting for a portrait. Debating whether to hurry to Georgia, Mrs. Roosevelt decided first to keep an appointment of long standing at the Sulgrave Club; she was reluctant to draw public attention to a possible crisis. She was called back from the meeting to the White House, where in her study Steve Early and Marvin McIntyre told her that the President was dead. The press secretary told newsmen that she had replied: "I am more sorry for the people of this country and of the world than I am for ourselves." Later Mrs. Roosevelt thought she probably had not said it, but the statement—one of those that seemed so true it was hard to disclaim—became a kind of theme for the sad occasion.

Vice President Harry S. Truman was concluding his day of presiding in the Senate when called to the White House, with the request that he go at once to Mrs. Roosevelt's study. He had no idea why he had been summoned. When Mrs. Roosevelt told him what had happened, Truman later wrote, "That was the first inkling I had of the seriousness of the situation." Was there anything he could do for her? Eleanor Roosevelt replied, "Is there anything *we* can do for *you*? For you are the one in trouble now."[55]

The news soon circulated. Flags began sinking to half-mast. Radios droned the few available facts, awaiting further details from Warm Springs and Washington. In the Cabinet Room, Truman was sworn in as President, the ceremony taking, according to his recollections, precisely one minute, 7:08–7:09 p.m. The room was filled with Cabinet members and officials. Truman's wife and daughter stood near him; Woodrow Wilson's portrait over the mantelpiece gazed over the assemblage. Members of the White House and office staffs crowded outside on the porch, looking in through the glass doors.

Mrs. Roosevelt, meanwhile, had gone to Georgia by air and the next day began the long trip back to Washington by train with Roosevelt's body. As the *Ferdinand Magellan* moved along day and night, slowing at towns and stations so the thousands of people waiting could draw close and see the flag-covered coffin through the lighted windows, Mrs. Roosevelt was reminded of what she had read of Abraham Lincoln's funeral train. The procession from Union Station to the White House was a long and somber display of military prowess and civilian grief. President Roosevelt's coffin was mounted on a caisson, as Harding's had been. Servicemen marched in formation before and behind it. Military airplanes flew overhead, also in formation. At least 500,000 people watched silently in the hot April sun.

The coffin was brought into the White House and placed before the great east window of the East Room, with the crimson curtains behind it closed against the sun. It was Saturday, April 14, 1945; Roosevelt's body would remain here for about five hours. Flowers, which had been arriving in great numbers, had been hung on the walls of the East Room to envelop it in fragrant blossoms. At the brief service at four in the afternoon, the new President's daughter, Margaret, felt sickened by the heat and the heavy scent of the flowers.[56]

Two hundred mourners were seated in the East Room. Large numbers found places in the state parlors, in the two dining rooms, and in the basement's central hallway, library, and china room, as well as in the glazed corridor and the movie theater in the East Wing. All the areas were wired for sound and tightly crowded with chairs. At the west end of the basement corridor a White House policeman stood at the door to the Map Room, a lone reminder that the war was still in progress.

Uncounted thousands crowded the iron fences outside, watching the windows of the East Room. At about 5 p.m. the coffin was brought out of the White House and returned by procession to Union Station for the trip to Hyde Park. In funeral instructions discovered among Roosevelt's papers after it was too late to follow most of them, he had asked that his coffin be placed before the fireplace in the library of his cherished home, so that he could spend one last night under that roof. His remains were not taken inside the house. But his request not to lie in state had been scrupulously observed.

Franklin D. Roosevelt was buried in the rose garden at Hyde Park as he specified. At the White House, workers took down the funeral flowers that remained. Nor did Mrs. Roosevelt delay. Returning to the White House after the graveside service, she began packing, and in five days her work was done. In the oval room she invited members of the staff to select mementoes from among the swarms of little things with which FDR had liked to surround himself.

Thirteen Army trucks departed for Hyde Park on April 20, 1945, carrying the Roosevelts' personal belongings.[57] That afternoon in the East Room Mrs. Roosevelt said good-bye first to the office staff, then to the household employees. Train ticket and satchel in hand, she left Washington for New York City.

42

History

The departure of the Roosevelts ended an era for the White House. With the war a new period had begun which would culminate in its virtual demolition and rebuilding. The origin of this development can be dated precisely in the week after Pearl Harbor, when the Secret Service investigation of the wartime safety of the White House stressed its structural vulnerability, especially to fire. The report made those who managed the house mindful for the first time of its hidden perils; henceforward they watched constantly for evidence of crumbling and decay. The gentle sagging, the jiggling wood floor, the unmendable plaster, and a hundred other features spoke no longer of beloved venerability, but of danger. Into this situation came a new President with a taste—indeed a hearty appetite—for building.

President Truman

Harry S. Truman burst upon the American scene. Though he had been a United States senator, as well as Vice President, he had not been a familiar figure in the national news. Even more than most Vice Presidents, he had been overshadowed by the man in the White House. He seemed, at first glance, unequal to the job before him. The antithesis of the Olympian FDR, he was striking more for his ordinariness than anything else. He looked to be in his early to middle 50s, gray hair notwithstanding, although he turned 61 within a month after being sworn in. His ready grin was that of a common man; his language was simple, without drama, and nearly always perfectly clear. His physical liveliness was almost overwhelming, considering that for 12 years the President had been able to move only with assistance. Truman was bouncy and agile; he was a great walker, who loved exercise and moved fast. A natty dresser, he wore suits tailored to his trim build, ties tied perfectly, handkerchiefs folded carefully, trousers creased sharply.

On the day after Roosevelt's burial at Hyde Park, Truman addressed the Congress, to continual ovations. He promised to carry forward the ideals of the late President. Having served in the Senate for a decade, he was one of them, as Roosevelt had never been. That afternoon he moved from his apartment on Connecticut Avenue to Blair House. This was his decision, but made doubtless at the urging of the Secret Service, for guarding him in an apartment building was not easy on him, the service, or the other tenants in the building. As it turned out, he would return to Blair House and live there longer than in the White House. During his administration of nearly eight years, he occupied the White House less than almost any other President.

There were only three in this family, the President, his wife, Bess, who was 60, and their daughter, Margaret, 21, who was studying history and international affairs at George Washington University. They were very close; as one staff member wrote, "The Trumans were the closest family who lived in the White House during the twenty-eight years I worked there." They spent evenings together as often as they could, reading and playing or listening to music.[1]

Although the glare of publicity, while greater than ever before, was not particularly new to them, the Trumans determined to maintain their privacy, insisting that their domestic life change as little as possible. Margaret Truman remembered that after her father became President, "we still tried to get together as frequently as we had before. For example, we all still made a point of having breakfast together," and when Margaret decided that she might like to have her breakfast in bed, "mother soon took care of that daydream, and made it clear that there would be no breakfast in bed for me except when I was sick."[2] The significance of Mrs. Truman in the family circle became increasingly clear to everyone at the White House. A woman of few public words, and with none of Mrs. Roosevelt's interest in pursuing causes, Mrs. Truman stayed in the background. Looking every year of her age, she dutifully performed the duties required by her position, yet scrupulously reserved her private life, which she devoted to the President, her daughter, and an abundance of relatives at home in Missouri, including her aged mother in Independence.

Truman, an enthusiastic reader of world history, was surprised in later years to discover Mrs. Truman at the fireplace burning letters. They had been prodigious letter writers through their years together, especially during his time as President. "You shouldn't be doing that," Truman said to his wife.

"Why not?" she asked, "I've read them several times."

"But think of history," Truman said.

"I have," she replied, and continued her work.[3]

Patching

When the Trumans moved in, 12 years of hard use had made the White House shabby. Much of the western half of the second floor looked sparse when the Roosevelts' personal belongings were removed; the many pictures left white spots on the walls, where they had shielded plaster and paper from dust and grime. Some of the draperies had rotted, and most of the carpets and rugs were furrowed by paths that had once skirted large pieces of furniture.

The deterioration of the house during the Roosevelt occupancy was no more noticeable than the shabbiness of Hyde Park or any other old family home loaded with generations of furnishings. It was part of a total picture; people familiar with such places feel wholly at home and often detest the intrusion of applied freshness. For example, when her study had been repainted at one point, Mrs. Roosevelt had demanded that a chart be made of the locations of the thick groupings of framed photographs and drawings on the walls, so that they could be put back exactly as they had been before.

Although President and Mrs. Truman had lived in an old house all their married lives, they were not interested in autobiographical clutter. They were sincerely concerned about the rundown look of the White House. Even Mrs. Roosevelt had given it some thought, but her husband's brief fourth term had offered little time to carry out any ideas she might have had. In anticipation of the end of the war and the return of the house to public functions, she had invited Mrs. Harold I. Pratt to the White House early in 1945 and asked her for ideas on how the state rooms might be improved. The President's death had ended this effort, and any changes were left to the Trumans.

When he went to live at the White House in the spring of 1945, Truman had no idea of the mark he would ultimately make on it. Coping with the heavy demands upon a new President, he and his family were only interested in moving into the house with some degree of comfort.

Howell Crim assigned to the task his chief assistant, J. B. West, a small, engaging man who had come to the White House shortly before Pearl Harbor. Himself a Midwesterner, West was delighted with Mrs. Truman and eager to please her. He liked her directness and gentle charm, but was embarrassed to show her the White House, which, he said, looked like an "abandoned hotel."[4]

The $50,000 appropriation usual to each administration since Coolidge's time had not been touched by Mrs. Roosevelt. Mrs. Truman decided to make do for the time. With West, she selected furnishings from many rooms and assembled them in the family quarters. Washing the white woodwork and painting the walls was her solution to the general seediness. She selected soft colors: lavender and gray for her bedroom and study, the southwest rooms used also by Mrs. Roosevelt; green and blue for the President's room; with beige for the oval room. The Lincoln bed was taken down the hall to the Lincoln Study, which now became the Lincoln Bedroom. The traditional Lincoln Suite on the northwest was reborn as Margaret Truman's sitting room and bedroom, the former Wedgwood blue and the latter raspberry pink.[5]

Mrs. Truman ordered the restoration of Mrs. Hoover's Monroe Room, with all the reproductions of President Monroe's furniture which Mrs. Roosevelt had moved out. This was perhaps to please Herbert Hoover, who was invited by the President to the White House late in May, his first visit since his bitter departure 12 years before. New window hangings and bedspreads arrived from Keith & Company, a decorating firm Mrs. Truman knew in Kansas City. The reupholstering, where necessary, was done in Washington, some of it by employees of the National Park Service. Mrs. Truman said she wanted to move on May 8, the President's birthday, so the rush was on. From their apartment the Trumans moved only their piano and their clothing.

The Bomb

On the morning of May 8, President Harry S. Truman awoke for the first time in the White House. The previous several days had brought continuing news of the German surrender to the British on May 4 and to the Americans on May 7. Early in the morning of the 8th Truman received word that the Germans had surrendered to the Russians, completing the capitulation of the Third Reich. That morning he wrote to his mother, "This will be an historical day. At 9:00 this morning I must make a broadcast to the country announcing the German surrender. The papers were signed yesterday morning and hostilities will cease on all fronts at midnight tonight. Isn't that some birthday present?"[6]

He proclaimed May 8 V-E Day for the victory in Europe. In his address he called on Japan to surrender. But although Americans moved victoriously through the Pacific islands, the Japanese continued to resist fiercely. This led to discussions of the atomic bomb as a means of forcing the surrender of Japan. Tests were made during the summer of 1945. As the war in the Pacific dragged on, Truman was occupied with great public events. On June 18 he received a triumphant General Dwight D. Eisenhower at the White House; eight days later he witnessed the signing of the United Nations Charter in San Francisco, after weeks of quarreling between the Russians and the Americans.

On July 7 he sailed from Newport News, bound for Potsdam, near Berlin, for the final meeting of the Big Three. He went reluctantly, believing the American public was uncomfortable with such distant meetings. The atomic bomb was dropped on Hiroshima on August 5, while Truman was at sea, returning to the United States. A second bomb was delivered four days later at Nagasaki, and that day the Japanese offered to surrender. On the 14th the Japanese surrendered unconditionally; the surrender was formally accepted on September 2, which Truman proclaimed V-J Day.

In four months World War II had ended, and the Cold War, which was to become the predominant theme in international affairs, had begun. That summer Truman wrote to his wife in Missouri, "Well I'm getting better organized now. My office force soon will be shaken down and so will my Cabinet when I've gotten State straightened out. War and Navy I shall let alone until the Japanese are out of the picture. It won't be long until I can sit back and study the whole picture and tell 'em what is to be done in each department. When things come to that stage there'll be no more to this job than there was to running Jackson County and not any more worry."[7]

Best Laid Schemes

Truman's first venture into building at the White House was an effort to enlarge the West Wing. In this he failed, because a vocal opposition arose against him, but he learned some lessons about getting his way in such matters that were to serve him in far more significant projects later on. When he went to the White House he could look back through the long Roosevelt years on an almost continuous program of building. His own first attempt was merely an extension of the course of improvement his predecessor had followed.

The Executive Office housed 225 employees when Truman was inaugurated. While the new President increased the staff only very slowly, he was immediately displeased with its working conditions. "The burden of the President has increased to such an extent," he wrote, "that now the basement, of the so-called office wing, is full of workers—it is the poorest place in the world for people to work. . . . The President has no place where these clerks, who have to be available for his call at any time, can possibly work except by an addition to the office wing." Lorenzo Winslow was directed to make sketches for an expansion of the Executive Office Building to the south. The addition would contain some 15,000 square feet, to accommodate an auditorium, facilities for the press, office space, and, at the suggestion of Edith Helm, a staff cafeteria. Most of the additional space would be devoted to the auditorium, which would be used primarily for the press conferences, at which some 200 reporters routinely appeared. The Oval Office was no longer adequate to receive them.[8]

Winslow remembered, "With the active advice and interest of the President in all the various details, sketches were prepared for an addition to the [office building] extending southward along West Executive Avenue." A new entrance was designed on West Executive, giving into the basement. The theater was to seat 375; it had a small stage accessible from the Oval Office and equipment for radio and television broadcasting. Roosevelt's and Truman's use of the Diplomatic Reception Room for radio addresses had been unhappy experiences: "With the intense heat and inadequate ventilation," remembered Winslow, "both Presidents suffered intensely."[9]

Externally, the addition was in Winslow's usual vein. Projected to be built of brick covered with stucco, it followed the original barren neoclassicism of the West Wing in a heavy ell-shaped mass, with bows at the two extremities recalling that of the Oval Office. In relation to the grounds, the projected addition seemed too large, although plantings might have reduced the apparent ill effects. The West Executive Avenue facade, however, pressed its lofty bulk close to the avenue, narrowing the space between the State, War, & Navy Building and the White House grounds into an almost tunnel-like passage. Truman had insisted only that the addition not be seen from Pennsylvania Avenue, for he thought the East Wing, which could be seen, a "monstrosity."[10]

The architect and his staff were putting final touches on a proposal for the Congress seven months after Truman took office. There was more to the request than the West Wing addition, but the office expansion was the major feature. Perhaps to sugarcoat the project, President Roosevelt's museum project for the East Wing, thwarted by the wartime need to use the spaces as offices, was revived. The museum would be filled with White House memorabilia of all kinds, including china, furniture, First Ladies' dresses, and original documents. For the White House proper, some furnishings were to be purchased both for the state rooms and upstairs. Substantial repairs were to be carried out in the family quarters, including the installation of new flooring; the President disliked the old boards because they were loose and sometimes moved beneath his feet. The heating system, most of it installed in 1902, was to be replaced.

By the end of November, Winslow's office had assembled charcoal sketches and skeletal specifications. Views had been made of the projected new wing from the south, east, and west. On November 30 Winslow presented the project for consideration to the Commission of Fine Arts. Reserving the right to discuss and alter "certain details of the design by the Architect," the commission gave its approval. Gilmore D. Clarke wrote in his letter to the President, "The Commission were pleased to note that the further extension of the West Wing to the south will not seriously encroach upon the grounds of the White House; in fact, the nature of the proposed extension of the West Wing will serve to provide the grounds near the House with greater seclusion than has been possible heretofore."[11]

Truman's formal request to the Congress was warmly received, and was approved December 3, 1945. An appropriation of $1,650,000 was tacked onto the last deficiency bill for the year, granting the President all he had requested. Two weeks later he put Winslow in charge: "In view of the fact that I am most interested in all of this new work, and as it must necessarily be carried forward with my active personal attention, I have appointed Mr. Lorenzo S. Winslow, who, as Architect of the White House, will act for me in all matters that concern the direct supervision of the design and the execution of all of the various projects." Winslow was ordered to begin preparation of the West Wing for its additions and to ready the site for construction immediately after New Year's. The architect duly commenced his preparations, breaking ground and starting demolition: "Workmen swarmed over the West Wing of the White House," reported Newsweek, "removing windows and tearing down the iron fence along West Executive Avenue to make way for President Truman's . . . addition."[12]

The project received extensive press coverage, usually accompanied by an illustration showing one of Winslow's drawings. Clearly the enlarged Executive Office would be a giant mass, and while not as tall as the White House, would cover a greater area. Winslow was interviewed on national radio and pressured to describe the new wing as an "addition" to the White House. "May I emphasize," said Winslow, "that there will be no addition to the White House? The new building is an extension to the south of the Executive Office . . . the *West Wing* of the White House!"[13]

But the idea that the White House was being added to became immediately and firmly fixed in the public's mind. "Unfortunately," said J. Leonard Reinsch, Truman's radio adviser, "the architect announced it as an addition to the White House. If he'd said it was an addition to the President's office or said that an executive office was being built, we would today have this conference room [auditorium] which is badly needed. . . . Once it was announced as an addition, all hell broke loose." Winslow's project for the expansion was published widely in the press in the second week of January. Letters of protest began to arrive in great numbers. The Commission of Fine Arts was accused in the press of "toadying to Presidential whims in indorsing the plans." Officials of the American Home Builders Association charged that the addition to the White House would use up valuable and scarce materials needed by veterans to build new homes. At last the American Institute of Architects issued its protest, proclaiming its stewardship over the White House as granted by Theodore Roosevelt. In the Congress both Democrats and Republicans questioned an expansion program that might result in damaging the White House; Congressman Howard W. Smith of Virginia called for a joint resolution to halt construction until the Congress had examined the plans.[14]

Not all the objection was external. Secretary of the Interior Harold L. Ickes—most durable of the holdovers from FDR's Cabinet—wrote to Truman that he was "deeply concerned about the proposal to add to the office space at the White House. My own conception is, and there is a historical reason for this, that the White House was intended to be in a very literal sense 'the President's house.' It is the most famous and highly cherished building in the whole country. . . . As you know, before the war, thousands of people came every day to see it as they would visit a shrine. Indeed the White House is a shrine, not only because it houses the Chief Executive of the Nation but for what it represents in the hearts of the people." He asked the President to slow down, to contact leading architects and ask their opinions "before such a drastic change in policy could be determined upon." Secretary Ickes reminded the President that Roosevelt's Reorganization Act of 1933 had put the White House and its grounds under the administration of the National Park Service. Since the Service was part of the Department of the Interior, Ickes felt personally responsible for the historic place; he did "not believe that the White House, as part of an office building, would be the White House that the people have come to love and respect."[15]

Ickes's letter annoyed the President, as did the growing opposition to his plan. He had also been surprised by the reaction, for he believed the Roosevelts had nearly ruined the White House with their additions and remodelings, yet the public had not arisen to defend the house from them. In comparison he felt that his proposed addition was of no consequence. "I am going forward with this construction," the President wrote tersely to Ickes, "because it is absolutely necessary." He had sponsored public buildings before, against what also seemed powerful odds. As presiding judge of Jackson County, Missouri, in the late 1920s he had built a skyscraper courthouse in Kansas City and had transformed the mid-19th-century courthouse in his hometown of Independence into a neo-Georgian pile that became the "colonial" climax of its main square. During the West Wing controversy he wrote: "I am sort of an 'architectural nut' myself."[16]

The controversy boiled in the newspapers, and at a press conference on January 24, the President threatened to move staff into the state rooms of the White House if he could not build his new wing. He showed the plans to the reporters, pointing out the precise location of the wing and telling its dimensions. "It will not be visible to the public except from the air and on West Executive Avenue. . . . The White House will not be changed or altered in any manner—exterior or interior." When asked about congressional enemies of his plan, President Truman said that there were few. Yet that same day the deficiency act was amended in the House by a standing vote of 110 to 41 to remove $883,660 from the appropriation. The deleted money was the exact amount specified for the addition to the West Wing.[17]

The office question died slowly. Acting on a suggestion from Secretary Ickes, the President ordered a model made of the Executive Office with the addition, to show that it would harmonize with the White House. Truman wrote of receiving "a great many suggestions about the office space" from other people, not the least the American Institute of Architects, which reminded him that the Executive Office had been from the first a temporary structure and that it should be removed from the grounds in its entirety as soon as possible. The A.I.A. recommended construction of a second temporary structure "raised over West Executive Avenue" between the White House grounds and the State, War, & Navy Building. To this idea President Truman responded curtly, "I rather think that building office space in the street is unique to say the least. I think it would be better to use the rooms in the White House itself . . . rather than to block one of the Washington streets."[18]

In the executive sessions of the A.I.A. and within many interested arts and antiquarian organizations, the issue of new construction at the White House was broader than the proposed Executive Office. It was obvious that great changes might soon take place in the area around the White House. Already there were preliminary plans to build a new State Department across from State, War, & Navy; the historic Decatur House as well as the Blair House and the old Corcoran Gallery of Art, then in use as a court building, were scheduled for demolition. Thus it was not just the White House that was threatened so much by the pressing post-war need for office space, but also its setting: If all the ideas then current had actually materialized, the White House could well have become dwarfed by a complex of federal buildings. The new East Wing—much disliked—had risen safely under the veil of war, or it would have met opposition. But with the war over, any move to change the White House was an alarm bell to those who considered themselves the guardians of the historic scene.

The model was exhibited and discussions were held over adding to the Executive Office, but official interest in the project waned. It seems to have been generally understood that any attempt to add to the building would raise a furor, and that no plan would be acceptable that did not call for the eventual removal of the Executive Office from the White House grounds. Meanwhile, a large part of the President's staff was shifted to the State, War, & Navy Building, where Winslow remodeled numerous rooms on the south and east sides. West Executive Avenue remained closed to traffic, to provide easy communication between the two buildings. Tranquillity returned, as the President, defeated, put these particular architectural plans to rest.

The Truman Balcony

A devoted student of history and a constant reader, Truman searched chronicles of the past for patterns that might repeat themselves: "there is not really anything new," he said, "if you know what has gone before. What is new to people is what they do not know about their history or the history of the World." He preferred the romantic works of the 19th-century historians he had read since his youth; he shared their view that history moved through the lives of great men. He often argued political points with examples from history and had decided opinions on the merits and shortcomings of his presidential predecessors.[19]

Although neither a sentimentalist nor an antiquarian, Truman felt affection for the White House as well as interest in its occupants. Lorenzo Winslow, close at hand, took every opportunity to cultivate this fondness. Winslow was intrigued with the past of the White House, having delved into the old records of the commissioners and officers of public buildings until he knew many details of the early days. His explorations were neither orderly nor scholarly, but the result of a curiosity developed over more than a decade of working with the old building. Shortly after Truman took office, Winslow got a mine detector from the Corps of Engineers and went on a quest for the cornerstone, with its brass plate. Laid with Masonic ceremonies, this stone fascinated Truman, who had been grand master of the Grand Lodge of the Masons of Missouri. He hoped that the cornerstone would be found during his administration. When a stone lintel in one of the basement windows had to be taken out and repaired, a second smoke-blackened bit of stone was revealed behind it, and Winslow had it chiseled out for the President, as a memento of the British burning of the White House in 1814.[20]

Truman decided in the summer of 1947 that the appearance of the south front and the livability of the family quarters would profit from the addition of a second-floor balcony behind the columns of the portico. He believed his idea was consistent with the tradition to which the White House belonged. The President made a speech in Charlottesville, Virginia, on the tranquil and lovely Fourth of July, 1947. During his visit, he took special interest in the upstairs galleries or porches—he called them "porticoes"—on the columned pavilions of the campus Thomas Jefferson had designed.

Already enamored of porches, he decided to build one at the White House that would open off both the oval room and his bedroom. Winslow had told him that the columned porticoes had been planned during Jefferson's Presidency, long before they were actually built, and Truman learned at Charlottesville that Jefferson had no objection to second-story porches. In fact, said the President, he possibly had such porches in mind; to build one might realize an old dream.[21]

Truman presented the idea to Howell Crim and Lorenzo Winslow as soon as he was home from Charlottesville. Both listened in great discomfort, knowing that, despite the President's historical justification, an attempt at such a bold alteration of the appearance of the White House proper would stir opposition. But Truman overrode their objections and entered his second architectural controversy.

The chief usher telephoned David E. Finley, director of the National Gallery of Art and a member of the Commission of Fine Arts, and explained the President's wishes. Finley suggested a conference on the scene, and on July 29, 1947, he, Crim, Winslow, Gilmore D. Clarke, chairman of the commission, and commission member Frederick V. Murphy stood before the south portico discussing the balcony. They studied the long shafts of the Ionic columns, uninterrupted in their dramatic rise to the half-round roof of the porch. About 12 feet up, new canvas awnings had been fixed between them every spring, column to column, for 40 years or more; these offended the President with their disorderly appearance and their inevitable mildew. The meeting appears to have been difficult for everyone, for the balcony would, of course, disrupt the facade. The President, however, had expressed his wishes in strong terms. To Crim and Winslow the visitors suggested that an architect of note, who had previously worked on the White House, be consulted; Eric Gugler and William Adams Delano were the obvious candidates, and Delano ultimately was called in.[22]

This was reported to the President, who mistakenly thought that he had thereby gained approval for his balcony from the Commission of Fine Arts, with the single stipulation that he hire Delano. Happy with this progress, he told Winslow to make contact with Delano and followed this up by having his appointments secretary, Matthew J. Connelly, write a letter to Delano: "The President would consider it a special favor if you would see your way clear to become the architect and supervise the proposed construction. He feels it will require a man of your outstanding professional attainments to satisfactorily accomplish this work, and your acceptance of this assignment would go a long way towards appeasing the small group who invariably oppose any additions or changes to the Executive Mansion."[23]

The commission had, however, suggested calling Delano merely as a strategy to avoid a confrontation with the President. Delano, though a former member of the Commission of Fine Arts, was an outsider, from all appearances unbiased; the commissioners were certain he would oppose the balcony and easily get them off the hook. The plan backfired. On August 28 the commissioners, in session, were "astonished . . . that Mr. Delano gave his endorsement to the proposed project and indicated that, in his judgment, the porch would not in any way detract from the dignity of the south portico." Delano had taken an enlarged photograph of the portico and drawn a balcony behind the columns in pen and ink. The commissioners did not like it and, though not officially asked for a verdict, voted that they "cannot approve any plan which will destroy the original design of an historic monument of the importance of the White House." Chief Usher Crim was informed by Chairman Clarke in a carefully written letter, explaining why the position was taken.[24]

For nearly a month nothing was heard of the balcony by the commissioners, then Gilmore Clarke, at his summer home in upstate New York, was telephoned by Howell Crim, who told him that the President "wished to proceed" with his balcony. Did Clarke think the commissioners might change their minds, "if formally asked to pass judgment in the matter by the President?" Clarke made it clear to him that the verdict would not change, but that the commission did not wish to embarrass the President in any way and would "not issue any statement to the Press with respect to the matter unless called upon to do so." At the same time he warned that if asked by reporters, he would have to say that the commission's rejection of the balcony was unanimous. "I stated," wrote Clarke in his notes on the call, "that I hoped that, in the event the President should insist on making the change in the design of the south front . . . the services of Mr. Wm Adams Delano be secured, since the plans for any change should be prepared only by a thoroughly competent architect familiar with the White House and with the period of architecture it represents."[25]

In November, Clarke wrote to the President explaining the commission's actions. The response came within a week: "My understanding was when the matter was discussed with you with regard to the arrangement on the south portico that when Mr. Delano made up his mind, the situation would be satisfactory to you. Now you confess that you hoped he would make up his mind in a manner that you approved of and that you didn't enter into the matter at all with an open mind—that is a great statement for the Chairman of the Commission of Fine Arts to send to the President. I can't understand your viewpoint when those dirty awnings are a perfect eyesore with regard to that south portico. I have had them painted; I have had them washed and they have been renewed every year and still they look like hell when they are on the porch. Of course, I wouldn't expect you to take into consideration the comfort and convenience of the Presidential family in this arrangement. . . . I certainly would like to have your reasons for preferring the dirty awnings to the good looking convenient portico and then maybe I'll come to a conclusion on the subject. I don't make up my mind in advance. However, I'll have to be convinced."[26]

He was not persuaded to the commission's views. Clarke wrote one more letter, which prompted a brief, chilly reply. Delano and Winslow completed working drawings in November. No new funds were needed from the Congress, the estimated $15,000—ultimately $16,050.74—being easily covered in the general appropriation. By mid-November,

Winslow was obtaining estimates for construction, although he and Delano debated certain details of design and construction. It is significant with regard to the subsequent reconstruction of the house that Delano opposed Winslow's plan to cut all five window openings on the balcony to the floor, so they could receive French doors. The window openings were left as they had been since the house was built; Delano argued that the original stone fabric of the house was sacrosanct. A compromise was reached in his favor: The lone door to the balcony was to be a slim metal one, introduced subtly into one of the windows, leaving most of the old wooden sash and carved stone trimming intact. Only a small amount of stone was removed to allow the door to extend to the floor. These seemingly minor discussions about cutting into the original stone walls may have established the concern for preservation that was soon to save the walls from demolition.

By March 1948 the work was nearing completion, accompanied beyond the iron fence by a blast of newspaper protest. Much of this centered ostensibly on what one paper called President Truman's "lamentable penchant for meddling with a historic structure," but the real target was Truman himself. The building of the "Truman balcony" appeared to symbolize his blustery presidential style, his hardheadedness, his unbending certainty that he was right. Truman persistently claimed that the addition of the porch had nothing to do with his personal comfort, but was an effort to perfect the appearance of the White House. He believed the columns on the south were clumsy and ill-proportioned and that the balcony would help correct this. "When the job is finished," he wrote, "everyone will like it."[27]

It was the first significant change in the main block of the White House since the completion of the north portico early in the administration of Andrew Jackson. Winslow and Delano had made the balcony—though it was in fact more a porch—as unobtrusive as possible. Where Winslow had wanted a stone balustrade to match the parapet, Delano insisted upon a thin one, very plain, of iron, painted white, instead of the black used on the iron railings of the double staircase below. The floor was concrete poured on a steel frame, all slightly slanted from the walls to the columns to shed water; the floor itself had a plastic surface. To replace the baggy, mildewed awnings of the past, Delano designed new canvas awnings rather like window shades that rolled onto reels out of sight behind simple valances on both upper and lower porches.

The furor died down. Some experts on historical architecture actually expressed admiration for the balcony, although the approbation was not epidemic. Time's passage made the new addition seem perfectly natural. The only casualty was the Commission of Fine Arts, which earned the President's contempt: He was not to forget what he considered ill-treatment from the commission when the time came to make far more significant changes in the historic White House.

The Social Schedule Returns

Truman's balcony was under construction in February 1948 when Sidney M. Shalett went to the White House to research an article for *American Magazine* on how the house operated. He stood with Howell Crim in the State Dining Room, then quiet and not in use, and Crim remarked, "I'm just as thrilled standing here today as when I first came here twenty years ago." It took such a man to be chief usher. He loved the house. Behind the scenes he had watched the President's building schemes with some anxiety, and although he was the agent for getting the work going, it is fairly clear that he did not approve of such a major change in the appearance of the White House. Crim presided over a staff of 46, in addition to two assistant ushers. Two electricians, five engineers, five carpenters, seven gardeners, and two plumbers made up the permanent maintenance staff. A housekeeper, six cooks, three butlers and a maître d'hôtel, seven doormen, four housemen, five maids, and several typists and messengers served the Trumans and their guests. [28]

It was an enormous establishment. On social matters and many others, Crim worked in close association with Edith Helm, who had been kept by Mrs. Truman as social secretary and answered directly to the First Lady. He remained in close contact with officials at the State Department, principal among whom was Chief of Protocol Stanley Woodward. Raymond Muir, Crim's predecessor as chief usher and an old friend, was the liaison between protocol and the White House. The social office was on the second floor of the East Wing, on the east side of the hall near Winslow's drafting room. Legally this was under the auspices of the Executive Office, but in practice it functioned as part of the house. Its chief was Adrian B. Tolley, the former calligrapher who had been summoned from the Treasury Department many years before to write invitations for Jessie Wilson's wedding. In addition to his full-time assistant, Sanford Fox, the tall, thin, soft-spoken Tolley had on his staff several part-time "engrossers," or calligraphers.

No "season" had been held at the White House since 1939. Dinners, luncheons, and some receptions had continued throughout the war, but the formal schedule of state dinners and receptions had been canceled. When in September 1946, nearly a year and a half after

Truman became President, Edith Helm released a schedule of state events for specified Tuesday evenings November through January, it created considerable attention. The 1946 season was to open with diplomatic dinners; next would come the judicial reception, then a Cabinet dinner and a diplomatic reception. To this were added other receptions, some smaller dinners, and a few musicales. Washington society had always arranged its own schedules for the winter season around that of the White House. After Mrs. Helm's announcement, a social column in the *Washington Post* proclaimed: "Hostesses may now get to work on their own pet social projects. They will cast their eyes over the White House schedule, see on which night a state dinner or reception is scheduled and make their plans accordingly."[29]

The President's decision to reintroduce the social season was made with the knowledge that he could have ordered radical modifications, if he had wished. The seven years from 1939 to 1946 covered so dramatic a time of change as to seem a generation. To one society columnist, the reappearance of the season "is a definite sign that the conversion cycle from war to peace is all but complete." Perhaps this is what the President had in mind, for as Margaret Truman recalled, "he hated to do it," because of the strain on himself and Mrs. Truman. But he saw the "traditional ceremony" as "a dramatic statement of the power and prestige of the presidency." Because of the renovation soon to come, the 1946-47 social season was to be the only one the Trumans would hold, full-scale, in the White House.[30]

Since the establishment of ceremonial forms at the White House in 1902, little had been changed. Some Presidents had rejected Theodore Roosevelt's grand march down the stair in favor of the elevator. Franklin D. Roosevelt, of course, had used the elevator, so the march had not been known for many years. Happily for Truman, Mrs. Helm had known White House ceremony in its heyday and could recall all the particulars. In addition, copious written materials were on file in the State Department. Archie Butt's heavy volumes of notes on state functions, complete with samples of invitations and seating charts, were well thumbed.

Directives for social forms were traditionally written as instructions to military aides. For example, those prepared in 1940 and 1943, the last under Roosevelt, curtly detailed the traffic patterns for crowds, the timing of various ceremonies, and the signals for starting or ending the various phases of the evening. Special attention was given to how the aides were to address the President, the First Lady, and the guests, a feature not present in the instructions of Theodore Roosevelt's time. Truman's instructions of November and December of 1946 were similar in content, but their tone was quite different: Where the earlier ones demanded military sharpness, Truman's encouraged a warmer, although not informal, interaction between the aides and the guests. "It is the desire of the President and the First Lady," read the orders of November, "that an atmosphere of cordial and dignified hospitality prevail at social functions. . . . Guests should leave the White House distinctly pleased with the courtesy of their reception."

A list of available military aides was kept in the social office, and the men were requisitioned as needed. Nineteen was a typical number at large receptions, but occasionally more were required; for a dinner party four or five might suffice. To be chosen as an aide was an honor for military men stationed in the Washington area. All were bachelor officers. "Smartness of appearance, soldierly bearing, attention to duty and *savoir faire* are important qualities in determining selections for the honor of serving at the White House," said an information sheet for aspiring aides. "A knowledge of languages, especially Spanish and French, is a valuable asset." There were usually ten regular "social aides" from the Army and ten from the Navy; they were picked by the President's military staff, who were with him daily at the White House.[31]

Formal social functions were generally divided into two categories, dinners and receptions. A state dinner during the Truman administration usually had about 85 guests, including members of the household; the dining room seated a maximum of 104 when the pine horseshoe table was brought in. A set procedure was always followed at state dinners. Most of the guests entered the house from the east side, where they left their wraps in the movie room. Each male guest was shown a seating chart, elaborately drawn in ink on a large card, and given an envelope containing his dinner partner's name and a smaller version of the seating chart with their places marked. Aides then directed the company upstairs to the state floor, where the Marine Band was playing in the entrance hall. At small dinners the guests went to the Blue Room, at large parties the East Room; in any case, their names were announced as they entered. Aides, moving quickly in the crowd, arranged all the guests in a circle, according to rank, with the highest ranking person to the immediate right of the doorway. During this process as many introductions were made as possible in an attempt to connect dinner partners, who would join later for the march to the State Dining Room.

At eight o'clock, if the circle was ready—and it was seldom much delayed—the Trumans descended in the elevator with the President's two military aides, who escorted them to the room where the guests were assembled. Their presence in the hallway announced by the playing of

"Hail to the Chief," the President and First Lady stopped just inside the door to the room, which was closed behind them. With his Army aide, General Harry H. Vaughan, announcing to the President's left, the circle of guests began to pass one by one, hardly stopping at all, until the last guest had shaken hands. Meanwhile, aides assisted in pairing up dinner partners. When the receiving line ended, the dinner partners of the President and First Lady were brought to them, and with the military aides in the lead and the band playing the President's march, the company marched two-by-two, as company at the White House had for almost a century, to the dining room, this time between a double row of aides forming a corridor on the crimson carpet of the transverse hall.

The Trumans added a new twist to after dinner forms. In the past, the men had remained in the State Dining Room while the women left, later to join them in the Red Room. Starting in 1946, when dinner was over, Mrs. Truman rose from her chair. Aides immediately went to her and the President, who were usually seated across the table from each other, and the two led the crowd into the Red Room, where the men left the ladies and walked through the Blue Room to the Green Room for coffee and cigars. The occupants of both the Red and Green Rooms were free to go to the rest rooms downstairs. In the Green Room with the President the men's conversation was informal, but it was understood that there were likely to be only a few the President felt he particularly needed to have conversations with, so no one approached him unless taken by an aide. Men and women joined in the Blue Room at about ten o'clock and conversed for a while before the President and Mrs. Truman bade them goodnight.[32]

State receptions were little more than opportunities to shake the President's hand. They had never been true entertainments, although during the war the Roosevelts had introduced dancing in the East Room after the receiving line had broken up and the President had retired upstairs. The Trumans continued this practice. All receptions were by invitation, the last public reception having been held on New Year's Day of 1932 by President Hoover. A typical large state reception in Truman's time included about 1,500 guests; since by 1946 the Washington diplomatic corps was 1,150 strong, the diplomatic reception, to which wives were also invited, had to be held on two different evenings, the guest list carefully ordered by diplomatic rank. Refreshments were served in the State Dining Room on Theodore Roosevelt's long table, which was crowned with Monroe's mirrored plateau, massed with flowers and surrounded by fancy foods, brimming punch bowls, and wine glasses, all constantly replenished by the butlers. A Truman innovation for smaller receptions was an open whiskey bar, set up for the first time in the East Room when the President received General Eisenhower and his staff on June 18, 1945. Cocktails had been served heretofore only for small dinners, and they had always been made out of sight in the pantry, with no liquor bottles in view.[33]

A typical reception of the first social season after World War II was held for the press. The press receptions had begun under Franklin D. Roosevelt early in his administration, reflecting somewhat the idea of the diplomatic receptions. Never a part of the official season, they were discontinued, like the other social functions, during the war. Truman resumed the custom on Friday evening, December 6, 1946, and more than a thousand attended. The hour was eight o'clock, as usual. Cabinet members and their wives were admitted at the north door, beginning at about 7:30, and walked up the grand staircase to the family quarters. In this Truman reverted to a pre-FDR practice, for under Roosevelt the Cabinet had assembled downstairs in the private dining room. Truman's Cabinet went to the second-floor Monroe Room. Meanwhile, a larger number of special guests, considered part of the "household," had arrived by the north door and been shown into the Green Room. The doors were then closed behind them.

The invited press corps had begun to arrive at the east entrance. As at state dinners, they were shown along the long glass corridor to the stairs to the state floor. The Marine Band was in its place between the columns of the hall, playing softly. On the second floor, as eight o'clock approached, four military men lined up before their commander in chief at the door to the oval room to request the colors—the American flag and the President's flag—which stood at each side of the President's desk. With the flags in hand, these "four horsemen," as the color guard was nicknamed at the White House, took their positions at the head of the grand staircase; behind them the President's military aides fell in line; then came the President and Mrs. Truman; last came the Cabinet officers and their wives, two abreast. On a signal the presidential party descended with no fanfare; Truman disliked the long stretch of "dangerous" staircase, which kept people looking awkwardly at their feet lest they stumble. He would one day remedy the situation.[34]

Three paces from the foot of the stair the procession stopped. The horsemen stepped forward as the iron gates were rolled back. In the hallway at the foot of the stair, with trumpet flourishes, honors were rendered in a little military ceremony visible to only a portion of those assembled in the East Room. At the instant this was completed, the horsemen stood in formation to lead the President and the First Lady forward. A crash of the drums introduced "Hail to the Chief," which the band played vigorously as the presidential party marched to the Blue Room. The Trumans stopped just inside the double mahogany doors, which were pulled shut behind them. They then went to the south end of the room. Standing between the two flags placed by the horsemen, they received first the special guests from the Green Room, then the line that started flowing from the East Room. When the line was finished, the Trumans elected not to return immediately upstairs. Instead, they mingled for a while with the newspaper and radio people. When they left they were accompanied to the elevator door by the military aides. Soon after, the colors were returned ceremonially to the oval room, leaving the guests free to remain for several hours, enjoying the food and drink in the State Dining Room or dancing in the East Room, to the music of a "dance orchestra" from the Marine Band.

Under Truman, much of the flutter and pressure of the Roosevelt era came to an end. Alonzo Fields, the maître d'hôtel, recalled that the White House "quieted down so much you couldn't believe it was the same place." Mrs. Truman was well organized and absolutely clear in her objectives, wanting to give as little time to the work as possible. Fields remembered, "The First Lady would not stand for fakers, shirkers or flatterers, and the only way you could gain her approval would be by doing your job to the best of your ability. This done, you would not want a more understanding person to work for." Crim assigned the assistant usher, J. B. West, to deal directly with the Trumans, and he met with Mrs. Truman every morning as her "main contact with the operations of the White House." He admired her wit, as well as her businesslike habits: "Mrs. Truman was very conscious of economy in housekeeping. She kept her own books, went over the bills with a finetoothed comb, and wrote every check herself."[35]

She knew well that the financial burdens of White House entertaining could easily become ruinous, even with an appropriation provided for some of it. The Trumans were not rich, and she watched their money carefully, although both insisted that appropriate standards of presidential living be met. Gone were the unappetizing meals of Roosevelt's time. Mrs. Nesbitt was apparently encouraged into retirement, having shown resistance to change in the kitchen. Food of what West called the "American" type was served to the family informally, usually in the solarium on the third floor, three times a day. For dinner parties, of course, Mrs. Truman consulted the chef and ordered more varied menus.

Mrs. Helm had not intended to remain at the White House after the Roosevelts left, yet she proved so useful and got along with Mrs. Truman so well that she remained until 1953, when the administration ended. She was the reigning expert on White House entertaining. Not bound by a regular schedule, she usually appeared for work upstairs in the morning, but seldom remained after lunch, unless a tea was being held. At such times, she seated herself at one end of the tea table and poured, a tradition started by the first social secretary, Belle Hagner. At the outset she drew up most of the Trumans' guest lists. J. B. West recalled that she "knew social Washington from one end to the other." While the "made" list of other times was gone, it was replaced by other lists. On Edith Helm's desk were the New York Social Register and the Social List of Washington, D.C. (the Green Book), as well as a well-worn copy of Emily Post's volume on etiquette.[36]

Since Mrs. Truman did not wish to hold press conferences as Mrs. Roosevelt had, this job fell to the social secretary. Mrs. Helm met regularly with women reporters to announce social schedules and answer questions about the Truman family and its habits. No large social staff served Mrs. Truman, as it had Mrs. Roosevelt. Mrs. Helm had one assistant, who was also personal secretary to Mrs. Truman; Reathel Odum had been Truman's secretary when he was in the Senate. Closer to the family than Mrs. Helm, Reathel Odum became a girl Friday for Mrs. Truman. Since the First Lady wrote most of her own letters, the secretary performed many services outside the office, not the least being to accompany Margaret Truman on her concert tours.

Mrs. Helm remembered society in the brief time the Trumans actually lived in the White House as brilliant in its formality, "the very peak of official entertaining." It was a contrast to the everyday informality of President Truman, which, to most of the American people, set the tone of the administration. To White House intimates, the President was relaxed and even casual in manner. "He was on very friendly terms with everybody," General Vaughan recalled. "He spoke to everybody as he walked through—the gardener, the painters, and had something to say about what was going on. . . . [he] knew all of his Secret Service men by their first names and would talk to them when he'd go walking with them and betting them a dollar whether it would or would not rain. . . ."[37]

History

Truman's quest to correct the past was an oft-repeated theme of his administration, and it influenced his treatment of the White House. The newspapers in the spring of 1945 described the redecorated family quarters as "modern," and modern was what Truman wished to be. He feared that some American traditions would prove dangerous in the postwar world. For example, he opposed the tradition of disarming in peacetime, believing that military strength was essential if the United States were to take a leading role in diplomacy.

Truman's labors to improve on the past included from 1948 to 1952 the demolition of the White House to its stone shell and the reconstruction of its inner parts in concrete and steel. In a sense he destroyed the past; in another he preserved the White House as the home of the Presidents. The end of 1947 also saw the end of the two full years the Trumans lived in the White House. In the fall of 1948 he returned victorious to Washington from his home in Missouri, where he had remained during the presidential election. He occupied not the White House but Blair House across the street, where he would remain until the last year of his administration, when the White House rebuilding was complete.

43

The Symbol

By the close of World War II, 153 years had elapsed since Hoban and the commissioners had laid the cornerstone of the White House. According to American standards in 1945 the house was very old, and, we have seen, it had known hard and continuous use. All its sufferings did not necessarily show: A small army of attendants lovingly saw to its needs, swarming over it daily, mending, polishing, and exerting many other efforts to keep up appearances. The white painted walls shone in the sun; yet wooden windows had so deteriorated in some places that the putty alone held the panes of glass; some iron grilles and railings were rusty and broken; marble floors were cracked and loose; the delicate ornaments—the roses, the guilloche, and the acanthus leaves—carved by the Scotsmen were covered so thickly with paint that they had lost their depth and clarity. In the lofty rooms layer upon layer of wallpaper, plaster, paint, and flooring chronicled the years of frequent, hasty change, as each presidential generation had adjusted the stage to suit its purposes.

Timbers sagged; pipes leaked onto the old clay brick, stone, and wood; plaster walls cracked, were repaired, then cracked again. The great symbol of the Presidency had heretofore overpowered its crumbling feet of clay: Plans to replace the house had always yielded to plans for renovation. But the results of many years of poor construction and the needs of the modern Presidency made it clear by the late 1940s that something drastic would have to be done to save the structure. The decision would be the most significant since James Madison, in 1815, ordered the White House rebuilt when only the fire-blackened shell remained.

Creaks and Groans

During the last months of 1947 President Truman grew increasingly concerned about vibrations in the floors of certain rooms in the family quarters. He was accustomed to the creaking sounds of old houses when all else was quiet at night, but this seemed different to him, especially in the oval room, where he sometimes held meetings and informal parties. In January 1948 he asked the commissioner of public buildings, W. E. Reynolds, to bring in engineers and check the floor of the oval study for safety. The floor's structure, installed in 1902, was found to be overstressed, and the commissioner advised that no more than 15 people be allowed in the room at once.[1]

As a result, the President ordered an analysis of the wooden framework of the entire second floor; the study revealed serious problems within the walls. On February 3, 1948, Truman appointed a committee to review the situation. Aware that he might be at the beginning of a long and costly program of renovation, he appointed his small committee with great caution, remembering previous controversies. Winslow and Reynolds were joined by Richard E. Dougherty, president of the American Society of Civil Engineers, and Douglas W. Orr, president of the American Institute of Architects.

The special committee quickly realized that the entire house needed a thorough structural survey. This would require time and money and would interfere with the normal functioning of the house. President Truman, who had cast his hat in the ring for the upcoming presidential race, would not agree to move, but said that since Mrs. Truman would be in Missouri for the summer, the work could begin in June. The committee submitted an estimate of $50,000, and the Congress made the appropriation on May 10, 1948, to include not only an investigation of the structure, but also plans and specifications for modernizing the house and replacing all wooden framing on the second floor with "a fire-resistant type of construction." Returning to Washington from a trip on August 3, the President wrote in his diary: "Found the White House 'falling down.' My daughter's sitting room floor had broken down into the family dining room. How very lucky we are the thing did not break when Margie and Annette Wright were playing two piano duets where the floor broke."[2]

The rooms were emptied one by one, and holes torn in the walls to examine the structural members. Since the walls were not actually taken apart, a full survey was impossible. The worst conditions were found on the west end, with structural deterioration so severe that the engineers wondered how the interior had remained intact. The main cause of the problem was McKim's 1902 expansion of the State Dining Room into the adjacent stair hall. When the partition—a bearing wall—was removed, the support for the original wooden ceiling joists of the dining room was taken away and replaced by a heavy steel beam. This beam, carrying the tremendous weight of the floors above it, gained a measure of stability by being socketed into the existing walls at each end, but its major support came from steel tie-rods that suspended it from the wooden structural systems of the roof. When the attic and roof had been rebuilt in 1927, the tie-rods were introduced into the new steel skeleton; but President Coolidge's upper structure of steel and concrete proved too heavy for the house below it, and a shifting of walls had begun. The most serious manifestation of damage was in the bulky structure hanging over the State Dining Room.

A remarkable transferral of stresses took place as the third floor bore down on the house beneath it. Old mortise-and-tenon timbers made for lesser purposes assumed new structural roles for which they were inadequate. One result of this process by 1948 was the weakness of the floor of Margaret Truman's bedroom. A leg of her grand piano sank into the floor, causing the plaster ceiling in the private dining room below it to fall. Likewise, in the Blue Room and the East Room, the chandeliers swayed slightly from time to time, moved by tremors from some unknown source, perhaps halfway across the house. Showers of plaster dust had fallen on the shoulders of Howell Crim's black suit. To the fear of fire in the White House was added the fear that at any time it might collapse.[3]

Remedies

"The White House is being closed immediately to all sightseers," announced the *Washington Post*, "because of its precarious physical condition." The paper speculated that the Trumans would move to Blair House, but the Trumans had made no statement to that effect. As soon as it was clear that the house was unsafe, Howell Crim got the President's permission to move. Initially, Crim reserved suites for the Trumans at the Carlton Hotel, lest Blair House not be ready by the time they returned from Missouri. But with the help of Charles T. Haight, head of the design department of B. Altman and Company, New York, Crim got it ready. Warehouses were scavenged; White House furnishings were moved across the street; window hangings from the White House were hemmed to fit Blair House; painters worked night and day. Blair House received the Trumans in time for Thanksgiving in 1948.[4]

The consultants on the structural condition of the White House met there on January 14, 1949, to consider what to do next. They learned that Lorenzo Winslow had mapped out an entire program, under the President's watchful eye. The external stone walls were to be preserved, together with the Coolidge-era third floor, but all else would go. Who came up with the idea is uncertain. The President wrote to a member of Congress: "My suggestion is that we do not tear down the present building. The outside walls are in good condition . . . . I believe with the right sort of a contractor and with proper supervision, the interior can be removed and . . . .We could put a steel and concrete structure inside the walls and restore the inside of the house to its original condition. We are saving all the doors, mantels, mirrors and things of that sort so that they will go back just as they were."[5]

The diary of the White House architect reveals that drawings were being made early in January 1949. Before the meeting on the 14th, Winslow noted a conference on the 11th with President Truman, which also included Reynolds, Major General Philip B. Fleming, the federal works administrator, and Edward F. Neild, a prominent architect from Shreveport, Louisiana. He had designed Truman's great skyscraper courthouse in Kansas City, and he was to serve as the President's personal architectural adviser during the renovation of the White House. At that session, the idea of saving the old stone walls and underpinning them was discussed, and Winslow showed a project for a new grand staircase, which Truman said he liked.

Of the meeting on the 14th, Winslow noted, "After some discussion we all agreed on the final work to be done in the White House. Complete program approved." With the earlier objectives confirmed by the consultants, Commissioner Reynolds, helped by Winslow and Fleming, as well as the President's staff, prepared a proposal to send to the Congress. Lorenzo Winslow wrote a long letter to Reynolds later that month describing Truman's goals: "It is the President's desire that this restoration be made so thoroughly complete that the structural condition and all principal and fixed architectural finishes will be permanent for many generations to come."[6]

The document sent to Congress called for a complete modernization, with special emphasis on fireproofing. It proposed 15 categories of improvement, giving high priority to four: 1) underpinning the foundations of the outer stone walls, putting the building on a secure stratum of sand and gravel at a level much below the existing footings; 2) removing all the interior walls; 3) building a freestanding structural steel frame within the old shell of stone and supporting it with concrete piers set in the same lower stratum of sand and gravel that would support the exterior walls; 4) transferring to the new independent interior structural steel frame "the weight of the structure and its contents except, principally, the weight of the exterior walls."[7]

In addition, sub-basements were to be built, with vaults to hold air-conditioning and other machinery. As much innovation as desirable was to be realized in the secondary and service spaces, but the program was to ensure "The retention and perpetuation. . . . of the first and second floors. . . . basic proportions, space dispositions, finishes, details and motifs. . . . " Moreover, "The exterior appearance of the building will not be changed."

The consultants had made a strong statement about what they believed was the symbolic value of the house: "No work is proposed in scope or detail that will alter the architectural or cultural features or impair the integrity of the building in its role of a National Shrine. In all respects the historic and traditional symbolism of the Nation's most revered mansion must be preserved to the greatest degree consistent with the use of modern materials and equipment that will be incorporated into the project." They emphasized that "No consideration has been given to the alternative of demolishing the present structure and replacing it with a new and modern building."[8]

Commissioner Reynolds presented the report, entitled "Elimination of Structural and Fire Hazards, Executive Mansion" to General Fleming on February 8 "for transmission to the Congress through the President." Two days later, the director of the Bureau of the Budget presented the final document to the President for approval, along with the estimate of $5,400,000 needed to accomplish the work. Within a week Truman sent the proposal to the Congress. He followed it in late March with a request that the Congress establish a commission "which would exercise general supervision and direction of all construction work involved in the renovation and modernization of the Mansion, including the approval of plans and the selection of contractors." Originally he had thought the work could be conducted "under my personal direction," however, that had been at a time when he had expected the work to be "confined to the second floor." When the project was expanded, wrote the President, "I . . . came to the conclusion that such a major renovation should have the participation of representatives of both Houses of the Congress as well as the Chief Executive because of the historical importance of the White House."[9]

The Commission for the Renovation of the Executive Mansion was established by an act of Congress on April 14, 1949, with the appropriation bill still in committee. The President hastened to appoint his six commissioners, including Richard E. Dougherty and Douglas W. Orr from the original committee of structural investigation. The four others were Senator Kenneth D. McKellar of Tennessee, at 80 years of age the president pro tempore of the Senate; Senator Edward Martin of Pennsylvania, one year McKellar's junior, venerable veteran of both world wars and the Republican representative from the Senate; representing the House were Congressman Louis C. Rabault of Michigan, a Democrat with background in the building business, and Congressman Frank B. Keefe, a banker and lawyer from Wisconsin, both in their 60s. Truman called the commissioners to the Cabinet Room at noon on June 3 for an informal session in which he gave his views on the work at hand.[10]

Commissioners

The appropriation was not approved until June 23, 1949, but by that time, with its orders in hand from the President, the commission had already been holding meetings. On June 16 it met in the Senate Office Building. President Truman, though not in attendance, was a looming presence; it was decided to enter into the minutes the fact that the Cabinet Room meeting with the President had taken place. Although the power of making appointments lay in the hands of the commissioners, Truman's hand was felt in nearly all of them. It is apparent that the President put Winslow in charge as architect, with the understanding that Winslow would deal directly with him. In setting up its rules of operation, the commissioners elected Orr as the liaison between themselves and Winslow. An accomplished architect from New Haven, Connecticut, Douglas W. Orr was a genial man who had a way of getting what he wanted. After Lorenzo Winslow announced at this meeting that the drawings for the White House renovation were 60 percent complete, Orr presented him with a long letter of requests for soil tests, analyses of antique mortars and materials, and other information relevant to construction.[11]

The consultants appointed that day were probably from a list provided by the President: William Adams Delano for design; Emil H. Praeger, an engineer, was a partner in Madigan & Hyland Co., New York; Ernest E. Howard, also an engineer, was president of Howard, Needles, Tammen & Bergendorf, Consulting Engineers, Kansas City, Missouri, and New York. The two engineers soon collaborated on a structural survey of the White House. For its executive director, the commission considered Major General Glenn E. Edgerton, recently retired from the office of the Army chief of staff, and also undoubtedly a recommendation of Truman's. Edgerton had demonstrated his managerial capabilities over nearly 40 years of military service in Panama, Alaska, Mexico, and in the Pacific. No man in public service was more highly respected by his peers. Edgerton knew his way around in the intricate system of the government in the capital.

The renovation commission took its work very seriously and functioned cohesively for the three years that it existed. Senator McKellar was elected chairman, and while he held his gavel firmly, he had little to say. The most outspoken was Congressman Rabault, who often took exception to what might otherwise have been unanimous decisions of the commission. Crusty and strong-minded, he opposed, for example, the retention of the external stone walls. An announcement had been made in the press that the walls would stay, but in August 1949 the commission had not yet made a formal resolution to that effect. Letters were pouring in favoring retention, and on August 3, the chairman wanted a final decision, so he could make it public. Rabault stood firm in his philosophical objection: "when we speak of retaining the exterior walls, we hold to a principle that we completely ignore in removing the interior of the first and second floors, which include the historical and sentimental features of the building. True, the fireplaces, the famous doors and exquisite panelling and other features are to be replaced—why should not the same consideration be given to the exterior walls? . . . We cling to the word 'preservation' in one sense, and entirely disregard it in another."[12]

The arguments this raised occupied the better part of the day. Billy Delano urged that the commissioners save the walls. Winslow protested that he had worked for a year and a half on plans incorporating the old walls, and to tear them down would delay the work from eight to ten months. Orr argued that most of the interior had been replaced by McKim, Mead, & White, that the external walls were original, while those inside the shell were, in most cases, not. The question was brought to a vote and passed in favor of saving the walls, with Congressman Rabault the lone dissenter.

After a few initial meetings in the Senate Office Building, General Edgerton moved to offices of his own in the White House. First occupying the ground floor library, he moved to the movie theater in the East Wing when demolition started in the main structure, then finally moved out to a separate building set up for the purpose among the carpentry sheds. Edgerton proved an able director, working closely with Winslow. He had as his assistant Colonel Douglas H. Gillette, Winslow's colleague and the engineer who had helped build Roosevelt's swimming pool in

1933. The office staff was thus a tight-knit group, most of them old acquaintances. Their main relationships with the commission on renovation were through Orr and Dougherty, both of whom were actively engaged in every aspect of the work.[13]

Design

Lorenzo Simmons Winslow, the architect of the reconstruction, holds a position in the chronicles of the White House with Hoban and McKim. He has not, however, enjoyed the fame of the other two; the glory of the remodeler has less luster than that of the creator. He owned valuable rental property in Georgetown, as well as a fine 18th-century house which he had restored; he shared it with his wife, Garnett, who was blind, and his daughters. At the time of the rebuilding, Winslow was a character of note about town. Having been an important staff member at the White House for some years, he was recognized as a man of influence, and people sought him out. He smoked a corncob pipe and drove about in an old automobile, which he kept in perfect order himself, sometimes devoting an entire Sunday to making repairs. Outside all this, Winslow had a secret life. He tumbled into amorous adventures with a succession of women. During the reconstruction of the White House he recorded his infidelities in his diary. Yet another secret side of him was fascinated by the occult. Winslow communed with spirits and claimed that he talked to the dead, including former Presidents.[14]

As architect of the White House, Winslow had a staff of three draftsmen and one secretary. They worked in a single room at the south end of the East Wing, overlooking the south grounds; the drawings for the reconstruction of the White House were made on large wooden drafting tables lighted by fluorescent lamps overhead and from tall windows shaded by venetian blinds. Winslow's chief draftsman was Horbin S. Chandler, a gifted delineator, whom he mentioned occasionally in his diary. Although it is generally assumed that most of the ideas for the reconstruction originated with Winslow and were put on paper by the draftsmen, it seems probable that Chandler often served as more than a draftsman, as when Winslow noted on New Year's Day 1949, "Chandler finished new stair design."[15]

Designs made in Winslow's office were approved by the President and Billy Delano before they were taken before the commission. Because of failing health, Delano was not much on the scene, and after 1949 he participated largely from his office in Manhattan. Lorenzo Winslow usually rode up on the Pullman, arriving in New York in time for a relatively early appointment and also an early return to Washington. Now and then Delano and Winslow crossed swords, but in general the consulting architect was as agreeable as ever, realizing, no doubt, that to buck the President was likely to be futile. It was better, he felt, to remain on the job, securing as much as possible of what he believed was right. By and large Delano seems to have been pleased, as was Orr, with the plans that eventually developed.

Nearly all the design decisions were made by the close of 1949. As announced, the house was unchanged on the outside. Inside, the state floor was more or less the same in plan as McKim had left it in 1902, the only radical change being the location and character of the grand stair-case. Truman had ardently disliked the old grand stair; long before there was a White House commission, he had encouraged Winslow to design a new grand stair that would be perfectly suited to the procession of the President and his guests. The old stair happened to be situated near a structural column, buried within the walls, that was crucial to the sup-port of that part of the White House. At first, Winslow designed around the column. When the decision was made to gut the house, the column was no longer an obstacle, and Truman demanded the perfect solution to the stair problem.

At last, in the fall of 1949, Winslow produced a stair design that suited the President, who may have approved the idea for it as early as January 1948. The commission, in any case, saw it for the first time on September 30, 1949, and Billy Delano objected to it so strongly that he took the train down from New York to register his opposition. Winslow had designed the stair to land in the east side of the entrance hall instead of the transverse corridor; he had removed the screen of columns that had divided the entrance hall from the transverse hall. The stair itself descended gently from the second floor to a landing, then to a second landing, then, finally, to a platform only a few steps above the floor of the entrance hall. The stage created by the platform made an appropriate setting for the presidential entrance. Delano felt that it wholly changed the character of the house. Since the President would not proceed with-out Delano's imprimatur, two concessions were made to the indomitable Billy. The columns were restored, and Winslow agreed to design a large opening from the new stair looking out on the transverse hall. Approval was unanimous.[16]

The ground floor's groin-vaulted hall was to be faithfully repro-duced—though wainscoted in marble—and the plan of rooms would reflect that of the original house, with the old kitchen beneath the en-trance hall re-created, complete to the stone arches and the two great fireplaces. On the second floor the arrangement remained the same, except that the bathrooms were more conveniently located and there were more closets. The long central cross corridor was divided by great arches into three parts, with the giant lunette windows east and west. Off this hallway opened bedrooms and sitting rooms, and at the center to the south was the oval room, the President's study. Where the house was to be remarkably different was in the areas beyond the familiar ground floor, state floor, and family floor. In the "new" areas, as much space was borrowed as possible for service rooms. Mezzanine levels were introduced at the far ends of the house. Two served the pantry off the State Dining Room; another served the ushers' office beside the north door; others at the east end of the house contained ample rest rooms for guests and were reached by elegant curving staircases.

Winslow's plan was of far greater extent than the public realized: The building was to be vast, with all of the new parts out of sight. A reproduction of the three floors of the original house was to be built in the midst of an institutional complex, which would make the White House functional as a modern residence of state.[17]

Beneath what had always been called the "basement" were to be two sub-basements. This lower area was to be linked to the rest of the house by elevators, the terminal of traffic for the servants being the pantry on the northwest corner. The various levels were all connected by stairs. Halls divided ranges of small, simply furnished rooms which would house the laundry, cleaning services, carpenters' and plumbers' shops, and storage. This anthill of domestic management was to be presided over as ever by the chief usher from the venerable office to the right of the north door. In addition Howell Crim was to have a hideaway in a little mezzanine above his office, a cozy retreat lighted by a bit of one of the great front windows.

Although the new areas seem never to have given the architect much trouble, he worried over the historic parts. In the design, Winslow's knowledge of the White House past appeared everywhere. Forced by the dictates of the law, the commissioners, and his own inclination to make heavy use of modern permanent and fireproof materials, he also appreciated the old, and from the outset urged the careful conservation and reuse of paneling, window sash, molding, and doors. As it happened, most of this could not be reused; Winslow, however, saved what he could. He planned to finish the basement rooms in pine paneling made from timbers used in the old house frame. Fragments of early plaster moldings found in the walls were copied for some rooms, replacing the trimmings put up by McKim, Mead, & White. Wherever possible, the new, he believed, should reflect the old, yet he also felt that he must "restore," in the sense that the house should conform to the taste of the Federal era when James Hoban rebuilt it. For this purpose he spent much time copying or adapting interior detailing from historic houses in the region.[18]

In May 1949 Winslow took his drawings to Williamsburg, where he met with the resident architect of the restoration, A. Edwin Kendrew. Kendrew and his colleague Bela Norton took Winslow through the Brush house, a restored colonial cottage, and the Governor's Palace, a reconstructed mansion, the original of which had been well known to Washington and Jefferson. The palace, built entirely new, must have foreshadowed to Winslow the reconstructed White House. Winslow's visit to the Governor's Palace at Williamsburg seems to have convinced him of the importance of preserving the original White House woodwork and decorations, for they alone would provide the patina of age. A month after his return from Williamsburg he addressed the commission: "There is a matter which I consider to be of vital importance . . . . This is the careful dismantling, removal and storage of all interior and exterior finish materials . . . which are intended to be restored when necessary and then to be reinstalled in the reconstructed building."[19]

He further occupied himself and his staff making measured drawings of the ornamental plaster of the state rooms. He urged the commission to contract with "a local ornamental plaster sculptor to make casts in place of all existing ornamental plaster work that is not easily removable in one complete piece. . . . Much of the ornamental plaster, I have had very accurate measured drawings made, together with rubbings in place."[20]

To some extent, the architect was granted his wish. With pressures from all sides to hurry along, the commissioners attended to matters they thought more urgent than a delicate dismantling. Winslow was the only one involved who had a sincere interest in preserving the old materials; the others were saving not a house but a symbol. On November 3, 1949, at their 13th meeting, the commissioners selected John McShain, Inc., of Philadelphia as the low bidder on the job of reconstruction. Builder of the Jefferson Memorial, Roosevelt's library at Hyde Park, and the Pentagon—the biggest job it had ever handled—the McShain company was held in high regard in Washington. On December 12 a subcontractor, Spencer, White & Prentis, Inc., of New York, began the process of underpinning the stone walls.

The next day, December 13, the dismantling of the interior began, with Winslow supervising much of it. This took a little more than two months, with the interruption of the Christmas holiday. The paneling of the East Room was pulled away from the wall, numbered, crated, and hauled to storage in a federal warehouse at Seventh and D Streets; window and door trimming, mantelpieces, hearths, chair rails, baseboards, wainscoting, even window sash and reveals, were carefully taken down. It was not easy work; panels split and door frames broke as they were pried from their places, the wood dry and often brittle, the paint peeling away in long strips.

Winslow felt that the oak paneling in the State Dining Room was the most important and saved it until last, only to have the commission turn the work over to the contractor and urge the architect back to his drafting tables. Wood flooring was pulled up, numbered, and crated. Winslow reported to the commission on February 16, 1950, that about half the sash on the first floor and two-thirds of that on the second had been removed, the sockets of the windows covered over for protection. On the 17th the commission declared the dismantling completed, except for some window sash. Little was said about what happened to the materials, for Winslow took the responsibility for storage and moving, assisted toward the end by Howell Crim.

The commissioners were far more interested in creating relics for sale and distribution from the timbers and discarded plaster decorations than in rescuing anything for reuse. On January 30, 1950, a plan by General Edgerton for the disposal of old materials, using ideas from many sources, had been presented to the President. Truman approved it on February 17, and a quantity of relic "kits" became available. Kit number one, for example, cost $2 and contained enough pine to make a gavel; kit number two, the same price, offered pine in sufficient quantity to make a walking stick; kit number four provided a small piece of sandstone and a square nail; kit number ten contained "one brick, as nearly whole as practicable." For $100 enough brick or stone could be bought to face a fireplace. "The entire operation," the commissioners wrote in their final report, "was designed to be self-supporting and it turned out to be so, by a considerable margin."[21]

The Vessel Is Emptied

The demolition and rebuilding of the White House within stone walls was a remarkable achievement. Hoban had built his walls on a shallow stratum of clay and gravel, and over 157 years some shifting had taken place. He had made the foundations for the interior bearing walls only half the width of the walls themselves, and they had become more heavily burdened than the external shell. The outside sandstone walls, lined inside with several layers of brick and sealed with whitewash and paint since they were first laid, represented a mixture of work done in the 1790s and during the 1815–17 rebuilding; only the south front had remained relatively intact from the earliest years. Aquia sandstone is highly porous and this old stonework showed its age, but otherwise the walls were in good condition.

Spencer, White & Prentis was the leading engineering firm in the United States specializing in the stabilization of old buildings. Edmund Astley Prentis and Lazarus White, the two partners directly involved with the White House work, wrote during construction that their company "was awarded the sub-contract for what might be called the structural work—that is, underpinning, excavation, and new foundations." In concert with the commission's consulting engineers, Ernest E. Howard and Emil H. Praeger, their first effort was the underpinning of the old walls. Winslow's borings, and those of Professor D. M. Burmister, showed that a firm stratum of gravel about 20 feet thick lay about 25 feet below the surface; this would be adequate to hold the renewed White House, with its added basements and concrete and steel inner structure. Underpinning the walls required digging pits about four feet square at intervals down to this gravel stratum, then filling the pits with reinforced concrete, which created a powerful column of supports. Some 126 of these were dug over a period of about six months.[22]

The underpinning and the dismantling of the interior started at about the same time in December 1949. Several weeks later, at the beginning of the new year, the shoring process commenced. Its purpose was to hold the stone walls together as a shell, as well as to support the heavy steel and concrete structure of the third floor and roof while the interior was removed below it. In the simplest terms, steel "towers"—groups of steel columns—extended up through the house, and a system of crossbeams and diagonal bracing rods provided lateral stability for these. The initial tower was begun in the center of the house as soon as the Blue Room was dismantled.

Winslow angrily complained that the engineers were rushing his removal of the fine finish materials, noting that in the hurry to vacate the Blue Room, someone stole the bronze ornaments from the marble mantel. But this changed nothing; speed was essential, and a hole was torn from the basement to the third floor, about 12 feet by 25, to receive the first group of shoring columns. Another great shoring hole was cut in the East Room, sub-basement level to attic, and another between the State Dining Room and the private dining room—all more or less in an east-to-west line running across the house. Some of the shoring towers contained temporary columns; others were permanent, so located as to be eventually hidden in the walls of the restored transverse halls.

A sharp distinction was made between "dismantling" and "demolition." When the former was completed on March 23, 1950, the latter, which had already begun slowly, increased to a fast pace. No particular care was taken to preserve anything intact during demolition, except the thick pine framing timbers which were later to be milled for paneling the ground floor rooms. Plaster moldings that had been measured and cast for reproduction fell into the category of debris, as did wall plaster and wood and metal lath, subflooring, pine flooring in secondary rooms, and many secondary doors. The windows had become empty sockets with temporary and easily removable covers, their old mahogany sash removed to storage. Much of the wreckage was thrown into trucks through wooden chutes outside convenient windows. Some of the wood, bits of plaster ornament, and as many square nails as could be rescued were set aside to sell in relic kits. Winslow picked up a brick with the imprint of a dog's paw, the record of an animal's venture into the drying yard a century and a half before.

As the interior of the house slowly vanished, new steel framing became more evident, defining the five levels that were to comprise the rebuilt house: two sub-basements, the basement or ground floor, the second and third floors, in addition to the small mezzanines at the east and west ends. The flooring was to be reinforced concrete poured on steel bedding, making each room in a sense a cage of steel; this structural material would, however, be buried behind plaster and fine surface finishes. In the autumn of 1950 the Washington *Evening Star* reported, "A massive steel structure of skyscraper strength was near completion today within the once unstable walls of the White House. . . . the mansion rests upon completely new and reinforced foundations, extending 24 feet below the old, and an extraordinarily heavy steel frame . . . has assumed the load once borne by the stone walls."[23]

Once the immense rectangular box was cleaned of its historic insides, it was an awesome sight, a great hollow space some 85 feet north to south, 165 feet east to west, and 70 or 80 feet high. Crossed by the steel framing, the vast shell could be viewed from catwalks at all levels. Trucks and tractors entered through a passage on the northeast, left open in the side of the new sub-basements, well beneath the old stone walls. Before the excavations that created this entrance had begun, a tractor for digging had been brought through an existing doorway in pieces and reassembled, because the President would not allow an opening cut into the original stone.[24]

The old stone walls attracted a great deal of attention. They had never been seen from this perspective, even when new. Steel construction had stripped them of the interior they once embraced and exposed their naked insides. Most of what was revealed was the brick backing, soft bricks, low fired, that crumbled easily when rubbed. The outer steel members were erected near them, leaving a slight space. In November 1950 the weight of the structure was transferred entirely to the new steel skeleton, leaving the old stone walls to support only their own dead weight. They were battered-looking inside, with channels for gas and water pipes, gravity heating ducts, and hand-powered service bell systems, the luxuries of ages gone by. Truman found them not only picturesque but fascinating as well, and he liked to travel the high catwalks, where he could study the stones at close range.

The President quickly began to notice the marks of identification left by the original stonemasons, the curious chisel designs described in the early pages of this book. He pronounced the marks "Masonic"—which was in part correct, as it turned out—and ordered all he could see extracted, some to be set into the walls of the restored ground floor kitchen and the rest sent to the grand lodges of the Masonic orders of every state in the Union, along with a letter which read in part: "I place in your hands a stone taken from the walls of The White House. . . . These evidences of the number of members of the Craft who built the President's official residence so intimately aligns Freemasonry with the formation and the founding of our Government that I believe your Grand Lodge will cherish this link between the Fraternity and the Government of the Nation, of which the White House is a symbol."[25]

Interiors

The commission usually assembled at the White House every ten days, meeting in some part of the East Wing, which, like the West Wing and Executive Office, was still in regular use. Already in the spring of 1950, when the inside of the White House was an echoing chasm, the subject of the interiors and their design began to come up regularly. At this juncture, Howell Crim asserted himself, claiming responsibility, indeed demanding, as chief usher, substantial control. Crim was particularly worried that the $200,000 appropriated would be inadequate to decorate the house. David E. Finley, the new chairman of the Commission of Fine Arts, wondered whether those in charge had the good taste to restore the interiors as he thought they should be.[26]

It was a time in world affairs when anyone was likely to worry, especially those concerned with the White House. During the early summer of 1950 the invasion of South Korea by North Korean forces raised the specter of a third world war. The military and the Secret Service convinced Truman to make the lower of the two new sub-basements bombproof, and the commission was informed of this, no questions asked, on August 16: "The President has authorized certain protective measures at basement level in and adjacent to the wings of the White House. Plans for this work are now being developed by the Architect of the White House and Public Buildings Service." The work was to include "strengthening the [concrete] walls of the basement corridor; increasing the thickness of the [concrete] floor above it, and thickening the mezzanine floor over the three northeast rooms of the basement." Additional costs were to be borne by the commissioner of public buildings.[27]

On November 1 an attempt was made on Truman's life by two members of the Puerto Rican nationalist movement who tried to enter Blair House under gunfire. A brief and bloody scene on the sidewalk outside resulted in the deaths of one of the would-be assassins and a White House guard. Security around the President was intensified, but the incident had no immediate effect upon the plans for the White House. The Korean War, however, was quite another matter. Through the autumn of 1950 prices for building materials soared, and supplies were sparse; there was an average working force of 250 men. The contractor, John McShain, wrote to Commissioner Reynolds: "Because of the world and our country's related unsettled conditions and the preparedness and defense programs now in progress in our country, both materials and labor are in such short supply that the resulting conditions make it impossible to properly schedule and complete construction work."[28]

The commission pressed McShain to quicken his pace, and he obligingly continued to work, protesting both high prices and federal controls on the sale of building materials, and accusing the architect of not producing working drawings quickly enough. Winslow asked for more draftsmen, and was denied. The pressures became extreme, until, after much effort and with assistance from the President, the Office of Price Administration granted the commission a limited priority on purchasing, on the basis that since this was to be the President's house, his protection was an essential feature of the project; thus the renovation was classed as a defense effort, an aspect of security for the commander in chief. The special exception was to prove valuable in moving the effort toward completion in 1952.

Meanwhile, the persistent Crim and Finley interjected something about the interior decoration at nearly every commission meeting. Crim, who had official status, rarely missed a session, but it was necessary for Finley to wangle an invitation. He was chairman of a new and largely Truman-appointed Commission of Fine Arts, which had nevertheless not yet been asked to approve the plans for the White House. But David Finley doggedly surmounted this embarrassing slight. Possessed of a deceptively meek appearance, he was a small man with pale to pinkish skin, and a soft falsetto voice; in his conversation—which was nearly constant—he was witty, southern-style, a fountain of funny stories. A fellow South Carolinian who knew him well remarked that in getting his way, "he has the persistence of a team of mules." He was determined to have a hand in the redecoration of the White House because he believed that by law the Commission of Fine Arts had the authority to make the decisions. If Truman blocked the commission's exercise of its legal functions, he would achieve the same end himself, entering as it were through a side door.[29]

The old advisory committee, made up of people known to Finley, was also anxious to take part in the renovation. Mrs. Pratt had met with Mrs. Truman early and they had corresponded pleasantly in 1945. After the renovation began, she and other committee members began to push for recognition through Billy Delano. In late August 1950 Delano wrote a letter on the subject to Douglas Orr, and a copy found its way to the President, whose response suggested that he was annoyed: "I want it distinctly understood that this matter will be closely watched by me and that there is going to be no special privileged people allowed to decide what will be done with the refurnishing of the White House. . . . I am very much interested in the proper replacement of the furniture in the White House in the manner in which it should be placed, and since I am the only President in fifty years who has had any interest whatever in the rehabilitation of the White House, I am going to see that it is done properly and correctly. . . . I do know something about the proper arrangement in interior decoration, particularly as it affects the White House and I am going to see that it is done in the proper manner."[30]

The subject was brought up no more. Delano, who had avoided White House conflicts even while in his prime, had no intention of starting to fight in old age. Furnishing the house was the responsibility of the building commission, and already Howell Crim was urging that a contract be given to B. Altman & Company. The formal proposal from Altman's was submitted on September 21, 1950, with the president of the Manhattan department store, John S. Burke, making the presentation himself. He assured the commission that "If called upon to furnish furniture, rugs, draperies, accessories or any other furnishings for the

White House, the firm of B. Altman & Co. will be happy to supply these goods at absolute cost. Cost in this instance consists of the invoice billing to B. Altman & Co. from any of its manufacturers or suppliers, including any expenses incurred for installation and shipping, without any additional overhead added thereto. The only other costs that may enter into a situation of this kind would be any taxes that we would be compelled to pay and any out of pocket expenses that may be incurred."[31]

Most of Altman's competitors probably would have made a similar offer, but they never got the chance. Altman's was trusted at the White House as a result of past services and that tipped the scale in its favor; John Burke wrote " . . . we do not enter into any work of this kind with the thought that we wish to use this contact for publicity or profit in any form, but offer our facilities rather in a spirit of helpfulness, taking pride only in the fact that we may be of service."

The long and happy relationship between Altman's and the White House was personified in the chief of the design department, Chuck Haight, who was liked by everyone from the President down. A native of Minneapolis, he had been educated as a decorator first at Parsons in New York, then for five years in Paris; he liked to recall, half-amused, half in awe, how his teacher Frank Alvah Parsons had taken him again and again to Versailles to rhapsodize over the taste of the 17th and 18th centuries. Parsons never failed to say: "It was never better at any time in the history of the world." Chuck Haight attended the September meeting, where he presented an impressive report.[32]

At that time the commission hoped to have the Trumans back in the White House within about a year, by the fall of 1951. Haight was asked, given that all approvals were in by January 1951, if he could meet the deadline. He replied that he could. Haight described some of the major projects of Altman's, the Morris Inn at Notre Dame, C. B. Whitney's residence on Long Island, which, said the decorator, "is a gorgeous place where they made reproductions of great value." Asked by commission member Dougherty, the civil engineer, if Altman's had ever done restoration work at Williamsburg, Haight's reply was negative, but he added that he had recently been asked to reconstruct and decorate the ballroom at Gadsby's Tavern, an old landmark over in Alexandria, approximately the age of the White House. When called upon to talk about his art, Haight was silver-tongued, masking somewhat the steely pragmatism of a good merchandiser.[33]

The commissioners began asking Haight questions. From Douglas Orr: How would you proceed, if you got the contract? "It was a big invitation to speak up," remembered Haight, and he asked in return, "do you want a contemporary overtone with some old things, or should [the White House] be as I think, with antiques of the period?" He reviewed the materials in storage. "There is not much of top calibre. There are things you'd better not use at all. Which brings up the question of how much can you spend for what *should* be in the White House. You have to tell me a great many things before I can answer you."

"Mr. Haight," said Orr, "we have $210,000 left for furnishings and interior decoration."

"My God," said Haight, "do you know how many rooms you have—I mean even a little space with a door and a window? My count is 210 rooms. You could spend your $210,000 in the blinking of an eye—on one or two rooms. I can spend your $210,000 the best it could be spent and Altman's will not make a penny. But it is not enough."

The rumble of conversation that followed this was interrupted by Delano. He spoke in a low voice—Haight remembered it sounded like that of "a professor of grammar"—and admonished the commission, "I don't think it's fair to ask Mr. Haight to come up with an opinion of how, when and where this house shall be done. It's a monumental question. *We* must make decisions."

Under pressure from Crim, who was obviously representing the views of the President and Mrs. Truman, Altman's got the contract, with the understanding all around that Charles T. Haight would be the principal on the job. Haight later admitted that he found the terms "vague." The budget was to cover everything—painting, finishing of the floors, curtains, refinishing of the old furniture. "I have no idea how far your money will go," he told the commissioners.[34]

He got to work at once. Winslow provided architectural drawings, and Delano offered an open door to his home or office whenever Haight needed help or advice. They became close friends, the younger Haight gaining a respect for Delano that amounted almost to hero worship. Several times when he called, Harriet Pratt was with Delano, and she looked over Haight's plans with relish: Haight found her "A square of the squarest sort, but a great lady." His and Finley's paths eventually crossed in Washington. At first he tried to avoid the chairman of the Commission of Fine Arts, but because Finley made it his business to become close to Howell Crim, he found himself meeting with him more and more, at Crim's request. Personally Haight found Finley "A very arrogant individual. He seemed always to say 'who is this man coming down from that department store telling us how to furnish the White House?' "[35]

To simplify the decision-making on the furnishings, the commission for the rebuilding appointed Delano and Orr in January 1951 to be the final authorities on the interior decoration. With the same stroke it specified that these two would consider the views of the following: the Truman family, the chief usher, the commissioner of public buildings, Winslow, and David Finley, as chairman of the Commission on Fine Arts. Finley had thus established more than a foot in the door, and Haight had no choice but to deal with him. Apart from minor discourtesies, Haight and Finley got along well after that. After the commission's January clarification of the relationships on the interiors, the work was able to move faster. On the 26th Finley, Delano, Winslow, and Crim met at the National Gallery to select the furniture they believed needed to be sent on to New York for restoration by B. Altman & Company.

At the next meeting, January 23, both Haight and Delano read prepared statements. Haight announced that the color schemes for the state rooms should be approved by all parties within three weeks; floor plans and "water color perspective drawings" of the rooms should be ready by mid-February, together with samples of all proposed materials. "We have been urged," he continued, "and are attempting. . . . to plan the entire first floor as nearly as possible in accordance with past traditions and to expend the principal sums of money in the east room, blue room, green room, red room, State dining room, President's dining room and halls." Delano's report followed, in which he went floor by floor, giving his opinion about mantels, chandeliers, rugs, and what new furniture he felt was necessary. "The Lincoln Room should be preserved as a historic monument," he wrote, "and could be furnished with its old pieces and perhaps a few others in character."[36]

By March most of the perspectives had been completed, and on the 15th Orr reported to the commission his delight with what he had seen. He also introduced a rather tender subject that had already come up among those working on the interiors, the painting of the English oak paneling of the State Dining Room. Orr explained to the commissioners that though the interior had actually been built only in 1902, it had been "done in the period of the building of the White House." The idea for painting it pale green came from either Haight or Delano during one of their sessions in New York, because they thought painted wood more appropriate to the 18th-century style than natural oak. Winslow and Finley had agreed.[37]

Most of the salvaged wood finish materials, including the paneling from the State Dining Room, was in the shop of Knipp & Co., the finish woodwork subcontractor. Knipp's had been known for many years for its fine marine carpentry and joinery; since the war it had branched out into interior woodwork and furnishings, including the House and Senate chambers, which it had rebuilt. The Knipp brothers took exception to painting the paneling of the State Dining Room because "crotch marks, blemishes and tool marks which offer an asset in the natural finish may show up as a liability in the painted finish." Samples of the oak painted were brought forward. After some debate, the commission took the views of its own advisers and stuck to the plan for painting the walls pale green, one of those chilly whitish greens of the early days of air-conditioning.[38]

In the course of these discussions David Finley seems to have been less interested in the rooms than in the idea of having the Commission of Fine Arts play a part in their decoration. Accordingly, he invited various people to study plans with him and give their views, notably Mrs. Dwight Davis and Mrs. Pratt. Delano was always available to consult in New York, but seldom came to Washington, unless absolutely necessary. As often as possible Haight met with him and felt that he learned something new about architecture and design every time.

Douglas Orr intervened in decisions on the interiors very little. He agreed that the State Dining Room paneling should be painted. When woodwork costs got too high, he supported Knipp's suggestion that "pressed wood ornament" be used, saying "when it is painted it will look just like the carved wood." Piece by piece the original woodwork was declared unreusable. First the chair rails, then the door framing and many of the doors, and finally most of the paneling for the East Room. At last the commissioners agreed to use "machine carved wood ornaments in all places except the State Dining Room." The mahogany sash, so carefully removed at the outset, was found to be in such poor condition that the commission decided to have it copied. Of the original wood finish material, only that of the State Dining Room survived in any semblance of completeness, and it was heavily supplemented and repaired.[39]

Crim, sometimes with Haight, took all designs to Mrs. Truman soon after he received them. Mrs. Truman made it clear that she was leaving most of the decorating to the professionals: "It would be unfair to the next First Lady to impose too many of my ideas upon the house." Haight remembered that Mrs. Truman, and occasionally Margaret Truman, went over the drawings and inspected the samples "rather ceremonially." He gave them many alternatives and combinations, but "pushed the key fabrics." Even as the design was in progress, Haight and his assistant Margaret Watts were "dealing with the business" in New York, trying to get fabrics and other materials at cost. "We laughed our way into it," he remembered. Franco Scalamandré pulled out bolts of silk for Haight to inspect; what the decorator wanted was $30 per yard, but after an appeal to Scalamandré on behalf of the nation's first house, he yielded: "we paid Scalamandré $3.50 a yard." Chuck Haight observed a quarter of a century later that he and Miss Watts had "robbed our friends blind."[40]

In the end the commission genuinely appreciated the hard work of David Finley. He had no official role; he was simply an adviser who happened to be chairman of the Commission of Fine Arts. Finley at last got what he wanted—recognition—for his commision on June 19, 1951, when, at the suggestion of Crim, Winslow, and Reynolds, the White House commission decided to seek approval of all its design plans from the Commission of Fine Arts, which had not been consulted directly since 1949. It was, however, a bit after the fact, for the White House was well along toward completion, and no plans were likely to be changed. When Finley was informed of this decision, he decided to be a little obstinate, insisting that his fellow commissioners must first walk through the building and study the plans on the site before they could vote. He took his time; he made his point. Afterward he wrote a gracious letter to the President, fully approving all that had been planned, all that had been carried out, and all that would be brought to fruition in the months of construction that lay ahead.[41]

The Pressures Mount

Repeated change-orders and the difficulty of altering working drawings caused delays, and further time was lost in trying to acquire building materials, especially metals. But the wheels of construction did turn. The arduous process of building the original house bore no parallel in the rebuilding. The new house materialized from all parts of the steel skeleton, the third floor being constructed at the same time as the first. The great stone shell, once empty save for steel supports beneath the heavy roof and third floor, soon gained horizontal levels of concrete, articulating once again the original four floors of the house and the two new ones below the old basement; unfamiliar levels forecast the mezzanines, relatively small "stacks" of low-ceilinged areas east and west.

On a cold Saturday morning toward the end of 1950, Truman took the journalist John Hersey on a tour. "We found ourselves in an eerie space," wrote Hersey, entering the ground floor. "Hemmed in by thick, ancient masonry walls, which were patinated with old plasters and paints of many faded shades, we stood nevertheless on a raw concrete floor, and we looked up and saw over our heads another bare concrete slab, supported by rows of naked concrete columns. There were as yet no partitions. Directly before us, along what would evidently become a hallway, were suspended from above, at about chest height, some very big galvanized-metal hot-air ducts. The scene was anachronistic; it was as if someone had decided to set up a modern office inside a deserted castle."[42]

It had become evident to the commissioners not long before Hersey's tour that their original objective of completing the White House a year hence, in October 1951, was impossible. The contractor received most of the blame, unjustly, and resented it. On New Year's Day 1951 McShain saw the President at the Army-Navy football game, and while walking along with him in good spirits, said that he would have the White House finished in five months. The President conveyed this to the commission, which erupted in anger at McShain for making such a promise. While McShain did apologize, the commission had to live with the result: Truman wanted the project to speed up. He would be in office only until January 1953, and he wished to live in the White House for as long as possible. He set a new deadline, Christmas 1951.

The pace quickened on all fronts. A caravan of trucks rolled from the White House to Fort Myer and back for 22 days, hauling building debris to be used as landfill. This was done in some secrecy, to avoid bad publicity, and was under the direction of Douglas Gillette. Other materials were donated to the wood shops of military installations and to schools and correctional facilities in the Washington area. Most of the surplus bricks were given to Mount Vernon for use in the reconstruction of George Washington's greenhouse, although bricks were also sent in some quantity to other historical sites. Mount Vernon received the Seneca sandstone from the original double stairs to the south portico, which were replaced in granite. Yet greater quantities of stone and brick seem to have become part of the landfill, along with doors, paneling, and other more perishable materials.[43]

In the winter of 1951 the work force rose at times to 300, and in spite of strikes, which pulled some workers off the job for short periods, the progress was remarkable. Most interior partitions were completed by the summer, with at least the mud coat of plaster on all of them. Teams of plasterers did their work even faster than had been anticipated, although they struck for two weeks beginning August 3. From the plaster casting shed on the grounds the moldings were brought in and put in place, a process that would continue for many months.

Winslow was given several more draftsmen, bringing his office staff to seven, with a secretary and himself. Hours were long. Trying to satisfy both the commission and the President exhausted him, and in addition he faced daily difficulties with the contractor's supervisors. On his own, Douglas Gillette took charge of the new designs for security measures in the sub-basement, but Gillette was sure he would be called away on active Army duty to Korea, so the threat of having to assume his work load hung over Winslow. To intensify pressures, the architect was deeply entangled in a love affair. He stole time to be with her whenever he could, no matter what the time of day; in the evenings the two of them shared an interest in the occult over a Ouija board or in seances: "I went . . . to Seance on materialization. John Faber called and stated he was the designer of the W. H. for Hoban. F.D.R. appeared and presented a rose to me as did Andrew [Jackson]. . . . Very wonderful."[44]

The interiors began to take shape, and by late spring of 1951 the state rooms had reassumed their familiar contours. Parquet flooring was being laid; wood trimmings were going up, and some mantels had been brought in. Haight and Margaret Watts were on the scene for a day in nearly every week, taking measurements to double-check those in the plans, and meeting with Finley and Crim. The historic rooms were to be restored to more or less what they had been; the same pattern of silk was ordered from Schumacher, Inc., for the walls of the parlors. Offstage, the house could as easily have been a modern hotel, for the new service areas bore no resemblance to the former White House. They were purely utilitarian, finished in an institutional style with asphalt tile floors and unadorned architecture.

On August 7, 1951, the commissioners were told that Billy Delano might be ill for a long time. They became anxious to have every detail on paper so that he could give his approvals as soon as possible. Haight was ordered to make a "color plan" of all the rooms in the house, and this he produced three days later. The decorator's design boards were passed around. Though Haight presented most of the colors as being of the late 18th century, they were nearly all adapted, showing the strident hues of the postwar years. For the Blue Room the dark blue of McKim was somewhat lightened toward a royal blue; the Red Room's color was similar to the one Mrs. Franklin D. Roosevelt had put there, not as dark as McKim's, and in damask instead of the velvet of 1902; the Green Room, which Haight had rehung in silk not long before the renovation, was put back in exactly the same bright color. Window hangings were to be the same material as that on the walls. Elsewhere in the house Haight's plans called for more modern colors in the lively palette of the time, together with large-scale patterns in damask, printed linen, and polished cotton.[45]

That same summer, the commissioners returned to the Congress for more money. Orr wrote to the President: "A careful review of the costs of the work to date on the project for the renovation of the White House and of estimates of the costs yet to be incurred shows that it will not be possible to complete the project satisfactorily within the present appropriation. It is estimated that additional funds to the amount of $225,000 will be required. The over-run is principally attributable to the effects of the Korean war. Costs have risen rapidly during the past year. . . . when the effects of the war became evident the Commission had the entire project reviewed and the specifications modified to reduce costs by every practical substitution of materials and simplification of work that would permit savings without very serious detriment to the quality needed in this special project." The funding was achieved with little difficulty, but on July 17 Crim was given the unhappy task of telling Truman that he would not be in the White House by Christmas. He "reluctantly" told him that March 1952 was his guess, and it proved correct.[46]

Entering the autumn of 1951, the White House project employed some 300 workmen, not counting government officials involved in various ways. Most of the plastering was finished, some of it already covered with canvas in preparation for painting or upholstering. The new Doric columns of Westland cream, a lightly clouded Vermont marble, were being put up in the entrance hall; installation of flooring started in September and would continue with constant difficulty for six months. Most of the lighting fixtures sent for repair to Edward Caldwell in New York were delayed. Those for the East Room, originally reduced in scale by McKim, were being reduced again. Ordinary lighting fixtures were being rewired in Washington, and when the chandelier for the private dining room arrived wired and with light bulbs Winslow rose in protest: The chandelier in that room had always burned candles and the tradition should be kept; at the direction of the commission, it was.

The difficulty of getting appropriate marble had troubled the commissioners for many months. It had been decided to replace the East Room mantels with red marble ones of Knoxville marble, in honor of the chairman, Senator McKellar of Tennessee. On November 2, 1951, it was reported that 15 men were working full time at the quarry on the four East Room mantels. Winslow, who had designed the mantels himself, was sent there several times to inspect the progress. He made every effort to save and reuse the Joliet stone flooring from the entrance hall, but the contractor opposed it and most of it joined the caravan to Fort Myer. The marble for the grand staircase was changed after half of it had been cut, and the resulting delay ran into months. Winslow was criticized for this by the commissioners on September 21, although they must have known that he was acting on his chief's orders. Pressure was beginning to bear upon everyone.

Winslow seems to have suffered the most. Had he simply taken orders, his ride would have been smoother, but the drawings were produced in his office, and most of the decisions at the paper stage were his. He had to defend many of his solutions. His frequent stand against the disposal of old materials—which may have been made with the President's encouragement—met with annoyance on the part of the contractor's representatives, who preferred to work with new materials. The commissioners usually took the side of the contractor, although their relationship with him was anything but comfortable.

Through the fall of 1951 the window sash was put into place. Doors were hung inside. By the end of the year the two main obstacles to completion were the lighting fixtures, which were still being restored, and the wood flooring. Most of the latter had not been installed, and that which had needed time-consuming hand finishing. To save time the commission authorized leveling the floors with machine sanders, then finishing the job by hand. On January 25, 1952 the commission was informed that the fine parquet flooring had been installed in most of the rooms of the second and third floors, the Red and the Blue Rooms, and that it was under way in the East Room.

Eighteen painters worked through the winter. David Finley opposed the bright yellow of the old kitchen, now the Broadcast Room, feeling that "a more dignified, severe type of decoration should be used—such as may be found in a gentleman's office or library." He heartily approved the black leather sofa and chairs. But the commission stuck to its decisions on all the rooms, making changes only when they were suggested by Crim, for the President. The work stopped only on Sundays, continuing steadily six days a week.[47]

The President was an increasing presence in the decision-making. Crim had taken Winslow's place as his main liaison, perhaps because of Crim's enormous capacity for organization, perhaps because of Truman's increasing annoyance over Winslow's private life. When the electricians prepared to hang McKim's old lantern in the entrance hall, Truman stopped them, saying he preferred a chandelier. He located one he liked on the second floor, and it was put in the entrance hall. Truman complained frequently about the old gas fixtures from the White House being in the Capitol. He had tried to get them back, with no success; had he been able to, he would have hung General Grant's mighty gasoliers in the East Room.[48]

Furniture in crates arrived daily. By late February it was being unloaded in the house and where possible taken to the rooms where it belonged, according to Haight's inventory. Crim was the final authority on this work. The upholsterers covered the walls of the state parlors with silk in February and early March; the five coats of white paint on the reproduced woodwork gleamed in contrast. In middle March the construction fences and shacks were dismantled and removed, leaving the ground sodden where they had been, and ancient boxwoods—some of them seven feet tall—were transplanted across the front of the north portico, "old bushes carefully selected to conform to the age of the Executive Mansion. . . ." Deep in the new sub-basement engineers turned on the electrical systems, heat and air-conditioning sufficient to serve a skyscraper. In the laundry and ironing rooms the machinery was tested; the great freezers, ranges, and equipment of the kitchens and pantries were put in order. On March 22, the regular White House staff, with Haight, Margaret Watts, and Crim, began pulling dustcovers and wrappers off the furniture and pictures. Vacuum cleaners hummed over the carpets and parquet. Workmen polished the windowpanes.[49]

Home Again

On March 27, 1952, President Truman was in the presidential plane, heading home from Key West. He had written a speech to be delivered two days later, announcing that he would not seek reelection. In his absence his belongings had been moved to the White House from Blair House. The members of the Commission for the Renovation of the Executive Mansion gathered in the conference room of the East Wing, prior to making a final tour of inspection. After a hard job had been done, it was time to reminisce and congratulate. The original commissioners had done the same 152 years before, on the day that President John Adams moved in.

They walked through the state rooms, the East Room, the Green, Blue, and Red Rooms, and the State Dining Room, brighter and fresher than before, but also still the same. There were 54 rooms now, instead of the 48 there had been. Steel, 660 tons of it, strengthened the concrete inner walls and floors; to the lowest basement had been added $868,000 worth of structural solidity. The commissioners found nearly all the furniture in place in the state rooms and family quarters. They paused in their tour to vote to have iron grilles made to cover the glass doors at the top of the grand staircase, to appease the Secret Service. Objection had been raised at the last minute over the openness of the stair, which seemed to invite people to climb it.[50]

A little ceremony had been arranged to greet the President when he arrived. A small group of staff members, the commissioners, and a gathering of officials were waiting when his car turned into the driveway and pulled into the shelter of the north portico. The President of the United States left the car and mounted the steps. Forty photographers recorded the scene; several hundred spectators stood on the sidewalk, looking through the iron fence, applauding and cheering. President Truman was presented with a gold key, which he held high for everyone to see. Then he turned, and at 6:20 p.m. walked briskly through the glass doors. The President was again at home in the White House.

Epilogue

Thirty-four years later, the White House is essentially the house Harry S. Truman rebuilt. Seven more presidents have lived there. Architectural changes have been few, and they have had virtually no effect upon the appearance of the whole. Change has come in other ways. Since Truman's renovation, the symbolic role of the White House has assumed far greater importance. No sooner had Roosevelt and his fireside chats passed from the scene than television began to offer new possibilities for mass communication. Truman took newsman Walter Cronkite on a televised tour of the renovated house soon after moving back in. The result was like a home movie: The two walked uncomfortably through the rebuilt rooms, camera jiggling along behind, as the 33rd President pointed out those things that interested him about the history of the house. In the former basement kitchen, with its two great fireplaces, he showed stones from the original walls. He had ordered them set into the new walls for display. They bore chiseled mason's marks left by the Scotsmen who had shaped them a century and a half before.

The President already knew the power of television. On many occasions during the rebuilding of the house, he had addressed the nation, walking across the street and using the White House, not his Blair House residence, as his backdrop. His successor, Dwight D. Eisenhower, made even more frequent use of television. He found a particularly dramatic example of its impact in the 1955 Little Rock crisis. Millions had watched televised confrontations between citizens and soldiers over the enforcement of public-school integration in the Arkansas capital. Unrest over the violence spread nationwide. President Eisenhower, on a golfing vacation in Newport, Rhode Island, first dismissed the idea that his going back to the White House would calm the waters. When he finally yielded and returned to Washington, proclaiming his presence in a television broadcast, the soothing effect upon the country was profound.

In the years since the 1950s, television has proved a valuable asset to the work of the Presidency. With its aura of reality and immediacy, it has strengthened the Chief Executive's presence in American life. Likewise, the increasing sophistication and effectiveness of all mass media have brought Americans closer to the President and to the events that affect him and with which he must contend. The slow process that spread the news of Pearl Harbor in 1941 could hardly be imagined today.

The White House itself has become an ever stronger part of the

President's identity. Largely through television, it is the best known house in the world, the instantly familiar symbol of the Presidency, flashed daily on millions and millions of TV screens everywhere. The house is more a stage than ever, and the audience inconceivably greater. Yet the basic character of the life there remains much the same.

The broad exposure of the White House has made people increasingly curious about it. Jefferson opened the President's House to the public for the first time in 1801 and, except for brief periods, it has been open on a regular basis since. But as the house gained new meaning through the later 1950s, there was a feeling that it should be more than simply a house and a place of official entertainment, that when people toured or visited there they should sense in their surroundings the strong continuity and stability of the Presidency. This possibility has not yet been fully explored in the philosophical sense, but it found expression in the 1960s in the renewal of an old trend chronicled in this book.

It will be remembered that through the years, especially after 1925, there had been an interest both inside and outside the White House in furnishing the rooms with antiques or reproductions which seemed appropriate to a historic house. Harriet Barnes Pratt and her advisory committee tried for a quarter of a century to gain control over the interior decoration of the state rooms and effect such a furnishings scheme. To some extent the intrusion was tolerated, if only because the committee was ready with money, and the Congress provided very little. The committee approached President Truman, hoping to become involved in his renovation, but he rejected the offer. Those who rebuilt the White House for him wanted to use antiques, but they had neither the money nor the resources for raising funds through contributions. During the later 1950s, Mamie Eisenhower revived the antiques trend when she sponsored the redecoration of the Diplomatic Reception Room as a Federal-style parlor.

But not until 1961, in the administration of John F. Kennedy, did a large-scale program of "historical" decoration begin. This paralleled, and to a large extent mirrored, the program in France under President Charles de Gaulle for reviving the interior splendor of state houses and palaces. Nine years had passed since Truman completed his work. Jacqueline Kennedy expressed her enthusiasm for the project in a televised tour of the house, a slick network special that showed how far television's techniques had advanced and fostered great public support for refurnishing the White House. The Kennedy program rallied around "restoration," a nobler word than "redecoration," as "repair" had seemed more politic to Madison than "reconstruct" when he rebuilt the White

House after the War of 1812. To speak of restoring the White House always brings up the question: "To what period?" Was laundry to be hung in the East Room?

In the broader sense, however, the word "restore" suited well, for the basic idea behind the furnishings program was to bring to the White House the aura of the past that had been lost in the post-World War II renovation. The chilly marble hallways, the lofty expanses of bright-colored silk, and the sparse rooms seemed by then too ordinary, something one might find in any hotel or country club of the time. This was not the image the restorers believed the American house of state should have. The way was paved by an act of Congress in September 1961 making all objects belonging to the White House "inalienable" parts of a permanent collection and recognizing the state rooms as having a museum character which was to be preserved and interpreted.

Although the work was interrupted by Kennedy's death late in 1963, the state floor was transformed, as well as several rooms upstairs. While carrying out her project, Mrs. Kennedy was advised by Henry Francis du Pont, well-known antiquarian and creator of the Winterthur museum of decorative arts in Delaware. The result was a compromise. American and European antiques were mixed with early White House furnishings, but the settings themselves—hangings, wallcoverings, and arrangements—were borrowed to a great extent from the restoration mode then popular in France. Never before had White House interiors been so affectionately hailed by the public. A White House was now presented that was unlike any seen before. It had become an elegant background for the Presidency, spiced with historical references through portraits and other objects associated with past administrations. It is important, however, to know that the ensembles were effective for their daily functions, thus subordinating the museum impulse to the dynamic purposes of the present.

The Kennedy program had a facet that made it unique. It was institutionalized in the founding of the White House Historical Association, a nonprofit organization dedicated to the historical interpretation of the White House. David Finley, undaunted by his earlier battles, served as its first chairman. The charter of the association provided that it engage in all the usual endeavors of historical societies, publishing, restoration, and museum collecting. As Jacqueline Kennedy's refurnishing materialized under her personal direction in 1961 and 1962, the White House Historical Association, in cooperation with the National Geographic Society, created a full-color guidebook describing the White House in terms of its architecture, furnishings, and history. *The White*

House: An Historic Guide was published in 1962. The book had phenomenal success. From its earnings the association made generous contributions to the Kennedy restoration work and remains today the major donor in every similar endeavor in the public rooms. For a quarter of a century its publishing program has continued to expand.

President Lyndon B. Johnson carried the Kennedy plans for the state rooms to completion. Lady Bird Johnson's interest in beautifying the American landscape was symbolized in the design of a new dinner service for the State Dining Room, the first in many years. It featured the American eagle and American wildflowers, harkening to the earlier themes of Lucy Webb Hayes and Caroline Scott Harrison.

In President Richard M. Nixon, the White House had an ardent devotee of history. With the guidance of White House curator Clement E. Conger, he sponsored the largest program of antiques acquisition before or since. The emphasis in the collection was on furniture of the early republic, prior to about 1840. The state rooms were redecorated and given the appearance they have today. Once again the influence of the Metropolitan Museum of Art was felt in the White House interior, for the designs followed a style of decoration espoused in the American Wing's 1970 exhibition on the decorative arts of the 19th century. Silk draperies in stripes and other patterns, or plain and lined in contrasting colors, were trimmed with borders and fringes; bright upholsteries and bolsters with tassels enriched antiques from the eras of Jefferson through Van Buren. A number of early White House furnishings have returned, notably parts of the French suite acquired in Paris for James Monroe in 1817. The museum-like settings suggest the early years of the house. In this decoration of the Nixon years, the design of the rooms was made to feature the fine furnishings, in contrast to the Kennedy interiors, in which the ensemble was the emphasis.

The hurried pace of collecting slowed after Nixon. Beginning during the Presidency of Gerald Ford, the interest shifted from furniture to artwork, and this continued into the administration of Jimmy Carter. Collecting fine paintings is usually a more costly endeavor than amassing antiques, so the acquisitions were fewer. In the Ford administration 26 works of art were brought to the White House, including landscapes by Frederick Church and Childe Hassam and, of greater interest here, the original wax portrait of James Hoban. President Carter acquired for the permanent collection the portrait of Washington by Charles Willson Peale that hangs over the mantelpiece in the Oval Office. He also approved the purchase of a portrait of Andrew Jackson by R.E.W. Earl, probably painted in 1835 in Earl's studio upstairs at the White House.

Perhaps the most important painting added in Carter's term was George Caleb Bingham's "Lighter Relieving a Steamboat Aground," painted around 1847 and acquired from descendants of the man who had bought it from Bingham.

Even before moving to the White House, President-elect and Mrs. Ronald Reagan decided to redecorate the family quarters. They themselves raised nearly a million dollars from friends and political supporters. The resulting work completed the last phase of the renovation begun in 1952. For lack of funds, the second and third floors had been decorated piecemeal since Truman's time. Presidents had brought some of their own furnishings to use alongside a large and diverse accumulation of White House furniture, and such as could be found in the White House warehouses across the river in Virginia.

Four rooms of the second floor family quarters are of a semi-state character. The oval room, previously a study or a library, was restyled under the Kennedy restoration the Yellow Oval Room, a formal drawing room with 18th-century French furnishings. It opens onto the Truman balcony, providing a magnificent view of the Jefferson Memorial and the Washington Monument. Next door, going east, the Treaty Room was the old Cabinet Room established by Andrew Johnson and used until Theodore Roosevelt moved the Cabinet to the West Wing. For many years a study, the Treaty Room has become a library and meeting room decorated with mementos of its distinguished past. On eastward, the Queen's Bedroom and the Lincoln Bedroom flank the central hallway.

It was the other parts of the large family quarters that the Reagans redecorated and refurnished in 1981 and 1982. On completion of this work, the two floors were at last brought together in a cohesive way. They do not represent any effort to create historical settings but reflect the present-day taste for informality and the mingling of many sorts of furnishings, old and new. Light contemporary colors and furniture arrangements supply an open quality to spaces which, because of security considerations, are decidedly confining.

Today the White House receives more than a million and a half visitors a year on public tours. Official guests at dinners and receptions add some 50,000. The state rooms have become museum rooms of a sort, designed for formal use, and to evoke a romantic past through their contents. All redecorations seem, when new, to be perfect and permanent solutions, as have these for more than a decade. This historical phase, however, has yet to be completed. It is a memorable episode in the history of the building, but, to be sure, not the last.

The White House was built to be changed. Washington said that it must be so, and time has proved him correct. He made his plans according to conditions of a life only he could have understood, for he was the first. Always past and present form a certain dichotomy at the White House. It is not an old, sagging edifice that creaks beneath footsteps; it is as sturdy as steel and concrete can make it. There is something very American in the way it has changed so much. The board floors trod by Lincoln are gone, and the plaster walls of FDR's Map Room have long since become landfill. Hoban's grand double staircase, down which James and Sarah Polk marched, is history, and the room where Garfield lay dying survives only in old photographs and drawings.

Those elements and many more have been revived again in this book. And life goes on every day. The East Room, still looking much as Charles McKim left it, is the scene of great events. The file of parlors—Green, Blue, Red—may well be filled tonight with the President's dinner guests; each presidential generation is surprised, as was Archie Butt's, to find that the State Dining Room is not big enough. Today's presidential families still gather upstairs before the great half-moon window, in the cheery west hall sitting room Julia Grant made from the old stairwell.

Within the sandstone walls the pace of living makes way for very little. Yet the walls have survived wear and fire and many renovations. To stand today in Lafayette Park, near Jackson's statue, and study the White House across the street is to see a physical presence remarkably intact. George Washington might hesitate a moment, but he would recognize it. This is the same house he saw built in the last decade of the 18th century, when the Old World seemed to be falling apart and the young republic's journey had just begun.

Bibliographical Note

Unpublished manuscripts of many kinds provided the main sources for *The President's House*. Forming the spine for the work were the public buildings records at the National Archives, which hold vast stores of written materials on the management and use of the White House from its inception in 1791 until about 1933. In 1933, after the transfer of the public buildings office to the National Park Service, the records ceased to be filed in the same archival series. They are now divided among the National Archives, the White House, and the current files of the National Park Service. This applies as well to drawings, photographs, and printed records.

The personal papers of the Presidents and their families, associates, and friends I questioned vigorously. These included letters, diaries, and other records. I have sought out the objects that each President used. White House domestic accounts were of great interest to me. They survive in surprising abundance, considering that in the past little importance was usually attached to preserving them.

I consulted the full scope of published scholarship. There are only a few serious books about the White House itself, but there are many excellent presidential biographies. While these seldom treat the house in the detail found in this history, they have been among the most useful secondary sources. Collections of published letters abound. They have been valuable in this study for all periods. The generation of the late 19th and early 20th century gave considerable energy to the writing of memoirs, thus providing sources for White House history. Tumultuous events, such as wars, always generate a lot of memoirs, and these I have mined for descriptions and points of view.

The chapter notes at the end of this bibliography direct the reader to most of my sources, be they manuscripts, interviews, published works, drawings, photographs, or maps. The following is a brief listing of materials, mainly books, which helped me significantly in writing these volumes. Without attempting to be comprehensive, I include them as the printed sources I consider the most useful.

Adams, Abigail. *Letters of Mrs. Adams, the Wife of John Adams*. Ed. Charles Francis Adams. Boston: C. C. Little and J. Brown, 1840.
Adams, Abigail. *New Letters of Abigail Adams, 1788–1801*. Ed. Stewart Mitchell. Boston: Houghton Mifflin Company, 1947.

Adams, John. *Diary and Autobiography of John Adams*. Eds. L. H. Butterfield, et al. Cambridge: Harvard University Press, 1961.

Adams, John. *Letters of John Adams Addressed to His Wife*. Ed. Charles Francis Adams. Boston: C. C. Little and J. Brown, 1841.

Adams, John Quincy. *The Diary of John Quincy Adams, 1794–1845*. Ed. Allan Nevins. New York: Longmans, Green and Company, 1928.

Adams, John Quincy. *Memoirs of John Quincy Adams*. Ed. Charles Francis Adams. Philadelphia: J. B. Lippincott & Company, 1876.

Aikman, Lonnelle. *The Living White House*. 7th edition. Washington: White House Historical Association, 1982.

Alexander, Holmes. *American Talleyrand: The Career and Contemporaries of Martin Van Buren*. New York: Harper & Brothers, 1935.

Ames, Mary Clemmer. *Ten Years in Washington*. Hartford: A. D. Worthington & Company, 1874.

Ammon, Harry. *James Monroe: The Quest for National Identity*. New York: McGraw-Hill Book Company, 1971.

Baker, Ray Stannard. *Woodrow Wilson: Life and Letters*. New York: Greenwood Press, 1968.

Baker, Ray Lyman. *The Memoirs of Ray Lyman Baker, 1875–1949*. Eds. Edgar Eugene Robinson and Paul Arnold Edwards. Palo Alto: Stanford University Press, 1960.

Barnard, Harry. *Rutherford B. Hayes and His America*. Indianapolis: Bobbs-Merrill Company, 1954.

Bemis, Samuel Flagg. *John Quincy Adams and the Union*. New York: Alfred A. Knopf, 1956.

Bierley, Paul E. *John Philip Sousa: American Phenomenon*. New York: Appleton-Century-Crofts, 1973.

Blaine, Mrs. James G. *Letters of Mrs. James G. Blaine*. Ed. Harriet S. Blaine Beale. 2 vols. New York: Duffield and Company, 1898.

Briggs, Emily Edson. *The Olivia Letters*. New York: Neale Publishing Company, 1906.

Brooks, Noah. *Washington in Lincoln's Time*. New York: Century Company, 1895.

Brown, Glenn. *Memories, 1860–1930*. Washington, D.C.: Press of W. F. Roberts Company, 1931.

Buchanan, James. *The Works of James Buchanan*. Ed. John Bassett Moore. 12 vols. Philadelphia: J. B. Lippincott Company, 1908–11.

Burke, Pauline W. *Emily Donelson of Tennessee*. 2 vols. Richmond: Garrett and Massie, 1941.

Butt, Archibald. *The Letters of Archie Butt, Personal Aide to President Roosevelt*. Ed. Lawrence F. Abbott. Garden City: Doubleday, Page

& Company, 1924.

―――. *Taft and Roosevelt: The Intimate Letters of Archie Butt.* 2 vols. Garden City: Doubleday, Doran & Company, 1930.

Caemmerer, H. Paul. *The Life of Pierre Charles L'Enfant.* Washington, D.C.: National Republic Publishing Company, 1950.

Carpenter, Francis B. *Six Months in the White House with Abraham Lincoln.* New York: Hurd & Houghton, 1866.

Carpenter, Frank. *Carp's Washington.* Ed. Frances Carpenter. New York: McGraw-Hill Book Company, 1960.

Clark, Allen. *Greenleaf and Law in the Federal City.* Washington, D.C.: Press of W. F. Roberts, 1901.

Clark, Allen. *Life and Letters of Dolly Madison.* Washington, D.C.: Press of W. F. Roberts, 1914.

Clay-Clopton, Virginia (Mrs. Clement C., Jr.). *A Belle of the Fifties.* Ed. Ada Sterling. New York: Doubleday, Page & Company, 1904.

Cleveland, Grover. *The Letters of Grover Cleveland.* Ed. Allan Nevins. 1935. Reprint. New York: DaCapo, 1970.

Collins, Herbert R. *Presidents on Wheels.* Washington, D.C.: Acropolis Books, 1971.

Commission for the Renovation of the Executive Mansion. *Acts and Estimates: Reconstruction of the White House,* and *Report.* Washington, D.C.: Government Printing Office.

Coolidge, Calvin. *The Autobiography of Calvin Coolidge.* New York: Cosmopolitan Book Corporation, 1929.

Coolidge, Grace G. "When I Became the First Lady." *American Magazine* CVIII (September 1929), 11–13, 104, 106, 108.

Crook, William H. *Memories of the White House.* Boston: Little, Brown, and Company, 1911.

Curtis, George Ticknor. *Life of James Buchanan.* New York: Harper & Brothers, 1883.

Daniels, Josephus. *The Wilson Era: Years of War and After.* Chapel Hill: University of North Carolina Press, 1946.

Davis, Varina Howell. *Jefferson Davis: A Memoir by His Wife.* New York: Belford Company, 1890.

Dawes, Charles G. *A Journal of the McKinley Years.* Ed. Bascom M. Timmons. Chicago: Lakeside Press, 1950.

DeGregorio, William. *The Complete Book of U.S. Presidents.* New York: Dembner Books, 1984.

Depew, Chauncey M. *My Memories of Eighty Years.* New York: Charles Scribner's Sons, 1922.

Dewitt, David M. *The Impeachment and Trial of Andrew Johnson.* 1903.

Reprint. Madison: State Historical Society of Wisconsin, 1967.

Dix, Dorothea, and Millard Fillmore. *The Lady and the President: The Letters of Dorothea Dix and Millard Fillmore.* Ed. Charles M. Snyder. Lexington: University Press of Kentucky, 1975.

Dyer, Brainerd. *Zachary Taylor.* New York: Barnes & Noble, 1967.

Fillmore, Millard. "Millard Fillmore Papers." Ed. Frank H. Severance. *Publications of the Buffalo Historical Society* X, XI (1907).

Foote, Henry S. *Casket of Reminiscences.* Washington, D.C.: Chronicle Publishing Company, 1874.

Foraker, Julia B. *I Would Live It Again: Memories of a Vivid Life.* New York: Harper & Brothers, 1932.

Freeman, Douglas Southall. *George Washington.* 7 vols. New York: Charles Scribner's Sons, 1948–57.

Freidel, Frank. *Franklin D. Roosevelt.* 4 vols. Boston: Little, Brown and Company, 1952–73.

Frémont, Jessie Benton. *Souvenirs of My Time.* Boston: D. Lothrop and Company, 1887.

Geer, Emily Apt. *First Lady: The Life of Lucy Webb Hayes.* Kent: Kent State University Press, 1984.

Gobright, L. A. *Recollection of Men and Things at Washington.* Philadelphia: Claxton, Remsen & Haffelfinger, 1869.

Goode, James M. *Capital Losses: A Cultural History of Washington's Destroyed Buildings.* Washington, D.C.: Smithsonian Institution Press, 1979.

Goode, James M. *The Outdoor Sculpture of Washington, D.C.* Washington, D.C.: Smithsonian Institution Press, 1974.

Grant, Jesse R. *In the Days of My Father, General Grant.* New York: Harper Brothers, 1925.

Grant, Julia Dent. *The Personal Memoirs of Julia Dent Grant.* Ed. John Y. Simon. New York: G. P. Putnam's Sons, 1975.

Grayson, Cary T. *Woodrow Wilson: An Intimate Memoir.* New York: Holt, Rinehart and Winston, 1960.

Green, Constance M. *Washington.* 2 vols. Princeton: Princeton University Press, 1962–63.

Green, James A. *William Henry Harrison: His Life and Times.* Richmond: Garrett and Massie, 1941.

Grimsley, Elizabeth Todd. "Six Months in the White House." *Illinois State Historical Society Journal* XIX (October 1926–January 1927), 43–73.

Griswold, Rufus Wilmot. *The Republican Court; or, American Society in the Days of Washington.* New York: D. Appleton & Company, 1864.

Hamilton, Holman. *Zachary Taylor: Soldier in the White House*. Indianapolis: Bobbs-Merrill Company, 1951.

Hamlin, Charles E. *The Life and Times of Hannibal Hamlin*. Cambridge: Riverside Press, 1899.

Hamlin, Talbot. *Benjamin Henry Latrobe*. New York: Oxford University Press, 1955.

Hay, John. *The Addresses of John Hay*. New York: Century Company, 1907.

Hayes, Rutherford Birchard. *Diary and Letters of Rutherford Birchard Hayes*. Ed. Charles R. Williams. Columbus: Ohio State Archaeological and Historical Society, 1922–26.

Helm, Edith Blenham. *The Captains and the Kings*. New York: G. P. Putnam's Sons, 1954.

Hersey, John. "Mr. President: Ghosts in the White House." *The New Yorker* XXVII (April 28, 1951), 36–38, 40, 42–50, 53–55.

Hesseltine, William B. *Ulysses S. Grant: Politician*. New York: Dodd, Mead & Company, 1935.

Hickok, Lorena A. *Eleanor Roosevelt: Reluctant First Lady*. New York: Dodd, Mead & Company, 1962.

Hobart, Mrs. Garret A. *Second Lady*. Mount Vernon, New York: W. E. Rudge, 1933.

Hoover, Herbert. *Memoirs*. 3 vols. New York: Macmillan Company, 1951–52.

Hoover, Irwin H. *Forty-Two Years in the White House*. Boston: Houghton Mifflin Company, 1934.

Howe, George Frederick. *Chester A. Arthur: A Quarter Century of Machine Politics*. New York: Dodd, Mead & Company, 1934.

Humphreys, Francis L. *Life and Times of David Humphreys*. 2 vols. New York: G. P. Putnam's Sons, 1917.

Hunt-Jones, Conover. *Dolley and the "Great Little Madison."* Washington, D.C.: American Institute of Architects Foundation, 1977.

Jaffray, Elizabeth. *Secrets of the White House*. New York: Cosmopolitan Book Corporation, 1927.

James, Marquis. *Andrew Jackson: Portrait of a President*. Indianapolis: Bobbs-Merrill Company, 1937.

Jefferson, Thomas. *Memoir, Correspondence and Miscellanies From the Papers of Thomas Jefferson*. Ed. Thomas Jefferson Randolph. Charlottesville: F. Carr and Company, 1829.

Jensen, Amy Lafollette. *The White House and Its Thirty-five Families*. New York: McGraw-Hill Book Company, 1970.

Keckley, Mrs. Elizabeth Hobbs. *Behind the Scenes, or, Thirty Years a Slave and Four Years in the White House.* 1868. Reprint. New York: Arno Press, 1968.

Kendall, Amos. *Autobiography of Amos Kendall.* Ed. William Stickney. Boston: Lee and Shepard, 1872.

Kimball, Marie. "The Original Furnishings of the White House." *Antiques* XV (June 1929), 481–86; and XVI (July 1929), 33–37.

King, Horatio. *Turning On the Light: A Dispassionate Study of President Buchanan's Administration, From 1860 to Its Close.* Philadelphia: J. B. Lippincott Company, 1895.

Kite, Elizabeth. *L'Enfant and Washington, 1791–1792.* Institut Français de Washington. Cahier III. Baltimore: Johns Hopkins Press, 1929.

Klapthor, Margaret Brown. "Benjamin Latrobe and Dolley Madison Decorate the White House." *Contributions From the Museum of History and Technology* Paper 49 (1965), 153–54.

————. *Official White House China: 1789 to the Present.* Washington, D.C.: Smithsonian Institution Press, 1975.

Klein, Philip S. "Harriet Lane: Our Republican Queen." *Valleys of History* II (Autumn 1966), 1–6.

————. *President James Buchanan.* University Park: Pennsylvania State University Press, 1962.

Koch, Robert. *Louis C. Tiffany: Rebel in Glass.* New York: Crown Publishers, 1964.

Lash, Joseph. *Eleanor and Franklin: The Story of Their Relationship, Based on Eleanor Roosevelt's Private Papers.* New York: W. W. Norton and Company, 1971.

Lathem, Edwin C., ed. *Meet Calvin Coolidge; the Man Behind the Myth.* Brattleboro: Stephen Greene Press, 1960.

Leech, Margaret. *In the Days of McKinley.* New York: Harper & Row, 1959.

————. *Reveille in Washington, 1860–1865.* New York: Harper & Brothers, 1941.

————, and Harry J. Brown. *The Garfield Orbit.* New York: Harper & Row, 1978.

Leish, Kenneth W. *The White House.* New York: Newsweek Book Division, 1972.

Link, Arthur S. *Wilson.* 5 vols. Princeton: Princeton University Press, 1947–65.

Logan, Mary Simmerson Cunningham (Mrs. John A.). *Thirty Years in Washington.* Hartford: A. D. Worthington & Company, 1901.

Lomask, Milton. *Andrew Johnson: President on Trial.* New York: Farrar, Strauss and Cudahy, 1960.

Longworth, Alice Roosevelt. *Crowded Hours*. New York: Charles Scribner's Sons, 1933.

Lorant, Stefan. *The Glorious Burden: The American Presidency*. New York: Harper & Row, 1968.

Lynch, Denis Tilden. *An Epoch and a Man: Martin Van Buren and His Times*. New York: Horace Liveright, 1929.

McAdoo, Eleanor Wilson, and Margaret Y. Gaffey. *The Woodrow Wilsons*. New York: Macmillan Company, 1937.

McClure, Alexander. *Recollections of Half a Century*. Salem: Salem Press, 1902.

McDaniel, James I. "Stone Walls Preserved." *White House History* (White House Historical Association) I (1983), 38–45.

McElroy, Robert. *Grover Cleveland: The Man and the Statesman*. New York: Harper & Brothers, 1923.

Macrae, David. *The Americans at Home*. New York: E. P. Dutton & Company, 1952.

Malone, Dumas. *Jefferson and His Time*. 5 vols. Boston: Little, Brown and Company 1948–70.

Miles, Edwin A. "The First People's Inaugural—1829." *Tennessee Historical Quarterly* XXXVII (Fall 1978).

Monkman, Betty C. "The White House: 1873–1902." *Nineteenth Century* III (Spring 1978), 81–84.

Moore, Charles. *The Life and Times of Charles Follen McKim*. Boston: Houghton Mifflin Company, 1929.

Morgan, H. Wayne. *William McKinley and His America*. Syracuse: Syracuse University Press, 1963.

Morgan, Ted. *F.D.R.* New York: Simon and Schuster, 1985.

Morris, Sylvia Jukes. *Edith Kermit Roosevelt: Portrait of a First Lady*. New York: Coward, McCann & Geoghegan, 1980.

Murray, Robert K. *The Harding Era: Warren G. Harding and His Administration*. Minneapolis: University of Minnesota Press, 1969.

Nelson, Anson and Fanny. *Memorials of Sarah Childress Polk, Wife of the Eleventh President of the United States*. New York: A. D. F. Randolph & Company, 1892.

Nesbitt, Henrietta. *White House Diary*. Garden City: Doubleday & Company, 1948.

Nevins, Allan. *Grover Cleveland: A Study in Courage*. New York: Dodd, Mead & Company, 1933.

Nichols, Roy. *Franklin Pierce: Young Hickory of the Granite Hills*. Philadelphia: University of Pennsylvania Press, 1958.

Niven, John. *Martin Van Buren: The Romantic Age of American Politics*.

New York: Oxford University Press, 1983.

O'Brien, Robert Lincoln. *Grover Cleveland as Seen by His Stenographer.* Boston: Massachusetts Historical Society, 1951.

Padover, Saul K., ed. *Thomas Jefferson and the National Capital.* Washington, D.C.: Government Printing Office, 1946.

Pendel, Thomas F. *Thirty-six Years in the White House.* Washington, D.C.: Neale Publishing Company, 1902.

Peskin, Allan. *Garfield.* Kent: Kent State University Press, 1978.

Poore, Ben Perley. *Perley's Reminiscences of Sixty Years in the National Metropolis.* 2 vols. Philadelphia: Hubbard Brothers, 1886.

Porter, David Dixon. *Incidents and Anecdotes of the Civil War.* New York: D. Appleton & Company, 1885.

Pringle, Henry F. *The Life and Times of William Howard Taft.* 2 vols. New York: Farrar & Rinehart, 1939.

Pryor, Sara A. R. *Reminiscences of Peace and War.* New York: Macmillan Company, 1905.

Quaife, Milo Milton. *The Diary of James K. Polk During His Presidency, 1845 to 1849.* 4 vols. Chicago: A. C. McClurg and Company, 1910.

Randall, Ruth Painter. *Mary Lincoln: Biography of a Marriage.* Boston: Little, Brown and Company 1953.

Randolph, Mary. *Presidents and First Ladies.* New York: D. Appleton-Century Company, 1936.

Reeves, Thomas C. *Gentleman Boss: The Life of Chester Alan Arthur.* New York: Alfred A. Knopf, 1975.

Remini, Robert V. *Andrew Jackson.* 3 vols. New York: Harper & Row, 1977–84.

Robinson, Corinne Roosevelt. *My Brother, Theodore Roosevelt.* New York: Charles Scribner's Sons, 1921.

Rogers, Lillian Parks, with Frances Spatz Leighton. *My Thirty Years Backstairs at the White House.* New York: Fleet Publishing Corp., 1961.

Roosevelt, Eleanor. *This I Remember.* New York: Harper & Brothers, 1949.

————, and Anna Roosevelt. *Mother and Daughter: The Letters of Eleanor and Anna Roosevelt.* Ed. Bernard Asbell. New York: Coward, McCann & Geoghegan, 1982.

Roosevelt, Elliott and James Brough. *A Rendezvous With Destiny: The Roosevelts of the White House.* New York: G. P. Putnam's Sons, 1975.

Roosevelt, Nicholas. *Theodore Roosevelt: The Man as I Knew Him.* New York: Dodd, Mead & Company, 1967.

Roosevelt, Theodore. *The Letters of Theodore Roosevelt*. Ed. Elting Morison. 8 vols. Cambridge: Harvard University Press, 1951–54.

————. *Theodore Roosevelt's Letters to His Children*. Ed. Joseph Bucklin Bishop. Charles Scribner's Sons, 1919.

Ross, Ishbel. *An American Family: The Tafts ~ 1678 to 1964*. New York: World Publishing Company, 1964.

————. *The General's Wife: The Life of Mrs. Ulysses S. Grant*. New York: Dodd, Mead & Company, 1959.

————. *Grace Coolidge and Her Era: The Story of a President's Wife*. New York: Dodd, Mead & Company, 1962.

Russell, Francis. *The Shadow of Blooming Grove: Warren G. Harding in His Times*. New York: McGraw-Hill Book Company, 1968.

Ryan, William, and Desmond Guinness. *The White House: An Architectural History*. New York: McGraw-Hill Book Company, 1980.

Sandburg, Carl. *Abraham Lincoln: The Prairie Years and the War Years*. New York: Harcourt, Brace, 1954.

————, and Paul Angle. *Mary Lincoln: Wife and Widow*. New York: Harcourt, Brace, 1932.

Saunders, Frances W. *Ellen Axson Wilson: First Lady Between Two Worlds*. Chapel Hill: University of North Carolina Press, 1985.

Schlesinger, Arthur M., Jr. *The Age of Jackson*. Boston: Little, Brown and Company 1946.

————. *The Age of Roosevelt*. 4 vols. Boston: Houghton Mifflin Company, 1957–64.

Seager, Robert II. *And Tyler, Too: A Biography of John & Julia Gardiner Tyler*. New York: McGraw-Hill Book Company, 1963.

Sherwood, Robert E. *Roosevelt and Hopkins: An Intimate History*. New York: Harper & Brothers, 1948.

Sievers, Harry J. *Benjamin Harrison: Hoosier President*. Indianapolis: Bobbs-Merrill Company, 1968.

Sinclair, Andrew. *The Available Man: The Life Behind the Masks of Warren Gamaliel Harding*. New York: Macmillan Company, 1965.

Singleton, Esther. *The Story of the White House*. 2 vols. New York: McClure Company, 1907.

Slayden, Ellen Maury. *Washington Wife: Journal of Ellen Maury Slayden From 1897–1919*. Ed. Walter Prescott Webb. New York: Harper & Row, 1962.

Smalley, E. V. "The White House." *Century Magazine* XXVIII (April 1884), 802–815.

Smith, Margaret Bayard. *The First Forty Years of Washington Society*. 1906. Ed. Gaillard Hunt. Reprint. New York: F. Ungar Publishing

Company, 1965.

Smith, Page. *John Adams.* 2 vols. Garden City: Doubleday & Company, 1962.

Smith, Theodore Clarke. *The Life and Letters of James Abram Garfield.* 2 vols. New York: Yale University Press, 1925.

Starling, Edmund W., with Thomas Sugrue. *Starling of the White House.* New York: Simon and Schuster, 1946.

Strode, Hudson. *Jefferson Davis: American Patriot, 1808–1861.* 3 vols. New York: Harcourt, Brace and Company, 1955.

Sullivan, Mark. *Our Times: 1900–1925.* New York: Charles Scribner's Sons, 1926.

Taft, Charles S. "The Last Hours of Abraham Lincoln." *Medical and Scientific Reporter* (December 1865), 452–54.

Taft, Helen. *Recollections of Full Years.* New York: Dodd, Mead & Company, 1914.

Taylor, Tim. *The Book of Presidents.* New York: Arno Press, 1972.

Thayer, William Roscoe. *The Life and Letters of John Hay.* 2 vols. Boston: Houghton Mifflin Company, 1915.

Thomas, Lately [Robert V. Steele]. *The First President Johnson.* New York: William Morrow & Company, 1968.

Truman, Harry S. *Dear Bess: The Letters From Harry to Bess Truman, 1910–1959.* Ed. Robert H. Ferrell. New York: W. W. Norton and Company, 1983.

_____. *Letters From Father: The Truman Family's Personal Correspondence.* Ed. Margaret Truman. New York: Arbor House, 1981.

_____. *Memoirs.* 2 vols. Garden City: Doubleday & Company, 1955–56.

Truman, Margaret. *Harry S. Truman.* New York: William Morrow & Company, 1973.

Tugwell, Rexford. *The Democratic Roosevelt: A Biography of Franklin D. Roosevelt.* Garden City: Doubleday & Company, 1957.

Tully, Grace. *FDR, My Boss.* New York: Charles Scribner's Sons, 1949.

Tumulty, Joseph P. *Woodrow Wilson as I Know Him.* New York: Doubleday, Page & Company, 1921.

Turner, Justin G., and Linda Lovitt Turner. *Mary Todd Lincoln: Her Life and Letters.* New York: Alfred A. Knopf, 1972.

Tyler, Lyon G. *The Letters and Times of the Tylers.* 3 vols. Richmond: Whittet & Shepperson, 1884–96.

Van Deusen, Glyndon G. *The Jacksonian Era, 1828–48.* New York: Harper & Brothers, 1959.

Verheyen, Egon. "James Hoban's Design for the White House in the

Context of the Planning of the Federal City." *Architectura* II (1981), 66–82.

———. "The Splendor of Its Empire: Reconsidering Jefferson's Role in the Planning of Washington." in *Festschrift Herbert Siebenhüner.* Würzburg: Ferdinand Schöningh, 1978.

Viola, Herman J. *Diplomats in Buckskin: A History of Indian Delegations in Washington City.* Washington, D.C.: Smithsonian Institution Press, 1981.

Washington, George. *The Diaries of George Washington, 1748–1799.* Ed. John C. Fitzpatrick. 4 vols. Boston: Houghton Mifflin, 1925.

———. *The Writings of George Washington.* Ed. John C. Fitzpatrick. 39 vols. Washington, D.C.: Government Printing Office, 1931–44.

Weed, Thurlow. *Thurlow Weed's Memoirs.* Ed. Harriet A. Weed. 1883. Vol. I of *Life of Thurlow Weed.* Boston: Houghton, Mifflin and Company, 1883–84.

West, J. B., with Mary Lynn Kotz. *Upstairs at the White House: My Life With the First Ladies.* New York: Coward, McCann & Geoghegan, 1973.

White, William Allen. *The Autobiography of William Allen White.* New York: Macmillan Company, 1946.

White House Historical Association. *The White House: An Historic Guide.* 15th ed. Washington, D.C.: White House Historical Association, 1982.

Wilson, Edith Bolling. *My Memoir.* Indianapolis: Bobbs-Merrill Company, 1938.

Wilson, Joan Hoff. *Herbert Hoover: Forgotten Progressive.* Boston: Little, Brown and Company, 1975.

Wilson, Major L. *The Presidency of Martin Van Buren.* Lawrence: University Press of Kansas, 1984.

Wilson, Woodrow. *The Papers of Woodrow Wilson.* Ed. Arthur S. Link, David Hirst, and John Little. 48 vols. to date. Princeton: Princeton University Press, 1956–.

———, and Ellen Axson Wilson. *The Priceless Gift: The Love Letters of Woodrow Wilson and Ellen Axson Wilson.* Ed. Eleanor Wilson McAdoo. New York: McGraw-Hill Book Company, 1962.

Wiltse, Charles. *The New Nation, 1800–1845.* New York: Hill & Wang, 1961.

Winston, Robert W. *Andrew Johnson: Plebeian and Patriot.* 1928. Reprint, New York: AMS Press, 1970.

Wirth, Conrad L. *Parks, Politics and the People.* Norman: University of Oklahoma Press, 1980.

Notes

The following abbreviations will be found in the Notes:

L.C.: Library of Congress
CHS *Records:* Columbia Historical Society, *Records*
OCWH: Office of the Curator, the White House
OCPB: Officer In Charge of Public Buildings, National Archives
OPBP: Office of Public Buildings and Parks, National Archives
NCP: National Park Service, National Capital Parks

VOLUME I

Chapter 1: The Palace

1. Jefferson to L'Enfant, Philadelphia, March, [2], 1791, in Julian P. Boyd, ed., *The Papers of Thomas Jefferson* (Princeton: Princeton University Press, 1974), vol. 19, 355–56.

2. L'Enfant's grand productions for the Federalists in New York and Philadelphia are described in H. Paul Caemmerer, *The Life of Pierre Charles L'Enfant* (Washington: National Republic Publishing Company, 1950); see also Elizabeth S. Kite, *L'Enfant and Washington: Institut Français de Washington* (Baltimore: Johns Hopkins Press, 1929); and Alain-Charles Gruber, *Les Grandes Fêtes Et Leurs Décors à L'Epoque de Louis XVI* (Geneva: Librairie Droz, 1972).

3. See William Hindley, "Federal Hall," unpublished ms., Hindley Papers, Avery Architecture Library, Columbia University; and Louis Torres, "A Construction History of the City Hall on Wall Street, 1699–1788," unpublished historic structure report, National Park Service, 1962; and Torres, "Federal Hall Revisited," *Journal of the Society of Architectural Historians,* vol. XXIX (December 1970): 327–38.

4. Edgar Erskine, *General Washington's Correspondence Concerning the Society of the Cincinnati* (Baltimore: Johns Hopkins Press, 1941), 146–49, 242–85.

5. L'Enfant to Washington, New York,

September 11, 1789, L'Enfant Papers, Library of Congress.

6. Cora Bacon-Foster, "Early Chapters in the Development of the Potomac Route to the West," Columbia Historical Society *Records,* vol. XV (1912): 96–322; L'Enfant to Washington, New York, September 11, 1789, L'Enfant Papers, L.C.; Commissioners of the Federal District, Proceedings, April 12–14, 1791, Records of the Commissioners of the District of Columbia, National Archives; Washington to Jefferson, Mount Vernon, March 31, 1791, CHS *Records,* vol. XVII (1914): 15.

7. L'Enfant to Jefferson, [Georgetown, Maryland], March 11, 1791, L'Enfant Papers, L.C.

8. *Ibid.*

9. Harold Donaldson Eberlein, "190 High Street, Below Market and Sixth: The House of Washington and Adams, 1790–1800," *American Philosophical Society Transactions,* vol. 43 (1953): 161–78.

10. Washington to James Madison, Mount Vernon, March 30, 1789, in John C. Fitzpatrick, ed., *Writings of Washington, 1745–1799,* (Washington: Government Printing Office, 1939), vol. 30, 255.

11. *Gazette of the United States,* May 2, 1789.

12. Washington, "Queries on a Line of Conduct to be Pursued By the President," New York, May 10, 1791, in Fitzpatrick, *Writings of Washington,* vol. 30, 319–321.

13. Hamilton to Washington, New York, May 5 [or 15], 1789, in Henry Cabot Lodge, ed., *Works of Alexander Hamilton* (New York: Putnam, 1904), vol. VIII, 83–84.

14. Adams to Washington, New York, [May 17, 1789?], Washington Papers, L.C.

15. Jared Sparks, ed., *Letters and Recollections of George Washington, Being Letters to Tobias Lear and Others Between 1790–1799* (New York: Doubleday, 1906), 25–26; Esther Singleton, *The*

Story of the White House (New York: The McClure Company, 1907), vol. I, 19; Douglas Southall Freeman, *George Washington: Patriot and President* (New York: Charles Scribner's Sons, 1954), vol. 6, 199–204.

16. R.W. Griswold, *The Republican Court* (New York: D. Appleton & Co., 1867), 163–66; Francis L. Humphreys, *Life and Times of David Humphreys* (New York: Putnam's, 1917), vol. II, 126; William Sullivan, *Public Men of the Revolution* (Philadelphia: Carey, 1847), 120; Freeman, *George Washington: Patriot and President*, vol. 6, 199–204.

17. Edgar Maclay, ed., *Journal of William Maclay* (New York: Appleton & Co., 1890), 69.

18. Washington to Commissioner David Stuart, Philadelphia, November 20, 1791, Fitzpatrick, *Writings of Washington,* vol. 31, 419–23.

19. Fitzpatrick, ed., *Diaries of George Washington, 1748–1799* (Boston: Houghton Mifflin, 1925), vol. IV, 152–55.

20. L'Enfant to Washington, Georgetown, June 22, 1791, CHS *Records,* vol. II (1899), 38.

21. *Ibid.*

22. Washington to Jefferson, Mount Vernon, March 31, 1791, Fitzpatrick, *Writings of Washington, vol. XXXI,* 155–56.

23. Jefferson to L'Enfant, Philadelphia, April 10, 1791, Jefferson Papers, L.C.

24. L'Enfant to Jefferson, Georgetown, April 4, 1791, L'Enfant Papers, L.C.

25. John Trumbull, *Autobiography, Reminiscences, and Letters* (New York: Wiley & Putnam, 1841), 168–69; that L'Enfant was drawing plans was also confirmed by the merchant George Walker, see Washington to Jefferson, Philadelphia [received by Jefferson February 22, 1792], in Fitzpatrick, *Writings of Washington,* vol. XXXI, 482–83.

26. Jefferson to Commissioners, Philadelphia, March 21, 1792, Commission-ers' letters received, Records of the Commissioners of the District of Columbia, National Archives; Commissioners to Jefferson, Georgetown, March 14, 1791, Commissioners' letters sent, Records of the Commissioners of the District of Columbia, National Archives; for information on the Charleston statehouse itself, see A. S. Salley, *The State Houses of South Carolina, 1751–1936* (Columbia: Historical Commission of South Carolina, n.d. [1936], 6–7; the Columbia statehouse is described in Henry-Russell Hitchcock and William Seale, *Temples of Democracy: The State Capitols of the USA* (New York: Harcourt Brace Jovanovich, 1976), 48–51; see also the *Charleston City Gazette,* February 7 and March 4, 1788, and the *Charleston Columbian Herald,* February 7 and 11, 1788. Nearly all of the early public building records of Charleston were burned during the Civil War. Thus documents on the Charleston statehouse are extremely few, and relate to the legislature's £3,500 appropriation on February 11, 1789 (six days after the fire), to contribute to building a court house on the site. The building of the Columbia statehouse is covered sporadically in the state archives records of South Carolina, naming carpenters, bricklayers, etc., see Commissioners of Columbia, Accounts, 1788–1794. James Douglass was the principal builder on the Columbia structure, but no name survives in official records for that in Charleston. Unlikely but early tradition ascribes the Charleston building to Admiralty Judge William Drayton, a member of the building committee, who died in 1790 and was replaced on the committee by his son. James Hoban's name does not appear in the documents of either building.

27. Washington to Commissioners, Charleston, May 17, 1791, in Fitzpatrick, *Writings of Washington,* vol. XXXI, 286.

28. L'Enfant to Washington, Georgetown, June 22, 1791, CHS *Records,* vol. II, 32–37.

29. *Ibid.*

30. Washington, diary, June 28–29, 1791, in "Writings of Washington Relating to the National Capital," CHS *Records*, vol. XVII (1914): 27–28.

31. Affidavit of L'Enfant in regard to the theft of his trunk of papers, etc., listing the sort of materials the trunk contained, Washington, February 8, 1803, cited in J.D. Morgan, "Maj. Pierre Charles L'Enfant," CHS *Records*, vol. II: 139–40.

32. David Stuart to Washington, Georgetown, January 1792, quoted in Kite, *L'Enfant and Washington*, 137; L'Enfant to Washington, Georgetown, August 19, 1791, quoted in Morgan, "L'Enfant," 40–41; L'Enfant to Isaac Roberdeau, Philadelphia, December 16, 1791, L'Enfant Papers, Library of Congress.

33. Dennis C. Kurjack, "Who Designed the President's House?" *Journal of the Society of Architectural Historians*, vol. XII, no. 2, (1952): 27–28; New York "Government House" project by John McComb, New-York Historical Society; see also Fiske Kimball, *Domestic Architecture of the American Colonies and of the Early Republic* (New York: Scribner's, 1922), 279.

34. This "L'Enfant Map" is in the Geography and Map Division, L.C.

35. L'Enfant to Washington, Georgetown, June 22, 1791, in Morgan, "L'Enfant," 32–37.

36. Jefferson to the Commissioners, Philadelphia, August 28, 1791, Commissioners' letters received.

37. Daniel Carroll to Jefferson, Georgetown, [received August 29, 1791], in Saul K. Padover, ed., *Thomas Jefferson and the National Capital* (Washington: Government Printing Office, 1946), 66.

38. Both maps, Geography and Map Division, L.C.

39. L'Enfant, "Memorial to the Honorable Senate and the Honorable House of Representatives of the United States," Washington, December 7, ?, in Caemmerer, *L'Enfant*, 389.

40. Jefferson to Thomas Johnson, Philadelphia, March 8, 1792, in Padover, *Jefferson and the National Capital*, 109–12.

41. L'Enfant to the Commissioners, Washington, May 30, 1800, in Caemmerer, *L'Enfant*, 402.

42. L'Enfant, "Observations Explanatory to the Plan," L'Enfant Plan.

43. Jeanne and Alfred Marie, *Marly* (Paris: Edit Tel, 1947); Emile Magne, *Le Château de Marly* (Paris: Edit Calmann-Lévy, 1934); André Mellerio, *Marly-le-Roi* (Paris: Imprimière Léon Desveaud, 1926).

44. L'Enfant to the Commissioners, May 30, 1800, *op. cit.*

45. Washington to Jefferson, Philadelphia, November 30, 1791, in Padover, *Jefferson and the National Capital*, 79–80; Jefferson to L'Enfant, Philadelphia, December 1, 1791, and L'Enfant to Roberdeau, Georgetown, December 16 and 25, 1791, L'Enfant Papers, L.C.; Washington to Jefferson, Philadelphia, January 18 and February 22, 1792, Fitzpatrick, *Writings of Washington*, vol. XXXI, 462–83.

46. Washington to David Stuart, Philadelphia, November 20, 1791, in Caemmerer, *L'Enfant*, 175–76.

47. L'Enfant to the Commissioners, May 30, 1800, *op. cit.*

Chapter 2: The House

1. Washington to Jefferson, Philadelphia, February 15, 1792, and Washington to L'Enfant, Philadelphia, February 28, 1792, in Fitzpatrick, *Writings of Washington*, vol. XXXI, 480–89; Jefferson to Daniel Carroll, Philadelphia, March 1, 1792, George Walker to Jefferson, Georgetown, March 9, 1792, and Andrew Ellicott to Jefferson, Georgetown, April 3, 1792, in Padover, *Jefferson and the National Capital*, 102, 113, 131.

2. L'Enfant to Roberdeau, Georgetown, December 16, 1791, L'Enfant Papers, L.C.; L'Enfant to Washington, "Operations Intended . . . in the Federal City," Philadelphia, January 17, 1792, in Caemmerer, *L'Enfant*, 196–98; Nicholas King to Jefferson, Washington, September 1803, Jefferson Papers, L.C.; Commissioners' Proceedings, September 1791–March 1792; Commissioners to Washington, Georgetown, January 3 and July 13, 1792, Commissioners' letters sent.

3. David Stuart to Washington, Georgetown, February 26, 1792, Commissioners' letters received; Washington's response, Philadelphia, March 8, 1792, Washington Papers, L.C.

4. Samuel Davidson to the Commissioners, Washington, January 31, 1797, Commissioners' letters received; Washington to the Commissioners, Philadelphia, February 20, 1797, Washington Papers, L.C.; Attorney General John Breckenridge to Jefferson, Washington, April 5, 1806, in Padover, *Jefferson and the National Capital*, 366–70.

5. Commissioners to George Brent, Georgetown, November 18 and December 23, 1791, and to Washington, Georgetown, December 21, 1791, Commissioners' letters sent.

6. Commissioners to Jefferson, November 1791 and April 14, 1792, Commissioners' letters sent; Commissioners' agreement with Francis Cabot, November 26, 1791, and Cabot to Commissioners, Philadelphia, December 11, 1791, Commissioners' letters received.

7. Jefferson to Commissioners, Philadelphia, March 6, 1792, Commissioners' letters received; Commissioners to Jefferson, Georgetown, March 14, 1792, Commissioners' letters sent.

8. Jefferson to Commissioners, Philadelphia, March 6 and April 5, 1792, Commissioners' letters received.

9. Jefferson, draft of advertisement, "A Premium," Philadelphia, March 13, 1792, Commissioners' letters received. President Washington's comments are written in pencil on this document.

10. Commissioners' Proceedings, March 22, 1792.

11. Commissioners to Jefferson, Georgetown, March 1792, Commissioners' letters sent.

12. Commissioners' Proceedings, April 12 and August 29, 1792; Collen Williamson to Jefferson, Washington, June 11, 1801, Jefferson Papers, L.C.

13. Washington to Commissioners, Philadelphia, June 8, 1792, Commissioners' letters received. Hoban's references besides Henry Laurens were the legislator Jacob Read and the fiery Irishman Judge Aedanus Burke. All were prominent in state politics and strong advocates of keeping Charleston the state capital. Laurens was directly involved in building the Charleston statehouse, while the others were peripherally connected to it. See Read to Washington, May 24, 1792, and Burke to Washington, May 12, 1792, both Charleston, Commissioners' letters received. Probably because of the importance of these references Hoban seems to have felt little hesitation in going directly to Washington in Philadelphia. His partner Pierce Purcell went at about the same time to the Potomac, where one of the Commissioners showed him the sites of the public buildings.

14. Commissioners to Jefferson, Washington, July 5, 1792, Commissioners' letters sent.

15. Samuel Blodget, Jr., to Jefferson, Boston, June 25, 1792; *U.S. vs. Smith*, cited in Padover, *Jefferson and the National Capital*, 147.

16. Commissioners' Proceedings, July 17 and 18, 1792; Commissioners to Washington, Georgetown, July 19, 1792, Commissioners' letters sent.

17. Washington to Commissioners, Philadelphia, March 3, 1793, Washington Papers, L.C.; Commissioners to Jefferson, Washington, January 5, 1793, Commissioners' letters received.

18. Commissioners' Proceedings, October 22, 1793; Hoban to Joseph Elgar, Washington, January 1829, Commissioner of Public Buildings, letters received, National Archives.

19. Section and plan by James Hoban, Jefferson Papers, Massachusetts Historical Society. See vol. I, plate 4.

20. Commissioners to Washington, Georgetown, July 17, 1792, Commissioners' letters received.

21. Washington to Alexander White, Philadelphia, May 17, 1795, in Fitzpatrick, *Writings of Washington*, vol. XXXIV, 201–3.

22. Washington to Commissioners, Mount Vernon, July 23 [1792], Washington Papers, L.C.

23. Commissioners to Washington, Georgetown, July 19, 1792, Commissioners' letters sent.

24. Commissioners to Mr. Johnson, Georgetown, August 3, 1792, Commissioners' letters sent.

25. *The Gazette and Daily Advertiser*, Charleston, August 9, 1792.

26. Commissioners' Proceedings, October 20, 1792; *Charleston City Gazette*, November 15, 1792.

Chapter 3: The Builders

1. Commissioners to Jefferson, Georgetown, April 11, 1792, Commissioners' letters sent.

2. John Laird to Commissioners, Georgetown, July 5 and November 15, 1792, Commissioners' letters received.

3. Commissioners' Proceedings, September 24, 1791, and April 13, 1792.

4. Commissioners to Washington, March 23, 1794, Commissioners' letters sent.

5. Commissioners' Proceedings, October 6, 1791, April 12, June 1 and 6, 1792; Commissioners to Elisha Owen Williams, Georgetown, January 10, 1792, Commissioners' letters sent. The best account of the workmen's huts involve their removal and demolition, see Commissioners' Proceedings, October 20, 1800, May 16, August 18, September 12, November 12, 1801, and February 3 and May 6, 1802.

6. Commissioners, agreement with William Knowles, Georgetown, April 12, 1792, Commissioners' Proceedings of that date.

7. Commissioners' order to Leonard Harbaugh, Commissioners' Proceedings, April 12, 1792; see also order to John Mountz, January 10 and March 30, 1792, also in the Proceedings.

8. Hoban's birth record is apparently lost, for the registry of the Parish of Cuffe Grange survives no earlier than 1819 and the relevant Ossory wills, County Kilkenny, were destroyed in a fire; U.S. Census, Charleston, 1790; Washington D.C., Census of 1820 lists him and his wife as being over 45; U.S. District Court, Charleston, "Aliens Admitted," Book A, "James Hoban [age not given] from Ireland, no present address given, Architect, admitted September 23, 1791."

9. *Charleston City Gazette*, May 4, 1790.

10. Proprietors of the Irish Traveller, *The Compleat Irish Traveller* (London: Proprietors, 1788), vol. 1, 123; see also the original wax profile of Hoban, White House Collection. See vol. I, plate 8.

11. Margaret M. Phelan, research notes on Hoban, Kilkenny; Gertrude Higgins, "Monument to an Architect," unpublished ms., Dublin, 1976; Earl of Desart and Lady Sybl Lubbock, *A Page From the Past: Memories of the Earl of Desart* (London: Privately Printed, 1936).

12. Earl of Desart and Lady Lubbock, *A Page From the Past*, 188–91; Thomas U. Sadleir and Page L. Dickinson, *Georgian Mansions in Ireland* (Dublin: 1915), 55–60; Iris Origo, *Images and Shadows* (Frome and London: 1970), 40–41.

13. Royal Dublin Society, *Proceedings* (November 23, 1780).

14. Hoban wrote to the Commissioners of the District of Columbia, December 1, 1792: "Being universally acquainted with men in the Building line in Ireland, Particularly with many stonecutters

in Dublin with whom I have been concerned in building, as the Royal Exchange, New[comen's] Bank, and Custom House, all of which buildings were done in the same Stile as the [buildings of Washington]." Commissioners' letters received.

15. See Edward McParland, *Thomas Ivory, Architect* (Dublin: August 1973).

16. Royal Dublin Society, "By-Laws and Ordinances," *Proceedings,* (June 5, 1777).

17. Royal Dublin Society, *Proceedings,* Dublin, November 23, 1780: "In the School for Drawing in Architecture. . . . 2nd Prem. ____ Hoban. . . ." There being no surviving manuscripts of the proceedings after 1745, the original cannot be checked against the printed version, but James Hoban, in America, did claim to have won the prize and did possess a medal from the Society.

18. *Philadelphia Post,* May 25, 1785.

19. Latrobe to Philip Mazzei, Washington, May 29, 1806, in Thomas E. Jeffrey, ed., *The Microfilm Edition of the Papers of Benjamin Henry Latrobe* (Clifton: James T. White and Company, 1976), 52/59. Latrobe Papers, L.C.; see also [Augustus Foster] "Foster's Notes on the United States," *The Quarterly Review,* London (1841): 24. The disclaimer of the Leinster House attribution appeared in Fiske Kimball, "The Genesis of the White House," *Century Magazine,* vol. 95 (February 1918): 523–28. Kimball believed Hoban's model was plate 51 of *Book of Architecture,* published by James Gibbs, 1728. Although the north elevation as built did strikingly resemble the plate in question, the original project bore no resemblance to it, nor did any other feature of the building as finally built. The White House, it will be seen, developed through various modifications of the original 1792 project, not an adherence to a plate in an architectural design book.

20. Robert Pool and John Cash, *Views of the Most Remarkable Public Buildings, Monuments and Other Edifices in the City of Dublin* (Royal Dublin Society: 1780).

21. It might be noted that the first statehouse at Columbia, South Carolina, attributed to Hoban, had hooded windows similar to those of Leinster House and the White House.

22. Commissioners to Washington, Washington, January 5, 1793, Commissioners' letters sent; Hoban's original estimate, Georgetown, January 1793, Commissioners' letters received.

23. Washington to the Commissioners, Philadelphia, March 3, 1793, Washington Papers, L.C.

24. *Ibid.*

25. Commissioners to Hoban, Georgetown, March 14, 1793, Commissioners' letters sent.

26. Commissioners' Proceedings, September 22–25, 1793.

27. *Ibid.,* October 22, 1793; see also Hoban to Commissioners, Washington, October 15, 1793, Commissioners' letters received. It is possible, of course, that at this point Hoban turned to Gibbs, *Book of Architecture,* for ideas, or at least to reassure his client of the merits of the new design. While the north façade as revised could have been devised without recourse to a pattern book, the appearance of the main-floor window hoods might be a reference to Gibbs, even though they also appear at Leinster House.

28. Hoban elevation, north front, President's House, Latrobe Papers, Maryland Historical Society. This is probably the original drawing, reflecting the October 22, 1793, change order.

29. Washington to the Commissioners, Philadelphia, March 30, 1792, in Fitzpatrick, *Writings of Washington,* vol. XXXII, 14.

30. While this cannot be wholly substantiated for lack of a complete record of houses built, no surviving houses before the late 1860s rival its scale, and the White House was, until the 1870s, larger than most state capitols.

31. Commissioners to Jefferson, Georgetown, June 2, 1792, and January 5, 1793, to the Municipality of Bordeaux, Washington, January 4, 1793, to Van Slophords and Hubbard, Washington, July 4, 1792, to James Fenwick, Washington, January 4, 1793, to [James] Traquair, Washington, January 2, 1793, Commissioners' letters sent; Hoban to the Commissioners, Washington, December 1, 1792, Commissioners' letters received.

32. Jefferson to the Commissioners, Philadelphia, December 23, 1792, Commissioners' letters received.

33. Joseph Fenwick to the Commissioners, Bordeaux, April 4, 1793, and James Traquair to the Commissioners, Philadelphia, January 13, 1793, Commissioners' letters received.

34. Baptism record, "Colin" Williamson, June 13, 1727, Register of Births, Parish of Moy and Dyke, Register House, Edinburgh; kinship with John Suter is established in Commissioners to Williamson, Georgetown, April 12, 1792, Commissioners' letters sent; see also Commissioners' Proceedings, August 29, 1792.

35. Collen Williamson to Mr. Grant of Grant, April 17, 1766; Gustavus Scott and William Thornton to Secretary of State Edmund Randolph, July 13, 1795, Commissioners' letters sent; George A. Dixon to Ierne Grant, Edinburgh, March 25 and 30, 1979, White House Historical Association.

36. Collen Williamson, plans and elevations for Moy House, Moray, ca. 1755–1758; Robert Adam, plans for remodeling Moy House, 1763–1765; John Adam to John Grant of Grant, Edinburgh, April 14 and 30 and May 14, 1763, also February 13, March 11, and June 27, 1765, Seafield Estate Papers, on deposit, Scottish Record Office.

37. Jefferson to the Commissioners, Philadelphia, December 23, 1793, Commissioners' letters received.

38. Jefferson to the Commissioners, Philadelphia, December 17, 1792, and

Traquair to the Commissioners, Philadelphia, January 13, 1793, Commissioners' letters received; see also Traquair to Jefferson, Philadelphia, November 29? 1792, and Jefferson's memorandum on Traquair, Philadelphia, December 5, 1792, Jefferson Papers, L.C.

39. Commissioners' Proceedings, May 1–4, 1792.

40. Agreement between Kale and Blodget, Philadelphia, entered in the Commissioners' Proceedings, March 14, 1793.

41. Commissioners' Proceedings, March, April, and May 1792 and *passim* 1792–1798.

42. The most readily accessible early White House bricks are in the walls of the reconstructed greenhouse at Mount Vernon. These were removed from the White House in 1949 and 1950 during the Truman renovation, and while most are probably post-1814, some appear to be earlier, judging from the size.

43. Commissioners' Proceedings, May 1–4, 1792.

44. Washington to the Commissioners, Philadelphia, December 16, 1793, Commissioners' letters received.

45. Commissioners' Proceedings, September–December 1792 and March–October 1793, *passim.*

46. Commissioners to Washington, Georgetown, April 14, 1792, Commissioners' letters sent.

47. Commissioners' Proceedings, December 4, August 3 and 29, 1792, and January 6, August 1 and 29, and October 22, 1793.

48. Commissioners' Proceedings, draft of the advertisement, November 5, 1792, and March 6, 1793; Commissioners to William A. Washington, Georgetown, December 14, 1792, Commissioners' letters sent.

49. Commissioners to Hoban, Washington, July 31, 1793, and to Jonah Thompson, Washington, February 6, Commissioners' letters sent.

50. Commissioners to William Washington, Washington, December 14, 1792, and January 2, 1793, Commissioners' letters sent.

51. Hoban and Henry Lee, agreement, December 12, 1793, Commissioners' Proceedings, December 16–24, 1793, and February 25 and March 15, 1795; also Commissioners to Henry Lee, Washington, March 12, 1795, and April 12, 1796.

52. Frederick R. Goff, ed., "The Federal City in 1793: James Kent's Account of a Journey From New York to the City of Washington, December 5, 1793–January 3, 1794," in Walter W. Ristow, ed., A La Carte: Selected Papers on Maps and Atlases (Washington: Library of Congress, 1972), 146.

53. See McKim, Mead, & White construction photographs, 1902, Sagamore Hill, National Park Service, Oyster Bay, New York; also demolition photographs by Abbie Rowe, 1949–51, Office of the Curator, the White House.

54. Williamson to Jefferson, Washington, June 11, 1801, Jefferson Papers, L.C.; also see Williamson to the Commissioners, Washington, June 5, 1794, Commissioners' letters received.

55. Commissioners to Williamson, Washington, June 3, 1795, Commissioners' letters sent; James Traquair to Commissioners, Philadelphia, January 13, 1793, Commissioners' letters received.

56. In Britain the law "to prevent artificers in the manufactures of Great Britain being seduced into foreign parts" passed in 1750. A subsequent law in 1782 strengthened the first. Both were repealed in 1824.

57. Helen I. Cowan, "British Emigration to British North America 1783–1837," University of Toronto Studies, vol. IV (1928): 14–22. Cowan observes that "Ships went out from the Western coast [of Scotland] to America in war as in peace."

58. Commissioners to the Municipality of Bordeaux, Washington, January 4, 1793, Commissioners' letters sent.

59. Traquair to Jefferson, Philadelphia, November 29? 1792, Jefferson Papers, L.C.

60. Allen C. Clark, Greenleaf and Law in the Federal City (Washington: Press of W.F. Roberts, 1901), 156.

61. George Walker, "A Description of the Situation and Plan of the City of Washington, Now Building, for the Metropolis of America and Established as the Permanent Residence of the Congress after the Year 1800," broadside (London: York Hotel, Bridge Street, Blackfriars, March 12, 1793), Commissioners' letters received.

62. Draft of advertisement to send to foreign newspapers, Commissioners' Proceedings, January 3, 1793.

63. Ibid.

64. Traquair to Jefferson, Philadelphia, November 29? 1792, op.cit.; see also Scottish Records Society, The Burgesses and Guild Brethren of Edinburgh 1751–1846 (Edinburgh: 1935) and P. Williamson, Williamson's Directory for the City of Edinburgh (Edinburgh: 1783).

65. Today's street numbers for these houses are 64 and 66 Queen Street. For an account of the New Town development see A. J. Youngson, The Making of Classical Edinburgh, 1750–1840 (Edinburgh: University Press, 1966).

66. Mark Book of Lodge No. 8, entries 1788–1793, Grand Lodge of Masons, Edinburgh.

67. Washington to Alexander White, Philadelphia, May 17, 1795, Washington Papers, L.C.

68. Washington to Robert Morris, Mount Vernon, September 14, 1795, Washington Papers, L.C.

69. Commissioners' Proceedings, May 4, 1792, March 10 and July 31, 1793, July 30, 1795, February 26, 1799, June 14, October 20, 22, and 24, and November 12, 1800, February 3 and May

2, 1801; see also various citizens' letters to the Commissioners in the fall of 1800, especially November 10, 1800, Commissioners' letters received.

70. Williamson to the Commissioners, Washington, March 11, 1796, and Hoban to the Commissioners, Washington, October 15, 1793, Commissioners' letters received; Commissioners' Proceedings, *passim*; Commissioners to Washington, Washington, August 11, 1793, Commissioners' letters sent.

71. Commissioners' Proceedings, April 10, 1793, and November 10, 1797; Commissioners to Betsy Dunnoho, Washington, July 17, 1795, Commissioners' letters sent. Betsy Dunnoho's house was pulled down about July 20, 1795, according to the Proceedings of three days before.

72. Commissioners' Proceedings, January 15, 1799.

73. Commissioners to Drs. Crocker, Cunningham, and Worthington, Washington, April 17, 1794, and Thomas Munroe to Bennett Fenwick, Washington, June 8, 1796, and Commissioners to William M. Duncan, Washington, January 18, 1797, Commissioners' letters sent; Commissioners' Proceedings, September 26, 1797, and January 11, February 6, April 5, and August 13, 1798.

74. Redmund Purcell to the Commissioners, Washington, March 20, 1798, Commissioners' letters received. This letter lists some of the carpenters by nationality, 11 born in the British Isles, 10 native to North America, but it is difficult to tell which were at the White House and which at the Capitol.

75. List of apprentices, December 5, 1797, Commissioners' Proceedings, shows only 7 apprentices at the White House. The last mention of apprentices in the Proceedings is November 14, 1799, presumably at the White House.

76. Commissioners' Proceedings, April 12, 1792.

77. Commissioners' letters sent and received, annual inventories, *passim*.

78. Stones bearing these marks were removed in 1949 and 1950 during the Truman renovation and with the exception of about 18 were distributed to Masonic lodges throughout North America. A survey made of these marks, with assistance from the some 75 lodges, formed the basis of identifying most of the Scottish stonemasons.

79. Washington to the Commissioners, Philadelphia, February 20, 1797, Washington Papers, L.C.

80. Washington to the Commissioners, Philadelphia, February 15, 1797, Washington Papers, L.C.

81. Commissioners' Proceedings, March 29, 1795; see also Alexander White to the Commissioners, Philadelphia, April 6, 1796, Commissioners' letters received; Commissioners to Col. Deakins, Washington, March 29, 1796, Commissioners' letters sent.

82. Commissioners' Proceedings, November 16, 1797, and May 7, 1798; Commissioners to Alexander White, Washington, February 5, 1796, and March 16, 1798; Commissioners to Washington, Washington, October 1, 1796, Commissioners' letters sent.

83. Commissioners to Washington, Washington, January 31, 1797, Commissioners' letters sent.

84. Commissioners to Washington, Washington, February 20, 1797, Commissioners' letters sent.

85. Commissioners to Washington, Washington, January 31, 1797, Commissioners' letters sent.

86. *The Washington Gazette,* March 15, 1797.

87. White to the Commissioners, Philadelphia, March 8, 1798, Commissioners' letters sent.

88. Commissioners' Proceedings, November 19 and December 12, 1798, and April 11, 1799; Commissioners to Leonard Harbaugh and William Lovering, Washington, May 9, 1799, Commissioners' letters sent; Washington to David

Humphreys, Mount Vernon, June 26, 1797, Washington Papers. L.C.

89. Commissioners' Proceedings, February 20, 1797. This decision was made quietly, in anticipation of Washington's retirement two weeks later. Washington had warmly opposed an earlier effort that same month to suspend work on the White House.

90. Commissioners' Proceedings, December 5, 1797; Peter Lennox, monthly reports 1800, Commissioners' letters received, *passim;* Commissioners to Philip Gadsden, Washington, April 25, 1797, Commissioners' letters sent.

91. Commissioners' Proceedings, April 16, 17, 21, 23, 1798; Commissioners to the stonecutters, Washington, April 16, 1798, Commissioners' letters sent.

92. Commissioners' Proceedings, May 10 and 28, August 21, and September 22–25, 1798.

93. Commissioners' Proceedings, March 17, 1799.

94. Commissioners' Proceedings, April 15, 1800.

95. Commissioners' Proceedings, December 1799–October 1800, *passim;* Commissioners to Harrison & Mayndier, Washington, April 2, 1800, and to Benjamin Stoddert, Washington, April 8, 1800, Commissioners' letters sent; Hugh Densley to the Commissioners, Washington, December 8, 1798, Commissioners' letters received.

96. Commissioners to Harrison and Mayndier, Washington, October 15, 1799, and to Samuel Blodget, Washington, June 2, 1800, Commissioners' letters sent; hardware invoice, September 10, 1799, Commissioners' miscellaneous papers.

97. Commissioners' Proceedings, May 23 and June 4, 1800; Alexander White, memorial to the Commissioners, Washington, June 14, 1800, Commissioners' letters received.

98. White to the Commissioners, Phila-

delphia, March 22, 1798, Commissioners' letters received.

99. Commissioners to Stoddert, Washington, April 19, 1800, Commissioners' letters sent.

100. Stoddert to William Thornton, Philadelphia, January 20 and 30, 1800, William Thornton Papers, L.C.

101. Commissioners' Proceedings, March-November 1800, *passim;* Diary of Mrs. Thornton, CHS *Records,* vol. X (1907): 153.

102. Commissioners to Washington, Washington, October 1, 1796, Commissioners' letters sent.

103. Stuart's authorship of the Washington portrait has been contested since soon after it was hung in the White House. Mrs. Thornton noted in a letter to Dolley Madison, Washington, August 24, 1802, that Stuart went to see the picture in the President's House and denied it (Madison Papers, University of Virginia Library). The controversy first appeared in print in 1834 in William Dunlap, *A History of the Rise and Progress of the Arts of Design of the United States* (Boston: C.E. Goodspeed & Co., reprint 1918), vol. I, 193–239. A rather constant stream of pros and cons followed until a definitive study was made of the documents and the portrait itself when it was restored 1977–1978. The conclusion was that stylistically and technically the portrait was indeed a Stuart and not a copy by William Winstanley, said to have been made ca. 1800. See Marion F. Mecklenburg and Justine Wimsatt, "The White House Full Length Portrait of George Washington by Stuart: Conservation Treatment Report and Commentary" (Kensington, Maryland, Washington Conservation Studio, October 1978, unpublished ms., OCWH). But the debate has doubtless not ended. See vol. I, plate 1.

104. Commissioners to George Andrews, Washington, November 1, 1800, Commissioners' letters sent.

105. Diary of Mrs. Thornton, *op. cit.,* 207–8.

106. John Adams to Mrs. Adams, President's House, Washington, November 2, 1800, in Charles Francis Adams, ed., *Letters of John Adams Addressed to His Wife* (Boston: Little, Brown & Co., 1841), 267. The original of this letter is in the Adams Papers, Massachusetts Historical Society.

Chapter 4: Anachronism

1. Abigail Adams to "dear child," Washington, November 21, 1800, in Charles Francis Adams, *Letters of Mrs. Adams, the Wife of John Adams* (Boston: Little & Brown, 1840), vol. II, 201.

2. Mrs. Adams to her sister, Philadelphia, November 10, 1800, in Stewart Mitchell, ed., *New Letters of Abigail Adams* (Boston: Houghton Mifflin Co., 1947), 254–55.

3. *The Times and District of Columbia Daily Advertiser*, March 16, 1801; Mrs. Adams to Adams, Quincy, February 11, 1784, and to Mrs. Cranch, February 10, 1788, in L. H. Butterfield *et al*, eds., *Diary and Autobiography of John Adams* (Cambridge: Harvard University Press, 1961), vol. III, 156.

4. Commissioners' Proceedings, November 1800-March 1801, *passim*.

5. Mrs. Adams to her sister, Philadelphia, April 28, 1798, *New Letters of Abigail Adams*, 167–68.

6. Inventory of the President's House, February 27, 1801, Commissioners' miscellaneous papers, also Legislative Records, Sixth Congress, Senate, National Archives.

7. *Ibid.*; Marie G. Kimball, "The Original Furnishings of the White House," *Antiques*, vol. IV (July 1929): 482–84; Abigail Adams to "dear child," *op. cit.*

8. *Washington Federalist*, November 27, 1800; *National Intelligencer*, November 28, 1800, notes that when the House called, "A considerable number of members remained behind."

9. *Ibid.*; J. B. Osborne, "Removal of the Government," CHS *Records*, vol. III (1900): 136–60.

10. Gouvernor Morris to Princess de la Tour et Taxis, Washington, December 14, 1800, in Anne Cary Morris, ed., *The Diary and Letters of Gouvenor Morris* (New York: Scribner's, 1888), vol. II, 394–95; Mrs. Adams to her sister, Philadelphia, June 23, 1797, in *New Letters of Abigail Adams*, 98–99.

11. Mrs. Adams to her sister, Washington, December 8, 1800, *New Letters of Abigail Adams*, 261–62.

12. Diary of Mrs. Thornton, 219.

13. Margaret Brown Klapthor, "A First Lady And A New Frontier, 1800," *Historic Preservation*, vol. XV (1963): 88–93.

14. Mrs. Adams to her sister, Washington, January 15, 1801, *New Letters of Abigail Adams*, 262–64; see also Page Smith, *John Adams* (New York: Doubleday & Co., 1962), vol. II, 1060.

15. Jefferson to Benjamin Rush, Monticello, January 16, 1811, in Andrew A. Lipscomb, *Writings of Jefferson* (Charlottesville: Thomas Jefferson Memorial Association, 1904), vol. XIII, 1–9. Versions of this encounter and its location vary. Jefferson's letter relates his own response, but does not set the scene.

16. Page Smith, *John Adams*, vol. II, 1067.

17. Jefferson to Mrs. Adams, Washington, June 13, 1804, Adams Papers, Massachusetts Historical Society.

18. Gaillard Hunt, ed., *The First 40 Years of Washington Society in the Family Letters of Margaret Bayard Smith* (New York: F. Ungar Publishing Company, 1965), 60.

19. Mrs. Harrison Smith [Margaret Bayard Smith] "The President's House Forty Years Ago," *Godey's Lady's Book*, (November 1843): 212–13.

20. *National Intelligencer*, March 11, 1801.

21. Adams to Jefferson, Washington, February 20, 1801, in Lester J. Cappon, ed., *The Adams-Jefferson Letters*, 2 vols., (Chapel Hill: Institute of Early American History and Culture, 1959), 263.

22. Commissioners' Proceedings, March 10, 1801; Commissioners to Mr. Thompson, Washington, April 30, 1801, and to William Blodget, March 12, 1801, Commissioners' letters sent.

23. The south door openings intended for the great open gallery or porch overlooking the river remain cut into the wall of the White House, and are filled with windows and wooden jib-doors in the Green, Blue, and Red Rooms.

24. William Claxton, inventory of the President's House, [February 19, 1809], "small dining room, S. front," Jefferson Papers, L.C.

25. Commissioners' Proceedings, March 13, May 22, September 22, and November 19, 1801.

26. Thornton to Lord Hawkesbury, Washington, December 9, 1801, see transcripts, British ministers to the U.S.A. writing to the Foreign Office, vol. V, 32, L.C.

27. Jefferson to Richard M. Johnson, Washington, March 10, 1808, Lipscomb, vol. XII, 9–10.

28. Cranch to Shaw, Washington, May 15, 1801, Cranch Papers, Massachusetts Historical Society.

29. Jefferson to Lewis, Washington, February 23, 1801, in Richard Dillon, *Meriwether Lewis* (New York: Coward-McCann, 1965), 25–26.

30. Cranch to Shaw, Washington, May 15, 1801, *op. cit.*; see also Commissioners' Proceedings, March 13, 1801.

31. Margaret Smith, *Society*, 383–87.

32. Lewis to his mother, Washington, July 2, 1802, in *The Virginia Magazine of History and Biography*, vol. XLV, (October 1937): 331–32; Dillon, *Meriwether Lewis*, 55.

33. Zebulon M. Pike to Jefferson, 10° C.A.M. [October 29, 1807] in Donald Jackson, ed., *The Journals of Zebulon Montgomery Pike* (Norman: University of Oklahoma Press, 1966), 275–76; Jefferson to Caspar Wistar, Washington,

March 20, 1808, Jefferson Papers, L.C.; Richard Beale Davis, ed., *Augustus John Foster: Jeffersonian America* (San Marino: Huntington Library, 1954), 12. "The room we were shown into [at the White House] was filled—furnished. There were some Indian ornaments and a Hooker pipe lying on the table. . . . "

34. Pike to Jefferson, Washington, February 3, 1808, in Jackson, *Pike*, 292–94.

35. Jefferson to Charles Willson Peale, Washington, February 6, 1808, in Jackson, *Pike*, 294.

36. Jefferson to Lewis, Washington, June 20, 1803, in Donald Jackson, ed., *Letters of the Lewis and Clark Expedition* (Urbana: University of Illinois Press, 1962), 61–66.

37. Margaret Smith, *Society*, 401–02.

38. *National Intelligencer*, May 26, 1804; see Herman J. Viola, *Diplomats in Buckskins: A History of Indian Delegations in Washington City* (Washington: Smithsonian Institution Press, 1981).

39. Augustus John Foster, Bart., *Jeffersonian America* (San Marino: The Huntington Library, 1954), 31–32.

40. White House inventory, 1809, *op. cit.*

41. *Ibid.*

42. Etienne Lemaire, account book, December 18, 1806–March 1809, Huntington Library; bill of Charles Craig, blacksmith, April 12, 1802, Commissioners' letters received.

43. Jefferson to Mary Jefferson Eppes, Monticello, April 11, 1801, in Thomas Jefferson Randolph, *Memoir, Correspondence and Miscellanies From the Papers of Thomas Jefferson* (Charlottesville: F. Carr & Co., 1829), 236; LeMaire account book, *passim*; Margaret Smith, *Society*, 313–14.

44. Lemaire account book; Jefferson to John W. Eppes, Monticello, August 7, 1804, in Randolph, *Memoir*, 264–65; bill of Thomas Carpenter for servants' livery, Washington, March 31, 1801, Thomas Jefferson Memorial Foundation.

45. Lemaire account book.

46. Commissioners' Proceedings, August 8, 1801; see also building contract between the Commissioners, John Caton, and Bartholomew Crowley, same date, Commissioners' miscellaneous papers.

47. Augustus Foster, "Letters," 28; Margaret Smith, Society, 30–31 and 386–90; see also Marie Kimball, "The Epicure of the White House," Virginia Quarterly Review, vol. VIV (January 1933): 71–81. There were several dumbwaiters in Jefferson's White House. Only one was built in permanently and that is said to have been in the small dining room, today's Green Room. It is very unlikely that this was the case, since the "mechanical" dumbwaiter—pivoted more than likely like the one at Monticello—filled a door opening, and the small dining room had only two doors, one into the transverse hall and a second into the unfinished East Room. In all probability the spinning dumbwaiter was actually attached to Jefferson's state dining room, today's family dining room, turning into the doorkeeper's lodge, thus giving the servants easy access to the service stair that connected the basement with the upper floors of the house.

48. Jefferson to Mary Eppes, Washington, October 26, 1801, Randolph, Memoir, 239.

49. Jefferson to Thomas Jefferson Randolph, Washington, November 24, 1808, Randolph, Memoir, 274.

50. Augustus Foster, "Letters," 26–27; Dumas Malone, Jefferson and His Time: Jefferson the President (Boston: Little, Brown, 1970), vol. 4, 378–81.

51. Paul Leicester Ford, ed., The Works of Thomas Jefferson (New York: G.P. Putnam's Sons, 1905), vol. X, 66.

52. Ibid.

53. Ford, ed., The Works of Jefferson, vol. X, 47–48.

54. Margaret Smith, Society, 398–400; Major Edwin N. McClellan, "How the Marine Band Started," United States Naval Institute Proceedings, vol. 49 (April 1923): 581–86. The Marine Band was often called the "Italian band" in the early 1800s, since it was composed almost entirely of Italian military band performers brought to the United States to play in the band. See National Intelligencer, July 20, 1804; also Marine Corps letterpress books for this period, National Archives; and Narrative of Gaetano Carusi in Support of His Claim Before the Congress of the United States (Washington: U.S. Government, n.d. [ca. 1818]).

55. Margaret Smith, Society, 398–400.

56. L'Enfant to Jefferson, Washington, November 3 and March 12, 1802; Jefferson's response, Washington, March 14, 1802, Jefferson Papers, L.C.

57. Hoban to the Commissioners, Washington, June 23, 1801, Commissioners' letters received; Commissioners' Proceedings, April-July 1801, passim.

58. Latrobe to Jefferson, Wilmington, May 5, 1805, in Padover, Jefferson and the National Capital, 360; also Latrobe, Report on the Public Buildings (Washington: Government Printing Office, 1806), 4.

59. A sketch in Jefferson's hand shows his projected ideas for the White House grounds. Cartographic Division, L.C. This further shows the relative scale of the two pavilions in outline. It is clear that a large archway was to have been on the east, but nothing is known of the western pavilion but its ground outline. Among Jefferson's unidentified drawings is an elevation for a garden house, which would probably have served the spot in the west wing. It is two story, entered on higher grade on the second level on one side, and on its lower floor on the other; thus it was designed to serve a sharply declining grade. And it was to be set north/south. The upper floor Jefferson described as "Entrance to garden," on the north, while the lower floor, on the south, he called the "ground floor greenhouse." Rooms inside

are labeled "lodges." It has been speculated that this building was for the vegetable garden at Monticello. A more
likely designation might be the west
wing of the White House, to balance
the arched gate on the east. The original drawing, in pencil, is in the Jefferson Papers, Massachusetts Historical
Society (#K153).

60. Commissioners' Proceedings, October 13, 1801; ground plan in Jefferson's
hand; Robert King and Nicholas King,
field notes for surveying in the President's Park, Cartographic Division, L.C.;
Latrobe, *Report* (Washington: Government Printing Office, May 23, 1808)
describes the walkways Jefferson and he
had proposed; Jefferson to Latrobe, Monticello, June 2, 1808, in Padover, *Jefferson and the National Capital*, 429–32.

61. Latrobe's report, May 23, 1808, *op.
cit.*

62. Jefferson sketches, "eastern and
western offices," Jefferson Papers, Massachusetts Historical Society.

63. Talbot Hamlin, *Benjamin Henry
Latrobe* (New York: Oxford University
Press, 1955), 300.

64. Jefferson's sketches for the wings,
op. cit.; Jefferson's 1809 inventory;
"memorandum for Mr. Lenthall," unsigned but in Jefferson's hand, July 14,
1805, and Latrobe to Lenthall, Ironhill,
July 29, 1805, Latrobe Papers, L.C.

65. Jefferson to Latrobe, Monticello,
April 22, 1807, and Latrobe's response,
Philadelphia, May 21, 1807, in Padover,
Jefferson and the National Capital, 386–
87, 390–92.

66. Latrobe to Lenthall, Wilmington,
May 3, 1805, in Hamlin, *Latrobe*, 294.

67. Latrobe to Lenthall, Wilmington,
May 11, 1805; also Jefferson to Lenthall,
Washington [May 5, 1805], Latrobe Pa-
pers, L.C.

68. Jefferson, *Message From the President
of the United States Communicating a Report of the Surveyor of Public Buildings*
(Washington: A. & G. Way, Printers
[Government Printing], 1805), 7.

69. Latrobe to Lenthall, Philadelphia,
December 31, 1806, in Hamlin, *Latrobe*,
295.

70. Hamlin, *Latrobe*, 285.

71. Latrobe to Lenthal, Ironhill, July
29, 1805, Latrobe Papers, L.C.

72. Latrobe's several projects for this
remodeling, south front, east end, and
plan, 1807 (although this date may have
been added later), Latrobe Papers, Library of Congress.

73. Jefferson to Latrobe, Monticello,
June 2, 1808, in Padover, *Jefferson and
the National Capital*, 429–32.

Chapter 5: The Trial

1. Hamlin, *Latrobe*, 333.

2. Latrobe to Jefferson, Washington,
September 1, 1807, in Jeffrey, *Latrobe
Microfiche*, 192/B9.

3. Latrobe to John Lenthall, Washington, May 3, 1805, *Ibid.*, 178/F13.

4. Allen Clark, *Life and Letters of Dolly
Madison* (Washington: Press of W.F.
Roberts, 1914), 141, *passim*; Conover
Hunt-Jones, *Dolley and the "Great Little
Madison,"* (Washington: The American
Institute of Architects Foundation,
1977), 11–27, *passim*.

5. Latrobe to Mrs. Madison, April 21,
May 7, September 28, November 23,
December 7, 1809, Latrobe Papers, L.C.

6. John H. McCormick, "The First
Master of Ceremonies of the White
House," CHS *Records*, vol. VII (1904):
171–94.

7. Clark, *Life and Letters of Dolly Madison*, 222.

8. G. Franklin Edwards and Michael R.
Winston, eds., "A Colored Man's Reminiscences of James Madison [1865],"
White House History, vol. I (1983): 46–
51.

9. Latrobe to Madison, Washington,
March 14, 1809, Latrobe Papers L.C.;
Latrobe to Munroe, Washington, June 1,

1809, Commissioner's letters received; Latrobe to Mrs. Madison, Washington, September 8, 1809, White House Collection; Margaret Brown Klapthor, "Benjamin Latrobe and Dolley Madison Decorate the White House," *Contributions From the Museum of History and Technology*, paper 49 (1965): 153–64; Claude G. Bowers, ed., *The Diary of Elbridge Gerry, Jr.* (New York: Brentano's, 1927), 179.

10. Latrobe to Mrs. Madison, Washington, September 8, 1809, *op. cit.*; see also various bills for goods and services in the Commissioner's records, National Archives and the Latrobe Papers, Maryland Historical Society.

11. Latrobe to Jacob Mark, Washington, August 1, 1809, Latrobe Papers, Maryland Historical Society.

12. Ethel Lewis, *The White House* (New York: Dodd, Mead & Company, 1937), 69–70. This source is rather uncertain, for Lewis's own sources are not given; yet it is the only real description of the parlor now known as the Red Room, as Madison knew it. The purchase orders, while not complete, do not call for a large quantity of yellow material, although Mary Sweeney could have dyed the fabric. Because the description has a strong ring of accuracy I have used it, but the Lewis description cannot be considered absolute.

13. Latrobe to Madison, Washington, July 5, 1809, Madison Papers, L.C.; Latrobe to Mrs. Madison, Washington, September 8, 1809, White House Collection.

14. For details of decorating the oval drawing room under Madison, see Klapthor, "Benjamin Latrobe and Dolley Madison Decorate the White House," *op. cit.*

15. Note Hoban's plan, vol. I, plate 4.

16. John and Hugh Finley to Latrobe, Baltimore, September 16, 1809, bill cited in Klapthor, "Benjamin Latrobe and Dolley Madison Decorate the White House," 158. Latrobe's inspiration for the furniture is sometimes ascribed to Thomas Hope's *Household Furniture* (London: Hope, May 1807); if indeed Latrobe found his models in a book or books, the Sheraton attribution seems to me more plausible, both in point of its Grecian-style contents and the earlier date. Latrobe's Blue Room chairs, with their heavy stretchers, and certainly his sofas, reflect more the taste of Sheraton than of Hope. The Grecian mode was well established when he left England for America. His own personal interest in the subject of Grecian design was firmly entrenched in the 1790s, when he studied the drawings of the British sculptor John Flaxman. His own drawings in the late 1790s in America show his predilection for the neoclassical. See Charles E. Brownell, "An Introduction to the Art of Latrobe's Drawings," in Edward C. Carter, II, John C. Van Horne, and Charles E. Brownell, eds., *Latrobe's View of America, 1795-1820* (New Haven: Yale University Press, 1985), 17–40.

17. Latrobe, drawing of the oval drawing room mantel and overmantel mirror with lambrequin decorations, Latrobe Papers, Maryland Historical Society.

18. Latrobe to Joseph Norris, Washington, June 6, 1809, Latrobe Papers, Maryland Historical Society.

19. Latrobe to Mrs. Madison, April 21, 1809, Latrobe Papers, New York Public Library.

20. Lewis Deblois to the commissioner of public buildings, Washington, October 29, 1813; Daniel Kennedy to the commissioner, Philadelphia, February 13 and December 13, 1813, bill for 2,000 common bricks bought "for stove," October 29, 1813, Commissioner's letters received; see also description of the workings of the Pettibone furnace in Daniel Pettibone, *Description of the Improvements of the Rarifying Air-Stove for Warming and Ventilating* (Philadelphia: by the author, 1810) and Daniel Pettibone, *Pettibone's Economy of Fuel* (Philadelphia: by the author, 1812).

21. Margaret Smith, *Society*; Hunt-

Jones, Dolley and the "Great Little Madison"; Clark, Life and Letters of Dolly Madison, passim; see also Singleton, The White House, vol. I, 63.

22. Singleton, The White House, vol. I, 64; Frances Jeffrey, "Journal of a Trip to the U.S. in 1813," typescript of the ms., ocwh.

23. Mrs. William Seaton, diary, November 12, 1812, in Josephone Seaton, ed., William Winston Seaton of the National Intelligencer (Boston: James R. Osgood & Co., 1871), 84–86.

24. Eliza Cope Harrison, ed., Philadelphia Merchant: The Diary of Thomas P. Cope, 1800–1851 (South Bend: Gateway Editions, Ltd., 1978), 261.

25. Mrs. Seaton, diary, January 2, 1814, in Seaton of the Intelligencer, 113; see also David Gantt to Sam Lane, Philadelphia, June 7, 1807, sends "2 bottles of snuff" of the sort he has "often supplied Mrs. Madison with," Commissioner's letters received.

26. Irving, quoted in Singleton, The White House, 65.

27. Preston's letter is quoted in Clark, Life and Letters of Dolly Madison, 141.

28. Harrison, Diary of Thomas P. Cope, 262.

29. Jeffrey, "Journal, 1813."

30. George Poindexter to William C. Mead, Washington, April 10, 1812, in Bernard Mayo, ed., Henry Clay: Spokesman of the New West (Boston: Houghton Mifflin Co., 1937).

31. That Madison signed the declaration of war in the Green Room is likely, but ultimately only my supposition.

32. John Betts's bill, August 2, 1813, Commissioner's letters received.

33. Mrs. Madison to Hannah Gallatin, Washington, July 28 and August 9, 1814, in Carl E. Prince, ed., The Papers of Albert Gallatin, microfilm edition, 1970; also see Mrs. Madison to her sister, August 23, 1814, [copy ca. 1804], Dolley Madison Papers, l.c.

34. Monroe's warning of the morning of August 22 appears in Committee Appointed to Investigate the Capture of Washington, Report (Washington: 13th Congress, 1815).

35. Jennings, "A Colored Man's Reminiscences," 48.

36. Mrs. Madison to her sister, Washington, August 23, 1814, op. cit.

37. Ibid.; Jennings, "A Colored Man's Reminiscences," 48.

38. Mrs. William Jones to Mrs. Madison, Washington, August 22, 1814, in Clark, Life and Letters of Dolly Madison, 105–6; James Scott, Recollections of a Naval Life (London: R. Bentley, 1834), 130–31.

39. Jennings, "A Colored Man's Reminiscences," 48–49.

40. Mrs. Madison to her sister, Washington, August 23, 1814, op. cit.

41. Mrs. Madison to Mrs. Latrobe, Washington, December 3, 1814, in Hamlin, Latrobe, 303–4.

42. Jennings, "A Colored Man's Reminiscences," 48.

43. George McCue, The Octagon (Washington: American Institute of Architects, 1976), 59.

44. "Nace his Rhodes" to "dear sir," Washington? April 24, 1815, "President's plate . . . urns, branch candlesticks, waiters & c." Commissioner's letters received.

45. Scott, Naval Recollections, 130; "Memoir of Major-General Robert Ross," The United Service Journal and Naval and Military Magazine, (London: Henry Colburn, 1829), part 1, 414.

46. Margaret Smith, Society, 111–12; G. R. Gleig, A Narrative of the Campaigns of the British Army at Washington and New Orleans (London: Murray, 1826), 70–74; London Courier, October 3, 1814.

47. Mrs. Thornton's eyewitness account as told to Mrs. Smith, Mrs. Smith to

Mrs. Kilpatrick, Washington, August 30, 1814, in Margaret Smith, *Society*, 111–112.

48. *Ibid.*; the principal work of burning the White House was carried out by Midshipman Samuel Decimus Davies and four sailors, all from Admiral Cockburn's flagship *Albion*, see Samuel Decimus Davies to his mother, H.M.S. *Albion*, Chespeak Bay North America, August 31, 1814, quoted in S. B. Davies, *The Rise and Fall of a Regency Dandy* (Oxford: Oxford University Press, 1981), 223–25.

49. Washington *City Gazette*, September 19, 1814; Hunt-Jones, *Dolley and the "Great Little Madison,"* 54–57; William Noland, inventory made in March 1825, reprinted as House Document 2, May 22, 1840, Commissioner's records say that Madison "hastily" collected furniture at auction houses and that they "never suited" the White House but were bought for smaller, temporary housing.

50. Margaret Smith, *Society*, 110–11; Mrs. Thornton's diary, 178–79. Mrs. Thornton also noted that the Madisons were guarded at all times and that the guards slept on straw: "even dogs have kennels," she wrote, 179.

Chapter 6: The Phoenix

1. Payment to Sioussat, [October] 1814, Commissioner's letters sent. The gully, which appears on all the early topographical maps, is today the site of the White House swimming pool. In the course of building the pool in the Ford administration in 1975, an archaeological analysis was made of the large quantity of dirt removed from the location and it revealed thousands of broken household items, including shards of Madison's china. See J. M. Young, "Archaeological Analysis of Excavations at the White House, Washington, D.C., A Preliminary Report," ms., Department of Anthropology, Montgomery College, Rockville, Maryland, May 13, 1977.

2. Hadfield's report, October 15, 1814, Commissioner's letters received.

3. Madison to the Commissioners, Montpelier, May 23, 1815, Madison Papers, l.c.; Commissioners' Proceedings, March 14, 1815.

4. Commissioners' Proceedings, March 23, 1815.

5. Latrobe to Munroe, Pittsburgh, February 16, 1815, Commissioners' letters received.

6. Hamlin, *Latrobe*, 434–36.

7. Sam Lane to Lewis Condict, Washington, February 15, 1817, Commissioner's letters sent.

8. Commissioners' Proceedings, March to May 1815, *passim*.

9. Commissioners' Proceedings, March 1815 to October 1816, *passim*.

10. Lane, *Report* (Washington: by the government, 1816), also draft of the report in commissioner's letters sent.

11. Report of James Hoban, ms. [1816], Harry and Mary Dalton Papers, Duke University Library.

12. Abstract of disbursements for rebuilding "or Repairing" the President's House, April 1, 1815, to July 1, 1817, *passim*, Commissioner's records.

13. Hoban to the Commissioners, August 12 and August 16, 1816, Commissioner's letters received.

14. Commissioners' proceedings, 1815-1816, *passim*.

15. Peter Lennox to Lane, Washington, October 22, 1816, Commissioner's letters received.

16. Lennox to Lane, April 28, 1817; bill of John McComb for mahogany veneering, New York, August 3, 1815, Commissioner's letters received; James Webb to Lane, Washington, April 10 and 12, 1818, Commissioner's miscellaneous warrants.

17. Harry Ammon, *James Monroe: The Quest for National Identity* (New York: McGraw-Hill Book Company, 1971), 139.

18. Monroe to Lane, Washington, April 4, 1817, Monroe Papers, Library of Congress.

19. William Thakara, Jr., to Lane, Washington, April 10, 1817, Commissioner's letters received.

20. Lennox to Lane, Washington, June 26, 1817.

21. Peter Lennox, report to Lane, Washington, June 26, 1817; Lennox's bill for trip to Elizabethtown, N.C., Washington, May 6, 1817, Commissioner's letters received.

22. Lennox report, June 26, 1817, *op. cit.*

23. Hoban to Lane, Washington, February 8, 1817, Commissioner's letters sent; Hoban report, [1818] in *Report of the Committee on the Expenditures of the Public Buildings* (Washington: Government Printing Office, April 3, 1818). Apparently the marble mantels were bought through a London agent, Baring Brothers & Co. Twenty-five "statuary marble" mantels arrived at the Potomac River landing and were delivered to the White House February 23, 1819, shipped by Purviance, Nichols & Co., Leghorn, Italy, August 22, 1817, see invoice and bills of lading, Commissioner's letters received. The white marble mantels in the Red and Green Rooms today were among those in this shipment.

24. James Martin to Lane, Washington, May 1, 1817, miscellaneous Treasury accounts, National Archives.

25. The bills of Alexandre and Perdreauville, sometimes undated, are numerous and apparently complete in the miscellaneous Treasury warrants, April 1817-December 1818.

26. Ammon, *James Monroe*, 366, 396–405; the President's eagerness to move in and his minute attention to furnishings reveal the importance he attached to the restoration of the Presidency and the White House.

27. John Quincy Adams, diary, December 29, 1817, in Singleton, *The White House*, vol. I, 132.

28. *National Intelligencer*, January 3, 1818.

29. P. Mauro to Lane, Washington, January 1, 1818, miscellaneous Treasury warrants.

30. At least some of this moving about was carried out by Alexandre, see bills, *passim*, in miscellaneous Treasury warrants for the year 1818.

31. Charles and T. P. Andrews to Lane, Washington, October 9, 1818, miscellaneous Treasury warrants.

32. Purviance, Nichols & Co., to Lane, Leghorn, August 22, 1817, and October 13, 1818, Commissioner's letters received.

33. Josiah Condor, *The Modern Traveller: A Description of the Various Countries of the Globe* (London: Thomas Tegg and James Duncan, 1828), vol. XXIV, 77; Hoban to Lane, Washington, December 28, 1818; Hoban, report to the commissioners, Washington, December 23, 1819; John McComb to Lane, New York, April 9, 1819, Commissioner's letters received; John Kennedy to Lane, Washington, August 12, 1819; payroll for November 1819, miscellaneous Treasury warrants.

34. The four buildings were demolished later in the 19th century and replaced with the present Treasury on the east and State, War, & Navy (Executive Office Building) on the west. The original columns of the War Department were made into the Sheridan Gate at Arlington and are presently in storage. They are Roman Ionic, like the columns of the White House.

35. Hoban to Lane, Washington, February 8, 1817, Commissioner's letters sent (misfiled); Lane, *Report of the Committee on the Expenditure of Public Buildings*.

36. Lane, *Report of the Committee on the Public Buildings* (Washington: January 7, 1819); Hoban, report to Lane, Washing-

ton, December 23 and 28, 1818, Commissioner's letters received; miscellaneous Treasury warrants, December 1818–October 1820, *passim.*

37. James Neilson to Lane, Baltimore, March 11, 1818, miscellaneous Treasury warrants.

38. This furniture can be seen today in the James Monroe Law Office Museum in Fredericksburg, Virginia.

39. *Statement of William Lee, Esquire, Agent for Procuring Furniture for the President's House* (Washington: E. DeKrafft, February 24, 1818.)

40. Hans Huth, "The White House Furniture at the Time of Monroe," *Gazette Des Beaux Arts,* vol. 29 (January 1946): 24–25.

41. *Statement of William Lee,* (Washington: by the government, March 9, 1818.)

42. Russell & LaFarge to James Monroe, Havre, n.d., [probably postscript to a letter of September 15, 1817] File on Monroe's furnishings, Commissioner's correspondence and papers.

43. *Ibid.*

44. Margaret Brown Klapthor, *Official White House China: 1789 to the Present* (Washington: Smithsonian Institution Press, 1975), 40–46.

45. William Lee to Joseph Russell, Washington, January 1, 1818, Commissioner's letters sent.

46. Robert Donaldson, "A Tour of Recreation," 1818, ms., University of North Carolina Library.

47. Alexander Macomb to Jane Kennedy, Washington, November 6, 1825, Burton Historical Collection, Detroit Public Library.

48. *Ibid.*

49. This comes from various sources, including the household inventory completed March 24, 1825, Rene Perdreauville's bills for April 17, 1817, Alexandre's for January 29, 1819, and James Yard's for January 23, 1818, mis-

cellaneous Treasury warrants and the Commissioner's letters received.

50. Inventory of March 24, 1825; Alexandre's bills from May to October for work in the house, miscellaneous Treasury warrants.

51. Charles and T. P. Andrews, bills for plaster work, Washington, October 9 and November 29, 1817; also Andrews's bills July 1, 7, 17, 18, 20, 1819, miscellaneous Treasury warrants; Margaret Smith, *Society,* 72; Captain Basil Hall, *Travels in North America in the Years 1827 and 1828* (Philadelphia: Carey, Lea & Carey, 1829), 127.

52. A fine collection of Mrs. Monroe's dresses and jewelry is in the James Monroe Law Office Museum, Fredericksburg, Virginia.

53. Ammon, *James Monroe,* 406–7.

54. Bills for payment of Thomas Conlon, 1819–1822, miscellaneous Treasury warrants, *passim.*

55. John Quincy Adams, "Procedures at the President's House," March 13, 1819, in Singleton, *The White House,* vol. I, 139; *National Intelligencer,* 1818–1825, *passim.*

56. James Fennimore Cooper, *Notions of the Americans* (New York: Stringer & Townsend, 1850), 60.

57. John Vanderlyn to Lane, New York, March 26, 1819, proposals and estimates, Commissioner of Public Buildings records, National Archives; Vanderlyn scholar William T. Oedel finds no other mention of the painter's decoration of the East Room, but point to two large allegorical drawings of justice and war, pricked for chalk dust transfer to another surface, in the manner of fresco art. These are "unique in Vanderlyn's work, but it would seem that they were intended as wall decoration rather than preparatory studies for paintings." While the possibility remains fascinating, no documents have been found that connect them to the East Room. Oedel to the author, Media, Pennsylvania, March 29, 1979.

Chapter 7: End of the Old Order

1. Caemmerer, *L'Enfant*, 402.

2. *Ibid.*

3. The date or general time of the first use of the name White House has been debated for many years. That it was in use before the fire is well established. The house was whitewashed in 1797 even before it was complete; that it was white before the British visit is documented visually in William Strickland's engraving, "A View of the President's House in the City of Washington," 1815, showing the house burned out, but the uniformity of the exterior unbroken by the ashlar and made cohesive by the whitewash, which is documented in written records of the Commissioners. See vol. I, plate 18. See Wilhelmus B. Bryan, "The Name White House," CHS *Records*, vol. 34–35 (1932): 308, who quotes this written by Congressman Abijah Bigelow, March 18, 1812, "There is much trouble at the White House, as we call it, I mean the President's."

4. Stephen V. Van Rensselaer to Elgar, Washington, n.d., [January 1819]; Hoban to Lane, Washington, December 12, 1818, and Hoban memorandum, n.d., [1802?], Commissioner's letters received.

5. The north portico was brought to completion under Andrew Jackson.

6. *National Intelligencer*, December 9, 1831.

7. Samuel Flagg Bemis, *John Quincy Adams and the Union* (New York: Alfred A. Knopf, 1956), 92–124; Allan Nevins, ed., *The Diary of John Quincy Adams* (New York: Longmans, Green & Co., 1929), *passim*.

8. Charles Francis Adams, ed., *Memoirs of John Quincy Adams* (Philadelphia: Lippincott, 1876), vol. VIII, 108–9.

9. Bemis, *John Quincy Adams*, 122–23; John Quincy Adams, *Diary, passim*; see also miscellaneous Treasury warrants for the Adams administration.

10. Bizet's payment records begin December 16, 1817, miscellaneous Treasury warrants. He received $50 fees at random intervals, so the circumstances of his employment are unclear. He is probably the same John Buzelet, who advertised himself as a "gardener from France" in the *Virginia Gazette and Alexandria Advertiser*, April 22, 1790.

11. Paullus Hedl to Lane, Washington, September 11, 1819, and November 18, 1822; Tobias Martin to Alex Borland, Washington, July 17, 1825, contracts file, Commissioner of Public Buildings Records, National Archives.

12. Bulfinch to Lane, Washington, June 30, 1818, payment for a "plan of President's square," miscellaneous Treasury warrants.

13. "Abstract of disbursements Made by Saml. Lane between June 24, 1818, and December 5, 1821"; F. C. DeKrafft to Lane, Washington, June 23, 1818, miscellaneous Treasury warrants; numerous bills of this kind are in the same record group, fully documenting the early development of the park.

14. William Noland to whom it may concern, Washington, May 1, 1840, Commissioner's letters received.

15. Orders for trees, miscellaneous Treasury warrants, *passim*; Rudolph Clark to Noland, Washington, August 1825, and William Yeats to "Commissioner," Washington, August 8, 1825, Commissioner's letters received.

16. John Quincy Adams, *Diary*, June 13, 1827.

17. *Ibid.*, June 12, 1827.

18. Inventory, March 24, 1825, Commissioner's letters sent.

19. John Quincy Adams, *Diary*, December 1, 3, 4, and 9, 1828.

Chapter 8: Democracy

1. Hoban to Elgar, February 10? 1829, Commissioner's letters received.

2. There were actually three wheeled pumping machines at the White House,

2 "first class fire engines" and "1 Domestic or garden Engine with pipe," see bill Perkins & Baker to Lane, Philadelphia, paid January 31, 1820, miscellaneous Treasury warrants.

3. J. Q. Callan to Elgar, Washington, January 29, 1829. Commissioner's letters received.

4. Margaret Smith, *Society*, 259–60.

5. Two different versions of the Jackson marriage controversy are in Marquis James, *Andrew Jackson* (New York: Bobbs-Merrill Company, 1938) and Robert V. Remini, *Andrew Jackson*, 3 vols. (New York: Harper & Row, Publishers, 1977, 1981, and 1984).

6. Amos Kendall to Francis Blair, Washington, March 7, 1829, Princeton University Library.

7. John Quincy Adams, *Diary*, vol. VIII, 103–4.

8. John Quincy Adams, *Memoirs*, vol. VIII, 141.

9. The U.S. Census of 1830 lists 14 slaves in Jackson's White House household. Guista is listed as "head" of 19, which is, alas, not explained and could refer to slaves hired as servants from outside.

10. Washington *United States Telegraph*, March 5, 1829; Margaret Smith, *Society*, 284; *Argus of Western America*, March 18, 1829.

11. Margaret Smith, *Society*, 294.

12. *Ibid.*; James Hamilton, Jr., to Martin Van Buren, Washington, March 5, 1829, Van Buren Papers, L.C.; *National Intelligencer*, March 7, 1829; Edwin A. Miles, "The First People's Inaugural— 1829," *Tennessee Historical Quarterly*, vol. XXXVII (fall 1978): 296.

13. Margaret Smith, *Society*, 290–98; Miles, "People's Inaugural," *passim*.

14. *National Intelligencer*, March 17, 1829; in spite of the several eyewitness accounts of damage being done to the White House, costs for repair are not noted in the public records or in Jackson's. It will be seen, however, that a

major redecorating program soon followed; the portrait of Mrs. Jackson by Earl hangs in Jackson's bedroom at the Hermitage, as it did when he was in residence there.

15. Pauline W. Burke, *Emily Donelson of Tennessee* (Richmond: Garrett and Massie, Inc., 1941), vol. I, 174.

16. Margaret Smith, *Society*, 307–8; David Campbell to his wife, May 28 and June 3, 1829, quoted in James, *Andrew Jackson*, vol. II, 515; see also James, *Andrew Jackson*, vol. II, 614, 669, *passim*.

17. John Quincy Adams, *Memoirs*, vol. VIII, 141.

18. Various bills for fitting up and repairing the basement rooms March–July 1829; James A. Hamilton, *Reminiscences* (New York: Charles Scribner & Co., 1869), 150, "[The President] then called his mulatto servant, who slept on a rug in his room. . . . "

19. John R. Montgomery to Letitia A. Montgomery, Washington, February 20, 1834, in "Documents 1834: Letter of Robert C. Caldwell, Contributed by George M. Whicher," *American Historical Review*, vol. XXVII (January 1922): 271–81.

20. The designations of the rooms at the White House in Jackson's time were noted by Charles Alexandre in May when he went room by room removing curtains and rugs for the summer and in October, when he returned those things from storage. See miscellaneous Treasury accounts.

21. Burke, *Emily Donelson*, vols. I and II, *passim*.

22. Alexandre's bills, *op. cit.*

23. *Ibid.*, for March 20, 1833, designates the north bedroom as the "Yellow Room upstairs" and the oval room across from it the "Green Room."

24. *Ibid.*, *passim*; Bryan & Wood, Washington, March 1, 1834, bill for "iron bars, locks, latches, fastenings on windows," miscellaneous Treasury warrants.

25. Louis Veron & Company, estimate for decorating the state rooms of the White House, Philadelphia, n.d. [before November 1829], miscellaneous Treasury accounts.

26. L. Veron & Co., to commissioner, Philadelphia, November 25, 1829, miscellaneous Treasury warrants.

27. Alexandre hung the picture. Exactly which of Jackson's portraits this was is uncertain, and it may have been one that has vanished. Earl did a thriving business painting Jackson's portrait from his room upstairs in the White House. One wonders if the picture in question was not the one of him standing on the south portico, with the gate and the willow trees in the distance, or at least some cartoon of it. Ben Perley Poore, who wrote about seeing the picture, gave few details.

28. Margaret Smith, Society, 248–49.

29. James, Andrew Jackson, vol. II, 491, 509, 517.

30. Ibid., 519.

31. Emily Donelson to Mrs. John Coffee, Washington, March 27, 1829, Andrew Jackson Donelson Papers, L.C..

32. Emily Donelson to Mrs. Eaton. Washington, April 10, 1829, Donelson Papers, L.C..

33. James Parton, Life of Andrew Jackson (New York: Mason Bros., 1861), vol. III, 202–5.

34. James, Andrew Jackson, vol. II, 536.

35. Mrs. Eaton to Jackson, Washington, June 9, 1830, Donelson Papers, L.C.

36. Jackson's appearance and clothes were often described by contemporaries, but the best visual accounts are in Earl's portraits, which convey the flavor of the man.

37. Remini, Andrew Jackson, vol. III, 393–94.

38. Caldwell, "Washington in 1834," op. cit.

39. John Quincy Adams, Diary, November 28, 1840.

40. Lewis to Jackson, Washington, August 13, 1833, Andrew Jackson Papers, the Hermitage.

41. Ben Perley Poore, Perley's Reminiscences of Sixty Years In the National Metropolis (Philadelphia: Hubbard Brothers, 1886), vol. I, 179.

42. Inventory of the White House, 1809 and 1825, op. cit.

43. Bryan & Wood, Washington, April 3, 1835, invoice and bid, miscellaneous Treasury warrants.

44. Alexandre, bills for disrobing the house for the summer, 1833–1834, passim; James Green to U.S.A., Alexandria, Va., n.d., 1833, for furniture; Alexandre for carpet, curtains, and wallpapers, March 20, 1833, miscellaneous Treasury accounts.

45. Bryan & Wood, Washington, April 3, 1835, op. cit.

46. Lewis to Jackson, Washington, August 13, 1833, op. cit.

47. J. Howard and H. Shortent to J. Belanger, Washington, n.d., 1833; Alexandre and Louis Labeille to the Commissioner, Washington, March 9, 1834, Commissioner's letters received.

48. William P. Elliott, building contract for stable and bill for making an elevation of stable (the elevation is now lost), Washington, March 12, 1833, Commissioner's contracts; abstract of expenses for stable, n.d., Commissioner's receipted accounts.

49. Robert Brown to the Commissioner, Georgetown, paid January 7, 1835, for work done in 1834, miscellaneous Treasury warrants.

50. Commissioner William Noland, Report (Washington: by the government, November 1833); abstract of expenditures for completing the waterworks at the President's House, August 16, 1834, miscellaneous Treasury accounts.

51. L. R. Walter to Noland, Washington, September 5, 1834, miscellaneous Treasury warrants.

52. Lewis to Jackson, Washington, August 13, 1833, op. cit.

53. C. Buckingham to Noland, Washington, October 4, 1834, miscellaneous Treasury warrants.

54. Ousley was called "gardener to the President," and paid monthly. The entire gardening payroll in 1835 was $2,850, which, besides Ousley's $450 per annum, included "laborers . . . and for planting." See Commissioner's letters received and sent.

55. Poore, Reminiscences, vol. I, 193.

56. James Maher to Noland, orders for trees and shrubbery, Washington, March 20, 1835; also orders to Bloodgood & Co., Prince & Sons, both Flushing, Long Island, spring and fall 1833 and 1834; William Radcliff to Noland, May 1834, gravel walks; Robert Mills, measurement of walks laid by contractors Murphy & [Drummond], Washington, September 13, 1833, miscellaneous Treasury accounts.

57. Elgar to Noland, Washington, February 26, 1834, Commissioner's letters received.

58. Ibid.

59. Noland, statement of accounts, August 25, 1834, Commissioner's letters sent.

60. Frances Kemble, Journal (Philadelphia: Carey, Lea, & Blanchard, 1835, vol. II, 95–97; Maher, bill for trees, March 22, 1834; James Birth to Noland, Washington, March 25, 1829, miscellaneous Treasury warrants.

61. Original daguerreotype, Eastman House, Rochester, New York, see vol. I, plate 29.

62. With the exception of an idealized view of the garden in an engraving published in Jackson's time, see plate 24, there are no views of the "old garden," although there are many of the White House itself. The watch box was in place by July 1834 and in need either of painting or repainting.

63. A long photograph survives of this arbor, taken to show construction on the Treasury building, but catching also a glimpse of the garden ca. 1858, Division of Prints and Photographs, Treasury Building Construction Records, National Archives; Bryan & Wood, invoice, March 14, 1834, miscellaneous Treasury warrants.

64. Richard Wright to Noland, Washington, November 11, 1835, miscellaneous Treasury warrants.

65. Jessie Benton Fremont, Souvenirs of My Time (Boston: D. Lothrop and Co., 1887), 95.

66. Legend has long held that Jackson patterned the Hermitage driveway on Mrs. Jackson's guitar, but it is clear that with his love of Washington's relics, paralleling himself somewhat to Washington, his rebuilt Hermitage was an echo of Mount Vernon, complete to the colonnade and driveway.

67. No drawings of the orangery survive, although the bills for its conversion in the spring and summer of 1836 are probably complete in the Treasury warrants. A photograph of the garden side of it in about 1858, op. cit., shows the façade, while two other photographs from the same source show the north or rear side during the Treasury construction.

68. National Intelligencer, January 3, 1832.

69. See chapter 2 on the subject of siting the White House, vol. I, pp. 33–35.

70. National Intelligencer, July 6, 1834.

71. Washington Globe, February 22, 1837; National Intelligencer, February 22, 1837.

72. National Intelligencer, February 25, 1837; the coach burned many years later, but today is restored from the surviving parts and is on display at the Hermitage.

Chapter 9: Elegance

1. Major L. Wilson, *The Presidency of Martin Van Buren* (Lawrence: University Press of Kansas, 1984), 21–42; see also Charles Wiltse, *The New Nation* (New York: Hill & Wang, 1961).

2. Denis Tilden Lynch, *Martin Van Buren: An Epoch and a Man* (New York: Horace Liveright, Inc., 1929), 416, 455; also Holmes Alexander, *American Talleyrand: The Career and Contemporaries of Martin Van Buren, Eighth President* (New York: Harper & Brothers, 1935), 340–54; Glyndon G. Van Deusen, *The Jacksonian Era, 1828–1848* (New York: Harper & Row, 1959), 147–48.

3. L. A. Gobright, *Recollection of Men and Things at Washington* (Philadelphia: Claxton, Remsen & Haffelfinger, 1869), 50.

4. Charles Ogle, "Speech of Mr. Ogle of Pennsylvania On the Regal Splendor of the President's Palace," *Congressional Globe*, April 14, 1840.

5. Jessie Benton Fremont, *Souvenirs*, 98; Holmes, *American Talleyrand*, 350; S. W. Jackson, ed., *Captain Frederick Marryat: A Diary in America With Remarks On Its Institutions* (London: 1839), vol. I, 156; Ogle, "Regal Splendor," spoke of a "Democratic peacock in full court costume, strutting. . . . "

6. Bills of John Thomas, Baltimore, Campbell and Hoyle, Washington, Alexandre, Washington, J. Lyambur (?), Joseph Lowe, Webb & Tinson, Canfield, Brothers, Pares & Faye, James Pators & Co., May–October 1837, miscellaneous Treasury warrants.

7. Alexandre's bills for May 14 and December 12, 1837, and June and July 1838; William Thompson's bills for May 1837 and May 1839, miscellaneous Treasury warrants.

8. The room was changed from crimson to blue. The original bill from James Pators & Co., New York, for fabrics supplied to the "circular room first story" was submitted December 12, 1837, for goods sent the previous March and described "sattin medallion," "plain sattin," etc., with no mention of color. But on May 30, 1837, Alexandre presented his bill for making curtains and hanging paper, and he calls the room the Blue Room, as well as specifying "blue silk taffeta" and "silver paper" with top and bottom borders. Miscellaneous Treasury warrants.

9. John Skinring to Joel Poinsett, Washington, March 17, 1840, proposal for central heating system, Commissioner's letters received; Robert Mills to William Noland, Washington, July 26, 1837, and to Thomas L. Smith, Washington, July 1837, asking for payment of $20 for "Drawings of plan of the President's House," which may have had something to do with the heating system and the screen, miscellaneous Treasury warrants.

10. John Skinring, contract with Noland, April 1837, Commissioner's contracts.

11. Commissioner's miscellaneous Treasury warrants, *passim*; Ogle, "Regal Splendor," contains numerous references to the grounds, which he obviously gleaned from these same public records then kept, of course, in Noland's office.

12. Jessie Benton Fremont, *Souvenirs*, 98; *Boston Post*, May 12, 1939; Holmes, *American Talleyrand*, 281.

13. Jessie Benton Fremont, *Souvenirs*, 98–100.

14. Ogle, "Regal Splendor," 11–12.

15. Capt. Marryat, *Diary in America*, 156–57; also miscellaneous Treasury accounts, *passim*, bills for services by guards; on the other hand, an English visitor in March 1838 found "neither guards without the gate, or sentries within." In Singleton, *The White House*, vol. I, 262.

16. Singleton, *The White House*, vol. I, 266; *National Intelligencer*, July 6, 1839; New York *Advertiser*, July 5, 1839.

17. *Congressional Globe*, April 14, 1840.

18. Ogle, "Regal splendor," *passim*.

19. Noland, statement, June 12, 1840, Commissioner's letters sent.

20. Jessie Benton Fremont, *Souvenirs*, 29.

21. John Niven, *Martin Van Buren: The Romantic Age of American Politics* (New York: Oxford University Press, 1983), 480.

Chapter 10: Stage and Players

1. Gobright, *Recollection*, 38.

2. James A. Green, *William Henry Harrison: His Life and Times* (Richmond: Garrett and Massie, 1941), *passim*.

3. Gobright, *Recollection*, 39–40.

4. Alexander B. Hagner, "History and Reminiscences of St. John's Church, Washington, D.C.," CHS *Records*, vol. XII (1909):110–11.

5. J. K. Paulding to Van Buren, Washington, March 22, 1841, Van Buren Papers, L.C.

6. Lyon G. Tyler, *The Letters and Times of the Tylers* (Richmond: Whittet & Shepperson, 1885), vol. II, 11.

7. Henry D. Gilpin to Van Buren, Washington, March 18, 1841, Van Buren Papers, L.C.

8. J. K. Paulding to Van Buren, Washington, March 22, 1841, *op. cit.*

9. Green, *William Henry Harrison*, 397; work was done on the "cow house" in late March 1841, see Commissioner's miscellaneous warrants.

10. Hagner, "St. John's Church," 111–12.

11. Dr. Thomas Miller, on the treatment and death of President Harrison, *Boston Medical and Surgical Journal*, vol. 25, (August 1841), 25–32.

12. Washington *Globe*, April 3, 4, and 5, 1841; *National Intelligencer*, April 1, 3, and 6, 1841.

13. N. P. Willis's poem commemorating the first death of a president in the White House was widely circulated through newspapers at the time. I have

quoted only a part of the final stanza. See Green, *William Henry Harrison*, 403.

14. Alexander Hunter, Marshal, etc., to Daniel Webster, Secretary of State, itemized listing of funeral expenses, August 12, 1841, House Document 55, August 16, 1841.

15. *National Intelligencer*, April 6, 1841; Washington *Globe*, April 5, 1841.

16. *National Intelligencer*, April 9 and 12, 1841.

17. *Ibid*, April 12.

18. John Williamson to Alexander Hunter, Washington, April 5, 1841, lists the materials necessary to make the funeral car; the funeral car was illustrated in a lithograph published in 1841 by N. Currier, New York.

19. Green, *William Henry Harrison*, 404.

20. Tyler, in retirement, also objected when addressed as "ex-vice president," see Tyler to James Buchanan, Sherwood Forest, Virginia, October 16, 1848, in Tyler, *Life and Times*, vol. II, 13.

21. *Ibid.*, 33–34.

22. Washington *Madisonian*, August 19, 1841.

23. Gobright, *Recollection*, 63–65.

24. Payments for guards and "watches," miscellaneous Treasury warrants.

25. Russel Young and James L. Feeney, *The Metropolitan Police Department: Official History* (Washington: Metropolitan Police, 1908), 22–26. The first Washington police force went on the job December 6, 1808. Replacing the single constable, the first police were called the "constables." Tyler's White House force had a captain and three guards and functioned in 1842 under an appropriation of $7,000.

26. Priscilla Tyler to her sisters, Williamsburg, October 1839, Elizabeth Tyler Coleman Papers, University of Alabama Library.

27. Priscilla Tyler to Mary Grace

Raoul, Washington, April 29, 1841, Coleman Papers.

28. Priscilla Tyler, fragment of a letter to Mary Grace Raoul, Washington, May 1841, Coleman Papers.

29. Priscilla Tyler, "journal," January 2, 1842, Coleman Papers.

30. Priscilla Tyler to her sisters, Washington, October 1842, Coleman Papers.

31. Act of May 22, 1826, specified that furnishings for the White House be of American manufacture "so far as may be practical," etc. The act was passed largely in reaction to Monroe's French purchases. Jackson's East Room purchases were in support of the act.

32. Bills of William Cupps and W. W. Wood for office furniture, Washington, November 19, 1842, miscellaneous Treasury warrants.

33. Robert Seager, II, *And Tyler, Too: A Biography of John & Julia Gardiner Tyler* (New York: McGraw Hill, 1963), 208; Oliver Perry Chitwood, *John Tyler: Champion of the Old South* (New York: Russell and Russell, Inc., 1964 reprint of the 1939 edition), 415–17. Tyler practiced all sorts of economies, not the least sending to New York for groceries at large discounts through relatives. He seems to have tried to save money until his marriage to Julia Gardiner, when he became a free-spender and in the months of their occupancy of the White House nearly broke himself.

34. Cincinnati *Graphic News*, June 25, 1887; Richmond *Dispatch*, July 21, 1889.

35. Seager, *And Tyler, too*, 208.

36. Priscilla Tyler to the President, [Philadelphia], June 26 or 28, 1844, Coleman Papers.

37. Seager, *And Tyler, Too*, 10; Jessie Benton Fremont, *Souvenirs*, 99.

Chapter 11: Imperial House

1. Seager, *And Tyler, Too*, 277.

2. Anson and Fanny Nelson, *Memorials of Sarah Childress Polk: Wife of the Elev-* enth *President of the United States* (New York: Anson D.F. Randolph & Company, 1892), 81.

3. *Ibid.*, 94.

4. Poore, *Reminiscences*, vol. I, 331–32.

5. The Jefferson statue is in the Capitol today. Cast in bronze, it had been commissioned and given to the government some years earlier by Navy Lieutenant Uriah P. Levy, owner of Monticello and an ardent admirer of Jefferson. It stood along the wall in the Capital rotunda until Polk ordered it moved to the north lawn of the White House. See James M. Goode, *The Outdoor Sculpture of Washington, D.C.*, (Washington: Smithsonian Institution Press, 1974), 521.

6. Milo Milton Quaife, *Diary of James K. Polk* (Chicago: McClurg Co., 1910), vol. I, 382.

7. Polk, *Diary*, vol. 1, 391.

8. *Ibid.*, vol. I, 392.

9. *Ibid.*, vol. I, 391–92.

10. William Seale, editorial, *Nineteenth Century Magazine*, vol. II (Spring 1976): 4–5

11. The original daguerreotype, quite a large one, is in the collection of the James K. Polk Memorial Auxiliary, Columbia, Tennessee. It was exhibited at the National Portrait Gallery in 1978.

12. Mrs. Richard Cutts to Mrs. Chubb, Washington[?], n.d., Dolley Madison Papers, Chicago Historical Society.

13. Jennings, *Reminiscences*, 50.

14. Commissioner's letters sent, May-October 1845, *passim*; see also Polk's financial records in the Polk Papers, L.C., note draft of July 20, 1846, two for January 9, 1847, February 2, 1847, and January 1, n.d., for the purchase of slaves.

15. The title "steward" had been used occasionally, beginning in the 1830s. In the Commissioner's records and private papers of Polk, it becomes a regular title as early as May 1845.

16. Polk, *Diary*, vol. II, 344, notes the

death of one Smith, a free "colored man." See also B. B. French, White House inventory, January 1, 1849, Commisioner's letters received.

17. Polk, *Diary, passim.*

18. Polk accounts, *passim,* James K. Polk Memorial Auxiliary.

19. *Ibid.*

20. Nelson, *Memorials,* 92–93.

21. Polk accounts.

22. Letters of Joanna Lucinda Rucker, James K. Polk Papers, Tennessee State Archives.

23. Rucker to Bet [Elizabeth C. Price], Washington, October 17, 1845, Polk Papers, Tennessee State Archives.

24. Rucker to Bet, Washington, October 18, 1845, Polk Papers, Tennessee State Archives.

25. Rucker to Bet, Washington, January 7, 1846, Polk Papers, Tennessee State Archives.

26. Rucker to Bet, Washington, May 30, 1846, Polk Papers, Tennessee State Archives.

27. Polk, *Diary,* vol. I, 264–65; Rucker to Bet, Washington, September 9, 1846, Polk Memorial Auxiliary.

28. Rucker to "dear cousin," Washington, April 7, 1846, Polk Memorial Auxiliary.

29. Polk Memorial Auxiliary, "Articles in the James K. Polk Home—Columbia, Tennessee—used in the White House During Polk's Presidency," ms., [1976].

30. Mrs. J. E. Dixon, diary, December 21, 1845, typescript copy, OCWH.

31. Henry Bowman, receipt, September 1, 1846; Mary Louise Corcoran to Mrs. Polk, New York, November 5, 1847, Polk Papers, Tennessee State Archives. Further correspondence regarding the Polk-Corcoran relationship is in the archives, Corcoran Gallery of Art.

32. J. J. W. Meeks bills, New York, May 31 and November 1, 1845, for "Louis XV" furniture and "Gothic"

chairs; B. Gardiner bills, New York, April 25, 1845, and November 12, 1846, Commissioner's vouchers.

33. Mrs. Dixon's diary, December 6, 1845.

34. *Ibid.;* see also the inventory of 1849.

35. The Rev. John C. Smith to Mrs. Polk, Washington, n.d., Polk Papers, Tennessee State Archives; bill of David Baird, Commissioner's vouchers.

36. Mrs. Dixon's diary, December 19, 1845; also see Poore, *Reminiscences,* and Jessie Benton Fremont, *Souvenirs, passim.*

37. No source contemporary to Mrs. Polk's tenure in the White House credits her with starting "Hail to the Chief" as a march, but the march did first appear at the White House during her time. If she did not originate the idea, she gave it her approval.

38. Haygood, Fox & Co., to Noland, Baltimore, May 30, 1845; Haygood, Fox & Co., contract, Baltimore, June 14, 1845, Commissioner's letters received. The contract specified the repair of Van Buren's furnace and the installation of four new ones.

39. Charles Douglas, *Report of the Commissioner of Public Buildings* (Washington: by the government, January 16, 1849). The 1848 appropriation of $25,000 included laying gas pipes and purchasing the lighting fixtures for the Capital and its grounds, Pennsylvania Avenue, and the President's House.

40. Nelson, *Memorials,* 118.

41. Commissioner's vouchers, *passim,* contain extensive records, bills, receipts, orders for plants and equipment and payrolls for the grounds.

42. Nelson, *Memorials,* 99–100.

43. *Ibid.,* 1–12.

44. Polk, *Diary,* vol. III, 397.

45. Mrs. Dixon's diary, December 6, 1845.

46. *Ibid.;* see also, Klapthor, *White House China,* 66–73.

47. Polk, *Diary*, vol. III, 345.

48. Portrait of Cortés hung in one of the state parlors and is now in the Polk Memorial Auxiliary, Columbia, Tennessee.

49. H.H. Bancroft, *History of California* (San Francisco: The History Company, 1884–90), vol. XVII, 114–17; *National Intelligencer*, September 21, December 13 and 15, 1848; John Walton Caughey, *The California Gold Rush* (Berkeley: University of California Press, 1948), 40–41; Ferol Egan, *Fremont: Explorer For a Restless Nation* (New York: Doubleday & Co., 1977), 269–432; Polk, *Diary*, 224–25; Stephen Bonsal, *Edward Fitzgerald Beale: A Pioneer In the Path of Empire* (New York: Putnam's, 1912), 30–63.

50. Bancroft, *History of California*, vol. XVII, 114–15.

51. Polk, *Diary*, vol. IV, 372–74.

Chapter 12: Mid-Century

1. Appointment of Ignatius Mudd, Washington, March 7, 1849, Commissioner's letters received.

2. J. B. Mower to John McLean, Washington, August 16, 1847, Manuscript Division, miscellaneous manuscripts, L.C.

3. Poore, *Reminiscences*, vol. I, 357–58; also Brainerd Dyer, *Zachary Taylor* (New York: Barnes & Noble, 1967), *passim*.

4. Holman Hamilton, *Zachary Taylor: Soldier In the White House* (New York: Bobbs-Merrill, 1951), 221.

5. Dyer, *Zachary Taylor*, 399–400; see also Robert L. Preston, "Zachary Taylor," *Magazine of the Society of the Lees of Virginia*, vol. IV (May 1926): 44.

6. Commissioner Mudd to Col. Bliss, Washington, December 31, 1849, Commissioner's letters received; U.S. Census of 1850.

7. Commissioner's letters sent and received make it clear that all White House operations were carried out under Bliss's direction.

8. Polk inventory, 1849; see also John

Wagner to Commissioner, August–November 1849; J. & J.W. Meeks to the Commissioner, October 30, 1849, Commissioner's letters received.

9. Ignatius Mudd, *Annual Report* (Washington: by the government, January 24, 1850); correspondence of Mudd about the gas fraud, October 1849–February 1850, Commissioner's letters sent.

10. Poore, *Reminiscences*, vol. I, 381–82.

11. *Daily National Intelligencer*, July 14, 1849; Dyer, *Zachary Taylor*, 400; for descriptions of Dolley Madison in her last years see Mrs. Dixon's diary, December 6, 1845, and Jessie Benton Fremont, *Souvenirs*, 112.

12. Hudson Strode, *Jefferson Davis: American Patriot, 1808–1861* (New York: Harcourt Brace & Co., 1955), 136.

13. Dyer, *Zachary Taylor*, 401–4.

14. Harriet A. Weed, ed., *Thurlow Weed's Memoirs* (Boston: Houghton, Mifflin & Co., 1884), vol. I, 176–77; Charles E. Hamlin, *The Life and Times of Hannibal Hamlin* (Cambridge: Oxford University Press, 1899), 201.

15. Silas Bent McKinley and Silas Bent, *Old Rough and Ready* (New York: Vanguard Press, 1946), 284–91; Dyer, *Zachary Taylor*, 403; *Washington Republic*, July 6, 1850.

16. Strode, *Jefferson Davis*, 227-28.

17. *Ibid.*, 228.

18. Poore, *Reminiscences*, 381; *Washington Republic*, July 12 and 15, 1850.

19. Charles M. Snyder, ed., *The Lady and the President: The Letters of Dorothea Dix and Millard Fillmore* (Lexington: University of Kentucky Press, 1975), 42–47.

20. Henry McCall Holmes, journal, ms., Wilmont Holmes Papers, Southern History Collection, University of North Carolina Library; Poore, *Reminiscences*, vol. 1, 379.

21. Snyder, ed., *The Lady and the President*, 51.

22. David A. Baird, accounts with the U.S.A., Washington, April 29, 1852; "Statement of Appropriations For the Purchase of a Library to be Preserved in the Executive Mansion, September 30, 1850, to March 3, 1851, Commissioner's letters sent; the bookcases for the oval room were ordered January 27, 1851, from William M. L. Cripps, "two Circular Bookcases and one Center." Two other long bookcases were bought from Cripps August 30. Commissioner's vouchers. The bookcases remained in the White House until they were sold at auction by Theodore Roosevelt in 1902.

23. Inventory of books purchased, General Accounting Office, vouchers filed March 11, 1853, Treasury records, National Archives.

24. William Easby to Robert Mills, Washington, May 26, 1851, Commissioner's letters sent; Mills was dismissed on July 29, 1851, and it was noted that the dismissal was made "in consultation with the President." See A. H. H. Steuart to Robert Mills, Washington, July 29, 1851, Commissioner's letters received.

25. Mudd, *Annual Report* (Washington: by the government, 1850), 599–647.

26. Downing to Joseph Henry, Newburgh, June 14, 1851, Henry Papers, Smithsonian Institution.

27. Easby to Alexander H. H. Stewart, Washington, July 12, 1851, Commissioner's letters sent; Stewart to Downing, Washington, July 18, 1851, copy in Commissioner's letters received.

28. Original plan is in the Geography and Map Division, L.C.

29. Downing's text of the plan, *op. cit.*

30. A. K. Craig to Easby, Ordinance Office, Washington, April 20, 1851, Commissioner's letters received.

31. Downing to Fillmore, Newburgh, March 3, 1851, Commissioner's letters received.

32. Downing to Henry, June 14, 1851, *op. cit.*

33. Easby to Downing, Washington, March 27, 1851, and Downing's response, which went directly to the President, Commissioner's letters sent.

34. Easby to Ousley, Washington, January 19, 1852, Commissioner's letters sent.

35. Watt's appointment as "gardener for the kitchen," Washington, January 31, 1852; inventory of tools, n.d., Commissioner's letters received.

36. Mrs. Jerediah Horsford to "My dear children all," Washington, March 24, 1852, National Museum of American History.

37. Commissioner's vouchers and letters received detail the work on Lafayette Park in the spring and summer of 1852. The Manhattan newspapers of July 30–August 5, 1852, chronicle in full detail the beaching and burning of the *Henry Clay* and the loss of Downing and his companions. The *Henry Clay* caught fire in the course of a race on the Hudson with the steamer *Armenia*, about two miles below Yonkers. Many New York socialites were on board, en route home from Saratoga Springs. Downing's body turned up the next day, July 28, when the river was dragged. Most of the baggage was apparently lost, including his materials on Washington improvements.

38. Fillmore to S. P. Chase, Washington, July 23, 1850, in Frank H. Severance, ed., "Millard Fillmore Papers," *Publications of the Buffalo Historical Society*, vol. X, XI (1907): 296–97.

39. Quoted in Gobright, *Recollections*, 126.

40. Fillmore to Mrs. Brooks, Washington, November 27, 1850, in "Millard Fillmore Papers," 304.

41. Fillmore to Mudd, Washington, January 27, 1851, Commissioner's letters received.

42. Alexander bills, Commissioner's letters received, May to October each year during the Fillmore administration, *passim;* Mrs. Horsford to Eliza Horsford,

Washington, February 26, 1852. Note that the Alexandres have by the 1850s dropped the French spelling of their name, in favor of "Alexander."

Chapter 13: Watershed

1. Varina Howell Davis, *Jefferson Davis: A Memoir By His Wife* (New York: Belford, 1890), vol. I, 540.

2. Roy Nichols, *Franklin Pierce: Young Hickory of the Granite Hills* (Philadelphia: University of Pennsylvania Press, 1958), 234, 241.

3. Thomson and Davis, bill for draping the house in "black cambric & crepe," Washington, June 15, 1853, Commissioner's miscellaneous accounts; Poore, *Reminiscences*, vol. I, 468–69.

4. Nichols, *Franklin Pierce*, 241; see also household accounts, as many are endorsed by William H. Snow. "Peter" is probably Peter Vermereu, who was to work as butler until the Lincoln administration (see page 395).

5. Benjamin B. French Papers, L.C.

6. Varina Howell Davis, *Davis*, vol. 1, 534.

7. Nichols, *Franklin Pierce*, 230.

8. Goode, *Outdoor Sculpture*, 377–78; Constance M. Green, *Washington: Village and Capital* (Princeton: Princeton University Press, 1962), 203; preparation of the park is chronicled in the accounts of the Commissioner, May–November 1853.

9. Meher to B. B. French, Washington, April 28, 1855, Commissioner's letters received.

10. The operations of the orangery are documented in the various bills and papers from Jackson's time, when it was developed, to that of Pierce, Commissioner's miscellaneous Treasury accounts and letters received. The most notable periods of activity are March through May.

11. Mrs. Clement C. Clay, Jr., *A Belle of the Fifties* (New York: Doubleday, Page & Co., 1904), 29.

12. See Commissioner's miscellaneous accounts, May–August 1853, and the "measurement" that determined the final cost, August 11, 1853.

13. Thomas Stanby to French, order for "36 glasses—red, blue, purple, amber," Baltimore, August 1, 1853, Commissioner's miscellaneous accounts.

14. James Kelly, bill for plumbing, August 10, 1853; bill of John Turton (?) for making flower boxes, lattice, etc., Washington, May 31, 1853; Thomas Stanley also provided similar items and did all the painting, which was white, trimmed in green.

15. See bills of Peter MacKenzie, James Maher, Richard Andrews, June 1853, Commissioner's miscellaneous accounts.

16. Thomas Stanley to French, Baltimore, August 1, 1853; Albion Hurdle to John Watt, Washington, bill paid November 23, 1853, Commissioner's miscellaneous accounts.

17. The accounts of crowds at the White House are numerous. Note the *National Intelligencer*, January 4, February 22, March 1, 1853; see also Poore, *Reminiscences*, Varina Howell Davis, *Davis*, and Mrs. Clay, *Belle of the Fifties*.

18. Thomas U. Walter, notebook labeled "Executive Mansion," n.d. [May or June 1853], Thomas U. Walter Papers, The Athenaeum of Philadelphia.

19. Easby to A. H. H. Stewart, Washington, December 15, 1853, Commissioner's letters sent; Walworth & Nason, Boston, contract to build the heating system, June 1853, Commissioner's letters received.

20. Walworth & Nason, contract, *op. cit.*

21. Thomas U. Walter, Executive Mansion notebook, *op. cit.*

22. *Ibid.*, the "Roman" character refers to the French furniture President Monroe had bought for the room through agents in France in 1818.

23. Linen bills, variously April–

December 1853, Commissioner's miscellaneous Treasury warrants.

24. Walter drawings for the White House, Walter Papers, the Athenaeum of Philadelphia.

25. Washington *Daily Union,* January 3, 1854.

26. Mrs. Clay, *Belle of the Fifties,* 106.

27. Nichols, *Franklin Pierce,* 299 and *passim.*

28. Easby served as Commissioner from March 1851 until June 1853. His good and bad points are reflected in the records of his work in the Commissioner's letters sent and received. He clashed repeatedly with other officials, notably Downing, who had the President's devoted patronage.

29. Nichols, *Franklin Pierce,* 241–42.

30. Poore, *Reminiscences,* 436.

31. As with most presidencies, the Pierce administration's registration books were not kept after his term of office, but were apparently thrown out. Those which were retained in various administrations were kept as souvenirs by staff members. They were considered as having no value.

32. Garden records for the Pierce administration are extensive and are scattered through the Commissioner's letters and the miscellaneous Treasury warrants. Papers concerning most of the specific projects are usually together.

Chapter 14: An Explosion

1. Mrs. Clay, *Belle of the Fifties,* 27–29.

2. Nichols, *Franklin Pierce,* 469. It might be noted that Pierce had added clusters of large gas lanterns to the columns of the north portico of the White House in the winter of 1853. They may have had something to do with his practice of making speeches from an upstairs window, for they did illuminate the inner part of the portico. The lanterns were in place until 1902.

3. Mrs. Clay, *Belle of the Fifties,* 61.

4. Samuel E. Morrison, *Old Bruin: Commodore Matthew Galbraith Perry* (Boston: Little, Brown, 1967), 353.

5. Varina Howell Davis, *Davis,* vol. I, 341. The official report of the expedition calls the dog a spaniel "of the small spaniel breed." Three of the dogs were brought back by Perry. See Francis L. Hawks, *Narrative of the Expedition of an American Squadron to the China Seas and Japan, 1852–1853, and 1854* (Washington: by the government, 1856), 78.

6. Morrison, *Perry,* 336; R. M. McClelland to French, Washington, March 27, 1855, Commissioner's letters received.

7. Mrs. Clay, *Belle of the Fifties,* 88–95.

8. Poore, *Reminiscences,* vol. I, 223–27.

9. *National Intelligencer,* February 4, 1857; New York *Daily Tribune,* February 10, 1857.

10. Nichols, *Franklin Pierce,* 501–2.

11. Varina Howell Davis, *Davis,* vol. I, 222–23.

12. David Dixon Porter, *Incidents and Anecdotes of the Civil War* (New York: D. Appleton & Co., 1885), 11.

13. Philip S. Klein, "Harriet Lane: Our Republican Queen," *Valleys of History,* vol. II (Autumn 1966): 1–6; letter of James Buchanan Henry describing his life as his uncle's secretary, in George Ticknor Curtis, *Life of James Buchanan* (New York: Harper & Brothers, 1883), vol. II, 235–40.

14. Klein, "Harriet Lane," 3.

15. *Ibid.,* 2.

16. Curtis, *James Buchanan,* 235.

17. *Ibid.,* 237.

18. *Ibid.,* 2361.

19. Easby, *Annual Report* (Washington: by the government, 1853), 6.

20. John B. Blake to secretary of the interior, Washington, April 21, 1857, Commissioner's letters sent.

21. U.S. Census field notes, National Archives.

22. Curtis, *James Buchanan*, 273–74.

23. *Ibid.*, 236–37. Most of the office decorations were added by Pierce in 1853, although the actual office furniture was an accumulation of things going back as early as Jefferson's time. Purchases for the office, oilcloth, water coolers, etc., are traced in the Commissioner's miscellaneous accounts.

24. Curtis, *James Buchanan*, 236–37.

25. Philip Shriver Klein, *President James Buchanan* (University Park: Pennsylvania State University Press, 1962), 274.

26. Blake to Chickering & Sons, Washington, July 3, 1857, Commissioner's letters received.

27. Buchanan to Harriet Lane, Washington, May 20, 1858, in Curtis, *James Buchanan*, 240–41.

28. Bills of Gottlieb Vollmer, May and June 1860; see also various bills for upholstery, Commissioner's miscellaneous accounts.

29. The circular divan remains in the White House Collection.

30. James C. McGuire & Co., "Sales for the Commissioner of Public Buildings," Washington, January 17, 1860, Commissioner's letters received.

31. *The New York Times*, January 31, 1859.

32. John Sassford, *Annual Reports* (Washington: by the government, 1851–1855); R. M. McClelland to Blake, Washington, July 6 and 13, 1855; James Guthrie to McClelland, Washington, July 6, 1855, Commissioner's letters received; see also various bills for moving earth, Commissioner's miscellaneous accounts.

33. Alexander H. Bowman to McClelland, Washington, February 2, 1857, Commissioner's letters sent.

34. Edward Clark to McClelland, Washington, February 14, 1857, in *Miscellaneous House Document #64, 34th Congress, 3rd Session*.

35. *Ibid.*

36. Edward Clark to Blake, payment to workmen on the president's greenhouse, Washington, January 5, 1858, Commissioner's letters received. No plans exist of the 1857/1858 greenhouse, although some descriptions can be gleaned from the construction records and photographs, ca. 1860, associated with the Treasury building.

37. P. Kraus to Dr. Black [Blake], Baltimore, January 8, 1858, Commissioner's letters received; William Pinkney Whyte to Blake, Baltimore, n.d., 1858, Commissioner's miscellaneous accounts, recommends Kraus for honesty and says he went to the site, measured the openings for the glass and hand-painted each pane himself. The "transparencies" were exhibited at the Capitol before being installed.

38. Orders for pots, treillage, repair and moving of plants, Commissioner's miscellaneous accounts, *passim*.

39. Sara A. R. Pryor, *Reminiscences of Peace and War* (New York: MacMillan Company, 1905), 5.

40. *Ibid.*

41. Mrs. Clay, *Belle of the Fifties*, 120.

42. Order of reception, notes of George Nicolay, March 1861, detailing White House procedures under Buchanan, as a guide to the incoming Lincoln. George Nicolay Papers, L.C.

43. Mrs. Clay, *Belle of the Fifties*, 114.

44. *Ibid.,*; Varian Howell Davis, *Davis;* Sara Pryor, *Reminiscences;* Poore, *Reminiscences;* see also Commissioner's miscellaneous accounts, *passim*.

45. French to H. F. French, Washington, May 20, 1860, French Papers, L.C.

46. Curtis, *James Buchanan*, 230.

47. James M. Goode, notes on the Soldiers' Home, ms. Smithsonian Institution; the outfitting of the cottage is well documented in the Commissioner's miscellaneous accounts. The cottage still stands.

48. Klein, *James Buchanan*, 334–35.

49. Curtis, *James Buchanan*, 330–51. The speech was delivered on December 3, 1860.

50. U.S. Census, 1860; Boulanger's restaurant is noted in all the city directories and papers of the time and in Poore, *Reminiscences*, vol. I, 179.

51. See Singleton, *The White House*, vol. II, 40.

52. Buchanan to James Gordon Bennett, Washington, December 20, 1860, in John Bassett Moore, ed., *The Works of James Buchanan* (New York: Antiquarian Press, 1960, reprint of 1908–1911 edition), vol. XI, 69–70.

53. Sara Pryor, *Reminiscences*, 111–12.

54. Mrs. Jacob Thompson to Mrs. Howell Cobb, Washington, December 15, 1860, in U. B. Phillips, ed., *The Correspondence of Robert Toombs, Alexander H. Stephens and Howell Cobb* (Washington: American Historical Association, Annual Report, 1911), vol. II, 522–24.

55. E. F. Elliot, *Court Circles of the Republic* (Hartford: Hartford Publishing Company, 1869), 514.

56. Albert D. Kirwan, *John J. Crittenden: The Struggle For the Union* (Lexington: University of Kentucky Press, 1962); Henry S. Foote, *A Casket of Reminiscences* (Washington: Chronicle Publishing Co., 1874); Amos Kendall, *Autobiography* (Boston: Lee & Shepard, 1872); Phillips, *Correspondence of Toombs, Stephens, and Cobb*; Strode, *Jefferson Davis*.

57. Horatio King, *Turning On the Light: A Dispassionate Survey of President Buchanan's Administration from 1860 Until its Close* (Philadelphia: J.B. Lippincott Company, 1895), 283.

Chapter 15:
Cannon Across the Potomac

1. Davis to Pierce, Washington, January 20, 1861, in Hudson Strode, ed., *Jefferson Davis: Private Letters, 1823–1889* (New York: Harcourt, Brace & World, 1966), 122.

2. Mrs. Clay, *Belle of the Fifties*, 119.

3. Harriet Lane to Sophie Plitt, February 24, 1861, Buchanan Papers, L.C.

4. French to Judge Henry French, Washington, March 6, 1861, French Papers, L.C.

5. Nicolay made guest lists and planned the festivities. He was advised by the President and the secretary of state; the Commissioner of public buildings usually managed the logistics. Little is written on the subject specifically. Nicolay's notes on Buchanan's entertaining survive, *op. cit.* On December 31, 1861, writing to his fiancée, he observed, "I have been engaged yesterday and to-day fixing things for the New Year's reception to-morrow." Mrs. Lincoln's cousin Lizzie Grimsley, acknowledged the secretaries' work of planning in her recollections, see Elizabeth Todd Grimsley, "Six Months in the White House," *Illinois State Historical Society Journal*, vol. 19 (October 1926–January 1927): 62. On page 49 Mrs. Grimsley notes the first conflict between Mrs. Lincoln and Secretary of State Seward on social matters. The battles with Mrs. Lincoln were numerous for everyone involved with social functions at the White House. See, for example, Nicolay to Hay, Washington, January 29, 1864, Nicolay Papers, L.C.

6. Grimsley, "Six Months," 47.

7. Nicolay to Therena Bates, Washington, March 5, 1861, Nicolay Papers, L.C.

8. *Ibid.*, also to Therena Bates, March 31 and April 14, 1861; John Hay, *The Addresses of John Hay* (New York: Century Company, 1907), 322–23.

9. Grimsley, "Six Months," 50–51.

10. Mrs. Lincoln's difficulties are the most revealingly chronicled in her own words, see Justin and Linda Lovitt Turner, *Mary Todd Lincoln: Her Life and Letters* (New York: Alfred A. Knopf, 1972).

11. Richard N. Current, *Lincoln and the First Shot* (Philadelphia: J.B. Lippincott Company, 1963), 76.

12. Nicolay's notes on this dinner are in the Nicolay Papers, *op. cit.*; see also Fletcher Pratt, ed., *Sir William H. Russell: My Diary North and South* (New York: Harper & Row, 1954), vol. I, 60–66.

13. Grimsley, "Six Months," 50–51.

14. John G. Nicolay and John Hay, *Abraham Lincoln: A History* (New York: The Century Company, 1914), vol. III, 394–95.

15. John B. Baldwin, *Interview Between President Lincoln and John B. Baldwin* (Staunton: D.E. Strasburg, 1866), 13.

16. F. B. Carpenter, *Six Months in the White House with Abraham Lincoln* (New York: Hurd & Houghton, 1866), 63.

17. Lincoln to Ellsworth, Washington, April 15, 1861, in Emmanuel Hertz, *Abraham Lincoln: A New Portrait* (New York: Liveright, 1931), vol. II, 828.

18. Nicolay to Therena Bates, April 8, 1861, Nicolay Papers, L.C.

19. John Hay's diary, April 18, 1861, in Helen Nicolay, ed., *Lincoln's Secretary* (Westport: Greenwood Press, 1970), 96.

20. Grimsley, "Six Months," 56.

21. *Ibid.*, 55; Singleton, *The White House*, vol. II, 78; John G. Nicolay, *The Army In the Civil War* (New York: Scribner's, 1885), 105–14.

22. Nicolay to Therena Bates, Washington, May n.d., 1861, Nicolay Papers, L.C.

23. Sandburg, *Abraham Lincoln: The Prairie Years and the War Years* (New York: Harcourt, Brace, 1954), 244.

24. Sketch of the stand with Lincoln and Scott reviewing the troops, Alfred and William Waud Collection, L.C., see vol. I, plate 39.

25. Nicolay to Therena Bates, Washington, July 7, 1861, Nicolay Papers, L.C.; Grimsley, "Six Months," 65–67.

26. Nicolay to Therena Bates, Washington, July 21, 1861, Nicolay Papers, L.C.

27. Nicolay to Therena Bates, Washington, July 21, 1861, *op. cit.*

Chapter 16: Turmoil

1. Thomas F. Pendel, *Thirty-Six Years in the White House* (Washington: Neale Publishing Company, 1902), 4–6; William H. Crook, *Memories of the White House* (Boston: Little, Brown, 1911), 2–4; see also the doorkeepers' quarterly payrolls; Poore, *Reminiscences*, vol. II, 105, notes that the Metropolitan Police "appeared for the first time in uniform" at the White House at Lincoln's first New Year's levee; Commissioner's miscellaneous accounts, *passim*.

2. Margareta Spalding Gerry, ed., *Through Five Administrations: Reminiscences of Colonel William H. Crook* (New York: Harper & Brothers, Publishers, 1907), 2.

3. Pendell, *Thirty-Six Years*, 179.

4. George Alfred Townsend, *The Life, Crime and Capture of John Wilkes Booth* (New York: Dick and Fitzgerald, 1865), 58.

5. David Macrae, *The Americans At Home* (New York: E.P. Dutton & Co., Inc., 1952), 102–10; Crook, *Memories*, 22; Mrs. Lincoln to Andrew Johnson, Washington, April 29, 1865, in Carl Sandburg and Paul Angle, *Mary Lincoln: Wife and Widow* (New York: Harcourt Brace and Company, 1932), 229.

6. William Dove to Blake, estimate for plumbing work, Washington, January 1, 1861, Commissioner's letters received; see also Commissioner's report, ms., October 29, 1862, Commissioner's letters sent.

7. A small number of orders for books survives in the Commissioner's records, see for example, Commissioner to Daniel Appleton & Co., New York, September 5, 1861; to A. Boyd, Washington, December 30, 1863, and to Hudson & Taylor, Washington, March 1, 1864; see

also Dr. Louis Warren, "A. Lincoln's Executive Mansion Library," *Antiquarian Bookman,* (February 11, 1950), 11–15; for the furnishings of the library see French's inventory of the White House made in May 1863, Commissioner's miscellaneous papers.

8. See Nicolay to Therena Bates, Washington, February 2, 1862, and to Hay, Washington, January 29, 1864, Nicolay Papers, L.C.; John Hay, *Addresses,* 335–36.

9. Of these sources, those of the two women present the fairest appraisals. Both acknowledged her emotional deterioration, but saw strong and good qualities as well. Mrs. Elizabeth Hobbs Keckley, *Behind the Scenes, or Thirty Years a Slave, and Four Years in the White House* (New York: Arno Press, 1968, centennial edition of the 1868 edition).

10. *Frank Leslie's Illustrated Newspaper,* February 5, 1862.

11. Keckley, *Behind the Scenes,* 101.

12. *Ibid.*

13. Grimsley, "Six Months," 58–59; Carryl bills, October and December 1861, Commissioner's miscellaneous accounts.

14. The Commissioner maintained a running account more or less with Alexander. The Lincoln account began June 27, 1861, when the house was disrobed for the summer, Commissioner's miscellaneous accounts; see also Harry E. Pratt and Ernest E. East, "Mrs. Lincoln Refurbishes the White House," *Lincoln Herald,* (February 1945): 13–22.

15. Grimsley, "Six Months," 58.

16. Hay to Nicolay, Washington, August 7, 1862, John Hay Papers, L.C.

17. John Eaton, *Grant, Lincoln and the Freedman* (New York: Longmans, Green, 1907), 535.

18. Mary Clemmer Ames, *Ten Years In Washington* (Hartford: A. D. Worthington & Company, 1874), 171.

19. Grimsley, "Six Months," 59.

20. *Ibid.;* Carryl bills, October-December 1861; French's inventory of the White House, May 1865, Commissioner's records.

21. *Mary Lincoln's Letters,* 102.

22. French to Judge Henry French, Washington, March 14, 1861, French Papers, L.C.

23. French to Mrs. Lincoln, Washington, July 5, 1861, French Papers, L.C.

24. French, journals, September 4 and 7, 1861, French Papers, L.C.

25. *Ibid.,* December 16, 1861.

26. French to his sister Pamela, Washington, October 13 and December 24, 1861, French Papers, L.C.

27. Bennett to Mrs. Clay, quoted in *Belle of the Fifties,* 87.

28. Alexander McKerichar, bill, September 16, 1861, Commissioner's miscellaneous accounts.

29. Grimsley, "Six Months," 61–62; Mrs. Lincoln to Hannah Shearer, Washington, July 11, 1861, *Mary Lincoln's Letters,* 94.

30. Thomas J. Sutton to J. B. Blake, Washington, July 9, 1860; Moses Kelly to R. M. McClelland, Washington, June 6, 1854, Commissioner's letters received.

31. Mrs. Lincoln to Caleb B. Smith, Washington, September 8, 1861, *Mary Lincoln's Letters,* 101–2.

32. *Ibid.*

33. *Ibid.,* footnote, 103; furnishings bills October–December 1861, Commissioner's miscellaneous accounts.

34. French, journal, September 13 and 14, 1862.

35. Mrs. Lincoln to Representative John F. Potter, Washington, September 13, [1862], *Mary Lincoln's Letters,* 103–4.

36. Watt was made a second lieutenant in August 1861. This commission was suspended because of suspicions of his Confederate sympathies.

37. Mrs. Lincoln to Simon Cameron, Washington, October 15, 1862, *Mary Lincoln's Letters*, 103.

38. Nicolay to Hay, Springfield, October 21, 1861, Nicolay Papers, L.C.

39. Mrs. Lincoln to Brig. Gen. George Sykes, Washington, November 10, 1862, in *Mary Lincoln's Letters*, 118; see also doorkeeper's quarterly payrolls, Commissioner's miscellaneous papers and contracts.

40. Mary Wall to Buchanan, Washington, August 26, 1867, in Klein, *James Buchanan*, 425–26.

41. Keckley, *Behind the Scenes* and *Mary Lincoln's Letters*, *passim*.

42. Noah Brooks, *Abraham Lincoln* (New York: Putnam's, 1888), 420.

43. Ruth Painter Randall, *Mary Lincoln: Biography of a Marriage* (Boston: Little, Brown, 1953), 377–79.

44. Nicolay, diary, February 18, 1862, Nicolay Papers, L.C.

45. French, journal, March 2, 1862, French Papers, L.C.

46. French to Judge Henry French, Washington, February 27, 1862, French Papers, L.C.

47. *Mary Lincoln's Letters*, 125.

Chapter 17: Good News

1. Horace Greeley, *Recollections of a Busy Life* (New York: J.B. Ford and Company, 1868), 409.

2. Helen Nicolay, *Lincoln's Secretary: A Biography of John G. Nicolay* (New York: Longmans, Green and Company, 1949), 155–56.

3. Macrae, *Americans At Home*, 109–10.

4. French, journal, March 23, 1862, French Papers, L.C.

5. See William O. Stoddard, *Inside the White House in Wartimes* (New York: C.L. Webster & Co., 1890).

6. French, journal, French Papers, L.C.; Laura Wood Roper, *Frederick Law Olm-sted* (Baltimore: Johns Hopkins University Press, 1973), 175; Carpenter, *With Lincoln*, 143; Secretary of the Navy to the Marine Band, Washington, June 8, 1863, Commissioner's letters received.

7. French, journal, February 15, 1863, French Papers, L.C.

8. Singleton, *The White House*, vol. II, 77–78; bills for services, Commissioner's miscellaneous accounts; also see Carl Holliday, "Lincoln's First Levee," *Illinois Historical Society Journal*, vol. 11 (October 1918), 386–90.

9. Pendel, *Thirty-Six Years*, 33–34.

10. Nicolay to Therena Bates, Washington, June 15, 1862, Nicolay Papers, L.C.

11. *Mary Lincoln's Letters*, 150; Ruth Painter Randall, *Mary Lincoln*, 319–20.

12. Mrs. Lincoln to James Gordon Bennett, Washington, October 4, 1862, in *Mary Lincoln's Letters*, 138.

13. Carpenter, *With Lincoln*, 90.

14. Singleton, *The White House*, vol. II, 86–87; the Tyler marble-top table was used for many years as a barrier behind which the President and First Lady could retreat from the crowds. The first mention of its use in this way is by Polk. Lincoln used it in the Blue Room. The table disappeared at about the time of World War I.

15. Carpenter, *With Lincoln*, 87.

16. Sandburg, *Prairie and War Years*, 344–46.

17. Noah Brooks, *Washington in Lincoln's Time* (New York: The Century Company, 1895), 285–86.

18. Randall, *Mary Lincoln*, 324–25.

19. Sandburg, *Prairie and War Years*, 415.

20. Brooks, *Abraham Lincoln*, 449.

21. Hay to Nicolay, Washington, August 7, 1863, in *Letters of John Hay and Extracts From Diary* (Washington: "printed but not published," 1908), vol. I, 90.

22. Ruth Painter Randall, *Mary Lincoln*, 335; see also Katherine Helm, *Mary, Wife of Lincoln* (New York: Harper Bros., 1928), 226.

23. Pendel, *Thirty-Six Years*, 14; see also Hay, "Life in the White House in the Time of Lincoln," 330–31.

24. Diary of Emilie T. Helm in Helm, *Wife of Lincoln*, 222. Emilie Helm: "The room I occupied had been fitted up for the visit of the Prince of Wales. The purple hangings seem gloomy and funereal though brightened with yellow cords."

25. *Ibid.*

26. Pendel, "Thirty-Six Years," 14.

27. Lincoln's visits to the vault were occasionally mentioned in the newspapers of the day and the implication was that on occasion the door was opened and the President went inside. See George L. Kackley, *Notable Persons at Oak Hill Cemetery* (Washington: Kackley, 1983).

28. *National Intelligencer*, February 11, 1864.

29. *National Intelligencer*, February 13 and 15, 1864; Abel P. Upshur to French, March 9 and 17 and April 2, 1864, Commissioner's letters received; see also Herbert R. Collins, *Presidents On Wheels* (New York: Bonanza Books, 1971), 203.

30. French, report to the committee on public buildings, 1864, Commissioner's letters sent.

31. Carpenter, *With Lincoln*, 163.

32. Allen C. Clark, "Abraham Lincoln In the National Capital," CHS *Records*, vol. 27, (1925): 21–22.

33. Carpenter, *With Lincoln*, 30.

34. *Ibid.*, 350–52.

35. William Roscoe Thayer, *The Life and Letters of John Hay* (Boston: Houghton Mifflin Co., 1915); Helen Nicolay, *John G. Nicolay, op. cit.*; see also Wayne C. Temple, ed., "Sketch of 'Tad' Lincoln," *Lincoln Herald*, vol. 60, (fall 1958), 79–81.

36. John Hay, diary, November 8, 1864, in *Letters of John Hay and Extracts From His Diary* (New York: Gordian Press, 1969, reprint of 1902 edition).

37. Thayer, *Life and Letters of Hay*, vol. I, 216.

38. Sandburg, *Abraham Lincoln: The War Years* (New York: Harcourt, Brace & Co., 1939), vol. III, 570.

39. Carpenter, *With Lincoln*, 205.

40. Nicolay to Therena Bates, Washington, March 5, 1865, Nicolay Papers, L.C.

41. French, journal, April 9, 1865, French Papers, L.C.

42. Crook, *Memories*, 61–62.

43. Brooks, *Abraham Lincoln*, 450.

44. Philip Van Doren Stern, *The Man Who Killed Lincoln* (New York: Forum Books, 1939), 15.

45. Mrs. Lincoln to F. B. Carpenter, Chicago, November 15, [1865], *Mary Lincoln's Letters*, 217–18.

Chapter 18: The Rescue

1. Leonard J. Farwell to Senator James R. Dolittle, Washington, February 8, 1866, Dolittle Papers, State Historical Society of Wisconsin.

2. Benn Pitman, ed., *The Assassination of President Lincoln and the Trial of the Conspirators* (New York: Funk & Wagnalls, 1954, reprint of the 1865 edition), 144–53.

3. French, journal, April 15 and May 24, 1865, French Papers, L.C.

4. Charles S. Taft, "The Last Hours of Abraham Lincoln," *Medical and Scientific Reporter*, December 1865, 452–54; see also J. J. Woodward to General J. K. Barnes, Surgeon General, Washington, April 18, 1865, in *Surgery Gynecology and Obstetrics* vol. 93 (1951): 645–53.

5. French, journal, April 15, 1865, French Papers, L.C.

6. Dorothy Meserve Kunhardt and Philip B. Kunhardt, Jr., *Thirty Days* (New York: Harper & Row, 1965), 95.

7. Bill of John Alexander, May 1865; B. Oertly, acting assistant architect of the Treasury, to French, Washington, November 11, 1865, Commissioner's letters received and warrants; see also abstract for the funeral expenses, a total $29,032.31, in the Commissioner's miscellaneous accounts.

8. French, journal, April 17, 1865, French Papers, L.C.

9. Keckley, *Behind the Scenes*, 191–92.

10. *National Intelligencer*, April 21, 1865; Kunhardt and Kunhardt, *Twenty Days*, passim.

11. Bills for clothing, April 17, 1865, Commissioner's letters received; Hitchcock and Seale, *Temples of Democracy*, 146.

12. Townsend, *The Life, Crime and Capture of John Wilkes Booth*, 57–59.

13. French, inventory of the White House, May 26, 1865, Commissioner's miscellaneous correspondence.

14. *Mary Lincoln's Letters*, 328.

15. Keckley, *Behind the Scenes*, 208.

16. Inventory of May 26, 1865, *op. cit.*

17. Margarita S. Gerry, ed., "Andrew Johnson in the White House, Being the Reminiscences of William H. Crook," *The Century*, vol. 76 (September–October 1908), 655.

18. *Ibid.*

19. Lately Thomas [Robert V. Steele], *The First President Johnson* (New York: William Morrow & Co., 1968), 530.

20. There are invoices for carpentry and some decorations in the President's office from John Alexander and William S. Mitchell, submitted in the fall of 1865, but most of the President's work of remodeling the offices consisted of moving furniture. Some new office furniture was built in the Treasury carpentry shop, see B. Oertly to French, Washing-

ton, November 11, 1865, Commissioner's letters received. In 1866 the Congress appropriated $2,000 for "alterations. . . in the business offices" and one suspects this covered the cost of only the telegraph office.

21. Milton Lomask, *Andrew Johnson: President on Trial* (New York: Farrar, Straus & Cudhay, 1960), 106.

22. Macrae, *Americans At Home*, 111–12.

23. Colonel William G. Moore, diary, Thursday, May 7, 1868, Andrew Johnson Papers, L.C.

24. French, journal, July 5, 1865, French Papers, L.C.

25. Thomas, *The First President Johnson*, 223, 230, 238, 242–43.

26. Inventory made by William Slade, February 28, 1867, and see also bills for furnishings and decoration, 1865–69, Commissioner's letters received.

27. Crook, *Five Administrations*, 88.

28. Ames, *Ten Years*, 245.

29. Edward McPherson, *The Political History of the United States of America During the Period of Reconstruction* (Washington: Solomons & Chapman, 1875), 60–61.

30. Stevenson to [House Committee on Public Buildings?], Washington, November 23, 1869; French "to Whom it May Concern," printed notice, Washington, January 24, 1867, Commissioner's letters received.

31. Crook, *Memories*, 47; Stevenson's bill, September 19, 1868; painting bill of Hubert Schutter, October 18, 1866; bills of A. Rutherford, November–May 1866/ 1867; Commissioner's *Report* (Washington: by the government, October 1866).

32. James Kelly to French, Washington, June 25, 1865, Commissioner's letters received; Commissioner's October *Report*.

33. Commissioner's October *Report*; see also photograph taken at the conclusion of the work, Eastman House.

34. Commissioner's October *Report;* Alfred Mullett, "Preliminary Specifications" for the new greenhouse; payroll of B. F. Burns, April–June 1867; George W. Goodall, bill for steam heating plant, October 18, 1866, Commissioner's letters received; see also architectural drawings, Cartographic Division, National Archives; and Edgar T. Welles, ed., *Diary of Gideon Welles,* (New York: Houghton Mifflin Co., 1911), 22.

35. Hubert & Schutter, paint contractors, bill, August 15, 1866; Singleton, *The White House,* vol. II, 109–11; Poore, *Reminiscences,* 215–16: "the halls had been paneled with gilt moldings."

36. Ames, *Ten Years,* 251; see also Betty C. Monkman, "The Acquisition of Portraits of the Presidents for the Executive Mansion in the 19th Century," unpublished ms., 1979, OCWH; bill for hanging "16 pictures in the upper rooms and Hall," September 19, 1868, Commissioner's letters received.

37. Crook, *Memories,* 62; Pendel, *Thirty-Six Years,* 54–58; French, journal, *passim.*

38. Singleton, *The White House,* vol. II, 111.

39. J. A. Stevenson's bill for "cutting, hemming and mending 166 yds. crash" and "putting out and in Carpet on Porch at Receptions," Washington, September 19, 1868, Commissioner's letters received.

40. William J. Rhees to French, Washington, February 22, 1866, Commissioner's letters received.

41. Servants' payrolls; undated tally of number of meals served at the White House each day, late 1867 or early 1868, Johnson Papers, L.C.

42. Steward of the Executive Mansion, 4th Section, Appropriation Act of July 23, 1866, Acts, First Session 39th Congress, 207: "provides for the appointment by the President of a steward who shall have the custody of the plate, furniture and other public property in the President's House."

43. See Washington city directories; a William Slade is listed as early as 1853 as a federal employee, but this may not be the same man. He first appeared in Andrew Johnson's employ in August 1865, having bought $256 in meats and $84.10 in vegetables and fruits as well as paying the servants. He is called "steward" in January 1866 by Johnson, but in his own hand he wrote that he became steward August 1, 1865. Bills, letters, laundry, and tailoring invoices, Johnson Papers, L.C.

44. Ames, *Ten Years,* 246.

45. Moore, diary, August 1–3, 1868, Johnson Papers, L.C.

46. Robert W. Winston, *Andrew Johnson: Plebeian and Patriot* (New York: Holt Co., 1928), 363–71.

47. *Ibid.,* 368–69.

48. David Miller Dewitt, *The Impeachment and Trial of Andrew Johnson* (Madison: State Historical Society reprint of the 1903 edition); Milton Lomask, *Andrew Johnson.*

49. Lomask, *President On Trial,* 275.

50. Moore, diary, April 9, 1868.

51. *Ibid.,* January 6, 1870.

52. Gerry, ed., "Crook's Reminiscences," 869–70; Pendel, *Thirty-Six Years,* 60.

53. Gerry. ed., "Crook's Reminiscences," 873; Gideon Welles noted in his diary, December 30, 1868, that "General Grant the President-elect, would not permit his children to attend this party of innocent youths. . . ." vol. 3, 494; a full account of the costs of the party and the various details can be gleaned from the records that survive in the Johnson Papers, L.C.

54. Gerry, ed., "Crook's Reminiscences," 867–68; James L. Thomas's employment began May 1, 1868, and Mrs. Slade served in emergencies until he was hired, Johnson Papers, L.C.

55. Charles Ruppert to Slade, Washington, February 8, 1867; Slade to French,

Washington, February 12, 1867, Commissioner's auditor's accounts.

56. Records and payrolls of servants, Johnson Papers, L.C.

57. "Bill of fare for 4th dinner," n.d., in Slade's hand, Johnson Papers, L.C.

58. Lomask, *Andrew Johnson*, 105–11, 143–47; see also Commissioner's auditor's accounts for various expenses of running Johnson's social functions.

59. While plants had been purchased during the summer, Alexander McKericher went to Philadelphia and New York buying plants for the conservatory in October and November 1868 and General Nathaniel Michler followed toward the close of November, visiting Baltimore, New York, and Boston. The plants sent back to the White House were numerous and more varied than the earlier stock. See Commissioner's auditor's accounts.

60. Gerry, ed., "Crook's Reminiscences," 881.

Chapter 19: The Glasshouse

1. William B. Hesseltine, *Ulysses S. Grant, Politician* (New York: Dodd, Mead & Company, 1935), 160–63; New York *Tribune*, March 9, 1869.

2. A. P. Upshur to French, Washington, February 29 and March 2 and 7, 1864, Commissioner's letters received. The records of the Commissioner of Public Buildings continue in the same record group at the National Archives. The title of the supervisor becomes the Officer in Charge of the Public Buildings. This title was to survive until 1934, but in the 19th century the "officer" was very often called the "commissioner." To simplify matters, however, I will take the official title of "officer," using in notes the letters OCPB. Most of the official workings of the White House were under him; thus his papers fall into the OCPB record group. However, in some instances records appear under the army, navy, or departmental records, as Department of the Interior.

3. General Michler, *Annual Report* (Washington: by the government, [February 13], 1867); Michler's various bills for his field trips and studies, January 1–31 and November 3–8, 1867; bill of Alexander Gardener for photographing 36 sheets of maps of possible sites for a new President's House, February 10 and July 9, 1868, Department of the Interior, vouchers, relevant dates, National Archives.

4. John Y. Simon, ed., *The Personal Memoirs of Julia Dent Grant* (New York: G. P. Putnam's Sons, 1975), 174.

5. *Ibid.*, 173–74; Pendel, *Thirty-Six Years*, 65.

6. Julia Grant, *Memoirs*, 174.

7. Crook, *Memories*, 98–99.

8. Julia Grant, *Memoirs*, 174.

9. Francis Lamb's bill for moving the picture and hanging it in the White House, March 22, 1869, first auditor's accounts, OCPB. The Grant family portrait is now at the National Museum of American History, Smithsonian Institution.

10. Julia Grant, *Memoirs*, 175.

11. *Ibid.*, 176.

12. *Ibid.*, 175.

13. Hesseltine, *Grant*, 301.

14. Ishbel Ross, *The General's Wife: The Life of Mrs. Ulysses S. Grant* (New York: Dodd, Mead & Company, 1959), 212; Jesse R. Grant, *In the Days of My Father General Grant* (New York: Harper Brothers Publishers, 1925), 66–67.

15. Bill of John J. Peabody, Washington, July 1, 1869; Horace Porter to Michler, Washington, January 15, 1870, OCPB letters received.

16. Ames, *Ten Years*, 123; Ross, *General's Wife*, 205.

17. Crook, *Memories*, 80–81.

18. White House monthly payrolls are spotty for some of the Grant years but enough survive to give a general idea about the size of the staff. At first the payrolls were in the OCPB letters, but beginning in 1871 they appear in the records of expenditures from the "appropriation for repairs, fuel, & c., Executive Mansion," first auditor's accounts.

19. Crook, *Memories*, 90; for an affectionate recollection of Albert Hawkins and the Grant family, see Jesse Grant, *In the Days of My Father General Grant*, 61–65.

20. Crook, *Memories*, 91.

21. *Ibid.*, 89–90.

22. Ross, *General's Wife*, 217.

23. *Ibid.*, 221; Pendel, *Thirty-Six Years*, 64; Adam Badeau, *Grant in Peace, From Appomattox to Mount McGregor: A Personal Memoir* (Hartford: S. S. Scranton & Company, 1887), 172–74.

24. Hesseltine, *Grant*, 210.

25. Emily Edson Briggs, *The Olivia Letters* (New York: Neale Publishing Company, 1906), 121–23; Badeau, *A Personal Memoir, passim*.

26. Julia Grant, *Memoirs*, 174.

27. William McLean's bills for carpentry, June 1–September 1, 1869, first auditor's accounts.

28. Crook, *Memories*, 93.

29. Briggs, *Olivia Letters*, 200–1.

30. Bill of Sommerville and Leitch for "altering flower stand," Washington, December 23, 1869, OCPB, letters received.

31. Klapthor, *White House China*, 90–96.

32. Bill of John R. Hunt, Washington, July 1, 1869; also William McLean's bills for lumber, September–October 1869, first auditor's accounts.

33. C. E. Creecey's bill, Washington, May 23, 1871, notes the chandelier is after a "Jacobson & Mabies Patent," first auditor's accounts. Pottier & Stymus decorated and refurnished the Cabinet

Room for Grant, and at this point Jefferson's long cabinet table, with drawers down both sides, was discarded.

34. Bills for fresco, Schutter & Rakeman, Washington, March 15, May 12, 1870, and Daniel Shanahan & Co., Washington, January 11, 1870; Browne, Spaulding & Co., n.p., May 14, 1870, first auditor's accounts.

35. J. L. Cowan's bill, n.p., February 11, 1870, first auditor's accounts.

36. Michler, "Statement of Expenditures," payment to Constantino Brumidi, December 3, 1869, OCPB, letters sent; see also Schutter & Rakeman's bill, Washington, August 25, 1870, first auditor's accounts; see also Washington *Critic*, December 4, 1869. The Brumidi cartouches, painted on canvas, were removed from the hall ceiling in 1902 and lost for some years. Two have been returned to the White House and are used today as framed pictures, hung on the wall.

37. Ezdorf was employed in the office of the Supervising Architect of the Treasury from the 1870s until the 1890s, and was considered one of the most gifted draftsmen on the staff. Little is known about him. He could use the title "count" in Europe, but he lived in relative obscurity in the U.S.A., his great hour being when he worked on State, War, & Navy. See Patrick Snadon, "The Second Empire Interiors of the Old Executive Office Building," unpublished ms., 1986, University of Kentucky; Ezdorf's career in Washington is outlined in his employment file, "Applications and Recommendations for Positions in the Washington Offices of the Treasury Department," Records of the Treasury Department, National Archives.

38. Expense progress report, March 23, 1875, New State, War, and Navy Department, Office of the Superintendant of Construction; Alex R. Shephard & Co., bill for hanging chandeliers, October 31, 1875; William B. Kendall, Bigelow Carpet Co., New York, bill for English Wilton carpeting, November 14,

1872, first auditor's accounts; see also Michler, "Statement of Expenditures," June–October, 1875, OCPB, letters sent.

39. Cornelius and Baker of Philadelphia manufactured the gas fixtures, see OCPB, letters received; see also Denys Peter Myers, *Gaslighting in America: A Guide For Historic Preservation* (Washington: Government Printing Office, 1978), 149.

Chapter 20: Flourishes

1. Mrs. John A. Logan [Mary Simmerson Cunningham Logan], *Thirty Years in Washington* (Hartford: A. D. Worthington & Co., 1901), 135.

2. Orville E. Babcock, "Condition, capacity and adaptability of the Executive Offices and Residence for the family of the President," Washington, January 18, 1873, OCPB, letters sent.

3. Briggs, *Olivia Letters*, 169.

4. *Ibid.*, 168.

5. *Ibid.*, 199–201.

6. Ames, *Ten Years*, 257–59; Mrs. A. Gaston charged $2.16 each for 7 tydie bows, October 31, 1870, first auditor's accounts. Tydie bows were large bows sewn in the desired configuration, and were placed usually at angles on the backs of chairs, the edges of mantelpieces, the sides of pianos and in other places to achieve that "personal" touch the Victorians loved. Mrs. Grant's were made of satin and the colors complemented the traditional colors of the state rooms.

7. John Stewart, ink and watercolor plan of the pinwheel parterre, 1874, Map Division, National Archives.

8. Mark Twain and Charles Dudley Warner, *The Gilded Age* (Hartford: American Publishing Company, 1873), 222.

9. OCPB miscellaneous accounts and letters received, *passim; Blue Book of Federal Employees*, 1869–70.

10. Singleton, *The White House*, vol. II, 142–43.

11. Charles G. Ball's bills, April and May 1869, OCPB, letters received.

12. Julia Grant, *Memories*, 181.

13. Singleton, *The White House*, 143.

14. Menu from Nellie Grant's wedding, OCWH.

15. New York *Herald*, May 22, 1874.

16. *Ibid.*; also, New York *Daily Graphic*, May 23, 1874.

17. *Ibid.*; see also photograph of the East Room decorated for the wedding, vol. I, plate 47.

18. New York *Herald*, May 22, 1874.

19. Unidentified newspaper clipping about the wedding, OCWH.

20. Menu, *op. cit.*

21. Bruce Catton, *U.S. Grant and the American Military Tradition* (Boston: Little, Brown, 1954), 165–67.

22. OCPB, letters sent and received, contracts, miscellaneous accounts, 1871–1875.

23. Julia Grant, *Memoirs*, 190–92.

24. *Ibid.*, 185–86.

Chapter 21: Peace and Plenty

1. Julia Grant, *Memoirs*, 189; see also bill from Gorham Manufacturing Company, New York, December 18, 1876, first auditor's accounts.

2. Harry Barnard, *Rutherford B. Hayes and His America* (New York: The Bobbs-Merrill Company, Inc., 1954), 403.

3. Hayes, diary, March 14, 1877, in Charles R. Williams, ed., *Diary and Letters of Rutherford Birchard Hayes* (Columbus: The Ohio State Archeological and Historical Society, 1926), vol. III, 426; Julia Grant, *Memoirs*, 195; Singleton, *The White House*, vol. II, 150–52.

4. Singleton, *The White House*, vol. II,

151; Cincinnati *Commercial*, March 3, 1877; *New York Tribune*, March 5, 1877.

5. Julia Grant, *Memoirs*, 197.

6. Emily Apt Greer, *First Lady: The Life of Lucy Webb Hayes* (Fremont: The Rutherford B. Hayes Presidential Center, 1984), 147–51.

7. New York *Daily Graphic*, April 25, 1877.

8. Frances E. Willard to Hayes, Stanstead, Vermont, July 5, 1880, *Hayes Center*.

9. Hayes to Huntington, March 3, 1881, Hayes Letterbook, Hayes Center.

10. *Resolute* file, OCWH; see also photo of the desk on exhibit to the tourists, Green Room, 1880, Hayes Center.

11. H. Wayne Morgan, *From Hayes to McKinley: National Party Politics, 1877–1896* (Syracuse: Syracuse University Press, 1969), 11.

12. Washington *National Republican*, October 27, 1877; W. H. Bernard to W. K. Rogers, Washington, October 21, 1880, copy, Hayes Center.

13. James Temple Brown's bill, February 4, 1880, General Accounting Office, vouchers, National Archives.

14. See office accounts, OCPB, letters received, March–December 1877.

15. Barnard, *Hayes*, 423.

16. Watt P. Marchman, "The 'memoirs' of Thomas Donaldson," *Hayes Historical Journal*, vol. II (1979): 243; see also bills of Demonet & Sons and Chapanis, miscellaneous accounts.

17. Gerry, ed., "Crook's Reminiscences," 644; Webb C. Hayes to William Dean Howells, Fremont, October 7, 1919, Hayes Center.

18. Payroll, Executive Mansion, OCPB, letters received.

19. Byron Paine, "Rutherford B. Hayes: The Age of Innocence in the White House," *Literary Digest*, vol. 92 (1920): 41–42; Donaldson memoirs, 237.

20. *Boston Herald*, March 28, 1878.

21. *Ibid.*

22. Grant commissioned the portrait from William Cogswell in the summer of 1869, see Horace Porter to Michler, Washington, June 23, 1869, and Michler to Cogswell, Washington, July 21, 1869, OCPB, letters received and sent.

23. James Daly to Mrs. Julia Gardiner Tyler, Washington, August 29, 1870, OCPB, letters sent.

24. A. R. Spofford to the President, Washington, November 19, 1878, Hayes Center.

25. Andrews correspondence, Corcoran Gallery of Art.

26. Gerry, ed., "Crook's Reminiscences," 646.

27. Portrait files, OCWH.

28. This portrait was painted by Daniel Huntington at Spiegel Grove.

29. Geer, *First Lady*, *passim*.

30. *Annual Report of the Chief of Engineers* (Washington: by the government, 1877), 1074.

31. Thomas Lincoln Casey, [work] force in Executive Mansion greenhouses, 1878, OCPB letters sent.

32. Babcock's records for improvements, 1871–1874 are rather full, OCPB records; see his annual report for 1871.

33. Casey, published annual reports, 1879–1880.

34. Bill of Sommerville & Leitch, Washington, May 29, 1871, first auditor's accounts.

35. Payroll, doormen, and guards, OCPB, letters received, also miscellaneous accounts, *passim*.

36. Washington *Evening Star*, April 20, 1878, and March 29, 1880; *Washington Post*, March 29, 1880.

37. G. M. Wright's bill for "1 rosewood billiard table, $350.00," April 3, 1877, first auditor's accounts.

38. Drawings, notes, and proposals for White House conservatories, 1879–1880, Cartographic and Architectural Branch, National Archives.

39. Unsigned, undated note in pencil describing the promenade and other dinner customs of the Hayeses. Probably the draft of a letter of instruction written to Garfield before he moved to the White House, Hayes Center.

40. Dora Scott's White House letters, December 1880–January 1881, Hayes Center.

41. Geer, *First Lady*, 228.

42. Klapthor, *White House China*, 97–121, 184–272; Mrs. Hayes to Davis, Washington, August 2, 1880, in Geer, *First Lady*, 220.

43. Barnard, *Hayes*, 496.

Chapter 22: Interlude

1. Pendel, *Thirty-Six Years*, 99.

2. Williams, ed., *Hayes Diary*, vol. III, 600–1, June 5, 1880.

3. Poore, *Reminiscences*, vol. II, 414; Marian West, "Our Republican Queens," *Munsey's Magazine*, vol. IV (September 1901): 895.

4. Hayes, memorandum to Garfield, Washington, January 17, 1881, in Williams, ed., *Hayes Diary*, vol. III, 639–40.

5. Allan Peskin, *Garfield: A Biography* (Kent: Kent State University Press, 1978), 546.

6. James C. Smith, *The Life and Letters of James Abram Garfield* (New Haven: Yale University Press, 1925), 1172–75.

7. Singleton, *The White House*, vol. II, 166–67.

8. Garfield to Joseph Rudolph, Washington, March 13, 1881, in Margaret Leech and Harry J. Brown, *The Garfield Orbit* (New York: Harper & Row, 1978), 313–14.

9. Smith, *Life and Letters of Garfield*,

vol. II, 1174; see also OCPB annual report for 1881.

10. Smith, *Life and Letters of Garfield*, vol. II, 1170.

11. Col. Rockwell's bill for reimbursement for the trip, May 20, 1881, miscellaneous accounts.

12. Peskin, *Garfield*, 573.

13. Crump to Hayes, Washington, June 7, 1881, Hayes Center.

14. *Ibid.*

15. Donaldson memoirs, 243–44; Casey to Otis Brothers & Co., March 19, 1881, OCPB, letters sent; and Casey and Rockwell, payrolls and records regarding the Metropolitan Police at the White House, March–May 1881, contracts. The idea of having an elevator in the White House predated Garfield's administration, although it may have come up in anticipation of his mother's moving there. The appropriation was made March 2, 1881.

16. Quoted in Smith, *Life and Letters of Garfield*, vol. II, 1170.

17. Garfield's diary, April 3, 1881, Garfield Papers, L.C.

18. Smith, *Life and Letters of Garfield*, vol. II, 1173–74; Garfield's diary, May and June 1881, *passim.*

19. H. G. and C. J. Hayes, *A Complete History of the Trial of Guiteau, Assassin of President Garfield* (Philadelphia: Lippincott, 1882), 589.

20. Crump's recollections of the event, ca. 1890, Lucretia Garfield Papers, L.C.; also Smith, *Life and Letters of Garfield*, vol. II, 1179–80.

21. Peskin, *Garfield*, 597–98; see also Crook, *Memories*, 149.

22. Peskin, *Garfield*, 597.

23. Crump to "dear sir," Washington, April 18, n.d., Garfield Papers, L.C.

24. Dr. William Tindall, "Echoes of a Surgical Tragedy," CHS *Records*, vol. 23 (1920): 147–66.

25. U.S. Navy Department, *Reports of Officers of the Navy On Ventilating and Cooling the Executive Mansion During the Illness of President Garfield* (Washington: by the Navy Department, 1882).

26. Crump's recollections.

27. Frank H. Trusdell to Genie Trusdell, Washington, August 16, 1881, copy, OCWH.

28. *Ibid.*

29. Bills for removal of Garfield to New Jersey, OCPB, letters received, July–September 1881.

30. Crump's recollections.

31. Thomas C. Reeves, *Gentleman Boss: The Life of Chester Alan Arthur* (New York: Alfred A. Knopf, 1975), 246–48.

Chapter 23: The Aesthetic House

1. *New York Times*, October 1, 1881.

2. Reeves, *Life of Arthur*, 268–76; see also George Frederick Howe, *Chester A. Arthur: A Quarter Century of Machine Politics* (New York: Dodd, Mead & Co., Inc., 1934).

3. Pendel, *Thirty-Six Years*, 125.

4. Moses contract, August 10, 1881, OCPB, letters received.

5. Rockwell, specifications for redecoration, Washington, July 27, 1881, OCPB, letters received.

6. Jacob (?) B. Solomon to Rockwell, New York, August 2, 1881, OCPB, letters received.

7. Crook, *Memories*, 160.

8. Waring report in *Papers From the President . . . In Relation to the Executive Mansion* (Washington: by the government, 1882), 3.

9. Manuscript of the Waring report, November 26, 1881, OCPB, letters received.

10. A. F. Rockwell to Brig. Gen. H.

G. Wright, Chief of Engineers, Washington, April 19, 1882, OCPB, letters sent.

11. Rockwell to the President, Washington, May 19, 1882, OCPB, letters sent.

12. Waring, "Report on Sanitary Conditions at the White House," in *U.S. vs. M. F. Morris et al.* (Washington: by the government, ca. 1882).

13. Crump to Hayes, Washington, April 29, 1882, and April ?, 1884 [1882?], Hayes Center; *Washington Post*, April 15, 1882.

14. See Robert Koch, *Louis C. Tiffany: Rebel In Glass* (New York: Crown Publishers, 1964), and Wilson H. Faude, "Associated Artists and the American Renaissance in the Decorative Arts," *Winterthur Portfolio 10* (Charlottesville: University of Virginia Press, 1975) 102–30.

15. A brief description of Tiffany's White House decorations in the aesthetic context is found in *Artistic Houses*, (New York: D. Appleton & Co., 1884), vol. II, 97–99. The "old colonial spirit" of the house is acknowledged, along with Tiffany's use of nationalistic emblems.

16. *The Chautauquan*, July 1884.

17. Bills for work on the White House, March 1881–October 1882; the Moses bills came in monthly, more or less, while Tiffany's work is covered in one very detailed invoice of October 2, 1882, OCPB, letters received.

18. E. V. Smalley, "The White House," *Century Magazine*, vol. VIII (April 1884): 802–10.

19. *Ibid.*, 808.

20. Harriet S. Blaine Beale, *Letters of Mrs. James G. Blaine*, (New York: Duffield & Co., 1908), vol. I, 309.

21. Reeves, *Life of Arthur*, 271.

22. *Ibid.*, 355.

23. Donaldson's memoirs, 246.

24. Mrs. McElroy is described in *The Knickerbocker Press*, March 16, 1913, and in her obituary in the New York *Evening Post*, January 9, 1917; Pendel, *Thirty-Six Years*, 126.

25. Singleton, *The White House*, vol. II, 175.

26. Donaldson's memoirs, 245.

27. Crump to Hayes, Southport, England, August 4, 1882, Hayes Center.

28. Beale, *Mrs. Blaine's Letters*, 310–11.

29. Seating charts, OCPB, letters sent and miscellaneous papers.

30. Paul E. Bierley, *John Philip Sousa: American Phenomenon* (Englewood Cliffs: Prentice-Hall, 1973), 42–45.

31. Collins, *Presidents on Wheels*, 99.

32. Alexander McClure, *Recollections of Half a Century* (Salem: Salem Press Co., 1902), 115.

33. Reeves, *Life of Arthur*, 317; see also obituary, New York *Sun*, November 19, 1886, and the New York *Mail and Express*, November 18, 1886.

34. New York *Evening Post*, April 23, 1883.

Chapter 24: The Blue Room

1. Crook, *Memories*; Pendel, *Thirty-Six Years*, passim.

2. Crook, *Memories*, 170.

3. Robert Marion LaFollette, *LaFollette's Autobiography* (Madison: LaFollette, 1913), 53.

4. Frances Carpenter, ed., *Carp's Washington*, by Frank G. Carpenter (New York: McGraw-Hill Book Co., 1960), 39.

5. Allan Nevins, *Grover Cleveland: A Study in Courage* (New York: Dodd, Mead & Co., 1933), 164.

6. Donaldson's memoirs, 258.

7. Robert McElroy, *Grover Cleveland:*

The Man and the Statesman (New York: Harper & Brothers, 1923), 37.

8. Cleveland to "Brother," Washington, March 27, 1885, Grover Cleveland Papers, L.C.

9. Carpenter, *Washington*, 40–41.

10. Nevins, *Cleveland*, 109–10.

11. *Ibid.*, 211.

12. Pendel, *Thirty-Six Years*, 131–32; Singleton, *The White House*, vol. II, 192–94; Nevins, *Cleveland*, 212–13; Mrs. Logan, *Thirty Years*, 698–700.

13. McElroy, *Cleveland*, 111.

14. Cleveland to G. F. Segar, Washington, October 25, 1886, in Allan Nevins, ed., *Letters of Grover Cleveland* (New York: DaCapo reprint, 1970, of the 1935 edition), 102. Tender letters between the President and his sisters Rose Cleveland and Mary Cleveland Hoyt demonstrate not only his deep attachment to them but their frequent visits to the White House.

15. Morgan, *From Hayes to McKinley*, 245–47.

16. Horace S. Merrill, *Bourbon Leader: Grover Cleveland and the Democratic Party* (Boston: Little, Brown, 1957), 89.

17. McElroy, *Cleveland*, 184.

18. Cleveland to Mrs. Hoyt, Washington, April 19, 1886, *Letters of Grover Cleveland*, 105–6.

19. Cleveland to Mrs. Hoyt, Washington, March 21, 1886, *Letters of Grover Cleveland*, 103–4.

20. *Ibid.*

21. Cleveland to Mrs. Hoyt, Washington, May 5, 1886, *Letters of Grover Cleveland*, 122.

22. Cleveland to Mrs. Hoyt, Washington, April 19, 1886, *Letters of Grover Cleveland*, 107.

23. Cleveland to Mrs. Hoyt, Washington, April 26, 1886, *Letters of Grover Cleveland*, 107.

24. Nevins, 303–7.

25. Cleveland to Vilas, Washington, May 28, 1886, *Letters of Grover Cleveland*, 109.

26. Crook, *Memories*, 178–79.

27. *Ibid.*, 179.

28. Charles Henlock (a White House gardener under Pfister) and Margaret Norris, "Flowers for First Ladies," *The Saturday Evening Post*, November 28, 1931, 13.

29. *Paris Morning News*, June 21, 1886, quoted in Wilbur Cross and Ann Novotny, *White House Weddings* (New York: David McKay, Co., 1967), 129–30.

30. Cleveland to Mrs. Hoyt, Washington, March 21, 1886, *Letters of Grover Cleveland*, 103–4.

31. James M. Goode, *Capital Losses: A Cultural History of Washington's Destroyed Buildings* (Washington: Smithsonian Institution Press, 1979), 103–5.

32. Crook, *Memories*, 195; Carpenter, *Washington*, 47.

33. Nevins, *Cleveland*, 310–11.

34. *Ibid.*, 309.

35. Mrs. Cleveland to Mrs. Maggie Nicodemus, Washington, June 3, 1888, in McElroy, *Cleveland*, vol. I, 285–86.

36. Singleton, *The White House*, vol. II, 203.

37. McElroy, *Cleveland*, vol. I, 304–5.

38. Crook, *Memories*, 197–98.

Chapter 25: Homecoming

1. See Harry Joseph Sievers, *Benjamin Harrison: Hoosier Warrior*, (1952 and 1960) and *Benjamin Harrison: Hoosier Statesman* both (New York: Bobbs-Merrill, Co.).

2. New York *Tribune*, March 14, 1889.

3. Harry Joseph Sievers, *Benjamin Harrison: Hoosier President* (New York: Bobbs-Merrill, Co., 1968), 33–35.

4. Pendel, *Thirty-Six Years*, 72.

5. Waring, "Report on Sanitary Conditions at the White House," n.d. [ca. 1882], OCPB, letters received.

6. See photographs of the corridors in the 1880s, OCWH and Eastman House.

7. Oswald H. Ernst, *Annual Reports*, 1889, 1890, 1891; John M. Wilson, *Annual Report*, 1892.

8. New York *Sun*, October 22, 1889.

9. Mrs. Logan, *Thirty Years*, 709; Carpenter, *Washington*, 302.

10. Carpenter, *Washington*, 300–1.

11. Klapthor, *White House China*, 126–30.

12. *Washington Post*, February 21, 1892; Benjamin Harrison, "The Social Life of the President," *The Ladies Home Journal*, vol. XIV (April 1897), 3–4.

13. See C. W. Bowen, ed., *The History of the Centennial Celebration of the Inauguration of George Washington as the First President of the United States* (New York: Appleton Publishers, 1892).

14. Sievers, *Hoosier President*, 69, 70, 70 n.

15. *House Reports*, 51st Congress, report #4042, "Extension of the Executive Mansion," March 2, 1891; Frederick D. Owen's resume to 1899 is found in a packet entitled, "authority to employ Fred D. Owen, June 25, 1900," OCPB, letters sent.

16. Randolph Keim and Frederick D. Owen, "The Executive Mansion: Suggestions by Mrs. Harrison for the Proposed Extension," *Architects and Builders' Magazine*, clipping OCWH.

17. *Ibid.*; Committee On Public Buildings and Grounds, *Report* (Washington: by the government, 1891).

18. New York *Sun*, August 24, 1890.

19. Notes on the Executive Mansion expansion project, typescript, Benjamin Harrison Papers, L.C.

20. Sievers, *Hoosier President*, 142–44.

21. New York *Sun*, October 22, 1889.

22. Carpenter, *Washington*, 302.

23. *Washington Evening Star*, June 8, 1889; *Washington Post* January 3, 1891; Singleton, *The White House*, vol. II, 225–28.

24. Mrs. Harrison presided as President-General at the Continental Congress of the Daughters of the American Revolution February 22, 1892. See Letitia Green (Mrs. Adlai E. Stevenson), *Brief History of the Daughters of the American Revolution* (Bloomington: [D.A.R.?], 1913), 27–30; see also Margaret Gibbs, *The DAR* (New York: Holt, Rinehart and Winston, 1969), 1, 2, 47–49, 58–59.

25. Donaldson's memoirs, 261.

26. E. S. Yergason, various specifications for work in the state rooms, January 15–June 2, 1891, Yergason Papers, OCWH.

27. Edison General Electric Company (F. S. Hastings), bill for "Introducing electric lamps into Executive Mansion," March 16, 1891, OCPB, letters received; also see Ernst, *Annual Report* (Washington: by the government, 1891) and draft, OCPB, letters sent.

28. Irwin H. Hoover, *Forty-Two Years In the White House* (Boston: Houghton Mifflin Co., 1934), 3–4.

29. Yergason specifications, June 2, 1891; see also photographs of the Blue Room as redecorated in 1891, OCWH.

30. Crook, *Memories*, 224–26; New York *World*, December 26, 1889; Hoover, *Forty Two Years*, 6–9; see also W. F. Dawson, *Christmas: Its Origin and Associations* (London: E. Stock, 1902), 313–14.

31. *Washington Post*, February 21, 1892.

32. Sievers, *Hoosier President*, 241–44.

33. Harrison to C. N. Bliss, Washington, November 16, 1892, Harrison Papers, L.C.

VOLUME II

Chapter 26: A Recollection of Roses

1. Crook, *Memories*, 198, 234–35; Edwin L. Godkin in *The Nation*, quoted in Stefan Lorant, *The Glorious Burden: The American Presidency* (New York: Harper & Row, 1968), 426.

2. McElroy, *Cleveland*, vol. II, 27–30; see also Robert Lincoln O'Brien, *Grover Cleveland As Seen By His Stenographer* (Boston: Massachusetts Historical Society, 1951), 7–8; and Cleveland to Dr. Kasson Gibson, Washington, October 14, 1893, *Letters of Grover Cleveland*, 338.

3. *Ibid.*, 27.

4. Elizabeth L. Banks, "Public Receptions at the White House," *Cassell's Magazine*, July 1898, 118–19.

5. *Ibid.*; Crook, *Memories*, 196; Singleton, *The White House*, vol. II, 242–43.

6. See various bills for setting up "hat boxes" and the ushers' office for social occasions, OCPB, letters received.

7. Social customs in Washington and at the White House were detailed at the time in Mary Pollok Nimmo, *Etiquette at the National Capital* (Washington: by the author, 1892).

8. Singleton, *The White House*, vol. II, 235–36; *Washington Post*, May 26, 1893.

9. Payrolls, 1893–1897, OCPB, letters received and sent and contract file, *passim*.

10. OCPB, letters sent and invoices, *passim*; Dubois before 1897 was always called a "doorman" in the payrolls.

11. Addee's reign as expert on protocol extended from 1866 until his death in 1924. Few papers of this remarkable official have been located; the Addee collection at the L.C. is small and of relatively little consequence. The best account of his work is in Henry Bartholomew Cox, "The Protocol Function in United States Foreign Relations: Its

Administration and Development, 1776–1968," unpublished ms., Historical Studies Division, History Office, Bureau of Public Affairs, Department of State; see also Cox, "The Protocol Function As An Aspect of Executive Responsibility," unpublished, ms., Law School Library, The George Washington University.

12. Crook, *Memories*, 191.

13. Bill of Johnson & Kennedy, Washington, September 14, 1893, for "Removing all old decorations, redecorating and frescoing ceiling, frieze, dado and side walls of the Red Parlor," and for some new woodwork and cutting new doors between the Red and Blue Rooms and cutting down and fixing with double mahogany doors the east window of the Red Room, giving access to the South Portico. Also see bills of W.H. Houghton Mfg. Co., July 1893, OCPB, letters received.

14. In 1986 "Love and Life" was hanging rather anonymously in the Grand Salon of the Renwick Gallery (old Corcoran Gallery of Art on Pennsylvania Avenue), Smithsonian Institution. In the late 19th and early 20th centuries it had a notorious career of going back and forth to the White House. It was much in the newspapers and frequently condemned as evil in subject matter by moralists.

15. Bill of A.H. Davenport, Boston, December 26, 1894, OCPB, letters received.

16. "Memories," *The New Yorker*, vol. 37 (January 27, 1962): 27.

Chapter 27: 1898

1. McElroy, *Cleveland*, vol. II, 253.

2. Crook, *Memories*, 242.

3. Quoted in H. Wayne Morgan, *William McKinley and His America* (Syracuse: Syracuse University Press, 1963), 305.

4. Mrs. Garret A. Hobart, *Second Lady* (New York: privately printed, 1933), 8.

5. Mrs. Logan, *Thirty Years*, 732.

6. Walter Prescott Webb, ed., *Washing-ton Wife: Journal of Ellen Maury Slayden From 1897 to 1919* (New York: Harper & Row, 1962), 8.

7. Harold Dean Cater, ed., *Henry Adams and His Friends* (New York: Octagon Books, 1970), 352.

8. Margaret Leech, *In the Days of McKinley* (New York: Harper & Brothers, 1959), 129.

9. *Washington Post*, January 20, 1898.

10. Written orders and bills for services, OCPB, correspondence.

11. Leech, *In the Days of McKinley*, 166.

12. Crook, *Memories*, 260–61.

13. L. White Busbey, ed., *Uncle Joe Cannon: The Story of a Pioneer American* (New York: Henry Holt and Company, 1927), 186–89.

14. Hoover, *Forty Two Years*, 22–23.

15. George Cortelyou, diary, April 20, 1898, Cortelyou Papers, L.C.

16. *Ibid.*

17. *Washington Post*, May 24, 1898; see also Cortelyou, diary, May 22, 1898.

18. Cortelyou, diary, April 20, 1898.

19. Leech, *In the Days of McKinley*, 126–29.

20. Payrolls 1898, OCPB correspondence; Frances Benjamin Johnston photographed the office and staff during the war, Johnston Collection, Prints and Photographs Division, L.C.

21. Cortelyou, diary, *passim*, spring 1898.

22. *Ibid.*, March 25, 1898.

23. Weldon Fawcett, "The War Room at the White House," *World's Work*, vol. III (March 1902): 1841–1843; see also Johnston photographs, *op. cit.*

24. Cortelyou, diary, June 8, 1898.

25. Hoover notebooks, Irwin H. Hoover Papers, L.C.

26. Leech, *McKinley*, 287–91; see also Cortelyou, diary, August 3–12, 1898.

Chapter 28: Grand Schemes

1. Morgan, *McKinley*, 527.

2. George Grantham Blair to Bingham, Washington, November 20, 1899, OCPB letters received.

3. See Mary Foote Henderson, *Proposed Executive Mansion* (Washington: privately printed, 1898).

4. Charles Moore, *The Life and Times of Charles Follen McKim* (Boston: Houghton Mifflin Co., 1921), 204.

5. *Washington Post*, December 13, 1900; *Washington Star*, June 30, 1900; *New York Evening Post*, November 23, 1899; *Philadelphia Press*, November 26, 1899; *New York Times*, December 16, 1900.

6. Silk fabric cuttings, Yergason Papers, OCWH.

7. Bills of W.B. Moses & Sons and E.E. Yergason, May–October 1899, OCPB, letters received.

8. Julia B. Foraker, *I would Live It Again: Memories of A Vivid Life* (New York: Harper & Brothers, 1932), 258–59; McKinley White House inventory, in the Chief of Engineers, U.S. Army, *Annual Report* (Washington: Army, 1901).

9. *Message of the President of the United States Transmitting the report of the Proceedings of the Commission Appointed in Conformity with an Act of Congress Entitled 'An Act to Provide for an Appropriate National Celebration of the Establishment of the Seat of Government in the District of Columbia* (Washington: Government Printing Office, 1900).

10. Bingham to the Hon. Joshua Wilbur, Washington, January 20 and May 4, 1900, OCPB, letters sent; to Thomas Manly Deane, Washington, March 5, 1900. See also photographs of the Owens model, Theodore Bingham Papers, L.C.

11. *Washington Post*, December 13, 1900.

12. Printed copy of the address, "History of the Executive Mansion During the Century 1800–1900," Bingham Papers, L.C.; Glenn Brown, *Memories, 1860–1930* (Washington: Press of W.F. Roberts, 1931), 106–8.

13. *Ibid.*, 108.

14. American Institute of Architects, *Journal of Proceedings*, 1900, 88–89, 112, and 1901, 46–47, 90–91; minutes of the Architectural League of New York, executive committee, December 21, 1899; "Enlargement of the White House," *Century Magazine*, vol. LXI (February 1901), 365–66; see also Brown, *Memories, passim*.

15. Bingham to M[ontgomery] Schuyler, Washington, December 20, 1900, OCPB, letters sent.

16. Pendel, *Thirty-Six Years*, 102; Crook, *Memories*, 264.

17. Bills for expenses of decorations, etc., OCPB, letters received; notes on funeral, Bingham Papers, L.C.; Cortelyou, diary, September 1901, L.C.

18. Leech, *McKinley*, 600–3; Bascom M. Timmons, ed., *A Journal of the McKinley Years By Charles G. Dawes* (Chicago: The Lakeside Press, 1950), 282–83.

19. Corinne Roosevelt Robinson, *My Brother Theodore Roosevelt* (New York: Charles Scribner's Sons, 1921), 206–7.

Chapter 29: An Image Refined

1. Bingham, notes on the White House, random typescript pages, n.d., Bingham Papers, L.C.

2. Alice Roosevelt Longworth, *Crowded Hours* (New York: Charles Scribner's Sons, 1933), 46–50; Chauncey M. Depew, *My Memories of Eighty Years* (New York: Charles Scribner's Sons, 1922), 169; see also letters between Roosevelt and Mrs. Roosevelt, 1901–1902, Roosevelt Papers, L.C.

3. Bingham, notes on the White House, *op. cit.*

4. Dewey W. Grantham, Jr., "Dinner At the White House: Theodore Roosevelt, Booker T. Washington and the South," *Tennessee Historical Quarterly*,

vol. XVIII (June 1958): 112–30; Louis R. Harlan, *Booker T. Washington: The Making of a Black Leader* (New York, Oxford University Press, 1972), 304–24; Samuel R. Spencer, Jr., *Booker T. Washington and the Negro's Place in American Life* (Boston: Little, Brown, and Co., 1955), 132–35; Roosevelt to Charles Washburn, Washington, November 20, 1915, Roosevelt Papers, L.C.

5. [Glenn Brown] "Enlargement of the White House," *Century Magazine, op. cit.*; see also the article probably by Brown in *The American Architect and Building News*, October 12, 1901.

6. Cortelyou to John Hay, Washington, October 17, 1901. Roosevelt Papers, L.C.

7. Charles Moore, paper written on the White House renovation, ms., n.d., [ca. 1928], Washington Literary Society Papers, L.C.; Glenn Brown, *Memories*, 106–8.

8. Charles Moore, *Daniel Burnham: Architect, Planner of Cities* (Boston: Houghton Mifflin Company, 1921), 136–38.

9. Moore, *McKim*, 204–5.

10. Bingham, notes on the White House, *op. cit.*

11. Moore, *McKim*, 208–9.

12. *Ibid.*, 205–6.

13. McKim to Charles Moore, New York, April 16, 1902, Charles Moore Papers, L.C.

14. See letters between McKim and Bingham, OCPB, letters sent and received; also McKim, Mead & White Papers and Drawings, New-York Historical Society.

15. Roosevelt to McKim, Washington, June 16, 1902, OCPB, letters received.

16. Moore, *McKim*, 210–11.

17. Brown, *Memories*, 115; also Moore to Eric Gugler in Gugler's notes on the White House, Century Club, New York, ca. 1935, OCWH.

18. Moore, *McKim*, 208.

19. McKim wrote very little about his thought process in developing the plan of the White House. His decisions were made very quickly, in the main. The concept, with detailed drawings, is found in *The Restoration of the White House*, Senate Document 197, 57th Congress, 2nd Session (Washington: Government Printing Office, 1903).

20. Roosevelt to McKim, Washington, May 10, 1902, Roosevelt Papers, L.C.

21. Moore, *McKim*, 207–9.

22. McKim to Moore, New York, June 18, 1902, Moore Papers, L.C.

23. Pfister to Mrs. Roosevelt, Washington, June 25, 1902, Roosevelt Papers, L.C.

24. Roosevelt to Bingham, Washington, June 28, 1902, OCPB, letters received.

25. Bingham to Mrs. Roosevelt, Washington, June 30, 1902, Roosevelt Papers, L.C.

26. Moore, *McKim*, 215.

27. "Treaty of Oyster Bay," typescript, July 2, 1902, Moore Papers, L.C.; in the considerable correspondence involved in the greenhouse controversy, Henry Pfister's letter to Mrs. Roosevelt dated Washington, June 25, 1902, *op. cit.* is the most emotional of all; it touched the First Lady and very nearly convinced her to save the glasshouses. It is not impossible that Col. Bingham helped Pfister write this letter. A copy is in the OCPB, correspondence.

28. McKim to Thomas Newbold, New York, July 1, 1902, in Moore, *McKim*, 214–15.

29. Brown, *Memories*, 117–18.

30. McKim had the project photographed from start to finish, showing various stages of the work. A set is at Sagamore Hill, the Theodore Roosevelt National Historic Site, and copies are in the historical files, White House Liaison, National Park Service, Washington, D.C.

31. "Papers relating to the remodeling of the White House, 1902," OCPB correspondence. The construction papers are

apparently intact and remain isolated from the other materials in the record group.

32. Mrs. Roosevelt to McKim, Washington, October 5, 1902, Roosevelt Papers, L.C.

33. Mrs. Roosevelt to McKim, Washington, September 18, 1902, Roosevelt Papers, L.C.

34. Invoices of Herter Brothers, Leon Marcotte Co., and A.H. Davenport & Co., August–December 1902, OCPB, letters received.

35. Drawings for furniture, A.H. Davenport & Co., Davenport Collection, Boston; copies in the OCWH files. See also Betty C. Monkman, "The White House: 1873–1902," *Nineteenth Century* (Spring 1978), p. 81.

36. What appears to be the complete inventory of the Caldwell lighting fixtures remains in the White House Collection.

37. Statement of Expenditures on Account of Appropriation of June 28, 1902, carbon copy, OCPB, letters received.

38. For all the ready destruction of the historic fabric of the White House in 1902, "history" was also brought in. When Narcross Bros. did restoration work on the Old South Meeting House in Boston, famed rendezvous site of the "Indians" of the Boston Tea Party, the company's officials ordered some of the oak beams salvaged and stored in the Narcross lumberyard. In 1902 some of these timbers were re-milled as finish paneling and used in the White House elevator. A great point was made of this being historical wood. When the elevator was replaced in 1951, the old car was set up in the National Museum of American History in the First Ladies' Hall, where it can be seen today.

39. See *Restoration of the White House, passim;* various work orders and invoices, remodeling papers, 1902, OCPB files on the renovation; Mrs. Roosevelt to McKim, Oyster Bay [summer] and Sep-

tember 18, 1902, and Washington, October 5, 1902; McKim, "Questions Referred to Mrs. Roosevelt," n.d., Roosevelt Papers, L.C.

40. "The New White House," *Harpers Weekly*, vol. XLVI (November 22, 1902): 1734.

41. Roosevelt to Kermit Roosevelt, Washington, December 4, 1902, in Etting E. Morison, *The Letters of Theodore Roosevelt* (Cambridge: Harvard University Press, 1951), 389.

42. Moore, *McKim*, 221.

43. Roosevelt to William Mitchell Kendall [of McKim, Mead & White], Washington, December 8, 1908, Roosevelt Papers, L.C.

44. Apparently the Guerin originals are lost. Reproductions are found in the *Restoration of the White House* and in the *Harper's Weekly* "The New White House," both *op. cit.* In both instances those which survived were too deteriorated to use here. No pictures better illustrate McKim's vision for the renewed White House.

Chapter 30: Protocol

1. *New York Times*, December 4, 1902; contents of the box inventoried when the house was rebuilt 1948–1950, see minutes, Commission for the Renovation of the Executive Mansion, January 6, 1950, and the news release on the subject dated the same day, National Archives.

2. Roosevelt, executive order, December 1902, copy in the Cortelyou Papers, L.C.

3. Cortelyou had held the post of secretary in all but name since the Spanish-American War. Porter left the office temporarily at the beginning of the summer 1900, and on his death December 15, Cortelyou became McKinley's secretary. Roosevelt kept him on, and soon grew to rely upon him as much as had McKinley.

4. Book of regulations governing presidential railroad trips, untitled, n.d. (printed), Cortelyou Papers, L.C.

5. See copy, Cortelyou Papers, L.C.

6. *Ibid.*

7. *Ibid.*

8. Newspaper clipping marked "1903," unidentified, Abby Gunn Baker Papers, OCWH.

9. Busbey, *Uncle Joe Cannon*, 216–17.

10. Washington *Evening Star*, December 16, 1902.

11. Most of the domestic staff were listed in the government's *Official Register*, along with their salaries and the date when each was hired. Note "Executive" section. For Roosevelt's staff, a typescript in the OCPB letters sent shows many more employees than are listed in the *Official Register*. See "White House Staff, Regular and Detailed."

12. *Official Registers*, 1881–1901; Crook, *Memories* and Pendel, *Thirty-Six Years*, *passim*; work orders, endorsements of receipts, and correspondence with the public buildings officer reveal much about the distribution of power in actual practice. OCPB, letters sent and received and miscellaneous accounts, *passim*.

13. Ike Hoover, *Forty-Two Years*, 239.

14. *Ibid.*, 33; see also Lawrence F. Abbott, ed., *The Letters of Archie Butt: Personal Aide to President Roosevelt* (New York: Doubleday, Page & Company, 1924), *passim*. Noted below as Butt (1924).

15. "White House Staff," typescript, *op. cit.*

16. *Ibid.*; various of Kennedy's bills are found in OCPB, letters received.

17. Roosevelt was not an admirer of the Secret Service, and said to Speaker Cannon that as far as he was concerned, "the principal purpose of the Secret Service men in travelling with the President was to pose for their pictures as his protectors . . ." in Busbey, *Uncle Joe Cannon*, 230–42.

18. Ike Hoover, *Forty-Two Years*, 36; Sylvia Jukes Morris, *Edith Kermit Roosevelt: Portrait of the First Lady* (New York: Coward, McCann & Geoghegan, 1980), 224–25.

19. Belle Hagner, memoirs, typescript, Isabella Hagner Papers, OCWH.

20. *Ibid.*, *passim*; see bound volumes, "Social Functions," 1902–1916, containing a full account of each major social event at the White House during those years, including invitation and seating lists, acceptances, automobile tickets, etc. OCPB papers.

21. Notes on order of rank at the White House, n.d., Bingham Papers, L.C.

22. "Social Functions," *passim*.

23. *Ibid.*; Ellen M. Slayden, *Washington Wife*, 52–54; Singleton, *The White House*, vol. II, 252–56.

24. "Social Functions." See also William E. Cutler, suggestions for future receptions, January 15, 1903, OCPB, letters received.

25. Singleton, *The White House*, 266; see also Florence Howe Hall, *Social Usages at Washington* (New York: Harper & Bros., 1906).

26. "Social Functions."

27. Bingham, note in "Social Functions," January 9, 1903.

28. Bingham to Cannon, Washington, February 1903, OCPB, letters sent; see also Hagner, memoirs.

29. Ike Hoover, *Forty-Two Years*, 27–28.

30. "Social Functions," *passim*.

31. Bromwell, notes on menu [December 1903], OCPB, letters sent.

32. "Social Functions," 1903–1909, *passim*.

33. Frederick R. Goff to author, Washington, spring 1980.

34. "Social Functions," 1903–1909, *passim*.

35. *Ibid.*

36. Samuel Whitaker Pennypacker, *The Autobiography of A Pennsylvanian* (Philadelphia: The John C. Winston Company, 1918), 476.

37. Invitations, in "Social Functions."

38. Butt (1924), 29–30, 164, 299; Hagner, memoirs.

39. Hagner, memoirs.

40. Mrs. George B. Cortelyou, memoirs, ms., p. 15, Cortelyou Papers, L.C.

41. "Social Functions," December 26, 1903.

42. The few documents that survive relative to the colonial garden suggest that it was built by the White House grounds staff or perhaps gardeners borrowed from the Agriculture Department. No great expense seems to have gone into its planting. Several excellent photographs survive, showing its paths and beds brimming with flowers. Photographs, OCWH.

43. Hall, *Social Usages*, 12.

44. "Social Functions," February 17, 1906.

45. *Washington Post*, interview with Alice Roosevelt Longworth, [1967], clipping, OCWH.

Chapter 31: Chronicles

1. Abby Gunn Baker, "The White House of the Twentieth Century," *The Independent*, vol. 55 (October 22, 1903): 2507.

2. Roosevelt to Abbott, Washington, March 14, 1904, Roosevelt Papers, L.C.

3. Henry E. Rood to Mr. Powell, n.p., November 7, 1950, Henry Edward Rood Papers, Duke University Library.

4. Singleton, *The White House*, vol. II, 303.

5. Butt (1924), 2.

6. *Ibid.*, 1.

7. *Ibid.*, 5.

8. *Ibid.*, 6, the date of the event is wrong. It was May, not April.

9. Gen. Frank Ross McCoy to Lawrence F. Abbott, see Butt (1924), xxii–xxiii.

10. David F. Sinclair, "The Monarchical Manners of the White House," *Harper's Weekly*, vol. LIV (June 13, 1908), 12–15.

11. Butt (1924), 7.

12. *Ibid.*, 69.

13. *Ibid.*, 215.

14. Hagner, memoirs; Collins, *Presidents on Wheels*, 119–27. The brougham, by Studebaker, is in the Henry Ford Museum, Dearborn, Michigan.

15. A copy of this booklet is in the Cortelyou Papers, L.C. and in OCPB, miscellaneous printed matter.

16. "Social Events," December 28, 1908.

17. Butt (1924), 260.

18. *Ibid.*, 257–58.

19. *Ibid.*, 355–56; the bison heads were installed after Roosevelt's departure, see three bills for the work: design, McKim, Mead, & White; sculpting, A. P. Proctor; and marble carving, Robert C. Fisher, Co., July 14, 1909, OCPB, letters received. See also Roosevelt to William M. Kendall, Washington, December 18, 1908, *op. cit.*, which recognizes architects Cass Gilbert and S. B. P. Trowbridge as having consulted on the redesigning of the mantelpiece.

20. Roosevelt to Harris, Washington, June 9, 1902, in Joseph Bucklin Bishop, ed., *Theodore Roosevelt's Letters To His Children* (New York: Charles Scribner's Sons, 1919), 34.

21. Butt (1924), 233.

22. Ishbel Ross, *An American Family* (New York: The World Publishing Company, 1964), 194.

23. Butt (1924), 240.

24. *Ibid.*, 234.

25. *Ibid.*, 206.

26. *Ibid.*, 205–6.

27. *Ibid.*, 234–35.

28. *Ibid.*, 235.

29. *Ibid.*, 238; Washington *Star*, August 23, 1908.

30. Butt (1924), 360; Hagner, memoirs.

31. Hoover, *Forty Two Years*, 39.

32. Mrs. William Howard Taft, *Recollections of Full Years* (New York: Dodd, Mead & Company, 1914), 347–50, 326–28.

33. Henry F. Pringle, *The Life and Times of William Howard Taft* (New York: Holt, Rinehart and Winston, Inc., 1939), vol. I, 396; see also "Social Events," March 1909.

34. Butt (1924), 382.

Chapter 32: Summer Days

1. Archibald Butt, *Taft and Roosevelt: The Intimate Letters of Archie Butt* (New York: Doubleday, Doran & Company, 1930), vol. I, 8–9. Cited hereafter as Butt (1930).

2. *Ibid.*, 12–14.

3. Elizabeth Jaffray, *Secrets of the White House* (New York: Cosmopolitan Book Corporation, 1926), 8–9.

4. Mrs. Taft, *Recollections*, 347–50.

5. Jaffray, *Secrets*, 5.

6. Mrs. Taft, *Recollections*, 347–64.

7. *Ibid.*, 349.

8. Katherine Graves Busbey, "Mrs. Taft's Home-Making," clipping from *Good Housekeeping Magazine*, Mrs. L. A. Jaffray's scrapbook, Martin Luther King, Jr., Library, Washington.

9. Various projects and work orders for the White House, designating rooms as "servants' dining room," etc., OCPB, letters received; Hoover, *Forty Two Years*, 282–84; see entry for Arthur Brooks in Rayford W. Logan and Michael R. Winston, eds., *Dictionary of American Negro Biography* (New York: W.W. Norton & Co., 1983), 61–62.

10. Lillian Parks Rogers in conversation with the author, spring 1980.

11. Jaffray, *Secrets*, 19–20.

12. Butt (1930), vol. I, 172.

13. Butt (1930), vol. I, 186.

14. Mrs. Taft to Helen Taft, Washington, May 16, 1909, William Howard Taft Papers, L.C.

15. Butt (1930), vol. I, 169.

16. *Ibid.*, 173.

17. Mrs. Taft, *Recollections*, 336.

18. Busbey, "Mrs. Taft's Home-Making," 592.

19. Butt (1930), vol. I, 327, 623; Mrs. Taft, *Recollections*, 361.

20. Helen Taft Manning in conversation with the author, Bryn Mawr, October 15, 1983; Jaffray, *Secrets*, 27–28.

21. Mrs. Taft, *Recollections*, 350.

22. Jaffray, *Secrets*, 13–15; Taft, "living expenses," grocery breakdown average, April, May, and December 1909, William Howard Taft Papers, L.C.

23. Butt (1930), vol. I, 152–53.

24. *Ibid.*, 54.

25. Mrs. Taft, *Recollections*, 361–62; Butt (1930), vols. I and II, *passim*.

26. Butt (1930), vol. I, p. 40.

27. Theodora Ozaki to Mrs. Taft, Tokyo, February 26, 1911, Taft Papers, L.C.

28. Mrs. Taft, *Recollections*, 356.

29. Butt (1930), vol. I, 33–35.

30. *Ibid.*, 34.

31. *Ibid.*, 34.

32. *Ibid.*, 35.

33. "Social Events," after March 1909, *passim*.

34. Mrs. Taft, *Recollections*, 366–68.

35. *Ibid.*, 369.

36. *Ibid.*, 378.

37. Butt (1930), vol. I, 88.

38. *Ibid.*, 340–42.

39. Frederick D. Owen, "Mr. Wyeth's Plan," [May 13, 1909]; "Comparison of Competition Plans of Wood, Donn & Fleming and N. C. Wyeth," [May 15, 1909]; McKim, Mead & White to Spencer Cosby, New York, April 14, 1909, ocpb, letters received.

40. Cosby to Wyeth, Washington, April 17, 1909; Owen, "Mr. Wyeth's Plan," ocpb, letters received.

41. Wyeth to Cosby, Washington, April 29, 1909, ocpb, letters received.

42. George A. Fuller Co., to Wyeth, Washington, August 2, 1909, ocpb, letters received. Two "air cooling devices" are mentioned, one from Johnson & Morris, $1170.00 and another from Biggs Heating Co., $1223.00. See also Butt (1930), vol. II, 659.

43. Cosby to John C. Knipp & Sons, Interior Decorators, Washington, September 8, 1909, ocpb, letters sent; also Knipp's specifications, Washington, August 18, 1909, ocpb, letters received.

44. "Social Events," June 19, 1911.

45. Clipping describing the event, undated and otherwise unidentified, in "Social Events," June 19, 1911.

46. Butt (1930), vol. II, 679.

47. Clippings about Butt's death were pasted into "Social Events" books probably in late April 1912, and the unsigned account written into the book describes the effect the event had on the White House, as well as Taft's attending the memorial services at the National Theater in Washington and the Opera House in Augusta, Georgia, Butt's hometown; also, Mrs. Taft, *Recollections*, 359.

48. Pringle, *Taft*, vol. I, 474.

49. Garrison Norton in conversation with the author, Washington, spring, 1982.

50. Taft to Mrs. Taft, Washington, July 14, 1912, Taft Papers, l.c.

51. Mrs. Taft, *Recollections*, 393.

52. Ike Hoover, *Forty-Two Years*, 52–53; Helen Taft Manning in conversation with the author and Judith W. Frank, Bryn Mawr, October 15, 1983.

Chapter 33: Thresholds

1. Ike Hoover, *Forty-Two Years*, 53–54; payrolls of the White House, ocpb, fiscal records, *passim*.

2. Jaffray, *Secrets*, 36–37.

3. Eleanor W. McAdoo, with Margaret Y. Gaffey, *The Woodrow Wilsons* (New York: Macmillan Company, 1937), 209.

4. Sladen, *Washington Wife*, 199–200.

5. Hagner, memoirs.

6. Eleanor W. McAdoo, *The Woodrow Wilsons*, 223.

7. *Ibid.*, 205.

8. Mrs. Wilson to Wilson, President's Cottage, Cornish, New Hampshire, July 28, [1913], in Eleanor W. McAdoo, ed., *The Priceless Gift* [letters of Woodrow and Ellen Wilson] (New York: McGraw Hill Book Co., 1962), 285–86.

9. *Ibid.*, 278.

10. Col. William W. Harts, *Report for Fiscal Year Ending June 30, 1914* (Washington: Government Printing Office, 1914), *passim*; invoice of John C. Knipp & Sons, Baltimore, December 4, 1913; Robert S. Talmage to Cosby, New York, July 8, September 2, 25, and December 2, 1913, ocpb, letters received; James A. Robinson, "Artistic Weaving in the Mountains of North Carolina," *The Art World*, vol. V (August 1917): 485.

11. Harts, *Report*, 1914; correspondence between Harts and the Boyle-Robertson Construction Company, Inc., and Wyeth, during the summer of 1913, ocpb, letters received and sent.

12. Eleanor W. McAdoo, *The Woodrow Wilsons*, 215.

13. Harts, *Report*, 1914; invoice of Robert S. Talmadge, New York, September 25, 1913, ocpb, letters received; Robinson, "Artistic Weaving," 485.

14. Eleanor W. McAdoo, *The Woodrow Wilsons*, 212-13.

15. Eleanor W. McAdoo, *The Priceless Gift*, 277.

16. Paula V. Graff, "The Keeper of the President's Trees," [interview with the gardener Charles Henlock] *American Forests*, vol. 37 (May 1931): 236; see also drawings for the garden and the President's walk, Cartographic and Architectural Branch, National Archives.

17. Beatrix Ferrand, plan for "southeast garden," 1913, Map Division, National Archives.

18. George Burnap, schematics and plan for southwest garden, 1913; a west elevation in ink shows a long trellis with paintings hanging on it: "Lattice end of southwest garden, White House, Prepared from Suggestions of Mrs. Wilson by George Burnap," Cartographic and Architectural Branch, National Archives.

19. Eleanor W. McAdoo, *The Woodrow Wilsons*, 237.

20. Wilson to Mrs. Wilson, Washington, October 5, 1913, in Eleanor W. McAdoo, *The Priceless Gift*, 310-11.

21. *Official Register*, 1913, "Executive Department."

22. Arthur Walworth, *Woodrow Wilson* (Boston: Houghton Mifflin Co., 1965), 284.

23. Cary T. Grayson, *Woodrow Wilson: An Intimate Memoir* (New York: Holt Rinehart and Winston, 1960).

24. Katharine Woodrow Kirkland in conversation with the author, Summerville, South Carolina, May 14, 1982.

25. Hagner, memoirs.

26. *Ibid.*; Eleanor W. McAdoo, *The Woodrow Wilsons*, 236-37.

27. James Borchert, "The Rise and Fall of Washington's Inhabited Alleys, 1852–1972," chs *Records*, vol. 48 (1971–1972): 268-81.

28. Quoted in "The Home-Maker of the White House," *The Survey*, vol. XXXIII (October 3, 1914): 19-22; Eleanor W. McAdoo, *The Woodrow Wilsons*, 236-37; see also Frances W. Saunders, *Ellen Axson Wilson: First Lady Between Two Worlds* (Chapel Hill: University of North Carolina Press, 1985), 244-47, 263.

29. Katharine Woodrow Kirkland to author, *op. cit.*

30. "Social Events," November 25, 1913, and May 7, 1914, gives full details of the two weddings, including plans of the state floor, showing the paths followed by the guests to and from the receiving line. See also Saunders, *Ellen Axson Wilson*, 262-63, 271-72.

31. Eleanor W. McAdoo, *The Woodrow Wilsons*, 287.

32. *Ibid.*, 290.

33. Grayson, *Wilson*, 33-34.

34. Eleanor W. McAdoo, *The Priceless Gift*, 316.

35. Jaffray, *Secrets*, 50.

36. Diary of Edward M. House, April 27, 1914, in Charles Seymour, ed., *The Intimate Papers of Colonel House* (Boston: Houghton Mifflin Co., 1926-1928), 124.

Chapter 34: 1917

1. Grayson, *Wilson*, 34; Eleanor W. McAdoo, *The Woodrow Wilsons* 291.

2. Eleanor W. McAdoo, *The Woodrow Wilsons*, 295.

3. Lillian Rogers Parks in conversation with the author, Washington, July 23, 1982; Hagner, memoirs.

4. Hagner, memoirs.

5. Eleanor Wilson McAdoo, *The Woodrow Wilsons*, 223.

6. *Washington Post,* January 26, 1915; Ike Hoover, note on the first transcontinental call, January 1915? I. H. Hoover Papers, L.C.

7. Katharine Woodrow Kirkland in conversation with the author, *op. cit.*

8. Edith Bolling Wilson, *My Memoir* (Indianapolis: Bobbs Merrill Company, 1938), 61.

9. *Ibid.*

10. Wilson to Mrs. Galt, Washington, May 27, 1915, in Edwin Tribble, ed., *A President in Love: The Courtship Letters of Woodrow Wilson and Edith Bolling Galt* (Boston: Houghton Mifflin Company, 1981), 34.

11. Alexander L. George and Juliette L. George, *Woodrow Wilson and Colonel House: A Personality Study* (New York: The John Day Co., 1956), 184–86.

12. Thomas Sugrue, ed., *Starling of the White House, by Colonel Edmund W. Starling* (Chicago: Peoples Book Club, 1946), 56.

13. Joseph P. Tumulty, *Woodrow Wilson As I Know Him* (New York: Doubleday, Page & Co., 1921), 250.

14. Jaffray, *Secrets,* 57–58.

15. Edith Wilson, *My Memoir,* 79.

16. Hagner, memoirs; Edith Blenham Helm, *The Captains and the Kings* (New York: Putnam, 1954), 54.

17. Edith Wilson, *My Memoir, passim.*

18. *Ibid.,* 96.

19. Grayson, *Wilson,* 52.

20. Arthur S. Link, *The Papers of Woodrow Wilson* (Princeton: Princeton University Press, 1981), vol. 37, 46–54.

21. *Ibid.,* 113–17.

22. Edith Wilson, *My Memoir,* 121.

23. Link, ed., *The Papers of Woodrow Wilson,* vol. 40, 293, quoting a letter from House to Wilson, New York, December 20, 1916.

24. Starling, *White House,* 84; Seymour, *Papers of Colonel House,* vol. I, 471–72 and vol. II, 468.

25. Seymour, ed., *Intimate Papers of Col. House,* vol. 2, 469.

26. Starling, *White House,* 87.

27. *Ibid.,* 88–89.

Chapter 35: Distant Drums

1. Starling, *White House,* 34; Jaffray, *Secrets,* 60–61; F. B. Butler, memorandum to [Theodore] Joslin, Washington, June 1, 1931.

2. Inventory of the President's study, June 30, 1917, OCPB, letters received; photo of study ca. 1915–1920, OCWH.

3. Hoover, *Forty Two Years,* 267.

4. Wilson to J. K. M. Norton, Washington, [May] 1917, in Ray Stannard Baker, *Woodrow Wilson: Life and Letters,* (New York: Greenwood Press Publishers, 1968), vol. 7, 71.

5. Edith Wilson, *My Memoir,* 123.

6. Wilson to Jessie Wilson Sayre, Mayflower [August?] 1917, and to House at about the same time, in Baker, *Woodrow Wilson,* 71.

7. Edward W. Bok, *Twice Thirty* (New York: Scribner's, 1925), 347–50.

8. Edith Wilson, *My Memoir,* 137.

9. *Ibid.*

10. "Position list," Congressional Joint Commission on Reclassification of Salaries, Wilson Papers, L.C.

11. Names of some of the servants can be gleaned from the OCPB, see Jaffray to Cosby, January–November 1916, letters concerning servants and salaries; also descriptions and comments on the various names mentioned in the letters made by Lillian Rogers Parks to the author, Washington, May 1982, and various times thereafter by telephone.

12. *Ibid.*

13. "Position list." See also invoices, vouchers and correspondence, 1917, OCPB, *passim*.

14. *Ibid.*; Elizabeth Jaffray, "For 17 Years I Ran the White House," *Hearst's International-Cosmopolitan*, January 1926, Jaffray scrapbook, *op. cit.* The Congress did provide some of the servants' salaries in the Annual Legislative, Executive, and Judicial Appropriation. It was seldom adequate and in 1914, for example, extra funds were taken from the subsequent Sundry Civil Act appropriation to raise certain salaries. White House salaries were usually low for servants, but probably better than the pay in some private service. A ladies' maid, for example, made $35/month in 1914, a laundress about the same and a butler $60/month. "House cleaners" made $47.50/month. See Cosby to the Judge Advocate General, Washington, July 22, 1914, OCPB, correspondence.

15. Eleanor W. McAdoo, *The Woodrow Wilsons*, 217.

16. Starling, *White House*, 81.

17. *Washington Post*, December 16, 1917; White House Diary, a daily account of the Wilsons' activities outside the White House, OCPB, papers, correspondence.

18. Edith Wilson, *My Memoir, passim*; D. W. Griffith to Wilson, Los Angeles, May 4, 1916, and Wilson to Tumulty, [Washington?] n.d., Wilson Papers, L.C.

19. *Washington Post*, December 7, 1916, and January 2 and 6, 1917.

20. Edith Wilson, *My Memoir*, 160; Charles A. Selden, "Mrs. Woodrow Wilson: Wife, Nurse, and Secretary, Who Kept the President Alive During the World's Greatest Crisis," *Ladies' Home Journal*, October 1921, clipping, OCWH; also Graff, "The Keeper of the President's Trees," 287–88.

21. New York *Tribune*, January 27, 1918.

22. Edith Wilson, *My Memoir*, 183.

23. Secretary of the Navy to command-ing officer, USS *George Washington*, Washington, November 22, 1918; memorandum to Captain Edward McCauley, Jr., November 25, 1918; log of the *George Washington*, November 25–December 4, 1918, Wilson Papers, L.C.

24. Slayden, *Washington Wife*, 349.

25. Log of the *George Washington*, December 24, 1918.

26. Edith Wilson, *My Memoir*, 272.

27. Tumulty, *Wilson As I Know Him*, 422–24.

28. Grayson, *Wilson*, 95.

29. Edith Wilson, *My Memoir*, 274–87.

30. Grayson, *Wilson*, 96–100.

31. Edith Wilson, *My Memoir*, 286–89; Grayson, *Wilson*, 100; Ike Hoover, *Forty-Two Years*, 100–1.

32. Edith Wilson, *My Memoir*, 289–94; Grayson, *Wilson*, 102–7.

33. Starling, *White House*, 156–57; Ike Hoover, *Forty-Two Years*, 107; Jaffray, *Secrets*, 71.

Chapter 36: Limelight

1. Edith Wilson, *My Memoir*, 316.

2. Harding to W. W. Moffett, Marion, December 27, 1920, Warren G. Harding Papers, L.C.

3. See Robert K. Murray, *The Harding Era* (Minneapolis: University of Minnesota Press, 1969), 111–22, 515–37; and Elizabeth Stevenson, *Babbits and Bohemians: The American 1920s* (New York: The Macmillan Company, 1967), 81–83.

4. Longworth, *Crowded Hours*, 223–24.

5. Andrew Sinclair, *The Available Man: The Life Behind the Masks of Warren Gamaliel Harding* (New York: Macmillan Company, 1965), 104–5.

6. Mark Sullivan, *Our Times: The United States 1900–1925* (New York: Charles Scribner's Sons, 1937), vol. VI, 243–44.

7. *Washington Post*, January 1, 1922.

8. *New York Times,* March 14, 1921; see 1923–1926 inventory of Harding furnishings and also packed goods which were returned to Ohio after the President's death. Harding Papers, Ohio Historical Society.

9. *Washington Post,* January 1, 1922.

10. *Ibid.*

11. Starling, *White House,* 169.

12. *Washington Post,* January 1, 13, 27, and February 3, 1922.

13. Lily Haxworth Wallace, editor-in-chief, *The New American Etiquette* (New York: Books, Inc., 1941), 576; customs in Washington surrounding the White House had not changed much since Hall, *Usages at Washington, op. cit.,* except that the automobile had streamlined some of the formalities of entering the White House grounds and the social wing on the east. Rather than walking to the portico, as in the old days, by the 1920s, the automobiles simply lingered beneath the portico's shelter, leaving their motor going, and a butler came to the car to receive the calling card. This was pure and simple convenience for both parties.

14. Directions for preparing White House events, typescript; "Social Functions," and see also the various bills for services December–May in any given year, OCPB, correspondence.

15. Seating charts, correspondence files, OCPB records.

16. Directions for preparing White House events, *op. cit., passim;* "Official Functions," a partial record of social functions, but by no means as complete as the earlier "Social Functions" books.

17. Lillian Rogers Parks to author, telephone, May 1983; and John Ficklin to author, Washington, January 1983. The chandelier ball had died out. According to Mrs. Parks: "Each year maybe you brought somebody or somebody else brought the wrong person. You know how it got everywhere after the war. So the chandelier ball was just stopped.

There wasn't a reason to have it any more." To author, July 23, 1982.

18. Procedures approved by Harding, typescript, "Official Functions," [1922]; also "Official Functions," *passim.*

19. *Ibid.;* Hagner, memoirs.

20. William Allen White, *Autobiography* (New York: Macmillan, 1946), 619.

21. Murray, *The Harding Era,* 114, 419; Francis Russell, *The Shadow of Blooming Grove: Warren G. Harding In His Times* (New York: McGraw-Hill Book Co., 1968), 461.

22. Starling, *White House,* 195–96.

23. Baltimore & Ohio Railroad Company, Police Department, "observations," on the president's tour to Alaska, Baltimore, September 11, 1923, Harding Papers, L.C.; *Washington Post,* August 7, 1922.

Chapter 37: Hearth and Home

1. Hoover, diary, August 8, 1923, Hoover Papers, L.C.; *Washington Post,* August 8, 1923; see also Edgar Eugene Robinson and Paul Arnold Edwards, eds., *The Memoirs of Ray Lyman Wilbur, 1875–1949* (Palo Alto: Stanford University Press, 1960), 379–81.

2. *Washington Post,* August 8, 1923.

3. *Washington Post* and *New York Times,* August 9, 1923.

4. Warren G. Harding Papers, "Introduction and Provenance," typescript, L.C.

5. Grace Coolidge, "When I Became the First Lady," *The American Magazine,* vol. CVIII (September 1929).

6. Mary Randolph, *Presidents and First Ladies* (New York: D. Appleton-Century Company, Inc., 1936), 94–95.

7. "Official Functions" for the Coolidge years, *passim;* Edward C. Lathem, ed., *Meet Calvin Coolidge* (Brattleboro: Stephen Greene Press, 1960), 90–93; Grace Coolidge, "How I Spent My Days in the White House," *The Ameri-*

can Magazine, vol. CVIII (October 1929): 17-19, 128-31; see also Cox, "The Protocol Function," *op. cit.*, 51–54.

8. Cox, "The Protocol Function As An Aspect of Executive Responsibility," *op. cit.*, 64–67.

9. Calvin Coolidge, *The Autobiography of Calvin Coolidge* (New York: Cosmopolitan Book Corporation, 1929), 190.

10. Randolph, *Presidents and First Ladies*, 83-84.

11. John T. Lambert, "When the President Wept," in Lathem, *Meet Calvin Coolidge*, pp. 139–41.

12. Grace Coolidge, "Making Ourselves At Home in the White House," *The American Magazine*, vol. CVIII (November 1929): 215–16.

13. Sherrill, resume of all work done or underway at the White House, OCPB, letters sent. The joint resolution was approved February 28, 1925, authorizing the White House to accept antiques on behalf of the nation and for the officer in charge of public buildings and parks to appoint a nine-member advisory committee subject to the president's approval. Colonel Sherrill made his recommendations March 14, 1925, and they were approved the 17th, see Sherill to Coolidge, Washington, the above date, OCPB, correspondence.

14. J. C. Mehaffey to Sherrill, Washington, October 1, 1925; J. C. Nagle, Chief, Engineering Section, Supervising Architect's Office, Washington, August 13, 1925; Capt. Ellis E. Haring and Earl G. Marsh to Sherrill, Washington, February 3, 1925; W. C. Lyon to the supervising architect, report, Washington, April 11, 1923. By act of February 26, 1925, the officer in charge of the public buildings was removed from the Corps of Engineers and made a separate executive agency called the Office of Public Buildings and Parks of the National Capital. Originally under the State Department, the agency had been under the executive from 1804 until 1849, when it was

placed under the new Department of the Interior. In 1867 it was put under the Army Corps of Engineers, where it remained until the act of 1925. Its chief, although still a military man, was now styled the "director." The actual transfer took place early in 1926. The new agency was to last 10 years and 4 months, before being put under the National Park Service. In note references the office will be symbolized by OPBP.

15. *New York Times*, July 3, 1925; Washington *Evening Star*, July 9, 1925; and the New York *Herald Tribune*, July 13, 1925.

16. The original of this letter, widely quoted in the press in June and July 1925, is in the library of the American Institute of Architects, Washington.

17. *New York Times*, July 8, 1925; see also *Washington Post*, August 3, 1925.

18. Kemper to Coolidge, Washington, July 11, 1925, OCPB, letters received.

19. "What Artists Think of the White House," *Literary Digest*, vol. LX (August 15, 1925): 26.

20. *New York Times*, August 16, 1925.

21. Mrs. Coolidge, "Making Ourselves At Home in the White House," and Randolph, *Presidents and First Ladies, passim*; see also, "Official Functions," which is complete to 1927.

22. Mrs. Coolidge, "Making Ourselves At Home in the White House," *op. cit*; Lillian Parks Rogers in *My Thirty Years Backstairs at the White House* (New York: Fleet Publishing Co., 1961), 194, attributes the interest in a new roof to the disastrous collapse of the snow-piled Knickerbocker Theater on January 22, 1922, killing 98 and injuring 136. This was one of Washington's greatest disasters, and it did create a general concern over wood-framed roofs all over the city. Parks recalled, "Every time there was a big snowfall, the men would have to rush [up to the roof] and shovel it off, because they feared it couldn't hold the weight."

23. Mehaffey, memorandum to Sherrill, October 1, 1925, ocpb, letters received.

24. Grant to William Adams Delano, Washington, November 4, 1927, ocpb, letters sent; see also other Grant and Delano letters about the reconstruction process, same source.

25. Bids, opbp, bids and contract files, 1926–1927.

26. Grant, "The Reconstruction of the White House Roof," unpublished ms., Columbia Historical Society; *Annual Report of the Director of Public Buildings and Public Parks of the National Capital* (Washington: Government Printing Office, 1927), 31; various invoices involving the packing, opbp, letters received, relative to the project, 1927.

27. Grant. "Reconstruction."

28. Mrs. Coolidge. "Making Ourselves At Home in the White House," 215–16.

29. Ishbel Ross, *Grace Coolidge: The Story of a President's Wife* (New York: Dodd, Mead & Co., 1962), 230; Randolph, *Presidents and First Ladies*, 71–72. The "Black Hills Affair" was widely covered in the press during that summer.

30. New York *Herald Tribune*, February 28, 1928; *Time* Magazine, December 26, 1927, reported that when asked why she put "1929" on the bedspread instead of "1933" she replied, "I know what I'm doing." See Joan Hoff Wilson, *Herbert Hoover: Forgotten Progressive* (Boston: Little, Brown & Co., 1975), 124.

31. Delano to Grant, New York, February 3, 1927, opbp, letters sent.

32. Grant to Delano, Washington, July 17, 1928, opbp, letters sent.

33. *Ibid.*

34. Pratt, "Report, [to] the Commission of Fine Arts by Mrs. Pratt," March 14, 1949, copy, ocwh.

35. Mrs. Coolidge, "Making Ourselves At Home in the White House," 215–16.

36. Pratt, "Report," 1949, *op. cit.*; various bills for work on the state rooms, opbp, letters received, redecoration file.

37. Pratt to Grant, New York, December 22, 1928, ocwh.

38. Dare Stark McMullin, "Hoover Furniture Study," 1932, typescript, p. 151, Herbert Hoover Library.

39. Starling, *White House,* 279–80.

Chapter 38: Irony

1. Mrs. Hoover to "Herbert and Allen— and all their children!" Washington, July 1932, Hoover Library.

2. Ike Hoover, *Forty-Two Years,* 180.

3. Raymond Henle, interview with Mildred Hall Campbell, Los Angeles, September 24, 1966, Hoover Library.

4. *Ibid.*; typescript on President and Mrs. Hoover, n.d., Mildred Hall Campbell, Hoover Library.

5. Joseph Coy Green to author, Washington, spring 1977; Ruth Fesler Lipman to Margaret Brown Klapthor, Berkeley, October 25, 1978, National Museum of American History; Ava Long, "900,000 Callers a Year!" *The American Magazine,* vol. CVVIII (June 1933): 90.

6. West Hall photograph, ca. 1930, ocwh; Long, "Callers," 90.

7. Campbell typescript; see also interview with Campbell (1966) and Lipman (1967), Hoover Library.

8. Herbert Hoover, *The Personal Memoirs of Herbert Hoover, Collier's,* vol. XI (March 17, 1951): 45; Ike Hoover, *Forty-Two Years,* 300–1. The strong resentment of the Hoover White House circle over the response of the press to Mrs. De Priest's invitation was evident decades later, see Raymond Henle, interview with Ruth Fesler Lipman, Stanford, September 26, 1967, Hoover Library.

9. Henle interview with Lipman, *op. cit.*

10. Hoover, *The Memoirs of Herbert Hoover: The Cabinet and the Presidency* (New York: Macmillan, 1952), 324.

11. New York *Herald Tribune,* April 4, 1929; also, New York *Evening Post,*

April 19, 1929; *New York Times,* May 5 and 12, 1929; *New York World,* April 6 and May 6, 1929.

12. *New York Times,* October 8, 1929; Dolly Gann, *Dolly Gann's Book* (New York: Doubleday, Doran & Company, Inc., 1933), 111–23.

13. Washington *Evening Star,* December 25, 1929.

14. *New York World,* December 25, 1929.

15. New York *Herald Tribune,* December 26, 1929.

16. *New York World,* December 25, 1929; Ike Hoover, notes on the fire, Irwin H. Hoover Papers, l.c.; Charles Morrissey, interview with George E. Akerson, Jr., Boston, March 11, 1969, Hoover Library.

17. Plan for reconstructing the Executive Office Building, March 14, 1929, Hoover Library.

18. Invitation and specifications for bid, December 27, 1929, and amendment #1, December 28, 1929, and amendment #2, December 31, 1929; Grant, correspondence about bidding, December 1929–May 1930, opbp, correspondence.

19. Washington *Evening Star,* December 26, 1929.

20. Plans for reconstructing the Executive Office Building, *op. cit.*; construction invoices and correspondence between Grant and the Charles H. Tompkins Co., file on the reconstruction of the Executive Office Building, opbp.

21. "List of Employees on Detail to the White House and Executive Office," 1930–1932, Hoover Library.

22. Hoover, "Personal Memoirs," 45–46.

23. Hastings, ms. on Hoover presidency, George Aubrey Hastings Papers, Hoover Library.

24. Hoover, "Personal Memoirs," 46;

Grant to Lewis H. Lane, Washington, November 21, 1930; see also Lewis H. Lane to the Hon. Charles A. Eaton, Plainfield, New Jersey, November 10, 1930, and Eaton to Grant, Washington, November 15, 1930, opbp correspondence.

25. Lillian Rogers Parks to author, Washington, July 1982.

26. Ava Long, "900,000 Callers," 48.

27. Long, "Presidents At Home," *Ladies Home Journal,* clipping ocwh.

28. Ava Long, "900,000 Callers," 90.

29. While the system of recording was extremely casual, the "official count of parlor visitors" (tourists) for 1929 was 111,393, with a peak of 35,253 in April, less than half the number in May and a low of 1,543 in December. See Lawrence Richey to Roy Harris, Washington, April 30, 1930, Hoover Library. The approximate figure of 900,000 for 1931 includes receptions, social occasions, and office callers. The figure is undoubtedly too high, but the increase was nevertheless said to be very sharp. See also Allen Campbell and Mildred Hall Campbell, memoirs, Los Angeles, November 30, 1971, Hoover Library.

30. By the 20th century the White House receptions had become real burdens to the presidents. Only the New Year's reception was counted an obligation, and sooner or later it had to go. President's hands had been badly bruised from thousands of handshakes. George Hastings, a Hoover speechwriter, recalled that "on one occasion" the President's hand "was cut until it bled by a ring on a guest's hand."

31. Starling, *White House,* 289.

32. Roger Daniels, *The Bonus March* (Westport: Greenwood Publishing Company, 1971), 175; Hoover, *The Memoirs of Herbert Hoover: The Great Depression* (New York, Macmillan, 1952), 225–32.

33. Hoover, *Memoirs: The Great Depression,* 230–32.

34. Christopher D. Morley, "What the

President Reads," *Saturday Review of Literature*, vol. 9 (September, 24, 1934): 117–20.

35. Ike Hoover, *Forty-Two Years*, 190–91.

36. McMullin, "Hoover Furniture Study"; Raymond Henle, interview with Dare Stark McMullin, Palo Alto, September 11, 1967, Hoover Library.

37. McMullin interview; see also letters between McMullin and Grant, May 12, 29, June 4 and 19, 1933, and Mrs. Hoover and Grant, May 29 and June 17, 1933, OPBP, correspondence.

38. Mrs. Hoover to Grant, Palo Alto, May 29, 1933, OCPB, correspondence.

39. McMullin, "Hoover Furniture Study."

40. *Ibid.*; Delano to Cecil Davis, New York, February 24, 1930, OPBP, correspondence; Stanley W. McClure, historian, to Mrs. Pratt, Washington, June 10, 1952; Mrs. Pratt to McClure, New York, June 18, 1952, National Park Service Papers, OCWH.

41. McMullin, "Hoover Furniture Study"; Mrs. Hoover to Grant, Palo Alto, May 29, 1933, *op. cit.*

42. McMullin, "Hoover Furniture Study."

43. Starling, *White House*, 299.

44. Ike Hoover, *Forty-Two Years*, 227.

45. Frank Freidel, *Franklin D. Roosevelt: Launching the New Deal* (Boston: Little, Brown & Co., 1973), 192–93.

Chapter 39: Full House

1. Ike Hoover, *Forty-Two Years*, 228; Lorena A. Hickok, *Eleanor Roosevelt: Reluctant First Lady* (New York: Dodd, Mead & Co., 1962), 145.

2. Ike Hoover, *Forty-Two Years*, 224–25; Louis Howe (?), map of the public areas of the White House showing wheelchair routes, Franklin Delano Roosevelt Library, Hyde Park, New York.

3. Starling, *White House*, 305–6.

4. *New York Times*, May 28, 1957; Eleanor Roosevelt, *This I Remember* (New York: Harper & Brothers, 1949), 77–79.

5. Elliott Roosevelt and James Brough, *A Rendezvous with Destiny: The Roosevelts of the White House* (London: W. H. Allen, 1977), 29.

6. Frances Perkins interview, Columbia University, cited in Freidel, *Launching the New Deal*, 211.

7. Rexford Tugwell, *The Democratic Roosevelt: A Biography of Franklin D. Roosevelt* (Garden City: Doubleday & Company, 1957), 270–71.

8. George N. Peck and Samuel Crowther, *Why Quit Our Own?* (New York: D. Van Nostrand Co., 1936), 82.

9. Fireside chat, March 12, 1933, typescript draft, FDR Library.

10. Hickok, *Eleanor Roosevelt*, 1.

11. Eleanor Roosevelt, *This I Remember*, 81; Henrietta Nesbitt, *White House Diary* (New York: Doubleday & Co., 1948), 312.

12. Fred Pasley to Stephen T. Early, memorandum, New York, March 26, 1933, FDR Library.

13. Lorenzo Winslow, memoir, copy of ms., OCWH.

14. Unrealized project for the swimming pool, two views, interior and exterior, P. Haertl, FDR Library; specifications for the pool [March and April] 1933, OPBP, contracts.

15. Winslow memoirs; Ernest H. Brandt, Jr., "Mechanical Equipment in the White House Swimming Pool," *Heating and Ventilating*, clipping, FDR Library.

16. *Washington Post*, June 3, 1933.

17. Grant to Louis Howe, Washington, April 29, 1933, OPBP, correspondence.

18. Roosevelt and Brough, *Rendezvous*, 13.

19. Nesbitt, *White House Diary, passim.*

20. *Ibid.*, 78.

21. Joseph Lash, *Eleanor and Franklin: The Story of Their Relationship Based on Eleanor Roosevelt's Private Papers* (New York: W. W. Norton and Company, 1971), 501; Eleanor Roosevelt, *This I Remember*, 85.

22. Edith Helm, *The Captains and the Kings.* 144, 147, 148, 155.

23. Former President Hoover resented the publication of Ike Hoover's memoirs, *Forty-Two Years in the White House* and some of his associates blamed Mrs. Roosevelt personally for encouraging the publication—really an accumulation of his notes—as a means of discrediting the Hoovers. See Mildred Hall Campbell to Tom Thalker, Laguna Hills, April 8, 1978, and Campbell's written review of *Forty-Two Years*; Herbert Hoover to Everett Sanders, n.p., October 22, 1934, Hoover Library.

24. Frances Parkinson Keyes, *Capital Kaleidoscope* (New York: Harper & Brothers, 1937), 319–20.

Chapter 40: Sketchbooks

1. The medicine chest is in the collection of the FDR Library.

2. Eleanor Roosevelt, *This I Remember*, 102–3.

3. Keyes, *Capital Kaleidoscope*, 327.

4. Grace Tully, *FDR, My Boss* (New York: Scribner's Sons, 1949) 203–6.

5. Friedel, *New Deal*, 294–96; Hickok, *Eleanor Roosevelt*, 109–12.

6. Howe to Ickes, Washington, December 13, 1933, FDR Library; Winslow memoirs.

7. Winslow memoirs.

8. Frederick Delano to Lewis McHenry Howe, Washington, March 22, 1934, FDR Library.

9. Eric Gugler to Rex Scouten [1970], "The White House: The Executive Of-

fice Building," ocwh; see also Gugler, brief dialogue, Century Club, New York, Gugler Papers, FDR Library.

10. Gugler, "The Executive Office Building," ms., Gugler Papers, FDR Library.

11. Roosevelt to Mac [Marvin H. McIntyre], n.p., n.d., [ca. May 9, 1934], and Roosevelt to Moore, Washington, June 6, 1934, FDR Library; Ferdinand Eiseman to author in conversation, New York, March 30, 1984.

12. Winslow memoirs.

13. Fireside chat, June 28, 1934, typescript, FDR Library.

14. Roosevelt, memorandum to Edwin P. Lock, McIntyre, and Gugler, June 18, 1934, FDR Library.

15. Early, diary, October 29, 1934, FDR Library.

16. Gugler, sketches and descriptions, Executive Office Building, [1934], FDR Library.

17. *Ibid.*; see also invoices, Department of the Interior, National Capital Parks, Records of Alteration, Construction and Repair, National Archives, identified hereafter as NCP.

18. *Ibid.* The tribunal was never built. It did remain a possibility until West Executive Avenue was closed during World War II, but once the street became part of the executive complex, there was no longer a reason to build the tribunal.

19. Moore to Gugler, Boston, October 27, 1934, FDR Library.

20. Mrs. Gugler to the author, telephone interview, Palisades, New York, March 30, 1984; Gugler to Mrs. Roosevelt, New York, June 6 and 15, October 29, 1934; Gugler to Malvina Thompson, draft of a letter [New York, ca. summer 1934]; Gugler estimates, June 6, 1934, FDR Library.

21. Gugler to Mrs. Roosevelt, New York, October 29, 1931, FDR Library.

22. Gugler to Mrs. Pratt, New York, July 11, 1934, FDR Library.

23. Pratt to Delano, Dark Harbor, August 5, 1934, OCWH.

24. Gugler, memorandum to Mrs. Roosevelt, New York, July 23, 1935, FDR Library.

25. Ibid.

26. Pratt to Gugler, Glen Cove, Long Island, July 19, 1935, OCWH; Gugler to Lockwoos, [New York], July 29, 1935, and Lockwood to Gugler, New York, August 1, 1935, FDR Library.

27. Gugler to Mrs. Pratt [New York], September 23, 1935, FDR Library.

28. Pratt to Delano, [New York], December 19, 1935, OCWH.

29. Ibid.

30. Moore to Gugler, Washington, February 10, 1936, FDR Library.

31. Mrs. Roosevelt, memorandum, March 17, 1941, OCWH.

32. Pratt to Delano, Glen Cove, May 17, 1941, OCWH.

33. Pratt to Mrs. Roosevelt, Glen Cove [1937], OCWH. The plan never materialized; only a listing of objects was made, not really a catalog.

34. Winslow memoirs.

35. Washington Post, November 2, 1952. The tiles were not completed until after Roosevelt's death. They were installed during the Truman renovation, in 1952. Another fireplace was altered in 1940, that in the State Dining Room. The first Roosevelt had replaced the lion ornaments with stone bison heads (see pages 683 and 731, with relevant notes) and the second ordered John Adams's famous benediction (see page 81) carved there. Piccirilli Brothers, New York, did the job and billed $110 for it, November 9, 1940 (invoice, OCWH). The mantel was removed during the Truman renovation and is in the Truman Library, Independence, Missouri, while a copy is in the State Dining Room today, put there in 1962.

36. Winslow memoirs.

37. Ibid.; Eleanor Roosevelt, This I Remember, 86.

38. Ruth Van Deman, "U.S. Kitchen No. 1," Journal of Home Economics, vol. 28 (February 1936): 93–94.

39. Invoices for work in the basement and kitchen, NCP; see also miscellaneous vouchers, OCWH.

40. Gugler, sketches and descriptions, Executive Office Building; see also Pratt to Delano, Glen Cove, July 7 [1937?], OCWH.

41. Frederick Law Olmsted [Jr.], "Report on White House Grounds," [Brookline, Massachusetts], October 9, 1934; see also Olmsted to McIntyre, Brookline, June 12, 1934; McIntyre to Roosevelt, Washington, June 26, 1934; and Olmsted to Roosevelt, Brookline, October 16, 1934, FDR Library.

42. Olmsted to McIntyre, Brookline, June 12, 1934, op. cit.

43. E. P. Lock, Jr., memorandums of October 29, 1934; [Arno B. Cammerer], "Estimate for Planning and Execution of Comprehensive Landscape Development for the Grounds of the Executive Mansion," NCP.

44. Emil Ludwig, "House of a Democrat," Reader's Digest vol. 33 (September 1938): 59–60. This was from a book he would publish in 1941, Roosevelt: A Study in Fortune and Power (New York: Garden City Publishing Company).

45. Eleanor Roosevelt, This I Remember, 182.

46. Nesbitt, White House Diary, 233.

47. Ibid., 223–25; Bullitt, confidential memorandum, FDR Library.

48. Eleanor Roosevelt, This I Remember, 184.

49. Ibid., 188; see also New York Times, June 9, 1939; and G. Gordon Young, Voyage of State (London: Hodder and Stoughton, 1939), 222–29; and Early, diary, June 8, 1939, FDR Library.

50. Young, Voyage, 224 and 226.

51. Lizzie McDuffie, recollections, FDR Library.

Chapter 41: The Castle

1. Nesbitt, *White House Diary*, 268.

2. H. P. Hamlin, "Reminiscences of Franklin and Eleanor Roosevelt, 1893–1945," Sunday, December 7, 1941, ms., FDR Library.

3. Ted Morgan, *F.D.R., A Biography* (New York: Simon and Schuster, 1985), 614.

4. Robert E. Sherwood, *Roosevelt and Hopkins: An Intimate History* (New York: Harper & Brothers, 1948), 430–32; ushers' log, December 8, 1941, FDR Library.

5. Eleanor Roosevelt, *This I Remember*, 241, 244–47; Nesbitt, *White House Diary*, 269–70; Winston S. Churchill, *The Grand Alliance* (Boston: Houghton Mifflin Co., 1951), 691.

6. Sir John Martin to the author, interview, Oxford, England, October 10, 1977.

7. Henry Morgenthau, recorded telephone conversation with Secret Service officials, Washington, 9:49 a.m., December 15, 1941, FDR Library; Eleanor Roosevelt, *This I Remember*, 243; *Washington Post*, December 25, 1941.

8. Grace Tully, *FDR, My Boss*, 258.

9. Frank J. Wilson, report, Washington, December 14, 1941; memorandum from Mr. Gaston to Morgenthau, Washington, December 15, 1941; Michael F. Reilly to Wilson, Washington, December 16, 1941, FDR Library.

10. Roosevelt and Morgenthau, recorded telephone conversation, Washington, December 15, 1941, FDR Library.

11. Kirk M. Reid to Joe Bachman, Cleveland, December 14, 1941, and Reilly to Wilson, Washington, December 16, 1941; Hamlin, Reminiscences, December 16, 1942, FDR Library.

12. Reilly to Early, memorandum, Washington, December 12, 1941, FDR Library.

13. Grace Tully, *FDR, My Boss*, 305–6.

14. Winslow memoirs.

15. Gugler to Howard Ker, New York, March 29, 1938; Ker to Gugler, Washington, April 13, 1938; Ker to the President, Washington, April 28, 1938, and Roosevelt's memorandum in response, April 29, 1938, FDR Library.

16. Winslow memoirs.

17. Grace Tully, *FDR, My Boss*, 259.

18. Winslow memoirs.

19. Howell Crim, memorandum, October 15, 1942, FDR Library; orders for materials and some invoices, NCP.

20. Winslow's east wing drawings are deposited in the architect's office, White House Liaison, NCP. Some copies are in the OCWH.

21. Lester W. Bosley to the Charles H. Tompkins, Co., Washington, July 7, 1942, NCP; Winslow memoirs; see also *New York Times*, May 30, 1943.

22. Admiral Ben Moreell to Captain John L. McCrea, Washington, February 12, 1942; Crim to Roosevelt, Washington, February 14, 1942, FDR Library; see also *New York Times*, May 20, 1945.

23. Hamlin, Reminiscences, December 26, 1941.

24. Frank Freidel, *Franklin D. Roosevelt* (Boston: Little, Brown & Co., 1973).

25. Winslow memoirs.

26. Clare Boothe Luce to S. Dillon Ripley, Honolulu, May 19, 1976, Smithsonian Institution.

27. Howard W. Smith to the author, Fauquier County, Virginia, May 31, 1975.

28. Frances Perkins, *The Roosevelt I Knew* (New York: Viking Press, 1946), 65–66.

29. George M. Elsey to the author, interview Washington, October 1984.

30. George M. Elsey interviews, February 10 and 17, 1964, March 9, 1965, July 10 and 17, 1969, April 9, July 7, and July 10, 1970, Harry S. Truman Library; Grace Tully, *FDR, My Boss*, 262.

31. William M. Rigdon, with James Derieux, *White House Sailor* (New York: Doubleday & Company, 1962), 7; see also *Cincinnati Times Star*, September 15, 1949.

32. Reilly to Wilson, Washington, October 27, 1942, FDR Library.

33. Rigdon, *White House Sailor*, 9–10; George M. Elsey to the author in conversation, Washington, October 1984.

34. Mrs. Roosevelt to Anna Roosevelt Boettiger, New York, April 27, [1942], in Bernard Asbell, ed., *Mother and Daughter: The Letters of Eleanor and Anna Roosevelt* (New York: Coward, McCann & Geoghegan, 1982), 142.

35. Eleanor Roosevelt, *This I Remember*, 292.

36. Rigdon, *White House Sailor*, 8.

37. Roosevelt and Brough, *Rendezvous*, 291.

38. Belle Willard Roosevelt, diaries 1942–1945, Friday, June 12, 1942, Kermit Roosevelt Papers, L.C.

39. Ibid., June 8, 1942.

40. Rexford Tugwell, *F.D.R., Architect of An Era* (New York: The Macmillan Co., 1967), 215.

41. Eleanor Roosevelt, *This I Remember*, 239.

42. Ibid., 257.

43. Mrs. Roosevelt to Anna Boettiger, Washington, May 19, 1942, in Asbell, *Mother and Daughter*, 145; Elizabeth Hight to "family," Washington, August 30, 1942, FDR Library.

44. Raymond Muir went to the protocol office, where he remained for many years the liaison between protocol and the White House, see payroll records, NCP. The business papers of the White House show that Crim took a far more active role in management than had Muir before him. Muir's name rarely appeared in the documents, nor are there more than a few notes or memorandums from him. Crim, on the other hand, is ever present in the records.

45. Monthly operations record, White House garage, FDR Library.

46. Nesbitt, *White House Diary*, 281–82, 289; *New York Times*, May 9, 1943.

47. Lash, *Eleanor and Franklin*, 503.

48. Eleanor Roosevelt, *This I Remember*, 244–45.

49. J. L. Dettbarn, "History of the Presidential Mountain Retreat, Camp David, Maryland," unpublished ms., copy in Department of the Interior Library, Washington; Barbara M. Kirkconnell, interview with Conrad L. Wirth, Washington, March 10, 1986; see also Wirth, *Parks, Politics and the People* (Norman: University of Oklahoma Press, 1980), 200–4.

50. Roosevelt and Brough, *Rendezvous*, 320.

51. Lash, *Eleanor and Franklin*, 690.

52. Asbell, *Mother and Daughter*, 298.

53. Eleanor Roosevelt, *This I Remember*, 314.

54. Rexford Tugwell, *Roosevelt's Revolution* (New York: Macmillan Publishing Company, 1977), 203–4.

55. Harry S. Truman, *Year of Decision* (New York: Doubleday & Co., 1965), 15.

56. Margaret Truman, *Harry S. Truman* (New York: William Morrow & Company, Inc., 1973), 223.

57. Nesbitt, *White House Diary*, 312.

Chapter 42: History

1. J. B. West and Mary Lynn Kotz, *Upstairs At the White House: My Life With the First Ladies* (New York: Coward, McCann & Geoghegan, 1973), 63.

2. Margaret Truman, *Letters From Fa-*

ther: *The Truman Family's Personal Correspondence* (New York: Arbor House, 1981), 25.

3. *Ibid.*, 16.

4. West, *Upstairs*, 58.

5. Margaret Truman, *Harry S. Truman*, 241.

6. Truman to his mother, Washington, May 8, 1945, Harry S. Truman Library.

7. Truman to Mrs. Truman, Washington, June 6, 1945, Truman Library.

8. Truman to Harold L. Ickes, Washington, January 7, 1946, Truman Library.

9. Winslow memoirs.

10. See various projects by Winslow, OCWH; Truman to Ickes, Washington, January 7, 1946, Truman Library.

11. Gilmore T. Clarke, Chairman, Commission of Fine Arts, to Truman, Washington, January 10, 1946, Commission of Fine Arts.

12. Truman to Major General Philip B. Fleming, Washington, December 17, 1945, Truman Library; *Newsweek*, February 11, 1946.

13. "Outline of Radio Address," typescript, n.d., [January 1946], Truman Library.

14. J. Leonard Reinsch, interview, Atlanta, March 13 and 14, 1967, Truman Library; *Newsweek*, February 11, 1946; *Washington Post*, January 23 and 24, 1946.

15. Ickes to Truman, Washington, January 10, 1946, Truman Library.

16. Truman to Ickes, Washington, January 10, 1946, Truman Library.

17. "Memorandum of remarks by the President at his press and radio conference," Washington, January 24, 1946; see also press briefing paper, January 11, 1946, Truman Library.

18. James R. Edmunds, Jr., President, American Institute of Architects, to Truman, Washington, February 19, 1946, to which was appended the resolution of the A.I.A. executive committee three days before; Truman's response, Washington, February 26, 1946, Truman Library.

19. William Hillman, *Harry S. Truman In His Own Words* (New York: Bonanza Books, 1984), 81.

20. Winslow memoirs.

21. President Truman's Charlottesville appearance July 4, 1947, brought the largest and most enthusiastic turnout he had experienced thus far. He spoke at the University of Virginia, urging his listeners to support him in abandoning the outmoded foreign policies of the Founding Fathers and take a more active role in world affairs. In a sense the Truman balcony yet to come commemorated his triumph that day. He expressed his heady feelings in a letter to his wife [Charlottesville?] July 5, 1947, in Robert H. Ferrell, ed., *Dear Bess: The Letters From Harry to Bess Truman, 1910–1959* (New York: W.W. Norton & Co., 1983), 345–46; Gilmore D. Clarke spoke of the influence of the "colonial buildings . . . of the University of Virginia" on the President's decision to build a balcony on the south portico, see minutes, Commission of Fine Arts, August 28, 1947, Commission of Fine Arts.

22. Commission of Fine Arts, minutes, August 28, 1947.

23. Connelly to Delano, Washington, August 1, 1947, Truman Library.

24. Commission of Fine Arts, minutes, August 28, 1947; Clarke to Crim, Washington, August 28, 1947, copy in the commission's minutes, Commission of Fine Arts.

25. *Ibid.*

26. Truman to Clarke, Washington, December 2, 1947, Truman Library.

27. *Washington Post*, January 3 and 12, 1948; *New York Herald Tribune*, January 6 and 15, 1948; *New York Times*, January 6, 1948; *New York Journal American*, February 3, 1948; see also Truman memorandum for the press, January 5, 1948, Commission of Fine Arts; Truman to

George Rothwell Brown, Washington, January 20, 1948, Truman Library.

28. Crim, memorandum to the President on the subject of the White House staff, Washington, November 1, 1951, Truman Library.

29. *Washington Post*, September 22, 1946.

30. Margaret Truman, *Harry S. Truman*, 336.

31. "Information for aides at the White House," typescript, November 1, 1946, George M. Elsey Papers, Truman Library.

32. "State Dinners" [procedures] typescript, November 1, 1946, Elsey Papers, Truman Library.

33. Alonzo Fields, "Looking Over the President's Shoulder," *Ladies Home Journal*, vol. 77 (July 1960): 106.

34. The grand march was apparently reinstalled for the Press and Radio Reception, December 6, 1946. See memorandum for aides at that event, Elsey Papers, Truman Library.

35. Fields, "Over the President's Shoulder," 58; West, *Upstairs*, 73.

36. West, *Upstairs*, 341.

37. Reathel Odum to the author, telephone interview, St. John's Island, South Carolina, June 12, 1985; Helm, *The Captains and the Kings*, 270.

Chapter 43: The Symbol

1. W. E. Reynolds, Commissioner of Public Buildings, to Crim, Washington, January 13, 1948; Reynolds memorandum to the President, Washington, January 29, 1948, Truman Library.

2. Truman diary, August 3, 1948; Reynolds, Douglas William Orr, and R. E. Dougherty, "Report to the President on the *Structural Survey* Second floor, White House," n.d., [after February 3, 1948]; Reynolds, memorandum to the President, Washington, January 29, 1948, Truman Library.

3. Charles W. Barber to Reynolds, Washington, July 8, September 7, October 8 and 26, 1948; D. E. Parsons to Reynolds, Washington, September 17, 1948; General Philip B. Fleming to Truman, Washington, November 8, 1948, and William D. Hassett to Fleming, November 17, 1948; Fleming to the President, November 8, 1948, Truman Library. See also *Washington Post*, December 30, 1948; West, *Upstairs*, 98, 104–6.

4. Charles T. Haight to the author, interview, Greenwich, Connecticut, August 16, 1977; *Washington Post*, November 7, 1948.

5. Truman to Clarence Cannon, Washington, May 3, 1949, Truman Library.

6. Winslow diary, January 14, 1949, OCWH; Winslow to Reynolds, Washington, January 26, 1949, Truman Library.

7. The President to Frank Pace, Jr., Director of the Bureau of the Budget, Washington, February 10, 1949, in *Acts and Estimates: Reconstruction of the White House* (Washington: Government Printing Office, 1952), 13.

8. W. E. Reynolds, "Elimination of Structural and Fire Hazards, Executive Mansion," Washington, February 8, 1949, Truman Library.

9. Truman to the vice president and speaker of the House of Representatives, [Washington], March 25, 1949; Truman to Fleming, Washington, May 12, 1949, Truman Library.

10. Commission for the Renovation of the Executive Mansion, minutes, June 15, 1949 [describes Cabinet Room meeting held with the President on June 3], Records of the Commission for the Renovation of the Executive Mansion, National Archives.

11. Commission minutes are complete and provide details of the relationship between the President and the commissioners; for a useful account of Orr's career see William A. Wiedersheim, *Douglas W. Orr, F.A.I.A., Exhibition* (New

Haven: New Haven Colony Historical Society, 1980).

12. Commission minutes, August 2, 1949.

13. *Ibid., passim.*

14. Winslow diary, 1949–1950, *passim.*

15. *Ibid.*, January 1, 1949.

16. Delano to the President, New York, September 21, 1949; Truman, memorandum on the grand stairs, Washington, September 23, 1949; Orr to Truman, September 28, 1949; Delano to Truman, October 4, 1949; Winslow diary, September 12–30, 1949, shows intense discussion over the staircase. Diary October 25, 1949, shows that all of the 1902 marble stairs were to be discarded and the new stairs made of new materials.

17. Winslow's projects and drawings are in the architect's office, White House Liaison, NCP. Many are restricted by the Secret Service, although all were made available to the author for study, if not for reproduction.

18. Winslow to Commission, Washington, June 22, 1949, Commissioner's correspondence; see also Commission minutes, *passim.*

19. Winslow to Commission, June 22, 1949, *op. cit.*

20. *Ibid.*

21. A. E. Demaray to Senator Kenneth McKellar, Washington, August 10, 1949; memorandum relative to the disposition of the roofing materials from the 1927 renovation, December 5, 1949; Glen E. Egerton to Commission, Washington, December 5, 1949; press release announcing sale of "surplus memento material," January 13, 1951, Commission papers on the sale of surplus materials and souvenirs.

22. Commission minutes, January 1950–March 1951; see also Edmund Astley Printis and Lazarus White, *Underpinning: Its Practice and Applications* (New York: Columbia University Press, 1950), 333–37.

23. *Washington Evening Star*, October 7, 1950.

24. The gutting of the structure was photographed extensively by Abbie Rowe for the National Park Service. Hundreds of his photographs document the disappearance of the old interior and the building of the new. The pictures, moreover, provide a good source for studying the 1818 construction of the house. My descriptions of the Truman renovation are based in part on the Rowe collection. Prints are available for study at the Truman Library. The original bound books of the photographs are at NCP, White House Liaison.

25. Truman to the various lodges, Washington, November 1952. Other "Masonic stones" were set into the walls of the reconstructed kitchen, known after 1952 as the Broadcast Room and presently subdivided into three different offices and storage rooms. The Masonic lodges still retain the stones and kindly provided me with rubbings, drawings, photographs, and sketches of their souvenirs, and this information led to some of the discoveries of the nationalities and identities of the stonemasons who built the house in the 1790s, all described in Chapter 3.

26. Finley to Crim, Washington, January 25, 1951, Commissioners' correspondence.

27. Commission minutes, August 16, 1950; in Winslow's diary for August 15, 1950, he notes that he and Delano went that night to Little Oatlands, Finley's retreat near Leesburg, Virginia, and after this session, "I started the final plan for the shelter under the East Terrace."

28. McShain to Reynolds, Philadelphia, November 24, 1950, Commissioners' correspondence.

29. Commission minutes, September 14, 1950, record the decision to proceed with interior decoration plans, and by January Finley was attending the meetings, apparently on his own authority; Finley to Crim, Washington, January 25, 1951, and to Delano, Washington, November 22, 1950, Commissioners' correspondence.

30. Truman to Delano, Washington, August 25, 1950, Truman Library.

31. John S. Burke to Commission, New York, September 21, 1950, Commissioners' correspondence.

32. Haight to the author, interview, Greenwich, Connecticut, *op. cit.*

33. Commission minutes, September 21, 1950.

34. Haight to the author, Greenwich, Connecticut, *op. cit.*

35. *Ibid.*

36. Commission minutes, January 23, 1951.

37. Room perspectives, files of B. Altman & Company, New York; Commission minutes, March 15, 1951.

38. Commission minutes, May 22, 1951.

39. *Ibid.*, July 17, 1951.

40. Haight to the author, Greenwich, Connecticut, *op. cit.*

41. Commission minutes, June 19 and July 17, 1951; Finley to Winslow, Washington, July 20, 1951, and to the president, same day, Truman Library.

42. John Hersey, "Profiles: Mr. President, Ghosts In the White House," Part IV, *The New Yorker*, vol. 27 (April 28, 1951): 37.

43. Orr to the vice president, Washington, July 3, 1950; "Plan for the Disposition of Surplus Material From the White House," January 6, 1950, Commissioners' correspondence. It was the original intention of the Commission to save practically everything removed from the White House and reuse most of the parts. For various reasons—the attitudes of the era, the lack of knowledge about how to "recycle"—very little was reused. The problem of what to do with the materials haunted the commission and by the end of 1950, what had seemed to some almost sacred relics, became mere surplus material. The idea of museum re-creations of White House rooms using

the old woodwork, doors, windows, cornices, and mantels seems never to have come up. But it is clear that such a proposal would have been objectionable to the Commission: There was to be only one Blue Room, etc. The old materials had been classified in five categories, (see Commission memorandum of December 5, 1949, Commissioners' correspondence), two for destruction and the other three to provide for some use by the government or ultimate destruction. Realizing that the surplus could become a political hot potato, the Commission, deciding apparently informally, had nearly everything hauled away as landfill in 1951. As late as May 19, 1952, 43 crates of old doors and trimmings, some tile, wood flooring, and random timbers were at the D.C. Department of Corrections, Lorton, Virginia, and at Fort Myer, Virginia (see memorandum to Egerton from Gilette, Washington, May 19, 1952, Commissioners' correspondence). At this writing, almost 35 years later, a few pieces of "White House" wood could be located in the carpentry shop at Fort Myer, together with one "old metal-covered kitchen door." None of the wood was reported as surviving at Lorton.

44. Winslow diary, July 29, 1950.

45. Haight to the author, Greenwich, Connecticut, *op. cit.*; Commission minutes, August 17, 1951, and *passim*; news release, "Plans For Interior Decoration of the White House," [ca. October 20, 1951], Commissioners' correspondence. See also samples of draperies and upholstery, OCWH.

46. Orr to Truman, Washington, July 19, 1951, Commissioners' correspondence; Commission minutes, July 17, 1951.

47. Commission minutes, summer 1951–spring 1952, and January 25, 1952, *passim*.

48. Truman to Finley, Washington, June 26, 1950, Truman Library. Truman asked Finley to try and retrieve the chandeliers taken from the White House

to the Capitol in 1902. It was a sore
subject, for McKim had sent the elaborate Victorian gas fixtures to auction and
an outraged Congress had demanded
their return and hung them in the Capitol. In any case, Finley had no interest
in Victorian fixtures and had already
written to the President: "I know of your
deep interest . . . in securing chandeliers
of the proper period and scale for the

East Room." Finley to Truman, Washington, June 19, 1950, Truman Library.

49. Commission minutes, February–
April 1952, *passim*; Commission For the
Renovation of the Executive Mansion,
Report (Washington: Government Printing Office, 1952).

50. Commission minutes, March 27,
1952.

Index

Balconies, south facade: Jefferson tenure 92; Madison tenure 125, 129; oval drawing room (1800) 80; see also Truman balcony

Balfour, Arthur, diplomat: friendship with the Wilsons 817-818

Baltimore: and conspiracy to murder Lincoln (1861) 370; gas lighting 173; occupied by Union troops (1861) 372, 383, ensuing riots 383

Baltimore & Potomac Railroad station: Garfield assassination (1881) 521

Baltimore Gas Company: Capitol gas plant 268

Balustrade 71, 877

Bancroft, George, minister to the Court of St. James's (1846-1849) 254; Secretary of the Navy (1845-1846) 252, 254, disapproval of the Mexican War 252, 254, resignation (1846) 254, 306

Bancroft, Herbert Howe, historian 276-277

"banker marks" (stonemasons' trademarks) 70, 1038, 1052

Banneker, Benjamin, mathematician: surveyed site of federal district 15

Barlow, Joel, supplier of furniture 148

Barnes, B. F., aide, Theodore Roosevelt tenure 688

Barouches: given to Lincolns by New York merchants 374, 417; open barouche for Grant's inaugural parade 449

Basement: billiard room, Garfield tenure 518; construction 59-60; dimensions 59; fire of 1814 59, 138, 141, kitchen equipment salvaged 138; floor 59, 432, 439; furnace room 216-217, 315, 663-664, 674, 679; furnishings 438-439; gas lighting installed 283; hydrant installed (1833) 199; hydraulic pump for elevator 535; improvements (1891) 580-581, 594; laundry 196, 438; pantries, Taft tenure 754; rat infestation 432, campaign against 439; remodeling (1935) 957-960; renovation of 1902 672, 673-674, entrance for guests created through east corridor 664, 682, 699, formal rooms added 663-664, 674, groin-vaulted hall 438, 664, 672, household services confined to west end 663, 674; schoolroom, Andrew Johnson

tenure 438; servants' quarters 194, 384, 438, 692-693, abandonment recommended (1881) 536, dining rooms, Andrew Johnson tenure 437, 438, waiting room 437, 438; silver storage 195, vault 754, 845; slave quarters, Polk tenure 257, 258; steward's rooms 194, 195, 438, 754; wine cellar, Garfield tenure 514; see also Diplomatic Reception Room; Kitchens; Sub-basements

Bathing facilities: family quarters 215, 316; installed in east wing (1833 or 1834) 200, 215; permanent installation in family quarters (1853) 316

Bathrooms: additions, 19th century 873; equipped with barber's chair, Andrew Johnson tenure 429; family quarters, Benjamin Harrison tenure 579; improvements (1853) 315, 316; plans (1949) 1033; remodeled (1882) 538; renovation of 1902 800; Theodore Roosevelt family 650, after renovation (1902) 679; Rose Bedroom suite 906

Beale, Charles, butler, Taylor tenure 282

Bear cubs, brought to White House by Pike (1807) 97

Bedroom, presidential: John Adams tenure 84; Arthur's redecoration (1881) 534; balcony see Truman balcony; Cleveland tenure 561, 614; Garfield's sickroom 522, air-conditioning 523-525; Harding tenure 839, 841; Benjamin Harrison tenure 578; Hayes tenure 499; Lincoln Bed removed, Hoover tenure 887; McKinley tenure 619, 639-640; Theodore Roosevelt tenure 650, 678-679; Taft tenure 745-746; Truman tenure 1005

Bedrooms see Lincoln Bedroom; Prince of Wales Room; Rose Bedroom

Beds 906; Arthur's walnut bed 534; custom-made for Franklin Roosevelt at Val-Kill Industries 929; Theodore Roosevelt tenure 650; McKinley tenure 639-640; see also Lincoln bed

Belknap, William W., Secretary of War (1869-1876): resigned because of wife's graft 484-485

Belknap, Mrs. William W.: selling of appointments 484

portrait saved by Dolley Madison 255, 472

Burns, David: farm 23-24

Burns, Thomas, doorkeeper 363, 395

Burr, Aaron: election of 1800 87, 88

Butlers: Buchanan tenure 395; Harding tenure 843, 845; Lincoln tenure 363, 384; livery, Wilson tenure 819; part-time, Andrew Johnson tenure 445-446; Pierce tenure 308; Taft tenure 742; Taylor tenure 282; Truman tenure 1016, 1019; Wilson tenure 819

Butt, Major Archibald Wellington "Archie," aide 722, 723, 724-725, 727, 739, 763-764, 1017; arrival at White House (1908) 723-724; chief ceremonial officer, Taft tenure 748, 751, 754, 772; detailed to the Army Corps of Engineers 748; died on the *Titanic* (1912) 764; duties, Taft tenure 748, 754; horseback riding with Theodore Roosevelt 728; ill health (1912) 763; meeting with Helen Taft (1908) 733-734; opinion of Tafts 745, 748-749; and Potomac Drive project (1909) 750; and Edith Roosevelt 724, 727, 728, 734; scrapbooks 752, 753, 764

Byrd, Adolph, butler: Harding tenure 845; Wilson tenure 819

Cabinet: first woman secretary 918; role in receptions, Truman tenure 1020

Cabinet dinner: Cleveland tenure 610; Coolidge tenure 858; Taft tenure 745

Cabinet Room: constructed within unfinished East Room, Madison tenure 123; Andrew Johnson tenure 426; McKinley's use of 627, 631, 634-635; used by Theodore Roosevelt as a study 690, 758; see also Treaty Room

Cabinet Room, Executive Office Building 681, 690-691, 947, 984; swearing-in of Truman (1945) 999

Cabinet table, Grant's: placed in Theodore Roosevelt's study 680; used by McKinley as desk 631

Cabot, Francis, procurement agent: construction of the President's House 25

Cadillac limousine, 16-cylinder: known as

White House Car Number One and used on trips to Camp Rapidan, Hoover tenure 907

Caffrey, Anthony, priest: first to serve at St. Patrick's Church (1790s) 67

Calhoun, John C., Vice President (1829-1837): death 286; negotiations for the annexation of Texas 247; and "Peggy O'Neale Affair" (1829-1831) 190; slavery issue 286

California: admission to Union (1850) 290, debated 287; gold discovered (1848) 275, 276

Call bells 78, 84, 1038; electric, Grant tenure 469; hung (1801) 92; installed in steward's room, Grant tenure 457; mother-of-pearl, following renovation (1902) 680; President's office, Buchanan tenure 340; pulls replaced, Van Buren tenure 214; servants' waiting room, Andrew Johnson tenure 437, 438; system expanded (1861) 385; Taft tenure 743

Callan, Nicholas, foreman of laborers: rebuilding of White House 140, 142, 143

Callers, social: blacks 653; Lincoln tenure 376; McKinley tenure 619, 625-626

Callers to office: announced by doorman 263; Andrew Johnson tenure 427; registration of 258, 517; rules governing, Pierce tenure 324

Calligraphers 495; employed for White House invitations, first instance of 515; Truman tenure 1016

Calling, social see Social calling

Calling cards: custom of leaving at gate ended during World War II 977; delivered by car 843, by coachmen 843, on foot 843; redesigned by Cortelyou 689

Cambon, Jules, ambassador from France 634

Camellias: greenhouse 313; popularity (1850s) 312

Camp David, Maryland see Shangri-La

Camp Rapidan, Virginia: created by Hoover (1929) 906-907

Campbell, Mary, cook: brought from Hyde Park by Franklin Roosevelt 985

Campbell, R. G., secretary to Fillmore 302

631; after sinking of *Maine* 623
Porters *see* Doorkeepers
Porter's lodge *see* Doorkeeper's lodge
Porticoes 843; Latrobe's designs, Jefferson
    tenure 117, 118; Madison tenure 144;
    plans abandoned (1819) 151, 152; *see
    also* North portico; South portico
Portraits: Arthur 530; gallery of ex-
    Presidents 434, 472, 499, 500-502;
    Grant family, by Cogswell 454, 472;
    Lucy Hayes, by Huntington 493, 514;
    Hoban, acquired, Ford tenure 1055;
    Jackson, by Earl 182, 188, 1056;
    Lincoln, by Cogswell 472; Red Room
    selections (1934) 950, 955, 956; Tyler,
    by Healy 434; Washington, by Peale
    1055; Washington, by Stuart 80, 123,
    155, 377, 472, restoration, Andrew
    Johnson tenure 445, saved from British
    by Dolley Madison (1814) 133-134,
    255, 284, 472; Martha Washington
    501, 502
Post Office building: Polk tenure 275
Potomac (presidential yacht, Franklin
    Roosevelt tenure): assigned to combat
    duty, World War II 996
Potomac Drive 749, 750
Potomac River: John Quincy Adams's
    swim outings 166; cruise taken by
    Prince of Wales (1860) 352; cruise
    taken by Tyler Cabinet (1844) 245,
    deaths 245; development promoted by
    Washington 3
Potsdam Conference (1945) 1006
Potter, John Fox, chairman of House
    investigating committee 394
Powell, Alexander "Alec," personal
    employee of Arthur 544-545
Powell, John Wesley: assisted in building
    air-cooling machine for Garfield 524
Powers, Abigail *see* Fillmore, Mrs. Millard
Powers, Hiram: sculpture 347
Praeger, Emil H., engineer: reconstruction
    consultant (1949-1952) 1029, 1036
Pratt, Mrs. Harold I. (Harriet Barnes),
    chairman of advisory committee 864,
    880, 882-883, 949, 957, 1053;
    furnishings plans (1951-1952) 1042,
    1044; inspections of state rooms 953,
    956; meeting with Bess Truman (1945)
    1040; meetings with Eleanor Roosevelt

951-952, 1004; on redecoration
    controversy (1925) 867; search for
    Green Room chandelier 908, 910; state
    floor decorating (1935) 952-953, 966
Pratt, Mrs. John T.: Green Room
    redecoration donation 868
Prentis, Edmund Astley, engineer: and
    reconstruction (1949-1952) 1036
Presidency: Bureau of the Budget control
    transferred to, from Treasury
    Department (1939) 979; Centennial
    celebrations (1889) 584-585;
    ceremonial roles 8; diplomatic potency
    810; emergency powers given, World
    War I 810; executive authority
    expanded under Cleveland 571, 602;
    first President to die in office (1841)
    228, 234, 236, 237; presidential style
    366; procedures and conduct established
    5, 6, 7; salaries *see* Salaries, presidential;
    Margaret Bayard Smith quoted on
    changes in administrations 89; social
    entertainment precedent set 127; social
    obligations eased 5; succession question
    resolved (1841) 238; symbol of office
    149, 159
Presidential assassinations *see*
    Assassinations of Presidents
Presidential bedroom *see* Bedroom,
    presidential
Presidential entrance *see* Entrance
    ceremony
Presidential funerals *see* Funerals,
    presidential
Presidential mansion: replacement for
    White House proposed 452, 454
Presidential palace, designed by L'Enfant
    1, 4, 9, 16, 17, drawings lost 452;
    dimensions 18; inspiration for 19;
    models for, suggested by Jefferson 11,
    19; site 17, 18, maps 17-18
Presidential portraits: Arthur 530; gallery
    of ex-Presidents 434, 472, 499, 500-
    502; Lincoln, by Cogswell 472; Red
    Room selections (1934) 950, 955, 956;
    Tyler, by Healy 434; Washington, by
    Peale 1055; Washington, by Stuart 123,
    155, 377, 472, hung in White House
    (1800) 80, moved to East Room (1930)
    901, moved to East Room, Hayes tenure
    500, 501, moved to State Dining

993; marriage 921, 994; opposition to consumption of alcohol 930; pistol 937; press conferences 935-936, 950; radio program 938; retreat 921, 996; shown White House by Lou Hoover 915; study 1004; tours abroad, World War II 996; travels 936, 937; White House social events 930, 931, 971; women's rights 931; writings 936, 938, 954

Roosevelt, Franklin Delano, Jr., son of Franklin Roosevelt 928, 990

Roosevelt, Franklin, Cabinet: denied access to Map Room, World War II 988; first Cabinet meeting (1933) 918; reception for (1933) 917, 918

Roosevelt, Franklin Delano, tenure (1933-1945): basement remodeled (1935) 957-960; bomb shelter built 980, 981, 983; Bonus Army (1933) 932; chief ushers *see* Crim, Howell G.; Hoover, Irwin H.; Muir, Raymond Douglas; Churchill's visits, World War II 973-974, 984, 987; Declaration of the United Nations (1942) 985; dinners 994; East Wing built (1941-1942) 978-983; Executive Office Building reconstruction (1934) 938-949; executive office staff expanded 939, 979; family quarters redecorated 921; guests 926-927, 928, 990, 992, official guests 973-974, 984, 987, 989, 992, 997; housekeeper *see* Nesbitt, Henrietta; kitchen built, third floor (1938) 985; landscaping (1934-1937) 960-965; Map Room established 987-988; New Deal programs 919-920, 934-935, 938, 965; Office of Public Buildings and Public Parks of the National Capital dissolved (1933) 925; Pearl Harbor attacked (1941) 972-973; presidential retreat 995-996; presidential secretary *see* Howe, Louis McHenry; Prohibition ended (1933) 920; purchase of land surrounding Lafayette Park (1939) 979; sitting room created in West Hall 922; social events 930, 931, 994, 995, 996-997, "made list" abandoned 931; social seasons cancelled (1941-1945) 977; state rooms refurbished 949-957; swimming pool built (1933) 922-925, 930; theft of

goods from White House stores 993-994; United Nations Relief and Rehabilitation Administration created (1943) 997-998; visit of king and queen of Great Britain (1939) 965-970; war declared on Axis powers (1941) 973; wartime routine at White House 975; wartime security at White House 975-978; yacht 996

Roosevelt, James, son of Franklin Roosevelt 928, 973

Roosevelt, John, son of Franklin Roosevelt 928, 992; military service 990

Roosevelt, Quentin, son of Theodore Roosevelt: antics 650; at inauguration of Taft 738

Roosevelt, Sara Delano, mother of Franklin Roosevelt 930; control of Hyde Park household 926; death (1941) 985

Roosevelt, Theodore (1858-1919): assistant secretary of the Navy (1897-1898) 626; background 651; "big stick" policy 740; and Theodore Bingham 703; and William Jennings Bryan 725; and burial of time capsule (1902) 685, 686; and Archie Butt 723-724, 728; children 649, 650, 679, 815; at diplomatic reception (1903) 700, 701; flamboyance 740; guards 696; hero of San Juan Hill 633; horseback riding 728-729; interest in White House 650, 732; Charles McKim, meeting with (April 1902) 659; McMillan Commission, reaction to 656-657; personal characteristics 650; portrait 956; presidential entrance march 750, 772; presidential style 729-730, changes in 702-703, 717-718, 724, 730-731; press relations 691-692, 726-727, 740; Progressive Party nomination (1912) 764; public appearances 728, 849; Republican Party nomination sought (1912) 764; sisters 647, 648; study 680, 690; and William Howard Taft 732, 733, 735, 736, 737, 739, 740, 764, 769; threatening letters to 736; train travel 937; vice presidential candidate (1900) 637; view of remodeled White House 673; wedding of daughter Alice 714-716

Roosevelt, Mrs. Theodore (Edith Kermit Carow): attention to social details 696-

Library of Congress CIP Data

Seale, William.
    The president's house.

    Bibliography: p.
    Includes index.

    1. White House (Washington, D. C.)
2. Washington (D. C.)—Buildings, structures, etc.   3. Presidents—United States—Dwellings. I. Title.

F204.W5S43   1986   975   86-50504

ISBN 0-912308-28-1

ISBN 0-8109-1490-5 (Abrams)

Composition by York Graphic Services, York, Pa., and Photographic Services of the National Geographic Society, Washington, D. C. Printed and bound by Arcata/Fairfield, Fairfield, Pa. Printing of plates by McCollum Press, Inc., Rockville, Md. Film preparation by Catharine Cooke Studios, Inc., New York, N.Y. Separations by Lincoln Graphics, Inc., Cherry Hill, N.J.

Set in Goudy Old Style
Designed by Viviane Y. Silverman
Printed on 60-pound Glatfelter offset, acid free
Manufactured by P. H. Glatfelter Co.